SELECTED

PROSE

OF

BERNARD SHAW

Selected Plays of Bernard Shaw in three volumes

★

THE DOCTOR'S DILEMMA

PYGMALION

MAJOR BARBARA

HEARTBREAK HOUSE

CAPTAIN BRASSBOUND'S CONVERSION

THE MAN OF DESTINY

ANDROCLES AND THE LION

★ ★

BACK TO METHUSELAH

SAINT JOAN

JOHN BULL'S OTHER ISLAND

YOU NEVER CAN TELL

IN GOOD KING CHARLES'S GOLDEN DAYS

★ ★ ★

MRS. WARREN'S PROFESSION

ARMS AND THE MAN

CANDIDA

THE DEVIL'S DISCIPLE

CAESAR AND CLEOPATRA

MAN AND SUPERMAN

FANNY'S FIRST PLAY

THE DARK LADY OF THE SONNETS

★ ★ ★ ★

Selected Prose of Bernard Shaw

MUSIC

THEATRE

SOCIALISM

FICTION

AUTOBIOGRAPHY

BERNARD SHAW

SELECTED PROSE

SELECTED BY DIARMUID RUSSELL

Dodd, Mead & Company

NEW YORK

Library of Congress Catalog Card Number: 52-11523

PRINTED IN THE UNITED STATES OF AMERICA BY THE
VAIL-BALLOU PRESS, INC., BINGHAMTON, N. Y.

INTRODUCTION

Shaw's renown as a playwright and his energy—Shaw wrote more than forty plays—have left many unaware or indifferent to his prose. This is an oversight, for his prose and the prose prefaces to the plays contain all Shaw's ideas, set forth with great explicitness. Though Shaw was fertile as a playwright, he was even more productive as a prose writer. In the Standard Edition of his works nineteen volumes are given to his prose writing and fourteen to his plays—and approximately one-quarter of the contents of his play volumes consists of the prose prefaces.

What made Shaw preeminently notable was his intelligence. Shaw, in fact, was one of the most consistently intelligent writers that ever lived. He divorced emotion from his view of the universe and human beings. He remarks over and over again in his writing that the intellect is also a passion. Shaw was writing about himself when he said this, and I think he used the word passion as we would ordinarily use it—to denote that state where we willingly throw all other feelings and bonds aside in our pursuit of what we love.

Psychologically there must always be a balancing of accounts when all the forces of one's nature are bent on a particular end—just as true of Shaw in his pursuit of the intellect as it would be of some other man in the pursuit of riches. Shaw knew this, for he remarks in an article on Henry Irving that "Irving's art was the whole of himself; and that was why he sacrificed himself—and everybody and everything else—to his art. It is a curious piece of artistic psychology, this, and will be misunderstood by stupid people and Philistines." This passion for the intellect does give to Shaw's prose a cold feeling. It is not warming as much other prose is, a communication of emotion and affection for human beings. Shaw's passion was of the head, not the heart.

If coldness were all one could sense in Shaw's work—and some have, Katherine Mansfield for one—we would be repelled. But Shaw's prose has passion, a great feeling of force and energy. It is as eloquent, as witty and as lucid as any written in his lifetime. There is nothing he writes which does not stir the mind. Stir is the right word to use, for we cannot, as we might with many writers of intelligence, read and marvel at Shaw's work and not really be involved. All Shaw's prose is a debate with all the conviction and force of a debate, and all the arts and cunning of a skilled debater—which Shaw was. One cannot listen to a debate and not take sides. One is always for or against Shaw.

Shaw's intelligence covered many fields. In his prose writings there are books of musical and dramatic criticism, socialism, education, medicine, crime, the First World War, reviews of books, impressions of friends. There was almost no facet of society or social custom on which Shaw's critical ability was not exercised. If we except the musical and dramatic criticism, which involve to some degree technical knowledge, all Shaw's prose deals with ideas or customs with which we are familiar. How exasperating for the conventional mind to find Shaw disagrees with almost everything taken as settled—marriage, education, capitalism, medicine, government, social customs of all kinds. Shaw seldom departs far from facts and logic, and the assault on conventional thought is carried on with such skill and brilliance that the conventional mind is hard put to it to find an answer.

Shaw's first major works in prose were the five novels he wrote between 1879 and 1883—one a year—*Immaturity*, *The Irrational Knot*, *Love Among the Artists*, *Cashel Byron's Profession*, and *An Unsocial Socialist*, written in that order. These novels now, even seventy years later, seem odd but not outmoded. The oddness is Shaw, perceptible even in his twenties. The background material, the accessories, are those of the period. But the preoccupations of the early Shaw are apparent. He was then, as he was all his life, a critic of convention and more interested in ideas than in his characters. The freshness the novels still have is due to the ideas, not yet out of date. The characters are seldom human beings as we know them but act from an intellectual logic which is Shaw's alone. We expect fiction to stir our emotions but Shaw's novels leave us unmoved emotionally.

Immaturity, Shaw's first novel, is his least successful. The interest wavers from one character to another, almost as if Shaw wasn't clear in his mind what he wanted to write about, and there is no definite theme such as the other novels have. Probably Shaw, for his first novel, tried to write the kind of novel others at the time were writing—and by writing it learned quickly that this sort of thing wasn't for him. Still there is probably some value in *Immaturity* for Shaw enthusiasts. It may reasonably be supposed that it is, like many first novels, partly autobiographical and the young man who is the chief character may well have a good deal of the young Shaw in him.

Shaw's last novel *An Unsocial Socialist* is, as Shaw himself said, almost pure Marx. It was intended to be longer but Shaw gave up when the work was partly done, realizing that he had said all he had to say. What readers will feel—and what Shaw may have felt too, though he did not say it—is that novels too obviously trying to preach propaganda are seldom successful.

The most interesting of the novels for the ordinary reader are the three middle novels, in which Shaw found a balance between ideas and characters—and it is the ideas they represent which give importance and interest to Shaw's characters. *The Irrational Knot* is a study of the morality and customs of marriage; *Love Among the Artists* contrasts the habits and manners of the artistic mind with those of conventional society; *Cashel Byron's Profession*, the first published and possibly the best known of the Shaw novels, places a prizefighter among the complexities of society, which is rather baffled by the simplicity and directness of his thought. There is an interesting supplement to this novel in which Shaw discusses the prizefighting of the past with that of the present, in which Shaw indicates that fighting with gloves is possibly more dangerous than when they fought with bare fists for forty rounds or so.

The five novels were rejected by all publishers. Some later secured publication in periodicals and later still as books. With these rejections came Shaw's rejection of the novel. Shaw was probably becoming impatient with fiction and was casting around for another outlet for his talents. Novels seemed an obvious thing to try first but as they brought him no hearing, he cut his losses. In a review of an Arnold Bennett book in The Nation in 1916 he was to make it plain he thought a good deal of novel writing was atmospheric nonsense. There was just too much stuff in novels that had nothing to do with ideas. Look at the opening to *Cashel Byron's Profession:* "Moncrief House, Panley Common. Scholastic establishment for the sons of gentlemen, etc." That *etc.* is what Shaw would like to have used more often in his novels. He could then have settled down to writing relevant to his ideas.

In the year 1884 Shaw joined the newly formed Fabian Society. His own socialist ideas were now buttressed by those of the other members and resulted in a body of doctrine for Shaw to which he adhered all his life. He wrote a large number of the pamphlets the Fabian Society issued in an endeavor to alter the political and economic thought of England. The most important of the Shaw pamphlets are gathered together in the volume entitled *Essays in Fabian Socialism.* These are first class expositions of economic thought, easy to read, easy to understand, witty, ironic, persuasive. All the emotion Shaw was unable to bring to his fiction he was able to bring to his economics. If Shaw is compared to the writers of the economic classics, Adam Smith, Marx, Ricardo, Henry George, it can be seen that if Shaw is not a pioneer in economic thought, he is certainly the most readable and the most lucid. Sydney Webb supports this opinion in a preface written for a new edition (1920) of *Fabian Essays.* He referred to Shaw's essay

The Economic Basis of Socialism as being "a survey of the economic evolution of society which, for terse comprehensiveness and brilliant generalization, has not since been excelled in any language." Webb wrote this in 1919, thirty years after the essay had been written. It is interesting that this collection of *Fabian Essays,* first published in 1889, was reprinted in 1908, 1920, 1931 and again in 1948. The thought of the pioneer Fabians has endured well, and their essays are the intellectual background for English Socialism.

Socialism was Shaw's strongest intellectual belief—but so rigid that he would tolerate in the name of socialism actions he would detest in another form of society. Shaw's writings on socialism should be read, no matter what one's economic inclination. They are an unusually brilliant and persuasive presentation of socialism and are among the best of Shaw's prose work—if they are not the best.

The lecturing and writing Shaw did for the Fabian Society were unpaid. They were his contribution to the Fabian Society and to society in general. The various items that make up *Essays in Fabian Socialism* date from 1888 to 1904. During most of this time Shaw was earning his living writing musical and dramatic criticism. As Corno di Bassetto he covered London music for *The Star* from May 1888 to May 1890 and then later in that year and month moved over to *The World* and carried on musical criticism under his own initials till August 1894.

Journalism of this kind is hardly the material to stand the test of time. What was written last week is out of date and what was written last month is forgotten. Yet there is not a page of Shaw's criticism—and most of it deals with unfamiliar names and people long dead—that isn't highly entertaining and instructive. Shaw never despised journalism. He brought all the powers of his mind and writing ability, and they were great powers, to his weekly task. He remarks in his preface to *The Sanity of Art:*

"Journalism can claim to be the highest form of literature; for all the highest literature is journalism. The writer who aims at producing the platitudes which are 'not for an age, but for all time' has his reward in being unreadable in all ages: whilst Plato and Aristophanes trying to knock some sense into the Athens of their day, Shakespear peopling the same Athens with Elizabethan mechanics and Warwickshire hunts, Ibsen photographing the local doctors and vestrymen of a Norwegian parish, Carpaccio painting the life of St. Ursula exactly as if she was a lady living in the next street to him, are still alive and at home everywhere among the dust and ashes of many thousands of academic, punctilious, most archaeologically correct men of letters avoiding the journalist's vulgar obsession with the ephemeral. I also am a journalist, proud of it, deliberately cutting out of my works all that is not journalism, convinced that nothing that is not journalism will live long as literature, or be of any use whilst it does live."

Shaw would not have claimed his weekly column on music was literature. But his attitude, the care and attention he gave to the work, was the same as he gave to any other job he undertook, and the four volumes of musical criticism that resulted are more readable than most novels. What is in most hands a routine job was turned by Shaw into an opportunity for consideration of all aspects of music. It was not just a question with him whether the performer was good or bad—a dull, expert appraisal. He investigated the music itself, no matter how classical or famous it was, he had ideas about what kind of music should be performed, who should perform it—and for whom it should be performed. What he did, in fact, was to create his own set of standards, bringing to music a wider scope and more importance, pouring a half-savage, half-humorous invective on those who failed, in his opinion, to understand what music could and should do.

The musical criticism ended in August 1894, Shaw having resigned from *The World* when the editor, Edmund Yates, died. Shaw was worn out and worked out from the steady drain of being entertaining and instructive once a week for six years. It is likely also Shaw knew musical work could do no more for him. He could do it well but it led no further. In the meantime he had found his profession, playwriting. *Widower's Houses* was performed in 1892 and *Arms and the Man* in 1894. When he next resumed steady journalism it was as dramatic critic for *The Saturday Review*, acting for them from January 1895 to May 1898, which period saw the production of two more of his plays, *Candida* in 1895 and *The Devil's Disciple* in 1897—first performed in the Harmanns Bleeker Hall, Albany, New York.

I think Shaw's dramatic criticism is better than his musical criticism—though not by much. In music he was the highly intelligent and knowledgeable amateur, capable of bringing many new ideas and points of view to bear. In his dramatic work Shaw was the professional. He was a practicing playwright himself, involved in the whole business of writing plays, casting them, aiding in the production and, since Shaw was a first-rate business man, interested in the whole financial background. He could, and did, call on all these matters in his criticism of what went on in the London theatres and there is constant discussion of what playwrights can do, what can be expected of actors, of those who design the stage sets, of managers, of casting, of the theatre in all its manifold functioning. Even more than in music he brought to the theatre his own set of beliefs. He remarks about his criticism:

"They contained something like a body of doctrine, because when I criticized I really did know definitely what I wanted. Very few journalistic critics do. . . . Weariness of the theatre is the prevailing note of London criticism. Only the ablest critics believe that the theatre is really important; in my time none of them would claim for it, as I claimed for it, that it is as important as the Church was in the Middle Ages and much more important than the Church was in London in the years under review."

The dramatic criticism as well as the musical criticism is a model of what art criticism ought to be—but it will not often be easy to find writers of Shaw's attainments to do this kind of work.

Nor would it be easy to find people with Shaw's energy. While he was doing this weekly dramatic column he was writing and speaking for the Fabian Society and also turning out plays—and during this same period he also found time to write three long essays, *The Perfect Wagnerite, The Quintessence of Ibsenism* and *The Sanity of Art*, which are gathered together in the volume entitled *Major Critical Essays.*

All are decidedly worth reading, though they date back before 1900. Intelligence has an enduring quality. Wagner was a matter of controversy when Shaw was doing his musical criticism, and a good deal of that criticism is an attack on those people who could not see any value in Wagner's work. *The Perfect Wagnerite*, as it happens, is less about Wagner's music than it is about the story of the Ring Cycle, in which Shaw interpreted a social and economic doctrine much to his taste—socialism. It would be unfair to say his backing of Wagner's new form of operatic drama was due to the socialism he discerned in the mythological story of the Ring Cycle. Shaw knew enough about music to recognize something good, but it would be true that a disguised socialism would appeal not only to his intellect but also to his sense of humor. The interpretation, right or wrong, gives added richness to the story and is absorbing reading even for those who have only a smattering of musical knowledge.

The Quintessence of Ibsenism arose as a consequence of the Fabian Society in 1890 asking for summer lectures to fit in under the general theme of socialism in contemporary literature. Ibsen was even more of a controversial subject than Wagner—and so was a ready-made subject for Shaw. Ibsen's plays had been attacked in the most intemperate manner and in terms which fell little short of the language of the gutter. He was accused of obscenity, of attacking the sanctity of the home, the institution of marriage, the chastity of woman. It was a wonderful opportunity for Shaw. To him Ibsen was the new drama, the way the theatre must go, the realism that showed things as they were, that exposed hypocrisy. Shaw's own line of thought ran parallel to Ibsen's—and his plays later were to be similarly realistic and controversial. He was able to leap to Ibsen's defence with all his natural pleasure in debate. Ibsen's views do not seem as strange now as they did in 1890, not because the insight and perception is less true, but because familiarity and repetition has dulled our responses. Yet what Ibsen criticized is still with us and Shaw's essay is as stimulating now as when written.

The Sanity of Art is a defence of what is new in the arts against the attack of a German writer, Max Nordau. Shaw demolished Nordau with ease. Yet what is new in art does not need to be defended these days. The battle for the new has been won and, if anything, what we need is some defence for the past. While Shaw's essay is fun to read, the cause has been won. The real interest lies in the easy confidence of Shaw's manner as he knocks his opponent's position down in ruins.

The year 1898 is the year of publication of *The Perfect Wagnerite*. It is also the year when Shaw ended his dramatic criticism, the last time Shaw worked for regular pay. From then on he was to devote himself almost totally to plays. With anyone else this would have meant there was little energy or intellect left for other exertions. Shaw was an exception in his intellect and also in his energy. If we take 1900 as a rough dividing line between Shaw as a general writer and Shaw as a playwright, it is worth while adding up what Shaw had produced. In 1900 he was forty-four years old and by that time had written five novels, had done enough journalism to make four volumes of musical criticism and three of dramatic criticism. He had written the *Major Critical Essays* and the *Essays in Fabian Socialism* (only one of which, *The Commonsense of Municipal Trading*, dates after 1900) and had had six plays produced.

An ordinary writer might well feel proud of such productiveness, and at forty-four might have felt that few years of really creative writing were left. Shaw's career was only starting, with another thirty or so plays to come, and that almost total devotion to plays left Shaw with just enough of a loophole to engage in an continual debate in newspapers and magazines on anything that attracted his attention or anger. As a mere by-product we have four more volumes of prose, made up of Shaw's glancing at what was going on in the world. *Doctors' Delusions, Crude Criminology, Sham Education* make up one volume, the contents being obvious from the title, the most notable article being a magnificent essay on imprisonment. *What I Really Wrote About the War* is a collection of material about the First World War, dwarfed in interest today by the rush of world events. *Pen Portraits and Reviews* is largely made up of random book reviewing by Shaw. He was never content with being routine so even his casual reviewing is astonishingly lively and some of the pieces are first-rate Shaw—notably one on Wilde and a moving memoir of William Archer, the dramatic critic, with whom Shaw had been friends for forty years. Shaw was probably as friendly with Archer as he ever was with anyone and his memoir about Archer incidentally discloses a good bit about Shaw. *Short Stories, Scraps and Shavings* is a miscellany with a couple of amusing items, *Death of an Old Revolutionary* being an ironically funny character study of the kind of man who always haunts progressive movements.

Then come three more prose volumes, *The Intelligent Woman's Guide to Socialism and Capitalism* in 1928, *Everybody's Political What's What* in 1944; and with the appearance of *Sixteen Self Sketches* in 1949 Shaw is through with prose and almost through with life, being then ninety-three years old. The self sketches are interesting, as any information about a man like Shaw would be interesting;

but they tend to be rather fragmentary and far better autobiographical material is to be found in the prefaces to *Immaturity* and to the musical criticism by Corno di Basseto. *Everybody's Political What's What* is an astonishing feat for a man almost ninety, for it is an omnibus volume of all Shaw's thoughts—war, peace, doctors, the law, government, science, socialism, capitalism, religion. It is, however, a recapitulation of matters that Shaw has written about earlier in other prose volumes or in play prefaces. Shaw at this stage, and no wonder, was not capable of new ideas. It is a marvel that he could tackle, and achieve, such a lengthy and coherent account of what he had learned in his life, and tried to teach.

The Intelligent Woman's Guide to Socialism and Capitalism is the most important of these late works. It is a remarkable piece of writing, being a full examination of capitalism and an equally full exposition of Shaw's socialism, covering all aspects that might be affected, even to matters like eugenics and marriage. This work of Shaw's is both unusual and fascinating inasmuch as it brings socialism into the home and everyday life. It is neither laborious nor technical and taken together with Shaw's essays for the Fabian Society provides one of the most readable and lucid introductions to socialism available.

There is an obvious difference between Shaw's plays and his prose. The theatre for most people is entertainment and Shaw made himself as entertaining as he could while writing for the theatre, even though what lay at the back of his head were the ideas he wished to communicate. In his prose Shaw is not deliberately the entertainer. He is often, indeed usually, witty and amusing, but these are aids to debate, in which irony and wit are used to ridicule the opponent—which for Shaw is always the conventional and accepted thought of society. There is no marked style in his writing. What Shaw wanted from prose was clarity and effectiveness. He says, "I have never aimed at style in my life: style is a sort of melody that comes into my sentences by itself. If a writer says what he has to say as accurately and effectively as he can, his style will take care of itself, if he has a style." What Shaw wanted he got, a superbly effective prose, forceful and direct, easy to read and easy to understand. Vigor is possibly the best adjective to describe the feeling we get from his writing. Shaw's sentences have a brisk air of being on their way to some destination. There is no dallying around with ornamental flourishes.

It is natural that Shaw's plays—probably on the stage somewhere in the world every day in the year—should leave his prose in the background, but Shaw's ideas are set forth more directly in prose than they are in plays. In plays he had to pay attention to the needs of the theatre; in prose he is direct, a most skilled and redoubtable debater. Anyone who seeks to know what Shaw thought about music, the theatre, socialism, economics, education and a host of other subjects will find Shaw's prose writings the most rewarding source of information.

Shaw's temperament, in spite of long residence in England, remained Irish. He was an intellectual revolutionary, delighting in battle and controversy, and probably took some pleasure in using the English stage and English periodicals to assault English conventions. He has none of the English pleasure in compromise and convention and nothing of their urbanity or power to veil over unpleasant situations. The Irish mind, despite the popular attributes of romanticism and mysticism, is curiously cold and realistic. Shaw's intellect had these two qualities.

There exists in Ireland, more than in most countries, the fanatic who is dedicated to an idea or a cause and who is remorseless in his devotion. Shaw belongs to this group, for Shaw was a fanatic about his ideas, never changing or altering them in his lifetime. He was even more a fanatic about the intellect itself—"the intellect is also a passion"—with the result that his prose does, in spite of its wit, have an air of austerity about it, coming from the pure intellectual approach to all things, the shunning of any emotional intrusion. But there is an air of magnificence about it too, the thing that made Shaw a great man—the appeal to the intellect, the constant search for the truth as he saw it, the spurning of any kind of hypocrisy, the desire to examine all things, all ideas, no matter how well established, by the light of intelligence. Shaw was an apostle for socialism all his life, but even more he was an apostle for the intellect, believing only in that cold clear light would humanity find answers to its problems. In his own odd way, he descends from the line of those Irish saints who ventured abroad carrying the word of God. The intellect which Shaw made his passion was also his religion, for which I suspect he made many sacrifices.

* * *

The scope of this selection has been limited to the degree that no personal letters have been drawn on, nor have the prefaces of any plays been used. Neither of these limitations is really important. Personal letters are outside the intent of this volume, besides which Shaw's correspondence was so large as to need separate consideration and publication. The play prefaces, not unsurprisingly, really belong with the plays, and the only preface drawn on is part of that written for *The Shewing Up of Blanco Posnet*, and this part happens to be an insertion into the preface of Shaw's testimony * before a government committee on censorship and theatre licensing.

The selection is, as all selections must be, a matter of personal choice. Still it happened quite happily and without any devices that what seemed a natural selection ended up with the theatre taking the most space and socialism coming next—and these fairly represent Shaw's two chief interests. Shaw's many other interests are well shown by the rest of the material included.

There is no need to point out how extremely readable Shaw is. Yet Shaw is not exercising all his arts just to be

* More accurately non-testimony. The committee refused to hear Shaw's statement and it was subsequently published.

entertaining. Everything Shaw wrote was with the direct intention of converting readers to his point of view. Since Shaw's ideas are not the usual ideas, readers are going to get stirred up—and a very good thing, too. Our brains need to get shaken up every now and again and Shaw is the perfect writer for this job. We may, or we may not, agree with him, but nobody will emerge from a bout of reading Shaw with exactly the same ideas and thoughts with which he started. We may not have been converted, we may even have been battling Shaw mentally—but no matter what we do Shaw will have won his chief point, stirring our intellect so that we think for ourselves. All Shaw ever wanted was to have people thinking and readers will find the process as exhilarating as Shaw meant it to be.

DIARMUID RUSSELL

March, 1952

CONTENTS

BIOGRAPHY

FICTION

MUSIC

THEATRE

CONTENTS

SOCIALISM

MISCELLANEOUS

SELECTED PROSE OF BERNARD SHAW

BIOGRAPHY

PREFACE TO IMMATURITY

THE scene of one of Mr Arnold Bennett's novels is laid in a certain *cul de sac* off the Brompton Road, nearly opposite the West Brompton District Post Office. He calls it Alexandra Grove; but its actual name is Victoria Grove. As he describes it, the houses now contrive a double rent to pay, as the gardens have been fitted up with studios, thus quietly modernizing London by the back-to-back housing so vehemently denounced as a relic of barbarism in Leeds. When I arrived there as an Irish emigrant of 20, this intensification of population had not occurred. The houses were semi-detached villas with plenty of air space round them (you could call it garden). On the other side of the back wall were orchards; for the huge Poor Law Infirmary which now occupies this space, with its tower on the Fulham Road, was not yet built. The land between West Brompton and Fulham and Putney, now closely packed with streets and suburban roads, had still plenty of orchard and market garden to give it a countrified air and to make it possible to live there, as I did for years, without feeling that one must flee to the country or wither in the smoke. All the parallel Groves connected the Fulham Road with King's Road, Chelsea, where Cremorne Gardens, an unlaid ghost from the eighteenth century, was desperately fighting off its final exorcism as a rendezvous of the half world. Hence these now blameless thoroughfares were then reputed Bohemian, whilst Victoria Grove, as a blind alley, remained as respectable as Clapham.

I came to London from Dublin in the spring of 1876, and found my mother and my one surviving sister (I had no brothers) established in No. 13 Victoria Grove, trying to turn their musical accomplishments to account: my mother by teaching, my sister by singing. My father, left in Dublin, spared us a pound a week from his slender resources; and by getting into debt and occasionally extracting ourselves by drawing on a maternal inheritance of £4000 over which my mother had a power of appointment, and which therefore could be realized bit by bit as her three children came of age, we managed to keep going somehow.

Impecuniosity was necessarily chronic in the household. And here let me distinguish between this sort of poverty and that which furnishes an element of romance in the early lives of many famous men. I am almost tempted to say that it is the only sort of poverty that counts, short of the privations that make success impossible. We all know the man whose mother brought him up with nineteen brothers and sisters on an income of eighteen shillings a week earned by her own labor. The road from the log cabin to the White House, from the bench in the factory to the Treasury Bench, from the hovel to the mansion in Park Lane, if not exactly a crowded road, always has a few well fed figures at the end of it to tell us all about it. I always assure these gentlemen that they do not know what poverty and failure is. Beginning with as much as they expected or were accustomed to, they have known nothing but promotion. At each step they have had the income of the society in which they moved, and been able to afford its clothes, its food, its habits, its rents and rates. What more has any prince? If you would know what real poverty is, ask the younger son of a younger son of a younger son. To understand his plight you must start at the top without the income of the top, and curse your stars that you were not lucky enough to start at the bottom.

Our institution of primogeniture may have been a feudal necessity. It kept the baronies together; and the barons and their retainers kept the king and the country supplied with an army, a magistracy, and a network of local governments. But it took no account of the younger sons. These unhappy ones were brought up in the baronial castle. Let us represent the income of the barony by the figure 1000. Both sons and daughters were brought up to know no other mode of life than life at this figure. When the eldest took all, what was there left for the girls' dowries and the boys' allowances? Only the scrapings and leavings of the mother's dowry, and such charity as the new baron might choose (if he could afford it) to bestow on his poor relations. A younger son's figure, especially if he had many brothers, might easily be 20 or less, even to zero. What was the poor wretch to do, knowing no other way of living but the way that cost 1000? Easy to tell him that he must cut his coat according to his cloth. Impossible to do it without being trained to that measure from childhood. Impossible anyhow without dropping every relative and friend in the world, and stepping down, a mistrusted, ridiculous, incongruous stranger, into the social circle of his mother's maid and his brother's butler. Impossible often even to go into the army, where an officer cannot live on his pay unless he is a promoted ranker in a line regiment, and not even then with any ease. There is nothing for it but to live beyond one's income, to spunge, to beg, to take credit at the shops without means, to borrow without the prospect of being able to repay, and to blackmail the baron by presenting him with a choice between paying up and having his brother haled before the criminal courts for swindling. The alternative (to marry the daughter of a rich *parvenu*, American or British) is not always available. Who would be an Honorable on such terms if he could help it?

But think of his son, and of his son's son: the undisguised commoner, for whom, because it costs too much, there is not even the public school and university education of the baron's cadet, and who cannot avail himself of the public elementary and secondary schools because such a step would disclass the man of family! Think of the attempt to go into business with some pitiful little capital! think of the struggle to make the loathed occupation yield a living! think of the son for whom there is nothing but a clerkship in the office of some goodnatured business acquaintance! and bear in mind that the descent implies that every generation is, like the original younger son, brought up to a mode of life more expensive than its income can compass; so that it is condemned to pull the devil by the tail from its adolescence to its grave! My able and flourishing friend A tells me that he knows what poverty is and what drink is: was he not brought up in the Borough by a drunken mother? B, rolling in wealth, tells me that when he was a boy he had meat only twice a year. C, wallowing in fame, calls me a snob, after gleefully narrating his experiences in the kitchen of his father's small shop, and how he was enabled to study country house society by a childish privilege of visiting the servants' hall. How easily I cap these zests to success by the simple statement that my father was second cousin to a baronet, and my mother the daughter of a country gentleman whose rule was, when in difficulties, mortgage. That was my sort of poverty. The Shaws were younger sons from the beginning, as I shall shew when I reveal my full pedigree. Even the baronetcy was founded on the fortunes of a fifth son who came to Dublin and made that city his oyster. Let who will preen himself on his Mother Hubbard's bare cupboard, and play for sympathy as an upstart: I was a downstart and the son of a downstart. But for the accident of a lucrative talent I should today be poorer than Spinoza; for he at least knew how to grind lenses, whereas I could not afford to learn any art. Luckily Nature taught me one.

This social *degringolade* never stops in these islands. It produces a class which deserves a history all to itself. Do not talk of the middle class: the expression is meaningless except when it is used by an economist to denote the man of business who stands in the middle between land and capital on the one hand, and labor on the other, and organizes business for both. I sing my own class: the Shabby Genteel, the Poor Relations, the Gentlemen who are No Gentlemen. If you want to know exactly where I came in, you will get at such facts as that of my many uncles only one, the eldest, contrived to snatch a university education. The rest shifted as best they could without it (rather better than he, mostly). One distinguished himself as a civil servant. He had a gun, and went shooting. One made a fortune in business, and attained to carriage horses; but he lost the fortune in a premature attempt to develop the mineral resources of Ireland without waiting for the new railways produced by the late war. Two emigrated to Tasmania, and, like Mr Micawber, made history there. One was blind and dependent on his brothers: another became blind later, but remained independent and capable. One aunt married the rector of St Bride's (now demolished) in Dublin. The others married quite prosperously, except the eldest, whose conception of the family dignity was so prodigious (the family snobbery being unmitigated in her case by the family sense of humor) that she would have refused an earl because he was not a duke, and so died a very ancient virgin. Dead or alive, there were fourteen of them; and they all, except perhaps the eldest, must have had a very straitened time of it in their childhood after their father died, leaving my grandmother to bring up an unconscionable lot of children on very inadequate means. The baronet came to the rescue by giving her a quaint cottage, with Gothically pointed windows, to live in at Terenure (we called the place Roundtown). It stands in, or rather creeps picturesquely along, its little walled garden near the tram terminus to this day, though my grandfather's brass helmet and sword (he was in the Yeomanry or Militia as a gentleman amateur soldier) no longer hang in the hall. Professionally, he was some sort of combination of solicitor, notary public, and stockbroker that prevailed at that time. I suspect that his orphans did not always get enough to eat; for the younger ones, though invincibly healthy and long lived, were not athletic, and exhibited such a remarkable collection of squints (my father had a stupendous squint) that to this day a squint is so familiar to me that I notice it no more than a pair of spectacles or even a pair of boots.

On the whole, they held their cherished respectability in the world in spite of their lack of opportunity. They owed something, perhaps, to the confidence given them by their sense of family. In Irish fashion they talked of themselves as the Shaws, as who should say the Valois, the Bourbons, the Hohenzollerns, the Hapsburgs, or the Romanoffs; and their world conceded the point to them. I had an enormous contempt for this family snobbery, as I called it, until I was completely reconciled to it by a certain Mr Alexander Mackintosh Shaw, a clansman who, instead of taking his pedigree for granted in the usual Shaw manner, hunted it up, and published 100 copies privately in 1877. Somebody sent me a copy; and my gratification was unbounded when I read the first sentence of the first chapter, which ran: "It is the general tradition, says the Rev. Lachlan Shaw [bless him!], that the Shaws are descended of McDuff, Earl of Fife." I hastily skipped to the chapter about the Irish Shaws to make sure that they were my people; and there they were, baronet and all, duly traced to the third son of that immortalized yet unborn Thane of Fife who, invulnerable to normally accouched swordsmen, laid on and slew Macbeth. It was as good as being descended from Shakespear, whom I had been unconsciously resolved to reincarnate from my cradle.

Years after this discovery I was staying on the shores of Loch Fyne, and being cooked for and housekept by a lady named McFarlane, who treated me with a consideration which I at first supposed to be due to my eminence as an author. But she undeceived me one day by telling me that the McFarlanes and the Shaws were descended from the Thanes of Fife, and that I must not make myself too cheap. She added that the McFarlanes were the elder branch.

My uncles did not trouble about Macduff: it was enough for them that they were Shaws. They had an impression that the Government should give them employment, preferably sinecure, if nothing else could be found; and I suppose this was why my father, after essaying a clerkship or two (one of them in an ironworks), at last had his position recognized by a post in the Four Courts, perhaps because his sister had married the brother of a law baron. Anyhow the office he held was so undeniably superfluous that it actually got abolished before I was born; and my father naturally demanded a pension as compensation for the outrage. Having got it, he promptly sold it, and set up in business as a merchant dealing wholesale (the family dignity made retail business impossible) in flour and its cereal concomitants. He had an office and warehouse in Jervis Street in the city; and he had a mill in Dolphin's Barn on the country side of the canal, at the end of a rather pretty little village street called Rutland Avenue. The mill has now fallen to pieces; but some relics of it are still to be seen from the field with the millpond behind Rutland House at the end of the avenue, with its two stone eagles on the gateposts. My father used to take me sometimes to this mill before breakfast (a long walk for a child); and I used to like playing about it. I do not think it had any other real use; for it never paid its way; and the bulk of my father's business was commissioned: he was a middleman. I should mention that as he knew nothing about the flour business, and as his partner, a Mr Clibborn, having been apprenticed to the cloth trade, knew if possible less, the business, purchased readymade, must have proceeded by its own momentum, and produced its results, such as they were, automatically in spite of its proprietors. They did not work the industry: it worked them. It kept alive, but did not flourish. Early in its history the bankruptcy of one of its customers dealt it such a blow that my father's partner broke down in tears, though he was fortified by a marriage with a woman of property, and could afford to regard his business as only a second string to his bow. My father, albeit ruined, found the magnitude of the catastrophe so irresistibly amusing that he had to retreat hastily from the office to an empty corner of the warehouse, and laugh until he was exhausted. The business struggled on and even supported my father until he died, enabling him to help his family a little after they had solved a desperate financial situation by emigrating to London: or, to put it in another way, by deserting him. His last years were soothed and disembarrassed by this step. He never, as far as I know, made the slightest movement towards a reunion; and none of us ever dreamt of there being any unkindness in the arrangement. In our family we did not bother about conventionalities or sentimentalities.

Our ridiculous poverty was too common in our class, and not conspicuous enough in a poor country, to account wholly for our social detachment from my father's family, a large and (for Ireland) not unprosperous one. In early days the baronet, being a bachelor, was clannishly accessible: he entertained even his second cousins at Bushy Park, and was specially attentive to my mother. I was never at Bushy Park myself except once, on the occasion of his funeral (the Shaw funerals were prodigies of black pomp); but if my father had been able to turn his social opportunities to account, I might have had a quite respectable and normal social training. My mother, socially very eligible, was made welcome in all directions. She sang very well; and the Shaws were naturally a musical family. All the women could "pick out tunes" on the piano, and support them with the chords of the tonic, subdominant, dominant, and tonic again. Even a Neapolitan sixth was not beyond them. My father played the trombone, and could vamp a bass on it to any tune that did not modulate too distractingly. My eldest uncle (Barney: I suppose I was called Bernard after him; but he himself was Uncle William) played the ophicleide, a giant keyed brass bugle, now superseded by the tuba. Berlioz has described it as a chromatic bullock; but my uncle could make it moo and bellow very melodiously. My aunt Emily played the violoncello. Aunt Shah (Charlotte), having beautiful hands, and refinements of person and character to match them, used the harp and tambourine to display them. Modern readers will laugh at the picture of an evening at Bushy Park, with the bachelor Sir Robert and his clan seated round an ottoman on which my uncle Barney stood, solemnly playing Annie Laurie on the ophicleide. The present distinguished inheritor of the title may well find it incredible. But in those days it was the fashion for guests to provide their own music and gentlemen to play wind instruments as a social accomplishment: indeed that age of brass is still remembered and regretted by the few makers of musical instruments whose traditions go back far enough.

And now you will ask why, with such unexceptional antecedents and social openings, was I not respectably

brought up? Unfortunately or fortunately (it all depends on how you look at it) my father had a habit which eventually closed all doors to him, and consequently to my mother, who could not very well be invited without him. If you asked him to dinner or to a party, he was not always quite sober when he arrived; and he was invariably scandalously drunk when he left. Now a convivial drunkard may be exhilarating in convivial company. Even a quarrelsome or boastful drunkard may be found entertaining by people who are not particular. But a miserable drunkard—and my father, in theory a teetotaller, was racked with shame and remorse even in his cups—is unbearable. We were finally dropped socially. After my early childhood I cannot remember ever paying a visit at a relative's house. If my mother and father had dined out, or gone to a party, their children would have been much more astonished than if the house had caught fire.

How my mother rescued herself from this predicament by her musical talent I will tell elsewhere. My father reduced his teetotalism from theory to practice when a mild fit, which felled him on our doorstep one Sunday afternoon, convinced him that he must stop drinking or perish. It had no worse effect; but his reform, though complete and permanent, came too late to save the social situation; and I, cut off from the social drill which puts one at one's ease in private society, grew up frightfully shy and utterly ignorant of social routine. My mother, who had been as carefully brought up as Queen Victoria, was too humane to inflict what she had suffered on any child; besides, I think she imagined that correct behavior is inborn, and that much of what she had been taught was natural to her. Anyhow, she never taught it to us, leaving us wholly to the promptings of our blood's blueness, with results which may be imagined.

In England, if people are reasonably goodnatured and amiable, they are forgiven any sort of eccentricity of behavior if only they are unaffected and all of one piece. If when I came to London I had been merely shy provincially, with incorrect table manners and wrong clothes; if I had

eaten peas with a knife and worn a red tie with an evening suit, kind people would have taken me in hand and drilled me in spite of the infernal and very silly Irish pride which will never admit the need of such tuition. But my difficulties were not of that easily remediable kind. I was sensible enough to inform myself so exactly as to what I should do with a finger bowl when it was placed before me on a dessert plate, that I could give a lead in such matters to other novices who were hopelessly floored by that staggering problem. Clever sympathetic women might divine at a glance that I was mortally shy; but people who could not see through my skin, and who were accustomed to respect, and even veneration, from the young, may well have found me insufferable, aggressive, and impudent. When a young man has achieved nothing and is doing nothing, and when he is obviously so poor that he ought to be doing something very energetically, it is rather trying to find him assuming an authority in conversation, and an equality in terms, which only conspicuous success and distinguished ability could make becoming. Yet this is what is done, quite unconsciously, by young persons who have in them the potentiality of such success and ability. Napoleon could hardly have felt much reverence for his average French generals before the French Revolution, when he was apparently only a by-no-means irreproachable subaltern from Corsica. No such general could possibly have liked him or his manners at that time, though after Austerlitz even first rate generals blushed with gratification at the most condescending word of praise from him. It must have been intolerable in Stratford-on-Avon in 1584 for a local magnate of mature age, knight of the shire and justice of the peace, to be contemplated *de haut en bas* by a dissolute young poacher, and even to amuse him by intellectual inadequacy. I am sure Shakespear was too civil by nature to make any such demonstration consciously; but it is inconceivable that the future author of Lear, who was to die a landowning magnate, and be described in the parish register as a Gent., could have treated Sir Thomas Lucy

quite as an ordinary country gentleman of mature age expects to be treated by an ordinary poacher in his teens.

The truth is that all men are in a false position in society until they have realized their possibilities, and imposed them on their neighbors. They are tormented by a continual shortcoming in themselves; yet they irritate others by a continual overweening. This discord can be resolved by acknowledged success or failure only: everyone is ill at ease until he has found his natural place, whether it be above or below his birthplace. The overrated inheritor of a position for which he has no capacity, and the underrated nobody who is a born genius, are alike shy because they are alike out of place. Besides, this finding of one's place may be made very puzzling by the fact that there is no place in ordinary society for extraordinary individuals. For the worldly wiseman, with common ambitions, the matter is simple enough: money, title, precedence, a seat in parliament, a portfolio in the cabinet, will mean success both to him and his circle. But what about people like St Francis and St Clare? Of what use to them are the means to live the life of the country house and the west end mansion? They have literally no business in them, and must necessarily cut an unhappy and ridiculous figure there. They have to make a society of Franciscans and Poor Clares for themselves before they can work or live socially. It is true that those who are called saints are not saintly all the time and in everything. In eating and drinking, lodging and sleeping, chatting and playing: in short, in everything but working out their destiny as saints, what is good enough for a ploughman is good enough for a poet, a philosopher, a saint, or a higher mathematician. But Hodge's work is not good enough for Newton, nor Falstaff's conversation holy enough for Shelley. Christ adapted himself so amiably to the fashionable life of his time in his leisure that he was reproached for being a gluttonous man and a winebibber, and for frequenting frivolous and worthless sets. But he did not work where he feasted, nor flatter the Pharisees, nor ask the Romans to buy him with a sinecure.

He knew when he was being entertained, well treated, lionized: not an unpleasant adventure for once in a way; and he did not quarrel with the people who were so nice to him. Besides, to sample society is part of a prophet's business: he must sample the governing class above all, because his inborn knowledge of human nature will not explain the anomalies produced in it by Capitalism and Sacerdotalism. But he can never feel at home in it. The born Communist, before he knows what he is, and understands why, is always awkward and unhappy in plutocratic society and in the poorer societies which ape it to the extent of their little means: in short, wherever spiritual values are assessed like Income Tax. In his nonage he is imposed on by the prestige which the propertied classes have conferred on themselves and inculcated in the schools, and by the comfort and refinement and splendor of their equipment in contrast to the squalor of the proletariat. If he has been brought up to regard himself as one of the propertied classes, and has its whole equipment of false standards of worth, lacking nothing but the indispensable pecuniary equipment without which his education is utterly meaningless, his embarrassment and bewilderment are pitiable, and his isolation often complete; for he is left alone between the poor whom he regards as beneath him and the rich whose standards of expenditure are beyond his means. He is ashamed of his poverty, in continual dread of doing the wrong thing, resentfully insubordinate and seditious in a social order which he not only accepts but in which he actually claims a privileged part.

As I write, there is a craze for what is called psychoanalysis, or the cure of diseases by explaining to the patient what is the matter with him: an excellent plan if you happen to know what is the matter with him, especially when the explanation is that there is nothing the matter with him. Thus a bee, desperately trying to reach a flower bed through a window pane, concludes that he is the victim of evil spirits or that he is mad, his end being exhaustion, despair, and death. Yet, if he only knew, there is nothing wrong with him: all he has to do is go out as he came in, through open window or door. Your born Communist begins like the bee on the pane. He worries himself and everybody else until he dies of peevishness, or else is led by some propagandist pamphlet, or by his own intellectual impulses (if he has any), to investigate the economic structure of our society.

Immediately everything becomes clear to him. Property is theft: respectability founded on poverty is blasphemy: marriage founded on property is prostitution: it is easier for a camel to go through the eye of a needle than for a rich man to enter the kingdom of heaven. He now knows where he is, and where this society which has so intimidated him is. He is cured of his *mauvaise honte*, and may now be as much at his ease with the princes of this world as Caesar was with the pirates whom he intended to crucify when, as presently happened, the fortune of war made their captive their conqueror.

If he be not a born Communist, but a predatory combative man, eager to do the other fellow down, and happy in a contrast between his prosperity and the indigence of others, happy also in a robust contempt for cowards and weaklings, the very same discovery of the nature of our Capitalism will nerve him to play the Capitalist game for all it and he are worth. But for the most part men drift with the society into which they are born, and make the best of its accidents without changing its morals or understanding its principles.

As it happens, I was a born Communist and Iconoclast (or Quaker) without knowing it; and I never got on easy terms with plutocracy and snobbery until I took to the study of economics, beginning with Henry George and Karl Marx. In my twentieth year, at Victoria Grove, not being on Caesarian easy terms with the pirates or their retainers, I felt much as Caesar might have done if he had imagined the pirate ship to be the Mayflower, and was still more inclined to mistrust himself than to mistrust the crew, however little respect they might pay him. Not that my opinions were conventional. Read my preface to Back to Methuselah, and you will see me as the complete infidel of that day. I had read much poetry; but only one poet was sacred to me: Shelley. I had read his works piously from end to end, and was in my negations atheist and republican to the backbone. I say in my negations; for I had not reached any affirmative position. When, at a public meeting of the Shelley Society, I scandalized many of the members by saying that I had joined because, like Shelley, I was a Socialist, an atheist, and a vegetarian, I did not know that I could have expressed my position more accurately by simply saying that my conception of God was that insisted on in the first Article of the Church of England, then as now vehemently repudiated by all pious persons, who will have it that God is a substantial gentleman of uncertain and occasionally savage temper, and a spirit only in the sense in which an archbishop is a spirit. I had never thought of reading the Articles of the Church of England; and if I had I should still have used the word atheist as a declaration that I was on the side of Bradlaugh and Foote and others who, as avowed Secularists and Atheists, were being persecuted and imprisoned for my opinions. From my childhood I had been accustomed to regard myself as a sceptic outside institutional religion, and therefore one to whom the conventional religious observances were fair game for scoffing. In this my manners were no better and no worse than those of my class generally. It never occurred to pious ladies and gentlemen to respect a sceptic; and it never occurred to a sceptic to respect a believer: reprobation and ostracism were considered natural and even obligatory on the one side, like derision, even to blasphemy, on the other. In Ireland Protestants and Catholics despised, insulted, and ostracized one another as a matter of course. In England Church people persecuted Dissenters; and Dissenters hated the Church with a bitterness incredible to anyone who has never known what it is to be a little village Dissenter in a Church school. I am not sure that controversial manners are any better now; but they certainly were odious then: you thought it your right and your duty to sneer at the man who was a heretic to your faith if you could not positively injure him in some way. As my manners in this respect were no better than other people's, and my satirical powers much more formidable, I can only hope that my natural civility, which led me to draw back when I found I was hurting people's feelings, may have mitigated my offensiveness in those early days when I still regarded controversy as admitting of no quarter. I lacked both cruelty and will-to-victory.

It may be asked here how I came by my heterodox opinions, seeing that my father's alcoholic neurosis, though it accounts for my not going into society, does not account for my not going to church. My reply, if put in the conventional terms of that day, would be that I was badly brought up because my mother was so well brought up. Her character reacted so strongly against her strict and loveless training that churchgoing was completely dropped in our family before I was ten years old. In my childhood I exercised my literary genius by composing my own prayers. I cannot recall the words of the final form I adopted; but I remember that it was in three movements, like a sonata, and in the best Church of Ireland style. It ended with the Lord's Prayer; and I repeated it every night in bed. I had been warned by my nurse that warm prayers were no use, and that only by kneeling by my bedside in the cold could I hope for a hearing; but I criticised this admonition unfavorably on various grounds, the real one being my preference for warmth and comfort. I did not disparage my nurse's authority in these matters because she was a Roman Catholic: I even tolerated her practice of sprinkling me with holy water occasionally. But her asceticism did not fit the essentially artistic and luxurious character of my devotional exploits. Besides, the penalty did not apply to my prayer; for it was not a petition. I had too much sense to risk my faith by begging for things I knew very well I should not get; so I did not care whether my prayers were answered or not: they were a literary performance for the entertainment and propitiation of the Almighty; and though I should not have dreamt of daring to say that if He did not like them He might lump them (perhaps I was too confident of their quality to apprehend such a rebuff), I certainly behaved as if my comfort were an indispensable condition of the performance taking place at all.

The Lord's Prayer I used once or twice as a protective spell. Thunderstorms are much less common in Ireland than in England; and the first two I remember frightened me horribly. During the second I bethought me of the Lord's Prayer, and steadied myself by repeating it.

I continued these pious habits long after the conventional compulsion to attend church and Sunday School had ceased, and I no longer regarded such customs as having anything to do with an emancipated spirit like mine. But one evening, as I was wandering through the furze bushes on Torca Hill in the dusk, I suddenly asked myself why I went on repeating my prayer every night when, as I put it, I did not believe in it. Being thus brought to book by my intellectual conscience I felt obliged in common honesty to refrain from superstitious practices; and that night, for the first time since I could speak, I did not say my prayers. I missed them so much that I asked myself another question. Why am I so uncomfortable about it? Can this be conscience? But next night the discomfort wore off so much that I hardly noticed it; and the night after I had forgotten all about my prayers as completely as if I had been born a heathen. It is worth adding that this sacrifice of the grace of God, as I had been taught it, to intellectual integrity synchronized with that dawning of moral passion in me which I have described in the first act of Man and Superman. Up to that time I had not experienced the slightest remorse in telling lies whenever they seemed likely to help me out of a difficulty: rather did I revel in the exercise of dramatic invention involved. Even when I was a good boy I was so only theatrically, because, as actors say, I saw myself in the character; and this occurred very seldom, my taste running so strongly on stage villains and stage demons (I painted the whitewashed wall in my bedroom in Dalkey with watercolor frescoes of Mephistopheles) that I must have actually bewitched myself; for, when Nature completed my countenance in 1880 or thereabouts (I had only the tenderest sprouting of hair on my face until I was 24), I found myself equipped with the upgrowing moustaches and eyebrows, and the sarcastic nostrils of the operatic fiend whose airs (by Gounod) I had sung as a child, and whose attitudes I had affected in my boyhood. Later on, as the generations moved past me, I saw the fantasies of actors and painters come to life as living men and women, and began to perceive that imaginative fiction is to life what the sketch is to the picture or the conception to the statue. The world is full of ugly little men who were taken to the theatre to see the Yellow Dwarf or Rumpelstiltskin when they were children; and we shall soon have women in all directions with the features of Movie Vamps because in childhood they were taken to the picture palaces and inspired with an ambition to be serpents of Old Nile.

My father disapproved of the detachment of his family from the conventional observances that were associated with the standing of the Shaw family. But he was in the grip of a humorous sense of anticlimax which I inherited from him and used with much effect when I became a writer of comedy. The more sacred an idea or a situation was by convention, the more irresistible was it to him as the jumping-off place for a plunge into laughter. Thus, when I scoffed at the Bible he would instantly and quite sincerely rebuke me, telling me, with what little sternness was in his nature, that I should not speak so; that no educated man would make such a display of ignorance; that the Bible was universally recognized as a literary and historical masterpiece; and as much more to the same effect as he could muster. But when he had reached the point of feeling really impressive, a convulsion of internal chuckling would wrinkle up his eyes; and (I knowing all the time quite well what was coming) would cap his eulogy by assuring me, with an air of perfect fairness, that even the worst enemy of religion could say no worse of the Bible than that it was the damndest parcel of lies ever written. He would then rub his eyes and chuckle for quite a long time. It became an unacknowledged game between us that I should provoke him to exhibitions of this kind.

With such a father my condition was clearly hopeless as far as the conventions of religion were concerned. In essential matters his influence was as good as his culture permitted. One of my very earliest recollections is reading The Pilgrim's Progress to him, and being corrected by him for saying grievious instead of grievous. I never saw him, as far as I can remember, reading anything but the newspaper; but he had read Sir Walter Scott and other popular classics; and he always encouraged me to do the same, and to frequent the National Gallery, and to go to the theatre and the opera when I could afford it. His anticlimaxes depended for their effect on our sense of the sacredness he was reacting against: there would have been no fun whatever in saying that the Adventures of Munchausen (known to us as Baron Mun Chawzon) were a parcel of lies. If my mother's pastors and masters had had a little of his humor, she would not simply have dropped the subject of religion with her children in silent but implacable dislike of what had helped to make her childhood miserable, and resolved that it should not do the same to them. The vacuum she left by this policy had, I think, serious disadvantages for my two sisters (the younger of whom died just before I came to London); but in my case it only made a clear space for positive beliefs later on.

My mother, I may say here, had no comedic impulses, and never uttered an epigram in her life: all my comedy is a Shavian inheritance. She had plenty of imagination, and really lived in it and on it. Her brother, my uncle Walter, who stayed with us from time to time in the intervals of his trips across the Atlantic as a surgeon on the Inman Liners, had an extraordinary command of picturesque language, partly derived by memory from the Bible and Prayer Book, and partly natural. The conversation of the navigating staffs and pursers of our ocean services was at that time (whatever it may be today) extremely Rabelaisian and profane. Falstaff himself could not have held his own with my uncle in obscene anecdotes, unprintable limericks, and fantastic profanity; and it mattered nothing to him whether his audience consisted of his messmates on board ship or his schoolboy nephew: he performed before each with equal gusto. To do him justice, he was always an artist in his obscenity and blasphemy, and therefore never sank to the level of incontinent blackguardism. His efforts were controlled, deliberate, fastidiously chosen and worded. But they were all the more effective in destroying all my inculcated childish reverence for the verbiage of religion, for its legends and personifications and parables. In view of my subsequent work in the world it seems providential that I was driven to the essentials of religion by the reduction of every factitious or fictitious element in it to the most irreverent absurdity.

It would be the greatest mistake to conclude that this shocking state of affairs was bad for my soul. In so far as the process of destroying reverence for the inessential trappings of religion was indecent, it was deplorable; and I wish my first steps to grace had been lighted by my uncle's wit and style without his obscenity. My father's comedy was entirely decent. But that the process was necessary to my salvation I have no doubt whatever. A popular book in my youth was Mark Twain's New Pilgrim's Progress, which horrified the thoughtlessly pious by making fun of what they called sacred things. Yet Mark Twain was really a religious force in the world: his Yankee at the Court of King Arthur was his nearest approach to genuine blasphemy; and that came from want of culture, not from perversity of soul. His training as a Mississippi pilot must have been, as to religion, very like my training as the nephew of a Transatlantic surgeon.

Later on, I discovered that in the Ages of Faith the sport of making fun of the accessories and legends of religion was organized and practised by the Church to such an extent that it was almost part of its ritual. The people were instructed in spiritual history and hagiology by stage plays full of comic passages which might have been written by my uncle. For instance, my uncle taught me an elaborate conversation supposed to have passed between Daniel in the lion's den and King Darius, in which each strove to outdo the other in Rabelaisian repartee. The medieval playwright, more daring than my uncle, put on the stage comical conversations between Cain and his Creator, in which Cain's language was no more respectful than that of Fielding's Squire Western, and similarly indecent. In all Catholic countries there is a hagiology that is fit for publication and a hagiology that is not. In the Middle Ages they may have condemned a story as lewd or blasphemous; but it did not occur to them that God or His Church could be shaken by it. No man with any faith worth respecting in any religion worth holding ever dreams that it can be shaken by a joke, least of all by an obscene joke. It is Messieurs Formalist and Hypocrisy who feel that religion is crumbling when the forms are not observed. The truth is, humor is one of the great purifiers of religion, even when it is itself anything but pure.

The institution of the family, which is the centre of reverence for carefully brought-up children, was just the opposite for me. In a large family there are always a few skeletons in the cupboard; and in my father's clan there were many uncles and aunts and cousins, consequently many cupboards, consequently some skeletons. Our own particular skeleton was my father's drunkenness. It was combined with a harmlessness and humaneness which made him the least formidable of men; so that it was impossible for him to impress his children in the manner that makes awe and dread almost an instinct with some children. It is much to his credit that he was incapable of deliberately practising any such impressiveness, drunk or sober; but unfortunately the drunkenness was so humiliating that it would have been unendurable if we had not taken refuge in laughter. It had to be either a family tragedy or a family joke; and it was on the whole a healthy instinct that decided us to get what ribald fun was possible out of it, which, however, was very little indeed. If Noah had made a habit of drinking, his sons would soon have worn out the pious solicitude which they displayed on the occasion of his single lapse from sobriety. A boy who has seen "the governor," with an imperfectly wrapped-up goose under one arm and a ham in the same condition under the other (both purchased under heaven knows what delusion of festivity), butting at the garden wall in the belief that he was pushing open the gate, and transforming his tall hat to a concertina in the process, and who, instead of being overwhelmed with shame and anxiety at the spectacle, has been so disabled by merriment (uproariously shared by the maternal uncle) that he has hardly been able to rush to the rescue of the hat and pilot its wearer to safety, is clearly not a boy who will make tragedies of trifles instead of making trifles of tragedies. If you cannot get rid of the family skeleton, you may as well make it dance.

Then there was my Uncle William, a most amiable man, with great natural dignity. In early manhood he was not only an inveterate smoker, but so insistent a toper that a man who made a bet that he would produce Barney Shaw sober, and knocked him up at six in the morning with that object, lost his bet. But this might have happened to any common drunkard. What gave the peculiar Shaw finish and humor to the case was that my uncle suddenly and instantly gave up smoking and drinking at one blow, and devoted himself to his accomplishment of playing the ophicleide. In this harmless and gentle pursuit he continued, a blameless old bachelor, for many years, and then, to the amazement of Dublin, renounced the ophicleide and all its works, and married a lady of distinguished social position and great piety. She declined, naturally, to have anything to do with us; and, as far as I know, treated the rest of the family in the same way. Anyhow, I never saw her, and only saw my uncle furtively by the roadside after his marriage, when he would make hopeless attempts to save me, in the pious sense of the word, not perhaps without some secret Shavian enjoyment of the irreverent pleasantries with which I scattered my path to perdition. He was reputed to sit with a Bible on his knees, and an opera glass to his eyes, watching the ladies' bathing place in Dalkey; and my sister, who was a swimmer, confirmed this gossip as far as the opera glass was concerned.

But this was only the prelude to a very singular conclusion, or rather catastrophe. The fantastic imagery of the Bible so gained on my uncle that he took off his boots, explaining that he expected to be taken up to heaven at any moment like Elijah, and that he felt that his boots would impede his celestial flight. He then went a step further, and hung his room with all the white fabrics he could lay hands on, alleging that he was the Holy Ghost. At last he became silent, and remained so to the end. His wife, warned that his harmless fancies might change into dangerous ones, had him removed to an asylum in the north of Dublin. My father thought that a musical appeal might prevail with him, and went in search of the ophicleide. But it was nowhere to be found. He took a flute to the asylum instead; for every Shaw of that generation seemed able to play any wind instrument at sight. My uncle, still obstinately mute, contemplated the flute for a while, and then played Home Sweet Home on it. My father had to be content with this small success, as nothing more could be got out of his brother. A day or two later my uncle, impatient for heaven, resolved to expedite his arrival there. Every possible weapon had been carefully removed from his reach; but his custodians reckoned without the Shavian originality. They had left him somehow within reach of a carpet bag. He put his head into it, and in a strenuous effort to decapitate or strangle himself by closing it on his neck, perished of heart failure. I should be glad to believe that, like Elijah, he got the heavenly reward he sought; for he was a fine upstanding man and a gentle creature, nobody's enemy but his own, as the saying is.

Still, what sort of gravity could a boy maintain with a family history of this kind? However, I must not imply that all my uncles were like that. They were mostly respectable normal people. I can recall only two other exceptions to this rule. One of my uncles married an elegant and brilliant lady, from whom he separated after scandalizing the family by beating her; but as Job himself would have beaten her when she lost her very unstable temper, nobody who knew her intimately ever blamed him. Though the neurosis which produced my father's joyless craving for alcohol had the same effect, with the same curious recalcitrance and final impermanence, in one or two other cases, and was perhaps connected with occasional family paroxysms of Evangelical piety, and some share of my father's comedic love of anticlimax, yet on the whole our collection of skeletons was not exceptionally large. But as, compared with similar English families, we had a power of derisive dramatization that made the bones of the Shavian skeletons rattle more loudly; and as I possessed this power in an abnormal degree, and frequently entertained my friends with stories of my uncles (so effectively, by the way, that nobody ever believed them), the family, far from being a school of reverence for me, was rather a mine from which I could dig highly amusing material without the trouble of inventing a single incident. What idle fancy of mine could have improved on the hard facts of the Life and Death of Uncle William?

Thus the immediate result of my family training in my Victoria Grove days was that I presented myself to the unprepared stranger as a most irreverent young man. My Mephistophelean moustache and eyebrows had not yet grown; and there was nothing in my aspect to break the shock of my diabolical opinions. Later on, when I had made a public reputation as an iconoclast, people who met me in private were surprised at my mildness and sociability. But I had no public reputation then: consequently expectation in my regard was normal. And I was not at all reticent of the diabolical opinions. I felt them to be advantageous, just as I felt that I was in a superior position as an Irishman, without a shadow of any justification for that patriotic arrogance. As it never occurred to me to conceal my opinions any more than my nationality, and as I had, besides, an unpleasant trick of contradicting everyone from whom I thought I could learn anything in order to draw him out and enable me to pick his brains, I think I must have impressed many amiable persons as an extremely disagreeable and undesirable young man.

And yet I was painfully shy, and was simply afraid to accept invitations, with the result that I very soon ceased to get any. I was told that if I wanted to get on, I must not flatly refuse invitations—actually dinner invitations—which were meant to help me, and the refusal of which was nothing short of a social outrage. But I knew very well that introductions could be of no use to one who had no profession and could do nothing except what any clerk could do. I knew I was useless, worthless, penniless, and that until I had qualified myself to do something, and proved it by doing it, all this business of calling on people who might perhaps do something for me, and dining out without money to pay for a cab, was silly. Fortunately for me, the realism that made me face my own position so ruthlessly also kept before me the fact that if I borrowed money I could not pay it back, and therefore might more candidly beg or steal it. I knew quite well that if I borrowed £5 from a friend and could not pay it back, I was selling a friend for £5, and that this was a foolish bargain. So I did not borrow, and therefore did not lose my friends; though some of them, who could have had no illusions about my financial capacity, hinted that they were quite willing, and indeed anxious, to call a gift a loan.

I feel bound to confess here, in reference to my neglect of the few invitations and offers of introductions that reached me, that behind the conviction that they could lead to nothing that I wanted lay the unspoken fear that they might lead to something I did not want: that is, commercial employment. I had had enough of that. No doubt it would have been a great relief to my mother if I could have earned something. No doubt I could have earned something if I had really meant to. No doubt if my father had died, and my mother been struck dumb and blind, I should have had to go back to the office desk (the doom of shabby gentility) and give up all hope of acquiring a profession; for even the literary profession, though it exacts no academic course and costly equipment, does exact all one's time and the best of one's brains. As it was, I dodged every opening instinctively. With an excellent testimonial and an unexceptionable character, I was an incorrigible Unemployable. I kept up pretences (to myself as much as to others) for some time. I answered advertisements, not too offensively. I actually took a berth in a telephone Company (then a sensational novelty) and had some difficulty in extricating myself from the Company which bought it up. I can remember an interview with a bank manager in Onslow Gardens (procured for me, to my dismay, by an officious friend with whom I *had* dined) with a view to employment in the bank. I entertained him so brilliantly (if I may use an adverb with which in later years I was much plagued by friendly critics) that we parted on the best of terms, he declaring that, though I certainly ought to get something to do without the least difficulty, he did not feel that a bank clerkship was the right job for me.

I have said that I had an excellent testimonial as an employee in a business office. I had, as a matter of fact, spent four and a half years at a desk in Dublin before I emigrated. I have already given the economic reasons why boys of my class have to do without university education, just as they have to do without horses and guns. And yet I cannot deny that clergymen no better off than my father do manage somehow to start their sons in life with a university degree. They regard it as an absolute necessity, and therefore do not consider whether they can afford it or not. They must afford it. The need for it may be an illusion; but we are subject to such illusions: one man cannot live without a grand piano, another without a boat, another without a butler, another with out a horse, and so on through a whole range of psychological imperatives. I have known women set up orphanages because they could not do without children to beat. Place their necessities in any rational order, and you will find that many of them cannot afford these things. They get out of the difficulty by simply rearranging your rational order as a psychological order, and putting their fancies at the top and their needs at the bottom. It is no use telling a woman that she needs good food and plenty of it much more vitally than she needs a seven guinea hat, a bottle of hair dye, a supply of face powder and rouge, a puff and a haresfoot. She will live on tea and rashers for months rather than forego them. And men are just as unreasonable. To say that my father could not afford to give me a university education is like saying that he could not afford to drink, or that I could not afford to become an author. Both statements are true; but he drank and I became an author all the same. I must therefore explain, just as seriously as if my father had had fifty thousand a year, why I did not graduate at Trinity College, Dublin.

I cannot learn anything that does not interest me. My memory is not indiscriminate: it rejects and selects; and its selections are not academic. I have no competitive instinct; nor do I crave for prizes and distinctions: consequently I have no interest in competitive examinations: if I won, the disappointment of my competitors would distress me instead of gratifying me: if I lost, my self-esteem would suffer. Besides, I have far too great a sense of my own importance to feel that it could be influenced by a degree or a gold medal or what not. There is only one sort of school that could have qualified me for academic success; and that is the sort in which the teachers take care that the pupils shall be either memorizing their lessons continuously, with all the desperate strenuousness that terror can inspire, or else crying with severe physical pain. I was never in a school where the teachers cared enough about me, or about their ostensible profession, or had enough conviction and cruelty, to take any such trouble; so I learnt nothing at school, not even what I could and would have learned if any attempt had been made to interest me. I congratulate myself on this; for I am firmly persuaded that every unnatural activity of the brain is as mischievous as any unnatural activity of the body, and that pressing people to learn things they do not want to know is as unwholesome and disastrous as feeding them on sawdust. Civilization is always wrecked by giving the governing classes what is called secondary education, which produces invincible ignorance and intellectual and moral imbecility as a result of unnatural abuse of the apprehensive faculty. No child would ever learn to walk or dress itself if its hands and feet were kept in irons and allowed to move only when and as its guardians pulled and pushed them.

I somehow knew this when I began, as a boy entering on my teens, to think about such things. I remember saying, in some discussion that arose on the subject of my education, that T.C.D. men were all alike (by which I meant all wrong), and that I did not want to go through college. I was entirely untouched by university idealism. When it reached me later on, I recognized how ignorantly I had spoken in my boyhood; but when I went still further and learnt that this idealism is never realized in our schools and universities, and operates only as a mask and a decoy for our system of impressing and enslaving children and stultifying adults, I concluded that my ignorance had been inspired, and had served me very well. I have not since changed my mind.

However that may be, I decided, at thirteen or thereabouts, that for the moment I must go into business and earn some money and begin to be a grown-up man. There was at that time, on one of the quays in Dublin, a firm of cloth merchants, by name Scott, Spain, and Rooney. A friend of ours knew Scott, and asked him to give me a start in life with some employment. I called on this gentleman by appointment. I had the vaguest notion of what would happen: all I knew was that I was "going into an office." I thought I should have preferred to interview Spain, as the name was more romantic. Scott turned out to be a smart handsome man, with moustachios; and I suppose a boy more or less in his warehouse did not matter to him when there was a friend to be obliged: at all events, he said only a few perfunctory things and was settling my employment, when, as my stars would have it, Rooney appeared. Mr Rooney was much older, not at all smart, but long, lean, grave and respectable.

The last time I saw the late Sir George Alexander (the

actor) he described to me his own boyhood, spent in a cloth warehouse in Cheapside, where they loaded him with bales, and praised him highly for his excellent conduct, even rewarding him after some years to the extent of sixteen shillings a week. Rooney saved me from the bales. He talked to me a little, and then said quite decisively that I was too young, and that the work was not suitable to me. He evidently considered that my introducer, my parents, and his young partner, had been inconsiderate; and I presently descended the stairs, reprieved and unemployed. As Mr Rooney was certainly fifty then at least, he must be a centenarian if, as I hope, he still lives. If he does, I offer him the assurance that I have not forgotten his sympathy.

A year later, or thereabouts, my uncle Frederick, an important official in the Valuation Office, whom no land agent or family solicitor in Dublin could afford to disoblige, asked a leading and terribly respectable firm of land agents, carrying on business at 15 Molesworth Street, to find a berth for me. They did so; and I became their office boy (junior clerk I called myself) at eighteen shillings a month. It was a very good opening for anyone with a future as a land agent, which in Ireland at that time was a business of professional rank. It was utterly thrown away on me. However, as the office was overstaffed with gentlemen apprentices, who had paid large fees for the privilege of singing operatic selections with me when the principals were out, there was nothing to complain of socially, even for a Shaw; and the atmosphere was as uncommercial as that of an office can be. Thus I learnt business habits without being infected with the business spirit. By the time I had attained to thirty shillings a month, the most active and responsible official in the office, the cashier, vanished; and as we were private bankers to some extent, our clients drawing cheques on us, and so forth, someone had to take his place without an hour's delay. An elder substitute grumbled at the strange job, and, though an able man in his way, could not make his cash balance. It became necessary, after a day or two of confusion, to try the office boy as a stopgap whilst the advertisements for a new cashier of appropriate age and responsibility were going forward. Immediately the machine worked again quite smoothly. I, who never knew how much money I had of my own (except when the figure was zero), proved a model of accuracy as to the money of others. I acquired my predecessor's very neat handwriting, my own being too sloped and straggly for the cash book. The efforts to fill my important place more worthily slackened. I bought a tailed coat, and was chaffed about it by the apprentices. My salary was raised to £48 a year, which was as much as I expected at sixteen and much less than the firm would have had to pay to a competent adult: in short, I made good in spite of myself, and found, to my dismay, that Business, instead of expelling me as the worthless impostor I was, was fastening upon me with no intention of letting me go.

Behold me therefore in my twentieth year, with a business training, in an occupation which I detested as cordially as any sane person lets himself detest anything he cannot escape from. In March 1876 I broke loose. I gave a month's notice. My employers naturally thought I was discontented with my salary (£84, I think, by that time), and explained to me quietly that they hoped to make my position more eligible. My only fear was that they should make it so eligible that all excuse for throwing it up would be taken from me. I thanked them and said I was resolved to go; and I had, of course, no reason in the world to give them for my resolution. They were a little hurt, and explained to my uncle that they had done their best, but that I seemed to have made up my mind. I had. After enjoying for a few days the luxury of not having to go to the office, and being, if not my own master, at least not anyone else's slave, I packed a carpet bag; boarded the North Wall boat; and left the train next morning at Euston, where, on hearing a porter cry, in an accent quite strange to me (I had hardly ever heard an h dropped before) "Ensm' faw weel?" which I rightly interpreted as "Hansom or four wheel?" I was afraid to say hansom, because I had never been in one and was not sure that I should know how to get in. So I solemnly drove in a growler through streets whose names Dickens had made familiar to me, London being at its spring best, which is its very best, to Victoria Grove, where the driver accepted four shillings as a reasonable fare for the journey.

I did not set foot in Ireland again until 1905, and not then on my own initiative. I went back to please my wife; and a curious reluctance to retrace my steps made me land in the south and enter Dublin through the backdoor from Meath rather than return as I came, through the front door on the sea. In 1876 I had had enough of Dublin. James Joyce in his Ulysses has described, with a fidelity so ruthless that the book is hardly bearable, the life that Dublin offers to its young men, or, if you prefer to put it the other way, that its young men offer to Dublin. No doubt it is much like the life of young men everywhere in modern urban civilization. A certain flippant futile derision and belittlement that confuses the noble and serious with the base and ludicrous seems to me peculiar to Dublin; but I suppose that is because my only personal experience of that phase of youth was a Dublin experience; for when I left my native city I left that phase behind me, and associated no more with men of my age until, after about eight years of solitude in this respect, I was drawn into the Socialist revival of the early eighties, among Englishmen intensely serious and burning with indignation at very real and very fundamental evils that affected all the world; so that the reaction against them bound the finer spirits of all the nations together instead of making them cherish hatred of one another as a national virtue. Thus, when I left Dublin I left (a few private friendships apart) no society that did not disgust me. To this day my sentimental regard for Ireland does not include the capital. I am not enamored of failure, of poverty, of obscurity, and of the ostracism and contempt which these imply; and these were all that Dublin offered to the enormity of my unconscious ambition. The cities a man likes are the cities he has conquered. Napoleon did not turn from Paris to sentimentalize over Ajaccio, nor Catherine from St Petersburg to Stettin as the centre of her universe.

On this question of ambition let me say a word. In the ordinary connotation of the word I am the least ambitious of men. I have said, and I confirm it here, that I am so poor a hand at pushing and struggling, and so little interested in their rewards, that I have risen by sheer gravitation, too industrious by acquired habit to stop working (I work as my father drank), and too lazy and timid by nature to lay hold of half the opportunities or a tenth of the money that a conventionally ambitious man would have grasped strenuously. I never thought of myself as destined to become what is called a great man: indeed I was diffident to the most distressing degree; and I was ridiculously credulous as to the claims of others to superior knowledge and authority. But one day in the office I had a shock. One of the apprentices, by name C. J. Smyth, older than I and more a man of the world, remarked that every young chap thought he was going to be a great man. On a really modest youth this commonplace would have had no effect. It gave me so perceptible a jar that I suddenly became aware that I had never thought I was to be a great man simply because I had always taken it as a matter of course. The incident passed without leaving any preoccupation with it to hamper me; and I remained as diffident as ever because I was still as incompetent as ever. But I doubt whether I ever recovered my former complete innocence of subconscious intention to devote myself to the class of work that only a few men excel in, and to accept the responsibilities that attach to its dignity.

Now this bore directly on my abandonment of Dublin, for which many young Irishmen of today find it impossible to forgive me. My business in life could not be transacted in Dublin out of an experience confined to Ireland. I had to go to London just as my father had to go to the Corn Exchange. London was the literary centre for the English language, and for such artistic culture as the realm of the English language (in which I proposed to be king) could afford. There was no Gaelic League in those days, nor any sense that Ireland had in herself the seed of culture. Every Irishman who felt that his business in life was on the higher planes of the cultural professions felt that he must have a metropolitan domicile and an international culture: that is, he felt that his first business was to get out of Ireland. I had the same feeling. For London as London, or England as England, I cared nothing. If my subject had been science or music I should have made for Berlin or Leipsic. If painting, I should have made for Paris: indeed many of the Irish writers who have made a name in literature escaped to Paris with the intention of becoming painters. For theology I should have gone to Rome, and for Protestant philosophy to Weimar. But as the English language was my weapon, there was nothing for it but London. In 1914 the Germans, resenting my description of their Imperial political situation as Potsdamnation, denounced me as a fatherlandless fellow. They were quite right. I was no more offended than if they had called me unparochial. They had never reproached me for making pilgrimages to Bayreuth when I could as easily have made them to the Hill of Tara. If you want to make me homesick, remind me of the Thuringian Fichtelgebirge, of the broad fields and delicate airs of France, of the Gorges of the Tarn, of the Passes of the Tyrol, of the North African desert, of the Golden Horn, of the Swedish lakes, or even of the Norwegian fiords where I have never been except in imagination, and you may stir that craving in me as easily—probably more easily—as in any exiled native of these places. It was not until I went back to Ireland as a tourist that I perceived that the charm of my country was quite independent of the accident of my having been born in it, and that it could fascinate a Spaniard or an Englishman more powerfully than an Irishman, in whose feeling for it there must always be a strange anguish, because it is the country where he has been unhappy and where vulgarity is vulgar to him. And so I am a tolerably good European in the Nietzschean sense, but a very bad Irishman in the Sinn Fein or Chosen People sense.

For the first couple of years of my life in London I did nothing decisive. I acted as ghost for a musician who had accepted a berth as musical critic; and as such ghosts must not appear, and I was therefore cut off from the paper and could not correct proofs, my criticisms, mostly very ruthless ones, appeared with such misprints, such mutilations and venal interpolations by other hands, so inextricably mixed up with other criticisms most offensive to my artistic sense, that I have ever since hidden this activity of mine as a guilty secret, lest someone should dig out these old notices and imagine that I was responsible for everything in them and with them. Even now I can hardly bring myself to reveal that the name of the paper was The Hornet, and that it had passed then into the hands of a certain Captain Donald Shaw, who was not related to me, and whom I never met. It died on his hands, and partly, perhaps, at mine.

Then my cousin, Mrs Cashel Hoey, a woman of letters, daughter of the aunt who played the tambourine with her beautiful hands, gave me an introduction to Arnold White, then secretary to the Edison Telephone Company. He found a berth for me in the Way Leave Department of that shortlived company; and I presently found myself studying the topography of the east end of London, and trying to persuade all sorts of people to allow the Company to put insulators and poles and derricks and the like on their roofs to carry the telephone lines. I liked the exploration involved; but my shyness made the business of calling on strangers frightfully uncongenial; and my sensitiveness, which was extreme, in spite of the brazen fortitude which I simulated, made the impatient rebuffs I had to endure occasionally, especially from much worried women who mistook me for an advertisement canvasser, ridiculously painful to me. But I escaped these trials presently; for I soon had to take charge of the department, and organize the work of more thick-skinned adventurers instead of doing it myself. Further particulars will be found in the preface to my second novel, The Irrational Knot. The Edison Telephone Company was presently swallowed up by the Bell Telephone Company; and I seized the opportunity to recover my destitute freedom by refusing to apply for the employment promised by the amalgamation to the disbanded staff. This was the end of my career as a commercial employee. I soon dropped even the pretence of seeking any renewal of it. Except for a day or two in 1881, when I earned a few pounds by counting the votes at an election in Leyton, I was an Unemployable, an ablebodied pauper in fact if not in law, until the year 1885, when for the first time I earned enough money directly by my pen to pay my way. My income for that year amounted to £112; and from that time until the war of 1914–18 momentarily threatened us all with bankruptcy, I had no pecuniary anxieties except those produced by the possession of money, not by the lack of it. My penury phase was over.

The telephone episode occurred in 1879; and in that year I had done what every literary adventurer did in those days, and many do still. I had written a novel. My office training had left me with a habit of doing something regularly every day as a fundamental condition of industry as distinguished from idleness. I knew I was making no headway unless I was doing this, and that I should never produce a book in any other fashion. I bought supplies of white paper, demy size, by sixpennorths at a time; folded it in quarto; and condemned myself to fill five pages of it a day, rain or shine, dull or inspired. I had so much of the schoolboy and the clerk still in me that if my five pages ended in the middle of a sentence I did not finish it until next day. On the other hand, if I missed a day, I made up for it by doing a double task on the morrow. On this plan I produced five novels in five years. It was my professional apprenticeship, doggedly suffered with all the diffidence and dissatisfaction of a learner with a very critical master, myself to wit, whom there was no pleasing and no evading, and persevered in to save my self-respect in a condition of impecuniosity which, for two acute moments (I still recall them with a wry face), added broken boots and carefully hidden raggedness to cuffs whose edges were trimmed by the scissors, and a tall hat so limp with age that I had to wear it back-to-front to enable me to take it off without doubling up the brim.

I had no success as a novelist. I sent the five novels to all the publishers in London and some in America. None would venture on them. Fifty or sixty refusals without a single acceptance forced me into a fierce self-sufficiency. I became undiscourageable, acquiring a superhuman insensitiveness to praise or blame which has been useful to me at times since, though at other times it has retarded my business affairs by making me indifferent to the publication and performances of my works, and even impatient of them as an unwelcome interruption to the labor of writing their successors. Instead of seizing every opportunity of bringing them before the public, I have often, on plausible but really trivial pretexts, put off proposals which I should have embraced with all the normal author's keenness for publicity.

Thus, after five years of novel writing, I was a complete professional failure. The more I wrote and the better I wrote the less I pleased the publishers. This first novel of mine, though rejected, at least elicited some expressions of willingness to read any future attempts. Blackwood actually accepted and then revoked. Sir George Macmillan, then a junior, not only sent me a longish and evidently considered report by the firm's reader, John (afterwards Lord) Morley, but suggested to him that I might be of some use to him in his capacity as editor of the Pall Mall Gazette.

All such responses ceased with my second novel; and I had no means of knowing, and was too young and inexperienced to guess, that what was the matter was not any lack of literary competence on my part, but the antagonism raised by my hostility to respectable Victorian thought and society. I was left without a ray of hope; yet I did not stop writing novels until, having planned my fifth effort on a colossal scale, I found at the end of what were to me only the first two sections of it, that I had no more to say and had better wait until I had educated myself much farther. And when, after an interval of critical journalism, I resumed the writing of fiction, I did so as a playwright and not as a novelist.

Four of the five novels of my nonage, as I call them, at last got into print as described in the preface already cited. But the first of them never got published at all. Opening the old parcel, as I do now (it is like opening a grave that has been closed for forty-two years), I find a pile of cahiers of twenty pages each, and realize with some dismay that I am face-to-face with a novel containing nearly 200,000 words. The title is Immaturity. The handwriting, which slopes slightly backwards, has all the regularity and legibility of my old cash book. Unfortunately, the mice have eaten so much of two of the cahiers that the ends of the lines are missing. This is awkward; for I have just told myself that I must make no attempt to correct the work of the apprentice with the hand of the master; that such as it is it must remain; that I am too old now to touch it without producing new incongruities more disagreeable than any that are possible between the style of 1879 and the taste of 1921. Yet, if the mice have eaten much, I must play the sedulous ape, like Stevenson, and imitate my own youthful manner like any literary forger.

It may be asked why I should print the thing at all: why not let ill alone? I am quite disposed to do so; but somehow one must not do such things. If Beethoven had destroyed his septet for wind instruments when he had advanced to the ninth symphony and the Mass in D, many people who delight in the septet and cannot make head or tail of symphony or Mass would suffer a wanton deprivation; and though my early style now makes me laugh at its pedantry, yet I have a great respect for the priggish conscientiousness of my first efforts. They prove too that, like Goethe, I knew all along, and have added more to my power of handling, illustrating, and addressing my material than to the material itself.

Anyhow, I have little doubt that Immaturity will be at least readable by the easygoing bookbuyers who will devour anything in the shape of a novel, however ridiculously out of fashion it may be. I know that some readers will like it much better than my later works. There must be a certain quality of youth in it which I could not now recapture, and which may even have charm as well as weakness and absurdity. Having re-read the other four novels for publication and republication at one time or another, I can guarantee the propriety of my early style. It was the last thing in correctness. I have never aimed at style in my life: style is a sort of melody that comes into my sentences by itself. If a writer says what he has to say as accurately and effectively as he can, his style will take care of itself, if he has a style. But I did set up one condition in my early days. I resolved that I would write nothing that should not be intelligible to a foreigner with a dictionary, like the French of Voltaire; and I therefore avoided idiom. (Later on I came to seek idiom as being the most highly vitalized form of language). Consequently I do not expect to find the English of Immaturity idiomatic. Also, there will be nothing of the voice of the public speaker in it: the voice that rings through so much of my later work. Not until Immaturity was finished, late in 1879, did I for the first time rise to my feet in a little debating club called The Zetetical Society, to make, in a condition of heartbreaking nervousness, my first assault on an audience.

Perhaps I had better add a word as to the characters in the book. I do so with some reluctance, because it is misleading to mention even the smallest circumstance connecting a fictitious person with a living one. If Shakespear had happened to mention that he made the Prince of Denmark carry a set of tablets and make notes in them because he had seen Sir Walter Raleigh doing so, it would by this time be an invincible tradition in English literature that Raleigh was the original of Hamlet. We should have writers following up the clue, as they would call it, to the conclusion that Raleigh was the real author of the play. One day, as I was sitting in the reading room of the British Museum, beginning my fifth and last novel, An Unsocial Socialist, I saw a young lady with an attractive and arresting expression, bold, vivid, and very clever, working at one of the desks. On that glimpse of a face I instantly conceived the character and wrote the description of Agatha Wylie. I have never exchanged a word with that lady; never made her acquaintance; saw her again under the same circumstances but very few times; yet if I mention her name, which became well known in literature (she too was writing a novel then, probably, and perhaps had the hero suggested to her by my profile), she will be set down as Agatha Wylie to her dying day, with heaven knows how much more scandalous invention added to account for my supposed intimate knowledge of her character. Before and since, I have used living models as freely as a painter does, and in much the same way: that is, I have sometimes made a fairly faithful portrait founded on intimate personal intercourse, and sometimes, as in Agatha's case, developed what a passing glance suggested to my imagination. In the latter case it has happened sometimes that the incidents I have invented on the spur of such a glance have hit the facts so nearly that I have found myself accused of unpardonable violations of personal privacy. I hardly expect to be believed when I say that I once invented a servant for one of my models and found afterwards that he actually had just such a servant. Between the two extremes of actual portraiture and pure fancy work suggested by a glance or an anecdote, I have copied nature with many degrees of fidelity, combining studies from life in the same book or play with those types and composites and traditional figures of the novel and the stage which are called pure fictions. Many of the characters in this first novel of mine owed something to persons I had met, including members of my family (not to mention myself); but none of them are portraits; and with one exception the models are unknown to the public. That exception was Cecil Lawson, whose early death lost us the only landscape painter who ever reminded me of the spacious and fascinating experiments of Rubens in that branch of painting. When I lived at Victoria Grove the Lawsons:

father, mother, Malcolm, and two sisters, lived in one of the handsome old houses in Cheyne Walk, Chelsea. Cecil and another brother, being married, boarded out. Malcolm was a musician; and the sisters sang. One, a soprano, dark, quick, plump and bright, sang joyously. The other, a contralto, sang with heartbreaking intensity of expression, which she deepened by dressing esthetically, as it was called then, meaning in the Rossettian taste. Miss Lawson produced this effect, not by the ugly extravagances which made the fashionable milliners' version of the esthetic mode ridiculous, but by very simple grey and brown gowns which somehow harmonized with her habitual expression of sadness and even suffering; so that when she sang "Oh, dont deceive me: oh, never leave me," she produced a picture as well as a tone poem. Cecil, who had just acquired a position by the few masterpieces which remain to us, was very much "in the movement" at the old Grosvenor Gallery (now the Aeolian Hall), then new, and passing through the sensational vogue achieved by its revelations of Burne Jones and Whistler.

Malcolm was conducting a Gluck Society, at which I had discovered Gluck through a recital of Alceste, in which Theo Marzials, who had a charming baritone voice, sang the part of Hercules. My mother had met Marzials in the course of her musical activities: he introduced her to Malcolm Lawson: she lent him a hand in the chorus of the Gluck Society; and the result was that I found myself invited to visit the Lawsons, who were at home in Cheyne Walk every Sunday evening. I suffered such agonies of shyness that I sometimes walked up and down the Embankment for twenty minutes or more before venturing to knock at the door: indeed I should have funked it altogether, and hurried home asking myself what was the use of torturing myself when it was so easy to run away, if I had not been instinctively aware that I must never let myself off in this manner if I meant ever to do anything in the world. Few men can have suffered more than I did in my youth from simple cowardice or been more horribly ashamed of it. I shirked and hid when the peril, real or imaginary, was of the sort that I had no vital interest in facing; but when such an interest was at stake, I went ahead and suffered accordingly. The worst of it was that when I appeared in the Lawsons' drawingroom I did not appeal to the goodnature of the company as a pardonably and even becomingly bashful novice. I had not then tuned the Shavian note to any sort of harmony; and I have no doubt the Lawsons found me discordant, crudely self-assertive, and insufferable. I hope they, and all the others on whom I jarred at this time, forgave me in later years, when it turned out that I really had something to assert after all. The house and its artistic atmosphere were most congenial to me; and I liked all the Lawsons; but I had not mastered the art of society at that time, and could not bear making an inartistic exhibition of myself; so I soon ceased to plague them, and, except for an occasional chance meeting with Malcolm, passed out of their lives after touching them very lightly in passing.

Cecil Lawson was the spoilt child of that household. He pontificated on art in a wayward grumbling incoherent musing fashion of his own. When, following my youthful and very irritating system of contradicting everyone from whom I thought I could learn anything, I suggested that Whistler was something short of the greatest artist of all time, he could not form a sentence to crush me with, but groaned inarticulately for a moment, like a clock about to strike, and then uttered the words Titian Turner Rembrandt Velasquez Whistler. He was goodlooking, not a big man, but trimly built, with just enough crisply curled hair to proclaim the artist without compromising the man. I had seen his work in the public exhibitions (never in private); and, thanks to my boyish prowlings in the Dublin National Gallery (as a boy I wanted to be a painter, never a writer), I knew its value. His untimely death, which occurred soon after my visits, must have broken up the Sunday evenings at Cheyne Walk very badly. I did not venture to intrude after it.

I used him in Immaturity as a model for the artist Cyril

Scott, an invented name which has since been made famous by a British composer. I chose it because Cyril resembled Cecil metrically, and because I thought Lawson was a Scot (he was, I learn, born in Shropshire). But I must again warn the reader against taking the man in the book as an authentic portrait of the great painter, or inferring that his courtship and marriage or any of the circumstances I have invented for him, represent facts in Lawson's life. I knew nothing whatever about him except what I saw of him during my few visits to Cheyne Walk; and I have learnt nothing since. He set my imagination to work: that was all.

I have now told as much as seems to me necessary of the circumstances and relevant antecedents of my first book. It is the book of a raw youth, still quite out of touch with the country to which he had transported himself; and if I am to be entirely communicative on this subject, I must add that the mere rawness which so soon rubs off was complicated by a deeper strangeness which has made me all my life a sojourner on this planet rather than a native of it. Whether it be that I was born mad or a little too sane, my kingdom was not of this world: I was at home only in the realm of my imagination, and at my ease only with the mighty dead. Therefore I had to become an actor, and create for myself a fantastic personality fit and apt for dealing with men, and adaptable to the various parts I had to play as author, journalist, orator, politician, committee man, man of the world, and so forth. In this I succeeded later on only too well. In my boyhood I saw Charles Mathews act in a farce called Cool as a Cucumber. The hero was a young man just returned from a tour of the world, upon which he had been sent to cure him of an apparently hopeless bashfulness; and the fun lay in the cure having overshot the mark and transformed him into a monster of outrageous impudence. I am not sure that something of the kind did not happen to me; for when my imposture was at last accomplished, and I daily pulled the threads of the puppet who represented me in the public press, the applause that greeted it was not unlike that which Mathews drew in Cool as a Cucumber. Certainly the growls of resentful disgust with which my advances were resisted closely resembled those of the unfortunate old gentleman in the farce whose pictures and furniture the young man so coolly rearranged to his own taste. At the time of which I am writing, however, I had not yet learnt to act, nor come to understand that my natural character was impossible on the great stage of London. When I had to come out of the realm of imagination into that of actuality I was still uncomfortable. I was outside society, outside politics, outside sport, outside the Church. If the term had been invented then I should have been called The Complete Outsider. But the epithet would have been appropriate only within the limits of British barbarism. The moment music, painting, literature, or science came into question the positions were reversed: it was I who was the Insider. I had the intellectual habit; and my natural combination of critical faculty with literary resource needed only a clear comprehension of life in the light of an intelligible theory: in short, a religion, to set it in triumphant operation. It was the lack of this last qualification that lamed me in those early days in Victoria Grove, and that set limits to this ungainly first novel of mine, which you will not lose very much by skipping.

Ayot St Lawrence,
Summer, 1921.

LONDON MUSIC PREFACE

WHEN my maiden novel, called Immaturity, was printed fifty years after it was written, I prefaced it with some account of the unhappy-go-lucky way in which I was brought up, ending with the nine years of shabby genteel destitution during which my attempts to gain a footing in literature were a complete and apparently hopeless failure.

I was rescued from this condition by William Archer, who transferred some of his book reviewing work to me, and pushed me into a post as picture critic which had been pushed on him, and for which he considered himself unqualified, as in fact he was. So, as reviewer for the old Pall Mall Gazette and picture critic for Edmund Yates's then fashionable weekly, The World, I carried on until I found an opening which I can explain only by describing the musical side of my childhood, to which I made only a passing allusion in my Immaturity preface, but which was of cardinal importance in my education.

In 1888, I being then 32 and already a noted critic and political agitator, the Star newspaper was founded under the editorship of the late T. P. O'Connor (nicknamed Tay Pay by Yates), who had for his very much more competent assistant the late H. W. Massingham. Tay Pay survived until 1936; but his mind never advanced beyond the year 1865, though his Fenian sympathies and his hearty detestation of the English nation disguised that defect from him. Massingham induced him to invite me to join the political staff of his paper; but as I had already, fourteen years before Lenin, read Karl Marx, and was preaching Socialism at every street corner or other available forum in London and the provinces, the effect of my articles on Tay Pay may be imagined. He refused to print them, and told me that, man alive, it would be five hundred years before such stuff would become practical political journalism. He was too goodnatured to sack me; and I did not want to throw away my job; so I got him out of his difficulty by asking him to let me have two columns a week for a feuilleton on music. He was glad to get rid of my politics on these terms; but he stipulated that—musical criticism being known to him only as unreadable and unintelligible jargon—I should, for God's sake, not write about Bach in B Minor. I was quite alive to that danger: in fact I had made my proposal because I believed I could make musical criticism readable even by the deaf. Besides, my terms were moderate: two guineas a week.

I was strong on the need for signed criticism written in the first person instead of the journalistic "we"; but as I then had no name worth signing, and G.B.S. meant nothing to the public, I had to invent a fantastic personality with something like a foreign title. I thought of Count di Luna (a character in Verdi's Trovatore), but finally changed it for Corno di Bassetto, as it sounded like a foreign title, and nobody knew what a corno di bassetto was.

As a matter of fact the corno di bassetto is not a foreigner with a title but a musical instrument called in English the basset horn. It is a wretched instrument, now completely snuffed out for general use by the bass clarionet. It would be forgotten and unplayed if it were not that Mozart has scored for it in his Requiem, evidently because its peculiar watery melancholy, and the total absence of any richness or passion in its tone, is just the thing for a funeral. Mendelssohn wrote some chamber music for it, presumably to oblige somebody who played it; and it is kept alive by these works and by our Mr Whall. If I had ever heard a note of it in 1888 I should not have selected it for a character which I intended to be sparkling. The devil himself could not make a basset horn sparkle.

For two years I sparkled every week in The Star under this ridiculous name, and in a manner so absolutely unlike the conventional musical criticism of the time that all the journalists believed that the affair was a huge joke, the point of which was that I knew nothing whatever about music. How it had come about that I was one of the few critics of that time who really knew their business I can explain only by picking up the thread of autobiography which I dropped in my scrappy prefix to Immaturity. For the sake of those who have not read the Immaturity preface, or have forgotten it, I shall have to repeat here some of my father's history, but only so far as is necessary to explain the situation of my mother.

Technically speaking I should say she was the worst mother conceivable, always, however, within the limits of the fact that she was incapable of unkindness to any child, animal, or flower, or indeed to any person or thing whatsoever. But if such a thing as a maternity welfare centre had been established or even imagined in Ireland in her time, and she had been induced to visit it, every precept of it would have been laughably strange to her. Though she had been severely educated up to the highest standard for Irish "carriage ladies" of her time, she was much more like a Trobriand islander as described by Mr Malinowski than like a modern Cambridge lady graduate in respect of accepting all the habits, good or bad, of the Irish society in which she was brought up as part of an uncontrollable order of nature. She went her own way with so complete a disregard and even unconsciousness of convention and scandal and prejudice that it was impossible to doubt her good faith and innocence; but it never occurred to her that other people, especially children, needed guidance or training, or that it mattered in the least what they ate and drank or what they did as long as they were not actively mischievous. She accepted me as a natural and customary phenomenon, and took it for granted that I should go on occurring in that way. In short, living to her was not an art: it was something that happened. But there were unkind parts of it that could be avoided; and among these were the constraints and tyrannies, the scoldings and browbeatings and punishments she had suffered in her childhood as the method of her education. In her righteous reaction against it she reached a negative attitude in which, having no substitute to propose, she carried domestic anarchy as far as in the nature of things it can be carried.

She had been tyrannously taught French enough to recite one or two of Lafontaine's fables; to play the piano the wrong way; to harmonize by rule from Logier's Thoroughbass; to sit up straight and speak and dress and behave like a lady, and an Irish lady at that. She knew nothing of the value of money nor of housekeeping nor of hygiene nor of anything that could be left to servants or governesses or parents or solicitors or apothecaries or any other member of the retinue, indoor and outdoor, of a country house. She had great expectations from a humpbacked little aunt, a fairylike creature with a will of iron, who had brought up her motherless niece with a firm determination to make her a paragon of good breeding, to achieve a distinguished marriage for her, and to leave her all her money as a dowry.

Manufacturing destinies for other people is a dangerous game. Its results are usually as unexpected as those of a first-rate European war. When my mother came to marriageable age her long widowed father married again. The brother of his late wife, to whom he was considerably in debt, disapproved so strongly that on learning the date of the approaching ceremony from my mother he had the bridegroom arrested on his way to church. My grandfather naturally resented this manoeuvre, and in his wrath could not be persuaded that his daughter was not my granduncle's accomplice in it. Visits to relatives in Dublin provided a temporary refuge for her; and the affair would have blown over but for the intervention of my father.

My father was a very ineligible suitor for a paragon with great expectations. His family pretensions were enormous; but they were founded on many generations of younger sons, and were purely psychological. He had managed to acquire a gentlemanly post in the law courts. This post had been abolished and its holder pensioned. By selling the pension he was enabled to start in business as a wholesaler in the corn trade (retail trade was beneath his family dignity) of which he knew nothing. He accentuated this deficiency by becoming the partner of a Mr Clibborn, who had served an apprenticeship to the cloth trade. Their combined ignorances kept the business going, mainly by its own inertia, until they and it died. Many years after this event I paid a visit of curiosity to Jervis St. Dublin; and there, on one of the pillars of a small portico, I found the ancient inscription "Clibborn & Shaw" still decipherable, as it were on the tombs of the Pharaohs. I cannot believe that this business yielded my father at any time more than three or four hundred a year; and it got less as time went on, as that particular kind of business was dying a slow death throughout the latter half of the nineteenth century.

My father was in principle an ardent teetotaller. Nobody ever felt the disgrace and misery and endless mischief of drunkenness as he did: he impressed it so deeply on me in my earliest years that I have been a teetotaller ever since. Unfortunately his conviction in this matter was founded on personal experience. He was the victim of a drink neurosis which cropped up in his family from time to time: a miserable affliction, quite unconvivial, and accompanied by torments of remorse and shame.

My father was past forty, and no doubt had sanguine illusions as to the future of his newly acquired business when he fell in love with my mother and was emboldened by her expectations and his business hopes to propose to her just at the moment when marriage seemed her only way of escape from an angry father and a stepmother. Immediately all her relatives, who had tolerated this middle-aged gentleman as a perfectly safe acquaintance with an agreeable vein of humor, denounced him as a notorious drunkard. My mother, suspicious of this sudden change of front, put the question directly to my father. His eloquence and sincerity convinced her that he was, as he claimed to be, and as he was in principle, a bigoted teetotaller. She married him; and her disappointed and infuriated aunt disinherited her, not foreseeing that the consequences of the marriage would include so remarkable a phenomenon as myself.

When my mother was disillusioned, and found out what living on a few hundreds a year with three children meant, even in a country where a general servant could be obtained for eight pounds a year, her condition must have been about as unhappy and her prospects as apparently hopeless as her aunt could have desired even in her most vindictive moments.

But there was one trump in her hand. She was fond of music, and had a mezzo-soprano voice of remarkable purity of tone. In the next street to ours, Harrington Street, where the houses were bigger and more fashionable than in our little by-street, there was a teacher of singing, lamed by an accident in childhood which had left one of his legs shorter than the other, but a man of mesmeric vitality and force. He was a bachelor living with his brother, whom he supported and adored, and a terrible old woman who was his servant of all work. His name was George John Vandaleur Lee, known in Dublin as Mr G. J. Lee. Singing lessons were cheap in Dublin; and my mother went to Lee to learn how to sing properly. He trained her voice to such purpose that she became indispensable to him as an amateur prima donna. For he was a most magnetic conductor and an indefatigable organizer of concerts, and later on of operas, with such amateur talent, vocal and orchestral, as he could discover and train in Dublin, which, as far as public professional music was concerned, was, outside the churches, practically a vacuum.

Lee soon found his way into our house, first by giving my mother lessons there, and then by using our drawing-room for rehearsals. I can only guess that the inadequacies of old Ellen in the Harrington Street house, and perhaps the incompatibilities of the brother, outweighed the comparative smallness of our house in Synge Street. My mother soon became not only prima donna and chorus leader but general musical factotum in the whirlpool of Lee's activity. Her grounding in Logier's Thoroughbass enabled her to take boundless liberties with composers. When authentic band parts were missing she thought nothing of making up an orchestral accompaniment of her own from the pianoforte score. Lee, as far as I know, had never seen a full orchestral score in his life: he conducted from a first violin part or from the vocal score, and had not, I think, any decided notion of orchestration as an idiosyncratic and characteristic part of a composer's work. He had no scholarship according to modern ideas; but he could do what Wagner said is the whole duty of a conductor: he could give the right time to the band; and he could pull it out of its amateur difficulties in emergencies by sheer mesmerism. Though he could not, or at any rate within my hearing never did sing a note, his taste in singing was classically perfect. In his search for the secret of *bel canto* he had gone to all the teachers within his reach. They told him that there was a voice in the head, a voice in the throat, and a voice in the chest. He dissected birds, and, with the connivance of three medical friends, human subjects, in his search for these three organs. He then told the teachers authoritatively that the three voices were fabulous, and that the voice was produced by a single instrument called the larynx. They replied that musical art had nothing to do with anatomy, and that for a musician to practise dissection was unheard-of and disgusting. But as, tested by results, their efforts to teach their pupils to screech like locomotive whistles not only outraged his ear but wrecked the voices and often the health of their victims, their practice was as unacceptable to him as their theory.

Thus Lee became the enemy of every teacher of singing in Dublin; and they reciprocated heartily. In this negative attitude he was left until, at the opera, he heard an Italian baritone named Badeali, who at the age of 80, when he first discovered these islands, had a perfectly preserved voice, and, to Lee's taste, a perfectly produced one. Lee, thanks to his dissections, listened with a clear knowledge of what a larynx is really like. The other vocal organs and their action were obvious and conscious. Guided by this knowledge, and by his fine ear, his fastidious taste, and his instinct, he found out what Badeali was doing when he was singing. The other teachers were interested in Badeali only because one of his accomplishments was to drink a glass of wine and sing a sustained note at the same time. Finally Lee equipped himself with a teaching method which became a religion for him: the only religion, I may add, he ever professed. And my mother, as his pupil, learnt and embraced this musical faith, and rejected all other creeds as uninteresting superstitions. And it did not fail her; for she lived to be Badeali's age and kept her voice without a scrape on it until the end.

I have to dwell on The Method, as we called it in the family, because my mother's association with Lee, and the *ménage à trois* in which it resulted, would be unpleasantly misunderstood without this clue to it. For after the death of Lee's brother, which affected him to the verge of suicide, we left our respective houses and went to live in the same house, number one Hatch Street, which was half in Lower Leeson Street. The arrangement was economical; for we could not afford to live in a fashionable house, and Lee could not afford to give lessons in an unfashionable one, though, being a bachelor, he needed only a music room and a bedroom. We also shared a cottage in Dalkey, high up on Torca Hill, with all Dublin Bay from Dalkey Island to Howth visible from the garden, and all Killiney Bay with the Wicklow mountains in the background from the hall door. Lee bought this cottage and presented it to my mother, though she never had any legal claim to it and did not benefit by its sale later on. It was not conveniently situated for rehearsals or lessons; but there were musical neighbors who allowed me to some extent to run in and out of their houses when there was music going on.

The *ménage à trois*, alternating between Hatch St. and Dalkey, worked in its ramshackle way quite smoothly until I was fifteen or thereabouts, when Lee went to London and our family broke up into fragments that never got pieced together again.

In telling the story so far, I have had to reconstruct the part of it which occurred before I came into it and began, as my nurse put it, to take notice. I can remember the ante-Lee period in Synge St. when my father, as sole chief of the household, read family prayers and formally admitted that we had done those things which we ought not to have done and left undone those things which we ought to have done, which was certainly true as far as I was personally concerned. He added that there was no health in us; and this also was true enough about myself; for Dr Newland, our apothecary, was in almost continual attendance to administer cathartics; and when I had a sore throat I used to hold out for a sixpence before submitting to a mustard plaster round my neck. We children (I had two sisters older than myself and no brothers) were abandoned entirely to the servants, who, with the exception of Nurse Williams, who was a good and honest woman, were utterly unfit to be trusted with the charge of three cats, much less three children. I had my meals in the kitchen, mostly of stewed beef, which I loathed, badly cooked potatoes, sound or diseased as the case might be, and much too much tea out of brown delft teapots left to "draw" on the hob until it was pure tannin. Sugar I stole. I was never hungry, because my father, often insufficiently fed in his childhood, had such a horror of child hunger that he insisted on unlimited bread and butter being always within our reach. When I was troublesome a servant thumped me on the head until one day, greatly daring, I rebelled, and, on finding her collapse abjectly, became thenceforth uncontrollable. I hated the servants and liked my mother because, on the one or two rare and delightful occasions when she buttered my bread for me, she buttered it thickly instead of merely wiping a knife on it. Her almost complete neglect of me had the advantage that I could idolize her to the utmost pitch of my imagination and had no sordid or disillusioning contacts with her. It was a privilege to be taken for a walk or a visit with her, or on an excursion.

My ordinary exercise whilst I was still too young to be allowed out by myself was to be taken out by a servant, who was supposed to air me on the banks of the canal or round the fashionable squares where the atmosphere was esteemed salubrious and the surroundings gentlemanly. Actually she took me into the slums to visit her private friends, who dwelt in squalid tenements. When she met a generous male acquaintance who insisted on treating her she took me into the public house bars, where I was regaled with lemonade and gingerbeer; but I did not enjoy these treats, because my father's eloquence on the evil of drink had given me an impression that a public house was a wicked place into which I should not have been taken. Thus were laid the foundations of my lifelong hatred of poverty, and the devotion of all my public life to the task of exterminating the poor and rendering their resurrection for ever impossible.

Note, by the way, that I should have been much more decently brought up if my parents had been too poor to afford servants.

As to early education I can remember our daily governess, Miss Hill, a needy lady who seemed to me much older than she can really have been. She puzzled me with her attempts to teach me to read; for I can remember no time at which a page of print was not intelligible to me, and can only suppose that I was born literate. She tried to give me and my two sisters a taste for poetry by reciting "Stop; for thy tread is on an empire's dust" at us, and only succeeded, poor lady, in awakening our sense of derisive humor. She punished me by little strokes with her fingers that would not have discomposed a fly, and even persuaded me that I ought to cry and feel disgraced on such occasions. She gave us judgment books and taught us to feel jubilant when after her departure we could rush to the kitchen crying "No marks today" and to hang back ashamed when this claim could not be substantiated. She taught me to add, subtract, and multiply, but could not teach me division, because she kept saying two into four, three into six, and so forth without ever explaining what the word "into" meant in this connection. This was explained to me on my first day at school; and I solemnly declare that it was the only thing I ever learnt at school. However, I must not complain; for my immurement in that damnable boy prison effected its real purpose of preventing my being a nuisance to my mother at home for at least half the day.

The only other teaching I had was from my clerical Uncle William George (surnamed Carroll) who, being married to one of my many maternal aunts (my father had no end of brothers and sisters), had two boys of his own to educate, and took me on with them for awhile in the early mornings to such purpose that when his lessons were ended by my being sent to school, I knew more Latin grammar than any other boy in the First Latin Junior, to which I was relegated. After a few years in that establishment I had forgotten most of it, and, as aforesaid, learnt nothing; for there was only the thinnest pretence of teaching anything but Latin and Greek, if asking a boy once a day in an overcrowded class the Latin for a man or a horse or what not, can be called teaching him Latin. I was far too busy educating myself out of school by reading every book I could lay hands on, and clambering all over Killiney hill looking at the endless pictures nature painted for me, meanwhile keeping my mind busy by telling myself all sorts of stories, to puzzle about my vocabulary lesson, as the punishments were as futile as the teaching. At the end of my schooling I knew nothing of what the school professed to teach; but I was a highly educated boy all the same. I could sing and whistle from end to end leading works by Handel, Haydn, Mozart, Beethoven, Rossini, Bellini, Donizetti and Verdi. I was saturated with English literature, from Shakespear and Bunyan to Byron and Dickens. And I was so susceptible to natural beauty that, having had some glimpse of the Dalkey scenery on an excursion, I still remember the moment when my mother told me that we were going to live there as the happiest of my life.

And all this I owed to the meteoric impact of Lee, with his music, his method, his impetuous enterprise and his magnetism, upon the little Shaw household where a thoroughly disgusted and disillusioned woman was suffering from a hopelessly disappointing husband and three uninteresting children grown too old to be petted like the animals and the birds she was so fond of, to say nothing of the humiliating inadequacy of my father's income. We never felt any affection for Lee; for he was too excessively unlike us, too completely a phenomenon, to rouse any primitive human feeling in us. When my mother introduced him to me, he played with me for the first and last time; but as his notion of play was to decorate my face with moustaches and whiskers in burnt cork in spite of the most furious resistance I could put up, our encounter was not a success; and the defensive attitude in which it left me lasted, though without the least bitterness, until the decay of his energies and the growth of mine put us on more than equal terms. He never read anything except Tyndall on Sound, which he kept in his bedroom for years. He complained that an edition of Shakespear which I lent him was incomplete because it did not contain The School for Scandal, which for some reason he wanted to read; and when I talked of Carlyle he understood me to mean the Viceroy of that name who had graciously attended his concerts in the Antient Concert Rooms. Although he supplanted my father as the dominant factor in the household, and appropriated all the activity and interest of my mother, he was so completely absorbed in his musical affairs that there was no friction and hardly any intimate personal contacts between the two men: certainly no unpleasantness. At first his ideas astonished us. He said that people should sleep with their windows open. The daring of this appealed to me; and I have done so ever since. He ate brown bread instead of white: a startling eccentricity. He had no faith in doctors, and when my mother had a serious illness took her case in hand unhesitatingly and at the end of a week or so gave my trembling father leave to call in a leading Dublin doctor, who simply said "My work is done" and took his hat. As to the apothecary and his squills, he could not exist in Lee's atmosphere; and I was never attended by a doctor again until I caught the smallpox in the epidemic of 1881. He took no interest in pictures or in any art but his own; and even in music his interest was limited to vocal music: I did not know that such things as string quartets or symphonies existed until I began, at sixteen, to investigate music for myself. Beethoven's sonatas and the classical operatic overtures were all I knew of what Wagner called absolute music. I should be tempted to say that none of us knew of the existence of Bach were it not that my mother sang My Heart Ever Faithful, the banjo like obbligato of which amused me very irreverently.

Lee was like all artists whose knowledge is solely a working knowledge: there were holes in his culture which I had to fill up for myself. Fortunately his richer pupils sometimes presented him with expensive illustrated books. He never opened them; but I did. He was so destitute of any literary bent that when he published a book entitled The Voice, it was written for him by a scamp of a derelict doctor whom he entertained for that purpose, just as in later years his prospectuses and press articles were written by me. He never visited the Dublin National Gallery, one of the finest collections of its size in Europe, with the usual full set of casts from what was called the antique, meaning ancient Greek sculpture. It was by prowling in this gallery that I learnt to recognize the work of the old masters at sight. I learnt French history from the novels of Dumas *père*, and English History from Shakespear and Walter Scott. Good boys were meanwhile learning lessons out of schoolbooks and receiving marks at examinations: a process which left them pious barbarians whilst I was acquiring an equipment which enabled me not only to pose as Corno di Bassetto when the chance arrived, but to add the criticism of pictures to the various strings I had to my bow as a feuilletonist.

Meanwhile nobody ever dreamt of teaching me anything. At fifteen, when the family broke up, I could neither play nor read a note of music. Whether you choose to put it that I was condemned to be a critic or saved from being an executant, the fact remains that when the house became musicless, I was forced to teach myself how to play written music on the piano from a book with a diagram of the keyboard in it or else be starved of music.

Not that I wanted to be a professional musician. My ambition was to be a great painter like Michael Angelo (one of my heroes); but my attempts to obtain instruction in his art at the School of Design presided over by the South Kensington Department of Science and Art only prevented me from learning anything except how to earn five shilling grants for the masters (payment by results) by filling up ridiculous examination papers in practical geometry and what they called freehand drawing.

With competent instruction I daresay I could have become a painter and draughtsman of sorts; but the School of Design convinced me that I was a hopeless failure in that direction on no better ground than that I found I could not draw like Michael Angelo or paint like Titian at the first attempt without knowing how. But teaching, of art and everything else, was and still is so little understood by our professional instructors (mostly themselves failures) that only the readymade geniuses make good; and even they are as often as not the worse for their academic contacts.

As an alternative to being a Michael Angelo I had dreams of being a Badeali. (Note, by the way, that of literature I had no dreams at all, any more than a duck has of swimming.) What that led to was not fully explained until Matthias Alexander, in search, like Lee, of a sound vocal method, invented his technique of self-control.

I had sung like a bird all through my childhood; but when my voice broke I at once fell into the error unmasked by Alexander of trying to gain my end before I had studied the means. In my attempts to reproduce the frenzies of the Count di Luna, the sardonic accents of Gounod's Mephistopheles, the noble charm of Don Giovanni, and the supernatural menace of the Commendatore, not to mention all the women's parts and the tenor parts as well (for all parts, high or low, male or female, had to be sung or shrieked or whistled or growled somehow) I thought of nothing but the dramatic characters; and in attacking them I set my jaws and my glottis as if I had to crack walnuts with them. I might have ruined my voice if I had not imitated good singers instead of bad ones; but even so the results were wretched. When I rejoined my mother in London and she found that I had taught myself to play accompaniments and to amuse myself with operas and oratorios as other youths read novels and smoke cigarets, she warned me that my voice would be spoiled if I went on like that. Thereupon I insisted on being shewn the proper way to sing. The instructive result was that when, following my mother's directions, I left my jaw completely loose, and my tongue flat instead of convulsively rolling it up; when I operated my diaphragm so as to breathe instead of "blowing"; when I tried to round up my pharynx and soft palate and found it like trying to wag my ears, I found that for the first time in my life I could not produce an audible note. It seemed that I had no voice. But I believed in Lee's plan and knew that my own was wrong. I insisted on being taught how to use my voice as if I had one; and in the end the unused and involuntary pharyngeal muscles became active and voluntary, and I developed an uninteresting baritone voice of no exceptional range which I have ever since used for my private satisfaction and exercise without damaging either it or myself in the process.

Here I must digress for a moment to point a moral. Years after I learnt how to sing without spoiling my voice and wrecking my general health, a musician-reciter (Matthias Alexander aforesaid) found himself disabled by the complaint known as clergyman's sore throat. Having the true scientific spirit and industry, he set himself to discover what it was that he was really doing to disable himself in this fashion by his efforts to produce the opposite result. In the end he found this out, and a great deal more as well. He established not only the beginnings of a far reaching science of the apparently involuntary movements we call reflexes, but a technique of correction and self-control which forms a substantial addition to our very slender resources in personal education.

Meanwhile a Russian doctor named Pavlov devoted himself to the investigation of the same subject by practising the horrible voodoo into which professional medical research had lapsed in the nineteenth century. For a quarter of a century he tormented and mutilated dogs most abominably, and finally wrote a ponderous treatise on reflexes in which he claimed to have established on a scientific basis the fact that a dog's mouth will water at the sound of a dinner bell when it is trained to associate that sound with a meal, and that dogs, if tormented, thwarted, baffled, and incommoded continuously, will suffer nervous breakdown and be miserably ruined for the rest of their lives. He was also able to describe what happens to a dog when half its brains are cut out.

What his book and its shamefully respectful reception by professional biologists does demonstrate is that the opening of the scientific professions to persons qualified for them neither by general capacity nor philosophic moral training plunges professional Science, as it has so often plunged professional Religion and Jurisprudence, into an abyss of stupidity and cruelty from which nothing but the outraged humanity of the laity can rescue it.

In the department of biology especially, the professors, mostly brought up as Fundamentalists, are informed that the book of Genesis is not a scientific document, and that the tribal idol whom Noah conciliated by the smell of roast meat is not God and never had any objective existence. They absurdly infer that the pursuit of scientific knowledge: that is, of all knowledge, is exempt from moral obligations, and consequently that they are privileged as scientists to commit the most revolting cruelties when they are engaged in research.

Their next step in this crazy logic is that no research is scientific unless it involves such cruelties. With all the infinite possibilities of legitimate and kindly research open to anyone with enough industry and ingenuity to discover innocent methods of exploration, they set up a boycott of brains and a ritual of sacrifice of dogs and guinea pigs which impresses the superstitious public as all such rituals do. Thereby they learn many things that no decent person ought to know; for it must not be forgotten that human advancement consists not only of adding to the store of human knowledge and experience but eliminating much that is burdensome and brutish. Our forefathers had the knowledge and experience gained by seeing heretics burnt at the stake and harlots whipped through the streets at the cart's tail. Mankind is better without such knowledge and experience.

If Pavlov had been a poacher he would have been imprisoned for his cruelty and despised for his moral imbecility. But as Director of the Physiological Department of the Institute of Experimental Medicine at St. Petersburg, and Professor of the Medical Academy, he was virtually forced to mutilate and torment dogs instead of discovering the methods by which humane unofficial investigators were meanwhile finding out all that he was looking for.

The reaction against this voodoo is gathering momentum; but still our rich philanthropic industrialists lavish millions on the endowment of research without taking the most obvious precautions against malversation of their gifts for the benefit of dog stealers, guinea pig breeders, laboratory builders and plumbers, and a routine of cruel folly and scoundrelism that perverts and wastes all the scientific enthusiasm that might otherwise have by this time reduced our death and disease rates to their natural minimum. I am sorry to have to describe so many highly respected gentlemen quite deliberately as fools and scoundrels; but the only definition of scoundrelism known to me is anarchism in morals; and I cannot admit that the hackneyed pleas of the dynamiter and the assassin in politics become valid in the laboratory and the hospital, or that the man who thinks they do is made any less a fool by calling him a professor of physiology.

And all this because in 1860 the men who thought they wanted to substitute scientific knowledge for superstition really wanted only to abolish God and marry their deceased wives' sisters!

I should add that there is no reason to suppose that Pavlov was by nature a bad man. He bore a strong external resemblance to myself, and was wellmeaning, intelligent, and devoted to science. It was his academic environment that corrupted, stultified, and sterilized him. If only he had been taught to sing by my mother no dog need ever have collapsed in terror at his approach; and he might have shared the laurels of Alexander.

And now I must return to my story. Lee's end was more tragic than Pavlov's. I do not know at what moment he began to deteriorate. He was a sober and moderate liver in all respects; and he was never ill until he treated himself to a tour in Italy and caught malaria there. He fought through it without a doctor on cold water, and returned apparently well; but whenever he worked too hard it came back and prostrated him for a day or two. Finally his ambition undid him. Dublin in those days seemed a hopeless place for an artist; for no success counted except a London success. The summit of a provincial conductor's destiny was to preside at a local musical festival modelled on the Three Choirs or Handel Festivals. Lee declared that he would organize and conduct a Dublin Festival with his own chorus and with all the famous leading singers from the Italian opera in London. This he did in connection with an Exhibition in Dublin. My mother, of course, led the chorus. At a rehearsal the contralto, Madame de Meric Lablache, took exception to something and refused to sing. Lee shrugged his shoulders and asked my mother to carry on, which she did to such purpose that Madame Lablache took care not to give her another such chance.

At the Festivals Lee reached the Dublin limit of eminence. Nothing remained but London. He was assured that London meant a very modest beginning all over again, and perhaps something of an established position after fifteen years or so. Lee said that he would take a house in Park Lane, then the most exclusive and expensive thoroughfare in the west end, sacred to peers and millionaires, and—stupendous on the scale of Irish finance—make his pupils pay him a guinea a lesson. And this he actually did with a success that held out quite brilliantly for several seasons and then destroyed him. For whereas he had succeeded in Dublin by the sheer superiority of his method and talent and character, training his pupils honestly for a couple of years to sing beautifully and classically, he found that the London ladies who took him up so gushingly would have none of his beauty and classicism, and would listen to nothing less than a promise to make them sing "like Patti" in twelve lessons. It was that or starve.

He submitted perforce; but he was no longer the same man, the man to whom all circumstances seemed to give way, and who made his own musical world and reigned in it. He had even to change his name and his aspect. G. J. Lee, with the black whiskers and the clean shaven resolute lip and chin, became Vandaleur Lee, whiskerless, but with a waxed and pointed moustache and an obsequious attitude. It suddenly became evident that he was an elderly man, and, to those who had known him in Dublin, a humbug. Performances of Marchetti's Ruy Blas with my sister as the Queen of Spain, and later on of Sullivan's Patience and scraps of Faust and Il Trovatore were achieved; but musical society in London at last got tired of the damaged Svengali who could manufacture Pattis for twelve guineas; and the guineas ceased to come in. Still, as there were no night clubs in those days, it was possible to let a house in Park Lane for the night to groups of merrymakers; and Lee was holding out there without pupils when he asked me to draft a circular for him announcing that he could cure clergyman's sore throat. He was still at Park Lane when he dropped dead in the act of undressing himself, dying as he had lived, without a doctor. The postmortem and inquest revealed the fact that his brain was diseased and had been so for a long time. I was glad to learn that his decay was pathological as well as ecological, and that the old efficient and honest Lee had been real after all. But I took to heart the lesson in the value of London fashionable successes. To this day I look to the provincial and the amateur for honesty and genuine fecundity in art.

Meanwhile, what had happened to the *ménage à trois?* and how did I turn up in Park Lane playing accompaniments and getting glimpses of that artstruck side of fashionable society which takes refuge in music from the routine of politics and sport which occupies the main Philistine body?

Well, when Lee got his foot in at a country house in Shropshire whither he had been invited to conduct some private performances, he sold the Dalkey cottage and concluded his tenancy of Hatch Street. This left us in a house which we could afford less than ever; for my father's moribund business was by now considerably deader than it had been at the date of my birth. My younger sister was dying of consumption caught from reckless contacts at a time when neither consumption nor pneumonia were regarded as catching. All that could be done was to recommend a change of climate. My elder sister had a beautiful voice. In the last of Lee's Dublin adventures in amateur opera she had appeared as Amina in Bellini's La Sonnambula, on which occasion the tenor lost his place and his head, and Lucy obligingly sang most of his part as well as her own. Unfortunately her musical endowment was so complete that it cost her no effort to sing or play anything she had once heard, or to read any music at sight. She simply could not associate the idea of real work with music; and as in any case she had never received any sort of training, her very facility prevented her from becoming a serious artist, though, as she could sing difficult music without breaking her voice, she got through a considerable share of public singing in her time.

Now neither my mother nor any of us knew how much more is needed for an opera singer than a voice and natural musicianship. It seemed to us that as, after a rehearsal or two, she could walk on to the stage, wave her arms about in the absurd manner then in vogue in opera, and sing not only her own part but everybody else's as well, she was quite qualified to take the place of Christine Nilsson or Adelina Patti if only she could get a proper introduction. And clearly Lee, now in the first flush of his success in Park Lane, would easily be able to secure this for her.

There was another resource. My now elderly mother believed that she could renounce her amateur status and make a living in London by teaching singing. Had she not the infallible Method to impart? So she realized a little of the scrap of settled property of which her long deceased aunt had not been able to deprive her; sold the Hatch Street furniture; settled my father and myself in comfortable lodgings at 61 Harcourt St; and took my sisters to the Isle of Wight, where the younger one died. She then took a semi-detached villa in a *cul-de-sac* off the Fulham Road, and waited there for Lucy's plans and her own to materialize.

The result was almost a worse disillusion than her marriage. That had been cured by Lee's music: besides, my father had at last realized his dream of being a practising teetotaller, and was now as inoffensive an old gentleman as any elderly wife could desire. It was characteristic of the Shavian drink neurosis to vanish suddenly in this way. But that

Lee should be unfaithful! unfaithful to The Method! that he, the one genuine teacher among so many quacks, should now stoop to outquack them all and become a moustachioed charlatan with all the virtue gone out of him: this was the end of all things; and she never forgave it. She was not unkind: she tolerated Lee the charlatan as she had tolerated Shaw the dipsomaniac because, as I guess, her early motherless privation of affection and her many disappointments in other people had thrown her back on her own considerable internal resources and developed her self-sufficiency and power of solitude to an extent which kept her up under circumstances that would have crushed or embittered any woman who was the least bit of a clinger. She dropped Lee very gently: at first he came and went at Victoria Grove, Fulham Road; and she went and came at 13 Park Lane, helping with the music there at his At Homes, and even singing the part of Donna Anna for him (elderly prima donnas were then tolerated as matters of course) at an amateur performance of Don Giovanni. But my sister, who had quarrelled with him as a child when he tried to give her piano lessons, and had never liked him, could not bear him at all in his new phase, and, when she found that he could not really advance her prospects of becoming a prima donna, broke with him completely and made it difficult for him to continue his visits. When he died we had not seen him for some years; and my mother did not display the slightest emotion at the news. He had been dead for her ever since he had ceased to be an honest teacher of singing and a mesmeric conductor.

Her plans for herself came almost to nothing for several years. She found that Englishwomen do not wish to be made to sing beautifully and classically: they want to sing erotically; and this my mother thought not only horrible but unladylike. Her love songs were those of Virginia Gabriel and Arthur Sullivan, all about bereaved lovers and ending with a hope for reunion in the next world. She could sing with perfect purity of tone and touching expression

Oh, Ruby, my darling, the small white hand
Which gathered the harebell was never my own.

But if you had been able to anticipate the grand march of human progress and poetic feeling by fifty years, and asked her to sing

You made me love you.
I didnt want to do it.
I didnt want to do it,

she would have asked a policeman to remove you to a third-class carriage.

Besides, though my mother was not consciously a snob, the divinity which hedged an Irish lady of her period was not acceptable to the British suburban parents, all snobs, who were within her reach. They liked to be treated with deference; and it never occurred to my mother that such people could entertain a pretension so monstrous in her case. Her practice with private pupils was negligible until she was asked to become musical instructress at the North London College. Her success was immediate; for not only did her classes leave the other schools nowhere musically, but the divinity aforesaid exactly suited her new rôle as schoolmistress. Other schools soon sought her services; and she remained in request until she insisted on retiring on the ground that her age made her public appearances ridiculous. By that time all the old money troubles were over and forgotten, as my financial position enabled me to make her perfectly comfortable in that respect.

And now, what about myself, the incipient Corno di Bassetto?

Well, when my mother sold the Hatch Street furniture, it never occurred to her to sell our piano, though I could not play it, nor could my father. We did not realize, nor did she, that she was never coming back, and that, except for a few days when my father, taking a little holiday for the first time in his life within my experience, came to see us in London, she would never meet him again. Family revolutions would seldom be faced if they did not present themselves at first as temporary makeshifts. Accordingly, having lived since my childhood in a house full of music, I suddenly found myself in a house where there was no music, and could be none unless I made it myself. I have recorded elsewhere how, having purchased one of Weale's Handbooks which contained a diagram of the keyboard and an explanation of musical notation, I began my self-tuition, not with Czerny's five-finger exercises, but with the overture to Don Giovanni, thinking rightly that I had better start with something I knew well enough to hear whether my fingers were on the right notes or not. There were plenty of vocal scores of operas and oratorios in our lodging; and although I never acquired any technical skill as a pianist, and cannot to this day play a scale with any certainty of not foozling it, I acquired what I wanted: the power to take a vocal score and learn its contents as if I had heard it rehearsed by my mother and her colleagues. I could manage arrangements of orchestral music much better than piano music proper. At last I could play the old rum-tum accompaniments of those days well enough (knowing how they *should* be played) to be more agreeable to singers than many really competent pianists. I bought more scores, among them one of Lohengrin, through which I made the revolutionary discovery of Wagner. I bought arrangements of Beethoven's symphonies, and discovered the musical regions that lie outside opera and oratorio. Later on, I was forced to learn to play the classical symphonies and overtures in strict time by hammering the bass in piano duets with my sister in London. I played Bach's Inventions and his Art of Fugue. I studied academic textbooks, and actually worked out exercises in harmony and counterpoint under supervision by an organist friend named Crament, avoiding consecutive fifths and octaves, and having not the faintest notion of what the result would sound like. I read pseudo-scientific treatises about the roots of chords which candidates for the degree of Mus.Doc. at the universities had to swallow, and learnt that Stainer's commonsense views would get you plucked at Oxford, and Ouseley's pedantries at Cambridge. I read Mozart's Succinct Thoroughbass (a scrap of paper with some helpful tips on it which he scrawled for his pupil Sussmaier); and this, many years later, Edward Elgar told me was the only document in existence of the smallest use to a student composer. It was, I grieve to say, of no use to me; but then I was not a young composer. It ended in my knowing much more about music than any of the great composers, an easy achievement for any critic, however barren. For awhile I must have become a little pedantic; for I remember being shocked, on looking up Lee's old vocal score of Don Giovanni, to find that he had cut out all the repetitions which Mozart had perpetrated as a matter of sonata form. I now see that Lee was a century before his time in this reform, and hope some day to hear a performance of Mozart's Idomeneo in which nothing is sung twice over.

When I look back on all the banging, whistling, roaring, and growling inflicted on nervous neighbors during this process of education, I am consumed with useless remorse. But what else could I have done? Today there is the wireless, which enables me to hear from all over Europe more good music in a week than I could then hear in ten years, if at all. When, after my five years office slavery, I joined my mother in London and lived with her for twenty years until my marriage, I used to drive her nearly crazy by my favorite selections from Wagner's Ring, which to her was "all recitative," and horribly discordant at that. She never complained at the time, but confessed it after we separated, and said that she had sometimes gone away to cry. If I had committed a murder I do not think it would trouble my conscience very much; but this I cannot bear to think of. If I had to live my life over again I should devote it to the establishment of some arrangement of headphones and microphones or the like whereby the noises made by musical maniacs should be audible to themselves only. In Germany it is against the law to play the piano with the window open. But of what use is that to the people in the house? It should be made felony to play a musical instrument in any other than a completely soundproof room. The same should apply to loud speakers on pain of confiscation.

Readers with a taste for autobiography must now take my Immaturity preface and dovetail it into this sketch to complete the picture. My business here is to account for my proposal to Tay Pay and my creation of Bassetto. From my earliest recorded sign of an interest in music when as a small child I encored my mother's singing of the page's song from the first act of Les Huguenots (note that I shared Herbert Spencer's liking for Meyerbeer) music has been an indispensable part of my life. Harley Granville-Barker was not far out when, at a rehearsal of one of my plays, he cried out "Ladies and gentlemen: will you please remember that this is Italian opera."

I reprint Bassetto's stuff shamefacedly after long hesitation with a reluctance which has been overcome only by my wife, who has found some amusement in reading it through, a drudgery which I could not bring myself to undertake. I know it was great fun when it was fresh, and that many people have a curious antiquarian taste (I have it myself) for old chronicles of dead musicians and actors. I must warn them, however, not to expect to find here the work of the finished critic who wrote my volumes entitled Music in London, 1890–94, and Our Theatres in the Nineties. I knew all that was necessary about music; but in criticism I was only a beginner. It is easy enough from the first to distinguish between what is pleasant or unpleasant, accurate or inaccurate in a performance; but when great artists have to be dealt with, only keenly analytical observation and comparison of them with artists who, however agreeable, are not great, can enable a critic to distinguish between what everybody can do and what only a very few can do, and to get his valuations right accordingly. All artsmen know what it is to be enthusiastically praised for something so easy that they are half ashamed of it, and to receive not a word of encouragement for their finest strokes.

I cannot deny that Bassetto was occasionally vulgar; but that does not matter if he makes you laugh. Vulgarity is a necessary part of a complete author's equipment; and the clown is sometimes the best part of the circus. The Star, then a hapenny newspaper, was not catering for a fastidious audience: it was addressed to the bicycle clubs and the polytechnics, not to the Royal Society of Literature or the Musical Association. I purposely vulgarized musical criticism, which was then refined and academic to the point of being unreadable and often nonsensical. Editors, being mostly ignorant of music, would submit to anything from their musical critics, not pretending to understand it. If I occasionally carried to the verge of ribaldry my reaction against the pretentious twaddle and sometimes spiteful cliquishness they tolerated in their ignorance, think of me as heading one of the pioneer columns of what was then called The New Journalism; and you will wonder at my politeness.

You may be puzzled, too, to find that the very music I was brought up on: the pre-Wagner school of formal melody in separate numbers which seemed laid out to catch the encores that were then fashionable, was treated by me with contemptuous levity as something to be swept into the dustbin as soon as possible. The explanation is that these works were standing in the way of Wagner, who was then the furiously abused coming man in London. Only his early works were known or tolerated. Half a dozen bars of Tristan or The Mastersingers made professional musicians put their fingers in their ears. The Ride of the Valkyries was played at the Promenade Concerts, and always encored, but only as an insanely rampagious curiosity. The Daily Telegraph steadily preached Wagner down as a discordant notoriety-hunting charlatan in six silk dressing-gowns, who could not write a bar of melody, and made an abominable noise with the orchestra. In pantomime harlequinades the clown produced a trombone, played a bit of the pilgrims' march from Tannhäuser fortissimo as well as he could, and said: "The music of the future!" The wars of religion were not more bloodthirsty than the discussions of the Wagnerites and the Anti-Wagnerites. I was, of course, a violent Wagnerite; and I had the advantage of knowing the music to which Wagner grew up, whereas many of the most fanatical Wagnerites (Ashton Ellis, who translated the Master's prose works, was a conspicuous example) knew no other music than Wagner's, and believed that the music of Donizetti and Meyerbeer had no dramatic quality whatever. "A few arpeggios" was the description Ellis gave me of his notion of Les Huguenots.

Nowadays the reaction is all the other way. Our young lions have no use for Wagner the Liberator. His harmonies, which once seemed monstrous cacophonies, are the commonplaces of the variety theatres. Audacious young critics disparage his grandeurs as tawdry. When the wireless strikes up the Tannhäuser overture I hasten to switch it off, though I can always listen with pleasure to Rossini's overture to William Tell, hackneyed to death in Bassetto's time. The funeral march from Die Götterdämmerung hardly keeps my attention, though Handel's march from Saul is greater than ever. Though I used to scarify the fools who said that Wagner's music was formless, I should not now think the worse of Wagner if, like Bach and Mozart, he had combined the most poignant dramatic expression with the most elaborate decorative design. It was necessary for him to smash the superstition that this was obligatory; to free dramatic melody from the tyranny of arabesques; and to give the orchestra symphonic work instead of rosalias and rum-tum; but now that this and all the other musical superstitions are in the dustbin, and the post-Wagnerian harmonic and contrapuntal anarchy is so complete that it is easier technically to compose another Parsifal than another Bach's Mass in B Minor or Don Giovanni I am no longer a combatant anarchist in music, not to mention that I have learnt that a successful revolution's first task is to shoot all revolutionists. This means that I am no longer Corno di Bassetto. He was pre- and pro-Wagner; unfamiliar with Brahms; and unaware that a young musician named Elgar was chuckling over his irreverent boutades. As to Cyril Scott, Bax, Ireland, Goossens, Bliss, Walton, Schönberg, Hindemith, or even Richard Strauss and Sibelius, their idioms would have been quite outside Bassetto's conception of music, though today they seem natural enough. Therefore I very greatly doubt whether poor old Bassetto is worth reading now. Still, you are not compelled to read him. Having read the preface you can shut the book and give it to your worst enemy as a birthday present.

MID-ATLANTIC,
Sunday, 2nd June 1935.

A SUNDAY ON THE SURREY HILLS

(*From The Pall Mall Gazette*, 25 *April* 1888)

AS I am not a born cockney I have no illusions on the subject of the country. The uneven, ankle-twisting roads; the dusty hedges; the ditch with its dead dogs, rank weeds, and swarms of poisonous flies; the groups of children torturing something; the dull, toil-broken, prematurely old agricultural laborer; the savage tramp; the manure heaps with their horrible odour; the chain of milestones from inn to inn, from cemetery to cemetery: all these I pass heavily by until a distant telegraph pole or signal-post tells me that the blessed rescuing train is at hand. From the village street into the railway station is a leap across five centuries from the brutalizing torpor of Nature's tyranny over Man into the order and alertness of Man's organized dominion over Nature.

And yet last week I allowed myself to be persuaded by my friend Henry Salt and his wife to "come down and stay until Monday" among the Surrey hills. Salt, a man of exceptional intelligence on most subjects, is country mad, and keeps a house at a hole called Tilford, down Farnham way, to which he retires at intervals, subsisting on the fungi of the neighborhood, and writing articles advocating that line of diet and justifying the weather and the season to "pent-up" London. He entertained no doubt that a day at Tilford would convert me from rurophobia to rurolatry; and as he is a sensible companion for a walk and a talk—if only he would, like a sensible man, confine himself to the Thames Embankment—I at last consented to the experiment, and even agreed to be marched to the summit of a scenic imposture called Hindhead, and there shewn the downs of the South Coast, the Portsmouth Road (the Knightsbridge end of which I prefer), and, above all, the place where three men were hanged for murdering someone who had induced them to take a country walk with him.

London was clean, fresh, and dry as I made my way to Waterloo after rising at the unnatural hour of seven on Sunday morning. Opening a book, I took care not to look out of the window between the stations until, after traversing a huge cemetery and a huge camp, we reached Farnham. As usual in the country, it was raining heavily. I asked my way to Tilford, and was told to go straight on for four miles or so. As I had brought nothing that could hurt Salt's feelings by betraying my mistrust of his rustic paradise, I was without an umbrella; and the paradise, of course, took the fullest advantage of the omission. I do not know what the downs of the South Coast may be; but I can vouch for both ups and downs as far as the Surrey roads are concerned. Between Farnham and Tilford there are nearly half a dozen hills and not one viaduct. Over these I trudged uphill on my toes and pounded downhill on my heels, making at each step an oozy quagmire full of liquid gamboge. As the landscape grew less human, the rain came down faster, reducing my book to a pulp and transferring the red of the cover to my saturated grey jacket. Some waterproof variety of bird, screaming with laughter at me from a plantation, made me understand better than before why birds are habitually shot. The road presently passed a pine wood, with a gorgeous carpet of wet moss, and a notice that trespassers will be prosecuted. Truly it is worth while travelling thirty miles to be turned back by the curmudgeonism of a country gentleman. My sleeves by this time struck cold to my wrists. Hanging my arms disconsolately so as to minimize the unpleasant repercussion, I looked down at my clinging knees, and instantly discharged a pint of rain water and black dye over them from my hat brim. At this I laughed, much as criminals broken on the wheel used to laugh at the second stroke. A mile or two more of treadmill and gamboge churning, and I came to the outposts of a village, with a river hurrying over a bed of weeds of wonderful colors, spanned by a bridge constructed on the principle of the Gothic arch, so as to extort from horses the maximum of effort both when drawing carts up one side, and preventing the carts from overrunning them when slithering precipitously down the other.

This was Tilford, uninhabited as far as I could see except by one man, whose surly looks asked me, more plainly than words could, what the devil I wanted there. Then up another hill between meeting house and church, and out upon an exposed stretch of road where the rain and wind had an unobstructed final pelt at me. Salt is mistaken in supposing that he lives at Tilford: as a matter of fact he lives considerably beyond it; and I was on the point of turning whilst I had yet strength enough left to get back to London, when he hailed me from his door with a delighted shout of, "Here he is!" and beamed at me as if my condition left nothing to be desired, and Tilford had done itself the highest credit. In no time my clothes were filling the kitchen with steam; and I, invested in some garments belonging to Salt's brother-in-law, a promising poet whose figure is somewhat dissimilar to mine, was distending myself with my host's latest discoveries in local fungology.

My clothes dried fast. Quite early in the afternoon I put them on again, and found them some two inches shorter and tighter, but warm and desiccated. Nevertheless I had a fit of sneezing; and Mrs Salt produced a bottle of spirits of camphor. Unfamiliar with the violent nature of this remedy, I incautiously took a spoonful of it. It all but killed me; but I had the satisfaction, when I came to, of feeling tolerably sure that the influenza bacillus had not survived it. Then, the rain having ceased, we went out for a walk, and followed the road between the hills, which were like streaks of wet peat beneath the cloudy sky. Eventually we got out upon the uplands, where the mud was replaced by soft quicksand and heather already swept dry by the stark wind from the North Sea. Frensham Pond, like a waterworks denuded of machinery, lay to leeward of us, with a shudder passing over it from head to foot at every squall. I sympathized with it, and looked furtively at Salt, to see whether the ineffable dreariness of the scene had not dashed him. But he was used to it; and, when we got home, began to plan an excursion to Hindhead for the morrow. The mere suggestion brought on a fresh fit of sneezing. I positively declined further camphor; and Mrs Salt, by no means at the end of her resources, administered black currant jam and boiling water, which I rather liked.

Next morning I got up at eight to see the sun and hear the birds. I found, however, that I was up before them; and I neither saw nor heard them until I got back to the metropolis. Salt was jubilant because the wind was north-east, which made rain impossible. So after breakfast we started across the hills to Hindhead, through a mist that made the cows look like mammoths and the ridges like Alpine chains. When we were well out of reach of shelter the rain began. Salt declared that it would be nothing; that it could never hold out against the north-east wind. Nevertheless it did. When, after staggering and slipping up and down places which Salt described as lanes, but which were, in fact, rapidly filling beds of mountain mud torrents, we at last got upon Hindhead (which was exactly like all the other mounds), we could hardly see one another, much less the south coast, through the mist. I saw the place where the men were hanged; and I cannot deny that I felt a certain vindictive satisfaction in the idea of somebody having been served out there.

When we started homeward Salt was in the highest spirits. The discovery of a wet day in a north-east wind elated him as the discovery of a comet elates an astronomer. As for Mrs Salt, the conclusion she drew from it all was that I must come down another day. The rain gave her no more concern than if she had been a duck; and I could not help wondering whether her walking costume was not in reality a skilfully contrived bathing dress. She seemed perfectly happy, though the very sheep were bawling plaintively at the sky, and a cow to which I gave a friendly slap in passing was so saturated that the water squirted up my sleeve to the very armpit. Her chief theme whilst we were on the hills was the gentleness of her dog Nigger, whose movements in the direction of the sheep Salt was meanwhile carefully frustrating. Before we got home, my clothes contained three times as much water as they had gathered the day before. When I again resumed them they seemed to have been borrowed in an emergency from a very young brother.

I need not describe my walk back to Farnham after dinner. It rained all the way; but at least I was getting nearer to London. I have had change of air and a holiday; and I have no doubt I shall be able to throw off their effect in a fortnight or so. Should my experience serve to warn any tempted Londoner against too high an estimate of the vernal delights of the Surrey hills, it will perhaps not have been wasted.

FICTION

THE EDUCATION OF AN ACTRESS
(*Chap. VIII from Love Among the Artists*)

THE autumn passed; and the obscure days of the London winter set in. Adrian Herbert sat daily at work in his studio, painting a companion picture to the Lady of Shalott, and taking less exercise than was good either for himself or his work. His betrothed was at Windsor, studying Greek with Miss Cairns, and music with Jack. She had carried her point with Mrs Beatty as to the bandmastership; and Jack had been invited to apply for it; but he, on learning that a large part of his duty would be to provide the officers of the regiment with agreeable music whilst they dined, had unexpectedly repudiated the offer in an intemperate letter to the adjutant, stating that he had refused as an organist to be subject to the ministers of religion, and that he should refuse, as a conductor, to be the hireling of professional homicides. Miss Cairns, when she heard of this, in the heat of her disappointment reproached him for needlessly making an enemy of the colonel; embittering the dislike of Mrs Beatty, and exposing Mary to their resentment. Jack thereupon left Newton Villa in anger; but Miss Cairns learned next day that he had written a letter of thanks to the colonel, in which he mentioned that the recent correspondence with the adjutant had unfortunately turned on the dignity of the musical profession, and begged that it might be disassociated entirely from the personal feeling to which he now sought to give expression. To Miss Cairns herself he also wrote briefly to say that it had occurred to him that Miss Sutherland might be willing to join the singing class, and that he hoped she would be asked to do so. Over this double concession Miss Cairns exulted; but Mary, humiliated by the failure of her effort to befriend him, would not join, and resisted all persuasion, until Jack, meeting her one day in the street, stopped her, inquired after Charlie, and finally asked her to come to one of the class meetings. Glad to have this excuse for relenting, she not only entered the class, but requested him to assist her in the study of harmony, which she had recently begun to teach herself from a treatise. As it proved, however, he confused rather than assisted her; for, though an adept in the use of chords, he could make no intelligible attempt to name or classify them; and her exercises, composed according to the instructions given in the treatise, exasperated him beyond measure.

Meanwhile, Magdalen Brailsford, with many impatient sighs, was learning to speak the English language with purity and distinctness, and beginning to look on certain pronunciations for which she had ignorantly ridiculed famous actors, as enviable conditions of their superiority to herself. She did not enjoy her studies, for Jack was very exacting; and the romantic aspect of their first meeting at Paddington was soon forgotten in the dread he inspired as a master. She left Church Street after her first lesson in a state of exhaustion; and, long after she had become accustomed to endure his criticism for an hour without fatigue, she often could hardly restrain her tears when he emphasized her defects by angrily mimicking them, which was the most unpleasant, but not the least effective, part of his system of teaching. He was particular, even in his cheerful moods, and all but violent in his angry ones; but he was indefatigable, and spared himself no trouble in forcing her to persevere in overcoming the slovenly habits of colloquial speech. The further she progressed, the less she could satisfy him. His ear was far more acute than hers; and he demanded from her beauties of tone of which she had no conception, and refinements of utterance which she could not distinguish. He repeated sounds which he declared were as distinct as day from night, and raged at her because she could hear no difference between them. He insisted that she was grinding her voice to pieces when she was hardly daring to make it audible. Often, when she was longing for the expiry of the hour to release her, he kept her until Mrs Simpson, who was always present, could bear it no longer, and interfered in spite of the frantic abuse to which a word from her during the lesson invariably provoked him. Magdalen would have given up her project altogether, for the sake of escaping the burden of his tuition, but for her fear of the contempt she knew he would feel for her if she proved recreant. So she toiled on without a word of encouragement or approval from him; and he grimly and doggedly kept her at it, until one day, near Christmas, she came to Church Street earlier than usual, and had a long conference with Mrs Simpson before he was informed of her presence. When he came down from his garret she screwed her courage up to desperation point, and informed him that she had obtained an engagement for a small part in the opening of a pantomime at Nottingham. Instead of exploding fiercely, he stared a little, rubbed his head perplexedly, and then said, "Well, well: you must begin somehow: the sooner the better. You will have to do poor work, in poor company, for some time, perhaps; but you must believe in yourself, and not flinch from the drudgery of the first year or two. Keep the fire always alight on the altar, and every place you go into will become a temple. Dont be mean: no grabbing at money, or opportunities, or effects! You can speak already better than ninety-nine out of a hundred of them: remember that. If you ever want to do as they do, then your ear will be going wrong; and that will be a sign that your soul is going wrong too. Do you believe me, eh?"

"Yes," said Madge dutifully.

He looked at her very suspiciously, and uttered a sort of growl, adding, "If you get hissed occasionally, it will do you good; although you are more likely to get applauded and spoilt. Dont forget what I have taught you: you will see the use of it when you have begun to understand your profession."

Magdalen protested that she should never forget, and tried to express her gratitude for the trouble he had taken with her. She begged that he would not reveal her destination to any one, as it was necessary for her to evade her family a second time in order to fulfil her engagement. He replied that her private arrangements were no business of his, advising her at the same time to reflect before she quitted a luxurious home for a precarious and vagabond career, and recommending Mrs Simpson to her as an old hag whose assistance would be useful in any business that required secrecy and lying. "If you want my help," he added, "you can come and ask for it."

"She can come and pay for it, and no thanks to you," said Mrs Simpson, goaded beyond endurance.

Jack turned on her, purple and glaring. Madge threw herself between them. Then he suddenly walked out; and, as they stood there trembling and looking at one another in silence, they heard him go upstairs to his garret.

"Oh, Polly, how could you!" said Madge at last, almost in a whisper.

"I wonder what he's gone for," said Mrs Simpson. "Theres nothing upstairs that he can do any harm with. I didnt mean anything."

He came down presently, with an old wash-leather purse in his hand. "Here," he said to Madge. They knew perfectly well, without further explanation, that it was the money she had paid him for her lessons.

"Mr Jack," she stammered; "I cannot."

"Come, take it," he said. "She is right: the people at Windsor pay for my wants. I have no need to be supported twice over. Has she charged you anything for the room?"

"No," said Madge.

"Then the more shame for me to charge you for your lessons," said Jack. "I shall know better another time. Here, take the money, and let us think no more about it. Goodbye! I think I can work a little now, if I set about it at once." He gave her the purse, which she did not dare refuse, shook her hand with both his, and went out hurriedly, but humbly.

Three days after this, Adrian Herbert was disturbed at his easel by Mr Brailsford, who entered the studio in an extraordinarily excited condition.

"Mr Brailsford! I am very glad to— What is the matter?"

"Do you know anything of Magdalen? She is missing

again." Herbert assumed an air of concern. "Herbert: I appeal to you, if she has confided her plans to you, not to ruin her by a misplaced respect for her foolish secrets."

"I assure you I am as much surprised as you. Why should you suppose that I am in her confidence?"

"You were much in her company during your recent visits to us; and you are the sort of man a young girl would confide any crazy project to. You and she have talked together a good deal."

"Well, we have had two conversations within the last six weeks, both of which came about by accident. We were speaking of my affairs only. You know Miss Sutherland is a friend of hers. She is our leading topic."

"This is very disappointing, Herbert. Confoundedly so."

"It is unfortunate; and I am sorry I know nothing."

"Yes, yes: I knew you were not likely to: it was mere clutching at a straw. Herbert, when I get that girl back, I'll lock her up, and not let her out of her room until she leaves it to be married."

"When did she go?"

"Last night. We did not miss her until this morning. She has gone to disgrace herself a second time at some blackguard country theatre or other. And yet she has always been treated with the greatest indulgence at home. She is not like other girls who do not know the value of a comfortable home. In the days when I fought the world as a man of letters, she had opportunities of learning the value of money." Mr Brailsford, as he spoke, moved about constantly; pulled at his collar as if it were a stock which needed to be straightened; and fidgeted with his gloves. "I am powerless," he added, "I cannot obtain the slightest clue. There is nothing for it but to sit down and let my child go."

"Are you aware," said Herbert thoughtfully, "that she has been taking lessons in acting from a professor of music during the last few months?"

"No, sir, I certainly am not aware of it," said Brailsford

fiercely. "I beg your pardon, my dear Herbert; but she is a damned ungrateful girl; and her loss is a great trouble to me. I did not know; and she could not have done it if her mother had looked after her properly."

"It is certainly the case. I was very much surprised myself when Miss Sutherland told me of it, especially as I happened to have some knowledge of the person whom Miss Brailsford employed."

"Perhaps he knows. Who is he and where is he to be found?"

"His name is an odd one—Jack."

"Jack? I have heard that name somewhere. Jack? My memory is a wreck. But we are losing time. You know his address, I hope."

"I believe I have it here among some old letters. Excuse me whilst I search."

Herbert went into the anteroom. Mr Brailsford continued his nervous movements, bit his nails, and made a dab at the picture with his glove, smudging it. The discovery that he had wantonly done mischief sobered him a little; and presently Adrian returned with one of Jack's letters.

"Church Street, Kensington," he said. "Will you go there?"

"Instantly, Herbert, instantly. Will you come?"

"If you wish," said Adrian, hesitating.

"Certainly. You must come. This is some low villain who has pocketed the child's money, and persuaded her that she is a Mrs Siddons. I had lessons myself long ago from the great Young, who thought highly of me, though not more so than I did of him. Perhaps I am dragging you away from your work, my dear fellow."

"It is too dark to work much today. In any case the matter is too serious to be sacrificed to my routine."

Quarter of an hour later, Mrs Simpson's maid knocked at the door of Jack's garret, and informed him that two gentlemen were waiting in the drawing room to see him.

"What are they like?" said Jack. "Are you sure they

want me?"

"Certain sure," said the girl. "One of em's a nice young gentleman with a flaxy beard; and the other is his father, I think. Aint he a dapper old toff, too!"

"Give me my boots; and tell them I shall be down presently."

The maid then appeared to Mr Brailsford and Adrian, saying, "Mr Jax'll be down in a minnit," and vanished. Soon after, Jack came in. In an instant Mr Brailsford's eyes lit up as if he saw through the whole plot; and he rose threateningly. Jack bade good morning ceremoniously to Herbert, who was observing with alarm the movements of his companion.

"You know me, I think, sir," said Mr Brailsford threateningly.

"I remember you very well," replied Jack grimly. "Be pleased to sit down."

Herbert hastily offered Mr Brailsford a chair, pushing it against his calves just in time to interrupt an angry speech at the beginning. The three sat down.

"We have called on you, Mr Jack," said Adrian, "in the hope that you can throw some light on a matter which is a source of great anxiety to Mr Brailsford. Miss Brailsford has disappeared—"

"What!" cried Jack. "Run away again! Ha! ha! I expected as much."

"Pray be calm," said Herbert, as Mr Brailsford made a frantic gesture. "Allow me to speak. Mr Jack: I believe you have lately been in communication with the young lady."

"I have been teaching her for the last four months, if that is what you mean."

"Pray understand that we attach no blame to you in the matter. We merely wish to ascertain the whereabouts of Miss Brailsford; and we thought you might be able to assist us. If so, I feel sure you will not hesitate to give this gentleman all the information in your power."

"You may reassure yourself," said Jack. "She has got

an engagement at some theatre and has gone to fulfil it. She told me so a few days ago, when she came to break off her lessons."

"We particularly wish to find out where she has gone to," said Herbert slowly.

"You must find that out as best you can," said Jack, looking attentively at him. "She mentioned the place to me: but she asked me not to repeat it, and it is not my business to do so."

"Herbert," cried Mr Brailsford. "Herbert."

"Pray!" remonstrated Adrian. "Just allow me one word—"

"Herbert," persisted the other: "this is the fellow of whom I told you as we came along in the cab. He is her accomplice. You know you are," he continued, turning to Jack, and raising his voice. "Do you still deny that you are her agent?"

Jack stared at him imperturbably.

"It is a conspiracy," said Mr Brailsford. "It has been a conspiracy from the first; and you are the prime mover in it. You shall not bully me, sir. I will make you speak."

"There, there," said Jack. "Take him away, Mr Herbert."

Adrian stepped hastily between them, fearing that his companion would proceed to violence. Before another word could be spoken the door was opened by Mrs Simpson, who started and stopped short when she saw visitors in the room.

"I beg pardon— Why, it's Mr Brailsford," she added, reddening. "I hope I see you well, sir," she continued, advancing with a propitiatory air. "I am honored by having you in my house."

"Indeed!" said the old gentleman, with a look which made her tremble. "So it is you who introduced Miss Magdalen to this man. Herbert, my dear boy, the thing is transparent. This woman is an old retainer of ours. It was her sister who took Madge away before. I told you it was all a conspiracy."

"Lord bless us!" exclaimed Mrs Simpson. "I hope nothing aint happened to Miss Magdalen."

"If anything has, you shall be held responsible for it. Where has she gone?"

"Oh, dont go to tell me that my sweet Miss Magdalen has gone away again, sir!"

"You hear how they contradict one another, Herbert?"

Mrs Simpson looked mistrustfully at Jack, who was grinning at her with cynical admiration. "I dont know what Mr Jack may have put into your head about me, sir," she said cautiously; "but I assure you I know nothing of poor Miss Magdalen's doings. I havent seen her this past month."

"You understand, of course," remarked Jack, "that that is not true. Mrs Simpson has always been present at your daughter's lessons. She knows perfectly well that Miss Brailsford has gone to play at some theatre. She heard it in—"

"I wish youd mind your own business, Mr Jack," said the landlady sharply.

"When lies are needed to serve Miss Brailsford, you can speak," retorted Jack. "Until then, hold your tongue. It is clear to me, Mr Herbert, that you want this unfortunate young lady's address for the purpose of attempting to drag her back from an honorable profession to a foolish and useless existence which she hates. Therefore I shall give you no information. If she is unhappy or unsuccessful in her new career, she will return of her own accord."

"I fear," said Herbert, embarrassed by the presence of Mrs Simpson, "that we can do no good by remaining here."

"You are right," said Mr Brailsford. "I decline to address myself further to either of you. Other steps shall be taken. And you shall repent the part you have played on this occasion, Mrs Simpson. As for you, sir, I can only say I trust this will prove our last meeting."

"I shant repent nothink," said Mrs Simpson. "Why shouldnt I assist the pretty—"

"Come!" said Jack, interrupting her, "we have said

enough. Good evening, Mr Herbert." Adrian colored, and moved towards the door. "You shall be welcome whenever you wish to see me," added Jack; "but at present you had better take this gentleman away." Herbert bowed slightly and went out, annoyed by the abrupt dismissal, and even more by the attempt to soften it. Mr Brailsford walked stiffly after him, staring indignantly at Mrs Simpson and her lodger. Provoked to mirth by this demonstration, Jack, who had hitherto behaved with dignity, rubbed his nose with the palm of his hand, and grinned hideously through his fingers at his visitor.

"As I told you before," said Mr Brailsford, turning as he reached the threshold, "you are a vile kidnapper; and I will see that your trade is exposed and put a stop to."

"As I told you before," said Jack, removing his hand from his nose, "you are an old fool; and I wish you good afternoon."

"Sh—sh," said Mrs Simpson, as Mr Brailsford, with a menacing wave of his glove, disappeared. "You didnt ought to speak like that to an old gentleman, Mr Jack."

"His age gives him no right to be ill-tempered and abusive to me," said Jack angrily.

"Humph!" retorted the landlady. "Your own tongue and temper are none of the sweetest. If I was you, I wouldnt be so much took aback at seeing others do the same as myself."

"Indeed. And how do you think being me would feel like, Mrs Deceit?"

"I wouldnt make out other people to be liars before their faces, at all events, Mr Jack."

"You would prefer the truth to be told of you behind your back, perhaps. I sometimes wonder what part of my music will show the influence of your society upon me. My Giulietta Guicciardi!"

"Give me no more of your names," said Mrs Simpson shortly, "I dont need them."

Jack left the room slowly as if he had forgotten her.

Meanwhile Mr Brailsford was denouncing him to Herbert. "From the moment I first saw him," he said, "I felt an instinctive antipathy to him. I have never seen a worse face, or met with a worse nature."

"I certainly do not like him," said Herbert. "He has taken up an art as a trade, and knows nothing of the trials of a true artist's career. No doubts of himself; no aspirations to suggest them; nothing but a stubborn narrow self-sufficiency. I half envy him."

"The puppy!" exclaimed Mr Brailsford, not attending to Adrian: "to dare insult me! He shall suffer for it. I have put a bullet into a fellow—into a gentleman of good position—for less. And Magdalen—my daughter—is intimate with him—has visited him. Girls are going to the devil of late years, Herbert, going to the very devil. She shall not give me the slip again, when I catch her."

Mr Brailsford, however, did not catch Magdalen. Her good looks, and her clear delivery of the doggerel verses allotted to her in the pantomime, gained the favor of the Nottingham playgoers. Their applause prevented her from growing weary of repeating her worthless part nightly for six weeks, and compensated her for the discomfort and humiliation of living among people whom she could not help regarding as her inferiors, and with whom she had to cooperate in entertaining vulgar people with vulgar pleasantries, fascinating them by a display of the comeliness, not only of her face, but of more of her person than she had been expected to show at Kensington Palace Gardens. Her costume almost shocked her at first; but she made up her mind to accept it without demur, partly because wearing such things was plainly part of an actress's business, and partly because she felt that any objection on her part would imply an immodest self-consciousness. Besides, she had no moral conviction that it was wrong, whereas she had no doubt at all that petticoats were a nuisance. She could not bring herself to accept with equal frankness the society which the pantomime company offered to her. Miss Lafitte, the chief performer, was a favorite with the public on account of her vivacity, her skill in clog-dancing, and her command of slang, which she uttered in a piercing voice with a racy Whitechapel accent. She took a fancy to Magdalen, who at first recoiled. But Miss Lafitte (in real life Mrs Cohen) was so accustomed to live down aversion, that she only regarded it as a sort of shyness—as indeed it was. She was vigorous, loud spoken, always full of animal spirits, and too well appreciated by her audiences to be jealous. Magdalen, who had been made miserable at first by the special favor of permission to share the best dressing-room with her, soon found the advantage of having a good-natured and powerful companion. The drunken old woman who was attached to the theatre as dresser needed to be kept efficient by sharp abuse and systematic bullying, neither of which Magdalen could have administered effectually. Miss Lafitte bullied her to perfection. Occasionally some of the actors would stroll into the dressing-room, evidently without the least suspicion that Magdalen might prefer to put on her shoes, rouge herself, and dress her hair in private. Miss Lafitte, who had never objected to their presence on her own account, now bade them begone whenever they appeared, at which they seemed astonished, but, having no intention of being intrusive, retired submissively.

"You make yourself easy, deah," she said to Magdalen. "Awe-y-'ll take kee-yerr of you. Lor bless you, awe-y know wot you are. Youre a law-ydy. But youll get used to them. They dont mean no arm."

Magdalen, wondering what Jack would have said to Miss Lafitte's vowels, disclaimed all pretension to be more of a lady than those with whom she worked; but Miss Lafitte, though she patted the young novice on the back, and soothingly assented, nevertheless continued to make a difference between her own behavior in Magdalen's presence, and the coarse chaff and reckless flirtation in which she indulged freely elsewhere. On Boxing night, when Madge was nerving herself to face the riotous audience, Miss Lafitte told her that she looked beautiful; exhorted her cheerfully to keep up her pecker and never say die; and, ridiculing her fear of putting too much paint on her face, plastered her cheeks and blackened the margins of her eyes until she blushed through the mask of pigment. When the call came, she went with her to the wing, pushed her on to the scene at the right instant, and praised her enthusiastically when she returned. Madge, who hardly knew what had passed on the stage, was grateful for these compliments, and tried to return them when Miss Lafitte came to the dressing-room, flushed with the exertion of singing a topical song with seven encore verses, and dancing a breakdown between each.

"I'm used to it," said Miss Lafitte. "It's my knowledge of music-hall business that makes me what I am. You wouldnt catch me on the stage at all, only that my husband's a bit of a swell in his own way—he'll like you for that—and he thinks the theatre more respectable. It dont pay as well, I can tell you; but of course it's surer and lasts longer."

"Were you nervous at your first appearance?" said Madge.

"Oh, wawnt I though! Just a little few. I cried at havin to go on. I wasnt cold and plucky like you; but I got over it sooner. I know your sort: you will be nervous all your life. I dont care twopence for any audience now, nor ever did after my second night."

"I may have looked cold and plucky," said Madge, surprised. "I never felt more miserable in my life before."

"Yes. Aint it awful? Did you hear Lefanu?—stuck up little minx! Her song will be cut out tomorrow. She's a reglar duffer, she is. She gives herself plenty of airs, and tells the people that she was never used to associate with us. I know who she is well enough: her father was an apothecary in Bayswater. She's only fit to be a governess. Youre worth fifty of her, either on the boards or off."

Madge did not reply. She was conscious of having contemplated escape from Miss Lafitte by attaching herself to Miss Lefanu, who was a ladylike young woman.

"She looks like a print gown after five washings," continued Miss Lafitte; "and she dont know how to speak. Now you speak lovely—almost as well as me, if youd spit it out a bit more. Who taught you?"

When the pantomime had been played for a fortnight, Madge found herself contemptuously indifferent to Miss Lefanu, and fond of Miss Lafitte. When the latter invited her to a supper at her house, she could not refuse, though she accepted with misgiving. It proved a jovial entertainment—almost an orgie. Some of the women drank much champagne; spoke at the top of their voices; and screamed when they laughed. The men paid court to them with facetious compliments, and retorted their raillery with broad sarcasms. Madge got on best with the younger and less competent actors, who were mostly unpropertied gentlemen, with a feeble amateur bent for singing and acting, who had contrived to get on the stage, not because they were fit for it, but because society had not fitted them for anything else. They talked theatrical shop and green-room scandal in addition to the usual topics of young gentlemen at dances; and they shielded Magdalen efficiently from the freer spirits. Sometimes an unusually coarse sally would reach her ears, and bring upon her a sense of disgust and humiliation; but, though she resolved to attend no more suppers, she was able next day to assure her hostess with perfect sincerity that she was none the worse for her evening's experience, and that she had never enjoyed herself as much at any Kensington supper party. Miss Lafitte thereupon embraced her, and told her that she had been the belle of the ball, and that Laddie (a Gentile abbreviation of Lazarus, her husband's name) had recognized her as a real lady, and was greatly pleased with her. Then she asked her whether she did not think Laddie a handsome man. Madge, to gratify her, replied that she had been struck by his dark hair and eyes, and that his manners were elegant. "There is one thing," she added, "that puzzles me a little. I always call you Miss Lafitte here, but should I not call you by your real name at your house?

I dont know the etiquette, you see."

"Call me Sal," said Mrs Cohen, kissing her.

When the pantomime was over, and the company dispersed, the only member of it whose departure she felt as a loss was Miss Lafitte; and she never afterwards fell into the mistake of confounding incorrigible rowdyism and a Whitechapel accent with true unfitness for society. By her advice, Madge accepted an engagement as one of the stock company of the Nottingham theatre at the salary—liberal for a novice—of two pounds per week. For this she did some hard work. Every night she had to act in a farce, and in a comedy which had become famous in London. In it, as in the pantomime, she had to play the same part nightly for two weeks. Then came three weeks of Shakespeare and the legitimate drama, in which she and the rest of the company had to support an eminent tragedian, a violent and exacting man, who expected them to be perfect in long parts at a day's notice. When they disappointed him, as was usually the case, he kept them rehearsing from the forenoon to the hour of performance with hardly sufficient interval to allow of their dining. The stage manager, the musicians, the scene-painters and carpenters even, muttered sulkily that it was impossible to please him. He did not require the actors to enter into the spirit of their lines—it was supposed that he was jealous of their attempts at acting, which were certainly not always helpful—but he was inflexible in his determination to have them letter-perfect and punctual in the movements and positions he dictated to them. His displeasure was vented either in sarcasms or oaths; and often Madge, though nerved by intense indignation, could hardly refrain from weeping like many other members of the company, both male and female, from fatigue and mortification. She worked hard at her parts, which were fortunately not long ones, in order to escape the humiliation of being rebuked by him. Yet once or twice he excited her fear and hatred to such a degree that she was on the point of leaving the theatre, and abandoning her profession. It was far worse than what Jack had made her endure; for her submission to him had been voluntary; whilst with the tragedian she could not help herself, being paid to assist him, and ignorant of how to do it properly.

Towards the end of the second week her business became easier by repetition. She appeared as the player queen in Hamlet, the lady-in-waiting in Macbeth, and the widow of King Edward IV, and began to feel for the first time a certain respect for the silently listening, earnest audiences that crowded the house. It was the first dim stirring in her of a sense that her relation as an actress to the people was above all her other relations. If the tragedian had felt this as between the audience and the company of which he was but a part, he might have inspired them to work all together with a will to realize the plays to the people. But he was a "star," recognizing no part and no influence but his own. She and her colleagues were dwarfed and put out of countenance; their scenes were cut short and hurried through; the expert swordsman who, as Richmond and Macduff, slew the star thrice a week in mortal combat, was the only person who shared with him the compliment of a call before the curtain. Naturally, they all hated Shakespeare; and the audiences, distinctly prefering the tragedian to the poet, never protested against his palming off on them versions by Cibber or Garrick as genuine Shakespearean plays.

On the second Saturday, when Madge was congratulating herself on having only six days more of the national Bard to endure, the principal actress sprained her ankle; and the arrangements for the ensuing week were thrown into confusion. The manager came to Madge's lodging on Sunday morning, and told her that she must be prepared to play Ophelia, Lady Ann, and Marion Delorme (in Lytton's Richelieu) in the course of the following week. It was, he added, a splendid chance for her. Madge was distracted. She said again and again that it was impossible, and at last ventured to remind the manager that she was not engaged for leading parts. He disposed of this objection by promising her an extra ten shillings for the week, and urged upon her that she would look lovely as Ophelia; that the tragedian had made a point of giving the parts to her because he liked her elocution; that his fierceness was only a little way of his which meant nothing; that he had already consented to substitute Hamlet and Richelieu for Much Ado and Othello because he was too considerate to ask her to play Beatrice and Desdemona; and, finally, that he would be enraged if she made any objection. She would, said the manager, show herself as willing as old Mrs Walker, who had undertaken to play Lady Macbeth without a moment's hesitation. Madge, ashamed to shrink from an emergency, and yet afraid of failing to please the tyrant at rehearsal, resisted the manager's importunity until she felt hysterical. Then, in desperation, she consented, stipulating only that she should be released from playing in the farces. She spent that Sunday learning the part of Ophelia, and was able to master it and to persuade herself that the other two parts would not take long to learn, before she went to bed, dazed by study and wretched from dread of the morrow. Hamlet had been played twice already, and only the part of Ophelia and that of the player queen needed to be rehearsed anew. On Monday morning the tragedian was thoughtful and dignified, but hard to please. He kept Madge at his scene with Ophelia for more than an hour. She had intended to try and fancy that she was really Ophelia, and he really Hamlet; but when the time came to practise this primitive theory of acting, she did not dare to forget herself for a moment. She had to count her steps, and repeat her entrance four times before she succeeded in placing herself at the right moment in the exact spot towards which the tragedian looked when exclaiming "Soft you now! The fair Ophelia." For a long time she could not offer him the packet of letters in a satisfactory manner; and by the time this difficulty was mastered, she was so bewildered that when he said, "I loved you not," she, instead of replying, "I was the more deceived," said, "Indeed, my lord, you made me believe so," whereupon he started, looked at her for a moment, muttering imprecations between his teeth, and abruptly walked off the stage, leaving her there alone, wondering. Suddenly she bethought her self of what she had done; and her cheeks began to tingle. She was relieved by the return of Hamlet, who, unable to find words to express his feelings, repeated his speech without making any verbal comment on her slip. This time she made the proper answer; and the rehearsal proceeded. The new player queen suffered less than Madge had done a week before, the tragedian treating her with brief disdain. He was very particular about Ophelia's chair and fan in the play scene; but when these were arranged, he left the theatre without troubling himself about the act in which he did not himself appear. Madge, left comparatively to her own devices in rehearsing it, soon felt the want of his peremptory guidance, and regretted his absence almost as much as she was relieved by it. The queen, jealous, like the other actresses, of Madge's promotion, was disparaging in her manner; and the king rehearsed with ostentatious carelessness, being out of humor at having to rehearse at all. Everybody present showed that they did not consider the scene of the least importance; and Madge sang her snatches of ballads with a disheartening sense of being unpopular and ridiculous.

The performance made amends to her for the rehearsal. The tragedian surpassed himself; and Madge was compelled to admire him, although he was in his fiftieth year and personally disagreeable to her. For her delivery of the soliloquy following her scene with him, she received, as her share of the enthusiasm he had excited, a round of applause which gratified her the more because she had no suspicion that he had earned the best part of it. The scene of Ophelia's madness was listened to with favor by the audience, who were impressed by the intensely earnest air which nervousness gave Madge, as well as by her good looks.

Next day she had leisure to study the part of Lady Anne in Cibber's adaptation of Richard III, which was rehearsed on the Wednesday; and this time the tragedian was so overbearing, and corrected her so frequently and savagely, that when he handed her his sword, and requested her to stab him, she felt disposed to take him at his word. In the scene from Richard's domestic life in which he informs his wife that he hates her, he not only spoke the text with a cold ferocity which chilled her, but cursed at her under his breath quite outrageously. At last she was stung to express her resentment by an indignant look, which fell immediately before his frown. When the rehearsal, which, though incomplete, lasted from eleven to four, was over, Madge was angry and very tired. As she was leaving, she passed near Richard, who was conversing graciously with the manager and one of the actors. The night before, he had threatened to leave the theatre because the one had curtailed his stage escort by two men; and he had accused the other of intentionally insulting him by appearing on the stage without spurs.

"Who is that little girl?" he said aloud, pointing to Madge.

The manager, surprised at the question, made some reply which did not reach her, his voice and utterance being less sonorous and distinct than the tragedian's.

"Unquestionably she has played with me. I am aware of that. What is she called?"

The manager told him.

"Come here," he said to Madge, in his grand manner. She reddened, and stopped.

"Come here," he repeated, more emphatically. She was too inexperienced to feel sure of her right to be treated more respectfully, so she approached him slowly.

"Who taught you to speak?"

"A gentleman in London," she said coldly. "A Mr Jack."

"Jack!" The tragedian paused. "Jack!" he repeated. Then, with a smile, and a graceful action of his wrists, "I never heard of him." The other men laughed. "Would you like to tour through the provinces with me—to act with me every night?"

"Oho!" said the manager jocularly, "I shall have something to say to that. I cannot afford to lose her."

"You need not be alarmed," said Madge, all her irritation suddenly exploding in one angry splutter. "I have not the slightest intention of breaking my present engagement, particularly now, when the most unpleasant part of it is nearly over." And she walked away, pouting and scarlet. The manager told her next day that she had ruined herself, and had made a very ungrateful return for the kindness that she, a beginner, had received from the greatest actor on the stage. She replied that she was not conscious of having received anything but rudeness from the greatest actor on the stage, and that if she had offended him she was very glad. The manager shook his head and retired, muttering that a week's leading business had turned her head. The tragedian, who had been, for so terrible a person, much wounded and put out of heart by her attack, took no further notice of her, demanding no fresh rehearsal of Ophelia, and only giving her a few curt orders in the small part of Marion Delorme. At last he departed from Nottingham; and Madge, for the first time since his arrival, lay down to sleep free from care.

Her next part was that of a peasant girl in an Irish melodrama. She looked very pretty in her Connemara cloak and short skirt, but was hampered by her stage brogue, which only made her accent aggressively English. During this period, she was annoyed by the constant attendance in the stalls of a young gentleman who flung bouquets to her, followed her to her lodging, and finally wrote her a letter in which he called her a fairy Red Riding Hood, describing his position and prospects, and begging her to marry him. Madge after some hesitation as to the advisability of noticing this appeal, replied by a note declining his offer, and requesting him to discontinue his gifts of flowers, which, she said, were a source of embarrassment, and not of pleasure, to her. After this, the young gentleman, instead of applauding, as before, sat in his stall with folded arms and a gloomy expression. Madge, who was by this time sufficiently accustomed to the stage to recognize faces among the audience, took care not to look at him; and so, after a week, he ceased to attend and she saw him no more.

The Irish melodrama passed on to the next town; and an English opera company came in its place for a fortnight, during which Madge found the time hang heavy on her hands, as she took no part in the performances, though she went to the theatre daily from habit. She was glad when she was at work again in a modern play with which a popular actress was making the tour of the provinces. This actress was an amiable woman; and Madge enacted Celia in As You Like It at her benefit without any revival of the dread of Shakespeare which the tragedian had implanted in her. She was now beginning to tread the boards with familiar ease. At first, the necessity of falling punctually into certain prearranged positions on the stage, and of making her exits and entrances at prescribed sides, had so preoccupied her that all freedom of attention or identification of herself with the character she represented had been impossible. To go through her set task of speeches and manœuvres with accuracy was the most she could hope to do. Now, however, these mechanical conditions of her art not only ceased to distract her, but enabled her to form plans of acting which stood the test of rehearsal. She became used to learning parts, not from a book of the play, but from a mere list of the fragments which she had to utter; so that she committed her lines to memory first, and found out what they were about afterwards. She was what is called by actors a quick study; and in Nottingham, where, besides the principal piece, one and often two farces were performed nightly, she had no lack of practice. In four months, she was second in skill only to the low comedian and the old woman, and decidedly superior to the rest of the stock company, most of whom had neither natural talent nor even taste for the stage, and only earned their livelihood on it because, their parents having been in the profession, they had been in a manner born into it.

Madge's artistic experience thenceforth was varied, though her daily course was monotonous. Other tragedians came to Nottingham, but none nearly so terrible, nor, she reluctantly confessed, nearly so gifted, as he who had taught her the scene from Hamlet. Some of them, indeed, objected to the trouble of rehearsing, and sent substitutes who imitated them in every movement and so drilled the company to act with them. Occasionally a part in a comedy of contemporary life enabled Madge to profit by her knowledge of fashionable society and her taste in modern dress. The next week, perhaps, she would have to act in a sensational melodrama, and, in a white muslin robe, to struggle in the arms of a pickpocket in corduroys, with his clothes and hands elaborately begrimed. Once she had to play with the wreck of a celebrated actress, who was never free from the effects of brandy, and who astonished Madge by walking steadily on the stage when she could hardly stand off it. Then Shakespeare, sensation drama, Irish melodrama, comic opera or pantomime, new comedy from London over again, with farce constantly. Study, rehearsal, and performance became part of her daily habits. Her old enthusiasm for the mock passions of the stage left her, and was succeeded by a desire to increase her skill in speaking by acquiring as much resource in shades of meaning as Jack had given her in pure pronunciation, and to add as many effective gestures as possible to the stock she had already learnt. When she was not engaged at the theatre she was at her lodging, practising the management of a train, trying to acquire the knack of disposing her dress prettily in the act of sitting down, or arranging her features into various expressions before a mirror. This last branch of her craft was the most troublesome to her. She had learned from Jack, much to her surprise, that she could not make her face express anger or scorn by merely feeling angry or scornful. The result of that method was a strained frown, disagreeable to behold; and it was long before she attained perfect control of her features, and artistic judgment in exercising it. Sometimes she erred on the side of exaggeration, and failed to conceal the effort which her studied acting required. Then she recoiled into tameness and conventionality. Then, waking from this, she tried a modification of her former manner, and presently became dissatisfied with that too, and remodified it. Not until she had gone through two years of hard study and practice did she find herself mistress of a fairly complete method; and then indeed she felt herself an actress. She ridiculed the notion that emotion had anything to do with her art, and seriously began to think of taking a pupil, feeling that she could make an actress of any girl, the matter being merely one of training. When she had been some four months in this phase, she had a love affair with a young acting manager of a touring company. The immediate effect was to open her eyes to the fact that the people were tired of her complete method, and that she was tired of it too. She flung it at once to the winds for ever, and thenceforth greatly undervalued her obligations to the study it had cost her, declaring, in the teeth of her former opinion, that study and training were useless, and that the true method was to cultivate the heart and mind and let the acting take care of itself. She cultivated her mind by high reading and high thinking as far as she could. As to the cultivation of her heart, the acting manager taught her that the secret of that art was love. Now it happened that the acting manager, though pleasant-looking and good-natured, was by no means clever, provident, or capable of resisting temptation. Madge never could make up her mind whether he had entangled her or she him. In truth, love entangled them both; and Madge found that love suited her excellently. It improved her health; it enlarged her knowledge of herself and of the world; it explained her rôles to her, thawed the springs of emotion that had never flowed freely before either on or off the stage, threw down a barrier that had fenced her in from her kind, and replaced her vague aspirations, tremors, doubts, and fits of low spirits with an elate enjoyment in which she felt that she was a woman at last. Nevertheless, her attachment to the unconscious instrument of this mysterious change proved transient. The acting manager had but slender intellectual resources: when his courtship grew stale, he became a bore. After a while, their professional engagements carried them asunder; and as a correspondent he soon broke down. Madge did not feel the parting: she found a certain delight in being fancy-free; and before that was exhausted she was already dreaming of a new lover, an innocent young English-opera librettist, whom she infatuated and ensnared and who came nearer than she suspected to blowing out his brains from remorse at having, as he thought, ensnared her. His love for her was abject in its devotion; but at last she went elsewhere, and, as her letters also presently ceased, his parents, with much trouble, managed to convince him at last that she no longer cared for him.

It must not be supposed that these proceedings cost Madge her self-respect. She stood on her honor according to her own instinct, took no gifts, tolerated no advances from men whose affections were not truly touched, absorbed all her passion in her art when there were no such deserving claimants, never sold herself or threw herself away, would content herself at any time with poetry without love rather than endure love without poetry. She rather pitied her married colleagues, knowing perfectly well that they were not free to be so fastidious, reserved, and temperate as her instinct told her a great artist should always be. Polite society pretended to respect her when it asked her to recite at bazaars or charity concerts: at other times it did not come into contact with her, nor trouble itself as to her conformity to its rules, since she, as an actress, was out of polite society from the start. The ostracism which is so terrible to women whose whole aim is to know and be known by people of admitted social standing cannot reach the woman who is busily working with a company bound together by a common co-operative occupation, and who obtains at least some word or sign of welcome from the people every night. As to the Church, it had never gained any hold on Madge: it was to her only a tedious hypocrisy out of all relation with her life. Her idea of religion was believing the Bible because God personally dictated it to Moses, and going to Church because her father's respectability required her to comply with that custom. Knowing from her secular education that such belief in the Bible was as exploded as belief in witchcraft, and despising respectability as those only can who have tasted the cream of it, she was perfectly free from all pious scruples. Habit, prejudice, and inherited moral cowardice just influenced her sufficiently to induce her to keep up appearances carefully, and to offer no contradiction to the normal assumption that her clandestine interludes of passion and poetry were sins. But she never had a moment of genuine remorse after once discovering that such sins were conditions of her full efficiency as an actress. They had brought tones into her voice that no teaching of Jack's could have endowed herself with; and so completely did she now judge herself by her professional powers, that this alone brought her an accession instead of a loss of self-respect. She was humiliated only when she played badly. If one of the clergymen who occasionally asked her, with many compliments, to recite at their school fêtes and the like, had demanded instead what it could profit her to gain the whole world and lose her own soul, she might have replied with perfect sincerity from her point of view that she had given up the whole world of Mrs Grundy and gained her own soul, and that, whether he considered it judicious to mention it or not, the transaction in fact profited her greatly.

But all this belonged to a later period than the novitiate of two and a half years which began at Nottingham. These thirty months did not pass without many fits of low spirits, during which she despaired of success and hated her profession. She remained at Nottingham until July, when the theatre there was closed for a time. She then joined a travelling company and went through several towns until she obtained an engagement at Leeds. Thence she went to Liverpool, where she remained for three months, at the expiration of which she accepted an offer made her by the manager of a theatre in Edinburgh, and went thither with a salary of five pounds a week, the largest wage she had as yet received for her services. There she stayed until August in the second year of her professional life, when she acted in London for the first time, and was disgusted by the coldness of the metropolitan audiences, which were, besides, but scanty at that period of the year. She was glad to return to the provinces, although her first task there was again to support her old acquaintance the tragedian, with whom she quarrelled at the first rehearsal with spirit and success. Here, as leading lady, she attempted the parts of Beatrice, Portia, and Lady Macbeth, succeeding fairly in the first, triumphantly in the second, and only escaping failure by her insignificance in the third. By that time she had come to be known by the provincial managers as a trustworthy, hard-working young woman, safe in the lighter sorts of leading business, and likely to improve with more experience. They hardly gave her credit enough, she thought, for what seemed to her the slow and painful struggle which her progress had cost her. Those were the days in which she was building up the complete method which, though it was a very necessary part of her training, proved so short-lived. She had had to exhaust the direct cultivation of her art before she could begin the higher work of cultivating herself as the source of that art.

Shortly after her flight from Kensington, her twenty-first birthday had placed her in a position to defy the interference of her family; and she had thereupon written to her father acquainting him with her whereabouts, and with her resolve to remain upon the stage at all hazards. He had replied through his solicitor, formally disowning her. She took no notice of this; and the solicitor then sent her a cheque for one hundred pounds, and informed her that this was all she had to expect from her father, with whom she was not to attempt to establish any further communication. Madge was about to return the money, but was vehemently dissuaded from doing so by Mrs Cohen, who had not at that time quitted Nottingham. It proved very useful to her afterwards for her stage wardrobe. In defiance of the solicitor's injunction, she wrote to Mr Brailsford, thanking him for the money, and reproaching him for his opposition to her plans. He replied at great length; and eventually they corresponded regularly once a month, the family resigning themselves privately to Madge's being an actress, but telling falsehoods publicly to account for her absence. The donation of one hundred pounds was repeated next year; and many an actress whose family heavily burdened instead of aiding her, envied Madge her independence.

She wrote once to Jack, telling him that all her success, and notably her early promotion from the part of the player queen to that of Ophelia, was due to the method of delivering verse which he had taught her. He answered, after a long delay, with expressions of encouragement curiously mixed up with inconsequent aphorisms; but his letter needed no reply, and she did not venture to write again, though she felt a desire to do so.

This was the reality which took the place of Madge's visions of the life of an actress.

THE CONCERT

(*Chap. IX from Love Among the Artists*)

THE year after that in which Madge had her autumnal glimpse of the London stage began with a General Election, followed by a change in the Ministry, a revival of trade, a general fancy that things were going to mend, and a sudden access of spirit in political agitation, commercial enterprise, public amusements, and private expenditure. The wave even reached a venerable artistic institution called the Antient Orpheus Society, established nearly a century ago for the performance of orchestral music, and since regarded as the pioneer of musical art in England. It had begun by producing Beethoven's symphonies: it had ended by producing a typical collection of old fogeys, who pioneered backwards so fast and so far that they had not finished shaking their heads over the innovations in the overture to William Tell when the rest of the world were growing tired of the overture to Tannhäuser. The younger critics had introduced a fashion of treating the Antient Orpheus as obsolescent; and even their elders began to forebode the extinction of the Society unless it were speedily rejuvenated by the supercession of the majority of the Committee. But the warnings of the press, as usual, did not come until long after the public had begun to abstain from the Antient Orpheus concerts; and as the Society in its turn resisted the suggestions of the press until death or dotage reduced the conservative majority of the Committee to a minority, the credit of the Antient Orpheus was almost past recovery when reform was at last decided on. When the new members of the rejuvenated Committee —three of whom were under fifty—realized this, they became as eager to fill the concert programmes with new works as their predecessors had been determined to exclude them. But when the business of selecting the new works came to be considered, all was discord. Some urged the advisability of performing the works of English composers, a wilful neglect of which had been that one of the practices of the old committee of which the press had most persistently complained. To this it was objected that in spite of the patriotic complaints of critics, the public had showed their opinion of English composers by specially avoiding the few concerts to which they had been allowed to contribute. At last it was arranged that an English work should be given at the first concert of the season, and that care should be taken to neutralize its repellent effect on the public by engaging a young Polish lady, who had recently made an extraordinary success abroad as a pianist, to make her first appearance in England on the occasion. Matters being settled so far, question now arose as to what the new English work should be. Most of the Committee had manuscript scores of their own, composed thirty years before in the interval between leaving the academy and getting enough teaching to use up all their energy; but as works of this class had already been heard once or twice by the public with undisguised tedium, and as each composer hesitated to propose his own opus, the question was not immediately answered. Then a recently-elected member of the Committee, not a professional musician, mentioned a fantasia for pianoforte and orchestra of which he had some private knowledge. It was composed, he said, by a young man, a Mr Owen Jack. The chairman coughed, and remarked coldly that he did not recollect the name. A member asked bluntly who Mr Jack was and whether anybody had ever heard of him. Another member protested against the suggestion of a fantasia, and declared that if this illustrious obscure did not know enough about musical form to write a concerto, the Antient Orpheus Society, which had subsisted for nearly a century without his assistance, could probably do so a little longer. When the laughter and applause which this speech evoked had subsided, a good-natured member remarked that he had met a man of the name of Jack at somebody's place in Windsor, and had heard him improvise variations on a song of the hostess's in a rather striking manner. He therefore seconded the proposal that Jack's fantasia should be immediately examined with a view to its performance by the Polish lady at the next concert. Another member, not good-natured, but professionally jealous of the last speaker but one, supported the proposal on the ground that the notion that the Society could get on high-and-mightily without ever doing anything new was just what had brought it to death's door. This naturally elicited a defiant statement that the Society had never been more highly esteemed than at that hour; and a debate ensued, in the course of which Jack's ability was hotly attacked and defended in turn by persons who had never heard of him before that day. Eventually the member who had introduced the subject obtained permission to invite Mr Jack to submit his fantasia to the Committee.

At the next meeting an indignant member begged leave to call the attention of his colleagues to a document which had accompanied the score forwarded in response to the invitation by which the Antient Orpheus Society had honored Mr Owen Jack. It was a letter to the Secretary, in the following terms:—

"Sir—Herewith you will find the instrumental partition of a fantasia composed by me for pianoforte and orchestra. I am willing to give the use of it to the Antient Orpheus Society gratuitously for one concert, on condition that the rehearsal be superintended by me, and that, if I require it, a second rehearsal be held."

The member said he would not dwell on the propriety of this communication to the foremost musical society in Europe from a minor teacher, as he had ascertained Mr Jack to be. It had been sufficiently rebuked by the Secretary's reply, dispatched after the partition had been duly examined, to the effect that the work, though not destitute of merit, was too eccentric in form, and crude in harmonic structure, to be suitable for public performance at the concerts of the Society. This had elicited a second letter from Mr Jack, of which the member would say nothing, as he preferred to leave it to speak for itself and for the character of the writer.

"CHURCH STREET, KENSINGTON, W.

"Sir—Your criticism was uninvited, and is valueless except as an illustration of the invincible ignorance of the pedants whose mouthpiece you are. I am, sir, yours truly,

"OWEN JACK."

The most astute diplomatist could not have written a more effective letter in Jack's favor than this proved. The party of reform took it as an exquisite slap at their opponents, and at once determined to make the Secretary smart for rejecting the work without the authority of the whole Committee.

Jack's advocate produced a note from the Polish lady acknowledging the receipt of a pianoforte fantasia, and declaring that she should be enchanted to play for the first time to an English audience a work so poetic by one of their own nation. He explained that having borrowed a copy of the pianoforte part from a young lady relative of his who was studying it, he had sent it to the Polish artist, who had just arrived in England. Her opinion of it, he contended, was sufficient to show that the letter of the secretary was the result of an error of judgment which deserved no better answer than it had elicited. The secretary retorted that he had no right to avail himself of his private acquaintance with the pianist to influence the course of the Society, and stigmatized Jack's letter as the coarse abuse natural to the vulgar mind of a self-assertive charlatan. On the other hand, it was maintained that Jack had only shown the sensitiveness of an artist, and that to invite a composer to send in a work and then treat it as if it were an examination paper filled by a presumptuous novice, was an impertinence likely to bring ridicule as well as odium upon the Antient Orpheus. The senior member, who occupied the chair, now declared very solemnly that he had seen the fantasia, and that it was one of those lawless compositions unhappily too common of late years, which were hurrying the beautiful art of Haydn and Mozart into the abyss of modern sensationalism. Hereupon some one remarked that the gentleman had frequently spoken of the works of Wagner in the same terms, although they all knew that Richard Wagner was the greatest composer of that or any other age. This assertion was vehemently repudiated by some, and loudly cheered by others. In the hubbub which followed, Jack's cause became identified with that of Wagner; and a motion to set aside the unauthorized rejection of the fantasia was carried by a majority of the admirers of the Prussian composer, not one of whom knew or cared a straw about the English one.

"I am glad we have won the day," said Mr Phipson, the proposer of this motion, to a friend, as the meeting broke up; "but we have certainly experienced the truth of Mary's remark that this Jack creates nothing but discord in real life, whatever he may do in music."

Jack at first refused to have anything further to do with the Antient Orpheus; but as it was evident that his refusal would harm nobody except himself, he yielded to the entreaties of Mary Sutherland, and consented to make use of the opportunity she had, through Mr Phipson, procured for him.

So the negotiation proceeded; and at last, one comfortless wet spring morning, Jack got out of an omnibus in Piccadilly, and walked through the mud to St James's Hall, where, in the gloomy rooms beneath the orchestra, he found a crowd of about eighty men, chatting, hugging themselves, and stamping because of the cold; stooping over black bags and boxes containing musical instruments; or reluctantly unwinding woollen mufflers and unbuttoning greatcoats. He passed them into a lower room, where he found three gentlemen standing in courtly attitudes before a young lady wrapped in furs, with a small head, light brown hair, and a pale face, rather toil worn. She received them with that natural air of a princess in her own right which is so ineffectually striven for by the ordinary princess in other people's rights. As she spoke to the gentlemen in French, occasionally helping them to understand her by a few words of broken English, she smiled occasionally, apparently more from kindness than natural gaiety, for her features always relapsed into an expression of patient but not unhappy endurance. Near her sat an old foreign lady, brown skinned, tall, and very grim.

Jack advanced a few steps into the room; glanced at the gentlemen; and took a long look at the younger lady, who, like the rest, had had her attention arrested by his impressive ugliness. He scrutinized her so openly that she turned away displeased, and a little embarrassed. Two of the gentlemen stared at him stiffly. The third came forward, and said with polite severity, "What is your business here, sir?"

Jack looked at him for a moment, wrinkling his face hideously. "I am Jack," he said, in the brassiest tone of his powerful voice. "Who are you?"

"Oh!" said the gentleman, relaxing a little. "I beg your pardon. I had not the pleasure of knowing you by sight, Mr Jack. My name is Manlius, at your service." Mr Manlius was the conductor of the Antient Orpheus orchestra. He was a learned musician, generally respected because he had given instruction to members of the Royal family, and, when conducting, never allowed his orchestra to forget the restraint due to the presence of ladies and gentlemen in the sofa stalls.

Jack bowed. Mr Manlius considered whether he should introduce the composer to the young lady. Whilst he hesitated, a trampling overhead was succeeded by the sounding of a note first on the pianoforte and then on the oboe, instantly followed by the din of an indescribable discord of fifths from innumerable strings, varied by irrelevant chromatic scales from the wood wind, and a doleful tuning of slides from the brass. Jack's eyes gleamed. Troubling himself no further about Mr Manlius, he went out through a door leading to the stalls, where he found a knot of old gentlemen disputing. One of them immediately whispered something to the others; and they continued their discussion in a lower tone.

Jack looked at the orchestra for a few minutes, and then returned to the room he had left, where the elder lady was insisting in French that the pianoforte fantasia should be rehearsed before anything else, as she was not going to wait in the cold all day. Mr Manlius assured her that he had anticipated her suggestion, and should act upon it as a matter of course.

"It is oll thé same thinks," said the young lady in English. Then in French. "Even if you begin with the fantasia, monsieur, I shall assuredly wait to hear for the first time your famous band perform in this ancient hall."

Manlius bowed. When he straightened himself again, he found Jack standing at his elbow. "Allow me to present to you Monsieur Jack," he said.

"It is for Monsieur Jacques to allow," she replied. "The poor artist is honored by the presence of the illustrious English composer."

Jack nodded gravely as acknowledging that the young woman expressed herself becomingly. Manlius grinned covertly, and proposed that they should go up on the orchestra, as the band was apt to get out of humor when too much time was wasted. She rose at once, and ascended the steps on the arm of the conductor. She was received with an encouraging clapping of hands and tapping of fiddle backs. Jack followed with the elder lady, who sat down on the top stair, and began to knit.

"If you wish to conduct the rehearsal," said Manlius politely to Jack, "you are, of course, quite welcome to do so."

"Thank you," said Jack. "I will." Manlius, who had hardly expected him to accept the offer, retired to the pianoforte, and prepared to turn over the leaves for the player.

"I think I can play it from memory," she said to him, "unless Monsieur Jacques puts it all out of my head. Judging by his face, it is certain that he is not very patien— Ah! Did I not say so?"

Jack had rapped the desk sharply with his stick, and was looking balefully at the men, who did not seem in any hurry to attend to him. He put down the stick, stepped from the desk, and stooped to the conductor's ear.

"I mentioned," he said, "that some of the parts ought to be given to the men to study before rehearsal. Has that been done?"

Manlius smiled. "My dear sir," he said, "I need hardly tell you that players of such standing as the members of the Antient Orpheus orchestra do not care to have suggestions of that kind offered to them. You have no cause to be uneasy. They can play anything—absolutely anything—at sight."

Jack looked black, and returned to his desk without a word. He gave one more rap with his stick, and began. The players were attentive, but many of them tried not to look so.

For a few bars, Jack conducted under some restraint, apparently striving to repress a tendency to extravagant gesticulation. Then, as certain combinations and progressions sounded strange and far-fetched, slight bursts of laughter were heard. Suddenly the first clarinettist, with an exclamation of impatience, put down his instrument.

"Well?" shouted Jack. The music ceased.

"I cant play that," said the clarinettist shortly.

"Can *you* play it?" said Jack, with suppressed rage, to the second clarinettist.

"No," said he. "Nobody could play it."

"That passage *has* been played; and it must be played. It has been played by a common soldier."

"If a common soldier even attempted it, much less played it," said the first clarinettist, with some contemptuous indignation at what he considered an evident falsehood, "he must have been drunk." There was a general titter at this.

Jack visibly wrestled with himself for a moment. Then with a gleam of humor like a flash of sunshine through a black thundercloud, he said: "You are right. He *was* drunk." The whole band roared with laughter.

"Well, *I* am not drunk," said the clarinettist, folding

his arms.

"But will you not just try wh—" Here Jack, choked by the effort to be persuasive and polite, burst out raging: "It can be done. It shall be done. It must be done. You are the best clarinet player in England. I know what you can do."

And Jack shook his fists wildly at the man as if he were accusing him of some infamous crime. But the compliment was loudly applauded, and the man reddened, not altogether displeased. A cornist who sat near him said soothingly in an Irish accent, "Aye, do, Joe. Try it."

"You will: you can," shouted Jack reassuringly, recovering his self-command. "Back to the double bar. Now!" The music recommenced; and the clarinettist, overborne, took up his instrument, and, when the passage was reached, played it easily, greatly to his own astonishment. The brilliancy of the effect, too, raised him for a time into a prominence which rivalled that of the pianist. The orchestra positively interrupted the movement to applaud it; and Jack joined in with high good humor.

"If you are uneasy about it," said he, with an undisguised chuckle, "I can hand it over to the violins."

"Oh, no, thank you," said the clarinettist. "Now I've got it, I'll keep it."

Jack rubbed his nose until it glowed like a coal; and the movement proceeded without another stoppage, the men now seeing that Jack was in his right place

But when a theme marked *andante cantabile*, which formed the middle section of the fantasia, was commenced by the pianist, Jack turned to her, said "Quicker, quicker. *Plus vite*"; and began to mark his beat by striking the desk. She looked at him anxiously, played a few bars in the time indicated by him, and then threw up her hands and stopped.

"I cannot," she exclaimed. "I must play it more slowly or not at all."

"Certainly, it shall be slower if you desire it," said the elder lady from the steps. Jack looked at her as he sometimes looked at Mrs Simpson. "Certainly it shall not be slower, if all the angels desired it," he said, in well pronounced but barbarously ungrammatical French. "Go on; and take the time from my beat."

The Polish lady shook her head; folded her hands in her lap; and looked patiently at the music before her. There was a moment of silence, during which Jack, thus mutely defied, glared at her with distorted features. Manlius rose irresolutely. Jack stepped down from the desk; handed him the stick; and said in a smothered voice, "Be good enough to conduct this lady's portion of the fantasia. When *my* music recommences, I will return."

Manlius took the stick and mounted the desk, the orchestra receiving him with applause. In the midst of it Jack went out, giving the pianist a terrible look as he passed her, and transferring it to her companion, who raised her eyebrows and shoulders contemptuously.

Manlius was not the man to impose his own ideas of a composition on a refractory artist; and though he was privately disposed to agree with Jack that the Polish lady was misjudging the speed of the movement, he obediently followed her playing with his beat. But he soon lost his first impression, and began to be affected by a dread lest any one should make a noise in the room. He moved his stick as quietly as possible, and raised his left hand as if to still the band, who were, however, either watching the pianist intently or playing without a trace of the expert offhandedness which they had affected at first. The pleasure of listening made Manlius forget to follow the score. When he roused himself and found his place, he perceived that the first horn player was altering a passage completely, though very happily. Looking questioningly in that direction, he saw Jack sitting beside the man with a pencil in his hand. Manlius observed for the first time that he had an expressive face and remarkable eyes, and was not, as he had previously seemed, unmitigatedly ugly. Meanwhile the knot of old gentlemen in the stalls, who had previously chattered subduedly, became quite silent; and a few of them closed their eyes rapturously. The lady on the steps alone did not seem to care about the music. At last the flow of melody waned and broke into snatches. The pianoforte seemed to appeal to the instruments to continue the song. A melancholy strain from the violas responded hopelessly; but the effect of this was marred by a stir in the orchestra. The trombone and trumpet players, hitherto silent, were taking up their instruments and pushing up their moustaches. The drummer, after some hasty screwing round his third drum, poised his sticks; and a supernumerary near him rose, cymbals in hand, fixed his eye on Manlius, and apparently stood ready to clap the head of the trumpet player in front of him as a lady claps a moth flying from a woollen curtain. Manlius looked at the score as if he did not quite understand the sequel. Suddenly, as the violas ceased, Jack shouted in a startling voice, "Let it be an avalanche. From the top to bottom of the Himalayas"; and rushed to the conductor's desk. Manlius made way for him precipitately; and a tremendous explosion of sound followed. "Louder," roared Jack. "Louder. Less noise and more tone. Out with it like fifty million devils." And he led the movement at a merciless speed. The pianist looked bewildered, like the band, most of whom lost their places after the first fifty bars; but when the turn of each player came, he found the conductor glaring at him, and was swept into his part without clearly knowing how. It was an insensate orgie of sound. Gay melodies, daintily given out by the pianoforte, or by the string instruments, were derisively brayed out immediately afterwards by cornets, harmonized in thirds with the most ingenious vulgarity. Cadenzas, agilely executed by the Polish lady, were uncouthly imitated by the double basses. Themes constructed like ballads with choruses were introduced instead of orthodox "subjects." The old gentlemen in the stalls groaned and protested. The Polish lady, incommoded by the capricious and often excessive speed required of her, held on gallantly, Jack all the time grinding his teeth, dancing, gesticulating, and by turns shshsh-shing at the orchestra, or shouting to them for more tone and less noise. Even the lady on the steps had begun to nod to the impetuous rhythm, when the movement ended as suddenly as it had begun; and all the players rose to their feet, laughing and applauding heartily. Manlius, from whose mind the fantasia had banished all prejudice as to Jack's rank as a musician, shook his hand warmly. The Polish lady, her face transfigured by musical excitement, offered her hand too. Jack took it and held it, saying abruptly, "Listen to me. You were quite right; and I am a fool. I did not know what there was in my own music, and would have spoiled it if you had not prevented me. You are a great player, because you get the most beautiful tone possible from every note you touch, and you make every phrase say all that it was meant to say, and more. You are an angel. I would rather hear you play scales than hear myself play sonatas. And"—here he lowered his voice and drew her aside—"I rely on you to make my work succeed at the concert. Manlius will conduct the band; but you must conduct Manlius. It is not enough to be a gentleman and a contrapuntist in order to conduct. You comprehend?"

"Yes, monsieur; I understand perfectly, perfectly. I will do my best. I shall be inspired. How magnificent it is!"

"Allow me to congratulate you, sir," said one of the old gentlemen, advancing. "Myself and colleagues have been greatly struck by your work. I am empowered to say on their behalf that whatever difference of opinion there may be among us as to the discretion with which you have employed your powers, of the extraordinary nature of those powers there can no longer be a doubt; and we are thoroughly gratified at having chosen for performance a work which displays so much originality and talent as your fantasia."

"Ten years ago," said Jack, looking steadily at him, "I might have been glad to hear you say so. At present the time for compliments is past, unless you wish to congratulate me on the private interest that has gained my work a hearing. My talent and originality have been my chief obstacles here."

"Are you not a little hasty?" said the gentleman, disconcerted. "Success comes late in London; and you are still, if I may say so, a comparatively young man."

"I am not old enough to harp on being comparatively young. I am thirty-four years old; and if I had adopted any other profession than that of composer of music, I should have been earning a respectable livelihood by this time. As it is, I have never made a farthing by my compositions. I dont blame those who have stood between me and the public: their ignorance is their misfortune, and not their fault. But now that I have come to light by a chance in spite of their teeth, I am not in the humor to exchange pretty speeches with them. Understand, sir: I do not mean to rebuff you personally. But as for your colleagues, tell them that it does not become them to pretend to acknowledge spontaneously what I have just, after many hard years, forced them to admit. Look at those friends of yours shaking their heads over my score there. They have *heard* my music; but they do not know what to say until they *see* it. Would you like me to believe that they are admiring it?"

"I am confident that they cannot help doing so."

"They are showing one another why it ought not to have been written—hunting out my consecutive fifths and sevenths, and my false relations—looking for my first subject, my second subject, my working out, and the rest of the childishness that could be taught to a poodle. Dont they wish they may find them?"

The gentleman seemed at a loss how to continue the conversation. "I hope you are satisfied with the orchestra," he said after a pause.

"No, I am not," said Jack. "They are over civilized. They are as much afraid of showing their individuality as if they were common gentlemen. You cannot handle a musical instrument with kid gloves on. However, they did better than I hoped. They are at least not coarse. That young woman is a genius."

"Ye-es. Almost a genius. She is young, of course. She has not the—I should call it the gi*gan*tic power and energy of such a player, for instance, as—"

"Pshaw!" said Jack, interrupting him. "I, or anybody else, can get excited with the swing of a Chopin's polonaise, and thrash it out of the piano until the room shakes. But she! You talk of making a pianoforte sing—a child that can sing itself can do that. But she can make it speak. She has eloquence, the first and last quality of a great player, as it is of a great man. The *finale* of the fantasia is too coarse for her: it does violence to her nature. It was written to be played by a savage—like me."

"Oh, undoubtedly, undoubtedly! She is a remarkable player. I did not for a moment intend to convey—" Here Manlius rapped his desk; and Jack, with an unceremonious nod to his interlocutor, left the platform. As he passed the door leading to the public part of the hall, he heard the voice of the elder lady.

"My child, they seek to deceive you. This Monsieur Jacques, with whose music you are to make your *debût* here, is he famous in England? Not at all. My God! he is an unknown man."

"Be tranquil, mother. He will not long be unknown."

Jack opened the door a little way, thrust his face through, and smiled pleasantly at the pianist. Her mother, seeing her start, looked round and saw him grimacing within a yard of her.

"Ah, Lord Jesus!" she exclaimed in German, recoiling from him. He chuckled, and abruptly shut himself out of her view as the opening unison of the Coriolan overture sounded from the orchestra. The old gentleman who had congratulated him had rejoined the others in the stalls.

"Well," said one of them: "is your man delighted with himself?"

"N-no, I cannot say that he is—or rather perhaps he is

too much so. I am sorry to say that he appears to be rather morose—soured by his early difficulties, perhaps. He is certainly not an agreeable person to speak to."

"What did you expect?" said another gentleman coldly. "A man who degrades music to be the vehicle of his own coarse humor, and shews by his methods of doing it an ignorant contempt for those laws by which the great composers established order in the chaos of sounds, is not likely to display a courteous disposition and refined nature in the ordinary business of life."

"I assure you, Professor," said a third, who had the score of the fantasia open on his knees, "this chap must know a devil of a lot. He plays old Harry with the sonata form; but he must do it on purpose, you know, really."

The gentleman addressed as Professor looked severely and incredulously at the other. "I really cannot listen to such things whilst they are playing Beethoven," he said "I have protested against Mr Jack and his like; and my protest has passed unheeded. I wash my hands of the consequences. The Antient Orpheus Society will yet acknowledge that I did well when I counselled it to renounce the devil and all his works." He turned away, sat down on a stall a little way off, and gave all his attention ostentatiously to Coriolan.

The pianist came presently and sat near him. The others quickly surrounded her; but she did not speak to them, and shewed by her attitude that she did not wish to be spoken to. Her mother, who did not care for Coriolan, and wanted to go home, knitted and looked appealingly at her from time to time, not venturing to express her impatience before so many members of the Antient Orpheus Society. At last Manlius came down; and the whole party rose and went into the performers' room.

"How do you find our orchestra?" said Manlius to her as she took up her muff.

"It is magnificent," she replied. "So refined, so quiet, so convenable! It is like the English gentleman." Manlius smirked. Jack, who had reappeared on the outskirts of the group with his hat on—a desperately ill-used hat—added:

"A Lithuanian or Hungarian orchestra could not play like that, eh?"

"No, truly," said the Polish lady, with a little shrug. "I do not think they could."

"You flatter us," said Manlius, bowing. Jack began to laugh. The Polish lady hastily made her adieux, and went out into Piccadilly, where a cab was brought for her. Her mother got in; and she was about to follow when she heard Jack's voice again, at her elbow.

"May I send you some music?"

"If you will be so gracious, monsieur."

"Good. What direction shall I give your driver?"

"F—f—you call it Feetzroysquerre?"

"Fitzroy Square," shouted Jack to the cabman. The hansom went off; and he, running recklessly through the mud to a passing Hammersmith omnibus, which was full inside, climbed to the roof, and was borne away in the rain.

THE ENGAGEMENT

(*Chap. X from The Irrational Knot*)

NEXT morning Mr Lind rose before his daughter was astir, and went to his club, where he breakfasted. He then went to the offices in Queen Victoria Street. Finding the board-room unoccupied, he sat down there, and said to one of the clerks:

"Go and tell Mr Conolly that I desire to speak to him, if he is disengaged. And if any one wants to come in, say that I am busy here. I do not wish to be disturbed for half an hour or so."

"Yes, sir," said the clerk, departing. A minute later, he returned and said: "Mr Conly is disengaged; and he says will you be so good as to come to his room, sir."

"I told you to ask him to come here," said Mr Lind.

"Well, thats what he said, sir," said the clerk, speaking in official Board School English. "Shloy gow to him and tell him again?"

"No, no: it does not matter," said Mr Lind, and walked out through the office. The clerk held the door open for him, and carefully closed it when he had passed through.

"Ow, oy sy!" cried the clerk. "This is fawn, this is."

"Wot's the row?" said another clerk.

"Woy, owld Lind sends me in to Conly to cam in to him into the board-room. 'Aw right,' says Conly, 'awsk him to cam in eah to me.' You should 'a seen the owld josser's feaches wnoy towld im. 'Oyd zoyred jou to sy e was to cam in eah to me.' 'Shloy gow and tell him again?' I says, as cool as ennything. 'Now,' says he, 'Oll gow myself.' Thets wot Aw loike in Conly. He tikes tham fellers dahn wen they troy it on over im."

Meanwhile, Mr Lind went to Conolly's room; returned his greeting by a dignified inclination of the head; and accepted, with a cold "Thank you," the chair offered him. Conolly, who had received him cordially, checked himself. There was a pause, during which Mr Lind lost countenance a little. Then Conolly sat down, and waited.

"Ahem!" said Mr Lind. "I have to speak to you with

reference to—to a—a matter which has accidentally come to my knowledge. It would be painful and unnecessary—quite unnecessary, to go into particulars."

Conolly remained politely attentive, but said nothing. Mr Lind began to feel very angry, but this helped him to the point.

"I merely wish—that is, I quite wish you to understand that any intimacy that may have arisen between you and—and a member of my family must—must, in short, be considered to be at an end. My daughter is—I may tell you—engaged to Mr Sholto Douglas, whom you know; and therefore—you understand."

"Mr Lind," said Conolly decisively: "your daughter is engaged to me."

Mr Lind lost his temper, and rose, exclaiming, "I beg you will not repeat that, either here or elsewhere."

"Pray be seated," said Conolly courteously.

"I have nothing more to say, sir."

Conolly rose as though the interview were at an end, and seemed to wait for his visitor to go.

"We understand one another, I presume," said Mr Lind, dubiously.

"Not quite, I think," said Conolly, relenting. "I should suggest our discussing the matter in full, now that we have a favourable opportunity—if you will be so good."

Mr Lind sat down, and said with condescension, "I am quite willing to listen to you."

"Thank you," said Conolly. "Will you tell me what your objections are to my engagement with your daughter?"

"I had hoped, sir, that your common sense and knowledge of the world would have rendered an explanation superfluous."

"They havnt," said Conolly.

Mr Lind rose to boiling point again. "Oh, Mr Conolly, I assure you I have no objection to explain myself: none whatever. I merely wished to spare you as far as possible. Since you insist on my mentioning what I think you must be perfectly well aware of, I can only say that from the point of view of English society our positions are different; and therefore an engagement between you and any member of my family is unsuitable, and—in short—out of the question, however advantageous it might be to you. That is all."

Mr Lind considered he had had the better of that, and leaned back in his chair more confidently. Conolly smiled and shook his head, appreciative of the clearness with which Mr Lind had put his case, but utterly unmoved by it.

He considered for a moment, and then said, weighing his words carefully:

"Your daughter, with her natural refinement and delicate habits, is certainly not fit to be married to a foul-mouthed fellow, ignorant, dirty, besotted, and out of place in any company except at the bar in a public house. That is probably your idea of a workman. But the fact of her having consented to marry me is a proof that I do not answer to any such description. As you have hinted, it will be an advantage to me in some ways to have a lady for my wife, but I should have no difficulty in purchasing that advantage, even with my present means, which I expect to increase largely in the course of some years. Do you not underrate your daughter's personal qualities when you assume that it was her position that induced me to seek her hand?"

"I am quite aware of my daughter's personal advantages. They are additional reasons against her contracting an imprudent marriage."

"Precisely. But in what respect would her marriage with me be imprudent? I possess actual competence, and a prospect of wealth. I come of a long lived and healthy family. My name is beyond comparison, more widely known than yours. [Mr Lind recoiled.] I now find myself everywhere treated with a certain degree of consideration, which an alliance with your daughter will not diminish."

"In fact, you are conferring a great honour on my family by condescending to marry into it?"

"I dont understand that way of looking at things, Mr

Lind; and so I leave you to settle the question of honour as you please. But you must not condemn me for putting my position in the best possible light in order to reconcile you to an inevitable fact."

"What do you mean by an inevitable fact, sir?"

"My marriage, of course. I assure you that it will take place."

"But I shall not permit it to take place. Do you think to ignore me in the matter?"

"Practically so. If you give your consent, I shall be glad for the sake of Marian, who will be gratified by it. But if you withhold it, we must dispense with it. By opposing us, you will simply—by making Marian's home unbearable to her—precipitate the wedding." Conolly, under the influence of having put the case neatly, here relaxed his manner so far as to rest his elbows on the table and look pleasantly at his visitor.

"Do you know to whom you are speaking?" said Mr Lind, driven by rage and a growing fear of defeat into desperate self-assertion.

"I am speaking," said Conolly with a smile, "to my future father-in-law."

"I am a director of this company, of which you are the servant, as you shall find to your cost if you persist in holding insulting language to me."

"If I found any director of this company allowing other than strictly business considerations to influence him at the Board, I should insist on his resigning."

Mr Lind looked at him severely, then indignantly, then unsteadily, without moving him in the least. At last he said, more humbly: "I hope you will not abuse your position, Mr Conolly. I do not know whether you have sufficient influence over Marian to induce her to defy me; but however that may be, I appeal to your better feelings. Put yourself in my place. If you had an only daughter—"

"Excuse my interrupting you," said Conolly, gently; "but that will not advance the argument unless you put yourself in mine. Besides, I am pledged to Marian. If she asks me to break off the match, I shall release her instantly."

"You will bind yourself to do that?"

"I cannot help myself. I have no more power to make her marry me than you have to prevent her."

"I have the authority of a parent. And I must tell you, Mr Conolly, that it will be my duty to enlighten my poor child as to the effect a union with you must have on her social position. You have made the most of your celebrity and your prospects. She may be dazzled for the moment; but her good sense will come to the rescue yet, I am convinced."

"I have certainly spared no pains to persuade her. Unless the habit of her childhood can induce Marian to defer to your prejudice—you must allow me to call it so: it is really nothing more—she will keep her word to me."

Mr Lind winced, recollecting how little his conduct toward Marian during her childhood was calculated to accustom her to his influence. "It seems to me, sir," he said, suddenly thinking of a new form of reproach, "that, to use your own plain language, you are nothing more or less than a Radical."

"Radicalism is not considered a reproach amongst workmen," said Conolly.

"I shall not fail to let her know the confidence with which you boast of your power over her."

"I have simply tried to be candid with you. You know exactly how I stand. If I have omitted anything, ask me, and I will tell you at once."

Mr Lind rose. "I know quite as much as I care to know," he said. "I distinctly object to and protest against all your proceedings, Mr Conolly. If my daughter marries you, she shall have neither my countenance in society nor one solitary farthing of the fortune I had destined for her. I recommend the latter point to your attention."

"I have considered it carefully, Mr Lind; and I am satisfied with what she possesses in her own right."

"Oh! You have ascertained *that*, have you?"

"I should hardly have proposed to marry her but for her entire pecuniary independence of me."

"Indeed. And have you explained to her that you wish to marry her for the sake of securing her income?"

"I have explained to her everything she ought to know, taking care, of course, to have full credit for my frankness."

Mr Lind, after regarding him with amazement for a moment, walked to the door.

"I am a gentleman," he said, pausing there for a moment, "and too old-fashioned to discuss the obligations of good breeding with a Radical. If I had believed you capable of the cynical impudence with which you have just met my remonstrances, I should have spared myself this meeting. Good morning."

"Good morning," said Conolly, gravely. When the door closed, he sprang up and walked to and fro, chuckling, rubbing his hands, and occasionally uttering a short laugh. When he had sufficiently relieved himself by this exercise, he sat down at his desk, and wrote a note.

"THE CONOLLY ELECTRO-MOTOR COMPANY OF LONDON, LIMITED. QUEEN VICTORIA STREET, E.C.

"This is to let your ever-radiant ladyship know that I am fresh from an encounter with your father, who has retired in great wrath, defeated, but of opinion that he deserved no better for arguing with a Radical. I thought it better to put forth my strength at once so as to save future trouble. I send this post haste in order that you may be warned in case he should go straight home and scold you. I hope he will not annoy you much.—E. C."

Having despatched the office boy to Westbourne Terrace with this letter, Conolly went off to lunch. Mr Lind went back to his club, and then to Westbourne Terrace, where he was informed that the young ladies were together in the drawing-room. Some minutes later, Marian, discussing Conolly's letter with Elinor, was interrupted by a servant, who informed her that her father desired to see her in his study.

"Now for it, Marian!" said Nelly, when the servant was gone. "Remember that you have to meet the most unreasonable of adversaries, a parent asserting his proprietary rights in his child. Dont be sentimental. Leave that to him: he will be full of a father's anguish on discovering that his cherished daughter has feelings and interests of her own. Besides, Conolly has crushed him; and he will try to crush you in revenge."

"I wish I were not so nervous," said Marian. "I am not really afraid, but for all that, my heart is beating very unpleasantly."

"I wish I were in your place," said Elinor. "I feel like a charger at the sound of the trumpet."

"I am glad, for poor papa's sake, that you are not," said Marian, going out.

She knocked at his study door; and her father's voice, as he bade her come in, impressed her more than ever before. He was seated behind the writing-table, in front of which a chair was set for his daughter. She, unaccustomed from her childhood to submit to any constraint but that which the position of a guest, which she so often occupied, had trained her to impose on herself, was rather roused than awed by this magisterial arrangement. She sat down with less than her usual grace of manner, and looked at him with her brows knitted. It was one of the rare moments in which she reminded him of her mother. An angry impulse to bid her not dare look so at him almost got the better of him. However, he began prudently with a carefully premeditated speech.

"It is my duty, Marian," he said gravely, "to speak of the statement you made last night. We need not allude to the painful scene which took place then: better let that rest and be forgotten as soon as possible. But the discovery of what you have been doing without my knowledge has cost me a sleepless night and a great deal of anxiety. I wish to reason with you now quite calmly and dispassionately; and

I trust you will remember that I am older and have far more experience of the world than you, and that I am a better judge of your interests than you yourself can possibly be. Ahem! I have been this morning to the City, where I saw Mr Conolly, and endeavored to make him understand the true nature of his conduct toward me—and, I may add, toward you—in working his way clandestinely into an intimacy with you. I shall not describe to you what passed; but I may say that I have found him to be a person with whom you could not hope for a day's happiness. Even apart from his habits and tastes, which are those of a mere workman, his social (and, I fear, his religious) views are such as no lady, no properly-minded woman of any class, could sympathize with. You will be better able to judge of his character when I tell you that he informed me of his having taken care, before making any advances to you, to ascertain how much money you had. He boasted in the coarsest terms of his complete influence over you, evidently without a suspicion of the impression of venality and indelicacy which his words were calculated to make on me. Besides, Marian, I am sure you would not like to contract a marriage which would give me the greatest pain; which would offend my family; and which would have the effect of shutting you out from all good society."

"You are mistaken in him, papa."

"I beg you will allow me to finish, Marian. [He had to think for a moment before he could substantiate this pretence of having something more to say.] I have quite made up my mind, from personal observation of Mr Conolly, that even an ordinary acquaintance between you is out of the question. I, in short, refuse to allow anything of the kind to proceed; and I must ask you to respect my wishes in the matter. There is another subject which I will take this opportunity of mentioning; but as I have no desire to force your inclinations, I shall not press you for a declaration of your feelings at present. Sholto Douglas—"

"I do not want to hear *anything* about Sholto Douglas,"

Library of Congress

e), the man (a judge) says to Uncle Sam: "If Immigration was
sm, the Mafia and such kindred evils!"

epares to fashio
atmosphere where
rces (the modern
desire to reduce
role of Washington
my) collide with
rs (the old conser-
to promote thrift
icits). Meanwhile,
ntervenes inconve-
inconsistently, in
e process by, among
, expressing chang-
n provisions of the
(k) retirement sav-
ns.

alliance with the Obama White House on health care in 2010.

It is also a break with practice. In the last major tax overhaul, completed in 1986, the White House and Congress worked together. Indeed, it was a Republican president and a Democratic chairman of the House Ways and Means Committee who were the principals in the landmark measure. Ronald Reagan and Rep. Dan Rostenkowski presented an astonishing united front, with the Illinois lawmaker's public

If you're
lican" an
web brow
1.2 millio
vout beli
is a wea
strong R
be argue
have a pr
has a pro

David
tive edito
(dshribm
412-263-1

Justin Fox

ax break shouldn't be

icans benefit from it. Many more millions don

that ar
some pe
ers, it co
guaran
ment i
than to
There a
as buyi
retirem
ple do
401(k) s
encour

So w
giving
putting
Chetty
that au
employ
fective
ings. N

the words "Repub-
rack up" in your
you will find some
ries. Given my de-
t the United States
nation without a
lican Party, it can
t if the Republicans
n, the United States

*hribman is execu-
he Post-Gazette
post-gazette.com,*

acred

tter shared. Because
e die earlier than oth-
a lot less per person to
an adequate retire-
me for 1,000 people
it for just yourself.
ways around this, such
an annuity with one's
savings. But few peo-
t, and at present the
em isn't really set up to
it.

would be *better* than
ple a tax deduction for
oney in a 401(k)? Mr.
d his co-authors argue
natic contributions by
s are a much more ef-
ay of encouraging sav-
be we should put in a
ly for that. Or there's

American history. The election of 1800 pitted Thomas Jefferson against John Adams, in what turned out to be a very nasty contest. Allies of Jefferson accused Adams of being a crypto-monarchist, intent on destroying American democracy. Allies of Adams accused Jefferson of being an atheist and Jacobin, who wanted to bring the mindless bloodshed of the French Revolution to the United States. Feelings between the principals were bitter for a while. But after Jefferson retired from public life in 1809, the two struck up a correspondence that was collegial and warm. They both could look back with pride on their many accomplishments, and appreciate that their disagreements were borne of good faith.

That is a good lesson for all American citizens. Politics is inevitably about the things we disagree over. Matters on which there is broad consensus are addressed quickly, and so do not come up in public debates. When we obsess over politics, we can start to forget that, in fact, we have a lot in common.

The overwhelming majority of us support a free market economy, but with regulations to protect the environment, working conditions and consumer safety. We agree that the government should provide some kind of safety net for the less fortunate. We agree that education is very important, and that the government should have a role in it. We agree on the virtues of free speech. We agree that the government should stay out of religion. We agree on the rule of law, and do not think justice should be politicized. We agree that political debates should remain nonviolent, and that the victorious side should win by convincing the opposition of the

Deja vu all over again

An illustration by Grant E. Hamilton, 1891. In the caption (not legible
properly Restricted you would no longer be troubled with Anarchy, So

said Marian, rising.

"I expect you, Marian, to listen to what I have to say."

"On that subject I will not listen. I have felt very sore and angry ever since you told me last night to leave the room when Sholto insulted me, as if I were the aggressor."

"Angry! I am sorry to hear you say so to me."

"It is better to say so than to think so. There is no use in going on with this conversation, papa. It will only lead to more bitterness between us; and I had enough of that when I tasted it for the first time last night. We shall never agree about Mr Conolly. I have promised to marry him; and therefore I am not free to withdraw, even if I wished to."

"A promise made by you without my sanction is not binding. And—listen to me, if you please—I have obtained Mr Conolly's express assurance that if you wish to withdraw, he is perfectly willing that you should."

"Of course. He would not marry me if I did not wish it."

"But he is willing that you should withdraw. He leaves you quite free."

"Yes; and, as you told me, he is quite confident that I will keep faith with him; and so I will. I have had a letter from him since you saw him."

"What!" said Mr Lind, rising also.

"Dont let us quarrel, papa," said Marian, appealingly. "Why may I not marry whom I please?"

"Who wants to prevent you, pray? I have most carefully abstained from influencing you with regard to Sholto Douglas. But this is a totally different question. It is my duty to save you from disgracing yourself."

"Where is the disgrace? Mr Conolly is an eminent man. I am not poor, and can afford to marry any one I can respect. I can respect him. What objection have you to him? I am sure he is far superior to Sholto."

"Mr Douglas is a gentleman, Marian: Mr Conolly is not; and it is out of the question for you to ally yourself with a—a member of the proletariat, however skilful he may be in his handicraft."

"What *is* a gentleman, papa?"

"A gentleman, Marian, is one who is well born and well bred, and who has that peculiar tone and culture which can only be acquired by intercourse with the best society. I think you should know that as well as I. I hope you do not put these questions from a desire to argue with me."

"I only wish to do what is right. Surely there is no harm in arguing when one is not convinced."

"Humph! Well, I have said all that is necessary. I feel sure that you will not take any step calculated to inflict pain on me—at least an act of selfishness on your part would be a new and shocking experience for me."

"That is a very unfair way of putting it, papa. You give me no good reason for breaking my word, and making myself unhappy; and yet you accuse me of selfishness in not being ready to do both."

"I think I have already given you my assurance, weighted as it is by my age, my experience, my regard for your welfare, and, I hope, my authority as a parent, that both your honor and happiness will be secured by your obeying me, and forfeited by following your own headstrong inclinations."

Marian, almost crushed by this, hesitated a moment, twisting her fingers and looking pitiably at him. Then she thought of Conolly; rallied; and said: "I can only say that I am sorry to disagree with you; but I am not convinced."

"Do you mean that you refuse to obey me?"

"I cannot obey you in this matter, papa. I—"

"That is enough," said Mr Lind, gravely, beginning to busy himself with the writing materials. Marian for a moment seemed about to protest against this dismissal. Then she checked herself and went out of the room, closing the door quite quietly behind her, thereby unconsciously terrifying her father, who had calculated on a slam.

"Well," said Elinor, when her cousin rejoined her in the drawing room: "have you been selfish and disobedient?

Have you lacerated a father's heart?"

"He is thoroughly unfair," said Marian. "However, it all comes to this: he is annoyed at my wanting to marry Ned; and I believe there will be no more peace for me until I am in a house of my own. What shall we do in the meantime? Where shall we go? I cannot stay here."

"Why not? Uncle Reginald will sulk; sit at dinner without speaking to us; and keep out of our way as much as he can. But you can talk to me; we neednt mind him. It is he who will be out in the cold, biting his nose to vex his face. Such a state of things is new to you; but I have survived weeks of it without a single sympathizer, and been none the worse, except, perhaps, in temper. He will pretend to be inexorable at first: then he will come down to wounded affection; and he will end by giving in."

"No, Nelly, I couldnt endure that sort of existence. If people cannot remain friends they should separate at once. I will not sleep in this house tonight."

"Hurrah!" cried Miss McQuinch. "That will be beginning the war with spirit. If I were in your place, I would stay and fight it out at close quarters. I would make myself so disagreeable that nobody can imagine what life in this house would be. But your plan is the best—if you really mean it."

"Certainly I mean it. Where shall we go, Nelly?"

"H'm! I am afraid none of the family would make us very comfortable under the circumstances, except Marmaduke. It would be a splendid joke to go to West Kensington; only it would tell as much against us and Ned as against the Roman father. I have it! We will go to Mrs Toplis's in St Mary's Terrace: my mother always stays there when she is in town. Mrs Toplis knows us: if she has a room to spare she will give it to us without making any bother."

"Yes, that will do. Are you ready to come now?"

"If you can possibly wait five minutes I should like to put on my hat and change my boots. We will have to come back and pack up when we have settled about the room.

We cannot go without clothes. I should like to have a night-dress, at least. Have you any money?"

"I have the housekeeping money; but that, of course, I shall not take. I have thirty pounds of my own."

"And I have my old stocking, which contains nearly seventeen. Say fifty in round numbers. That will keep us going very comfortably for a month."

"Ridiculous! It will last longer than that. Oh!"

"Well?"

"We mustnt go, after all. I forgot *you*."

"What of me?"

"Where will you go when I am married? You cant live by yourself; and papa may not welcome you back if you take my part against him."

"He would not, in any case; so it makes no difference to me. I can go home if the worst comes to the worst. It does not matter: my present luxurious existence must come to an end some time or another, whether we go to Mrs Toplis's or not."

"I am sure Ned will not object to your continuing with me, if I ask him."

"No, poor fellow! He wont object—at first; but he might not like it. You have no right to inflict me on him. No: I stick to my resolution on that point. Send for the carriage. It is time for us to be off; and Mrs Toplis will be more impressed if we come in state than if we trudge afoot."

"Hush," said Marian, who was standing near the window. "Here is George, with a face full of importance."

"Uncle Reginald has written to him," said Elinor.

"Then the sooner we go, the better," said Marian. "I do not care to have the whole argument over again with George."

As they passed through the hall on their way out they met the clergyman.

"Well, George," said Elinor, "how are the heathen getting on in Belgravia? You look lively."

"Are you going out, Marian?" he said, solemnly, disregarding his cousin's banter.

"We are going to engage a couple of rooms for some errant members of the family," said Elinor. "May we give you as a reference?"

"Certainly. I may want to speak to you before I go, Marian. When will you return?"

"I do not know. Probably we shall not be long. You will have plenty of opportunities, in any case."

"Will you walk into the study, please, sir," said the parlormaid.

The Rev. George was closeted with his father for an hour. When he came out, he left the house, and travelled by omnibus to Westbourne Grove, whence he walked to a house in Uxbridge Road. Here he inquired for Mr Conolly, and, learning that he had just come in, sent up a card. He was presently ushered into a comfortable room, with a pleasant view of the garden. A meal of tea, wheatcakes, and fruit was ready on the table. Conolly greeted his visitor cordially, and rang for another cup. The Rev. George silently noted that his host dined in the middle of the day and had tea in the evening. Afraid though he was of Conolly, he felt strengthened in his mission by these habits, quite out of the question for Marian. The tea also screwed up his courage a little; but he talked about the electro-motor in spite of himself until the cloth was removed, when Conolly placed two easy chairs opposite one another at the window; put a box of cigarettes on a little table close at hand; and invited his visitor to smoke. But as it was now clearly time to come to business, the cigarette was declined solemnly. So Conolly, having settled himself in an easy attitude, waited for the clergyman to begin. The Rev. George seemed at a loss.

"Has your father spoken to you about an interview he had with me this morning?" said Conolly, good-naturedly helping him out.

"Yes. That, in fact, is one of the causes of my visit."

"What does he say?"

"I believe he adheres to the opinion he expressed to you. But I fear he may not have exhibited that self-control in speaking to you which I fully admit you have as much right to expect as any one else."

"It does not matter. I can quite understand his feeling."

"It does matter—pardon me. We should be sorry to appear wanting in consideration for you."

"That is a trifle. Let us keep the question straight before us. We need make no show of consideration for one another. I have shewn none toward your family."

"But I assure you our only desire is to arrange everything in a friendly spirit."

"No doubt. But when I am bent on doing a certain thing which you are equally bent on preventing, no very friendly spirit is possible except one of us surrender unconditionally.

"Hear me a moment, Mr Conolly. I have no doubt I shall be able to convince you that this romantic project of my sister's is out of the question. Your ambition—if I may say so without offence—very naturally leads you to think otherwise; but the prompting of self-interest is not our safest guide in this life."

"It is the only guide I recognize. If you are going to argue the question, and your arguments are to prevail, they must be addressed to my self-interest."

"I cannot think you quite mean that, Mr Conolly."

"Well, waive the point for the present: I am open to conviction. You know what my mind is. I have not changed it since I saw your father this morning. You think I am wrong?"

"Not wrong. I do not say for a moment that you are wrong. I—"

"Mistaken. Ill-advised. Any term you like."

"I certainly believe that you are mistaken. Let me urge upon you first the fact that you are causing a daughter to disobey her father. Now that is an awful fact. May I—appealing to that righteousness in which I am sure you are not naturally deficient—ask you whether you have reflected on that fact?"

"It is not half so awful to me as the fact of a father forcing his daughter's inclinations. However, awful is hardly the word for the occasion. Let us come to business, Mr Lind. I want to marry your sister because I have fallen in love with her. You object. Have you any other motive than aristocratic exclusiveness?"

"Indeed, you quite mistake. I have no such feeling. We are willing to treat you with every possible consideration."

"Then why object?"

"Well, we are bound to look to her happiness. We cannot believe that it would be furthered by an unsuitable match. I am now speaking to you frankly as a man of the world."

"As a man of the world you know that she has a right to choose for herself. You see, our points of view are different. On Sundays, for instance, you preach to a highly privileged audience at your church in Belgravia; whilst I lounge here over my breakfast, reading Reynolds' Newspaper. I have not many social prejudices. Although a workman, I dont look on every gentleman as a bloodsucker who seizes on the fruits of my labor only to pursue a career of vice. I will even admit that there are gentlemen who deserve to be respected more than the workmen who have neglected all their opportunities—slender as they are—of cultivating themselves a little. You, on the other hand, know that an honest man's the noblest work of God; that nature's gentlemen are the only real gentlemen; that kind hearts are more than coronets, and simple faith than Norman blood, and so forth. But when your approval of these benevolent claptraps is brought to such a practical test as the marriage of your sister to a workman, you see clearly enough that they do not establish the suitability of personal intercourse between members of different classes. That being so, let us put our respective philosophies of society out of the question, and argue on the facts of this particular case. What qualifications do you consider essential in a satisfactory brother-in-law?"

"I am not bound to answer that; but, primarily, I should consider it necessary to my sister's happiness that her husband should belong to the same rank as she."

"You see you are changing your ground. I am not in the same rank—after your sense—as she; but a moment ago you objected to the match solely on the ground of unsuitability."

"Where is the difference?" said the clergyman, with some warmth. "I have not changed my ground at all. It is the difference in rank that constitutes the unsuitability."

"Let us see, then, how far you are right—how far suitability is a question of rank. A gentleman may be, and frequently is, a drunkard, a gambler, a libertine, or all three combined."

"Stay, Mr Conolly! You shew how little you understand the only true significance—"

"One moment, Mr Lind. You are about to explain away the term gentleman into man of honor, honest man, or some other quite different thing. Let me put a case to you. I have a fellow at Queen Victoria Street working for thirty shillings a week, who is the honestest man I know. He is as steady as a rock; supports all his wife's family without complaining; and denies himself beer to buy books for his son, because he himself has experienced what it is to be without education. But he is not a gentleman."

"Pardon me, sir. He is a true gentleman."

"Suppose he calls on you tomorrow, and sends up his name with a request for an interview. You wont know his name; and the first question you will put to your servant is 'What sort of person is he?' Suppose the servant knows him, and, sharing your professed opinion of the meaning of the word, replies 'He is a gentleman.' On the strength of that you will order him to be shewn in; and the moment you see him you will feel angry with your servant for deceiving you completely as to the sort of man you were to expect by using the word gentleman in what you call its true sense. Or reverse the case. Suppose the caller is your cousin, Mr Marmaduke Lind, and your high-principled servant by mistaking the name or how not, causes you to ask the same question with respect to him. The answer will be that Mr Marmaduke—being a scamp—is not a gentleman. You would be just as completely deceived as in the other case. No, Mr Lind, you might as well say that this workman of mine is a true lord or a true prince as a true gentleman. A gentleman may be a rogue, and a knife-grinder may be a philosopher and philanthropist. But they dont change their ranks for all that."

The clergyman hesitated. Then he said timidly, "Even admitting this peculiar view of yours, Mr Conolly, does it not tell strongly against yourself in the present instance?"

"No; and I will presently shew you why not. When we digressed as to the meaning of the word gentleman, we were considering the matter of suitability. I was saying that a gentleman might be a drunkard, or, briefly, a scoundrel. A scoundrel would be a very unsuitable husband for Marian —I perceive I annoy you by calling her by her name."

"N—no. Oh, no. It does not matter."

"Therefore gentility alone is no guarantee of suitability. The only gentlemanliness she needs in a husband is ordinary good address, presentable manners, sense enough to avoid ridiculous solecisms in society, and so forth. Marian is satisfied with me on these points; and her approval settles the question finally. As to rank, I am a skilled workman, the first in my trade; and it is only by courtesy and forbearance that I suffer any man to speak of my class as inferior. Take us all, professions and trades together, and you will find by actual measurement round the head and round the chest, and round our manners and characters, if you like, that we are the only genuine aristocracy at present in existence. Therefore I meet your objection to my rank with a point-blank assertion of its superiority. Now let us have the other objections, if there *are* any others."

The clergyman received this challenge in silence. Then, after clearing his throat uneasily twice, he said:

"I had hoped, Mr Conolly, to have been able to persuade you on general grounds to relinquish your design. But as you are evidently not within reach of those considerations which I am accustomed to see universally admitted, it becomes my painful duty to assure you that a circumstance, on the secrecy of which you are relying, is known to me, and, through me, to my father."

"What circumstance is that?"

"A circumstance connected with Mr Marmaduke Lind, whom you mentioned just now. You understand me, I presume?"

"Oh! you have found that out?"

"I have. It only remains for me to warn my sister that she is about to contract a close relationship with one who is—I must say it—living in sin with our cousin."

"What do you suppose will be the result of that?"

"I leave you to imagine," said the clergyman indignantly, rising.

"Stop a bit. You do not understand me yet, I see. You have said that my views are peculiar. What if I have taken the peculiar view that I was bound to tell Marian this before proposing to her, and have actually told her?"

"But surely— That is not very likely."

"The whole affair is not very likely. Our marriage is not likely; but it is going to happen, nevertheless. She knows this circumstance perfectly well. You told her yourself."

"I! When?"

"The year before last, at Carbury Towers. It is worth your consideration, too, that by mistrusting Marian at that time, and refusing to give her my sister's address, you forced her to appeal to me for help, and so advanced me from the position of consulting electrician to that of friend in need. She knew nothing about my relationship to the woman in a state of sin (as you call it), and actually deputed me to warn your cousin of the risk he was running by his intimacy with her. Whilst I was away running this queer errand for her, she found out that the woman was my sister, and of course rushed to the conclusion that she had inflicted the deepest pain on me. Her penitence was the beginning of the sentimental side of our acquaintance. Had you recognized that she was a woman with as good a right as you to know the truth concerning all matters in this world which she has to make her way through, you would have answered her question, and then I suppose I should have gone away without having exchanged a word with her on any more personal matters than induction coils and ohms of resistance; and in all probability you would have been spared the necessity of having me for a brother-in-law."

"Well, sir," said the Rev. George dejectedly, "if what you say be true, I cannot understand Marian, I can only grieve for her. I shall not argue with you on the nature of the influence you have obtained over her. I shall speak to her myself; since you will not hear me."

"That is hardly fair. I have heard you, and am willing to hear more, if you have anything new to urge."

"You have certainly listened to my voice, Mr Conolly. But I fear I have used it to very little purpose."

"You will fail equally with Marian, believe me. Even I, whose ability to exercise influence you admit, never obtained the least over my own sister. She knew me too well on my worst side and not at all on my best. If, as I presume, your father has tried in vain, what hope is there for you?"

"Only my humble trust that a priest may be blessed in his appeal to duty even where a father's appeal to natural affection has been disregarded."

"Well, well," said Conolly, kindly, rising as his visitor disconsolately prepared to go, "you can try. *I* got on by dint of dogged faith in myself."

"And I get on by lowly faith in my Master. I would I could imbue you with the same feeling!"

Conolly shook his head, and they went downstairs in silence. "Hallo!" said he, as he opened the door, "it is raining. Let me lend you a coat."

"Thank you, no. Not at all. Good night," said the

clergyman, quickly, and hastened away through the rain from Conolly's civilities.

When he arrived at Westbourne Terrace, there was a cab waiting before the house. The door was opened to him by Marian's maid, who was dressed for walking.

"Master is in the drawing room, sir, with Miss McQuinch," she said, meaning, evidently, "Look out for squalls."

He went upstairs, and found Elinor, with her hat on, standing by the pianoforte, with battle in her nostrils. Mr Lind, looking perplexed and angry, was opposite to her.

"George," said Mr Lind, "close the door. Do you know the latest news?"

"No."

"Marian has run away!"

"Run away!"

"Yes," said Miss McQuinch. "She has fled to Mrs Toplis's, at St Mary's Terrace, with—as Uncle Reginald was just saying—a most dangerous associate."

"With—?"

"With *me*, in short."

"And you have counselled her to take this fatal step?"

"No. I advised her to stay. But she is not so well used to domestic discomfort as I am; so she insisted on going. We have got very nice rooms: you may come and see us, if you like."

"Is this a time to display your bitter and flippant humor?" said the Rev. George, indignantly. "I think the spectacle of a wrecked home—"

"Stuff!" interrupted Elinor, impatiently. "What else can I say? Uncle Reginald tells me I have corrupted Marian, and refuses to believe what I tell him. And now you attack me, as if it were my fault that you have driven her away. If you want to see her, she is within five minutes' walk of you. It is you who have wrecked her home, not she who has wrecked yours."

"There is no use in speaking to Elinor, George," said

Mr Lind, with the air of a man who had tried it. "You had better go to Marian, and tell her what you mentioned this afternoon. What has been the result of your visit?"

"He maintains that she knows everything," said the Rev. George, with a dispirited glance at Elinor. "I fear my visit has been worse than useless."

"It is impossible that she should know. He lies," said Mr Lind. "Go and tell her the truth, George, and say that I desire her—I order her—to come back at once. Say that I am waiting here for her."

"But, Uncle Reginald," began Elinor, in a softer tone than before, whilst the clergyman stood in doubt—

"I think," continued Mr Lind, "that I must request you, Elinor, to occupy the rooms you have taken, until you return to your parents. I regret that you have forced me to take this step; but I cannot continue to offer you facilities for exercising your influence over my daughter. I will charge myself with all your expenses until you go to Wiltshire."

Elinor looked at him as if she despaired of his reason. Then, seeing her cousin slowly going to the door, she said:

"You dont really mean to go on such a fool's errand to Marian, George?"

"Elinor!" cried Mr Lind.

"What else is it?" said Elinor. "You asserted all your authority yourself this morning, and only made matters worse. Yet you expect her to obey you at second hand. Besides, she is bound in honor not to desert *me* now; and I will tell her so, too, if I see any sign of her letting herself be bullied."

"I fear Marian will not pay much heed to what I say to her," said the clergyman.

"If you are coming," said Elinor, "you had better come in my cab. Good night, Uncle Reginald."

"Stay," said Mr Lind, irresolutely. "Elinor, I—you—Will you exercise your influence to induce Marian to return? I think you owe me at least so much."

"I will if you will withdraw your opposition to her

marriage and let her do as she likes. But if you can give her no better reason for returning than that she can be more conveniently persecuted here than at St Mary's Terrace, she will probably stay where she is, no matter how I may influence her."

"If she is resolved to quarrel with me, I cannot help it," said Mr Lind, pettishly.

"You know very well that she is the last person on earth to quarrel with any one."

"She has been indulged in every way. This is the first time she has been asked to sacrifice her own wishes."

"To sacrifice her whole life, you mean. It is the first time she has ever hesitated to sacrifice her own comfort, and therefore the first time you are conscious that any sacrifice is required. Let me tell her that you will allow her to take her own course, Uncle Reginald. He is well enough off; and they are fond of one another. A man of genius is worth fifty men of rank."

"Tell her, if you please, Elinor, that she must choose between Mr Conolly and me. If she prefers him, well and good: I have done with her. That is my last word."

"So now she has nobody to turn to in the world except him. That is sensible. Come, cousin George! I am off."

"I do not think I should do any good by going," said the clergyman.

"Then stay where you are," said Elinor. "Good night." And she abruptly left the room.

"It was a dreadful mistake ever to have allowed that young fury to enter the house," said Mr Lind. "She must be mad. What did *he* say?"

"He said a great deal in attempted self-justification. But I could make no impression on him. We have no feelings in common with a man of his type. No. He is evidently bent on raising himself by a good marriage."

"We cannot prevent it."

"Oh, surely we—"

"I tell you we *cannot* prevent it," repeated Mr Lind,

turning angrily upon his son. "How can we? What can we do? She will marry this—this—this—this beggar. I wish to God I had never seen her mother."

The clergyman stood by, cowed, and said nothing.

"You had better go to that woman of Marmaduke's," continued Mr Lind, "and try whether she can persuade her brother to commute his interest in the company, and go back to America, or to the devil. I will take care that he gets good terms, even if I have to make them up out of my own pocket. If the worst comes, *she* must be persuaded to leave Marmaduke. Offer her money. Women of that sort drive a hard bargain, but they have their price."

"But sir, consider my profession. How can I go to drive a bargain with a woman of evil reputation?"

"Well, I must go myself, I suppose."

"Oh no. I will go. Only I thought I would mention it."

"A clergyman can go anywhere. You are privileged. Come to breakfast in the morning: we can talk over matters then."

THE PARTING

(*Chap. XVII from The Irrational Knot*)

CONOLLY returned from Glasgow a little before eight on Monday evening. There was no light in the window when he entered the garden. Miss McQuinch opened the door before he reached it.

"What!" he said. "Going the moment I come in!" Then, seeing her face by the hall lamp, he put down his bag quickly, and asked what the matter was.

"I dont know whether anything is the matter. I am very glad you have returned. Come into the drawing room: I dont want the servants to hear us talking."

"There is no light here," he said, following her in. "Is it possible you have been waiting in the dark?"

He lit a candle, and was about to light a lamp when she exclaimed impatiently, "Oh, I did not notice it: what does it matter? Do let the lamp alone, and listen to me." He obeyed, much amused at her irritation. "Where has Marian gone to?" she asked.

"Is she out?" he said, suddenly grave. "You forget that I have come straight from Glasgow."

"I have been here since three o'clock. Marian sent me a note not to come on Sunday—that she should be out and that you were away. But they tell me that she was at home all yesterday, except for two hours when she was out with Sholto. She packed her trunks in the evening, and went away with them. She told the cabman to drive to Euston. I dont know what it all means, and I have been half distracted waiting here for you. I thought you would never come. There is a note for you on your dressing-table."

He pursed his lips a little and looked attentively at her, but said nothing.

"Wont you go and open it?" she said anxiously. "It must contain some explanation."

"I am afraid the explanation is obvious."

"You have no right to say that. How do you know? If you are not going to read her letter, you had better say so at once. I dont want to pry into it: I only want to know what has become of Marian."

"You shall read it by all means. Will you excuse me whilst I fetch it?"

She stamped with impatience. He smiled and went for the letter, which, after a brief absence, he placed unopened on the table before her, saying:

"I suppose this is it. I laid my hand on it in the dark."

"Are you going to open it?" she said, hardly able to contain herself.

"No."

He had not raised his voice; but it struck her that he was in a rage. His friendly look and quiet attitude first reassured, then, on second thoughts, exasperated her.

"Why wont you?"

"I really dont know. Somehow, I am not curious. It interests you. Pray open it."

"I will die first. If it lie there until I open it, it will lie there for ever."

He opened the envelope neatly with a paper cutter, and handed her the enclosure. She kept down her hands stubbornly. He smiled a little, still presenting it. At last she snatched it, much as she would have liked to snatch a handful of his hair. Having read it, she turned pale, and looked as she had used to in her childhood, when in disgrace and resolute not to cry. "I had rather have had my two hands cut off," she said passionately, after a pause.

"It is very sad for you," said Conolly, sympathetically. "He is an educated man, but I cannot think that he has much in him."

"He is a selfish, lying, conceited hound. Educated indeed! And what are *you* going to do, may I ask?"

"Eat my supper. I am as hungry as a bear."

"Yes, you had better, I think. Good evening."

He seemed to know that she would not leave, for he made no movement to open the door for her. On her way out, she turned, and so came at him with her fists clenched, that for a moment he was doubtful whether she would not bodily assault him.

"Are you a brute, or a fool, or both?" she said, letting her temper loose. "How long do you intend to stand there, doing nothing?"

"What *can* I do, Miss McQuinch?" he said, gently.

"You can follow her and bring her back before she has made an utter idiot of herself with that miserable blackguard. Are you afraid of him? If you are, I will go with you, and not let him touch you."

"Thank you," he said, good-humoredly. "But you see she does not wish to live with me."

"Good God, man, what woman do you think *could* wish to live with you! I suppose Marian wanted a human being to live with, and not a calculating machine. You would drive any woman away. If you had feeling enough to have kicked him out of the house, and then beaten her black and blue for encouraging him, you would have been more of a man than you are: she would have loved you more. You are not a man: you are a stone full of brains—such as they are! Listen to me, Mr Conolly. There is one chance left—if you will only make haste. Go after them; overtake them; thrash him within an inch of his life, and bring her back and punish her how you please so long as you shew her that you care. You can do it if you will only make up your mind: he is a coward; and he is afraid of you: I have seen it in his eye. You are worth fifty of him—if you would only not be so cold-blooded—if you will only go—*dear* Mr Conolly—youre not really insensible—you will, wont you?"

This, the first tender tone he had ever heard in her voice, made him look at her curiously. "What does the letter say?" he asked, still quietly, but inexorably.

She snatched it up again. "Here," she said. "'*Our marriage was a mistake. I am going away with Douglas to the other side of the world. It is all I can do to mend matters. Pray forget me.*' That is what her letter says, since you condescend to ask."

"It is too late, then. You felt that as you read it, I think?"

"Yes," she cried, sitting down in a paroxysm of grief, but unable to weep. "It is too late; and it is all your fault. What business had you to go away? You knew what was going to happen. You intended it to happen. You wanted it to happen. You are glad it has happened; and it serves you right. '*Pray forget her.*' Oh, yes, poor girl! she need not trouble about that. I declare there is nothing viler, meaner, cowardlier, selfisher on earth than a man. Oh, if we had only done what we always said we would do—kept free from you!"

"It was a good plan," said Conolly, submissively.

"Was it? How were we to know that you were not made of flesh and blood, pray? There, let me go. [The table was between them, but she rose and shook off an imaginary detaining hand.] I dont want to hear anything more about it. I suppose you are right not to care. Very likely she was right to go, too; so we are all right, and everything is for the best, no doubt. Marian is ruined, of course, but what does that matter to you? She was only in your way. You can console yourself with your—" Here Armande came in, and Elinor turned quickly to the fireplace and stood there, so that the housemaid should not see her face.

"Your dinner, sir," said Armande, with a certain artificiality of manner that was, under the circumstances, significant. "There is a nice fire in the laboratory."

"Thank you," said Conolly. "Presently, Armande."

"The things will spoil if you wait too long, sir. The mistress was very particular with me and cook about it."

And Armande, with an air of declining further responsibility, went out.

"What shall I do without Marian?" said Conolly. "Not one woman in a hundred is capable of being a mistress to her servants. She saved me all the friction of housekeeping."

"You are beginning to feel your loss," said Elinor, facing him again. "A pleasant thing for a woman of her talent to be thrown away to save you the friction of housekeeping. If you had paid half the attention to her happiness that she did to your dinners you would not be in your present predicament."

"Have you really calculated that it is twice as easy to make a woman happy as to feed a man?"

"Calc—! Yes, I have. I tell you that it is three times as easy—six times as easy: more fool the woman! You can make a woman happy for a week by a word or a kiss? How long do you think it takes to order a week's dinners? I suppose you consider a kiss a weakness?"

"I am afraid—judging by the result—that I am not naturally clever at kissing."

"No, I should think not, indeed. Then you had better go and do what you *are* clever at—eat your dinner."

"Miss McQuinch: did you ever see an unfortunate little child get a severe fall, and then, instead of a little kindly petting, catch a sound whacking from its nurse for daring startle her and spoil its clothes?"

"Well, what is the point of that?"

"You remind me a little of the nurse. I have had a sort of fall this evening."

"And now you are going to pretend to be hurt, I suppose, because you dont care to be told that it is your own fault. That is a common experience with children, too. I tell you plainly that I dont believe you are hurt at all, though you may not be exactly pleased—just for the moment. However, I did not mean to be uncivil. If you are really sorry, I am at least *as* sorry. I have not said all I think."

"What more?"

"Nothing of any use to say. I see I am wasting my time here—and no doubt wasting yours too."

"Well, I think you have had your turn. If you are not thoroughly satisfied, pray go on for ten minutes longer: your feelings do you credit, as the phrase goes. Still do not forget that you thought just the same of me a week ago, and that if you had said as much then you might have prevented what has happened. Giving me a piece of your mind now is of no use except as far as it relieves you. To

Marian or me or any one else it does no good. So when you have said your worst, we cannot do better, I think, than set our wits to work about our next move."

Elinor received this for a moment in dudgeon. Then she laughed sourly, and said, "There is some sense in that. I am as much to blame as anybody: I dont deny it—if that is any comfort to you. But as to the next move, you say yourself that it is too late to do anything, and I dont see that you can do much."

"That is so. But there are a few things to be faced. First, I have to set Marian and myself free."

"How?"

"Divorce her."

"Divorce!" Elinor looked at him in dismay. He was unmoved. Then her gaze fell slowly, and she said: "Yes: I suppose you have a right to that."

"She also."

"So that she may marry him from a sense of duty. That will be so happy for her!"

"She will have time, before she is free, to find out whether she likes him or not. There will be a great fuss in the family over the scandal."

"Do you care about that? *I* dont."

"No. However, thats a detail. Marian will perhaps write to you. If so, just point out to her that her five hundred a year belongs to her still, and makes her quite independent of him and of me. That is all, I think. You need take no pains now to conceal what has happened: the servants below know it as well as we: in a week it will be town talk."

Elinor looked wistfully at him, her impetuosity failing her as she felt how little effect it was producing. Yet her temper rather rose than fell at him. There was a much more serious hostility than before in her tone as she said: "You seem to have been thoroughly prepared for what has happened. I do not want any instructions from you as to what I shall write to Marian about her money affairs: I want to know, in case she takes it into her head to come back when she has found what a fool she had made of herself, whether I may tell her that you are glad to be rid of her, and that there is no use in her humiliating herself by coming to your door and being turned away."

"Shall I explain the situation to you from my point of view?" said he. At the sound of his voice she looked up in alarm. The indulgent, half-playful manner which she had almost lost the sense of because it was so invariable with him in speaking to ladies was suddenly gone. She felt that the real man was coming out now without ceremony. He was quick to perceive the effect he had produced. To soften it, he placed a comfortable chair on the hearthrug, and said, in his ordinary friendly way: "Sit nearer the fire: we can talk more comfortably. Now," he continued, standing with his back to the mantelpiece, "let me tell you, Miss McQuinch, that when you talk of my turning people away from my door you are not talking fair and square sense to me. I dont turn my acquaintances off in that way, much less my friends; and a woman who has lived with me as my wife for eighteen months must always be a rather particular friend. I liked her before I was her husband, and I shall continue to like her when I am no longer her husband. So you need have no fear on that score. But I wont remain her husband. You said just now that I knew what was going to happen; that I intended it to happen, wanted it to happen, and am glad it happened. There is more truth in that than you thought when you said it. For some time past Marian has been staying with me as a matter of custom and convenience only, using me as a cover for her philandering with Douglas, and paying me by keeping the house very nicely for me. I had asked myself once or twice how long this was to last. I was in no hurry for the answer; for although I was wifeless and had no one to live with who really cared for me, I was quite prepared to wait a couple of years if necessary, on the chance of our making it up somehow. But sooner or later I should have insisted on closing our accounts and parting; and I am not sorry now that the end has come, since it was inevitable, though I am right sorry for the way it has come. Instead of eloping in the conventional way, she should have come to an understanding with me. I could easily have taken her for a trip in the States, where we could have stopped a few months in South Dakota and got divorced without any scandal. I have never made any claims on her since she found out that she didnt care for me; and she might have known from that that I was not the man to keep her against her will and play dog in the manger with a fellow like Douglas. However, thats past praying for now. She has had enough of me, and I have had more than enough of her set and her family, except that I should like to remain good friends with you. You are the only one of the whole lot worth your salt. It is understood, of course, that you take Marian's part against me on all issues; but will you be friends as far as is consistent with that?"

"All right," said Nelly, shortly.

"Shake hands on it, and I'll tell you something else that will help you to understand me better," he said, holding out his hand. She gave hers; and when the bargain was struck, he turned to the fire and seated himself on the edge of the table.

"You know that when I married," he resumed, "I was promoted to mix in fashionable society for the first time. Of course you do: that was the whole excitement of the affair for the family. You know the impression I made on polite society better, probably, than I do. Now tell me: do you know what impression polite society made on me?"

"Dont understand."

"Perhaps it has never occurred even to you, sharp as you are, that I could have taken society otherwise than at its own valuation of itself, as something much higher, more cultivated and refined than anything that I had been accustomed to. Well, I never believed much in that at any time; but it was not until I had made a *mésalliance* for Marian's sake that I realized how infinitely beneath me and my class was the one I had married into."

"*Mésalliance!*—with Marian! I take back the shake hands."

"*Mésalliance* with her class, for her sake: I made the distinction purposely. Now what am I, Miss McQuinch? A worker. I belonged and belong to the class that keeps up the world by its millions of serviceable hands and serviceable brains. All the pride of caste in me settles on that point. I admit no loafer as my equal. The man who is working at the bench is my equal, whether he can do my day's work or not, provided he is doing the best he can. But the man who does not work anyhow, and the class that does not work, is a class below mine. When I annoyed Marian by refusing to wear a tall hat and cuffs, I did so because I wanted to have it seen as I walked through Piccadilly and St James's Street that I did not belong there, just as your people walk through a poor street dressed so as to shew that they dont belong there. To me a man like your uncle, Marian's father, or like Marmaduke or Douglas, loafing idly round spending money that has been made by the sweat of men like myself, are little better than thieves. They get on with the queerest makeshifts for self-respect: old Mr Lind with family pride, Douglas with personal vanity, and Marmaduke with a sort of interest in his own appetites and his own jollity. Everything is a sham with them: they have drill and etiquette instead of manners, fashions instead of tastes, small talk instead of intercourse. Everything that is special to them as distinguished from workers is a sham: when you get down to the real element in them, good or bad, you find that it is something that is common to them and to all civilized mankind. The reason that this isnt as clear to other workmen who come among them as it is to me is that most workmen share their ignorance of the things they affect superiority in. Poor Jackson, whom you all call the Yankee cad, and who is not a cad at all in his proper place among the engineers at our works, believes in the sham refinements he sees around him at the at-homes he is so fond of. He has no art in him—no trained ear for music or for fine diction, no trained eye for pictures and colors and buildings, no cultivated sense of dignified movement, gesture, and manner. But he knows what fashionable London listens to and looks at, and how it talks and behaves; and he makes that his standard, and sets down what is different from it as vulgar. Now the difference between me and him is that I got an artistic training by accident when I was young, and had the natural turn to profit by it. Before I ever saw a West End Londoner I knew beautiful from ugly, rare from common, in music, speech, costume, and gesture; for in my father's operatic and theatrical companies there did come now and then, among the crowd of third-raters, a dancer, an actor, a scene-painter, a singer, or a bandsman or conductor who was a fine artist. Consequently, I was not to be taken in like Jackson by made-up faces, trashy pictures, drawling and lounging and strutting and tailoring, drawing-room singing and drawing-room dancing, any more than by bad ventilation and unwholesome hours and food, not to mention polite dram drinking, and the round of cruelties they call sport. I found that the moment I refused to accept the habits of the rich as standards of refinement and propriety, the whole illusion of their superiority vanished at once. When I married Marian I was false to my class. I had a sort of idea that my early training had accustomed me to a degree of artistic culture that I could not easily find in a working girl, and that would be quite natural to Marian. I soon found that she had the keenest sense of what was ladylike, and no sense at all of what was beautiful. A drawing, a photograph, or an engraving sensibly framed without a white mount round it to spoil it pained her as much as my wrists without cuffs on them. No mill girl could have been less in sympathy with me on the very points for which I had preferred her to the mill girls. The end of it was that I felt that love had made me do a thoroughly vulgar thing—marry beneath me. These aristocratic idle gentlemen will never be shamed out of their laziness and low-mindedness until the democratic working gentlemen refuse to associate with them instead of running after them and licking their boots. I am heartily glad now to be out of their set and rid of them, instead of having to receive them civilly in my house for Marian's sake. The whole business was strangling me: the strain of keeping my feeling to myself was more than you can imagine. Do you know that there have been times when I have been so carried away with the idea that she must be as tired of the artificiality of our life as I was, that I have begun to speak my mind frankly to her; and when she recoiled, hurt and surprised and frightened that I was going to turn coarse at last, I have shut up and sat there apparently silent, but really saying under my breath: 'Why dont you go? Why dont you leave me, vanish, fly away to your own people? You must be a dream: I never married you. You dont know me: you cant be my wife: your lungs were not made to breathe the air I live in.' I have said a thousand things like that, and then wondered whether there was any truth in telepathy—whether she could possibly be having my thoughts transferred to her mind and thinking it only her imagination. I would ask myself whether I despised her or not, calling on myself for the truth as if I did not believe the excuses I made for her out of the fondness I could not get over. I am fond of her still, sometimes. I did not really—practically, I mean—despise her until I gave up thinking about her at all. There was a certain kind of contempt in that indifference, beyond a doubt: there is no use denying it. Besides, it is proved to me now by the new respect I feel for her because she has had the courage and grit to try going away with Douglas. But my love for her is over: nothing short of her being born over again—a thing that sometimes happens—will ever bring her into contact with me after this. To put it philosophically, she made the mistake of avoiding all realities, and yet marrying herself to the hardest of realities, a working man; so it was inevitable that she should go back at last to the region of shadows and mate with that ghostliest of all unrealities, the non-working man. Perhaps, too, the union may be more fruitful than ours: the cross between us was too violent. Now you have the whole story from my point of view. What do you—"

"Hush!" said Elinor, interrupting him. "What is that noise outside?"

The house bell began to ring violently, and they could hear a confused noise of voices and footsteps without.

"Can she have come back?" said Elinor, starting up.

"Impossible!" said Conolly, looking disturbed for the first time. They stood a moment listening, with averted eyes. A second peal from the bell was followed by roars of laughter, amid which a remonstrant voice was audible. Then the house door was hammered with a stick. Conolly ran downstairs at once and opened it. On the step he found Marmaduke reeling in the arms of the Rev. George.

"How are you, ol' fler?" said Marmaduke, plunging into the hall. "The parson is tight. I found him tumbling about High Street, and brought him along."

"Pray excuse this intrusion," whispered the Rev. George. "You see the state he is in. He accosted me near Campden Hill, and I really could not be seen walking with him into town. I wonder he was not arrested."

"He is the worse for drink; but he is sober enough to know how to amuse himself at your expense," said Conolly, aloud. "Come up to the laboratory. Miss McQuinch is there."

"But he is not fit," urged the clergyman. "Look at him trying to hang up his hat. How absurd—I should rather say how deplorable! I assure you he is perfectly tipsy. He has been ringing the bells of the houses, and requesting females to accompany us. Better warn Elinor."

"Nonsense!" said Conolly. "I have some news that will sober him. Here is Miss McQuinch. Are you going?"

"Yes," said Elinor. "I should lose my patience if I had to listen to George's comments, and I am tired. I would rather go."

"Not yet, Nelly. Wont um stay and talk to um's

Marmadukes?"

"Let me go," said Elinor, snatching away her hand, which he had seized. "You ought to be at home in bed. You are a sot." At this Marmaduke laughed boisterously. She passed him contemptuously, and left. The three men then went upstairs, Marmaduke dropping his pretence of drunkenness under the influence of Conolly's presence.

"Marian is not in, I presume," said the clergyman, when they were seated.

"No," said Conolly. "She has eloped with Douglas."

They stared at him. Then Marmaduke gave a long whistle, and the clergyman rose, pale. "What do you mean, sir?" he said.

Conolly did not answer, and the Rev. George slowly sat down again.

"Well, I'm damned sorry for it," said Marmaduke, emphatically. "It was a mean thing for Douglas to do, with all his brag about his honor."

The Rev. George covered his face with his handkerchief and sobbed.

"Come, shut up, old fellow, and dont make an ass of yourself," said Marmaduke. "What are you going to do, Conolly?"

"I must simply divorce her."

"Go for heavy damages, Conolly. Knock a few thousand out of him, just to punish him."

"He could easily afford it. Besides, why should I punish him?"

"My dear friend," cried the clergyman, "you must not dream of a divorce. I implore you to abandon such an idea. Consider the disgrace, the impiety! The publicity would kill my father."

Conolly shook his head.

"There is no such thing as divorce known to the Church. 'What God hath joined together, let no man put asunder.'"

"She had no right to bolt," said Marmaduke. "Thats certain."

"I was married by a registrar," said Conolly: "and as there is no such thing as civil marriage known to the Church, our union, from the ecclesiastical point of view, has no existence. We were not joined by God, in fact, in your sense. To deny her the opportunity of re-marrying would be to compel her to live as an adulteress in the eye of the law, which, by the by, would make me the father of Douglas's children. I cannot, merely because your people are afraid of scandal, take such a revenge on Marian as to refuse her the freedom she has sacrificed so much for. After all, since our marriage has proved a childless one, the only reason for our submitting to be handcuffed to one another, now that our hearts are no longer in the arrangement, is gone."

"The game began at Sark," said Marmaduke. "Douglas stuck to her there like a leech. He's been about the house here a good deal since she came back. I often wondered you didnt kick him out. But, of course, it was not my business to say anything. Was she huffed into going? You hadnt any row with her just before, had you?"

"We never had rows."

"That was your mistake, Conolly. You should have heard poor Susanna and me fighting. We always ended by swearing we would never speak to one another again. Nothing duller than a smooth life. If you had given Marian something to complain of, she would have been too much taken up with it to bother about Douglas."

"But have you ascertained whither they have gone?" said the clergyman, distractedly. "Will you not follow them?"

"I know nothing of their movements. Probably they are crossing to New York."

"But surely you ought to follow her," said the Rev. George. "You may yet be in time to save her from worse than death."

"Yah!" said Marmaduke. "Drop all that rot, George. Worse than death be hanged! Serves the family right! They are a jolly sight too virtuous: it will do them good to get shewn up a bit."

"If you have no respect for the convictions of a priest," exclaimed the Rev. George, shedding tears, "you might at least be silent in the presence of a heart-broken brother and husband."

"Oh, I dont want to shew any want of consideration for you or Conolly," said Marmaduke, sulkily. "No doubt it's rough on you. But as to the feelings of the family, I tell you flatly that I dont care if the whole crew were brought to the Old Bailey tomorrow and convicted of bigamy. It would take the conceit out of them."

"I know not how to break this wretched news to my father," said the Rev. George, turning disconsolately from his sottish cousin to Conolly.

"It is no such uncommon occurrence. The less fuss made about it the better. She is not to blame, and I shall not be heard crying out misery and disgrace. Your family can very well follow my example. I have nothing to say against her, and I believe she has nothing to say against me. Nothing can prevent such publicity as a petition for divorce must entail. Your father will survive it, never fear."

The clergyman, remembering how vainly he had tried to change Conolly's intention when Marian was to be married, felt that he should succeed no better now that she was to be divorced. Silent and cast down, he sat dangling his handkerchief between his knees and leaning forward on his elbow toward the fire.

"You must excuse me if I see my way straight through to the end. I daresay you would rather realize it gradually, inevitable as it is," added Conolly, looking down with some pity at his drooping figure. "I cannot help my habit of mind. When are you going to be married?" he continued, to Marmaduke.

"I dont know. The Countess is in a hurry. I'm not. But I suppose it will be some time in spring."

"You have made up your mind to it at last?"

"Oh, I never had any particular objection to it, only I

dont like to be hunted into a corner. Conny is a good little girl, and will make a steady wife. I dont like her mother; but as for herself, she is fond of me; and after all, I *did* lead her a dance long ago. Besides, old boy, the Earl is forking out handsomely; and as I have some notion of settling down to farm, his dust will come in conveniently as capital."

The clergyman rose, and slowly pulled on his woollen gloves.

"If youre going, I will see you part of the way," said Marmaduke. "I'll cheer you up. You know you neednt tell the governor until tomorrow."

"I had rather go alone, if you intend to behave as you did before."

"Never fear. I'm as sober as a judge now. Come along. Away with melancholy! Youll have Douglas for a brother-in-law before this time next year."

This seemed to have been in the clergyman's mind, for he shook hands with his host more distinctly than usual. When they were gone, Conolly went to the laboratory, and rang for his neglected dinner, which he ate with all a traveller's appetite. From the dinner table he went straight to the organ, and played until a little before midnight, when, after a brief turn in the open air, he retired to bed, and was soon quietly asleep.

DEATH OF AN OLD REVOLUTIONARY HERO

(*From The Clarion of the 24th March* 1905)

SO old Joe Budgett of Balwick—Stalwart Joe—is dead at last. The Socialist movement has seldom mourned a more typical thoroughgoer than dear old Joe. We all knew him; for he quarrelled with every one of us at one time or another; and yet is there one who is not sorry to lose him? Those who witnessed that simple funeral at Balwick last Thursday morning, when the remains of a poor workman in a cheap pine coffin were borne through the pelting sleet to their last resting-place on the shoulders of Robert Blatchford and H. M. Hyndman, Sidney Webb and Harold Cox, Jaurès (who had come from Paris expressly to pay this last sad duty to the veteran of the International) and myself, Mr Gerald Balfour and Lord Lansdowne, must have asked themselves what manner of man this was to receive a tribute from persons of such diverse views, and so far removed from him in social position.

Joseph Budgett was a heavily built man; and even at 90—his age when he died—he was no light weight. My heart was heavy as I helped to shoulder the coffin; but I confess that poor Joe seemed heavier still by the time we reached the grave; for we were not trained to the work; and there was a good deal of sugaring among the bearers: Harold, for instance, did nothing but shelter from the sleet under the pall after the first ten yards; Jaurès and Hyndman argued in French instead of attending to their work; Blatchford, after the manner of highly sympathetic literary geniuses with a strong susceptibility to incongruous humor, was so convulsed with suppressed laughter that his quiverings rattled Joe's bones over the stones without contributing anything to their support; and if it had not been for Webb and myself (Fabians doing the practical work as usual), Joe Budgett would never have got to his grave; for Gerald Balfour and Lord Lansdowne were too far forward to get their shoulders properly under the coffin.

Lord Lansdowne was evidently taken aback to find that there was to be no religious service (Joe having been an uncompromising atheist); but he spoke very feelingly at the graveside. "It was part of the tragedy of this man's career," he said, "that in all the seventy years of active political life during which he agitated ceaselessly on behalf of his own class, he never found either in the Liberal party or in the irregular groups which pretended to represent Labor and Socialism, that incorruptible spirit, that stainless purity of principle, that absolute integrity, aloof from all compromising alliances, which his honest character demanded as the sole and sufficient claim to his support. He regarded the Conservative party as an open enemy; but he rightly preferred an open enemy to a false or half-hearted friend; and so, if we never gained his theoretic approval, we at least always had what we valued far more: his practical support."

It was at this point that the accident of which so much has been made befell Blatchford. The account of it in the evening papers was much exaggerated. It is true that the editor of The Clarion broke down and covered his face with his handkerchief. It is also true that in an attempt to hurry away from the graveside with his eyes full of tears he tripped over the sexton's spade; but he did not fall into the grave, nor was an impression of the name-plate found on his person afterwards. The capitalist press naturally strives to belittle and make ridiculous the obsequies of a political opponent; but I cannot help thinking that it might have shown better taste than to choose a funeral for a display of its cockney facetiousness.

The rest of the speaking has been so fully reported in all the Labor papers that I need not give any account of it here, except that Webb's advice to the Progressive Municipalities to make Free Funerals a plank in the program of Municipal Socialism was quite practical and sincere, and was not, as The Deptford Times asserted, a thinly veiled threat of wholesale political assassination.

A good deal of misunderstanding has been caused by the

report that the reason I did not speak was that Mrs Budgett said it would be a mockery for a man who had done his best to kill her husband to make a speech over his grave, and that Joe would turn in his coffin at the sound of my voice. Now it is quite true that Mrs Budgett actually did say this, and that I took no part in the speaking in deference to her wishes. But the three Labor papers who have rebuked Mrs Budgett for making her husband's funeral the occasion of an attack on the Fabian Society are quite wrong in their interpretation of her remarks. She was not thinking of the Fabian Society at all. The truth is, I once did actually try to kill Joe; and as it happened a good many years ago, and he forgave me handsomely—though Mrs Budgett could never forget it—I may as well do penance now by describing the affair exactly as it happened.

I was quite a young Socialist then; and when I heard one day in spring that old Budgett was passing away whilst the earth was germinating all around, a lump came into my throat: the only one I have ever had. I got used to the news later on, because Joe began dying when he was 75, and never got out of his bed from that time forth except to address a meeting or attend a Socialist Congress. But, as I have just said, I was a young hand then; and an intense desire to see the old revolutionary hero before he returned to dust took hold of me. The end of it was that I found myself a couple of days later at his cottage at Balwick, asking Mrs Budgett whether he was strong enough to see me. She said he was not, as his heart was in such a state that the least excitement or any sudden noise might be fatal. But when she saw how disappointed I was, she added that he was so mortal dull that a little company would perhaps do him good; and so, if I would promise not to talk to him, and be careful not to make any noise, she would let me up for a while. I promised eagerly; and we went up together, she warning me not to trip over the high sills or dash my head against the low lintels of the sturdy old oak-framed cottage, and I doing the one at every door in my anxiety to avoid doing the other.

This is perhaps the best place for me to say that Mrs Budgett struck me even then as being extraordinarily devoted to Joe. In fact, I dont think she ventured to regard him as anything so familiar as a husband. She had known both toil and sorrow; for she had had to keep Joe and bring up a family of five by her own exertions. As a boy, Joe had been apprenticed to a bigginwainer, and had served his time and learnt the trade; but when a little thumbed and blackened volume containing Shelley's Queen Mab and Men of England, and Tom Paine's Age of Reason, came in his way, and he heard a speech from Orator Hunt, the famous Man in the White Hat, he threw up his bigginwaining and devoted his life to the cause of the people, entrusting all his business affairs to his faithful wife, who never let him know want. In course of time he almost forgot his trade; for I remember on one occasion, when William Morris, in his abrupt way, said to him "And what the devil is a bigginwainer?" Joe was quite at a loss, and could describe it only as a branch of the coopering. The consequence was that Mrs Budgett had to work pretty hard as a laundress; but she did not mind hard work: what weighed on her was the curious fatality that the five children all turned against Joe. They became strong chapelgoers and moneymakers, and made their quarrel with Joe an excuse for doing very little for her, because, they said, they did not want their earnings wasted in encouraging him. So there had been sorrow and strife enough even in that little household.

Joe was sitting up in bed when we entered; and I was struck at once by the lion-like mane of white hair, the firmly closed mouth with its muscles developed by half a century of public speaking, the serene brow, clear ruddy complexion, and keen bold eyes of the veteran. He gave my hand a strong hearty grip, and said, in tones that were still resonant (for he had not then acquired the senile whistling utterance that pierced the ears and hearts of the International Socialist Congress at Amsterdam), "Do I at last see before me that old and tried friend of the working classes, George Bernard

Shaw? How are you, George?"

Although I was not then old, and had no other feeling for the working classes than an intense desire to abolish them and replace them by sensible people, Joe's cordial manner encouraged and set me at ease. He invited me to sit down; and before my trousers had pressed the chair, he was deep in a flood of reminiscences.

"I served my apprenticeship to the revolution," he said, "in the struggle against the Reform Bill of 1832."

"*Against* it!" I cried.

"Aye, against it," he said. "Old as I am, my blood still boils when I think of the way in which a capitalist tailor named Place—one of the half-hearted Radical vermin—worked that infamous conspiracy to enfranchise the middle classes and deny the vote to the working men. I spoke against it on every platform in England. The Duke of Wellington himself said to me that he disapproved of revolutionists in general, but that he wished there were a few more in the country of my kidney. Then came Chartism with its five points to fool the people and keep them from going to the real root of the matter by abolishing kings, priests, and private property. I showed up its leaders, and had the satisfaction of seeing them all go to prison and come out without a single follower left to them. Then there was Bright and Cobden trailing the red herring of Free Trade across the trail of the emancipation of the working classes. I exposed them and their silly lies about cheap bread; and if I'd been listened to, no Englishman need ever have wanted bread again. Next came those black blots on our statute book, the Factory Acts, which recognized and regulated and legalized the accursed exploitation of the wives and children of the poor in the factory hells. Why, when I took the field against them, the very employers themselves said I was right and bid me God-speed in that campaign. Then came a worse swindle than the Reform Bill of 1832—the '67 Bill, that gave just a handful of votes to a few workmen to bolster up the lie that Parliament represents the people instead of the vampires that live by plundering them. Didnt I get this scar over my eye from a stone that hit me while I was speaking against that Bill? But it became law for all that; and it emboldened the capitalists so much that they brought in the Education Act to drive all our children into their prisons of schools, and drill them into submission, and teach them to be more efficient slaves to make profits for their bloodsuckers. I spoke against it until I lost my voice for a whole month; and the people were with me too, heart and soul. It ended, as all double-facedness ends, in the Compromise. But thank God—not that I believe in God, but I use the word in a manner of speaking—I never compromised; and I never will. I left the International because it would not support me against the school Bastilles. And it was high time I did; for the International was a rotten compromise itself—half mere Trade-Unionism, and the other half a little private game of a rare old dodger named Marx—not Harry Marks, you know, but Karl—a compromise between a German and a Jew, *he* was: neither one thing nor the other. Then came the Commune of Paris, that did nothing but get the people of Paris slaughtered like mad dogs, because as I pointed out at the time, it was too local, and stood for a city instead of for all the world. That put an end to everything for ten years; and then Socialism came up again with all the old mistakes and compromises: the half-hearted Chartist palliatives, the stooping to use the votes that the capitalists had bribed the people with, the pushing middle class men and autocratic swells at the head of it. I soon saw through Hyndman, and went with Morris into the Socialist League. But Morris was just as bad: all he wanted was our pennies to publish his poems—John Bull's Earthly Paradise and such tosh as that—in The Commonweal. I turned the League against him at last and took The Commonweal from him; and then he showed his true nature by leaving us without means to pay the rent or publish the paper. Nothing came of it but another Reform Bill in 1885. I said, 'Does it abolish the registration laws and establish Universal Suffrage?' 'No,' they said. 'Then have nothing to do with it,' I said; and I spoke against it and agitated against it as I never agitated before. But the spirit of the workers was broken: they submitted to it like sheep. I took to my bed then, and never came out of it until the Dock Strike of 1889."

"That roused you, did it?" I said, ambiguously; for I was now alive to the danger of jumping to any conclusions as to which side Joe might have taken.

"Could I lie here and see the people led away by a renegade like John Burns?" he exclaimed. "Oh what a degradation that was! what a spectacle of crawling slavery! to see freeborn men begging for sixpence an hour instead of insisting in a voice of thunder on the full product of their labor! That was what Burns's pretended Socialism came to when he was put to the test. Sixpence an hour! But I expected no more. I saw through him from the first, just as I saw through Francis Place, and Fergus O'Connor, and Bronterre O'Brien, and the hypocritical Christian Socialists, and George Odger and Charles Bradlaugh and Hyndman and Morris and Champion and the German wirepullers, Bebel and Liebknecht. Self-seeking humbugs, talkers and compromisers all of them. None of them thorough, none of them genuine right through. The Dock Strike was nothing but a conspiracy between Cardinal Manning and John Burns to get Manning made Pope and to get Burns into the County Council. From that day I resolved that Burns should be driven from the cause of the people if my tongue and pen could do it. I'm organizing the Socialist opposition to him at Battersea—the genuine real Socialist opposition—and we'll have him out at the next election, when the Albert Palace is rcplaced by flats full of Conservative voters."

"You are working for the Conservatives, then?"

"Young man: I have opposed the Tories all my life; but theres one thing I hate more than a Tory; and thats a traitor."

"Are all the Labor and Socialist leaders traitors?"

"Traitors! What puts such a thought into your mind?

There are hundreds of true men who *ought* to be leaders, and will be when the people come to their senses. But the men that put themselves forward as leaders—that organize strikes and tout for votes and win elections are all traitors and self-seekers, every man of them. It's the so-called unsuccessful men—the martyrs of the movement—the men that stand up for the people against everybody—mark that, against *everybody*: those are the real men, the salt of the people's cause, the glory of the revolution."

He paused to take a sip of Liebig from a cup his wife had brought him when we came in. He did it just as a speaker who is getting hoarse takes a sip of water on the platform. As his historical reminiscences had by this time come pretty well up to date, I thought he was done; but he suddenly switched off from history to moral exhortation.

"Look at me!" he said, "going on for eighty, and as sound as a bell, except for this complaint in my heart, brought on by its bleeding for the people and by overwork on the platform. Thats because I am a teetotaler, young man. And why am I a teetotaler? Because the cause of the people has been drink to me and stimulant to me and courage and warmth to me. Have I ever taken money for my principles? Never. The exploiting classes have offered over and over again to finance me. But I have never accepted a penny."

"Except from your wife," I remarked, thoughtlessly.

For a moment he was completely taken aback. Then he said, with indescribable majesty, "Never. It is a foul lie; and whoever told it to you lies in his black throat. Prove to me that my wife has ever accepted a farthing from any oppressor of the people—that she has ever possessed a coin that was not earned by her own honest toil—and I will never look on her face again."

"Thats not precisely what I mean," I said, rather lamely; for I perceived that he had missed my point; and I rather doubted whether an explanation would mend matters. But he went on impetuously, being constitutionally a bad listener.

"My wife is a crown of rubies to me," he said, with feeling. "But I have always kept her out of the rough and tumble of political strife. It has broken me up; but at least I have shielded *her* from it." Here he wiped away a tear. "And when I think," he went on, "that there are men who are at this present moment plotting to give the vote to middle class women and deny it to my wife, I feel that I could rise from my bed like a young man and fight with my last breath against it as I did against the abomination of 1832."

"All or nothing is your principle," I said.

"Thats it," he responded in a ringing voice, aglow with enthusiasm. "All or nothing."

"Well," I said, "as it is quite certain that you wont get All, you are practically the propagandist of Nothing: a Nihilist, in fact."

"I am not ashamed of the word Nihilist," he said. "The Nihilists are my brothers."

"To change the subject," I said: "is it really true that your heart is so bad that a sudden noise would kill you?"

"It is," he said proudly. "You could snuff me out like a candle by knocking that cup of Liebig's Extract over on to the floor."

I looked round. A grandfather's clock ticked peacefully in the silence; for Joe, having reminded himself of the Liebig, was now drinking it; and even he could not talk and drink at the same time.

"Mr Budgett," I said, rising, "I am not a Nihilist; and it is perfectly clear to me that nothing will ever be done as long as you are about. So here goes!" And I pulled the grandfather's clock right over.

It fell with an appalling crash, striking as it fell until its weights thundered on the boards. Terrified at my own deed, I looked fearfully at the dying man. But Joe did not die. Instead, he sprang out of bed and said, "What the —— —— are you doing?"

I thought it best, on the whole, to drop from the window

and make for the railway station. Next day I sent him £2—all I could spare—to pay for repairing the clock. But he sent it back to me with a letter of some thirty pages to say that he could do without a clock, but not without his self-respect.

That was why Mrs Budgett objected to my speaking at the funeral.

I confess, now that advancing years have mellowed my character, that I was wrong in trying to kill Joe. One must live and let live. He bore no malice whatever for the incident, and used to refer to it with the utmost good humor, always ending up with the assurance that he did not take me seriously, and knew that my real object was simply to give him a hearty laugh.

His end was undoubtedly hastened by his efforts to turn the Labor movement against the new Bill for the Enfranchisement of Women; and he was proud to number a Countess among his converts. He almost lost his temper with me because I said that I should support any Bill that would make a start by giving a parliamentary vote or seat to even one woman, though the property qualification were a million sterling. "All or nothing!" he said, with a fervor worthy of Ibsen's Brand.

The governing classes keep the mass of people enslaved by taking advantage of their sloth, their stupidity, their ignorance, their poverty, their narrowness, their superstition, and their vices. They could not enslave Joe by such means. He was energetic and clever; he was as well read as most cabinet ministers; he was sufficiently fed, clothed and housed (by his wife); he was a universalist in his breadth of view; he was an atheist; and he had practically no vices. And yet the governing classes tied Joe up with the principles of absolute morality tighter than they could tie a hooligan with a set of handcuffs.

After all, the principles of absolute morality were made for this very purpose; so Joe was hardly to be blamed.

MUSIC

BEETHOVEN'S CENTENARY

From the Radio Times, 18 March 1927

A HUNDRED years ago a crusty old bachelor of fifty-seven, so deaf that he could not hear his own music played by a full orchestra, yet still able to hear thunder, shook his fist at the roaring heavens for the last time, and died as he had lived, challenging God and defying the universe. He was Defiance Incarnate: he could not even meet a Grand Duke and his court in the street without jamming his hat tight down on his head and striding through the very middle of them. He had the manners of a disobliging steamroller (most steamrollers are abjectly obliging and conciliatory); and he was rather less particular about his dress than a scarecrow: in fact he was once arrested as a tramp because the police refused to believe that such a tatterdemalion could be a famous composer, much less a temple of the most turbulent spirit that ever found expression in pure sound. It was indeed a mighty spirit; but if I had written the mightiest, which would mean mightier than the spirit of Handel, Beethoven himself would have rebuked me; and what mortal man could pretend to a spirit mightier than Bach's? But that Beethoven's spirit was the most turbulent is beyond all question. The impetuous fury of his strength, which he could quite easily contain and control, but often would not, and the uproariousness of his fun, go beyond anything of the kind to be found in the works of other composers. Greenhorns write of syncopation now as if it were a new way of giving the utmost impetus to a musical measure; but the rowdiest jazz sounds like The Maiden's Prayer after Beethoven's third Leonora overture; and certainly no negro corobbery that I ever heard could inspire the blackest dancer with such *diable au corps* as the last movement of the Seventh Symphony. And no other composer has ever melted his hearers into complete sentimentality by the tender beauty of his music, and then suddenly turned on them and mocked them with derisive trumpet blasts for being such fools. Nobody but Beethoven could govern Beethoven; and when, as happened when the fit was on him, he deliberately refused to govern himself, he was ungovernable.

It was this turbulence, this deliberate disorder, this mockery, this reckless and triumphant disregard of conventional manners, that set Beethoven apart from the musical geniuses of the ceremonious seventeenth and eighteenth centuries. He was a giant wave in that storm of the human spirit which produced the French Revolution. He called no man master. Mozart, his greatest predecessor in his own department, had from his childhood been washed, combed, splendidly dressed, and beautifully behaved in the presence of royal personages and peers. His childish outburst at the Pompadour, "Who is this woman who does not kiss me? The Queen kisses me," would be incredible of Beethoven, who was still an unlicked cub even when he had grown into a very grizzly bear. Mozart had the refinement of convention and society as well as the refinement of nature and of the solitudes of the soul. Mozart and Gluck are refined as the court of Louis XIV was refined: Haydn is refined as the most cultivated country gentlemen of his day were refined: compared to them socially Beethoven was an obstreperous Bohemian: a man of the people. Haydn, so superior to envy that he declared his junior, Mozart, to be the greatest composer that ever lived, could not stand Beethoven: Mozart, more farseeing, listened to his playing, and said "You will hear of him some day"; but the two would never have hit it off together had Mozart lived long enough to try. Beethoven had a moral horror of Mozart, who in Don Giovanni had thrown a halo of enchantment round an aristocratic blackguard, and then, with the unscrupulous moral versatility of a born dramatist, turned round to cast a halo of divinity round Sarastro, setting his words to the only music yet written that would not sound out of place in the mouth of God.

Beethoven was no dramatist: moral versatility was to him revolting cynicism. Mozart was still to him the master of masters (this is not an empty eulogistic superlative: it means literally that Mozart is a composer's composer much more than he has ever been a really popular composer); but he was a court flunkey in breeches whilst Beethoven was a Sansculotte; and Haydn also was a flunkey in the old livery: the Revolution stood between them as it stood between the eighteenth and nineteenth centuries. But to Beethoven Mozart was worse than Haydn because he trifled with morality by setting vice to music as magically as virtue. The Puritan who is in every true Sansculotte rose up against him in Beethoven, though Mozart had shewn him all the possibilities of nineteenth-century music. So Beethoven cast back for a hero to Handel, another crusty old bachelor of his own kidney, who despised Mozart's hero Gluck, though the pastoral symphony in The Messiah is the nearest thing in music to the scenes in which Gluck, in his Orfeo, opened to us the plains of Heavens.

Thanks to broadcasting, millions of musical novices will hear the music of Beethoven this anniversary year for the first time with their expectations raised to an extraordinary pitch by hundreds of newspaper articles piling up all the conventional eulogies that are applied indiscriminately to all the great composers. And like his contemporaries they will be puzzled by getting from him not merely a music that they did not expect, but often an orchestral hurlyburly that they may not recognize as what they call music at all, though they can appreciate Gluck and Haydn and Mozart quite well. The explanation is simple enough. The music of the eighteenth century is all dance music. A dance is a symmetrical pattern of steps that are pleasant to move to; and its music is a symmetrical pattern of sound that is pleasant to listen to even when you are not dancing to it. Consequently the sound patterns, though they begin by being as simple as chessboards, get lengthened and elaborated and enriched with harmonies until they are more like Persian carpets; and the composers who design these patterns no longer expect people to dance to them. Only a whirling

Dervish could dance a Mozart symphony: indeed, I have reduced two young and practised dancers to exhaustion by making them dance a Mozart overture. The very names of the dances are dropped: instead of suites consisting of sarabands, pavanes, gavottes, and jigs, the designs are presented as sonatas and symphonies consisting of sections called simply movements, and labelled according to their speed (in Italian) as allegros, adagios, scherzos, and prestos. But all the time, from Bach's preludes to Mozart's Jupiter Symphony, the music makes a symmetrical sound pattern, and gives us the dancer's pleasure always as the form and foundation of the piece.

Music, however, can do more than make beautiful sound patterns. It can express emotion. You can look at a Persian carpet and listen to a Bach prelude with a delicious admiration that goes no further than itself; but you cannot listen to the overture to Don Giovanni without being thrown into a complicated mood which prepares you for a tragedy of some terrible doom overshadowing an exquisite but Satanic gaiety. If you listen to the last movement of Mozart's Jupiter Symphony, you hear that it is as much a riotous corobbery as the last movement of Beethoven's Seventh Symphony: it is an orgy of ranting drumming tow-row-row, made poignant by an opening strain of strange and painful beauty which is woven through the pattern all through. And yet the movement is a masterpiece of pattern designing all the time.

Now what Beethoven did, and what made some of his greatest contemporaries give him up as a madman with lucid intervals of clowning and bad taste, was that he used music altogether as a means of expressing moods, and completely threw over pattern designing as an end in itself. It is true that he used the old patterns all his life with dogged conservatism (another Sansculotte characteristic, by the way); but he imposed on them such an overwhelming charge of human energy and passion, including that highest passion which accompanies thought, and reduces the passion of the physical appetites to mere animalism, that he not only played Old Harry with their symmetry but often made it impossible to notice that there was any pattern at all beneath the storm of emotion. The Eroica Symphony begins by a pattern (borrowed from an overture which Mozart wrote when he was a boy), followed by a couple more very pretty patterns; but they are tremendously energized, and in the middle of the movement the patterns are torn up savagely; and Beethoven, from the point of view of the mere pattern musician, goes raving mad, hurling out terrible chords in which all the notes of the scale are sounded simultaneously, just because he feels like that, and wants you to feel like it.

And there you have the whole secret of Beethoven. He could design patterns with the best of them; he could write music whose beauty will last you all your life; he could take the driest sticks of themes and work them up so interestingly that you find something new in them at the hundredth hearing: in short, you can say of him all that you can say of the greatest pattern composers; but his diagnostic, the thing that marks him out from all the others, is his disturbing quality, his power of unsettling us and imposing his giant moods on us. Berlioz was very angry with an old French composer who expressed the discomfort Beethoven gave him by saying "*J'aime la musique qui me berce,*" "I like music that lulls me." Beethoven's is music that wakes you up; and the one mood in which you shrink from it is the mood in which you want to be let alone.

When you understand this you will advance beyond the eighteenth century and the old-fashioned dance band (jazz, by the way, is the old dance band Beethovenized), and understand not only Beethoven's music, but what is deepest in post-Beethoven music as well.

THE PERFECT WAGNERITE

(*Preface to the Fourth Edition*)

MUCH water, some of it deeply stained with blood, has passed under the bridges since this book was first published twenty-four years ago. Musically Wagner is now more old-fashioned than Handel and Bach, Mozart and Beethoven, whose fashions have perished though their music remains; whilst his own fashion has been worn to rags by young composers in their first efforts to draw the bow of Ulysses. Finally, it has been discarded as Homerically impossible; and England, after two centuries of imitative negligibility, has suddenly flung into the field a cohort of composers whose methods have made a technical revolution in musical composition so complete that the conductor does not dare to correct the most cacophonous errors in band parts lest the composer should have intended them, and looks in vain for key signatures because young men no longer write in keys but just mark their notes flat or sharp as they come. One can imagine Wagner trying to conduct the latest British tone poem, and exclaiming in desperation, "Is this music?" just as his own contemporaries did when they were confronted with the "false relations" in the score of Tristan. It is true that most of the modern developments, as far as they are really developments and not merely experimental eccentricities, are implicit in Parsifal. Indeed, for that matter, they are implicit in Bach: still, the first man to be scandalized by a new departure is usually he that found the path for it; and I cannot feel sure that Wagner would have encouraged Messrs Bax, Ireland, Cyril Scott, Holst, Goossens, Vaughan Williams, Frank Bridge, Boughton, Holbrooke, Howells and the rest (imagine being able to remember offhand so many names of British composers turning out serious music in native styles of their own!!!) any more than Haydn encouraged Beethoven. Wagner, after his 1855 London season as conductor of the Philharmonic, would not have believed that such a thing could happen in England. Had he been told that within two years a British baby Elgar would arrive who would attain classic rank as a European composer, he would hardly have kept his temper. Yet all this has happened very much as it happened before in Shakespear's time; and the English people at large are just as unconcerned about it, and indeed unconscious of it, as they were then.

Also the English have taken, as I said in this book they might, to Wagner singing and acting; and there is now no question of going to Bayreuth or importing German singers when we wish to hear The Ring or Parsifal; for much better performances of both can be heard now from English companies in England than Wagner ever heard at Bayreuth; and even a transpontine theatre like the Old Vic. thinks no more of doing Tannhäuser than it would have thought of doing Black-Eyed Susan half a century ago.

Another change has outmoded my description of the Bayreuth Festival Playhouse as an ultra modern theatre. Bayreuth has a pictorial stage framed by a proscenium, and the framed picture stage is not now in the latest fashion. When the monarchy and the theatre were restored in England simultaneously on the accession of Charles II, the representation of Shakespear's plays as he planned them was made impossible by the introduction of pictorial scenery and of the proscenium with its two curtains, the act drop and the final green baize, to divide the plays into acts and hide the stage for intervals during which elaborate scenes were built up on it. His plays had to be chopped into fragments; divided into acts; re-written and provided with new endings to make effective "curtains", in which condition they were intolerably tedious except as mere pedestals for irresistibly attractive actors and actresses.

Thus the pictorial stage not only murdered Shakespear, and buried the old Athenian drama, but dictated the form of opera (which grew up with it) and changed the form of the spoken drama. Wagner submitted to it as inevitable; but when he conceived the performances of The Ring, and planned a theatre for them, he made a desperate effort to elaborate its machinery so as to enable complete changes of scene to be made without stopping the performance and keeping the audience staring idly for fifteen minutes at a dropped curtain, or scrambling to and from their seats to fill up the time by smoking cigarets and drinking. One of his devices was to envelop the stage in mists produced by what was called a steam curtain, which looked exactly like what it really was, and made the theatre smell like a laundry. By its aid The Rhine Gold was performed without a break instead of in three acts with long intervals between each.

One had to admit at Bayreuth that here was the utmost perfection of the pictorial stage, and that its machinery could go no further. Nevertheless, having seen it at its best, fresh from Wagner's own influence, I must also admit that my favorite way of enjoying a performance of The Ring is to sit at the back of a box, comfortable on two chairs, feet up, and listen without looking. The truth is, a man whose imagination cannot serve him better than the most costly devices of the imitative scenepainter, should not go to the theatre, and as a matter of fact does not. In planning his Bayreuth theatre, Wagner was elaborating what he had better have scrapped altogether.

But as this did not occur to him, he allowed his technical plan of The Ring to be so governed by pictorial visions that it is as unreasonable to ask Bayreuth to scrap the Wagner tradition as it would be to ask the Théâtre Français to scrap the Molière tradition. Only, I must now treat that tradition as old-fashioned, whereas when this book was first published it was the latest development. What has happened since in England is that an Englishman, Mr Harley Granville-Barker, developing certain experiments made from time to time by Mr William Poel, another Englishman, inaugurated twentieth century Shakespear by a series of performances in which the plays were given with unprecedented artistic splendor without the omission of a single decently presentable line, undivided into acts, without the old pictorial scenery, and with, as a result, a blessed revelation of Shakespear as the Prince of Entertainers instead of the most dreaded of bores, and a degree of illusion which the pictorial theatre had not only failed to attain, but had sedulously destroyed, nowhere more effectively than (save only in certain scenes of pure ritual in Parsifal) at Bayreuth.

Almost simultaneously with Mr Granville-Barker's revolutionary restoration of Shakespear, the pictorial stage triumphantly announced that at the English Bayreuth, which is the Shakespear Memorial Theatre at Stratford-on-Avon, the play of Coriolanus had been, by a climax of Procrustean adaptation, cut down to a performance lasting only one hour, in which state it was humbly hoped that the public would steel itself to bear it just once or twice for the sake of our national playwright. That was too much. Mr Bridges Adams, who had started with Mr Granville-Barker, took the new method to Stratford, where the former victims of the pictorial stage now find to their amazement that three hours of unabbreviated Shakespear fly faster than one hour of Procrusty Coriolanus. And at the Old Vic. in London, where the reform was adopted by Mr Atkins, Shakespear now draws better than would-be popular melodrama.

Thus have Englishmen left Wagner behind as to methods, and made obsolete all that part of this book which presents him as a pioneer. I must add that nobody who knows the snobbish contempt in which most Englishmen hold one another will be surprised when I mention that in England the exploits of Poel, Granville-Barker, Bridges Adams, Atkins, and the English designers and painters who have worked for them, are modestly attributed to Herr Reinhardt, their eminent German contemporary. The only Englishman who is given any credit by his countrymen is Mr Gordon Craig, a fascinating propagandist who still loves the stage picture better than the stage play, and, living in the glamor of the Continent, seldom meddles with the actual theatre except to wipe his boots on it and on all the art that grows on its boards.

As to the sociological aspect of The Ring, which is unaffected by the rapid ageing of its technical aspect as a musical composition and a theatrical spectacle, it seems to challenge the so-called Great War to invalidate it if it can.

Gross as the catastrophe has been, it has not shaken Bayreuth. But post-war contemplation of The Ring must not make us forget that all the progress Wagner saw was from the revolutions of 1848, when he was with the barricaders, to the Imperialist climax of 1871, when he sang:

Hail, hail, our Cæsar!
Royal William!
Rock and ward of German freedom!

What would he have said had he lived to see 1917 in Russia and 1918 in Germany, with England singing "Hang, hang that Kaiser!" and Germany sympathizing to such an extent that the grandson of Wagner's William had to seek safety in Holland? Rhine maidens walking out with British Tommies, Senegalese negroes in Goethe's house, Marx enthroned in Russia, pistolled Romanoffs, fugitive Hapsburgs, exiled Hohenzollerns marking the ruins of empires with no more chance of restoration than the Stuarts and Bourbons: such a Götterdämmerung, in short, as in its craziness can be fitted into no allegory until its upshot becomes plainer than it now is: all this has so changed the political atmosphere in which Wagner lived, and in which this book was written, that it says much for the comprehensiveness of his grasp of things that his allegory should still be valid and important. Indeed the war was more a great tearing off of masks than a change of face: the main difference is that Alberic is richer, and his slaves hungrier and harder worked when they are so lucky as to have any work to do. The Ring ends with everybody dead except three mermaids; and though the war went far enough in that conclusive direction to suggest that the next war may possibly kill even the mermaids with "depth charges", the curtain is not yet down on our drama, and we have to carry on as best we can. If we succeed, this book may have to pass into yet another edition: if not, the world itself will have to be re-edited.

Ayot St Lawrence, 1922.

PREFACE TO THE THIRD EDITION

IN 1907 The Perfect Wagnerite was translated into German by my friend Siegfried Trebitsch. On reading through his version in manuscript I was struck by the inadequacy of the merely negative explanation given by me of the irrelevance of Night Falls on The Gods (Die Götterdämmerung) to the general philosophic scheme of The Ring. That explanation was correct as far as it went; but, put as I had put it, it seemed to me to suggest that the operatic character of Night Falls on The Gods was the result of indifference or forgetfulness produced by the lapse of twenty-five years between the first projection of The Ring and its completion. Now it is clear that in whatever other ways Wagner may have changed, he never became careless and never became indifferent. I therefore inserted in the first German edition a new section in which I shewed how the revolutionary history of Western Europe from the Liberal explosion of 1848 to the confused attempt at a popular and *quasi* Socialist military and municipal administration by the Commune of Paris in 1871 (that is to say, from the literary beginning of The Niblung's Ring by Wagner to the long-delayed musical completion of Night Falls on The Gods) had demonstrated practically that the passing away of the present capitalistic order was going to be a much more complicated business than it appears in Wagner's dramatization.

Since 1907, then, the German edition has been more complete than the English one. I now, after six years' pure procrastination, for which I have no excuse except preoccupation with other work, add the German extension to the English text. It begins on page 251, and ends on page 258. Otherwise the book remains as it was.

I have sometimes been asked why anyone should read a philosophic treatise merely to find out the story of The Ring. I take this opportunity to reply publicly that there is, as far as I know, no reason why anyone should take any trouble in the matter at all unless they want to, and that the degree of trouble must be determined by the degree of want, which, again, will be determined by the wanter's capacity. But this I will say. Even for the purposes of the idlest Bayreuth tourist the story of The Ring must be told as Wagner's score tells it if it is to be of any real use to the visitor who cannot understand what the singers are saying. Anyone can, without knowing a bar of the score, string the events narrated in The Ring together in the order of their occurrence on the stage, add the names of the *dramatis personae* and a description of the scenes, and offer the result as a guide to The Ring. But such a mechanical account of the affair will hinder more than it will help. It will pass over as trivial, or even omit altogether, points to which Wagner has given immense weight and consequence, either by the length or intensity of his direct musical treatment or by the recurrence of themes connected with them; and it will rhetorically emphasize or spread itself descriptively over the more obvious matters which speak for themselves to the spectator and occupy little space and less depth in the musical fabric. People primed with such accounts sit waiting to see the bear or the dragon or the rainbow, or the transformation of Alberic into a snake and a toad, or the magic fire or the swimming feats of the Rhine daughters, and are bored because these exciting spectacles are so unconscionably delayed whilst Wotan, Fricka, Brynhild, Erda, Alberic and Loki discuss things of which the "synopsis" gives no hint.

Now the story as it is told in this book has its centres of gravity placed exactly where Wagner has placed them in his score. What Wagner has made much of, I have made much of; and I have explained why he made much of it. What he passed lightly over, I have passed lightly over. There is a good deal in The Ring which is on the surface of the score: nobody with ears and eyes can miss its significance at the performance. But there is also a good deal that was at the back of Wagner's mind, and that determined what I have called the centres of gravity; and this, which is neither in the score nor in the stage action, being assumed by Wagner to be part of the common consciousness of mankind, is what I have chiefly attended to. For this, obvious as it was to Wagner, and as it is to anyone who has reflected on human history and destiny in the light of a competent knowledge of modern capitalistic civilization, is an absolute blank to many persons who are highly susceptible to the musical qualities of Wagner's music and poetry, but have never reflected on human destiny at all, and have been brought up in polite ignorance of the infernal depths our human society descended to in the nineteenth century. Clearly none of your synopses or popular guides or lists of musical themes would be of the slightest use here. That, I take it, is why this little book remains, after some fifteen years, still in demand, and why I have found it necessary to complete it in this edition by a chapter dealing neither with music nor poetry, but with European history. For it was in that massive material, and not in mere crotchets and quavers, that Wagner found the stuff for his masterpiece. G.B.S.

AYOT ST LAWRENCE, 1913.

PREFACE TO THE SECOND EDITION

THE preparation of a Second Edition of this booklet is quite the most unexpected literary task that has ever been set me. When it first appeared I was ungrateful enough to remonstrate with its publisher for printing, as I thought, more copies than the most sanguine Wagnerite could ever hope to sell. But the result proved that exactly one person buys a copy on every day in the year, including Sundays; and so, in the process of the suns, a reprint has become necessary.

Save a few verbal slips of no importance, I have found nothing to alter in this edition. As usual, the only protests the book has elicited are protests, not against the opinions it expresses, but against the facts it records. There are people who cannot bear to be told that their hero was associated with a famous Anarchist in a rebellion; that he was proclaimed as "wanted" by the police; that he wrote revolutionary pamphlets; and that his picture of Niblunghome under the reign of Alberic is a poetic vision of unregulated industrial capitalism as it was made known in Germany in the middle of the nineteenth century by Engels's Condition of the Laboring Classes in England. They frantically deny these facts, and then declare that I have connected them with Wagner in a paroxysm of senseless perversity. I am sorry I have hurt them; and I appeal to charitable publishers to bring out a new life of Wagner, which shall describe him as a court musician of unquestioned fashion and orthodoxy, and a pillar of the most exclusive Dresden circles. Such a work would, I believe, have a large sale, and be read with satisfaction and reassurance by many lovers of Wagner's music.

As to my much demurred-to relegation of Night Falls on The Gods to the category of grand opera, I have nothing to add or withdraw. Such a classification is to me as much a matter of fact as the Dresden rising or the police proclamation; but I shall not pretend that it is a matter of such fact as everybody's judgment can grapple with. People who prefer grand opera to serious music-drama naturally resent my placing a very grand opera below a very serious music-drama. The ordinary lover of Shakespear would equally demur to my placing his popular catchpenny plays, of which As You Like It is an avowed type, below true Shakespearean plays like Measure for Measure. I cannot help that. Popular dramas and operas may have overwhelming merits as enchanting make-believes; but a poet's sincerest vision of the world must always take precedence of his prettiest fool's paradise.

As many English Wagnerites seem to be still under the impression that Wagner composed Rienzi in his youth, Tannhäuser and Lohengrin in his middle age, and The Ring in his later years, may I again remind them that The Ring was the result of a political convulsion which occurred when Wagner was only thirty-six, and that the poem was completed when he was forty, with thirty more years of work before him? It is as much a first essay in political philosophy as Die Feen is a first essay in romantic opera. The attempt to recover its spirit twenty years later, when the music of Night Falls on The Gods was added, was an attempt to revive the barricades of Dresden in the Temple of the Grail. Only those who have never had any political enthusiasms to survive can believe that such an attempt could succeed. G. B. S.

London, 1901.

PREFACE TO THE FIRST EDITION

THIS book is a commentary on The Niblung's Ring, Richard Wagner's chief work. I offer it to those enthusiastic admirers of Wagner who are unable to follow his ideas, and do not in the least understand the dilemma of Wotan, though they are filled with indignation at the irreverence of the Philistines who frankly avow that they find the remarks of the god too often tedious and nonsensical. Now to be devoted to Wagner merely as a dog is devoted to his master, sharing a few elementary ideas, appetites and emotions with him, and, for the rest, reverencing his superiority without understanding it, is no true Wagnerism. Yet nothing better is possible without a stock of ideas common to master and disciple. Unfortunately, the ideas of the revolutionary Wagner of 1848 are taught neither by the education nor the experience of English and American gentleman-amateurs, who are almost always political mugwumps, and hardly ever associate with revolutionists. The earlier attempts to translate his numerous pamphlets and essays into English resulted in ludicrous mixtures of pure nonsense with the absurdest distortions of his ideas into the ideas of the translators. We now have a translation which is a masterpiece of interpretation and an eminent addition to our literature; but that is not because its author, Mr Ashton Ellis, knows the German dictionary better than his predecessors. He is simply in possession of Wagner's ideas, which were to them inconceivable.

All I pretend to do in this book is to impart the ideas which are most likely to be lacking in the conventional Englishman's equipment. I came by them myself much as Wagner did, having learnt more about music than about anything else in my youth, and sown my political wild oats subsequently in the revolutionary school. This combination is not common in England; and as I seem, so far, to be the only publicly articulate result of it, I venture to add my commentary to what has already been written by musicians who are no revolutionists, and revolutionists who are no musicians.

PITFOLD, HINDHEAD, 1898 G.B.S.

THE PERFECT WAGNERITE

PRELIMINARY ENCOURAGEMENTS

A FEW of these will be welcome to the ordinary citizen visiting the theatre to satisfy his curiosity, or his desire to be in the fashion, by witnessing a representation of Richard Wagner's famous tetralogy: The Niblung's Ring.

First, The Ring, with all its gods and giants and dwarfs, its water-maidens and Valkyries, its wishing-cap, magic ring, enchanted sword, and miraculous treasure, is a drama of today, and not of a remote and fabulous antiquity. It could not have been written before the second half of the nineteenth century, because it deals with events which were only then consummating themselves. Unless the spectator recognizes in it an image of the life he is himself fighting his way through, it must needs appear to him a monstrous development of the Christmas pantomimes, spun out here and there into intolerable lengths of dull conversation by the principal baritone. Fortunately, even from this point of view, The Ring is full of extraordinarily attractive episodes, both orchestral and dramatic. The nature music alone—music of river and rainbow, fire and forest—is enough to bribe people with any love of the country in them to endure the passages of political philosophy in the sure hope of a prettier page to come. Everybody, too, can enjoy the love music, the hammer and anvil music, the clumping of the giants, the tune of the young woodsman's horn, the trilling of the bird, the dragon music and nightmare music and thunder and lightning music, the profusion of simple melody, the sensuous charm of the orchestration: in short, the vast extent of common ground between The Ring and the ordinary music we use for play and pleasure. Hence it is that the four separate music-plays of which it is built have become popular throughout Europe as operas. We shall presently see that one of them, Night Falls on The Gods, actually is an opera.

It is generally understood, however, that there is an inner ring of superior persons to whom the whole work has a most urgent and searching philosophic and social significance. I profess to be such a superior person; and I write this pamphlet for the assistance of those who wish to be introduced to the work on equal terms with that inner circle of adepts.

My second encouragement is addressed to modest citizens who may suppose themselves to be disqualified from enjoying The Ring by their technical ignorance of music. They may dismiss all such misgivings speedily and confidently. If the sound of music has any power to move them, they will find that Wagner exacts nothing further. There is not a single bar of "classical music" in The Ring—not a note in it that has any other point than the single direct point of giving musical expression to the drama. In classical music there are, as the analytical programs tell us, first subjects and second subjects, free fantasias, recapitulations, and codas; there are fugues, with counter-subjects, strettos, and pedal points; there are passacaglias on ground basses, canons ad hypodiapente, and other ingenuities, which have, after all, stood or fallen by their prettiness as much as the simplest folk-tune. Wagner is never driving at anything of this sort any more than Shakespear in his plays is driving at such ingenuities of verse-making as sonnets, triolets, and the like. And this is why he is so easy for the natural musician who has had no academic teaching. The professors, when Wagner's music is played to them, exclaim at once "What is this? Is it aria, or recitative? Is there no cabaletta to it—not even a full close? Why was that discord not prepared; and why does he not resolve it correctly? How dare he indulge in those scandalous and illicit transitions into a key that has not one note in common with the key he has just left? Listen to those false relations! What does he want with six drums and eight horns when Mozart worked miracles with two of each? The man is no musician." The layman neither knows nor cares about any of these things. If Wagner were to turn aside from his straightforward dramatic purpose to propitiate the professors with correct exercises in sonata form, his music would at once become unintelligible to the unsophisticated spectator, upon whom the familiar and dreaded "classical" sensation would descend like the influenza. Nothing of the kind need be dreaded. The unskilled, untaught musician may approach Wagner boldly; for there is no possibility of a misunderstanding between them: the Ring music is perfectly single and simple. It is the adept musician of the old school who has everything to unlearn; and him I leave, unpitied, to his fate.

THE NIBLUNG'S RING

THE Ring consists of four plays, intended to be performed on four successive evenings, entitled The Rhine Gold (a prologue to the other three), The Valkyrie, Siegfried, and Night Falls on The Gods; or, in the original German, Das Rheingold, Die Walküre, Siegfried, and Die Götterdämmerung.

THE RHINE GOLD

Let me assume for a moment that you are a young and good-looking woman. Try to imagine yourself in that character at Klondyke five years ago. The place is teeming with gold. If you are content to leave the gold alone, as the wise leave flowers without plucking them, enjoying with perfect naïveté its color and glitter and preciousness, no human being will ever be the worse for your knowledge of it; and whilst you remain in that frame of mind the golden age will endure.

Now suppose a man comes along: a man who has no sense of the golden age, nor any power of living in the present: a man with common desires, cupidities, ambitions, just like most of the men you know. Suppose you reveal to that man the fact that if he will only pluck this gold up, and turn it into money, millions of men, driven by the invisible whip of hunger, will toil underground and overground night and day to pile up more and more gold for him until he is master of the world! You will find that the prospect will not tempt him so much as you might imagine, because it involves some distasteful trouble to himself to start with, and because there is something else within his reach involving no distasteful toil, which he desires more passionately; and that is yourself. So long as he is preoccupied with love of you, the gold, and all that it implies, will escape him: the golden age will endure. Not until he forswears love will he stretch out his hand to the gold, and found the Plutonic empire for himself. But the choice between love and gold may not rest altogether with him. He may be an ugly, ungracious, unamiable person, whose affections may seem merely ludicrous and despicable to you. In that case, you may repulse him, and most bitterly humiliate and disappoint him. What is left to him then but to curse the love he can never win, and turn remorselessly to the gold? With that, he will make short work of your golden age, and leave you lamenting its lost thoughtlessness and sweetness.

In due time the gold of Klondyke will find its way to the great cities of the world. But the old dilemma will keep continually reproducing itself. The man who will turn his back on love, and upon all the fruitful, creative, life-pursuing activities into which the loftiest human energy can develop it, and will set himself single-heartedly to gather gold in an exultant dream of wielding its Plutonic powers, will find the treasure yielding quickly to his touch. But few men will make this sacrifice voluntarily. Not until the Plutonic power is so strongly set up that the higher human impulses are suppressed as rebellious, and even the mere appetites are denied, starved, and insulted when they cannot purchase their satisfaction with gold, are the energetic spirits driven to build their lives upon riches. How inevitable that course has become to us is plain enough to those who have the power of understanding what they see as they look at the plutocratic societies of our modern capitals.

FIRST SCENE

Here, then, is the subject of the first scene of The Rhine Gold. As you sit waiting for the curtain to rise, you suddenly catch the booming ground-tone of a mighty river. It becomes plainer, clearer: you get nearer to the surface, and catch the green light and the flights of bubbles. Then the curtain goes up and you see what you heard—the depths of the Rhine, with three strange fairy fishes, half water-maidens, singing and enjoying themselves exuberantly. They are not singing barcarolles or ballads about the Lorely and her fated lovers, but simply trolling any nonsense that comes into their heads in time to the dancing of the water and the rhythm of their swimming. It is the golden age; and the attraction of this spot for the Rhine maidens is a lump of the Rhine gold, which they value, in an entirely uncommercial way, for its bodily beauty and splendor. Just at present it is eclipsed, because the sun is not striking down through the water.

Presently there comes a poor devil of a dwarf stealing along the slippery rocks of the river bed, a creature with energy enough to make him strong of body and fierce of passion, but with a brutish narrowness of intelligence and selfishness of imagination: too stupid to see that his own welfare can only be compassed as part of the welfare of the world, too full of brute force not to grab vigorously at his own gain. Such dwarfs are quite common in London. He comes now with a fruitful impulse in him, in search of what he lacks in himself, beauty, lightness of heart, imagination, music. The Rhine maidens, representing all these to him, fill him with hope and longing; and he never considers that he has nothing to offer that they could possibly desire, being by natural limitation incapable of seeing anything from anyone else's point of view. With perfect simplicity, he offers himself as a sweetheart to them. But they are thoughtless, elemental, only half real things, much like modern young ladies. That the poor dwarf is repulsive to their sense of physical beauty and their romantic conception of heroism, that he is ugly and awkward, greedy and ridiculous, disposes for them of his claim to live and love. They mock him atrociously, pretending to fall in love with him at first sight, and then slipping away and making game of him, heaping ridicule and disgust on the poor wretch until he is beside himself with mortification and rage. They forget him when the water begins to glitter in the sun, and the gold to reflect its glory. They break into ecstatic worship of their treasure; and though they know the parable of Klondyke quite well, they have no fear that the gold will be wrenched away by the dwarf, since it will yield to no one who has not forsworn love for it, and it is in pursuit of love that he has come to them. They forget that they have poisoned that desire in him by their mockery and denial of it, and that he now knows that life will give him nothing that he cannot wrest from it by the Plutonic power. It is just as if some poor, rough, vulgar, coarse fellow were to offer to take his part in aristocratic society, and be snubbed into the knowledge that only as a millionaire could he ever hope to bring that society to his feet and buy himself a beautiful and refined wife. His choice is forced on him. He forswears love as thousands of us forswear it every day; and in a moment the gold is in his grasp, and he disappears in the depths, leaving the water-fairies vainly screaming "Stop thief!" whilst the river seems to plunge into the darkness and sink from us as we rise to the cloud regions above.

And now, what forces are there in the world to resist Alberic, our dwarf, in his new character of sworn plutocrat? He is soon at work wielding the power of the gold. For his gain, hordes of his fellow-creatures are thenceforth condemned to slave miserably, overground and underground, lashed to their work by the invisible whip of starvation. They never see him, any more than the victims of our "dangerous trades" ever see the shareholders whose power is nevertheless everywhere, driving them to destruction. The very wealth they create with their labor becomes an additional force to impoverish them; for as fast as they make it it slips from their hands into the hands of their master, and makes him mightier than ever. You can see the process for yourself in every civilized country today, where millions of people toil in want and disease to heap up more wealth for our Alberics, laying up nothing for themselves, except sometimes horrible and agonizing disease and the certainty of premature death. All this part of the story is frightfully real, frightfully present, frightfully modern; and its effects on our social life are so ghastly and ruinous that we no longer know enough of happiness to be discomposed by it. It is only the poet, with his vision of what life might be, to whom these things are unendurable. If we were a race of poets we would make an end of them before the end of this miserable century. Being a race of moral dwarfs instead, we think them highly respectable, comfortable and proper, and allow them to breed and multiply their evil in all directions. If there were no higher power in the world to work against Alberic, the end of it would be utter destruction.

Such a force there is, however; and it is called Godhead. The mysterious thing we call life organizes itself into all living shapes, bird, beast, beetle and fish, rising to the human marvel in cunning dwarfs and in laborious muscular giants, capable, these last, of enduring toil, willing to buy love and life, not with suicidal curses and renunciations, but with patient manual drudgery in the service of higher powers. And these higher powers are called into existence by the same self-organization of life still more wonderfully into rare persons who may by comparison be called gods, creatures capable of thought, whose aims extend far beyond the satisfaction of their bodily appetites and personal affections, since they perceive that it is only by the establishment of a social order founded on common bonds of moral faith that the world can rise from mere savagery. But how is this order to be set up by Godhead in a world of stupid giants, since these thoughtless ones pursue only their narrower personal ends and can by no means understand the aims of a god? Godhead, face to face with Stupidity, must compromise. Unable to enforce on the world the pure law of thought, it must resort to a mechanical law of commandments to be enforced by brute punishments and the destruction of the disobedient. And however carefully these laws are framed to represent the highest thoughts of the framers at the moment of their promulgation, before a day has elapsed that thought has grown and widened by the ceaseless evolution of life; and lo! yesterday's law already fallen out with today's thought. Yet if the high givers of that law themselves set the example of breaking it before it is a week old, they destroy all its authority with their subjects, and so break the weapon they have forged to rule them for their own good. They must therefore maintain at all costs the sanctity of the law, even when it has ceased to represent their thought; so that at last they get entangled in a network of ordinances which they no longer believe in, and yet have made so sacred by custom and so terrible by punishment, that they cannot themselves escape from them. Thus Godhead's resort to law finally costs it half its integrity—as if a spiritual king, to gain temporal power, had plucked out one of his eyes—and it finally begins secretly to long for the advent of some power higher than itself which will destroy its artificial empire of law, and establish a true republic of free thought.

This is by no means the only difficulty in the dominion of Law. The brute force for its execution must be purchased; and the mass of its subjects must be persuaded to respect the authority which employs this force. But how is such respect to be implanted in them if they are unable to comprehend the thought of the lawgiver? Clearly, only by associating the legislative power with such displays of splendor and majesty as will impress their senses and awe their imaginations. The god turned lawgiver, in short, must be crowned Pontiff and King. Since he cannot be known to the common folk as their superior in wisdom, he must be known to them as their superior in riches, as the dweller in castles, the wearer of gold and purple, the eater of mighty feasts, the commander of armies, and the wielder of powers of life and death, of salvation and damnation after death. Something may be done in this way without corruption whilst the golden age still endures. Your gods may not prevail with the dwarfs; but they may go to these honest giants who will give a day's work for a day's pay, and induce them to build for Godhead a mighty fortress, complete with hall and chapel, tower and bell, for the sake of the homesteads that will grow up in security round that church-castle. This only, however, whilst the golden age lasts. The moment the Plutonic power is let loose, and the loveless Alberic comes into the field with his corrupting millions, the gods are face to face with destruction; since Alberic, able with invisible hunger-whip to force the labor of the dwarfs and to buy the services of the giants, can outshine all the temporal shows and splendors of the golden age, and make himself master of the world, unless the gods, with their bigger brains, can capture his gold. This, the dilemma of the Church today, is the situation created by the exploit of Alberic in the depths of the Rhine.

SECOND SCENE

From the bed of the river we rise into cloudy regions, and finally come out into the clear in a meadow, where Wotan, the god of gods, and his consort Fricka lie sleeping. Wotan, you will observe, has lost one eye; and you will presently learn that he plucked it out voluntarily as the price to be paid for his alliance with Fricka, who in return has brought to him as her dowry all the powers of Law. The meadow is on the brink of a ravine, beyond which, towering on distant heights, stands Godhome, a mighty castle, newly built as a house of state for the one-eyed god and his all-ruling wife. Wotan has not yet seen this castle except in his dreams: two giants have just built it for him whilst he slept; and the reality is before him for the first time when Fricka wakes him. In that majestic burg he is to rule with her and through her over the humble giants, who have eyes to gape at the glorious castles their own hands have built from his design, but no brains to design castles for themselves, or to comprehend divinity. As a god, he is to be great, secure, and mighty; but he is also to be passionless, affectionless, wholly impartial; for Godhead, if it is to live with Law, must have no weaknesses, no respect for persons. All such sweet littlenesses must be left to the humble stupid giants to make their toil sweet to them; and the god must, after all, pay for Olympian power the same price the dwarf has paid for Plutonic power.

Wotan has forgotten this in his dreams of greatness. Not so Fricka. What she is thinking of is this price that Wotan has consented to pay, in token whereof he has promised this day to hand over to the giants Fricka's sister, the goddess Freia, with her golden love-apples. When Fricka reproaches Wotan with having selfishly forgotten this, she finds that he, like herself, is not prepared to go through with his bargain, and that he is trusting to another great world-force, the Lie (a European Power, as Lassalle said), to help him to trick the giants out of their reward. But this force does not dwell in Wotan himself, but in another, a god over whom he has triumphed, one Loki, the god of Intellect, Argument, Imagination, Illusion, and Reason. Loki has promised to deliver him from his contract, and to cheat the giants for him; but he has not arrived to keep his word: indeed, as Fricka bitterly points out, why should not the Lie fail Wotan, since such failure is the very essence of him?

The giants come soon enough; and Freia flies to Wotan for protection against them. Their purposes are quite honest; and they have no doubt of the god's faith. There stands their part of the contract fulfilled, stone on stone, port and pinnacle all faithfully finished from Wotan's design by their mighty labor. They have come undoubtingly for their agreed wage. Then there happens what is to them an incredible, inconceivable thing. The god begins to shuffle. There are no moments in life more tragic than those in which the humble common man, the manual worker, leaving with implicit trust all high affairs to his betters, and reverencing them wholly as worthy of that trust, even to the extent of accepting as his rightful function the saving of them from all roughening and coarsening drudgeries, first discovers that they are corrupt, greedy, unjust and treacherous. The shock drives a ray of prophetic light into one giant's mind, and gives him a momentary eloquence. In that moment he rises above his stupid gianthood, and earnestly warns the Son of Light that all his power and eminence of priesthood, godhood, and kingship must stand or fall with the unbearable cold greatness of the incorruptible lawgiver. But Wotan, whose assumed character of lawgiver is altogether false to his real passionate nature, despises the rebuke; and the giant's ray of insight is lost in the murk of his virtuous indignation.

In the midst of the wrangle, Loki comes at last, excusing himself for being late on the ground that he has been detained by a matter of importance which he has promised to lay before Wotan. When pressed to give his mind to the business immediately in hand, and to extricate Wotan from his dilemma, he has nothing to say except that the giants are evidently altogether in the right. The castle has been duly built: he has tried every stone of it, and found the work first-rate: there is nothing to be done but pay the price agreed upon by handing over Freia to the giants. The gods are furious; and Wotan passionately declares that he only consented to the bargain on Loki's promise to find a way for him out of it. But Loki says no: he has promised to find a way out if any such way exist, but not to make a way if there is no way. He has wandered over the whole earth in search of some treasure great enough to buy Freia back from the giants; but in all the world he has found nothing for which Man will give up Woman. And this, by the way, reminds him of the matter he had promised to lay before Wotan. The Rhine maidens have complained to him of Alberic's theft of their gold; and he mentions it as a curious exception to his universal law of the unpurchasable preciousness of love, that this gold-robber has forsworn love for the sake of the fabulous riches of the Plutonic empire and the mastery of the world through its power.

No sooner is the tale told than the giants stoop lower than the dwarf. Alberic forswore love only when it was denied to him and made the instrument for cruelly murdering his self-respect. But the giants, with love within their reach, with Freia and her golden apples in their hands, offer to give her up for the treasure of Alberic. Observe, it is the treasure alone that they desire. They have no fierce dreams of dominion over their superiors, or of moulding the world to any conceptions of their own. They are neither clever nor ambitious: they simply covet money. Alberic's gold: that is their demand, or else Freia, as agreed upon, whom they now carry off as hostage, leaving Wotan to consider their ultimatum.

Freia gone, the gods begin to wither and age: her golden apples, which they so lightly bargained away, they now find to be a matter of life and death to them; for not even the gods can live on Law and Godhead alone, be their castles ever so splendid. Loki alone is unaffected: the Lie, with all its cunning wonders, its glistenings and shiftings and mirages, is a mere appearance: it has no body and needs no food. What is Wotan to do? Loki sees the answer clearly enough: he must bluntly rob Alberic. There is nothing to prevent him except moral scruple; for Alberic, after all, is a poor, dim, dwarfed, credulous creature whom a god can outsee and a lie can outwit. Down, then, Wotan and Loki plunge into the mine where Alberic's slaves are piling up wealth for him under the invisible whip.

THIRD SCENE

This gloomy place need not be a mine: it might just as well be a match-factory, with yellow phosphorus, phossy jaw, a large dividend, and plenty of clergymen shareholders. Or it might be a whitelead factory, or a chemical works, or a pottery, or a railway shunting yard, or a tailoring shop, or a little gin-sodden laundry, or a bakehouse, or a big shop, or any other of the places where human life and welfare are daily sacrificed in order that some greedy foolish creature may be able to hymn exultantly to his Plutonic idol:

> Thou mak'st me eat whilst others starve,
> And sing while others do lament:
> Such unto me Thy blessings are,
> As if I were Thine only care.

In the mine, which resounds with the clinking anvils of the dwarfs toiling miserably to heap up treasure for their master, Alberic has set his brother Mime—more familiarly, Mimmy—to make him a helmet. Mimmy dimly sees that there is some magic in this helmet, and tries to keep it; but Alberic wrests it from him, and shows him, to his cost, that it is the veil of the invisible whip, and that he who wears it can appear in what shape he will, or disappear from view altogether. This helmet is a very common article in our streets, where it generally takes the form of a tall hat. It makes a man invisible as a shareholder, and changes him into various shapes, such as a pious Christian, a subscriber to hospitals, a benefactor of the poor, a model husband and father, a shrewd, practical, independent Englishman, and what not, when he is really a pitiful parasite on the commonwealth, consuming a great deal, and producing nothing, feeling nothing, knowing nothing, believing nothing, and doing nothing except what all the rest do, and that only because he is afraid not to do it, or at least pretend to do it.

When Wotan and Loki arrive, Loki claims Alberic as an old acquaintance. But the dwarf has no faith in these civil strangers: Greed instinctively mistrusts Intellect, even in the garb of Poetry and the company of Godhead, whilst envying the brilliancy of the one and the dignity of the other. Alberic breaks out at them with a terrible boast of the power now within his grasp. He paints for them the world as it will be when his dominion over it is complete, when the soft airs and green mosses of its valleys shall be changed into smoke, slag, and filth; when slavery, disease, and squalor, soothed by drunkenness and mastered by the policeman's baton, shall become the foundation of society; and when nothing shall escape ruin except such pretty places and pretty women as he may like to buy for the slaking of his own lusts. In that kingdom of evil he sees that there will be no power but his own. These gods, with their moralities and legalities and intellectual subtlety, will go under and be starved out of existence. He bids Wotan and Loki beware of it; and his "Hab' Acht!" is hoarse, horrible, and sinister. Wotan is revolted to the very depths of his being: he cannot stifle the execration that bursts from him. But Loki is unaffected: he has no moral passion: indignation is as absurd to him as enthusiasm. He finds it exquisitely amusing—having a touch of the comic spirit in him—that the dwarf, in stirring up the moral fervor of Wotan, has removed his last moral scruple about becoming a thief. Wotan will now rob the dwarf without remorse; for is it not positively his highest duty to take this power out of such evil hands and use it himself in the interests of Godhead? On the loftiest moral grounds, he lets Loki do his worst.

A little cunningly disguised flattery makes short work of Alberic. Loki pretends to be afraid of him; and he swallows that bait unhesitatingly. But how, enquires Loki, is he to guard against the hatred of his million slaves? Will they not steal from him, whilst he sleeps, the magic ring, the symbol of his power, which he has forged from the gold of the Rhine? "You think yourself very clever", sneers Alberic, and then begins to boast of the enchantments of the magic helmet. Loki refuses to believe in such marvels without witnessing them. Alberic, only too glad to shew off his powers, puts on the helmet and transforms himself into a monstrous serpent. Loki gratifies him by pretending to be frightened out of his wits, but ventures to remark that it would be better still if the helmet could transform its owner into some tiny creature that could hide and spy in the smallest cranny. Alberic promptly transforms himself into a toad. In an instant Wotan's foot is on him; Loki tears away the helmet; they pinion him, and drag him away a prisoner up through the earth to the meadow by the castle.

FOURTH SCENE

There, to pay for his freedom, he has to summon his slaves from the depths to place all the treasure they have heaped up for him at the feet of Wotan. Then he demands his liberty; but Wotan must have the ring as well. And here the dwarf, like the giant before him, feels the very foundations of the world shake beneath him at the discovery of his own base cupidity in a higher power. That evil should, in its loveless desperation, create malign powers which Godhead could not create, seems but natural justice to him. But that Godhead should steal those malign powers from evil, and wield them itself, is a monstrous perversion; and his appeal to Wotan to forego it is almost terrible in its conviction of wrong. It is of no avail. Wotan falls back again on virtuous indignation. He reminds Alberic that he stole the gold from the Rhine-daughters, and takes the attitude of the just judge compelling a restitution of stolen goods. Alberic, knowing perfectly well that the judge is taking the goods to put them in his own pocket, has the ring torn from his finger, and is once more as poor as he was when he came slipping and stumbling among the slimy rocks in the bed of the Rhine.

This is the way of the world. In older times, when the Christian laborer was drained dry by the knightly spendthrift, and the spendthrift was drained by the Jewish usurer, Church and State, religion and law, seized on the Jew and drained him as a Christian duty. When the forces of lovelessness and greed had built up our own sordid capitalist systems, driven by invisible proprietorship, robbing the poor, defacing the earth, and forcing themselves as a universal curse even on the generous and humane, then religion and law and intellect, which would never themselves have discovered such systems, their natural bent being towards welfare, economy, and life instead of towards corruption, waste, and death, nevertheless did not scruple to seize by fraud and force these powers of evil on pretence of using them for good. And it inevitably happens that when the Church, the Law, and all the Talents have made common cause to rob the people, the Church is far more vitally harmed by that unfaithfulness to itself than its more mechanical confederates; so that finally they turn on their discredited ally and rob the Church, with the cheerful co-operation of Loki, as in France and Italy for instance.

The twin giants come back with their hostage, in whose presence Godhead blooms again. The gold is ready for them; but now that the moment has come for parting with Freia the gold does not seem so tempting; and they are sorely loth to let her go. Not unless there is gold enough to utterly hide her from them—not until the heap has grown so that they can see nothing but gold—until money has come between them and every human feeling, will they part with her. There is not gold enough to accomplish this: however cunningly Loki spreads it, the glint of Freia's hair is still visible to Giant Fafnir, and the magic helmet must go on the heap to shut it out. Even then Fafnir's brother, Fasolt, can catch a beam from her eye through a chink, and is rendered incapable thereby of forswearing her. There is nothing to stop that chink but the ring; and Wotan is as greedily bent on keeping that as Alberic himself was; nor can the other gods persuade him that Freia is worth it, since for the highest god, love is not the highest good, but only the universal delight that bribes all living things to travail with renewed life. Life itself, with its accomplished marvels and its infinite potentialities, is the only force that Godhead can worship. Wotan does not yield until he is reached by the voice of the fruitful earth, that before he or the dwarfs or the giants or the Law or the Lie or any of these things were, had the seed of them all in her bosom, and the seed perhaps of something higher even than himself, that shall one day supersede him and cut the tangles and alliances and compromises that already have cost him one of his eyes. When Erda, the First Mother of life, rises from her sleeping-place in the heart of the earth, and warns him to yield the ring, he obeys her; the ring is added to the heap of gold; and all sense of Freia is cut off from the giants.

But now what Law is left to these two poor stupid laborers whereby one shall yield to the other any of the treasure for which they have each paid the whole price in surrendering Freia? They look by mere habit to the god to judge for them; but he, with his heart stirring towards higher forces than himself, turns with disgust from these lower forces. They settle it as two wolves might; and Fafnir batters his brother dead with his staff. It is a horrible thing to see and hear, to anyone who knows how much blood has been shed in the world in just that way by its brutalized toilers, honest fellows enough until their betters betrayed them. Fafnir goes off with his booty. It is quite useless to him. He has neither the cunning nor the ambition to establish the Plutonic empire with it. Merely to prevent others from getting it is the only purpose it brings him. He piles it in a cave; transforms himself into a dragon by the helmet; and devotes his life to guarding it, as much a slave to it as a jailor is to his prisoner. He had much better have thrown it all back into the Rhine and transformed himself into the shortest-lived animal that enjoys at least a brief run in the sunshine. His case, however, is far too common to be surprising. The world is overstocked with persons who sacrifice all their affections, and madly trample and batter down their fellows to obtain riches of which, when they get them, they are unable to make the smallest use, and to which they become the most miserable slaves.

The gods soon forget Fafnir in their rejoicing over Freia. Donner, the Thunder god, springs to a rocky summit and calls the clouds as a shepherd calls his flocks. They come at his summons; and he and the castle are hidden by their black legions. Froh, the Rainbow god, hastens to his side. At the stroke of Donner's hammer the black murk is riven in all directions by darting ribbons of lightning; and as the air clears, the castle is seen in its fullest splendor, accessible now by the rainbow bridge which Froh has cast across the ravine. In the glory of this moment Wotan has a great thought. With all his aspirations to establish a reign of noble thought, of righteousness, order, and justice, he has found that day that there is no race yet in the world that quite spontaneously, naturally, and unconsciously realizes his ideal. He himself has found how far short Godhead falls of the thing it conceives. He, the greatest of gods, has been unable to control his fate: he has been forced against his will to choose between evils, to make disgraceful bargains, to break them still more disgracefully, and even then to see the price of his disgrace slip through his fingers. His consort has cost him half his vision; his castle has cost him his affections; and the attempt to retain both has cost him his honor. On every side he is shackled and bound, dependent on the laws of Fricka and on the lies of Loki, forced to traffic with dwarfs for handicraft and with giants for strength, and to pay them both in false coin. After all, a god is a pitiful thing. But the fertility of the First Mother is not yet exhausted. The life that came from her has ever climbed up to a higher and higher organization. From toad and serpent to dwarf, from bear and elephant to giant, from dwarf and giant to a god with thoughts, with comprehension of the world, with ideals. Why should it stop there? Why should it not rise from the god to the Hero? to the creature in whom the god's unavailing thought shall have become effective will and life, who shall make his way straight to truth and reality over the laws of Fricka and the lies of Loki with a strength that overcomes giants and a cunning that outwits dwarfs? Yes: Erda, the First Mother, must travail again, and breed him a race of heroes to deliver the world and himself from his limited powers and disgraceful bargains. This is the vision that flashes on him as he turns to the rainbow bridge and calls his wife to come and dwell with him in Valhalla, the home of the gods.

They are all overcome with Valhalla's glory except Loki. He is behind the scenes of this joint reign of the Divine and the Legal. He despises these gods with their ideals and their golden apples. "I am ashamed," he says, "to have dealings with these futile creatures." And so he follows them to the rainbow bridge. But as they set foot on it, from the river below rises the wailing of the Rhine-daughters for their lost gold. "You down there in the water," cries Loki with brutal irony: "you used to bask in the glitter of your gold: henceforth you shall bask in the splendor of the gods." And they reply that the truth is in the depths and the darkness, and that what blazes on high there is falsehood. And with that the gods pass into their glorious stronghold.

BEFORE leaving this explanation of The Rhine Gold, I must have a word or two about it with the reader.

It is the least popular of the sections of The Ring. The reason is that its dramatic moments lie quite outside the consciousness of people whose joys and sorrows are all domestic and personal, and whose religions and political ideas are purely conventional and superstitious. To them it is a struggle between half a dozen fairytale personages for a ring, involving hours of scolding and cheating, and one long scene in a dark, gruesome mine, with gloomy, ugly music, and not a glimpse of a handsome young man or pretty woman. Only those of wider consciousness can follow it breathlessly, seeing in it the whole tragedy of human history and the whole horror of the dilemmas from which the world is shrinking today. At Bayreuth I have seen a party of English tourists, after enduring agonies of boredom from Alberic, rise in the middle of the third scene, and almost force their way out of the dark theatre into the sunlit pinewood without. And I have seen people who were deeply affected by the scene driven almost beside themselves by this disturbance. But it was a very natural thing for the unfortunate tourists to do, since in this Rhine Gold prologue there is no interval between the acts for escape. Roughly speaking, people who have no general ideas, no touch of the concern of the philosopher and statesman for the race, cannot enjoy The Rhine Gold as a drama. They may find compensations in some exceedingly pretty music, at times even grand and glorious, which will enable them to escape occasionally from the struggle between Alberic and Wotan; but if their capacity for music should be as limited as their comprehension of the world, they had better stay away.

And now, attentive Reader, we have reached the point at which some foolish person is sure to interrupt us by declaring that The Rhine Gold is what they call "a work of art" pure and simple, and that Wagner never dreamt of shareholders, tall hats, whitelead factories, and industrial and political questions looked at from the socialistic and humanitarian points of view. We need not discuss these impertinences: it is easier to silence them with the facts of Wagner's life. In 1843 he obtained the position of conductor of the Opera at Dresden at a salary of £225 a year, with a pension. This was a first-rate permanent appointment in the service of the Saxon State, carrying an assured professional position and livelihood with it. In 1848, the year of revolutions, the discontented middle class, unable to rouse the Church-and-State governments of the day from their bondage to custom, caste, and law by appeals to morality or constitutional agitation for Liberal reforms, made common cause with the starving wage-working class, and resorted to armed rebellion, which reached Dresden in 1849. Had Wagner been the mere musical epicure and political mugwump that the term "artist" seems to suggest to so many critics and amateurs—that is, a creature in their own lazy likeness—he need have taken no more part in the political struggles of his day than Bishop took in the English Reform agitation of 1832, or Sterndale Bennett in the Chartist or Free Trade movements. What he did do was first to make a desperate appeal to the King to cast off his bonds and answer the need of the time by taking true kingship on himself and leading his people to the redress of their intolerable wrongs (fancy the poor monarch's feelings!), and then, when the crash came, to take his side with the right and the poor against the rich and the wrong. When the insurrection was defeated, three leaders of it were especially marked down for vengeance: August Roeckel, an old friend of Wagner's to whom he wrote a well-known series of letters; Michael Bakoonin, afterwards a famous apostle of revolutionary Anarchism; and Wagner himself. Wagner escaped to Switzerland: Roeckel and Bakoonin suffered long terms of imprisonment. Wagner was of course utterly ruined, pecuniarily and socially (to his own intense relief and satisfaction); and his exile lasted twelve years. His first idea was to get his Tannhäuser produced in Paris. With the notion of explaining himself to the Parisians he wrote a pamphlet entitled Art and Revolution, a glance through which will show how thoroughly the socialistic side of the revolution had his sympathy, and how completely he had got free from the influence of the established Churches of his day. For three years he kept pouring forth pamphlets —some of them elaborate treatises in size and intellectual rank, but still essentially the pamphlets and manifestoes of a born agitator—on social evolution, religion, life, art, and the influence of riches. In 1853 the poem of The Ring was privately printed; and in 1854, five years after the Dresden insurrection, The Rhine Gold score was completed to the last drum tap.

These facts are on official record in Germany, where the proclamation summing up Wagner as "a politically dangerous person" may be consulted to this day. The pamphlets are now accessible to English readers in the translation of Mr Ashton Ellis. This being so, any person who, having perhaps heard that I am a Socialist, attempts to persuade you that my interpretation of The Rhine Gold is only "my socialism" read into the works of a dilettantist who borrowed an idle tale from an old saga to make an opera book with, may safely be dismissed from your consideration as an ignoramus.

If you are now satisfied that The Rhine Gold is an allegory, do not forget that an allegory is never quite consistent except when it is written by someone without dramatic faculty, in which case it is unreadable. There is only one way of dramatizing an idea; and that is by putting on the stage a human being possessed by that idea, yet none the less a human being with all the human impulses which make him akin and therefore interesting to us. Bunyan, in his Pilgrim's Progress, does not, like his unread imitators, attempt to personify Christianity and Valour: he dramatizes for you the life of the Christian and the Valiant Man. Just so, though I have shown that Wotan is Godhead and Kingship, and Loki Logic and Imagination without living Will (Brain without Heart, to put it vulgarly); yet in the drama Wotan is a religiously moral man, and Loki a witty, ingenious, imaginative and cynical one. As to Fricka, who stands for State Law, she does not assume her allegorical character in The Rhine Gold at all, but is simply Wotan's wife and Freia's sister: nay, she contradicts her allegorical self by conniving at all Wotan's rogueries. That, of course, is just what State Law would do; but we must not save the credit of the allegory by a quip. Not until she reappears in the next play (The Valkyries) does her function in the allegorical scheme become plain.

One preconception will bewilder the spectator hopelessly unless he has been warned against it or is naturally free from it. In the old-fashioned orders of creation, the supernatural personages are invariably conceived as greater than man, for good or evil. In the modern humanitarian order as adopted by Wagner, Man is the highest. In The Rhine Gold, it is pretended that there are as yet no men on the earth. There are dwarfs, giants, and gods. The danger is that you will jump to the conclusion that the gods, at least, are a higher order than the human order. On the contrary, the world is waiting for Man to redeem it from the lame and cramped government of the gods. Once grasp that; and the allegory becomes simple enough. Really, of course, the dwarfs, giants, and gods are dramatizations of the three main orders of men: to wit, the instinctive, predatory, lustful, greedy people; the patient, toiling, stupid, respectful, money-worshipping people; and the intellectual, moral, talented people who devise and administer States and Churches. History shows us only one order higher than the highest of these: namely, the order of Heroes.

Now it is quite clear—though you have perhaps never thought of it—that if the next generation of Englishmen consisted wholly of Julius Cæsars, all our political, ecclesiastical, and moral institutions would vanish, and the less perishable of their appurtenances be classed with Stonehenge and the cromlechs and round towers as inexplicable relics of a bygone social order. Julius Cæsars would no more trouble themselves about such contrivances as our codes and churches than a Fellow of the Royal Society will touch his hat to the squire and listen to the village curate's sermons. This is precisely what must happen some day if life continues thrusting towards higher and higher organization as it has hitherto done. As most of our English professional men are to Australian bushmen, so, we must suppose, will the average man of some future day be to Julius Cæsar. Let any man of middle age, pondering this prospect, consider what has happened within a single generation to the articles of faith his father regarded as eternal, nay, to the very scepticisms and blasphemies of his youth (Bishop Colenso's criticism of the Pentateuch, for example!); and he will begin to realize how much of our barbarous Theology and Law the man of the future will do without. Bakoonin, the Dresden revolutionary leader with whom Wagner went out in 1849, put forward later on a program, often quoted with foolish horror, for the abolition of all institutions, religious, political, juridical, financial, legal, academic, and so on, so as to leave the will of man free to find its own way. All the loftiest spirits of that time were burning to raise Man up, to give him self-respect, to shake him out of his habit of grovelling before the ideals created by his own imagination, of attributing the good that sprang from the ceaseless energy of the life within himself to some superior power in the clouds, and of making a fetish of self-sacrifice to justify his own cowardice.

Farther on in The Ring we shall see the Hero arrive and make an end of dwarfs, giants, and gods. Meanwhile, let us not forget that godhood means to Wagner infirmity and compromise, and manhood strength and integrity. Above all, we must understand—for it is the key to much that we are to see—that the god, since his desire is toward a higher and fuller life, must long in his inmost soul for the advent of that greater power whose first work, though this he does not see as yet, must be his own undoing.

In the midst of all these far-reaching ideas, it is amusing to find Wagner still full of his ingrained theatrical professionalism, and introducing effects which now seem old-fashioned and stagey with as much energy and earnestness as if they were his loftiest inspirations. When Wotan wrests the ring from Alberic, the dwarf delivers a lurid and bloodcurdling stage curse, calling down on its every future possessor care, fear, and death. The musical phrase accompanying this outburst was a veritable harmonic and melodic bogey to mid-century ears, though time has now robbed it of its terrors. It sounds again when Fafnir slays Fasolt, and on every subsequent occasion when the ring brings death to its holder. This episode must justify itself purely as a piece of stage sensationalism. On deeper ground it is superfluous and confusing, as the ruin to which the pursuit of riches leads needs no curse to explain it; nor is there any sense in investing Alberic with providential powers in the matter.

THE VALKYRIE

BEFORE the curtain rises on the Valkyrie, let us see what has happened since it fell on The Rhine Gold. The persons of the drama will tell us presently; but as we probably do not understand German, that may not help us.

Wotan is still ruling the world in glory from his giant-built castle with his wife Fricka. But he has no security for the continuance of his reign, since Alberic may at any moment contrive to recover the ring, the full power of which he can wield because he has forsworn love. Such forswearing is not possible to Wotan: love, though not his highest need, is a higher than gold: otherwise he would be no god. Besides, as we have seen, his power has been established in the world by and as a system of laws enforced by penalties. These he must consent to be bound by himself; for a god who broke his own laws would betray the fact that legality and conformity are not the highest rule of conduct—a discovery fatal to his supremacy as Pontiff and Lawgiver. Hence he may not wrest the ring unlawfully from Fafnir, even if he could bring himself to forswear love.

In this insecurity he has hit on the idea of forming a heroic bodyguard. He has trained his love children as war-maidens (Valkyries) whose duty it is to sweep through battle-fields and bear away to Valhalla the souls of the bravest who fall there. Thus reinforced by a host of warriors, he has thoroughly indoctrinated them, Loki helping him as dialectician-in-chief, with the conventional system of law and duty, supernatural religion and self-sacrificing idealism, which they believe to be the essence of his godhood, but which is really only the machinery of the love of necessary power which is his mortal weakness. This process secures their fanatical devotion to his system of government; but he knows perfectly well that such systems, in spite of their moral pretensions, serve selfish and ambitious tyrants better than benevolent despots, and that, if once Alberic gets the ring back, he will easily out-Valhalla Valhalla, if not buy it over as a going concern. The only chance of permanent security, then, is the appearance in the world of a hero who, without any illicit prompting from Wotan, will destroy Alberic and wrest the ring from Fafnir. There will then, he believes, be no further cause for anxiety, since he does not yet conceive Heroism as a force hostile to Godhead. In his longing for a rescuer, it does not occur to him that when the Hero comes, his first exploit must be to sweep the gods and their ordinances from the path of the heroic will.

Indeed, he feels that in his own Godhead is the germ of such Heroism, and that from himself the Hero must spring. He takes to wandering, mostly in search of love, from Fricka and Valhalla. He seeks the First Mother; and through her womb, eternally fertile, the inner true thought that made him first a god is reborn as his daughter, uncorrupted by his ambition, unfettered by his machinery of power and his alliances with Fricka and Loki. This daughter, the Valkyrie Brynhild, is his true will, his real self (as he thinks): to her he may say what he must not say to anyone, since in speaking to her he but speaks to himself. "Was Keinem in Worten unausgesprochen," he says to her, "bleib es ewig: mit mir nur rath' ich, red' ich zu dir."

But from Brynhild no hero can spring until there is a man of Wotan's race to breed with her. Wotan wanders further; and a mortal woman bears him twins: a son and a daughter. He separates them by letting the girl fall into the hands of a forest tribe which in due time gives her as wife to a fierce chief, one Hunding. With the son he himself leads the life of a wolf, and teaches him the only power a god can teach, the power of doing without happiness. When he has given him this terrible training, he abandons him, and goes to the bridal feast of his daughter Sieglinda and Hunding. In the blue cloak of the wanderer, wearing the broad hat that flaps over the socket of his forfeited eye, he appears in Hunding's house, the middle pillar of which is a mighty tree. Into that tree, without a word, he strikes a sword up to the hilt, so that only the might of a hero can withdraw it.

Then he goes out as silently as he came, blind to the truth that no weapon from the armory of Godhead can serve the turn of the true Human Hero. Neither Hunding nor any of his guests can move the sword; and there it stays awaiting the destined hand. That is the history of the generations between The Rhine Gold and The Valkyries.

THE FIRST ACT

This time, as we sit looking expectantly at the curtain, we hear, not the deep booming of the Rhine, but the patter of a forest downpour, accompanied by the mutter of a storm which soon gathers into a roar and culminates in crashing thunderbolts. As it passes off, the curtain rises; and there is no mistaking whose forest habitation we are in; for the central pillar is a mighty tree, and the place fit for the dwelling of a fierce chief. The door opens; and an exhausted man reels in: an adept from the school of unhappiness. Sieglinda finds him lying on the hearth. He explains that he has been in a fight; that his weapons, not being as strong as his arms, were broken; and that he had to fly. He desires some drink and a moment's rest; then he will go; for he is an unlucky person, and does not want to bring his ill-luck on the woman who is succoring him. But she, it appears, is also unhappy; and a strong sympathy springs up between them. When her husband arrives, he observes not only this sympathy, but a resemblance between them, a gleam of the snake in their eyes. They sit down to table; and the stranger tells them his unlucky story. He is the son of Wotan, who is known to him only as Wolfing, of the race of the Volsungs. The earliest thing he remembers is returning from a hunt with his father to find their home destroyed, his mother murdered, and his twin-sister carried off. This was the work of a tribe called the Neidings, upon whom he and Wolfing thenceforth waged implacable war until the day when his father disappeared, leaving no trace of himself but an empty wolfskin. The young Volsung was thus cast alone upon the world, finding most hands against him, and bringing no good luck even to his friends. His latest exploit has been the slaying of certain brothers who were forcing their sister to wed against her will. The result has been the slaughter of the woman by her brothers' clansmen, and his own narrow escape by flight.

His luck on this occasion is even worse than he supposes; for Hunding, by whose hearth he has taken refuge, is clansman to the slain brothers and is bound to avenge them. He tells the Volsung that in the morning, weapons or no weapons, he must fight for his life. Then he orders the woman to bed, and follows her himself, taking his spear with him.

The unlucky stranger, left brooding by the hearth, has nothing to console himself with but an old promise of his father's that he shall find a weapon to his hand when he most needs one. The last flicker of the dying fire strikes on the golden hilt of the sword that sticks in the tree; but he does not see it; and the embers sink into blackness. Then the woman returns. Hunding is safely asleep: she has drugged him. She tells the story of the one-eyed man who appeared at her forced marriage, and of the sword. She has always felt, she says, that her miseries will end in the arms of the hero who shall succeed in drawing it forth. The stranger, diffident as he is about his luck, has no misgivings as to his strength and destiny. He gives her his affection at once, and abandons himself to the charm of the night and the season; for it is the beginning of Spring. They soon learn from their confidences that she is his stolen twin-sister. He is transported to find that the heroic race of the Volsungs need neither perish nor be corrupted by a lower strain. Hailing the sword by the name of Nothung (or Needed), he plucks it from the tree as her bride-gift, and then, crying "Both bride and sister be of thy brother; and blossom the blood of the Volsungs!" clasps her as the mate the Spring has brought him.

THE SECOND ACT

So far, Wotan's plan seems prospering. In the mountains he calls his war-maiden Brynhild, the child borne to him by the First Mother, and bids her see to it that Hunding shall fall in the approaching combat. But he is reckoning without his consort, Fricka. What will she, the Law, say to the lawless pair who have heaped incest on adultery? A hero may have defied the law, and put his own will in its place; but can a god hold him guiltless, when the whole power of the gods can enforce itself only by law? Fricka, shuddering with horror, outraged in every instinct, comes clamoring for punishment. Wotan pleads the general necessity of encouraging heroism in order to keep up the Valhalla bodyguard; but his remonstrances only bring upon him torrents of reproaches for his own unfaithfulness to the law in roaming through the world and begetting war-maidens, "wolf-cubs," and the like. He is hopelessly beaten in the argument. Fricka is absolutely right when she declares that the ending of the gods began when he brought this wolf-hero into the world; and now, to save their very existence, she pitilessly demands his destruction. Wotan has no power to refuse: it is Fricka's mechanical force, and not his thought, that really rules the world. He has to recall Brynhild; take back his former instructions; and ordain that Hunding shall slay the Volsung.

But now comes another difficulty. Brynhild is the inner thought and will of Godhead, the aspiration from the high life to the higher that is its divine element, and only becomes separated from it when its resort to kingship and priestcraft for the sake of temporal power has made it false to itself. Hitherto, Brynhild, as Valkyrie or hero chooser, has obeyed Wotan implicitly, taking her work as the holiest and bravest in his kingdom; and now he tells her what he could not tell Fricka—what indeed he could not tell to Brynhild, were she not, as she says, his own will—the whole story of Alberic and of that inspiration about the raising up of a hero. She thoroughly approves of the inspiration; but when the story ends in the assumption that she too must obey Fricka, and help Fricka's vassal, Hunding, to undo the great work and strike the hero down, she for the first time hesitates to accept his command. In his fury and despair he overawes her by the most terrible threats of his anger; and she submits.

Then comes the Volsung Siegmund, following his sister bride, who has fled into the mountains in a revulsion of horror at having allowed herself to bring her hero to shame. Whilst she is lying exhausted and senseless in his arms, Brynhild appears to him and solemnly warns him that he must presently leave the earth with her. He asks whither he must follow her. To Valhalla, to take his place there among the heroes. He asks, shall he find his father there? Yes. Shall he find a wife there? Yes: he will be waited on by beautiful wish-maidens. Shall he meet his sister there? No. Then, says Siegmund, I will not come with you. She tries to make him understand that he cannot help himself. Being a hero, he will not be so persuaded: he has his father's sword, and does not fear Hunding. But when she tells him that she comes from his father, and that the sword of a god will not avail in the hands of a hero, he accepts his fate, but will shape it with his own hand, both for himself and his sister, by slaying her, and then killing himself with the last stroke of the sword. And thereafter he will go to Hell, rather than to Valhalla.

How now can Brynhild, being what she is, choose her side freely in a conflict between this hero and the vassal of Fricka? By instinct she at once throws Wotan's command to the winds, and bids Siegmund nerve himself for the combat with Hunding, in which she pledges him the protection of her shield. The horn of Hunding is soon heard; and Siegmund's spirits rise to fighting pitch at once. The two meet; and the Valkyrie's shield is held before the hero. But when he delivers his sword-stroke at his foe, the weapon shivers on the spear of Wotan, who suddenly appears between them and the first of the race of heroes falls with the weapon of the Law's vassal through his breast. Brynhild snatches the fragments of the broken sword, and flies, carrying off the woman with her on her war-horse; and Wotan, in terrible wrath, slays Hunding with a wave of his hand, and starts in pursuit of his disobedient daughter.

THE THIRD ACT

On a rocky peak, four of the Valkyries are waiting for the rest. The absent ones soon arrive, galloping through the air with slain heroes, gathered from the battle-field, hanging over their saddles. Only, Brynhild, who comes last, has for her spoil a live woman. When her eight sisters learn that she has defied Wotan, they dare not help her; and Brynhild has to rouse Sieglinda to make an effort to save herself, by reminding her that she bears in her the seed of a hero, and must face everything, endure anything, sooner than let that seed miscarry. Sieglinda, in a transport of exaltation, takes the fragments of the sword and flies into the forest. Then Wotan comes; the sisters fly in terror at his command; and he is left alone with Brynhild.

Here, then, we have the first of the inevitable moments which Wotan did not foresee. Godhead has now established its dominion over the world by a mighty Church, compelling obedience through its ally the Law, with its formidable State organization of force of arms and cunning of brain. It has submitted to this alliance to keep the Plutonic power in check—built it up primarily for the sake of that soul in itself which cares only to make the highest better and the best higher; and now here is that very soul separated from it and working for the destruction of its indispensable ally, the lawgiving State. How is the rebel to be disarmed? Slain it cannot be by Godhead, since it is still Godhead's own very dearest soul. But hidden, stifled, silenced it must be; or it will wreck the State and leave the Church defenceless. Not until it passes completely away from Godhead, and is reborn as the soul of the hero, can it work anything but the confusion and destruction of the existing order. How is the world to be protected against it in the meantime? Clearly Loki's help is needed here: it is the Lie that must, on the highest principles, hide the Truth. Let Loki surround this mountain top with the appearance of a consuming fire; and who will dare penetrate to Brynhild? It is true that if any man will walk boldly into that fire, he will discover it at once to be a lie, an illusion, a mirage through which he might carry a sack of gunpowder without being a penny the worse. Therefore let the fire seem so terrible that only the hero, when in the fulness of time he appears upon earth, will venture through it; and the problem is solved. Wotan, with a breaking heart, takes leave of Brynhild; throws her into a deep sleep; covers her with her long warshield; summons Loki, who comes in the shape of a wall of fire surrounding the mountain peak; and turns his back on Brynhild for ever.

The allegory here is happily not so glaringly obvious to the younger generations of our educated classes as it was forty years ago. In those days, any child who expressed a doubt as to the absolute truth of the Church's teaching, even to the extent of asking why Joshua told the sun to stand still instead of telling the earth to cease turning, or of pointing out that a whale's throat would hardly have been large enough to swallow Jonah, was unhesitatingly told that if it harbored such doubts it would spend all eternity after its death in horrible torments in a lake of burning brimstone. It is difficult to write or read this nowadays without laughing; yet no doubt millions of ignorant and credulous people are still teaching their children that. When Wagner himself was a little child, the fact that hell was a fiction devised for the intimidation and subjection of the masses was a well-kept secret of the thinking and governing classes. At that time the fires of Loki were a very real terror to all except persons of exceptional force of character and intrepidity of thought. Even thirty years after Wagner had printed the verses of The Ring for private circulation, we find him excusing himself from perfectly explicit denial of current superstitions, by reminding his readers that it would expose him to prosecution. In England, so many of our respectable voters are still grovelling in a gloomy devil worship, of which the fires of Loki are the main bulwark, that no Government has yet had the conscience or the courage to repeal our monstrous laws against "blasphemy."

SIEGFRIED

SIEGLINDA, when she flies into the forest with the hero's son unborn in her womb, and the broken pieces of his sword in her hand, finds shelter in the smithy of a dwarf, where she brings forth her child and dies. This dwarf is no other than Mimmy, the brother of Alberic, the same who made for him the magic helmet. His aim in life is to gain possession of the helmet, the ring, and the treasure, and through them to obtain that Plutonic mastery of the world under the beginnings of which he himself writhed during Alberic's brief reign. Mimmy is a blinking, shambling, ancient creature, too weak and timid to dream of taking arms himself to despoil Fafnir, who still, transformed to a monstrous serpent, broods on the gold in a hole in the rocks. Mimmy needs the help of a hero for that; and he has craft enough to know that it is quite possible, and indeed much in the ordinary way of the world, for senile avarice and craft to set youth and bravery to work to win empire for it. He knows the pedigree of the child left on his hands, and nurses it to manhood with great care.

His pains are too well rewarded for his comfort. The boy Siegfried, having no god to instruct him in the art of unhappiness, inherits none of his father's ill luck, and all his father's hardihood. The fear against which Siegmund set his face like flint, and the woe which he wore down, are unknown to the son. The father was faithful and grateful: the son knows no law but his own humor; detests the ugly dwarf who has nursed him; chafes furiously under his claims for some return for his tender care; and is, in short, a totally unmoral person, a born anarchist, the ideal of Bakoonin, an anticipation of the "overman" of Nietzsche. He is enormously strong, full of life and fun, dangerous and destructive to what he dislikes, and affectionate to what he likes; so that it is fortunate that his likes and dislikes are sane and healthy. Altogether an inspiriting young forester, a son of the morning, in whom the heroic race has come out into the sunshine from the clouds of his grandfather's majestic entanglements with law, and the night of his father's tragic struggle with it.

THE FIRST ACT

Mimmy's smithy is a cave, in which he hides from the light like the eyeless fish of the American caverns. Before the curtain rises the music already tells us that we are groping in darkness. When it does rise Mimmy is in difficulties. He is trying to make a sword for his nursling, who is now big enough to take the field against Fafnir. Mimmy can make mischievous swords; but it is not with dwarfmade weapons that heroic man will hew the way of his own will through religions and governments and plutocracies and all the other devices of the kingdom of the fears of the unheroic. As fast as Mimmy makes swords, Siegfried Bakoonin smashes them, and then takes the poor old swordsmith by the scruff of the neck and chastises him wrathfully. The particular day on which the curtain rises begins with one of these trying domestic incidents. Mimmy has just done his best with a new sword of surpassing excellence. Siegfried returns home in rare spirits with a wild bear, to the extreme terror of the wretched dwarf. When the bear is dismissed, the new sword is produced. It is promptly smashed, as usual, with, also, the usual effects on the temper of Siegfried, who is quite boundless in his criticisms of the smith's boasted skill, and declares that he would smash the sword's maker too if he were not too disgusting to be handled.

Mimmy falls back on his stock defence: a string of maudlin reminders of the care with which he has nursed the little boy into manhood. Siegfried replies candidly that the strangest thing about all this care is that instead of making him grateful, it inspires him with a lively desire to wring the dwarf's neck. Only, he admits that he always comes back to his Mimmy, though he loathes him more than any living thing in the forest. On this admission the dwarf attempts to build a theory of filial instinct. He explains that he is Siegfried's father, and that this is why Siegfried cannot do without him. But Siegfried has learned from his forest companions, the birds and foxes and wolves, that mothers as well as fathers go to the making of children. Mimmy, on the desperate ground that man is neither bird nor fox, declares that he is Siegfried's father and mother both. He is promptly denounced as a filthy liar, because the birds and foxes are exactly like their parents, whereas Siegfried, having often watched his own image in the water, can testify that he is no more like Mimmy than a toad is like a trout. Then, to place the conversation on a plane of entire frankness, he throttles Mimmy until he is speechless. When the dwarf recovers, he is so daunted that he tells Siegfried the truth about his birth, and for testimony thereof produces the pieces of the sword that broke upon Wotan's spear. Siegfried instantly orders him to repair the sword on pain of an unmerciful thrashing, and rushes off into the forest, rejoicing in the discovery that he is no kin of Mimmy's, and need have no more to do with him when the sword is mended.

Poor Mimmy is now in a worse plight than ever; for he has long ago found that the sword utterly defies his skill: the steel will yield neither to his hammer nor to his furnace. Just then there walks into his cave a Wanderer, in a blue mantle, spear in hand, with one eye concealed by the brim of his wide hat. Mimmy, not by nature hospitable, tries to drive him away; but the Wanderer announces himself as a wise man, who can tell his host, in emergency, what it most concerns him to know. Mimmy, taking this offer in high dudgeon, because it implies that his visitor's wits are better than his own, offers to tell the wise one something that *he* does not know: to wit, the way to the door. The imperturbable Wanderer's reply is to sit down and challenge the dwarf to a trial of wit. He wagers his head against Mimmy's that he will answer any three questions the dwarf can put to him.

Now here were Mimmy's opportunity, had he only the wit to ask what he wants to know, instead of pretending to know everything already. It is above all things needful to him at this moment to find out how that sword can be mended; and there has just dropped in upon him in his need the one person who can tell him. In such circumstances a wise man would hasten to show to his visitor his three deepest ignorances, and ask him to dispel them. The dwarf, being a crafty fool, desiring only to detect ignorance in his guest, asks him for information on the three points on which he is proudest of being thoroughly well instructed himself. His three questions are, Who dwell under the earth? Who dwell on the earth? and Who dwell in the cloudy heights above? The Wanderer, in reply, tells him of the dwarfs and of Alberic; of the earth, and the giants Fasolt and Fafnir; of the gods and of Wotan: himself, as Mimmy now recognizes with awe.

Next, it is Mimmy's turn to face three questions. What is that race, dearest to Wotan, against which Wotan has nevertheless done his worst? Mimmy can answer that: he knows the Volsungs, the race of heroes born of Wotan's infidelities to Fricka, and can tell the Wanderer the whole story of the twins and their son Siegfried. Wotan compliments him on his knowledge, and asks further with what sword Siegfried will slay Fafnir? Mimmy can answer that too: he has the whole history of the sword at his fingers' ends. Wotan hails him as the knowingest of the knowing, and then hurls at him the question he should himself have asked: Who will mend the sword? Mimmy, his head forfeited, confesses with loud lamentations that he cannot answer. The Wanderer reads him an appropriate little lecture on the folly of being too clever to ask what he wants to know, and informs him that a smith to whom fear is unknown will mend Nothung. To this smith he leaves the forfeited head of his host, and wanders off into the forest. Then Mimmy's nerves give way completely. He shakes like a man in delirium tremens, and has a horrible nightmare, in the supreme convulsion of which Siegfried, returning from the forest, presently finds him.

A curious and amusing conversation follows. Siegfried himself does not know fear, and is impatient to acquire it as an accomplishment. Mimmy is all fear: the world for him is a phantasmagoria of terrors. It is not that he is afraid of being eaten by bears in the forest, or of burning his fingers in the forge fire. A lively objection to being destroyed or maimed does not make a man a coward: on the contrary, it is the beginning of a brave man's wisdom. But in Mimmy, fear is not the effect of danger: it is a natural quality of him which no security can allay. He is like many a poor newspaper editor, who dares not print the truth, however simple, even when it is obvious to himself and all his readers. Not that anything unpleasant would happen to him if he did—not, indeed, that he could fail to become a distinguished and influential leader of opinion by fearlessly pursuing such a course, but solely because he lives in a world of imaginary terrors, rooted in a modest and gentlemanly mistrust of his own strength and worth, and consequently of the value of his opinion. Just so is Mimmy afraid of anything that can do him any good, especially of the light and the fresh air. He is also convinced that anybody who is not sufficiently steeped in fear to be constantly on his guard must perish immediately on his first sally into the world. To preserve Siegfried for the enterprise to which he has destined him he makes a grotesque attempt to teach him fear. He appeals to his experience of the terrors of the forest, of its dark places, of its threatening noises, its stealthy ambushes, its sinister flickering lights, its heart-tightening ecstasies of dread.

All this has no other effect than to fill Siegfried with wonder and curiosity; for the forest is a place of delight for him. He is as eager to experience Mimmy's terrors as a schoolboy to feel what an electric shock is like. Then Mimmy has the happy idea of describing Fafnir to him as a likely person to give him an exemplary fright. Siegfried jumps at the idea, and, since Mimmy cannot mend the sword for him, proposes to set to work then and there to mend it for himself. Mimmy shakes his head, and bids him see now how his youthful laziness and frowardness have found him out—how he would not learn the smith's craft from Professor Mimmy, and therefore does not know how even to begin mending the sword. Siegfried Bakoonin's retort is simple and crushing. He points out that the net result of Mimmy's academic skill is that he can neither make a decent sword himself nor even set one to rights when it is damaged. Reckless of the remonstrances of the scandalized professor, he seizes a file, and in a few moments utterly destroys the fragments of the sword by rasping them into a heap of steel filings. Then he puts the filings into a crucible; buries it in the coals; and sets to at the bellows with the shouting exultation of the anarchist who destroys only to clear the ground for creation. When the steel is melted he runs it into a mould; and lo! a sword-blade in the rough. Mimmy, amazed at the success of this violation of all the rules of his craft, hails Siegfried as the mightiest of smiths, professing himself barely worthy to be his cook and scullion; and forthwith proceeds to poison some soup for him so that he may murder him safely when Fafnir is slain. Meanwhile Siegfried forges and tempers and hammers and rivets, uproariously singing the while as nonsensically as the Rhine-daughters themselves. Finally he assails the anvil on which Mimmy's swords have been shattered, and cleaves it with a mighty stroke of the newly forged Nothung.

THE SECOND ACT

In the darkest hour before the dawn of that night, we find ourselves before the cave of Fafnir; and there we find Alberic, who can find nothing better to do with himself than to watch the haunt of the dragon, and eat his heart out in vain longing for the gold and the ring. The wretched Fafnir, once an honest giant, can only make himself terrible enough to keep his gold by remaining a venomous reptile. Why he should not become an honest giant again, and clear out of his cavern, leaving the gold and the ring and the rest of it for anyone fool enough to take them at such a price, is the first question that would occur to anyone except a civilized man, who would be too accustomed to that sort of mania to be at all surprised at it.

To Alberic in the night comes the Wanderer, whom the

dwarf, recognizing his despoiler of old, abuses as a shameless thief, taunting him with the helpless way in which all his boasted power is tied up with the laws and bargains recorded on the haft of his spear, which, says Alberic truly, would crumble like chaff in his hands if he dared use it for his own real ends. Wotan, having already had to kill his own son with it, knows that very well; but it troubles him no more; for he is now at last rising to abhorrence of his own artificial power, and looking to the coming hero, not for its consolidation but its destruction. When Alberic breaks out again with his still unquenched hope of one day destroying the gods and ruling the world through the ring, Wotan is no longer shocked. He tells Alberic that Brother Mime approaches with a hero whom Godhead can neither help nor hinder. Alberic may try his luck against him without disturbance from Valhalla. Perhaps, he suggests, if Alberic warns Fafnir, and offers to deal with the hero for him, Fafnir may give him the ring. They accordingly wake up the dragon, who condescends to enter into bellowing conversation, but is proof against their proposition, strong in the magic of property. "I have and hold," he says: "leave me to sleep." Wotan, with a wise laugh, turns to Alberic. "That shot missed," he says: "no use abusing me for it. And now let me tell you one thing. All things happen according to their nature; and *you* cant alter them." And so he leaves him. Alberic, raging with the sense that his old enemy has been laughing at him, and yet prophetically convinced that the last word will not be with the god, hides himself as the day breaks, and his brother approaches with Siegfried.

Mimmy makes a final attempt to frighten Siegfried by discoursing of the dragon's terrible jaws, poisonous breath, corrosive spittle, and deadly, stinging tail. Siegfried is not interested in the tail: he wants to know whether the dragon has a heart, being confident of his ability to stick Nothung into it if it exists. Reassured on this point, he drives Mimmy away, and stretches himself under the trees, listening to the morning chatter of the birds. One of them has a great deal to say to him; but he cannot understand it; and after vainly trying to carry on the conversation with a reed which he cuts, he takes to entertaining the bird with tunes on his horn, asking it to send him a loving mate such as all the other creatures of the forest have. His tunes wake up the dragon; and Siegfried makes merry over the grim mate the bird has sent him. Fafnir is highly scandalized by the irreverence of the young Bakoonin. He loses his temper; fights; and is forthwith slain, to his own great astonishment.

In such conflicts one learns to interpret the messages of Nature a little. When Siegfried, stung by the dragon's vitriolic blood, pops his finger into his mouth and tastes it, he understands what the bird is saying to him, and, instructed by it concerning the treasures within his reach, goes into the cave to secure the gold, the ring and the wishing cap. Then Mimmy returns, and is confronted by Alberic. The two quarrel furiously over the sharing of the booty they have not yet secured, until Siegfried comes from the cave with the ring and the helmet, not much impressed by the heap of gold, and disappointed because he has not yet learned to fear.

He has, however, learnt to read the thoughts of such a creature as poor Mimmy, who, intending to overwhelm him with flattery and fondness, only succeeds in making such a self-revelation of murderous envy that Siegfried smites him with Nothung and slays him, to the keen satisfaction of the hidden Alberic. Caring nothing for the gold, which he leaves to the care of the slain; disappointed in his fancy for learning fear; and longing for a mate, he casts himself wearily down, and again appeals to his friend the bird, who tells him of a woman sleeping on a mountain peak within a fortress of fire that only the fearless can penetrate. Siegfried is up in a moment with all the tumult of spring in his veins, and follows the flight of the bird as it pilots him to the fiery mountain.

THE THIRD ACT

To the foot of the mountain comes also the Wanderer, now nearing his doom. He calls up the First Mother from the depths of the earth, and begs counsel from her. She bids him confer with the Norns (the Fates). But they are of no use to him: what he seeks is some foreknowledge of the way of the Will in its perpetual strife with these helpless Fates who can only spin the net of circumstance and environment round the feet of men. Why not, says Erda then, go to the daughter I bore you, and take counsel with her? He has to explain how he has cut himself off from her, and set the fires of Loki between the world and her counsel. In that case the First Mother cannot help him: such a separation is part of the bewilderment that is ever the first outcome of her eternal work of thrusting the life energy of the world to higher and higher organization. She can show him no way of escape from the destruction he foresees. Then from the innermost of him breaks the confession that he rejoices in his doom, and now himself exults in passing away with all his ordinances and alliances, with the spear-sceptre which he has only wielded on condition of slaying his dearest children with it, with the kingdom, the power and the glory which will never again boast themselves as "world without end." And so he dismisses Erda to her sleep in the heart of the earth as the forest bird draws near, piloting the slain son's son to his goal.

Now it is an excellent thing to triumph in the victory of the new order and the passing away of the old; but if you happen to be part of the old order yourself, you must none the less fight for your life. It seems hardly possible that the British army at the battle of Waterloo did not include at least one Englishman intelligent enough to hope, for the sake of his country and humanity, that Napoleon might defeat the allied sovereigns; but such an Englishman would kill a French cuirassier rather than be killed by him just as energetically as the silliest soldier ever encouraged, by people who ought to know better, to call his ignorance, ferocity and folly, patriotism and duty. Outworn life may have become mere error; but it still claims the right to die a natural death, and will raise its hand against the millennium itself in self-defence if it tries to come by the short cut of murder. Wotan finds this out when he comes face to face with Siegfried, who is brought to a standstill at the foot of the mountain by the disappearance of the bird. Meeting the Wanderer there, he asks him the way to the mountain where a woman sleeps surrounded by fire. The Wanderer questions him, and extracts his story from him, breaking into fatherly delight when Siegfried, describing the mending of the sword, remarks that all he knew about the business was that the broken bits of Nothung would be of no use to him unless he made a new sword out of them right over again from the beginning. But the Wanderer's interest is by no means reciprocated by Siegfried. His majesty and elderly dignity are thrown away on the young anarchist, who, unwilling to waste time talking, bluntly bids him either show him the way to the mountain, or else "shut his muzzle." Wotan is a little hurt. "Patience, my lad," he says: "if you were an old man I should treat you with respect." "That would be a precious notion," says Siegfried. "All my life long I was bothered and hampered by an old man until I swept him out of my way. I will sweep you in the same fashion if you dont let me pass. Why do you wear such a big hat; and what has happened to one of your eyes? was it knocked out by somebody whose way you obstructed?" To which Wotan replies allegorically that the eye that is gone—the eye that his marriage with Fricka cost him—is now looking at him out of Siegfried's head. At this, Siegfried gives up the Wanderer as a lunatic, and renews his threats of personal violence. Then Wotan throws off the mask of the Wanderer; uplifts the world-governing spear; and puts forth all his divine awe and grandeur as the guardian of the mountain, round the crest of which the fires of Loki now break into a red background for the majesty of the god. But all this is lost on Siegfried Bakoonin. "Aha!" he cries, as the spear is levelled against his breast: "I have found my father's foe"; and the spear falls in two pieces under the stroke of Nothung. "Up then," says Wotan: "I cannot withhold you," and disappears forever from the eye of man. The fires roll down the mountain; but Siegfried goes at them as exultantly as he went at the forging of the sword or the heart of the dragon, and shoulders his way through them, joyously sounding his horn to the accompaniment of their crackling and seething. And never a hair of his head is singed. Those frightful flames which have scared mankind for centuries from the Truth have not heat enough in them to make a child shut its eyes. They are mere phantasmagoria, highly creditable to Loki's imaginative stage-management; but nothing ever has perished or will perish eternally in them except the Churches which have been so poor and faithless as to trade for their power on the lies of a romancer.

BACK TO OPERA AGAIN

And now, O Nibelungen Spectator, pluck up; for all allegories come to an end somewhere; and the hour of your release from these explanations is at hand. The rest of what you are going to see is opera, and nothing but opera. Before many bars have been played, Siegfried and the wakened Brynhild, newly become tenor and soprano, will sing a concerted cadenza; plunge on from that to a magnificent love duet; and end with a precipitous *allegro a capella*, driven headlong to its end by the impetuous semiquaver triplets of the famous finales to the first act of Don Giovanni or the coda to the Leonore overture, with a specifically contrapuntal theme, *points d'orgue*, and a high C for the soprano all complete.

What is more, the work which follows, entitled Night Falls on The Gods, is a thorough grand opera. In it you shall see what you have so far missed, the opera chorus in full parade on the stage, not presuming to interfere with the prima donna as she sings her death song over the footlights. Nay, that chorus will have its own chance when it first appears, with a good roaring strain in C major, not, after all, so very different from, or at all less absurd than the choruses of courtiers in La Favorita or "Per te immenso giubilo" in Lucia. The harmony is no doubt a little developed, Wagner augmenting his fifths with a G sharp where Donizetti would have put his fingers in his ears and screamed for G natural. But it is an opera chorus all the same; and along with it we have theatrical grandiosites that recall Meyerbeer and Verdi: *pezzi d' insieme* for all the principals in a row, vengeful conjurations for trios of them, romantic death song for the tenor: in short, all manner of operatic conventions.

Now it is probable that some of us will have been so talked by the more superstitious Bayreuth pilgrims into regarding Die Götterdämmerung as the mighty climax to a mighty epic, more Wagnerian than all the other three sections put together, as not to dare notice this startling atavism, especially if we find the trio-conjurations more exhilarating than the metaphysical discourses of Wotan in the three true music dramas of The Ring. There is, however, no real atavism involved. Die Götterdämmerung, though the last of The Ring dramas in order of performance, was the first in order of conception, and was indeed the root from which all the others sprang.

The history of the matter is as follows. All Wagner's works prior to The Ring are operas. The last of them, Lohengrin, is perhaps the best known of modern operas. As performed in its entirety at Bayreuth, it is even more operatic than it appears at Covent Garden, because it happens that its most old-fashioned features, notably some of the big set concerted pieces for principals and chorus (*pezzi d' insieme* as I have called them above), are harder to perform than the more modern and characteristically Wagnerian sections, and for that reason were cut out in preparing the abbreviated fashionable version. Thus Lohengrin came upon the ordinary operatic stage as a more advanced departure from current operatic models than its composer had made it. Still, it is unmistakably an opera, with chorus, concerted pieces, grand finales, and a heroine who, if she does not sing florid variations with flute obbligato, is none the less a very perceptible prima donna. In everything but musical technique the change from Lohengrin to The Rhine Gold is quite revolutionary.

The explanation is that Night Falls on The Gods came in between them, although its music was not finished until twenty years after that of The Rhine Gold, and thus belongs to a later and more masterful phase of Wagner's harmonic style. It first came into Wagner's head as an opera to be entitled Siegfried's Death, founded on the old Niblung Sagas, which offered to Wagner the same material for an effective theatrical tragedy as they did to Ibsen. Ibsen's Vikings in Helgeland is, in kind, what Siegfried's Death was originally intended to be: that is, a heroic piece for the theatre, without the metaphysical or allegorical complications of The Ring. Indeed, the ultimate catastrophe of the Saga cannot by any perversion of ingenuity be adapted to the perfectly clear allegorical design of The Rhine Gold, The Valkyries, and Siegfried.

SIEGFRIED AS PROTESTANT

THE philosophically fertile element in the original project of Siegfried's Death was the conception of Siegfried himself as a type of the healthy man raised to perfect confidence in his own impulses by an intense and joyous vitality which is above fear, sickliness of conscience, malice, and the makeshifts and moral crutches of law and order which accompany them. Such a character appears extraordinarily fascinating and exhilarating to our guilty and conscience-ridden generations, however little they may understand him. The world has always delighted in the man who is delivered from conscience. From Punch and Don Juan down to Robert Macaire, Jeremy Diddler and the pantomime clown, he has always drawn large audiences; but hitherto he has been decorously given to the devil at the end. Indeed eternal punishment is sometimes deemed too high a compliment to his nature. When the late Lord Lytton, in his Strange Story, introduced a character personifying the joyousness of intense vitality, he felt bound to deny him the immortal soul which was at that time conceded even to the humblest characters in fiction, and to accept mischievousness, cruelty, and utter incapacity for sympathy as the inevitable consequence of his magnificent bodily and mental health.

In short, though men felt all the charm of abounding life and abandonment to its impulses, they dared not, in their deep self-mistrust, conceive it otherwise than as a force making for evil—one which must lead to universal ruin unless checked and literally mortified by self-renunciation in obedience to superhuman guidance, or at least to some reasoned system of morals. When it became apparent to the cleverest of them that no such superhuman guidance existed, and that their secularist systems had all the fictitiousness of "revelation" without its poetry, there was no escaping the conclusion that all the good that man had done must be put down to his arbitrary will as well as all the evil he had done; and it was also obvious that if progress were a reality, his beneficent impulses must be gaining on his destructive ones. It was under the influence of these ideas that we began to hear about the joy of life where we had formerly heard about the grace of God or the Age of Reason, and that the boldest spirits began to raise the question whether churches and laws and the like were not doing a great deal more harm than good by their action in limiting the freedom of the human will. Four hundred years ago, when belief in God and in revelation was general throughout Europe, a similar wave of thought led the strongest-hearted peoples to affirm that every man's private judgment was a more trustworthy interpreter of God and revelation than the Church. This was called Protestantism; and though the Protestants were not strong enough for their creed, and soon set up a Church of their own, yet the movement, on the whole, has justified the direction it took. Nowadays the supernatural element in Protestantism has perished; and if every man's private judgment is still to be justified as the most trustworthy interpreter of the will of Humanity (which is not a more extreme proposition than the old one about the will of God) Protestantism must take a fresh step in advance, and become Anarchism. Which it has accordingly done, Anarchism being one of the notable new creeds of the eighteenth and nineteenth centuries.

The weak place which experience finds out in the Anarchist theory is its reliance on the progress already achieved by "Man." There is no such thing as Man in the world: what we have to deal with is a multitude of men, some of them great rascals, some of them great statesmen, others both, with a vast majority capable of managing their personal affairs, but not of comprehending social organization, or grappling with the problems created by their association in enormous numbers. If "Man" means this majority, then "Man" has made no progress: he has, on the contrary, resisted it. He will not even pay the cost of existing institutions: the requisite money has to be filched from him by "indirect taxation." Such people, like Wagner's giants, must be governed by laws; and their assent to such government must be secured by deliberately filling them with prejudices and practising on their imaginations by pageantry and artificial eminences and dignities. The government is of course established by the few who are capable of government, though, its mechanism once complete, it may be, and generally is, carried on unintelligently by people who are incapable of it, the capable people repairing it from time to time when it gets too far behind the continuous advance or decay of civilization. All these capable people are thus in the position of Wotan, forced to maintain as sacred, and themselves submit to, laws which they privately know to be obsolescent makeshifts, and to affect the deepest veneration for creeds and ideals which they ridicule among themselves with cynical scepticism. No individual Siegfried can rescue them from this bondage and hypocrisy; in fact, the individual Siegfried has come often enough, only to find himself confronted with the alternative of governing those who are not Siegfrieds or risking destruction at their hands. And this dilemma will persist until Wotan's inspiration comes to our governors, and they see that their business is not the devising of laws and institutions to prop up the weaknesses of mobs and secure the survival of the unfittest, but the breeding of men whose wills and intelligences may be depended on to produce spontaneously the social wellbeing our clumsy laws now aim at and miss. The majority of men at present in Europe have no business to be alive; and no serious progress will be made until we address ourselves earnestly and scientifically to the task of producing trustworthy human material for society. In short, it is necessary to breed a race of men in whom the life-giving impulses predominate, before the New Protestantism becomes politically practicable.[1]

[1] The necessity for breeding the governing class from a selected stock has always been recognized by Aristocrats, however erroneous their methods of selection. We have changed our system from Aristocracy to Democracy without considering that we were at the same time changing, as regards our governing class, from Selection to Promiscuity. Those who have taken a practical part in modern politics best know how farcical the result is.

The most inevitable dramatic conception, then, of the nineteenth century is that of a perfectly naïve hero upsetting religion, law and order in all directions, and establishing in their place the unfettered action of Humanity doing exactly what it likes, and producing order instead of confusion thereby because it likes to do what is necessary for the good of the race. This conception, already incipient in Adam Smith's Wealth of Nations, was certain at last to reach some great artist, and be embodied by him in a masterpiece. It was also certain that if that master happened to be a German, he should take delight in describing his hero as the Freewiller of Necessity, thereby beyond measure exasperating Englishmen with a congenital incapacity for metaphysics.

PANACEA QUACKERY, OTHERWISE IDEALISM

Unfortunately, human enlightenment does not progress by nicer and nicer adjustments, but by violent corrective reactions which invariably send us clean over our saddle and would bring us to the ground on the other side if the next reaction did not send us back again with equally excessive zeal. Ecclesiasticism and Constitutionalism send us one way, Protestantism and Anarchism the other; Order rescues us from confusion and lands us in Tyranny; Liberty then saves the situation and is presently found to be as great a nuisance as Despotism. A scientifically balanced application of these forces, theoretically possible, is practically incompatible with human passion. Besides, we have the same weakness in morals as in medicine: we cannot be cured of running after panaceas, or, as they are called in the sphere of morals, ideals. One generation sets up duty, renunciation, self-sacrifice as a panacea. The next generation, especially the women, wake up at the age of forty or thereabouts to the fact that their lives have been wasted in the worship of this ideal, and, what is still more aggravating, that the elders who imposed it on them did so in a fit of satiety with their own experiments in the other direction. Then that defrauded generation foams at the mouth at the very mention of duty, and sets up the alternative panacea of love, their deprivation of which seems to them to have been the most cruel and mischievous feature of their slavery to duty. It is useless to warn them that this reaction, if prescribed as a panacea, will prove as great a failure as all the other reactions have done; for they do not recognize its identity with any reaction that ever occurred before. Take for instance the hackneyed historic example of the austerity of the Commonwealth being followed by the licence of the Restoration. You cannot persuade any moral enthusiast to accept this as a pure oscillation from action to reaction. If he is a Puritan he looks upon the Restoration as a national disaster: if he is an artist he regards it as the salvation of the country from gloom, devil worship and starvation of the affections. The Puritan is ready to try the Commonwealth again with a few modern improvements: the Amateur is equally ready to try the Restoration with modern enlightenments. And so for the present we must be content to proceed by reactions, hoping that each will establish some permanently practical and beneficial reform or moral habit that will survive the correction of its excesses by the next reaction.

DRAMATIC ORIGIN OF WOTAN

We can now see how a single drama in which Wotan does not appear, and of which Siegfried is the hero, expanded itself into a great fourfold drama of which Wotan is the hero. You cannot dramatize a reaction by personifying the reacting force only, any more than Archimedes could lift the world without a fulcrum for his lever. You must also personify the established power against which the new force is reacting; and in the conflict between them you get your drama, conflict being the essential ingredient in all drama. Siegfried, as the hero of Die Götterdämmerung, is only the *primo tenore robusto* of an opera book, deferring his death, after he has been stabbed in the last act, to sing rapturous love strains to the heroine exactly like Edgardo in Donizetti's Lucia. In order to make him intelligible in the wider significance which his joyous, fearless, conscienceless heroism soon assumed in Wagner's imagination, it was necessary to provide him with a much vaster dramatic antagonist than the operatic villain Hagen. Hence Wagner had to create Wotan as the anvil for Siegfried's hammer; and since there was no room for Wotan in the original opera book, Wagner had to work back to a preliminary drama reaching primarily to the very beginnings of human society. And since, on this world-embracing scale, it was clear that Siegfried must come into conflict with many baser and stupider forces than those lofty ones of supernatural religion and political constitutionalism typified by Wotan and his wife Fricka, these minor antagonists had to be dramatized also in the persons of Alberic, Mime, Fafnir, Loki, and the rest. None of these appear in Night Falls on The Gods save Alberic, whose weird dream-colloquy with Hagen, effective as it is, is as purely theatrical as the scene of the Ghost in Hamlet, or the statue in Don Giovanni. Cut the conference of the Norns and the visit of Valtrauta to Brynhild out of Night Falls on The Gods, and the drama remains coherent and complete without them. Retain them, and the play becomes connected by conversational references with the three music dramas; but the connection establishes no philosophic coherence, no real identity between the operatic Brynhild of the Gibichung episode (presently to be related) and the daughter of Wotan and the First Mother.

THE LOVE PANACEA

We shall now find that at the point where The Ring changes from music drama into opera, it also ceases to be philosophic, and becomes didactic. The philosophic part is a dramatic symbol of the world as Wagner observed it. In the didactic part the philosophy degenerates into the prescription of a romantic nostrum for all human ills. Wagner, only mortal after all, succumbed to the panacea mania when his philosophy was exhausted, like any of the rest of us.

The panacea is by no means an original one. Wagner was anticipated in the year 1819 by a young country gentleman from Sussex named Shelley, in a work of extraordinary artistic power and splendor. Prometheus Unbound is an English attempt at a Ring; and when it is taken into account that the author was only 27, whereas Wagner was 40 when he completed the poem of The Ring, our vulgar patriotism may find an envious satisfaction in insisting upon the comparison. Both works set forth the same conflict between humanity and its gods and governments, issuing in the redemption of man from their tyranny by the growth of his will into perfect strength and self-confidence; and both finish by a lapse into panacea-mongering didacticism by the holding up of Love as the remedy for all evils and the solvent of all social difficulties.

The differences between Prometheus Unbound and The Ring are as interesting as the likenesses. Shelley, caught in the pugnacity of his youth and the first impetuosity of his prodigious artistic power by the first fierce attack of the New Reformation, gave no quarter to the antagonist of his hero. His Wotan, whom he calls Jupiter, is the almighty fiend into whom the Englishman's God had degenerated during two centuries of ignorant Bible worship and shameless commercialism. He is Alberic, Fafnir, Loki and the ambitious side of Wotan all rolled into one melodramatic demon who is finally torn from his throne and hurled shrieking into the abyss by a spirit representing that conception of Eternal Law which has been replaced since by the conception of Evolution. Wagner, an older, more experienced man than the Shelley of 1819, understood Wotan and pardoned him, separating him tenderly from all the compromising alliances to which Shelley fiercely held him; making the truth and heroism which overthrow him the children of his inmost heart; and representing him as finally acquiescing in and working for his own supersession and annihilation. Shelley, in his later works, is seen progressing towards the same tolerance, justice, and humility of spirit, as he advanced towards the middle age he never reached. But there is no progress from Shelley to Wagner as regards the panacea, except that in Wagner there is a certain shadow of night and death come on it: nay, even a clear opinion that the supreme good of love is that it so completely satisfies the desire for life that after it the Will to Live ceases to trouble us, and we are at last content to achieve the highest happiness of death.

This reduction of the panacea to absurdity was not forced upon Shelley, because the love which acts as a universal solvent in his Prometheus Unbound is a sentiment of affectionate benevolence which has nothing to do with sexual passion. It might, and in fact does, exist in the absence of any sexual interest whatever. The words mercy and kindness connote it less ambiguously than the word love. But Wagner sought always for some point of contact between his ideas and the physical senses, so that people might not only think or imagine them in the eighteenth century fashion, but see them on the stage, hear them from the orchestra, and feel them through the infection of passionate emotion. Dr Johnson kicking the stone to confute Berkeley is not more bent on common-sense concreteness than Wagner: on all occasions he insists on the need for sensuous apprehension to give reality to abstract comprehension, maintaining, in fact, that reality has no other meaning. Now he could apply this process to poetic love only by following it back to its alleged origin in sexual passion, the emotional phenomena of which he has expressed in music with a frankness and forcible naturalism which would possibly have scandalized Shelley. The love duet in the first act of The Valkyries is brought to a point at which the conventions of our society demand the precipitate fall of the curtain; whilst the prelude to Tristan and Isolde is such an astonishingly intense and faithful translation into music of the emotions which accompany the union of a pair of lovers that it is questionable whether the great popularity of this piece at our orchestral concerts really means that our audiences are entirely catholic in their respect for life in all its beneficently creative functions, or whether they simply enjoy the music without understanding it.

But however offensive and inhuman may be the superstition which brands such exaltations of natural passion as shameful and indecorous, there is at least as much common sense in disparaging love as in setting it up as a panacea. Even the mercy and loving-kindness of Shelley do not hold good as a universal law of conduct: Shelley himself makes extremely short work of Jupiter, just as Siegfried does of Fafnir, Mime, and Wotan; and the fact that Prometheus is saved from doing the destructive part of his work by the intervention of that very nebulous personification of Eternity called Demogorgon does not in the least save the situation, because, flatly, there is no such person as Demogorgon, and if Prometheus does not pull down Jupiter himself, no one else will. It would be exasperating, if it were not so funny, to see these poets leading their heroes through blood and destruction to the conclusion that, as Browning's David puts it (David of all people!), "All's Love; yet all's Law."

Certainly it is clear enough that such love as that implied by Siegfried's first taste of fear as he cuts through the mailed coat of the sleeping figure on the mountain, and discovers that it is a woman; by her fierce revolt against being touched by him when his terror gives way to ardor; by his manly transports of victory; and by the womanly mixture of rapture and horror with which she abandons herself to the passion which has seized on them both, is an experience which it is much better, like the vast majority of us, never to have passed through, than to allow it to play more than a recreative holiday part in our lives. It did not play a very large part in Wagner's own laborious life, and does not occupy more than two scenes of The Ring. Tristan and Isolde, wholly devoted to it, is a poem of destruction and death. The Mastersingers, a work full of health, fun and happiness, contains not a single bar of love music that can be described as passionate: the hero of it is a widower who cobbles shoes, writes verses, and contents himself with looking on at the sweetheartings of his customers. Parsifal makes an end of it altogether. The truth is that the love panacea in Night Falls on The Gods and in the last act of Siegfried is a survival of the first crude operatic conception of the story, modified by an anticipation of Wagner's later, though not latest, conception of love as the fulfiller of our Will to Live and consequently our reconciler to night and death.

NOT LOVE, BUT LIFE

The only faith which any reasonable disciple can gain from The Ring is not in love, but in life itself as a tireless power which is continually driving onward and upward—not, please observe, being beckoned or drawn by *Das Ewig Weibliche* or any other external sentimentality, but growing from within, by its own inexplicable energy, into ever higher and higher forms of organization, the strengths and the needs of which are continually superseding the institutions which were made to fit out former requirements. When your Bakoonins call out for the demolition of all these venerable institutions, there is no need to fly into a panic and lock them up in prison whilst your parliament is bit by bit doing exactly what they advised you to do. When your Siegfrieds melt down the old weapons into new ones, and with disrespectful words chop in twain the antiquated constable's staves in the hands of their elders, the end of the world is no nearer than it was before. If human nature, which is the highest organization of life reached on this planet, is really degenerating, then human society will decay; and no panic-begotten penal measures can possibly save it: we must, like Prometheus, set to work to make new men instead of vainly torturing old ones. On the other hand, if the energy of life is still carrying human nature to higher and higher levels, then the more young people shock their elders and deride and discard their pet institutions the better for the hopes of the world, since the apparent growth of anarchy is only the measure of the rate of improvement. History, as far as we are capable of history (which is not saying much as yet), shows that all changes from crudity of social organization to complexity, and from mechanical agencies in government to living ones, seem anarchic at first sight. No doubt it is natural to a snail to think that any evolution which threatens to do away with shells will result in general death from exposure. Nevertheless, the most elaborately housed beings today are born not only without houses on their backs but without even fur or feathers to clothe them.

ANARCHISM NO PANACEA

One word of warning to those who may find themselves attracted by Siegfried's Anarchism, or, if they prefer a term with more respectable associations, his neo-Protestantism. Anarchism, as a panacea, is just as hopeless as any other panacea, and will still be so even if we breed a race of perfectly benevolent men. It is true that in the sphere of thought, Anarchism is an inevitable condition of progressive evolution. A nation without Freethinkers—that is, without intellectual Anarchists—will share the fate of China. It is also true that our criminal law, based on a conception of crime and punishment which is nothing but our vindictiveness and cruelty in a virtuous disguise, is an unmitigated and abominable nuisance, bound to be beaten out of us finally by the mere weight of our experience of its evil and uselessness. But it will not be replaced by anarchy. Applied to the industrial or political machinery of modern society, anarchy must always reduce itself speedily to absurdity. Even the modified form of anarchy on which modern civilization is based: that is, the abandonment of industry, in the name of individual liberty, to the upshot of competition for personal gain between private capitalists, is a disastrous failure, and is, by the mere necessities of the case, giving way to ordered Socialism. For the economic rationale of this, I must refer disciples of Siegfried to a tract from my hand published by the Fabian Society and entitled The Impossibilities of Anarchism, which explains why, owing to the physical constitution of our globe, society cannot effectively organize the production of its food, clothes and housing, nor distribute them fairly and economically on any anarchic plan: nay, that without concerting our social action to a much higher degree than we do at present we can never get rid of the wasteful and iniquitous welter of a little riches and a great deal of poverty which current political humbug calls our prosperity and civilization. Liberty is an excellent thing: but it cannot begin until society has paid its daily debt to Nature by first earning its living. There is no liberty before that except the liberty to live at somebody else's expense, a liberty much sought after nowadays, since it is the criterion of gentility, but not wholesome from the point of view of the common weal.

SIEGFRIED CONCLUDED

In returning now to the adventures of Siegfried there is little more to be described except the finale of an opera. Siegfried, having passed unharmed through the fire, wakes Brynhild and goes through all the fancies and ecstasies of love at first sight in a duet which ends with an apostrophe to "leuchtende Liebe, lachender Tod!", which has been romantically translated into "Love that illumines, laughing at death," whereas it really identifies enlightening love and laughing death as involving each other so closely as to be virtually one and the same thing.

PROLOGUE

DIE GÖTTERDÄMMERUNG begins with an elaborate prologue. The three Norns sit in the night on Brynhild's mountain top spinning their thread of destiny, and telling the story of Wotan's sacrifice of his eye, and of his breaking off a bough from the World Ash to make a haft for his spear, also how the tree withered after suffering that violence. They have also some fresher news to discuss. Wotan, on the breaking of his spear by Siegfried, has called all his heroes to cut down the withered World Ash and stack its faggots in a mighty pyre about Valhalla. Then, with his broken spear in his hand, he has seated himself in state in the great hall, with the Gods and Heroes assembled about him as if in council, solemnly waiting for the end. All this belongs to the old legendary materials with which Wagner began The Ring.

The tale is broken by the thread snapping in the hands of the third Norn; for the hour has arrived when man has taken his destiny in his own hands to shape it for himself, and no longer bows to circumstance, environment, necessity (which he now freely wills), and all the rest of the inevitables. So the Norns recognize that the world has no further use for them, and sink into the earth to return to the First Mother. Then the day dawns; and Siegfried and Brynhild come, and have another duet. He gives her his ring; and she gives him her horse. Away then he goes in search of more adventures; and she watches him from her crag until he disappears. The curtain falls; but we can still hear the trolling of his horn, and the merry clatter of his horse's shoes trotting gaily down the valley. The sound is lost in the grander rhythm of the Rhine as he reaches its banks. We hear again an echo of the lament of the Rhine maidens for the ravished gold; and then, finally, a new strain, which does not surge like the mighty flood of the river, but has an unmistakable tramp of hardy men and a strong land flavor about it. And on this the opera curtain at last goes up—for please remember that all that has gone before is only the overture.

THE FIRST ACT

We now understand the new tramping strain. We are in the Rhineside hall of the Gibichungs, in the presence of King Gunther, his sister Gutruna, and Gunther's grim half brother Hagen, the villain of the piece. Gunther is a fool, and has for Hagen's intelligence the respect a fool always has for the brains of a scoundrel. Feebly fishing for compliments, he appeals to Hagen to pronounce him a fine fellow and a glory to the race of Gibich. Hagen declares that it is impossible to contemplate him without envy, but thinks it a pity that he has not yet found a wife glorious enough for him. Gunther doubts whether so extraordinary a person can possibly exist. Hagen then tells him of Brynhild and her rampart of fire; also of Siegfried. Gunther takes this rather in bad part, since not only is he afraid of the fire, but Siegfried, according to Hagen, is not, and will therefore achieve this desirable match himself. But Hagen points out that since Siegfried is riding about in quest of adventures, he will certainly pay an early visit to the renowned chief of the Gibichungs. They can then give him a philtre which will make him fall in love with Gutruna and forget every other woman he has yet seen.

Gunther is transported with admiration of Hagen's cunning when he takes in this plan; and he has hardly assented to it when Siegfried, with operatic opportuneness, drops in just as Hagen expected, and is duly drugged into the heartiest love for Gutruna and total oblivion of Brynhild and his own past. When Gunther declares his longing for the bride who lies inaccessible within a palisade of flame, Siegfried at once offers to undertake the adventure for him. Hagen then explains to both of them that Siegfried can, after braving the fire, appear to Brynhild in the semblance of Gunther through the magic of the wishing cap (or Tarnhelm, as it is called throughout The Ring), the use of which Siegfried now learns for the first time. It is of course part of the bargain that Gunther shall give his sister to Siegfried in marriage.

On that they swear blood-brotherhood; and at this opportunity the old operatic leaven breaks out amusingly in Wagner. With tremendous exordium of brass, the tenor and baritone go at it with a will, showing off the power of their voices, following each other in canonic imitation, singing together in thirds and sixths, and finishing with a lurid unison, quite in the manner of Ruy Gomez and Ernani, or Othello and Iago. Then without further ado Siegfried departs on his expedition, taking Gunther with him to the foot of the mountain, and leaving Hagen to guard the hall and sing a very fine solo which has often figured in the programs of the Richter concerts, explaining that his interest in the affair is that Siegfried will bring back the Ring, and that he, Hagen, will presently contrive to possess himself of that Ring and become Plutonic master of the world.

And now it will be asked how does Hagen know all about the Plutonic empire; and why was he able to tell Gunther about Brynhild and Siegfried, and to explain to Siegfried the trick of the Tarnhelm. The explanation is that though Hagen's mother was the mother of Gunther, his father was not the illustrious Gibich, but no less a person than our old friend Alberic, who, like Wotan, has begotten a son to do for him what he cannot do for himself.

In the above incidents, those gentle moralizers who find the serious philosophy of the music dramas too terrifying for them, may allegorize pleasingly on the philtre as the maddening chalice of passion which, once tasted, causes the respectable man to forget his lawfully wedded wife and plunge into adventures which eventually lead him headlong to destruction.

We now come upon a last relic of the tragedy of Wotan. Returning to Brynhild's mountain, we find her visited by her sister Valkyrie Valtrauta, who has witnessed Wotan's solemn preparations with terror. She repeats to Brynhild the account already given by the Norns. Clinging in anguish to Wotan's knees, she has heard him mutter that were the ring returned to the daughters of the deep Rhine, both

Gods and world would be redeemed from that stage curse of Alberic's in The Rhine Gold. On this she has rushed on her warhorse through the air to beg Brynhild to give the Rhine back its ring. But this is asking Woman to give up love for the sake of Church and State. She declares that she will see them both perish first; and Valtrauta returns to Valhalla in despair. Whilst Brynhild is watching the course of the black thundercloud that marks her sister's flight, the fires of Loki again flame high round the mountain; and the horn of Siegfried is heard as he makes his way through them. But the man who now appears wears the Tarnhelm: his voice is a strange voice: his figure is the unknown one of the king of the Gibichungs. He tears the ring from her finger, and, claiming her as his wife, drives her into the cave without pity for her agony of horror, and sets Nothung between them in token of his loyalty to the friend he is impersonating. No explanation of this highway robbery of the ring is offered. Clearly, this Siegfried is not the Siegfried of the previous drama.

THE SECOND ACT

In the second act we return to the hall of Gibich, where Hagen, in the last hours of that night, still sits, his spear in his hand, and his shield beside him. At his knees crouches a dwarfish spectre, his father Alberic, still full of his old grievances against Wotan, and urging his son in his dreams to win back the ring for him. This Hagen swears to do; and as the apparition of his father vanishes, the sun rises and Siegfried suddenly comes from the river bank tucking into his belt the Tarnhelm, which has transported him from the mountain like the enchanted carpet of the Arabian tales. He describes his adventures to Gutruna until Gunther's boat is seen approaching, when Hagen seizes a cowhorn and calls the tribesmen to welcome their chief and his bride. It is most exhilarating, this colloquy with the startled and hastily armed clan, ending with a thunderous chorus, the drums marking the time with mighty pulses from dominant to tonic, much as Rossini would have made them do if he had been a pupil of Beethoven's.

A terrible scene follows. Gunther leads his captive bride straight into the presence of Siegfried, whom she claims as her husband by the ring, which she is astonished to see on his finger: Gunther, as she supposes, having torn it from her the night before. Turning on Gunther, she says, "Since you took that ring from me, and married me with it, tell him of your right to it; and make him give it back to you." Gunther stammers, "The ring! I gave him no ring—er—do you know him?" The rejoinder is obvious. "Then where are you hiding the ring that you had from me?" Gunther's confusion enlightens her; and she calls Siegfried trickster and thief to his face. In vain he declares that he got the ring from no woman, but from a dragon whom he slew; for he is manifestly puzzled; and she, seizing her opportunity, accuses him before the clan of having played Gunther false with her.

Hereupon we have another grandiose operatic oath, Siegfried attesting his innocence on Hagen's spear, and Brynhild rushing to the footlights and thrusting him aside to attest his guilt, whilst the clansmen call upon their gods to send down lightnings and silence the perjured. The gods do not respond; and Siegfried, after whispering to Gunther that the Tarnhelm seems to have been only half effectual after all, laughs his way out of the general embarrassment and goes off merrily to prepare for his wedding, with his arm round Gutruna's waist, followed by the clan. Gunther, Hagen, and Brynhild are left together to plot operatic vengeance. Brynhild, it appears, has enchanted Siegfried in such a fashion that no weapon can hurt him. She has, however, omitted to protect his back, since it is impossible that he should ever turn that to a foe. They agree accordingly that on the morrow a great hunt shall take place, at which Hagen shall thrust his spear into the hero's vulnerable back. The blame is to be laid on the tusk of a wild boar. Gunther, being a fool, is remorseful about his oath of blood-brotherhood and about his sister's bereavement, without having the strength of mind to prevent the murder. The three burst into a herculean trio, similar in conception to that of the three conspirators in Un Ballo in Maschera; and the act concludes with a joyous strain heralding the appearance of Siegfried's wedding procession, with strewing of flowers, sacrificing to the gods, and carrying bride and bridegroom in triumph.

It will be seen that in this act we have lost all connection with the earlier drama. Brynhild is not only not the Brynhild of The Valkyries, she is the Hiordis of Ibsen, a majestically savage woman, in whom jealousy and revenge are intensified to heroic proportions. That is the inevitable theatrical treatment of the murderous heroine of the Saga. Ibsen's aim in The Vikings was purely theatrical, and not, as in his later dramas, also philosophically symbolic. Wagner's aim in Siegfried's Death was equally theatrical, and not, as it afterwards became in the dramas of which Siegfried's antagonist Wotan is the hero, likewise philosophically symbolic. The two master-dramatists therefore produce practically the same version of Brynhild. Thus on the second evening of The Ring we see Brynhild in the character of the truth-divining instinct in religion, cast into an enchanted slumber and surrounded by the fires of hell lest she should overthrow a Church corrupted by its alliance with government. On the fourth evening, we find her swearing a malicious lie to gratify her personal jealousy, and then plotting a treacherous murder with a fool and a scoundrel. In the original draft of Siegfried's Death, the incongruity is carried still further by the conclusion, at which the dead Brynhild, restored to her godhead by Wotan, and again a Valkyrie, carries the slain Siegfried to Valhalla to live there happily ever after with its pious heroes.

As to Siegfried himself, he talks of women, both in this second act and the next, with the air of a man of the world. "Their tantrums," he says, "are soon over." Such speeches do not belong to the novice of the preceding drama, but to the original Siegfried's Tod, with its leading characters sketched on the ordinary romantic lines from the old Sagas, and not yet reminted as the original creations of Wagner's genius whose acquaintance we have made on the two previous evenings. The very title "Siegfried's Death" survives as a strong theatrical point in the following passage. Gunther, in his rage and despair, cries, "Save me, Hagen: save my honor and thy mother's who bore us both." "Nothing can save thee," replies Hagen: "neither brain nor hand, but *Siegfried's Death*." And Gunther echoes with a shudder, "*Siegfried's Death!*"

A WAGNERIAN NEWSPAPER CONTROVERSY

The devotion which Wagner's work inspires has been illustrated lately in a public correspondence on this very point. A writer in The Daily Telegraph having commented on the falsehood uttered by Brynhild in accusing Siegfried of having betrayed Gunther with her, a correspondence in defence of the beloved heroine was opened in The Daily Chronicle. The imputation of falsehood to Brynhild was strongly resented and combated, in spite of the unanswerable evidence of the text. It was contended that Brynhild's statement must be taken as establishing the fact that she actually was ravished by somebody whom she believed to be Siegfried, and that since this somebody cannot have been Siegfried, he being as incapable of treachery to Gunther as she of falsehood, it must have been Gunther himself after a second exchange of personalities not mentioned in the text. The reply to this—if so obviously desperate a hypothesis needs a reply—is that the text is perfectly explicit as to Siegfried, disguised as Gunther, passing the night with Brynhild with Nothung dividing them, and in the morning bringing her down the mountain *through the fire* (an impassable obstacle to Gunther) and there transporting himself in a single breath, by the Tarnhelm's magic, back to the hall of the Gibichungs, leaving the real Gunther to bring Brynhild down the river after him. One controversialist actually pleaded for the expedition occupying two nights, on the second of which the alleged outrage might have taken place. But the time is accounted for to the last minute: it all takes place during the single night watch of Hagen. There is no possible way out of the plain fact that Brynhild's accusation is to her own knowledge false; and the impossible ways just cited are only interesting as examples of the fanatical worship which Wagner and his creations have been able to inspire in minds of exceptional power and culture.

More plausible was the line taken by those who admitted the falsehood. Their contention was that when Wotan deprived Brynhild of her Godhead, he also deprived her of her former high moral attributes; so that Siegfried's kiss awakened an ordinary mortal jealous woman. But a goddess can become mortal and jealous without plunging at once into perjury and murder. Besides, this explanation involves the sacrifice of the whole significance of the allegory, and the reduction of The Ring to the plane of a child's conception of The Sleeping Beauty. Whoever does not understand that, in terms of The Ring philosophy, a change from godhead to humanity is a step higher and not a degradation, misses the whole point of The Ring. It is precisely because the truthfulness of Brynhild is proof against Wotan's spells that he has to contrive the fire palisade with Loki, to protect the fictions and conventions of Valhalla against her.

The only tolerable view is the one supported by the known history of The Ring, and also, for musicians of sufficiently fine judgment, by the evidence of the scores; of which more anon. As a matter of fact Wagner began, as I have said, with Siegfried's Death. Then, wanting to develop the idea of Siegfried as neo-Protestant, he went on to The Young Siegfried. As a Protestant cannot be dramatically projected without a pontifical antagonist, The Young Siegfried led to The Valkyries, and that again to its preface The Rhine Gold (the preface is always written after the book is finished). Finally, of course, the whole was revised. The revision, if carried out strictly, would have involved the cutting out of Siegfried's Death, now become inconsistent and superfluous; and that would have involved, in turn, the facing of the fact that The Ring was no longer a Niblung epic, and really demanded modern costumes, tall hats for Tarnhelms, factories for Nibelheims, villas for Valhallas, and so on—in short, a complete confession of the extent to which the old Niblung epic had become the merest pretext and name directory in the course of Wagner's travail. But, as Wagner's most eminent English interpreter once put it to me at Bayreuth between the acts of Night Falls on The Gods, the master wanted to "Lohengrinize" again after his long abstention from opera; and Siegfried's Death (first sketched in 1848, the year before the rising in Dresden and the subsequent events which so deepened Wagner's sense of life and the seriousness of art) gave him exactly the libretto he required for that outbreak of the old operatic Adam in him. So he changed it into Die Götterdämmerung, retaining the traditional plot of murder and jealousy, and with it, necessarily, his original second act, in spite of the incongruity of its Siegfried and Brynhild with the Siegfried and Brynhild of the allegory. As to the legendary matter about the world-ash and the destruction of Valhalla by Loki, it fitted in well enough; for though, allegorically, the blow by which Siegfried breaks the god's spear is the end of Wotan and of Valhalla, those who do not see the allegory, and take the story literally, like children, are sure to ask what becomes of Wotan after Siegfried gets past him up the mountain; and to this question the old tale told in Night Falls on The Gods is as good an answer as another. The very senselessness of the scenes of the Norns and of Valtrauta in relation to the three foregoing dramas, gives them a highly effective air of mystery; and no one ventures to challenge their consequentiality, because we are all more apt to pretend to understand great works of art than to confess that the meaning (if any) has escaped us. Valtrauta, however, betrays her irrelevance by explaining that the gods can be saved by the restoration of the ring to the Rhine daughters. This, considered as part of the previous allegory, is nonsense; so that even this scene, which has a more plausible air of organic connection with The Valkyries than any other in Night Falls on The Gods, is as clearly part of a different and earlier conception as the episode which concludes it, in which Siegfried actually robs Brynhild of her ring, though he has no recollection of having given it to her. Night Falls on The Gods, in fact, was not even revised into any real coherence with the world-poem which sprang from it; and that is the authentic solution of all the controversies which have arisen over it.

THE THIRD ACT

The hunting party comes off duly. Siegfried strays from it and meets the Rhine maidens, who almost succeed in coaxing the ring from him. He pretends to be afraid of his wife; and they chaff him as to her beating him and so forth; but when they add that the ring is accursed and will bring death upon him, he discloses to them, as unconsciously as Julius Cæsar disclosed it long ago, that secret of heroism, never to let your life be shaped by fear of its end.[1] So he keeps the ring; and they leave him to his fate. The hunting party now finds him; and they all sit down together to make a meal by the river side, Siegfried telling them meanwhile the story of his adventures. When he approaches the subject of Brynhild, as to whom his memory is a blank, Hagen pours an antidote to the love philtre into his drinking horn, whereupon, his memory returning, he proceeds to narrate the incident of the fiery mountain, to Gunther's intense mortification. Hagen then plunges his spear into the back of Siegfried, who falls dead on his shield, but gets up again, after the old operatic custom, to sing about thirty bars to his love before allowing himself to be finally carried off to the strains of the famous Trauermarsch.

[1] "We must learn to die, and to die in the fullest sense of the word. The fear of the end is the source of all lovelessness; and this fear is generated only when love begins to wane. How came it that this love, the highest blessedness to all things living, was so far lost sight of by the human race that at last it came to this: all that mankind did, ordered, and established, was conceived only in fear of the end? My poem sets this forth."—Wagner to Roeckel, 25th Jan. 1854.

The scene then changes to the hall of the Gibichungs by the Rhine. It is night; and Gutruna, unable to sleep, and haunted by all sorts of vague terrors, is waiting for the return of her husband, and wondering whether a ghostly figure she has seen gliding down to the river bank is Brynhild, whose room is empty. Then comes the cry of Hagen, returning with the hunting party to announce the death of Siegfried by the tusk of a wild boar. But Gutruna divines the truth; and Hagen does not deny it. Siegfried's body is brought in; Gunther claims the ring; Hagen will not suffer him to take it; they fight; and Gunther is slain. Hagen then attempts to take it; but the dead man's hand closes on it and raises itself threateningly. Then Brynhild comes; and a funeral pyre is raised whilst she declaims a prolonged scena, extremely moving and imposing, but yielding nothing to resolute intellectual criticism except a very powerful and elevated exploitation of theatrical pathos, psychologically identical with the scene of Cleopatra and the dead Anthony in Shakespear's tragedy. Finally she flings a torch into the pyre, and rides her warhorse into the flames. The hall of the Gibichungs catches fire, as most halls would were a cremation attempted in the middle of the floor (I permit myself this gibe purposely to emphasize the excessive artificiality of the scene); but the Rhine overflows its banks to allow the three Rhine maidens to take the ring from Siegfried's finger, incidentally extinguishing the conflagration as it does so. Hagen attempts to snatch the ring from the maidens, who promptly drown him; and in the distant heavens the Gods and their castle are seen perishing in the fires of Loki as the curtain falls.

COLLAPSE OF THE ALLEGORY

In all this, it will be observed, there is nothing new. The musical fabric is enormously elaborate and gorgeous; but you cannot say, as you must in witnessing the Rhine Gold, The Valkyries, and the first two acts of Siegfried, that you have never seen anything like it before, and that the inspiration is entirely original. Not only the action, but most of the poetry, might conceivably belong to an Elizabethan drama. The situation of Cleopatra and Antony is unconsciously reproduced without being bettered, or even equalled in point of majesty and musical expression. The loss of all simplicity and dignity, the impossibility of any credible scenic presentation of the incidents, and the extreme staginess of the conventions by which these impossibilities are got over, are no doubt covered from the popular eye by the overwhelming prestige of Die Götterdämmerung as part of so great a work as The Ring, and by the extraordinary storm of emotion and excitement which the music keeps up. But the very qualities that intoxicate the novice in music enlighten the adept. In spite of the fulness of the composer's technical accomplishment, the finished style and effortless mastery of harmony and instrumentation displayed, there is not a bar in the work which moves us as the same themes moved us in The Valkyries, nor is anything but external splendor added to the life and humor of Siegfried.

In the original poem, Brynhild delays her self-immolation on the pyre of Siegfried to read the assembled choristers a homily on the efficacy of the Love panacea. "My holiest wisdom's hoard," she says, "now I make known to the world. I believe not in property, nor money, nor godliness, nor hearth and high place, nor pomp and peerage, nor contract and custom, but in Love. Let that only prevail; and ye shall be blest in weal or woe." Here the repudiations still smack of Bakoonin; but the saviour is no longer the volition of the full-grown spirit of Man, the Free Willer of Necessity, sword in hand, but simply Love, and not even Shelleyan love, but vehement sexual passion. It is highly significant of the extent to which this uxorious commonplace lost its hold of Wagner (after disturbing his conscience, as he confesses to Roeckel, for years) that it disappears in the full score of Night Falls on The Gods, which was not completed until he was on the verge of producing Parsifal, twenty years after the publication of the poem. He cut the homily out, and composed the music of the final scene with a flagrant recklessness of the old intention. The rigorous logic with which representative musical themes are employed in the earlier dramas is here abandoned without scruple; and for the main theme at the conclusion he selects a rapturous passage sung by Sieglinda in the third act of The Valkyries (p. 210, *ante*) when Brynhild inspires her with a sense of her high destiny as the mother of the unborn hero. There is no dramatic logic whatever in the recurrence of this theme to express the transport in which Brynhild immolates herself. There is of course an excuse for it, inasmuch as both women have an impulse of self-sacrifice for the sake of Siegfried; but this is really hardly more than an excuse; since the Valhalla theme might be attached to Alberic on the no worse ground that both he and Wotan are inspired by ambition, and that the ambition has the same object, the possession of the ring. The common sense of the matter is that the only themes which had fully retained their old hold on Wagner's intellectual conscience when he composed Night Falls on The Gods are those which are mere labels of external features, such as the Dragon, the Fire, the Water and so on. This particular theme of Sieglinda's is, in truth, of no great musical merit: it might easily be the pet climax of a popular sentimental ballad: in fact, the gushing effect which is its sole valuable quality is so cheaply attained that it is hardly going too far to call it the most trumpery phrase in the entire tetralogy. Yet, since it undoubtedly does gush very emphatically, Wagner chose, for convenience' sake, to work up this final scene with it rather than with the more distinguished, elaborate and beautiful themes connected with the love of Brynhild and Siegfried.

He would certainly not have thought this a matter of no consequence had he finished the whole work ten years earlier. It must always be borne in mind that the poem of The Ring was complete and printed in 1853, and represents the sociological ideas which, after germinating in the European atmosphere for many years, had been brought home to Wagner, who was intensely susceptible to such ideas, by the crash of 1849 at Dresden. Now no man whose mind is alive and active, as Wagner's was to the day of his death, can keep his political and spiritual opinions, much less his philosophic consciousness, at a standstill for quarter of a century until he finishes an orchestral score. When Wagner first sketched Night Falls on The Gods he was 35. When he finished the score for the first Bayreuth festival in 1876 he had turned 60. No wonder he had lost his old grip of it and left it behind him. He even tampered with The Rhine Gold for the sake of theatrical effect when stage-managing it, making Wotan pick up and brandish a sword to give visible point to his sudden inspiration as to the raising up of a hero. The sword had first to be discovered by Fafnir among the Niblung treasures and thrown away by him as useless. There is no sense in this device; and its adoption shows the same recklessness as to the original intention which we find in the music of the last act of The Dusk of the Gods.[1]

[1] Die Götterdämmerung means literally Godsgloaming. The English versions of the opera are usually called The Dusk of the Gods, or The Twilight of the Gods. I have purposely introduced the ordinary title in the sentence above for the reader's information.

WHY HE CHANGED HIS MIND

WAGNER, however, was not the man to allow his grip of a great philosophic theme to slacken, even in twenty-five years, had the theme stood the test of the world's experience. If the history of Germany from 1849 to 1876 had been the history of Siegfried and Wotan transposed into the key of actual life, Night Falls on The Gods would have been the logical consummation of The Rhine Gold and The Valkyrie instead of the operatic anachronism it actually is.

But, as a matter of fact, Siegfried did not arrive and Bismarck did. Roeckel faded into a prisoner whose imprisonment made no difference. Bakoonin broke up, not Valhalla, but The International, which petered out in an undignified quarrel between him and Karl Marx. The Siegfrieds of 1848 were hopeless political failures, whereas the Wotans and Alberics and Lokis were conspicuous political successes. Even the Mimes held their own as against Siegfried. With the single exception of Ferdinand Lassalle, there was no revolutionary leader who was not an obvious Impossibilist in practical politics; and Lasalle got himself killed in a romantic and quite indefensible duel after wrecking his health in a titanic oratorical campaign which convinced him that the great majority of the working classes were not ready to join him, and that the minority who were ready did not understand him. The International, founded in 1864 by Karl Marx in London, and mistaken for several years by nervous newspapers for a red spectre, was really only a turnip ghost. It achieved some beginnings of international Trade Unionism by inducing English workmen to send money to support strikes on the continent, and recalling English workers who had been taken across the North Sea to defeat such strikes; but on its revolutionary socialistic side it was a romantic figment. The suppression of the Paris Commune, one of the most tragic examples in history of the pitilessness with which capable practical administrators and soldiers are forced by the pressure of facts to destroy romantic amateurs and theatrical dreamers, made an end of melodramatic Socialism. It was as easy for Marx, with his literary talent, to hold up Thiers as the most execrable of living scoundrels, and to put upon Gallifet a brand indelible enough to ostracize him politically for ever, as it was for Victor Hugo to bombard Napoleon III. from his paper battery in Jersey. It was also easy to hold up Félix Pyat and Delescluze as men of much loftier ideals than Thiers and Gallifet; but the one fact that could not be denied was that when it came to actual shooting, it was Gallifet who got Delescluze shot and not Delescluze who got Gallifet shot, and that when it came to administering the affairs of France, Thiers could in one way or another get it done, whilst Pyat could neither do it nor stop talking and allow somebody else to do it. True, the penalty of following Thiers was to be exploited by the landlord and capitalist; but then the penalty of following Pyat was to be shot like a mad dog, or at best sent to New Caledonia, quite unnecessarily and uselessly.

To put it in terms of Wagner's allegory, Alberic had got the ring back again, and was marrying into the best Valhalla families with it. He had thought better of his old threat to dethrone Wotan and Loki. He had found that Nibelheim was a very gloomy place, and that if he wanted to live handsomely and safely, he must not only allow Wotan and Loki to organize society for him, but pay them very handsomely for doing it. He needed splendor, military glory, loyalty, enthusiasm, and patriotism; and his greed and gluttony were wholly unable to create them, whereas Wotan and Loki carried them all to their most triumphant climax in Germany in 1871, when Wagner himself celebrated the event with his Kaisermarsch, which sounded much more convincing than the Marseillaise or the Carmagnole.

How, after the Kaisermarsch, could Wagner go back to his idealization of Siegfried in 1853? How could he believe seriously in Siegfried slaying the dragon and charging through the mountain fire, when the immediate foreground was occupied by the Hôtel de Ville with Félix Pyat endlessly discussing the principles of Socialism whilst the shells of Thiers were already battering the Arc de Triomphe and ripping up the pavement of the Champs Elysées? Is it not clear that things had taken an altogether unexpected turn; that although The Ring may, like the famous Communist Manifesto of Marx and Engels, be an inspired guess at the historic laws and predestined end of our capitalistic-theocratic epoch, yet Wagner, like Marx, was too inexperienced in technical government and administration and too melodramatic in his hero-contra-villain conception of the class struggle, to foresee the actual process by which his generalization would work out, or the part to be played in it by the classes involved.

Let us go back for a moment to the point at which the Niblung legend first becomes irreconcilable with Wagner's allegory. Fafnir in the real world becomes a capitalist; but Fafnir in the allegory is a mere hoarder. His gold does not bring him in any revenue. It does not even support him: he has to go out and forage for food and drink. In fact, he is on the way to his drinking-pool when Siegfried kills him. And Siegfried himself has no more use for the gold than Fafnir: the only difference between them in this respect is that Siegfried does not waste his time watching a barren treasure that is useless to him, whereas Fafnir sacrifices his humanity and his life merely to prevent anybody else getting it. This contrast, true to human nature, is not true to modern economic development. The real Fafnir is not a miser: he seeks dividends, a comfortable life, and admission to the circles of Wotan and Loki. His only means of procuring these is to restore the gold to Alberic in exchange for scrip in Alberic's enterprises. Thus fortified with capital, Alberic exploits his fellow dwarfs as before, and also exploits Fafnir's fellow giants who have no capital. What is more, the competitive strategy and large-scaled enterprise the exploitation involves, and the self-respect and social esteem its success wins, effect a development in Alberic's own character which neither

Marx nor Wagner appears to have foreseen. He discovers that to be a dull, greedy, narrow-minded moneygrubber is not the way to make money on the modern scale; for though greed may suffice to turn tens into hundreds and even hundreds into thousands, to turn thousands into hundreds of thousands requires economic magnanimity and a will to power as well as to pelf. And to turn hundreds of thousands into millions, Alberic must make himself an earthly Providence for masses of workmen, creating towns, and governing markets. In the meantime, Fafnir, wallowing in the dividends he has done nothing to earn, may rot, intellectually and morally, from mere disuse of his energies and lack of incentive to excel; but the more impotent he becomes, the more dependent he is upon Alberic for his income, on Loki for his politics, and on Wotan for his respectability and safety from rebellion: Alberic, as the purse-bearer, being, under Destiny, the real master of the situation. Consequently, though Alberic in 1850 may have been merely the vulgar Manchester factory-owner portrayed in Friedrich Engels' Condition of the Working Classes, in 1876 he was well on the way towards becoming exoterically a model philanthropic employer and esoterically a financier.

Now, without exaggerating the virtues of such gentlemen, it will be conceded by everybody except perhaps those veteran Social-Democrats who have made a cult of obsolescence under the name of Marxism, that the dominant sort of modern employer is not to be displaced and dismissed so lightly as Alberic in The Ring. Wotan is hardly less dependent on him than Fafnir: the War-Lord visits his works, acclaims them in stirring speeches, and imprisons his enemies; whilst Loki does his political jobs in Parliament, making wars and commercial treaties for him at command. And he owns and controls a new god, called The Press, which manufactures public opinion on his side, and organizes the persecution and suppression of Siegfried.

The end cannot come until Siegfried learns Alberic's trade and shoulders Alberic's burden. Not having as yet done so, he is still completely mastered by Alberic. He does not even rebel against him except when he is too stupid and ignorant, or too romantically impracticable, to see that Alberic's work, like Wotan's work and Loki's work, is necessary work, and that therefore Alberic can never be superseded by a warrior, but only by a capable man of business who is prepared to continue his work without a day's intermission. Even though the proletarians of all lands were to become "class-conscious," and obey the call of Marx by uniting to rush the class struggle to a proletarian victory in which all capital should become common property, and all Monarchs, Millionaires, Landlords, and Capitalists become common citizens, the triumphant proletarians would have either to starve in anarchy next day or else do the political and industrial work which now gets itself done somehow under limited monarchs, despotic presidents, irresponsible financiers, and bourgeois parliaments. And in the meantime these magnates must defend their power and property with all their might against the revolutionary forces until these forces become positive, executive, administrative forces, instead of the conspiracies of protesting, moralizing, virtuously indignant amateurs who mistook Marx for a man of affairs and Thiers for a stage villain.

Now all this represents a development of which one gathers no forecast from Wagner or Marx. Both of them prophesied the end of our epoch; and, though in 1913 that epoch seemed so prosperous that the prophecy seemed ridiculously negligible, within ten years the centre had fallen out of Europe; and humane men could only shake their heads and shrug their shoulders when they were asked for another half-crown to help to save another ten million children from starvation. Alberic had prospered so greatly that he had come to believe himself immortal; and his alliances with Wotan had brought his sons and daughters under the influences, dangerous to commerce, of feudal militarist ideals. The abyss in his path had been pointed out to him not only by Wagner and Marx, but by men who, instead of vainly consulting the oracle in the pages of Das Kapital, had sought new and safe paths by the light of contemporary history and practical administrative experience. But Alberic would neither believe that the old path led to the abyss nor explore the new paths; and the masses knew nothing of paths and much of poverty. So he went faster and faster, at last marching sword in hand with his feudal sons-in-law, blasting his way with cyclopean explosives, at which point he crashed into the abyss he had not believed in, bringing down the civilization of Central and Eastern Europe along with him, and leaving the Bolshevists (ci-devant Marxists), Social-Democrats, Republicans and amorphous revolutionaries generally to extricate it as best they could, and to learn in the process the truth of these last few pages.

But Wagner did not live to see this reduction of Alberic to absurdity. What he did see was the reduction of Siegfried to absurdity. Siegfried had done nothing that promised success in his struggle with Alberic; and Alberic had not yet outdone Siegfried in ineptitude by committing suicide. Now Wagner was compelled by his profession to be, compared with Siegfried, a practical man. It is possible to learn more of the world by producing a single opera, or even conducting a single orchestral rehearsal, than by ten years reading in the library of the British Museum. Wagner must have learnt between The Rhine Gold and the Kaisermarsch that there are yet several dramas to be interpolated in The Ring after The Valkyrie before the allegory can tell the whole story. If anyone doubts the extent to which Wagner's eyes had been opened to the administrative childishness and romantic conceit of the heroes of the revolutionary generation that served its apprenticeship on the barricades of 1848–49, and perished on those of 1871 under Thiers' mitrailleuses, let him read Eine Kapitulation, that scandalous burlesque in which the poet and composer of Siegfried, with the levity of a schoolboy, mocked the French republicans who were doing in 1871 what he himself was exiled for doing in 1849. He had set the enthusiasm of the Dresden revolution to his own greatest music; but he set the enthusiasm of twenty years later in derision to the music of Rossini. There is no mistaking the tune he meant to suggest by his doggerel of Republik, Republik, Republik-lik-lik. The Overture to William Tell is there as plainly as if it were noted down in full score.

In the case of such a man as Wagner, you cannot explain this *volte-face* as mere jingoism produced by Germany's overwhelming victory in the Franco-Prussian war, nor as personal spite against the Parisians for the Tannhäuser fiasco. Wagner had more cause for personal spite against his own countrymen than he ever had against the Parisians: he was ten times bitterer against his respectable prosperity in Dresden than against his starvation in Paris. No doubt his outburst gratified the pettier feelings which great men have in common with small ones; but he was not a man to indulge in such gratifications or indeed to feel them as gratifications, if he had not become convinced of the administrative impotence of the agitators who were trying to wield Nothung, and who had done less for Wagner's own art than a single German king, and he, too, a mad one. Wagner had by that time done too much himself not to know that the world is ruled by deeds, not by good intentions, and that one efficient sinner is worth ten futile saints and martyrs.

I need not elaborate the point further in these pages. Like all men of genius, Wagner had exceptional sincerity, exceptional respect for facts, exceptional freedom from the hypnotic influence of sentimental popular movements, exceptional sense of the realities of political power as distinguished from the pretences and idolatries behind which the real masters of modern States pull their wires and train their guns. When he scored Night Falls on The Gods, he had accepted the failure of Siegfried and the triumph of the Wotan-Loki-Alberic trinity as a fact. He had given up dreaming of heroes, heroines, and final solutions, and had conceived a new protagonist in Parsifal, whom he announced, not as a hero, but as a fool, armed, not with a sword which cut irresistibly, but with a spear which he held only on condition that he did not use it: one who, instead of exulting in the slaughter of a dragon, was ashamed of having shot a swan. The change in the conception of the Deliverer could hardly be more complete. It reflects the change which took place in Wagner's mind between the composition of The Rhine Gold and Night Falls on The Gods; and it explains why he found it so easy to drop the Ring allegory and fall back on Lohengrinizing.

WAGNER'S OWN EXPLANATION

AND now, having given my explanation of The Ring, can I give Wagner's explanation of it? If I could (and I can) I should not by any means accept it as conclusive. Nearly half a century has passed since the tetralogy was written; and in that time the purposes of many half instinctive acts of genius have become clearer to the common man than they were to the doers. Some years ago, in the course of an explanation of Ibsen's plays, I pointed out that it was by no means certain or even likely that Ibsen was as definitely conscious of his thesis as I. All the stupid people, and some critics who, though not stupid, had not themselves written what the Germans call "tendency" works, saw nothing in this but a fantastic affectation of the extravagant self-conceit of knowing more about Ibsen than Ibsen himself. Fortunately, in taking exactly the same position now with regard to Wagner, I can claim his own authority to support me. "How," he wrote to Roeckel on the 23rd August 1856, "can an artist expect that what he has felt intuitively should be perfectly realized by others, seeing that he himself feels in the presence of his work, if it is true Art, that he is confronted by a riddle, about which he, too, might have illusions, just as another might?"

The truth is, we are apt to deify men of genius, exactly as we deify the creative force of the universe, by attributing to logical design what is the result of blind instinct. What Wagner meant by "true Art" is the operation of the artist's instinct, which is just as blind as any other instinct. Mozart, asked for an explanation of his works, said frankly "How do I know?" Wagner, being a philosopher and critic as well as a composer, was always looking for moral explanations of what he had created; and he hit on several very striking ones, all different. In the same way one can conceive Henry the Eighth speculating very brilliantly about the circulation of his own blood without getting as near the truth as Harvey did long after his death.

None the less, Wagner's own explanations are of exceptional interest. To begin with, there is a considerable portion of The Ring, especially the portraiture of our capitalistic industrial system from the socialist's point of view in the slavery of the Niblungs and the tyranny of Alberic, which is unmistakeable, as it dramatizes that portion of human activity which lies well within the territory covered by our intellectual consciousness. All this is concrete Home Office business, so to speak: its meaning was as clear to Wagner as it is to us. Not so that part of the work which deals with the destiny of Wotan. And here, as it happened, Wagner's recollection of what he had been driving at was completely upset by his discovery, soon after the completion of The Ring poem, of Schopenhauer's famous treatise "The World as Will and Representation." So obsessed did he become with this masterpiece of philosophic art that he declared that it contained the intellectual demonstration of the conflict of human forces which he himself had demonstrated artistically in his great poem. "I must confess," he writes to Roeckel, "to having arrived at a clear understanding of my own works of art through the help of another, who has provided me with the reasoned conceptions corresponding to my intuitive principles."

Schopenhauer, however, had done nothing of the sort. Wagner's determination to prove that he had been a Schopenhauerite all along without knowing it only shews how completely the fascination of the great treatise on The Will had run away with his memory. It is easy to see how this happened. Wagner says of himself that "seldom has there taken place in the soul of one and the same man so profound a division and estrangement between the intuitive or impulsive part of his nature and his consciously or reasonably formed ideas." And since Schopenhauer's great contribution to modern thought was to educate us into clear consciousness of this distinction—a distinction familiar, in a fanciful way, to the Ages of Faith and Art before the Renascence, but afterwards swamped in the Rationalism of that movement—it was inevitable that Wagner should jump at

Schopenhauer's metaphysiology (I use a word less likely to be mistaken than metaphysics) as the very thing for him. But metaphysiology is one thing, political philosophy another. The political philosophy of Siegfried is exactly contrary to the political philosophy of Schopenhauer, although the same clear metaphysiological distinction between the instinctive part of man (his Will) and his reasoning faculty (dramatized in The Ring as Loki) is insisted on in both. The difference is that to Schopenhauer the Will is the universal tormentor of man, the author of that great evil, Life; whilst reason is the divine gift that is finally to overcome this life-creating will and lead, through its abnegation, to cessation and peace, annihilation and Nirvana. This is the doctrine of Pessimism. Now Wagner was, when he wrote The Ring, a most sanguine revolutionary Meliorist, contemptuous of the reasoning faculty, which he typified in the shifty, unreal, delusive Loki, and full of faith in the life-giving Will, which he typified in the glorious Siegfried. Not until he read Schopenhauer did he become bent on proving that he had always been a Pessimist at heart, and that Loki was the most sensible and worthy adviser of Wotan in The Rhine Gold.

Sometimes he faces the change in his opinions frankly enough. "My Niblung drama," he writes to Roeckel, "had taken form at a time when I had built up with my reason an optimistic world on Hellenic principles, believing that nothing was necessary for the realization of such a world but that men should wish it. I ingeniously set aside the problem why they did not wish it. I remember that it was with this definite creative purpose that I conceived the personality of Siegfried, with the intention of representing an existence free from pain." But he appeals to his earlier works to shew that behind all these artificial optimistic ideas there was always with him an intuition of "the sublime tragedy of renunciation, the negation of the will." In trying to explain this, he is full of ideas philosophically, and full of the most amusing contradictions personally. Optimism, as an accidental excursion into the barren paths of reason on his own part, he calls "Hellenic." In others he denounces it as rank Judaism, the Jew having at that time become for him the whipping boy for all modern humanity. In a letter from London he expounds Schopenhauer to Roeckel with enthusiasm, preaching the renunciation of the Will to Live as the redemption from all error and vain pursuits: in the next letter he resumes the subject with unabated interest, and finishes by mentioning that on leaving London he went to Geneva and underwent "a most beneficial course of hydropathy." Seven months before this he had written as follows: "Believe me, I too was once possessed by the idea of a country life. In order to become a radically healthy human being, I went two years ago to a Hydropathic Establishment, prepared to give up Art and everything if I could once more become a child of Nature. But, my good friend, I was obliged to laugh at my own naïveté when I found myself almost going mad. None of us will reach the promised land: we shall all die in the wilderness. Intellect is, as some one has said, a sort of disease: it is incurable."

Roeckel knew his man of old, and evidently pressed him for explanations of the inconsistencies of The Ring with Night Falls on The Gods. Wagner defended himself with unfailing cleverness and occasional petulances, ranging from such pleas as "I believe a true instinct has kept me from a too great definiteness; for it has been borne in on me that an absolute disclosure of the intention disturbs true insight," to a volley of explanations and commentaries on the explanations. He gets excited and annoyed because Roeckel will not admire the Brynhild of Night Falls on The Gods; reinvents the Tarnhelm scene; and finally, the case being desperate, exclaims, "It is wrong of you to challenge me to explain it in words: you must feel that something is being enacted that is not to be expressed in mere words."

THE PESSIMIST AS AMORIST

Sometimes he gets very far away from Pessimism indeed, and recommends Roeckel to solace his captivity, not by conquering the will to live at liberty, but by "the inspiring influences of the Beautiful." The next moment he throws over even Art for Life. "Where life ends," he says, very wittily, "Art begins. In youth we turn to Art, we know not why; and only when we have gone through with Art and come out on the other side, we learn to our cost that we have missed Life itself." His only comfort is that he is beloved. And on the subject of love he lets himself loose in a manner that would have roused the bitterest scorn in Schopenhauer, though, as we have seen (p. 232), it is highly characteristic of Wagner. "Love in its most perfect reality," he says, "is only possible between the sexes: it is only as man and woman that human beings can truly love. Every other manifestation of love can be traced back to that one absorbingly real feeling, of which all other affections are but an emanation, a connection, or an imitation. It is an error to look on this as only one of the forms in which love is revealed, as if there were other forms coequal with it, or even superior to it. He who after the manner of metaphysicians prefers *unreality* to *reality*, and derives the concrete from the abstract—in short, puts the word before the fact—may be right in esteeming the idea of love as higher than the expression of love, and may affirm that actual love made manifest in feeling is nothing but the outward and visible sign of a pre-existent, non-sensuous, abstract love; and he will do well to despise that sensuous function in general. In any case it were safe to bet that such a man had never loved or been loved as human beings can love, or he would have understood that in despising this feeling, what he condemned was its sensual expression, the outcome of man's animal nature, and not true human love. The highest satisfaction and expression of the individual is only to be found in his complete absorption, and that is only possible through love. Now a human being is both *man* and *woman*: it is only when these two are united that the real human being exists; and thus it is only by love that man and woman attain to the full measure of humanity. But when nowadays we talk of a human being, such heartless blockheads are we that quite involuntarily we only think of man.

It is only in the union of man and woman by love (sensuous and supersensuous) that the human being exists; and as the human being cannot rise to the conception of anything higher than his own existence—his own being—so the transcendent act of his life is this consummation of his humanity through love."

It is clear after this utterance from the would-be Schopenhauerian, that Wagner's explanations of his works for the most part explain nothing but the mood in which he happened to be on the day he advanced them, or the train of thought suggested to his very susceptible imagination and active mind by the points raised by his questioner. Especially in his private letters, where his outpourings are modified by his dramatic consciousness of the personality of his correspondent, do we find him taking all manner of positions, and putting forward all sorts of cases which must be taken as clever and suggestive special pleadings, and not as serious and permanent expositions of his works. These works must speak for themselves: if The Ring says one thing, and a letter written afterwards says that it said something else, The Ring must be taken to confute the letter just as conclusively as if the two had been written by different hands. However, nobody fairly well acquainted with Wagner's utterances as a whole will find any unaccountable contradictions in them. As in all men of his type, our manifold nature was so marked in him that he was like several different men rolled into one. When he had exhausted himself in the character of the most pugnacious, aggressive, and sanguine of reformers, he rested himself as a Pessimist and Nirvanist. In The Ring the quietism of Brynhild's "Rest, rest, thou God" is sublime in its deep conviction; but you have only to turn back the pages to find the irrepressible bustle of Siegfried and the revelry of the clansmen expressed with equal zest. Wagner was not a Schopenhauerite every day in the week, nor even a Wagnerite. His mind changes as often as his mood. On Monday nothing will ever induce him to return to quill-driving: on Tuesday he begins a new pamphlet. On Wednesday he is impatient of the misapprehensions of people who cannot see how impossible it is for him to preside as a conductor over platform performances of fragments of his works, which can only be understood when presented strictly according to his intention on the stage: on Thursday he gets up a concert of Wagnerian selections, and when it is over writes to his friends describing how profoundly both bandsmen and audience were impressed. On Friday he exults in the self-assertion of Siegfried's will against all moral ordinances, and is full of a revolutionary sense of "the universal law of change and renewal": on Saturday he has an attack of holiness, and asks, "Can you conceive a moral action of which the root idea is not renunciation?" In short, Wagner can be quoted against himself almost without limit, much as Beethoven's adagios could be quoted against his scherzos if a dispute arose between two fools as to whether he was a melancholy man or a merry one.

THE MUSIC OF THE RING
THE REPRESENTATIVE THEMES

TO be able to follow the music of The Ring, all that is necessary is to become familiar enough with the brief musical phrases out of which it is built to recognize them and attach a certain definite significance to them, exactly as any ordinary Englishman recognizes and attaches a definite significance to the opening bars of God Save the Queen. There is no difficulty here: every soldier is expected to learn and distinguish between different bugle calls and trumpet calls; and anyone who can do this can learn and distinguish between the representative themes or "leading motives" (Leitmotifs) of The Ring. They are the easier to learn because they are repeated again and again; and the main ones are so emphatically impressed on the ear whilst the spectator is looking for the first time at the objects, or witnessing the first strong dramatic expression of the ideas they denote, that the requisite association is formed unconsciously. The themes are neither long, nor complicated, nor difficult. Whoever can pick up the flourish of a coach-horn, the note of a bird, the rhythm of the postman's knock or of a horse's gallop, will be at no loss in picking up the themes of The Ring. No doubt, when it comes to forming the necessary mental association with the theme, it may happen that the spectator may find his ear conquering the tune more easily than his mind conquers the thought. But for the most part the themes do not denote thoughts at all, but either emotions of a quite simple universal kind, or the sights, sounds and fancies common enough to be familiar to children. Indeed some of them are as frankly childish as any of the funny little orchestral interludes which, in Haydn's Creation, introduce the horse, the deer, or the worm. We have both the horse and the worm in The Ring, treated exactly in Haydn's manner, and with an effect not a whit less ridiculous to superior people who decline to take it good-humoredly. Even the complaisance of good Wagnerites is occasionally rather overstrained by the way in which Brynhild's allusions to her charger Grani elicit from the band a little rum-ti-tum triplet which by itself is in no way suggestive of a horse, although a continuous rush of such triplets makes a very exciting musical gallop.

Other themes denote objects which cannot be imitatively suggested by music: for instance, music cannot suggest a ring, and cannot suggest gold; yet each of these has a representative theme which pervades the score in all directions. In the case of the gold the association is established by the very salient way in which the orchestra breaks into the pretty theme in the first act of The Rhine Gold at the moment when the sunrays strike down through the water and light up the glittering treasure, hitherto invisible. The reference of the strange little theme of the wishing cap is equally manifest from the first, since the spectator's attention is wholly taken up with the Tarnhelm and its magic when the theme is first pointedly uttered by the orchestra. The sword theme is introduced at the end of The Rhine Gold to express Wotan's hero inspiration; and I have already mentioned that Wagner, unable, when it came to practical stage management, to forego the appeal to the eye as well as to the thought, here made Wotan pick up a sword and brandish it, though no such instruction appears in the printed score. When this sacrifice to Wagner's scepticism as to the reality of any appeal to an audience that is not made through their bodily sense is omitted, the association of the theme with the sword is not formed until that point in the first act of The Valkyries at which Siegmund is left alone by Hunding's hearth, weaponless, with the assurance that he will have to fight for his life at dawn with his host. He recalls then how his father promised him a sword for his hour of need; and as he does so, a flicker from the dying fire is caught by the golden hilt of the sword in the tree, when the theme immediately begins to gleam through the quiver of sound from the orchestra, and only dies out as the fire sinks and the sword is once more hidden by the darkness. Later on, this theme, which is never silent whilst Sieglinda is dwelling on the story of the sword, leaps out into the most dazzling splendor the band can give it when Siegmund triumphantly draws the weapon from the tree. As it consists of seven notes only, with a very marked measure, and a melody like a simple flourish on a trumpet or post horn, nobody capable of catching a tune can easily miss it.

The Valhalla theme, sounded with solemn grandeur as the home of the gods first appears to us and to Wotan at the beginning of the second scene of The Rhine Gold, also cannot be mistaken. It, too, has a memorable rhythm; and its majestic harmonies, far from presenting those novel or curious problems in polyphony of which Wagner still stands suspected by superstitious people, are just those three simple chords which festive students who vamp accompaniments to comic songs "by ear" soon find sufficient for nearly all the popular tunes in the world.

On the other hand, the ring theme, when it begins to hurtle through the third scene of The Rhine Gold, cannot possibly be referred to any special feature in the general gloom and turmoil of the den of the dwarfs. It is not a melody, but merely the displaced metric accent which musicians call syncopation, rung on the notes of the familiar chord formed by piling three minor thirds on top of one another (technically, the chord of the minor ninth, *ci-devant* diminished seventh). One soon picks it up and identifies it; but it does not get introduced in the unequivocally clear fashion of the themes described above, or of that malignant monstrosity, the theme which denotes the curse on the gold. Consequently it cannot be said that the musical design of the work is perfectly clear at the first hearing as regards all the themes; but it is so as regards most of them, the main lines being laid down as emphatically and intelligibly as the dramatic motives in a Shakespearean play. As to the coyer subtleties of the score, their discovery provides fresh interest for repeated hearings, giving The Ring a Beethovenian inexhaustibility and toughness of wear.

The themes associated with the individual characters get

stamped on the memory easily by the simple association of the sound of the theme with the appearance of the person indicated. Its appropriateness is generally pretty obvious. Thus, the entry of the giants is made to a vigorous stumping, tramping measure. Mimmy, being a quaint, weird old creature, has a quaint, weird theme of two thin chords that creep down eerily one to the other. Gutruna's theme is pretty and caressing: Gunther's bold, rough, and commonplace. It is a favorite trick of Wagner's, when one of his characters is killed on the stage, to make the theme attached to that character weaken, fail, and fade away with a broken echo into silence.

THE CHARACTERIZATION

All this, however, is the mere child's play of theme work. The more complex characters, instead of having a simple musical label attached to them, have their characteristic ideas and aspirations identified with special representative themes as they come into play in the drama; and the chief merit of the thematic structure of The Ring is the mastery with which the dramatic play of the ideas is reflected in the contrapuntal play of the themes. We do not find Wotan, like the dragon or the horse, or, for the matter of that, like the stage demon in Weber's Freischütz or Meyerbeer's Robert the Devil, with one fixed theme attached to him like a name plate to an umbrella, blaring unaltered from the orchestra whenever he steps on the stage. Sometimes we have the Valhalla theme used to express the greatness of the gods as an idea of Wotan's. Again, we have his spear, the symbol of his power, identified with another theme, on which Wagner finally exercises his favorite device by making it break and fail, cut through, as it were, by the tearing sound of the theme identified with the sword, when Siegfried shivers the spear with the stroke of Nothung. Yet another theme connected with Wotan is the Wanderer music which breaks with such a majestic reassurance on the nightmare terror of Mimmy when Wotan appears at the mouth of his cave in the scene of the three riddles. Thus not only are there several Wotan themes, but each varies in its inflexions and shades of tone color according to its dramatic circumstances. So, too, the merry horn tune of the young Siegfried changes its measure, loads itself with massive harmonies, and becomes an exordium of the most imposing splendor when it heralds his entry as full-fledged hero in the prologue to Night Falls on The Gods. Even Mimmy has his two or three themes: the weird one already described; the little one in triple measure imitating the tap of his hammer, and fiercely mocked in the savage laugh of Alberic at his death; and finally the crooning tune in which he details all his motherly kindnesses to the little foundling Siegfried. Besides this there are all manner of little musical blinkings and shamblings and whinings, the least hint of which from the orchestra at any moment instantly brings Mimmy to mind, whether he is on the stage at the time or not.

In truth, dramatic characterization in music cannot be carried very far by the use of representative themes. Mozart, the greatest of all masters of this art, never dreamt of employing them; and, extensively as they are used in The Ring, they do not enable Wagner to dispense with the Mozartian method. Apart from the themes, Siegfried and Mimmy are still as sharply distinguished from one another by the character of their music as Don Giovanni from Leporello, Wotan from Gutruna as Sarastro from Papagena. It is true that the themes attached to the characters have the same musical appropriateness as the rest of the music: for example, neither the Valhalla nor the spear themes could, without the most ludicrous incongruity, be used for the forest bird or the unstable, delusive Loki; but for all that the musical characterization must be regarded as independent of the specific themes, since the entire elimination of the thematic system from the score would leave the characters as well distinguished musically as they are at present.

One more illustration of the way in which the thematic system is worked. There are two themes connected with Loki. One is a rapid, sinuous, twisting, shifty semiquaver figure suggested by the unsubstantial, elusive logic-spinning of the clever one's braincraft. The other is the fire theme. In the first act of Siegfried, Mimmy makes his unavailing attempt to explain fear to Siegfried. With the horror fresh upon him of the sort of nightmare into which he has fallen after the departure of the Wanderer, and which has taken the form, at once fanciful and symbolic, of a delirious dread of light, he asks Siegfried whether he has never, whilst wandering in the forest, had his heart set hammering in frantic dread by the mysterious lights of the gloaming. To this, Siegfried, greatly astonished, replies that on such occasions his heart is altogether healthy and his sensations perfectly normal. Here Mimmy's question is accompanied by the tremulous sounding of the fire theme with its harmonies most oppressively disturbed and troubled; whereas with Siegfried's reply they become quite clear and straightforward, making the theme sound bold, brilliant, and serene. This is a typical instance of the way in which the themes are used.

The thematic system gives symphonic interest, reasonableness and unity to the music, enabling the composer to exhaust every aspect and quality of his melodic material, and, in Beethoven's manner, to work miracles of beauty, expression and significance with the briefest phrases. As a set-off against this, it has led Wagner to indulge in repetitions that would be intolerable in a purely dramatic work. Almost the first thing that a dramatist has to learn in constructing a play is that the persons must not come on the stage in the second act and tell one another at great length what the audience has already seen pass before its eyes in the first act. The extent to which Wagner has been seduced into violating this rule by his affection for his themes is startling to a practised playwright. Siegfried inherits from Wotan a mania for autobiography which leads him to inflict on everyone he meets the story of Mimmy and the dragon, although the audience have spent a whole evening witnessing the events he is narrating. Hagen tells the story to Gunther; and that same night Alberic's ghost tells it over again to Hagen, who knows it already as well as the audience. Siegfried tells the Rhine-maidens as much of it as they will listen to, and then keeps telling it to his hunting companions until they kill him. Wotan's autobiography on the second evening becomes his biography in the mouths of the Norns on the fourth. The little that the Norns add to it is repeated an hour later by Valtrauta. How far all this repetition is tolerable is a matter of individual taste. A good story will bear repetition; and if it has woven into it such pretty tunes as the Rhine-maidens' yodel, Mimmy's tinkling anvil beat, the note of the forest bird, the call of Siegfried's horn, and so on, it will bear a good deal of rehearing. Those who have but newly learnt their way through The Ring will not readily admit that there is a bar too much repetition.

But how if you find some anti-Wagnerite raising the question whether the thematic system does not enable the composer to produce a music drama with much less musical fertility than was required from his predecessors for the composition of operas under the old system!

Such discussions are not within the scope of this little book. But as the book is now finished (for really nothing more need be said about The Ring), I am quite willing to add a few pages of ordinary musical criticism, partly to please the amateurs who enjoy that sort of reading, and partly for the guidance of those who wish to obtain some hints to help them through such critical small talk about Wagner and Bayreuth as may be forced upon them at the dinner table or between the acts.

THE OLD AND THE NEW MUSIC

IN the old-fashioned opera every separate number involved the composition of a fresh melody; but it is quite a mistake to suppose that this creative effort extended continuously throughout the number from the first to the last bar. When a musician composes according to a set metrical pattern, the selection of the pattern and the composition of the first stave (a stave in music corresponds to a line in verse) generally completes the creative effort. All the rest follows more or less mechanically to fill up the pattern, an air being very like a wall-paper design in this respect. Thus the second stave is usually a perfectly obvious consequence of the first; and the third and fourth an exact or very slightly varied repetition of the first and second. For example, given the first line of Pop Goes the Weasel or Yankee Doodle, any musical cobbler could supply the remaining three. There is very little tune-turning of this kind in The Ring; and it is noteworthy that where it does occur, as in Siegmund's spring song and Mimmy's croon, "Ein zullendes Kind," the effect of the symmetrical staves, recurring as a mere matter of form, is perceptibly poor and platitudinous compared with the free flow of melody which prevails elsewhere.

The other and harder way of composing is to take a strain of free melody, and ring every variety of change of mood upon it as if it were a thought that sometimes brought hope, sometimes melancholy, sometimes exultation, sometimes raging despair and so on. To take several themes of this kind, and weave them together into a rich musical fabric passing panoramically before the ear with a continually varying flow of sentiment, is the highest feat of the musician: it is in this way that we get the fugue of Bach and the symphony of Beethoven. The admittedly inferior musician is the one who, like Auber and Offenbach, not to mention our purveyors of drawing room ballads, can produce an unlimited quantity of symmetrical tunes, but cannot weave themes symphonically.

When this is taken into account, it will be seen that the

fact that there is a great deal of repetition in The Ring does not distinguish it from the old-fashioned operas. The real difference is that in them the repetition was used for the mechanical completion of conventional metric patterns, whereas in The Ring the recurrence of the theme is an intelligent and interesting consequence of the recurrence of the dramatic phenomenon which it denotes. It should be remembered also that the substitution of symphonically treated themes for tunes with symmetrical eight-bar staves and the like, has always been the rule in the highest forms of music. To describe it, or be affected by it, as an abandonment of melody, is to confess oneself an ignoramus conversant only with dance tunes and ballads.

The sort of stuff a purely dramatic musician produces when he hampers himself with metric patterns in composition is not unlike what might have resulted in literature if Carlyle (for example) had been compelled by convention to write his historical stories in rhymed stanzas. That is to say, it limits his fertility to an occasional phrase, and three quarters of the time exercises only his barren ingenuity in fitting rhymes and measures to it. In literature the great masters of the art have long emancipated themselves from metric patterns. Nobody claims that the hierarchy of modern impassioned prose writers, from Bunyan to Ruskin, should be placed below the writers of pretty lyrics, from Herrick to Mr Austin Dobson. Only in dramatic literature do we find the devastating tradition of blank verse still lingering, giving factitious prestige to the platitudes of dullards, and robbing the dramatic style of the genuine poet of its full natural endowment of variety, force, and simplicity.

This state of things, as we have seen, finds its parallel in musical art, since music can be written in prose themes or in versified tunes; only here nobody dreams of disputing the greater difficulty of the prose forms and the comparative triviality of versification. Yet in dramatic music, as in dramatic literature, the tradition of versification clings with the same pernicious results; and the opera, like the tragedy, is conventionally made like a wall paper. The theatre seems doomed to be in all things the last refuge of the hankering after cheap prettiness in art.

Unfortunately this confusion of the decorative with the dramatic element in both literature and music is maintained by the example of great masters in both arts. Very touching dramatic expression can be combined with decorative symmetry of versification when the artist happens to possess both the decorative and dramatic gifts, and to have cultivated both hand in hand. Shakespear and Shelley, for instance, far from being hampered by the conventional obligation to write their dramas in verse, found it much the easiest and cheapest way of producing them. But if Shakespear had been compelled by custom to write entirely in prose, all his ordinary dialogue might have been as good as the first scene of As You Like It; and all his lofty passages as fine as "What a piece of work is Man!", thus sparing us a great deal of blank verse in which the thought is commonplace, and the expression, though catchingly turned, absurdly pompous. The Cenci might either have been a serious drama or might never have been written at all if Shelley had not been allowed to carry off its unreality by Elizabethan versification. Still, both poets have achieved many passages in which the decorative and dramatic qualities are not only reconciled, but seem to enhance one another to a pitch otherwise unattainable.

Just so in music. When we find, as in the case of Mozart, a prodigiously gifted and arduously trained musician who is also, by a happy accident, a dramatist comparable to Molière, the obligation to compose operas in versified numbers not only does not embarrass him, but actually saves him trouble and thought. No matter what his dramatic mood may be, he expresses it in exquisite musical verses more easily than a dramatist of ordinary singleness of talent can express it in prose. Accordingly, he too, like Shakespear and Shelley, leaves versified airs, like *Dalla sua pace*, or Gluck's *Che faro senza Euridice*, or Weber's *Leise, leise*, which are as dramatic from the first note to the last as the untrammelled themes of The Ring. In consequence, it used to be professorially demanded that all dramatic music should present the same double aspect. The demand was unreasonable, since symmetrical versification is no merit in dramatic music: one might as well stipulate that a dinner fork should be constructed so as to serve also as a tablecloth. It was an ignorant demand too, because it is not true that the composers of these exceptional examples were always, or even often, able to combine dramatic expression with symmetrical versification. Side by side with *Dalla sua pace* we have *Il mio tesoro* and *Non mi dir*, in which exquisitely expressive opening phrases lead to decorative passages which are as grotesque from the dramatic point of view as the music which Alberic sings when he is slipping and sneezing in the Rhine mud is from the decorative point of view. Further, there is to be considered the mass of shapeless "dry recitative" which separates these symmetrical numbers, and which might have been raised to considerable dramatic and musical importance had it been incorporated into a continuous musical fabric by thematic treatment. Finally, Mozart's most dramatic finales and concerted numbers are more or less in sonata form, like symphonic movements, and must therefore be classed as musical prose. And sonata form dictates repetitions and recapitulations from which the perfectly unconventional form adopted by Wagner is free. On the whole, there is more scope for both repetition and convention in the old form than in the new; and the poorer a composer's musical gift is, the surer he is to resort to the eighteenth century patterns to eke out his invention.

THE NINETEENTH CENTURY

WHEN Wagner was born in 1813, music had newly become the most astonishing, the most fascinating, the most miraculous art in the world. Mozart's Don Giovanni had made all musical Europe conscious of the enchantments of the modern orchestra and of the perfect adaptability of music to the subtlest needs of the dramatist. Beethoven had shown how those inarticulate mood-poems which surge through men who have, like himself, no exceptional command of words, can be written down in music as symphonies. Not that Mozart and Beethoven invented these applications of their art; but they were the first whose works made it clear that the dramatic and subjective powers of sound were enthralling enough to stand by themselves quite apart from the decorative musical structures of which they had hitherto been a mere feature. After the finales in Figaro and Don Giovanni, the possibility of the modern music drama lay bare. After the symphonies of Beethoven it was certain that the poetry that lies too deep for words does not lie too deep for music, and that the vicissitudes of the soul, from the roughest fun to the loftiest aspiration, can make symphonies without the aid of dance tunes. As much, perhaps, will be claimed for the preludes and fugues of Bach; but Bach's method was unattainable: his compositions were wonderful webs of exquisitely beautiful Gothic traceries in sound, quite beyond all ordinary human talent. Beethoven's far blunter craft was thoroughly popular and practicable: not to save his soul could he have drawn one long Gothic line in sound as Bach could, much less have woven several of them together with so apt a harmony that even when the composer is unmoved its progressions saturate themselves with the emotion which (as modern critics are a little apt to forget) springs as warmly from our delicately touched admiration as from our sympathies, and sometimes makes us give a composer credit for pathetic intentions which he does not entertain, just as a boy imagines a treasure of tenderness and noble wisdom in the beauty of a woman. Besides, Bach set comic dialogue to music exactly as he set the recitatives of the Passion, there being for him, apparently, only one recitative possible, and that the musically best. He reserved the expression of his merry mood for the regular set numbers in which he could make one of his wonderful contrapuntal traceries of pure ornament with the requisite gaiety of line and movement. Beethoven bowed to no ideal of beauty: he only sought the expression for his feeling. To him a joke was a joke; and if it sounded funny in music he was satisfied. Until the old habit of judging all music by its decorative symmetry had worn out, musicians were shocked by his symphonies, and, misunderstanding his integrity, openly questioned his sanity. But to those who were not looking for pretty new sound patterns, but were longing for the expression of their moods in music, he achieved a revelation, because, being single in his aim to express his own moods, he anticipated with revolutionary courage and frankness all the moods of the rising generations of the nineteenth century.

The result was inevitable. In the nineteenth century it was no longer necessary to be a born pattern designer in sound to be a composer. One had but to be a dramatist or a poet completely susceptible to the dramatic and descriptive powers of sound. A race of literary and theatrical musicians appeared; and Meyerbeer, the first of them, made an extraordinary impression. The frankly delirious description of his Robert the Devil in Balzac's short story entitled Gambara, and Goethe's astonishingly mistaken notion that he could have composed music for Faust, show how completely the enchantments of the new dramatic music upset the judgment of artists of eminent discernment. Meyerbeer was, people said (old gentlemen still say so in Paris), the successor of Beethoven: he was, if a less perfect musician than Mozart, a profounder genius. Above all, he was original and daring. Wagner himself raved about the duet in the fourth act of Les Huguenots as wildly as anyone.

Yet all this effect of originality and profundity was produced by a quite limited talent for turning striking phrases, exploiting certain curious and rather catching rhythms and modulations, and devising suggestive or eccentric instrumentation. On its decorative side, it was the same phenomenon in music as the Baroque school in architecture: an energetic struggle to enliven organic decay by mechanical oddities and novelties. Meyerbeer was no symphonist. He could not apply the thematic system to his striking phrases, and so had to cobble them into metric patterns in the old style; and as he was no "absolute musician" either, he hardly got his metric patterns beyond mere quadrille tunes, which were either wholly undistinguished, or else made remarkable by certain brusqueries which, in the true rococo manner, owed their singularity to their senselessness. He could produce neither a thorough music drama nor a charming opera. But with all this, and worse, Meyerbeer had some genuine dramatic energy, and even passion; and sometimes rose to the occasion in a manner which, whilst the imagination of his contemporaries remained on fire with the novelties of dramatic music, led them to overrate him with an extravagance which provoked Wagner to conduct a long critical campaign against his supremacy. In the eighteen-sixties this was inevitably ascribed to the professional jealousy of a disappointed rival. Nowadays young people cannot understand how anyone could ever have taken Meyerbeer's influence seriously. The few who remember the reputation he built on The Huguenots and The Prophet, and who now realize what a no-thoroughfare the path he opened proved to be, even to himself, know how inevitable and how impersonal Wagner's attack was.

Wagner was the literary musician par excellence. He could not, like Mozart and Beethoven, produce decorative tone structures independently of any dramatic or poetic subject matter, because, that craft being no longer necessary for his purpose, he did not cultivate it. As Shakespear, compared with Tennyson, appears to have an exclusively dramatic talent, so exactly does Wagner compared with Mendelssohn. On the other hand, he had not to go to third rate literary hacks for "librettos" to set to music: he produced his own dramatic poems, thus giving dramatic integrity to opera, and making symphony articulate. A Beethoven symphony (except the articulate part of the ninth) expresses noble feeling, but not thought: it has moods, but no ideas. Wagner added thought and produced the music drama. Mozart's loftiest opera, his Ring, so to speak, The Magic Flute, has a libretto which, though none the worse for seeming, like The Rhine Gold, the merest Christmas tomfoolery to shallow spectators, is the product of a talent immeasurably inferior to Mozart's own. The libretto of Don Giovanni is coarse and trivial: its transfiguration by Mozart's music may be a marvel; but nobody will venture to contend that such transfigurations, however seductive, can be as satisfactory as tone poetry or drama in which the musician and the poet are at the same level. Here, then, we have the simple secret of Wagner's pre-eminence as a dramatic musician. He wrote the poems as well as composed the music of his "stage festival plays," as he called them.

Up to a certain point in his career Wagner paid the penalty of undertaking two arts instead of one. Mozart had his trade as a musician at his fingers' ends when he was twenty, because he had served an arduous apprenticeship to that trade and no other. Wagner was very far from having attained equal mastery at thirty-five: indeed he himself has told us that not until he had passed the age at which Mozart died did he compose with that complete spontaneity of musical expression which can only be attained by winning entire freedom from all preoccupation with the difficulties of technical processes. But when that time came, he was not only a consummate musician, like Mozart, but a dramatic poet and a critical and philosophical essayist, exercising a considerable influence on his century. The sign of this consummation was his ability at last to play with his art, and thus to add to his already famous achievements in sentimental drama that lighthearted art of comedy of which the greatest masters, like Molière and Mozart, are so much rarer than the tragedians and sentimentalists. It was then that he composed the first two acts of Siegfried, and later on The Mastersingers, a professedly comedic work, and a quite Mozartian garden of melody, hardly credible as the work of the straining artificer of Tannhäuser. Only, as no man ever learns to do one thing by doing something else, however closely allied the two things may be, Wagner still produced no music independently of his poems. The overture to The Mastersingers is delightful when you know what it is all about; but only those to whom it came as a concert piece without any such clue, and who judged its reckless counterpoint by the standard of Bach and of Mozart's Magic Flute overture, can realize how atrocious it used to sound to musicians of the old school. When I first heard it, with the clear march of the polyphony in Bach's B minor Mass fresh in my memory, I confess I thought that the parts had got dislocated, and that some of the band were half a bar behind the others. Perhaps they were; but now that I am familiar with the work, and with Wagner's harmony, I can still quite understand certain passages producing that effect on an admirer of Bach even when performed with perfect accuracy.

THE MUSIC OF THE FUTURE

THE ultimate success of Wagner was so prodigious that to his dazzled disciples it seemed that the age of what he called "absolute" music must be at an end, and the musical future destined to be an exclusively Wagnerian one inaugurated at Bayreuth. All great geniuses produce this illusion. Wagner did not begin a movement: he consummated it. He was the summit of the nineteenth century school of dramatic music in the same sense as Mozart was the summit (the word is Gounod's) of the eighteenth century school. All those who attempted to carry on his Bayreuth tradition have shared the fate of the forgotten purveyors of second-hand Mozart a hundred years ago. As to the expected supersession of absolute music, Wagner's successors in European rank were Brahms, Elgar, and Richard Strauss. The reputation of Brahms rests on his absolute music alone: such works as his German Requiem endear themselves to us as being musically great fun; but to take them quite seriously is to make them oppressively dull. Elgar followed Beethoven and Schumann: he owes nothing essential to Wagner, and secured his niche in the temple by his symphonies and his Enigma Variations, which are as absolutely musical as any modern music can be. Although Strauss produced works for the musical theatre which maintained it at the level to which Wagner had raised it, his new departure was a form of musical drama, comic epic, and soul autobiography in which stage, singers, and all the rest of the theatrical material of Bayreuth save only the orchestra are thrown overboard, and the work effected by instrumental music alone, even Beethoven's final innovation of a chorus being discarded. Just the same thing happened when Elgar took as his theme Shakespear's Henry IV, with Falstaff as its chief figure. He made the band do it all, and with such masterful success that one cannot bear to think of what would have been the result of a mere attempt to turn the play into an opera.

The Russian composers whose vogue succeeded that of

Wagner were not in the least Wagnerian: they developed from the romantic school, from Weber and Meyerbeer, from Berlioz and Liszt, much as they might have done had Wagner never existed except as a propagandist of the importance of their art. A disparaging attitude towards Wagner resembling that of Chopin to Beethoven, and a very similar escape from his influence even in technique, was quite common among the composers whose early lives overlapped the last part of his. In England the composers who are the juniors of Elgar, but the seniors of (for example) Bax and Ireland, the most notable of whom are Mr Granville Bantock and Mr Rutland Boughton, were heavily Wagnerized in their youth, and began by Tristanizing and Götterdämmerunging heroically; but when they found themselves their Wagnerism vanished. The younger men do not begin with Wagner nor even with Strauss: they are mostly bent on producing curiosities of absolute music until they settle down into a serious style of their own. All that can be said for the Wagner tradition is that it finally killed the confusion between decorative pattern music and dramatic music which muddled Meyerbeer and imposed absurd repetitions on the heroes and heroines of Handel and Mozart. Even in absolute music, the post-Wagnerite sonata form has become so much less mechanical and thoughtless that the fact that it still persists in essentials is hardly worth asserting.

Writing before any of these developments had happened, I said in the first edition of this book that there was no more hope in attempts to out-Wagner Wagner in music drama than there had been in the old attempts to make Handel the starting point of a great school of oratorio. How true this was is now so obvious that my younger readers may wonder why I thought it worth while to say it. But if veterans did not indulge in these day-before-yesterdayisms Music would lose the thread of its history.

BAYREUTH

WHEN the Bayreuth Festival Playhouse was at last completed, and opened in 1876 with the first performance of The Ring, European society was compelled to admit that Wagner was "a success." Royal personages, detesting his music, sat out the performances in the row of boxes set apart for princes. They all complimented him on the astonishing "push" with which, in the teeth of all obstacles, he had turned a fabulous and visionary project into a concrete commercial reality, patronized by the public at a pound a head. It is as well to know that these congratulations had no other effect upon Wagner than to open his eyes to the fact that the Bayreuth experiment, as an attempt to evade the ordinary social and commercial conditions of theatrical enterprise, was a failure. His own account of it contrasts the reality with his intentions in a vein which would be bitter if it were not so humorous. The precautions taken to keep the seats out of the hands of the frivolous public and in the hands of earnest disciples, banded together in little Wagner Societies throughout Europe, had ended in their forestalling by ticket speculators and their sale to just the sort of idle globe-trotting tourists against whom the temple was to have been strictly closed. The money, supposed to be contributed by the faithful, was begged by energetic subscription-hunting ladies from people who must have had the most grotesque misconceptions of the composer's aims: among others, the Khedive of Egypt and the Sultan of Turkey!

Since then, subscriptions are no longer needed; for the Festival Playhouse pays its own way now, and is commercially on the same footing as any other theatre. The only qualification required from the visitor is money. A Londoner spends twenty pounds on a visit: a native Bayreuther spends one pound. In either case "the Folk," on whose behalf Wagner turned out in 1849, are effectually excluded; and the Festival Playhouse must therefore be classed as infinitely less Wagnerian in its character than Hampton Court Palace.

Nobody knew this better than Wagner; and nothing can be further off the mark than to chatter about Bayreuth as if it had succeeded in escaping from the conditions of our modern civilization any more than the Grand Opera in Paris or London.

Within these conditions, however, it effected a new departure in that excellent German institution, the summer theatre. Unlike the old opera houses, which are constructed so that the audience may present a splendid pageant to the delighted manager, it was designed to secure an uninterrupted view of the stage, and an undisturbed hearing of the music, to the audience. The dramatic purpose of the performances was taken with entire and elaborate seriousness as the sole purpose of them; and the management was jealous for the reputation of Wagner. The sightseeing globe-trotter no longer crowds out the genuine disciple: the audiences are now as genuinely devoted as Wagner could have desired: the disconcerted, bewildered, bored followers of fashion have vanished with the sportsman on a holiday: the atmosphere is the right one for the work. There is, apparently, an effective demand for summer theatres of the highest class. There is no reason why the experiment should not be tried in England. If our enthusiasm for Handel can support Handel Festivals, laughably dull, stupid and anti-Handelian as these choral monstrosities are, as well as annual provincial festivals on the same model, there is no likelihood of a Wagner Festival failing. Suppose, for instance, a Wagner theatre were built at Hampton Court or on Richmond Hill, not to say Margate pier, so that we could have a delightful summer evening holiday, Bayreuth fashion, passing the hours between the acts in the park or on the river before sunset, is it seriously contended that there would be any lack of visitors? If a little of the money that is wasted on grand stands, Eiffel towers, and dismal Halls by the Sea, all as much tied to brief annual seasons as Bayreuth, were applied in this way, the profit would be far more certain and the social utility prodigiously greater. Any English enthusiasm for Bayreuth that does not take the form of clamor for a Festival playhouse in England may be set aside as mere pilgrimage mania.

Besides, the early Bayreuth performances were far from delectable. The singing was sometimes tolerable, and sometimes abominable. Some of the singers were mere animated beer casks, too lazy and conceited to practise the self-control and physical training that is expected as a matter of course from an acrobat, a jockey or a pugilist. The women's dresses were prudish and absurd. It is true that after some years Kundry no longer wore an early Victorian ball dress with "ruchings," and that Freia was provided with a quaintly modish copy of the flowered gown of Spring in Botticelli's famous picture; but the mailclad Brynhild still climbed the mountains with her legs carefully hidden in a long white skirt, and looked so exactly like Mrs Leo Hunter as Minerva that it was quite impossible to feel a ray of illusion whilst looking at her. The ideal of womanly beauty aimed at reminded Englishmen of the barmaids of the seventies, when the craze for golden hair was at its worst. Further, whilst Wagner's stage directions were sometimes disregarded as unintelligently as at the old opera houses, Wagner's quaintly old-fashioned tradition of half rhetorical, half historical-pictorial attitude and gesture prevailed. The most striking moments of the drama were conceived as *tableaux vivants* with posed models, instead of as passages of action, motion, and life.

I need hardly add that the supernatural powers of control attributed by credulous pilgrims to Wagner's widow, and later on to his son, did not exist. Prima donnas and tenors were as unmanageable at Bayreuth as anywhere else. Casts were capriciously changed; stage business was insufficiently rehearsed; the audience was compelled to listen to a Brynhild or Siegfried of fifty when they had carefully arranged to see one of twenty-five, much as in any ordinary opera house. Even the conductors upset the arrangements occasionally. On the other hand, we could always feel assured that in thoroughness of preparation of the chief work of the season, in strenuous artistic pretentiousness, in pious conviction that the work was of such enormous importance as to be worth doing well at all costs, the Bayreuth performances would deserve their reputation. Their example raised the quality of operatic performances throughout the world, even in apparently incorrigible centres of fashion and frivolity.

BAYREUTH IN ENGLAND

In 1898 I purposely dwelt on the early shortcomings of Bayreuth to shew that there was no reason in the world why as good and better performances of The Ring should not be given in England, and that neither Wagner's widow nor his son could pretend to handle them with greater authority than any artist who feels the impulse to interpret them. Nobody will ever know what Wagner himself thought of the artists who established the Bayreuth tradition: he was obviously not in a position to criticize them. For instance, had Rubini survived to create Siegmund, Wagner could hardly have written so amusing and vivid a description as he did of his Ottavio in the old Paris days. Wagner was under great obligations to the heroes and heroines of 1876; and he naturally said nothing to disparage their triumphs; but there is no reason to believe that all or indeed any of them satisfied him as Schnorr of Carolsfeld satisfied him as Tristan, or Schröder Devrient as Fidelio. It was just as likely that the next Schnorr or Schröder would arise in England. Nowadays it seems odd that anyone should need to be told all this. British and American singers have long since replaced the Bayreuth veterans to considerable advantage.

WAGNERIAN SINGERS

No nation need have any difficulty in producing a race of Wagnerian singers. With the single exception of Handel, no composer has written music so well calculated to make its singers vocal athletes as Wagner. Abominably as the Germans sang in Wagner's day, it was astonishing how they throve physically on his leading parts. His secret is the

Handelian secret. Instead of specializing his vocal parts after the manner of Verdi and Gounod for shrieking sopranos, goat-bleating tenors, and tremulous baritones with an effective compass of about a fifth at the extreme tiptop of their ranges, and for contraltos with chest registers forced all over their compass in the manner of music hall singers, he employs the entire range of the human voice, demanding from everybody nearly two effective octaves. The bulk of the work lies easily in the middle of the voice, which is nevertheless well exercised all over, one part of it relieving the other healthily and continually. He uses the highest notes sparingly, and is ingeniously considerate in the matter of instrumental accompaniment. Even when the singer seems to dominate all the thunders of the full orchestra, a glance at the score will shew that he is well heard, not because of a stentorian voice, but because Wagner meant him to be heard. The old lazy Italian style of orchestral accompaniment as we find it in Rossini's Stabat or Verdi's Trovatore, where the strings play a rum-tum accompaniment whilst the whole wind band blares away, fortissimo, in unison with the singer, is somehow not so brutally opaque in practice as it looks on paper; but Wagner never condescends to it. Even in an ordinary opera house, with the orchestra ranged directly between the singers and the audience, his instrumentation is transparent to the human voice.

On every point, then, a Wagner theatre and Wagner festivals are much more generally practicable than the older and more artificial forms of dramatic music. A presentable performance of The Ring is a big undertaking only in the sense in which the construction of a railway is a big undertaking: that is, it requires plenty of work and plenty of professional skill; but it does not, like the old operas and oratorios, require those extraordinary vocal gifts which only a few individuals scattered here and there throughout Europe are born with. Singers who could never execute the roulades of Semiramis, Assur, and Arsaces in Rossini's Semiramide, could sing the parts of Brynhild, Wotan, and Erda without missing a note. Any Englishman can understand this if he considers for a moment the difference between a Cathedral service and an Italian opera at Covent Garden. The service is a much more serious matter than the opera. Yet provincial talent is sufficient for it, if the requisite industry and devotion are forthcoming. Even at the Opera I have seen lusty troopers and porters, without art or manners, accepted by fashion as principal tenors during the long interval between Mario and Jean de Reszke; and the two most extraordinary dramatic singers of the twentieth century, Chaliapin and Vladimir Rosing, are quite independent of the old metropolitan artificialities. Let us remember that Bayreuth has recruited its Parsifals from the peasantry, and that the artisans of a village in the Bavarian Alps are capable of a famous and elaborate Passion Play, and then consider whether any country is so poor in talent that its amateurs must journey to the centre of Europe to witness a Wagner Festival.

WAGNERISM WITH WAGNER LEFT OUT

In spite of the fact that my old suggestion of a Festival Playhouse on Richmond Hill has now been proved perfectly feasible as far as the availability of the necessary home talent is concerned, only one serious attempt to establish a Bayreuth in England has come to my knowledge; and that one, far from concerning itself with Wagner, owes its success to native British music with some early ultra-classical assistance from Gluck. Mr Rutland Boughton, who began his career as a composer when the influence of Wagner was at its height, has attempted to do in Somerset what Wagner did in Thuringia, with the very material difference that Wagner had the King of Bavaria at his back, and Mr Boughton had nothing material at his back at all. He selected Glastonbury as his Bayreuth; and has established an annual festival there which can already shew a remarkable record of work done. The very desperation of the enterprise has been its salvation. Had Mr Boughton been obsessed, as Wagner was, with the scale to which the Grand Operas of Paris, London, and Berlin work, he would have had to wait for a king to help him: that is, he would have waited for ever. Fortunately he remembered that Wagner was not only the highly professionalized royal conductor of Dresden, brought up in the belief that the only success that can hallmark an opera is a Meyerbeerian success at the Paris Opera: he was also the author of the saying that music is kept alive, not by the triumphs of fashionable commercial professionalism, but on the cottage piano of the amateur. Mr Rutland Boughton began in ordinary village halls in Somerset, with a piano and his own fingers for orchestra, his wife as scene painter and costumier, and a fit-up for a stage. The singing and acting was done by the villagers and by anyone else who would come; and a surprising number of quite distinguished talents did come. On these terms performances were achieved which in point of atmosphere and intimacy of interest were actually better than the performances at the enormously more pretentious Festival Playhouse in Bayreuth, or its copy the Prince Regent Theatre in Munich. There were friendly subscribers, not enough to prevent each festival from ruining Mr Boughton for six months or so, but enough to enable him to devote the remaining six months to preparation for another financial catastrophe, encouraged by the fact that the crashes were less and less disastrous as his enterprise became better and better known. His festival is now a yearly event in Avalon, once an island, now a city in a plain, Glastonbury, steeped in traditions which make it holy ground. But it still has no theatre, no electric light, no convenience for Wagnerian drama that every village does not possess. Yet it is here that the Wagnerist dream has been best realized in England.

That dream, truly interpreted, did not mean that the English soil should bring forth performances of Wagner's music copied from those at Bayreuth. It meant that the English soil should produce English music and English drama, and that English people should perform them in their own way. It is precisely because Mr Boughton has never performed a work of Wagner's, but, with the scholastic exception of an opera or two by Gluck, has composed his own music and had it and other English music sung in English ways, that he can claim to be a Perfect Wagnerite.

By this time there may be other and cognate experiments less known to me. During the twentieth century an important social development has transformed that costly and deleterious bore, the British holiday, into a genuinely recreative change. Under the title of Summer Schools, voluntary associations of artistically minded students of sociology, theosophy, science, history, and what not—shall we say people who take life, or some department of life, seriously, and cannot be happy unless they are using their brains and learning something in the intervals of dancing and singing for pure fun?—now appear every autumn in the prettiest country districts. These Schools are open to everybody; they afford intimate glimpses of more or less celebrated people who come and lecture to them for the sake of propaganda; and they are very much jollier, as well as substantially cheaper and more genial, than the so-called pleasure resorts in which irritable and overworked professional entertainers hypnotize credulous Britons into believing that they are enjoying themselves when they are only paying through the nose for being worried and pillaged. Where there were formerly only one or two elderly congresses, like the meetings of the British Association, with no activity but that of elderly lecturers all lecturing at the same time in different rooms, there are now dozens of smaller but more youthful and vital gatherings in which, whatever the main subject to be studied may be, Art is continually breaking in in one form or another.

I myself, after a larger experience of professionally and commercially organized art than most men can afford (for I had to earn my living as a critic of such art in my early days), find that it is at such gatherings and from such voluntary enterprises that I can oftenest recapture something of that magic which music and drama had for me in my childhood, and which it is so utterly impossible to preserve under commercial conditions. Commerce in art can save me from many ridiculous blunders and makeshifts that do not matter; but it seldom achieves the things that do matter, never indeed except when they are forced on it in spite of its teeth by some individual artist, mostly one heavily persecuted by it as Wagner was.

Amateur art is discredited art in so far only as the amateur is known as the ape of commercial art. Persons who go to the theatre and opera house only to be smitten with an infatuate ambition to reproduce in their own untrained persons what they see the great professional artists doing there, are mostly foredoomed to failure and ridicule. Here and there one of them succeeds, only to be absorbed by the commercial profession. But the countryside is full of stout characters with no such folly and no such ambition, who will do as much for any really gifted artistic leader as they have done for Mr Boughton and for the organizers of our provincial choirs and brass bands. If Little Bethel has raised the miners of England in a few generations from troglodyte savagery to pious respectability, Little Bayreuth may as easily raise them from pious respectability to a happy consciousness of and interest in fine art, without which all their piety and respectability will not save their children from resorting to cruel sports and squalid sensualities in their natural need for enjoyment. And so, good luck to Little Bayreuth; and may it be as successful as Little Bethel in demonstrating that the laughter of fools is as the crackling of thorns under a pot!

From LONDON MUSIC IN 1888–89 AS HEARD BY CORNO DI BASSETTO (LATER KNOWN AS BERNARD SHAW)

23 *January* 1889

MADAME PATTI kissed hands last night, in her artless way, to a prodigious audience come to bid her farewell before her trip to South America. The unnecessary unpleasantness of the most useful of Mr Louis Stevenson's novels makes it impossible to say that there is in Madame Patti an Adelina Jekyll and an Adelina Hyde; but there are certainly two very different sides to her public character. There is Patti the great singer: Patti of the beautiful eloquent voice, so perfectly produced and controlled that its most delicate pianissimo reaches the remotest listener in the Albert Hall: Patti of the unerring ear, with her magical *roulade* soaring to heavenly altitudes: Patti of the pure, strong tone that made God save the Queen sound fresh and noble at Covent Garden: Patti of the hushed, tender notes that reconcile rows of club-loving cynics to Home, sweet Home. This was the famous artist who last night sang *Bel raggio* and Comin' thro' the Rye incomparably. With Verdure Clad would also have been perfect but that the intonation of the orchestra got wrong and spoiled it. But there is another Patti: a Patti who cleverly sang and sang again some pretty nonsense from Delibes' Lakmé. Great was the applause, even after it had been repeated; and then the comedy began. Mr Ganz, whilst the house was shouting and clapping uproariously, deliberately took up his *bâton* and started Moszkowski's Serenata in D. The audience took its cue at once, and would not have Moszkowski. After a prolonged struggle, Mr Ganz gave up in despair; and out tripped the *diva*, bowing her acknowledgments in the character of a petted and delighted child. When she vanished there was more cheering than ever. Mr Ganz threatened the serenata again; but in vain. He appealed to the sentinels of the greenroom; and these shook their heads, amidst roars of protest from the audience, and at last, with elaborate gesture, conveyed in dumb show that they dare not, could not, would not, must not, venture to approach Patti again. Mr Ganz, with well-acted desolation, went on with the serenata, not one note of which was heard. Again he appealed to the sentinels; and this time they waved their hands expansively in the direction of South America, to indicate that the prima donna was already on her way thither. On this the audience showed such sudden and unexpected signs of giving in that the diva tripped out again, bowing, wafting kisses, and successfully courting fresh thunders of applause. Will not some sincere friend of Madame Patti's tell her frankly that she is growing too big a girl for this sort of thing, which imposes on nobody—not even on the infatuated gentlemen who write columns about her fans and jewels. No: the queens of song should leave the coquetry of the footlights to the soubrettes. How much more dignified was Madame Neruda's reception of the magnificent ovation which followed her playing of Bazzini's Ronde des Lutins!

It is unnecessary to say more of the rest of the programme than that *E che! fra voi la tema* brought back pleasantly the days when Mr Santley trod the stage, and that Wallace's ridiculous Let me like a Soldier Fall was treated as it deserves, even though it was Mr Edward Lloyd's breast that "expanded to the ball." Miss Gomez made a very favorable impression by her singing of Sir Arthur Sullivan's Sleep, my love, sleep. Madame Patti, it may be added, looks very well and strong, and her voice is as good as ever.

21 *February* 1889

ON Monday the editor of The Star summoned me to a private conference. "The fact is, my dear Corno," he said, throwing himself back in his chair and arranging his moustache with the diamond which sparkles at the end of his pen-handle, "I dont believe that music in London is confined to St James's Hall, Covent Garden, and the Albert Hall. People must sing and play elsewhere. Whenever I go down to speak at the big Town Halls at Shoreditch, Hackney, Stratford, Holborn, Kensington, Battersea, and deuce knows where, I always see bills at the door announcing oratorios, organ recitals, concerts by local Philharmonic and Orpheus societies, and all sorts of musical games. Why not criticise these instead of saying the same thing over and over again about Henschel and Richter and Norman Neruda and the rest?" I replied, as best I could, that my experience as a musical critic had left me entirely unacquainted with these outlandish localities and their barbarous minstrelsy; that I regarded London as bounded on the extreme north-east by Stonecutter Street, on the extreme south-west by Kensington Gore, on the south by the Thames, and on the north by the Strand and Regent-street. He assured me that the places he had mentioned actually existed; but that, as I was evidently hurt by the suggestion that I should condescend to visit them, he would hand the ticket he had just received for a Purcell-Handel performance at Bow, to Musigena. "What!" I exclaimed, "Purcell! the greatest of English composers, left to Musigena! to a man whose abnormal gifts in every other direction have blinded him to his utter ignorance of music!" "Well, the fact is" said the editor "Musigena told me only half an hour ago that he was at a loss to imagine how a writer so profound and accomplished as di Bassetto could be in music a mere superficial amateur." I waited to hear no more. Snatching the tickets from the editor's desk, I hastily ran home to get my revolver as a precaution during my hazardous voyage to the east end.

Then I dashed away to Broad-street, and asked the booking-clerk whether he knew of a place called Bow. He was evidently a man of extraordinary nerve, for he handed me a ticket without any sign of surprise, as if a voyage to Bow were the most commonplace event possible. A little later the train was rushing through the strangest places: Shoreditch, of which I had read in historical novels; Old Ford, which I had supposed to be a character in one of Shakespeare's plays; Homerton, which is somehow associated in my mind with pigeons; and Haggerston, a name perfectly new to me. When I got into the concert-room I was perfectly dazzled by the appearance of the orchestra. Nearly all the desks for the second violins were occupied by ladies: beautiful young ladies. Personal beauty is not the strong point of West-end orchestras, and I thought the change an immense improvement until the performance began, when the fair fiddlers rambled from bar to bar with a certain sweet indecision that had a charm of its own, but was not exactly what Purcell and Handel meant. When I say that the performance began, I do not imply that it began punctually. The musicians began to drop in at about ten minutes past eight, and the audience were inclined to remonstrate; but an occasional apology from the conductor, Mr F. A. W. Docker, kept them in good humor.

Dido and Eneas is 200 years old, and not a bit the worse for wear. I daresay many of the Bowegians thought that the unintentional quaintness of the amateurs in the orchestra were Purcellian antiquities. If so, they were never more mistaken in their lives. Henry Purcell was a great composer: a very great composer indeed; and even this little boarding-school opera is full of his spirit, his freshness, his dramatic expression, and his unapproached art of setting English speech to music. The Handel Society did not do him full justice: the work, in fact, is by no means easy; but the choir made up bravely for the distracting dances of the string quartet. Eneas should not have called Dido Deedo, any more than Juliet should call Romeo Ro-*may*-oh, or

Othello call his wife Days-*day*-mona. If Purcell chose to pronounce Dido English fashion, it is not for a Bow-Bromley tenor to presume to correct him. Belinda, too, was careless in the matter of time. She not only arrived after her part had been half finished by volunteers from the choir, but in Oft She Visits she lost her place somewhat conspicuously. An unnamed singer took Come away, fellow sailors, come away: that salt sea air that makes you wonder how anyone has ever had the face to compose another sailor's song after it. I quote the concluding lines, and wish I could quote the incomparably jolly and humorous setting:—

> Take a bowsy short leave of your nymphs on the shore;
> And silence their mourning
> With vows of returning,
> Though never intending to visit them more.

SAILORS (*greatly tickled*). Though never—!

OTHER SAILORS (*ready to burst with laughter*). Though never—!

ALL (*uproariously*). Inte-en-ding to vi-isit them more.

I am sorry to have to add that the Handel choir, feeling that they were nothing if not solemn, contrived to subdue this rousing strain to the decorum of a Sunday school hymn; and it missed fire accordingly. Of Alexander's Feast I need only say that I enjoyed it thoroughly, even though I was sitting on a cane-bottomed chair (Thackeray overrated this description of furniture) without adequate room for my knees. The band, reinforced by wind and organ, got through with a healthy roughness that refreshed me; and the choruses were capital. Mr Bantock Pierpoint, the bass, covered himself with merited glory, and Mr John Probert would have been satisfactory had he been more consistently careful of his intonation. Miss Fresselle acquitted herself fairly; but her singing is like that of the society generally: it lacks point and color. Mr Docker must cure his singers of the notion that choral singing is merely a habit caught in church, and that it is profane and indecorous to sing Handel's music as if it meant anything. That, however, is the worst I have to say of them. I am, on the whole, surprised and delighted with the East end, and shall soon venture there without my revolver. At the end of the concert, a gentleman, to my entire stupefaction, came forward and moved a vote of thanks to the performers. It was passed by acclamation, but without musical honors.

P.S. The Handel Society appeals urgently for tenors, a second bassoon, and horns. Surely every reader of The Star can at least play the second bassoon. Apply to Mr P. L. G. Webb, 3 Chandos Street, Cavendish Square, W.

31 *May* 1889

ELSEWHERE you will find a letter on The Music of the People, by Mr Marshall-Hall, a young composer who is much spoken of among the young lions of Mr Hamish McCunn's generation. At one of Mr Henschel's concerts Mr Santley sang some portions of an opera, the poem and music of which were by Mr Marshall-Hall. I was not at that concert, so I am quite out of it as far as Mr Marshall-Hall's music is concerned; but I am delighted to find him, as a representative of young genius, denouncing the stalls, trusting to the gallery, waving the democratic flag, and tearing round generally.

Young genius has rather a habit, by the way, of writing to my editor to denounce me as flippant and unenlightened, and to demand that I also shall tear round and proclaim the working man as the true knower and seer in Art. If I did, the working man would not think any the better of me; for he knows well enough that society is not divided into "animated clothes-pegs" on the one hand and lovers of Beethoven in ligatured corduroys on the other. For Beethoven purposes society is divided into people who can afford to keep a piano and go to operas and concerts, and people who cannot. Mr Marshall-Hall's idea that the people who cannot are nevertheless screwed up to concert pitch by honest, thorough, manly toil, shews that, though he be an expert in the music question, in the labor question he is a greenhorn.

Take a laborer's son; let him do his board-schooling mostly on an empty stomach; bring him up in a rookery tenement; take him away from school at thirteen; offer him the alternative of starvation or 12 to 16 hours work a day at jerry building, adulterated manufactures, coupling railway waggons, collecting tramway fares, field labor, or what not, in return for food and lodging which no "animated clothes-peg" would offer to his hunter; bully him; slave-drive him; teach him by every word and look that he is not wanted among respectable people, and that his children are not fit to be spoken to by their children. This is a pretty receipt for making an appreciator of Beethoven.

The truth is, that in the innumerable grades of culture and comfort between the millionaire on the one hand, and the casual laborer on the other, there is a maximum of relish for art somewhere. That somewhere is certainly not among the idle rich, whose appetites for enjoyment are not sharpened by work, nor is it among those who, worn out by heavy muscular toil, fall asleep if they sit quiet and silent for five minutes of an evening. Professional and business men of musical tastes who work hard, and whose brains are of such a quality that a Beethoven symphony is a recreation to them instead of an increased strain on their mental powers, are keen patrons of music, though, in outward seeming, they belong to the animated clothes-peg section. Middle-class young ladies, to whom there is no path to glory except that of the pianist or prima donna, frequent St James's Hall with astonishing persistence, and eventually form musical habits which outlast their musical hopes.

The musical public is the shilling public, by which I mean the people who can afford to pay not more than a shilling once a week or so for a concert without going short of more immediately necessary things. Music can be better nourished on shilling, sixpenny, and threepenny seats than on the St James's Hall scale. The laborers are so enormously numerous that the absolute number of their exceptional men—men who will buy books out of 13s. a week in the country and 18s. in a town, and find time to read them while working 12 hours a day—is considerable. The more comfortable members of the artisan class can often afford a shilling much better than the poorer middle-class families; but it has a certain customary and traditional scale of expenditure, in which concerts stand at threepence or sixpence, shillings being reserved for the gallery of a West-end theatre, and half-crowns for Sunday trips to Epping Forest and for extra refreshments.

After these come the innumerable "poor devils" of the middle class, always craving in an unaccountable way for music, and crowding the Promenade Concerts on classical nights, the Albert Hall gallery, and wherever else decent music is to be heard cheaply. To these three classes Mr Marshall-Hall must look for the little that is now possible in the way of a musical public. Even when we have supplied all three with as much music as they can stomach, the laborer in ligatured corduroys will still open his eyes to darkness, and the vapid snob grub like a blind puppy in the light. What we want is not music for the people, but bread for the people, rest for the people, immunity from robbery and scorn for the people, hope for them, enjoyment, equal respect and consideration, life and aspiration, instead of drudgery and despair. When we get that I imagine the people will make tolerable music for themselves, even if all Beethoven's scores perish in the interim.

Pending these millennial but perfectly practical measures, I must beg my readers not to blame me if the progress of the race makes it more and more apparent that the middle-class musical critic is the most ridiculous of human institutions. I do not take my function seriously, because it is impossible for an intelligent man to do so; and I am an eminently intelligent man. I often yield to quite romantic impulses. For instance, when Miss Adrienne Verity sent me a ticket for her concert at Collard's the other day, I went because Adrienne Verity struck me as being a pretty name. And I must own that I found her a pleasant-faced, well-grown lass, with refreshingly unceremonious ways and a healthy boisterousness which would make her the life and soul of a haymaking. But a singer! an artist! not yet. The way in which that young lady plunged into *Saper vorreste*, and rampaged through Be wise in time, and fired off Cherry Ripe at us, was bewildering. When ladies and children came forward with trophies of flowers, and did her floral homage as a Queen of Song, my brain reeled. And now I suppose that Miss Verity, having invited me to hear her sing, expects me to give her my opinion. My opinion is that she will either study hard with a competent teacher for a couple of years to come, learning to sing, to speak, to walk, to bow, and to abjure premature concerts and flower offerings, or else she will find a place in Mr D'Oyly Carte's or Mr Leslie's chorus, and there unskilfully scream her voice away in less than six months. And whoever gives her a more flattering opinion will do her a very cruel kindness.

Of the numerous concerts which I unavoidably missed, none caused me any particular regret, except the performance by pupils of the Royal Normal College for the Blind at the Crystal Palace, and a Board School contest at Hampstead, which the head master was quite right in bringing under my notice. It was, for example, much more important than Miss McKenzie's concert at Dudley House, which has been much written about, and concerning which I have nothing whatever to say except that it went off very successfully; that Mr Giddings amused me by his recitation; that the Dudley pictures interested me more than the music; and that the Dudley livery of black and yellow continually reminded me of the contrast between the gildings in Park-lane and the gloom of the coal pits wherein that gilding is made.

I need hardly say that my remarks about the Tonic Sol-Fa have brought letters upon me insisting on the attractive simplicity of the notation, and even inviting me to learn it myself forthwith. This reminds me of a sage whom I consulted in my youth as to how I might achieve the formation of a perfect character. "Young man," he said, "are you a vegetarian?" I promptly said "Yes" which took him aback. (I subsequently discovered that he had a weakness for oysters.) "Young man" he resumed "have you mastered Pitman's shorthand?" I told him I could write it very nearly as fast as longhand, but that I could not read it; and he admitted that this was about the maximum of human attainment in phonography. "Young man" he went on "do you understand phrenology?"

This was a facer, as I knew nothing about it; but I was determined not to be beaten, so I declared that it was my favorite pursuit, and that I had been attracted to him by the noble character of his bumps. "Young man" he continued "you are indeed high on the Mount of Wisdom. There remains but one accomplishment to the perfection of your character. Are you an adept at the Tonic Sol-Fa system?" This was too much. I got up in a rage, and said: "Oh, dash the Tonic Sol-Fa system!" Then we came to high words; and our relations have been more or less strained ever since. I have always resolutely refused to learn the Tonic Sol-Fa, as I am determined to prove that it is possible to form a perfect character without it.

From MUSIC IN LONDON 1890–94

13 *April* 1892

AT the Philharmonic Concert last week I went down during the interval to find out from the placards at the door whether the musical season was really so dull as I had gathered from the comparatively few concert invitations which had reached me. For I am never quite certain as to how much music may be going on behind my back. The people who only want puffs have given me up as a bad job; the concert-givers who cannot afford to have the truth told about their performances shun me like the plague; the spoiled children of the public are driven by a word of criticism into fits of magnificent sulking; the soft-hearted, uncritical patrons and patronesses, always regarding me as the dispenser of a great power of giving charitable lifts to hard-up people who have mistaken their profession, see plainly that since I reserve so much of my praise for comparatively well-to-do artists my favorable notices must be simply the outcome of invitations, chicken and champagne, smiles of beauty, five-pound notes and the like (I am far from wishing to discourage such realizable illusions); and the genuine enthusiasts, whenever I do not appreciate their pet artists and composers, will have it that I am an ignorant fellow, writing musical criticism for the gratification of my natural hatred of the sublime and beautiful. In brief, there is always a section of the musical world thoroughly convinced that, like the creditor who detained Sam Weller in the Fleet, I am "a malicious, badly disposed, vorldly-minded, spiteful, windictive creetur, with a hard heart as there aint no softnin." When a person, in passing through this harmless and transient madness, gives a concert or an opera, I am not invited; and as I never bias myself by reading advertisements or criticisms, I may quite easily, at any given moment, be the worst-informed man in London on every current musical topic except the quality of the performances I have actually attended.

Sometimes it is I who have to stand on the offensive, and exclude myself, in self-defence. The *entrepreneurs* who send me a couple of stalls the week before a concert, and a lawyer's letter the week after it, may be irascible gentlemen who must splutter in some direction from congenital inability to contain themselves, or they may be long-headed men of business who understand the overwhelming disadvantages at which the law of libel places every writer whose subject is completely outside the common sense of a British jury. But the effect on me is the same either way. The moment I understand that the appeal to law is not barred between myself and any artist or *entrepreneur*, I fly in terror from the unequal contest, and never again dare to open my lips, or rather dip my pen, about that litigious person.

No doubt, in the case of an *entrepreneur*, the fact that I dare not allude to the artists he brings forward is a disadvantage to them, to the public, and to myself; but I submit that the remedy is, not for me to defy the law and bring ruinous loss of time on myself and of money on my principals, nor for the artists, who are mostly foreigners and strangers, with no effective choice in the matter, to avoid litigious agents, but for the public, as electors and jurymen, to make criticism legal. Many innocent persons believe it to be so at present; but what are the facts?

Last season an opera-singer, of whom I am reminded by an uncomfirmed report of his death at Malta, had his performance criticized by my eminent colleague Mr Joseph Bennett in a manner which was almost culpably goodnatured. The artist, however, declared that the effect of the criticism was to open the eyes of impresarios to the undisputed fact that he was no longer in his prime; and, the paper in which the notice appeared being well able to pay any amount of damages, he sued it. The case was peculiarly favorable to the critic, as there was no difficulty in making even a jury see that the criticism erred only on the side of leniency. But one of the proofs of its justice was that it had depreciated the market value of the artist's services, as every unfavorable criticism must if it has any effect at all. The jury accordingly gave a verdict for the artist against the critic, putting the damages at a farthing to emphasize the fact that they considered that the critic would have been in the right if his occupation had been a lawful one. And if Mr. Bennett had called on me next day, and asked me in the common interests of our profession and of the public never to mention that artist's name again, he could have been indicted for conspiracy and imprisoned.

In spite of the adverse verdict, some critics expressed themselves as satisfied with the termination of the case, on the ground that the artist had a fine lesson, since he had gained nothing, and incurred both heavy costs and loss of reputation, not to mention such press boycotting as arises spontaneously from the *esprit de corps* of the critics without any express concert between them. No doubt this was so, though it does not offer the smallest set-off to the still heavier costs incurred by the defendants. But let us proceed from what actually happened on that occasion to what might have happened. Suppose the artist, instead of depending on his own resources, had been backed by a rich and influential impresario who had made up his mind to muzzle the press. If I were such an impresario I could do it in spite of all the boasted thunders of the Fourth Estate. First, I would take the young men; cultivate them; flatter them a little; wave my hand round the stalls, and say, "Come in whenever you like—always a place for you—always glad to see you." In this fashion I would make personal friends of them; invite them to garden-parties and introduce them to my artists; make them feel themselves a part of the artistic world of which I was the great solar centre; and give them hypnotic suggestions of my intentions in such a way as to create tremendous expectations of the artists I had in my managerial eye. No young man recently promoted from the uncomfortable obscurity of the amphitheatre or gallery, no matter how conceited he may be, knows enough of the value of his goodwill to suspect that a great impresario could have any motive beyond pure amiability in shewing so much kindness to a mere beginner in journalism. The old men would give me still less trouble. They would have learnt to live and let live: not a fault in my performances would they find that they had not pointed out over and over again twenty years ago, until they were tired of repeating themselves. I should not quarrel with them, nor they with me. What with the foolish critics who would think everything delightful as long as I made them happy, and the wise ones who would call everything beautiful as long as I made them comfortable, the ground would be cleared for my final *coup*. This, of course, would be struck at the few born critics—the sort of men who cannot help themselves, who know what good work is, crave for it, are tortured by the lack of it, will fight tooth and nail for it, and would do so even if the managers were their fathers and the prima donnas their sweethearts. These fellows would presently find their principals figuring as defendants in libel actions taken by my artists. They would learn from bitter experience that they must either hold their tongues about the shortcomings in my theatre, or else find themselves costing more in damages and lawyers' fees than any paper could afford to spend on its musical department alone; and the full accomplishment of this would not cost me a thousand pounds if I managed it adroitly. If one big manager can do this, what could not a ring of managers and concert-agents do by organizing a boycott against any obnoxious critic? They could drive him out of his profession, unless his danger roused his colleagues to the need for a counter-organization, which would not be easy in an occupation which employs so much casual and unskilled labor as musical criticism. In short, then, I pursue my present calling by sufferance—by a sort of informal Geneva convention, which puts actions-at-law in the same category with explosive bullets. When a combatant shews the least disposition to violate this convention, I prudently avoid him altogether. At the same time, I do not object to retorts in kind. The one manager with whom I feel on perfectly easy terms runs a paper of his own; and whenever I libel his enterprises in this column to the tune of £500 damages, he does not meanly take an action against me, but promptly fires off a round thousand worth of libels on me in his own paper. I appreciate his confidence as he appreciates mine; and we write reciprocally with complete freedom, whereas, if we suspected any possibility of litigiousness, we should never dare allude to one another.

I offer this little glimpse behind the scenes partly to explain to a bewildered public how it is that only the most desperate and ungovernable critics say half what they think about the shortcomings of the performances they sample, and partly to complete my reasons for going down to the entrance of St. James's Hall between the parts of the Philharmonic Concert to ascertain whether there was a tremendous eruption of musical activity going on unknown to me under the auspices of the gentlemen who shelter their enterprises from criticism beneath the shield of Dodson and Fogg.

But there was nothing of the sort: the season has not recovered from the discouragement of the failure of the concerts given by the Manchester band, and the recoil after the disastrous over-speculation of the year before last, when the program of each week was as long as the program for the month is now. At the Philharmonic concert in question, the chief attraction was Joachim, who played Bruch's new concerto badly—outrageously, in fact—for the first twenty bars or so, and then recovered himself and played the rest splendidly. The orchestra played Mr. Cowen's *suite de ballet*, entitled The Language of Flowers, very prettily, though the audience must have felt that, in the absence of any dancing, the performance was much as if Mr. Cowen had arranged the accompaniments of some of his songs for the band, and given them without the aid of a singer.

As to the other pieces, I am sorry to say that their execution shewed a relapse into the old Philharmonic faults from the standard reached at the Mozart Concert. The death-song from Tristan, with which Madame Nordica did so well at the London Symphony Concert under Henschel, fell flat:

every time the orchestra began to rise at it Mr. Cowen threw up his hand in agony lest the singer should be drowned. There was not the slightest danger of that. And, if there had been, she would probably have preferred to risk it rather than have her only chance at the concert spoiled, as it was, by being handled like a trumpery drawing room ballad. I call it her only chance; for I am quite sure that Madame Nordica will agree with me that she was not up to her highest standard of brilliancy and smoothness of execution in the polacca from Mignon.

For the rest, nothing but the *suite de ballet*, and perhaps the Cherubini overture, had been sufficiently rehearsed; and the old complaints of superficiality, tameness, dullness, and so on, have begun again. The fact is, that the Philharmonic thinks its band above the need for rehearsing as carefully as its rivals. But since superiority in London means superiority to first-rate competitors, it can only be secured by the hardest workers. And that is why the Philharmonic is the worst band of its class in London, and will remain so until it sets to work in earnest, instead of simply getting one of its directors to write Panglossian puffs for circulation among the audience, assuring them and the "bigoted" critics that the Society is the best of all possible societies, and the conductor the best of all possible conductors. It had much better give its conductor a fair chance, by either shortening its programs or multiplying its rehearsals, and insisting on a full attendance at each of them.

At the Crystal Palace concert last Saturday I heard a new note in the orchestra, and traced it to the first flute, Mr. Fransella, whom I have not, as far as I know, had the pleasure of hearing before, but who shewed himself a fine artist, fully worthy of the post he has just taken. Mr. Arthur Hervey's Overture in G has a Fate motive and a Love motive, transformable into one another; this being the latest development of double counterpoint, which used to mean merely that two simultaneously played parts would sound equally well when you turned them upside down. It shewed how easily a man of artistic taste and intelligence, with a dash of imagination, can turn out imposing tone-poems. Mr. Hervey handles the orchestra and manages his themes with such freedom and ingenuity that I hope he will try his hand at something more interesting to me than fate and love, for which, in the abstract, I do not care two straws. The pianist at this concert was Mr Lamond, who played a swinging concerto of Tchaikowsky's in the Cyclopean manner, impetuous and formidable, but a little deficient in eloquence of style and sensitiveness of touch.

Miss Gambogi sang Mercé dilette well enough to justify her in having attempted it, which is no small praise; whilst another singer, a gentleman who had evidently often brought off Dio possente with applause on the stage, discovered that the only operatic method known to the Crystal Palace audience was pure singing, which unluckily happened to be his weak point.

2 August 1893

SHALL SIR AUGUSTUS HAVE A TESTIMONIAL?

I HAVE received a circular letter, which I give here in full, although some of my readers will have already seen it elsewhere. Its reappearance in this column may be the means of adding a few more donations to the one which it announces.

Proposed Testimonial to Sir Augustus Harris

To the Editor

Sir,—As a very old musician, and one that admires talent, energy, and perseverance, I have watched with keen interest the extraordinary success which has attended the efforts of Sir Augustus Harris to establish in this country an opera worthy of the name, and in accordance with the best traditions of its history. This, in my own opinion, deserves some sort of public recognition, and I have therefore ventured to suggest that all lovers of high-class music, and all admirers of managerial enterprise, should be invited to subscribe towards an appropriate souvenir which shall serve as a testimonial to the Impresario of our Royal Opera House, who, for the reasons just stated, I cannot but regard as a benefactor to his country.

Except for the unceasing exertions of Sir Augustus Harris, and his persistent determination to revive our Covent Garden Opera at any personal cost or sacrifice, that time-honored institution would have long since died a natural death. Indeed, at one period it gave sufficient promise of becoming for ever extinct, in spite of the repeated attempts of La Porte, Lumley, E. T. Smith, Gye, and Mapleson to save it from this doom. At last people began to believe that the failures were due not so much to want of managerial enterprise as to want of operatic attractions, and it was said that the "palmy days" of opera—which I myself so well remember—were completely over, never to be revived again. This was, however, by no means the view taken by the present Manager of Covent Garden. In his own estimation, there were as many good fish in the operatic sea as were ever produced out of it. So Sir Augustus Harris betook himself to the Continent, and ransacked every leading opera-house there, with the result that he returned triumphant with a company which, regarded as a whole, I have no hesitation in pronouncing the completest and most brilliant that has ever yet appeared upon the boards of Covent Garden during her Majesty's reign.

It is in view of these circumstances that I have proposed to open the fund for the souvenir already referred to, under the title of "The Operatic Testimonial Fund," and I shall be pleased to head the list of subscribers to it by a donation of ten guineas. Should the readers of this letter be disposed to follow my example in any way, their contributions, whether in the form of cheques or otherwise, will be received by the National Bank, Oxford Street Branch, if sent on behalf of "The Operatic Testimonial Fund."—I am, Sir, yours, etc.

(Signed) HENRY RUSSELL.

18 Howley Place, Maida Vale, July 26th, 1893.

Now I have no objection on general grounds to a testimonial to Sir Augustus, though I would not, if I were Mr Russell, call it an "operatic" testimonial. Let it by all means be a genuine, enthusiastic, munificently subscribed and influentially patronized tribute; and since Sir Augustus knows what is due to himself, let us not insult him with anything meaner than a life-size statue of solid gold, with suitable quotations from the opera criticisms in the Sunday Times on the four sides of the pedestal. And let Mr Henry Russell, as the leader of the enterprise, inaugurate the monument by once more singing I am not mad; by heavens! I am not mad.

But it would be a mistake, as well as a very left-handed compliment, to attribute to our illustrious impresario any design to revive the palmy days. Mr Russell was born more than forty years before I was, and so belongs to a younger period of the world's history. I am therefore to all intents and purposes his senior; and I can assure him, as one who remembers the end of the palmy days, and whose youth was blighted by their accursed traditions, that they deserved their fate, and are not only dead, but—I use the word in the profoundest serious sense—damned. If you discuss them with one of their veteran admirers, you will find that all the triumphs which his memory fondles are not feats of management, but strokes of genius by individual artists. Indeed, so far is he from being able to conceive an operatic performance as an artistic whole, that he will describe the most absurd *contretemps* and the most disastrous shortcomings in the stage management, the band, chorus, dresses and scenery, as excellent jokes.

My readers will remember the examples of this which I was able to give from Santley's Student and Singer, culminating in his playing Don Giovanni for the first time after one rehearsal, at which the tenor (Mario) did not turn up until it was half over. As to the mutilations, the spurious scorings, the "additional accompaniments," and the dozen other violations of artistic good faith which were played off on palmy nights as a matter of course, you will find the average veteran either unconscious of them or utterly unconcerned about them. He is content to remember Ambrogetti as "the Don" (an almost centenarian reminiscence), Piccolomini as Zerlina, Taglioni as La Sylphide, Malibran as Amina, Grisi and Rubini, Tamburini and Lablache in the Puritani quartet; and so on up to Titiens and Giuglini, and those post-Giuglinian days when "the mantle of Mario" was tried on every trooper, porter, or ice-barrow man who could bawl a high C, until at last the jeremiads of Berlioz and Wagner were fulfilled, and palmy Italian opera, which had been corrupt even in its prime, openly putrified and had to be embalmed, in which condition its mummy still draws audiences in the United States and other back-eddies of civilization.

Mr Russell, under the impression that he is paying Sir Augustus a compliment, accuses him of having tried to play the resurrection-man. I believe this to be unjust. I admit that there are certain scattered materials for Mr Russell's case—tentative Favoritas, Lucias, and Trovatores (palmy style, with Signor Rawner as Manrico), which had a somewhat retrograde air; but they cannot outweigh the broad fact that the Italian operas which were the staple of the old repertory are the mere stopgaps and makeshifts of the new. If the testimonial is to be given for palminess, then let it be transferred to Colonel Mapleson, whose gallant attempt to revive the old repertory in competition with Sir Augustus a few years ago utterly failed. And the failure was so certain from the first, that for the sake of old times I refrained from attending a single performance, although I have no doubt that I could have had three or four rows of stalls any night for the asking. No, Covent Garden has its defects, as I have had occasionally to remark; but such as it is, it has been created by Sir Augustus, and is no mere revival of the palmy imposture which still takes in Mr Russell.

Is Sir Augustus then, as Mr Russell says, "a benefactor to his country"? The standard definition of a national benefactor is "the man who causes two blades of grass to grow where one grew before." Now Sir Augustus, on the contrary, has caused one opera-house to keep open where two kept open before. But I do not think he ought to be disqualified on so highly technical a point. He established an opera where, for the moment, there was no opera at all; and if this was not a benefaction I do not know what is.

Therefore, instead of churlishly asking why he should have a testimonial, let us rather ask why he should not have one, and why Mr D'Oyly Carte should not have one, and why Signor Lago should not have one, and why, above all, I should not have one? Signor Lago discovered Giulia Ravogli and Ancona, Orfeo and Cavalleria; and although Sir Augustus is no doubt right in preferring to take his own discoveries ready-made, still, the original discoverer is useful in his little way too, and should not be overlooked. Mr D'Oyly Carte founded a new school of English comic opera; raised operatic inscenation to the rank of a fine art; and finally built a new English Opera House, and made a magnificent effort to do for English grand opera what he had done for comic opera, with the result that Sir Augustus is now conducting a music-hall on the ruins of the enterprise.

As to my own claims, modesty forbids me to ask whose pen has done more to revive public interest in dramatic music during the past five or six years than mine. It is true that I have done it because I have been paid to do it; but even Sir Augustus does not play the public benefactor for nothing. A man must live. Take the case of August Manns, whose enormous services to music in England do not need the penetrating eye of an octogenarian to discover them: even he does not scorn to accept his bread-and-butter. If there is any spare cash left in the country when the Harris testimonial is fully subscribed, some little token—say a cheap conducting stick—might be offered to the untitled Augustus of Sydenham.

But now that I think of it, such a proceeding might be construed as a slight to the conducting staff at Covent Garden. And we must not thoughtlessly appear to undervalue what Sir Augustus has done for us in placing his orchestra in the hands of three such *chefs* as Mancinelli, Bevignani, and Randegger. Although they are so devoted to the traditions of the house that Sir Augustus has to send to Germany for help whenever the Nibelungen dramas are performed, yet Mancinelli can conduct Die Meistersinger and Bevignani Tannhäuser in a way that I am sure I for one can never forget. Why not give them testimonials? The stage manager, too—he who staged Gluck's Orfeo and Das Rheingold—that "damned pantomime," as somebody is said to have called it—why should not something be done for him! But I am opening up too vast a field. There are so many public benefactors about.

I should be less than candid on the subject, however, if I were to take the proposal quite uncritically. I do not see how it is possible for an impresario to maintain Covent Garden in such a fashion as to deserve a testimonial as a public benefactor. As I have often pointed out, fashionable grand opera does not pay its own expenses in London any more than it does in Paris or Berlin. A subvention is necessary; and if the State does not provide it, a body of private guarantors must. In England there are so many irrational people who think the National Gallery and the British Museum virtuous and Opera vicious (because it takes place in a theater), that the State leaves Covent Garden to a knot of rich people for whom Opera is not a form of art but simply an item of fashion. These people pay the piper; and they naturally expect to call the tune.

Now suppose an artist or a clique of artists get at the guarantors behind the impresario's back, they can make it very difficult for him to do anything that they disapprove of, whether it be in the public interest or not. To such means of resistance to the manager must be added the already enormous powers possessed by leading artists in virtue of their personal monopoly of voice and talent. The impresario's one defence is his own monopoly of the power of making London reputations. To preserve this monopoly and at the same time to provide for the danger always latent in the fact that London will support one guaranteed Opera handsomely, but not two, he must strain all his commercial genius to suppress competition; and this means not only taking every theatre large enough to be used as a rival house, but engaging several superfluous artists for the sole purpose of forestalling their possible engagement by someone else, the result being, of course, to waste their talents most frightfully.

Finally, he must by hook or crook, by conciliation or intimidation, gag independent criticism, because his greatest need is prestige, and this the press can mar if it chooses. His prestige is his life-blood: it convinces meddling guarantors and mutinous artists that he is the only possible man to run the Italian Opera; and it paralyses his competitors, making their attempts to raise a rival guarantee unavailing, and stamping them from the outset as second rate. And this prestige, which is at once his sword and shield, propagates itself by all the operations which he undertakes for its sake. The theatres leased and kept closed, or sublet on conditions which bar opera; the magnificent list of artists engaged apparently out of an insatiable artistic enthusiasm which takes no account of salaries; even the running of two sets of performances to prevent the superfluous artists from eating their heads off: all these master-moves, with the huge turnover of money they involve, heap prestige on prestige, until at last the public gets dazzled, and ancient men call for testimonials to the national benefactor.

Then there is only one enemy left; and that is the unhypnotizable critic who, having his own prestige to look after, persists in explaining the situation to the public and criticizing the performances for just what they are worth, and no more. And such critics are scarce, not because of their Roman virtue, but because they must have an eye for the economics of the situation; and a musical critic who is a bit of an economist as well is a very rare bird.

Under these circumstances I do not see how the public services of Sir Augustus as impresario can run to a testimonial. However high-mindedly and ably he may have struggled to do his best within the limits of his very narrow freedom of action, or however Napoleonically he may have faced and fought the opposing economic forces, the fact remains that Covent Garden, with all its boasted resources, could not put the four Nibelung dramas on the stage last year except by the pure showman's expedient of sending for a German company, orchestra, conductor and all.

I do not blame Sir Augustus for this: I pointed out again and again (before the event as well as after) that the real difficulty was the incorrigible *fainéantise* of the De Reszkes, with their perpetual schoolboy Faust and Mephistopheles,

Roméo and Frère Laurent, and their determination to make Covent Garden a mere special edition of the Paris Grand Opera. Sir Augustus did contrive to get one triumph out of Jean de Reszke and Lassalle—Die Meistersinger. But from the moment when Jean allowed Alvary to take Siegfried from him, and Edouard left Wotan to Grengg (I hope I have the name correctly), there was an end of all possibility of a testimonial for Covent Garden.

Give me one performance of Die Walküre or Siegfried by the De Reszkes, Calvé, and Giulia Ravogli, with the orchestral work done by the regular band of the house, and a competent conductor of the calibre of Richter or Faccio in permanent command, and then Mr Russell may apply again. At present I am not at home.

Let me point out, however, that there may be an opening on the dramatic side, as to which I, of course, cannot speak. Sir Augustus is famous for his pantomimes and popular dramas, in producing which he is unhampered by guarantors or tenors, and can face competition without misgiving. My duties as musical critic make me a stranger to his work in this department. There, where his qualities have fuller scope, no doubt they take effect in the high artistic temper and wholesome moral atmosphere of his productions. If so, perhaps my friend W. A. will give Mr Russell's project his blessing and his subscription.

10 *January* 1894

I AM, I suppose, in the west country, by which I mean generally any place for which you start from Paddington. To be precise, I am nowhere in particular, though there are ascertained localities within easy reach of me. For instance, if I were to lie down and let myself roll over the dip at the foot of the lawn, I should go like an avalanche into the valley of the Wye. I could walk to Monmouth in half an hour or so. At the end of the avenue there is a paper nailed to a tree with a stencilled announcement that The Penalt Musical Society will give a concert last Friday week (I was at it, as shall presently appear); and it may be, therefore, that I am in the parish of Penalt, if there is such a place. But as I have definitely ascertained that I am not in England either ecclesiastically or for the purposes of the Sunday Closing Act; as, nevertheless, Wales is on the other side of the Wye; and as I am clearly not in Ireland or Scotland, it seems to follow that I am, as I have honestly admitted, nowhere. And I assure you it is a very desirable place—a land of quietly beautiful hills, enchanting valleys, and an indescribable sober richness of winter coloring. This being so, need I add that the natives are flying from it as from the plague? Its lonely lanes, where, after your day's work, you can wander amid ghosts and shadows under the starry firmament, stopping often to hush your footsteps and listen to a wonderful still music of night and nature, are eagerly exchanged for sooty streets and gaslamps and mechanical pianos playing the last comic song but two. The fact is, wages in the district do not reflect the sufficiency of the scenery: hence ambitious young men forsake their birthplace to begrime themselves in "the tinworks," symbolic of the great manufacturing industries of the nation, which have all, figuratively speaking, the production of tin as their final cause. I cannot walk far without coming upon the ruins of a deserted cottage or farmhouse. The frequency of these, and the prevalence of loosely piled stone walls instead of hedges, gives me a sensation of being in Ireland which is only dispelled by the appearance of children with whole garments and fresh faces acquainted with soap. But even children are scarce, the population being, as far as I can judge, about one sixth of a human being per square mile. The only fit pleasures of the place are those of contemplation. Yet one day, as I was coasting a neighboring valley, the sylvan echoes were wakened by an abjectly monotonous Too Too too-too-too-too, Too Too too too-tooting on a poor sort of horn; and presently a huntsman appeared jogging along, followed by a pack of hounds full of eager excitement, which they had to waste, for want of anything else to do, in a restless wagging of their multitudinous tails which quite hid their bodies from me, exactly as the swordsman in the German tale kept himself dry in a shower of rain by waving his sword above his head. Then came some young gentlemen, their bored human instincts struggling with those which they shared with the pack. With them were many older men, of whom a few, if my observation is to be trusted, eke out their incomes by selling horses to the younger ones. Usually, when the hunt is up, my sympathies are with the fox, and I have nothing but contemptuous indignation for its pursuers; but on this occasion the foxless cortège, as it clattered slowly along, comforting itself with flasks and sandwiches, was such a hopeless failure that I pitied it, and would have even provided it with a quarry had I possessed a spirited young tiger or other carnivorous animal able to bring out the manly qualities which are the pride of the sportsman. Had these hunters been wise, they would have satiated their destructive instincts by criticizing musical performances in town, and devoted their country holidays to benevolence and poetry.

There is a band in this place. Two little cornets, four baritone saxhorns, and a euphonium, all rather wasted for want of a competent person to score a few airs specially for them; for the four saxhorns all play the same part in unison instead of spreading themselves polyphonically over the desert between the cornets and the tuba. When their strains burst unexpectedly on my ear on Christmas Day, I supposed, until I went cautiously to the window to reconnoitre, that there were only three instruments instead of seven. With a parish organist to set this matter right for them, and a parish bandmaster to teach them a few simple rules of thumb as to the manipulation of their tuning-slides, the seven musicians would have discoursed excellent music. I submit that, pending the creation of a Ministry of Music, the Local Government Board should appoint District Surveyors of Brass Bands to look after these things. There are also carol singers; but of them I have nothing to say except that the first set, consisting of a few children, sang with great spirit a capital tune which I shall certainly steal when I turn my attention seriously to composition. The second set came very late, and had been so hospitably entertained at their previous performances that they had lost that clearness of intention and crispness of execution which no doubt distinguished their earlier efforts.

But the great event of the Penalt season was the concert. It was taken for granted that I, as an eminent London critic, would hold it in ineffable scorn; and it was even suggested that I should have the condescension to stay away. But, as it happened, I enjoyed it more than any native did, and that, too, not at all derisively, but because the concert was not only refreshingly different from the ordinary London miscellaneous article, but much better. The difference began with the adventurousness of the attempt to get there. There were no cabs, no omnibuses, no lamps, no policemen, no pavement, and, as it happened, no moon or stars. Fortunately, I have a delicate sense of touch in my boot-soles, and this enabled me to discriminate between road and common in the intervals of dashing myself against the gates which I knew I had to pass. At last I saw a glow in the darkness, and an elderly countryman sitting in it with an air of being indoors. He turned out to be the bureau, so to speak; and I was presently in the concert-room, which was much more interesting than St James's Hall, where there is nothing to look at except the pictures of mountain and glacier accidentally made—like faces in the fire—by the soot and dust in the ventilating lunettes in the windows. Even these are only visible at afternoon concerts. Here there was much to occupy and elevate the mind pending the appearance of the musicians: for instance, there was St Paul preaching at Athens after Raphael, and the death of General Wolfe after West, with a masonic-looking document which turned out to be the school time-table, an extensive display of flags and paraffin lamps, and an ingenious machine on the window-blind principle for teaching the children to add up sums of money of which the very least represented about eleven centuries of work and wages at current local rates. It presently appeared that the Penalt Musical Society had adopted one of the most advanced suggestions in Wagner's famous Dresden plan for the reformation of the theatre: to wit, the constitution of a Concert and Theatre department under the Minister of Public Worship. In Penalt, accordingly, the music was under the supreme control of the clergyman. He was conductor, he was accompanist, he was *entrepreneur*, he was (in emergencies) leader of the choir, he was chairman, he was master of the ceremonies, and he had written and composed all the comic songs and trios on local topics. He even mingled the politician and sociologist with the composer—again reminding one of Wagner in Dresden; for one of his compositions dealt with the Parish Councils Bill, and another with the recent coal difficulties. Furthermore, he had rehearsed the concert thoroughly; and this is the beginning and the end of true righteousness.

The program shewed how varied are the resources of a country parish compared to the helplessness of a town choked by the density and squalor of its own population. We had glees—Hail, Smiling Morn, The Belfry Tower, etc.—by no means ill sung. We had feats of transcendent execution on the pianoforte, in the course of which the Men of Harlech took arms against a sea of variations, and, by opposing, ended them to the general satisfaction. But it was from the performances of the individual vocalists that I received the strongest sense that here, on the Welsh border, we were among a naturally musical and artistic folk. From the young lady of ten who sang When you and I were young, to the robust farmer-comedians who gave the facetious and topical interludes with frank enjoyment and humor, and without a trace of the vulgarity which is the heavy price we have to pay for professionalism in music, the entertainment was a genuine and spontaneous outcome of the natural talent of the people. The artists cost nothing: the pianoforte-tuner, the printer, and the carpenter who fixed the platform can have cost only a few shillings. Comparing the result with certain "grand concerts" at St James's Hall, which have cost hundreds of pounds, and left me in a condition of the blankest pessimism as to the present and future of music in England, I am bound to pronounce the Penalt concert one of the most successful and encouraging of the year.

If I dared, I should proceed to criticize the singers in detail. But only an experienced critic knows the frightful danger of doing this. Everywhere alike, in the most outlandish village and the greatest capital, amateur singers are the same—one incautious word of appreciation and they are off to study for the operatic stage, abandoning all their real opportunities in life for a doubtful chance of reaching that mirage which looks like the Albert Hall and the Opera, but which is really a huge casual ward of vagabonds and humbugs, whose punishment for having attempted to make Art their catspaw in snatching at riches and fame is perpetual envy and disappointment. Let me, therefore, explicitly forewarn all concerned that when I confess to having been touched and charmed by some of the songs—nay, to having caught a gleam of that "sacred fire" of which we used to talk long ago in the performance of He thinks I do not love him, and of Mr Blockley's old-fashioned setting of Tennyson's O swallow, swallow, I do not mean that if the singers had been transferred from the little schoolroom and the mild cottage-piano to the stage of Covent Garden or the platform of St James's Hall, with a full orchestra thundering round them, they could have produced the same effect. Suffice it that they did produce it in Penalt, and gave me thereby greater pleasure than I often get from singers with far greater pretensions. And in one respect their superiority was absolute as well as relative. All their voices were unspoiled. They sang in low keys and used their chest registers a good deal; but the moment the music went above the natural range of that register they unaffectedly quitted it for the comparatively light and unassertive, but sweet and pure falsetto. Need I add that they were untaught, though they probably do not know how heartily they are to be congratulated on that fact. One lady, who sang modern drawing room ballads by Stephen Adams and Weatherly, rather alarmed me at first by a very effective use of her lower notes, as if she were determined to rival Miss Mackenzie. Not that I objected to her using them effectively, but I feared that she would presently try to force that rich quality of tone all over her voice. But no: she also was content to have that quality only where Nature gave it to her; and when the concert was over and we all plunged again into the black void without, where we jostled one another absurdly in our efforts to find the way home, I had quite made up my mind to advise all our fashionable teachers of singing to go to the singers of Penalt, consider their ways, and be wise.

13 June 1894

DR VILLIERS STANFORD has been favoring us with his views on Some Aspects of Musical Criticism in England in the shape of a magazine article. I am very strongly tempted to quote it here at full length; for it is the best article I ever saw on the subject, unexceptionally judicious and accurate, and much better written than most musical criticisms are. I shall at least quote his exposition of his main point, as I cannot paraphrase it to any advantage:

"A new opera, which has been, perhaps, the work of years, and the outcome of the daily thought and labor of composer and librettist, is produced on a Monday night; and by 2 A.M. on Tuesday morning a critic, who has just made his first acquaintance with the composition, is expected to have completed a full and just chronicle of its merits and faults, its workmanship and its effect, fit to be put into print, and intended to instruct the public before breakfast as to what attitude they should be prepared to take when they find themselves in the audience. I say, as one who is, from much experience in the musician's craft, perhaps exceptionally quick in seizing the points of a new work at first hearing, that to expect the best possible criticism, or indeed criticism of any lasting value at all under such circumstances is grotesque; and the insistence upon such hot haste production is a hardship to the writer, an injury to the producer, and a mischief to the public."

True as this is, and deeply as I am touched by the tribute here implied, and elsewhere explicitly rendered, to the superiority of those weekly articles of which my own may be taken as examples, I am not sure that the opinion elaborated in a week is always so much more valuable than the impression made in a moment. The only musical compositions which will bear thinking of for more than half an hour are those which require an intimate acquaintance of at least ten years for their critical mastery. As to the weekly article being any more "just" than the daily one, I do not see how that can be sustained for a moment. Let us try to vivify our ideas on the subject by getting away from the abstraction "criticism" to the reality from which it is abstracted: that is, the living, breathing, erring, human, nameable and addressable individual who writes criticism.

To avoid getting into trouble I shall not cite any musical critics. The dramatic and parliamentary ones will serve my turn as well. Two of the best dramatic critics in London, Mr Clement Scott and Mr Walkley, write both weekly essays and two-o'clock-in-the-morning notices of new plays. Both write the immediate notice as impressionists. Mr Scott writes his deferred notice also as an impressionist, rubbing in his first impression, and as often as not spoiling it. Mr Walkley is an acute analyst; and in his case the gain in intellectual elaboration in the deferred notice is immense. But has anyone ever observed any gain in either case in the matter of justice? I certainly never have.

Take another case in point. I have for years urged upon editors the necessity of sending a fine critic into the House of Commons to write notices of the sittings of the House exactly as they send a critic to the Opera. The result of giving such a critic a brief for Lord Rosebery against Lord Salisbury is as absurd as it would be to give me a brief for Calvé as against Melba, or my colleague W. A. a brief for Mr Irving as against Mr Tree. Of late years the custom of prefacing the verbatim reports of the sittings of the House by a descriptive report has been developing parliamentary criticism on my lines.

For example, Mr Massingham, a typical parliamentary critic of the new kind, will, in criticizing a debate, praise the performances of Mr Balfour and Mr John Burns, and slate Sir William Harcourt and Mr Chamberlain, or vice versa, as if there were no such thing as party politics in the world. This sounds impartial; but does anybody find Mr Massingham "just"; or is it likely that he would be any the juster if his extraordinary small-hour performances were replaced by weekly ones? The fact is, justice is not the critic's business;

and there is no more dishonest and insufferable affectation in criticism than that impersonal, abstract, judicially authoritative air which, since it is so easy to assume, and so well adapted to rapid phrase stringing, is directly encouraged by the haste which Dr Stanford deprecates.

In Dr Stanford's article, which is a masterpiece in the way of tact, no individual critic now alive and working on the English press is talked either of or at. Instead, we have "the critic," "the musical correspondent," and so on. Now "the critic" is a very fine character. One can quite believe that if only the noble creature is given time to consider his utterances, he will hold the scales balanced to a hair's breadth. But just substitute for "the critic" the initials G. B. S. Instantly the realities of the case leap to light; and you see without any argument that the lapse of a few days between the performance and the notice, far from obliterating the writer's partialities and prejudices, his personal likes and dislikes, his bias, his temperament, his local traditions, his nationality—in a word, himself, only enables him to express them the more insidiously when he wishes to conceal their influence.

No man sensitive enough to be worth his salt as a critic could for years wield a pen which, from the nature of his occupation, is scratching somebody's nerves at every stroke, without becoming conscious of how monstrously indefensible the superhuman attitude of impartiality is for him. If the countless injustices which I have done in these columns had been perpetrated in that attitude I should deserve hanging. I therefore add to Dr Stanford's plea for the more considerate utterance of the weekly feuilleton, a further plea for sincerity of expression, not only of the critic's opinion, but of the mood in which that opinion was formed.

We cannot get away from the critic's tempers, his impatiences, his sorenesses, his friendships, his spite, his enthusiasms (amatory and other), nay, his very politics and religion if they are touched by what he criticizes. They are all there hard at work; and it should be his point of honor—

as it is certainly his interest if he wishes to avoid being dull—not to attempt to conceal them or to offer their product as the dispassionate dictum of infallible omniscience. If the public were to receive such a self exhibition by coldly saying, "We dont want to know the sort of person you are: we want to know whether such a work or artist or performance is good or bad," then the critic could unanswerably retort, "How on earth can you tell how much my opinion on that point is worth unless you know the sort of person I am?" As a matter of fact the public never does meet a good critic with any such rebuff. The critic who cannot interest the public in his real self has mistaken his trade: that is all.

Dr Stanford touches a painful point when he speaks of "the danger that editors who happen themselves to be ignorant of music, should engage the services of writers almost equally ignorant merely because they possess the gift of literary style." Here, for almost the only moment in his article, Dr Stanford speaks without inside knowledge of journalism. Editors, by some law of Nature which still baffles science, are *always* ignorant of music, and consequently always abjectly superstitious on the subject. Instead of looking the more keenly to the critic's other qualifications because they cannot judge of his musical ones, they regard him with an awe which makes them incapable of exercising any judgment at all about him.

Find me an editor who can tell at a glance whether a review, a leading article, a London letter, or a news paragraph is the work of a skilled hand or not, and who has even some power of recognizing what is money's worth and what is not in the way of a criticism of the Royal Academy or the last new play; and I, by simply writing that "the second subject, a graceful and flowing theme contrasting happily with the rugged vigor of its predecessor, appears unexpectedly in the key of the dominant," will reduce that able editor to a condition so abject that he will let me inundate his columns with pompous platitude, with the dullest plagiarisms from analytic programs, with shameless puffery, with bad grammar, bad logic, wrong dates, wrong names, with every conceivable blunder and misdemeanor that a journalist can commit, provided I do it in the capacity of his musical critic.

Not that my stuff will not bore and worry him as much as it will bore and worry other people; but what with his reluctance to risk a dispute with me on a subject he does not understand, and his habit of considering music as a department of lunacy, practised and read about by people who are not normally sane and healthy human beings, he will find it easiest to "suppose it is all right" and to console himself with the reflection that it does not matter anyhow. Dr Stanford says, "If editors appoint an incompetent person, public opinion is pretty sure, sooner or later, to find out and expose the ignoramus." This expectation is so entirely and desperately unwarranted by experience, that I may take it that Dr Stanford only offers it rather than leave the difficulty without at least a pretense of a solution.

But why not form a Vigilance Committee of musicians for the exposure of incompetent critics? The other day, as we all remember, five eminent musicians published a protest against a certain musical critic. Being new to their work, they did not do it well; and the critic got the best of it; but I sincerely hope the five will not be discouraged. After a few trials, a Vigilance Committee would learn to attack cautiously and effectively, and to avoid the professional weakness of exaggerating the importance of those blunders as to historic facts and musical technicalities which sometimes give a ludicrous air to really shrewd and essentially sound criticism.

Musical criticisms, like sermons, are of low average quality simply because they are never discussed or contradicted; and I should rejoice were such a committee to be formed, especially if Dr Stanford were to be chairman, and would undertake the drafting of such public protests as it might be deemed advisable to issue.

The Philharmonic orchestra has been distinguishing itself at the last two concerts in the hands of Grieg and Saint-Saëns. Grieg is so successful in getting fine work out of the band that if the directors were wise they would make him a handsome offer to take it in hand permanently.

Saint-Saëns also persuaded it to give him a very smooth and fine-drawn performance of his symphony for orchestra with pianoforte and organ, a model of elegant instrumentation, in which the effect of the adoption of what I may call the Lohengrin orchestra, with three wood wind instruments of each kind instead of two, is to my ear conclusive as to the advisability of its general employment in symphony. It is a pity that this particular work of Saint-Saëns degenerates so frightfully at the end. All that barren coda stuff, with its mechanical piling of instruments, its whipping of rhythms, and its ridiculous scraps of fugato, should be ruthlessly excised: it has no real theme, and only spoils the rest. Grieg's suite of entr'actes and incidental music is, for a composer of his pretension, trumpery stuff enough, except for a fanciful and delicate movement for muted violins pianissimo, with starts and shudders on the drum, representing somebody's uneasy dreams. Whether Grieg was clever enough to get all the rehearsal to himself I do not know; but a rather abject performance of Beethoven's eighth symphony suggested that he had not left much time to Dr Mackenzie, who, by the way, was exceptionally successful with Wagner's Faust overture at the next concert.

Mr Ben Davies self-sacrificingly added his name to the long list of tenors who have failed in Beethoven's Adelaida, which is virtually a sonatina for tenor voice, and should be treated accordingly. This was rather a drop after the clever singing of Mdlle Landi on the previous occasion.

Mr Bispham's Schumann concert last week was so prodigiously successful that I had to retreat unwillingly into the fresh air before it was quite over. Mr Bispham's artistic judgment served him well in his choice of Mrs Henschel and Miss Marguerite Hall as colleagues no less than in his own fine singing, which is getting almost too gentle in its touch for large popular audiences, and will probably be all the better for the greater sharpness of definition and vigor of stroke which Drury Lane will demand from him in the forthcoming German Opera season there.

Mr Henry Bird, in the very important position of Schumann accompanist, divided the honors with the singers, his only failure being in the scene from Faust, which requires a broad orchestral handling altogether different from that of the songs. However, I rejoice to find Mr Bispham turning his attention to this undeservedly neglected piece of Schumann's work; and I take the opportunity to repeat my old suggestion that he should be invited by the Philharmonic or Crystal Palace directors, or by Richter or Mottl, to take part in a performance of the whole of the middle section of the work, from the sunrise scene to the death of Faust.

20 *June* 1894

WHOEVER has not seen Miss Eames as Charlotte has not realized the full ſorce of Thackeray's picture of the young lady who, when she saw the remains of her lover

> Borne before her on a shutter,
> Like a well-conducted person,
> Went on cutting bread-and-butter.

I never saw such a well-conducted person as Miss Eames. She casts her propriety like a Sunday frock over the whole stage, and gives Mr Steadman's choir-boys, as she cuts the bread-and-butter for them, a soapy nosed, plastery haired, respectable-aged-mothered appearance which they totally lack in Carmen under the influence of Calvé. Like Goldsmith's hero in She Stoops to Conquer, I am ill at ease in the company of ladylike women; and during the first act of Werther at Covent Garden I grew shyer and more awkward in my stall, until, upon Charlotte informing Werther that she was another's, I felt ready to sink into the earth with confusion. In the third act, when Werther, breaking down under the strain of a whole year's unintermitted well-behavedness, desperately resolved to have a kiss, and to that end offered the young lady violence, the whole audience shared the chills with which he was visibly struggling. Never, since Miss Mary Anderson shed a cold radiance on the rebuked stage, have virtue and comeliness seemed more awful than they do at Covent Garden on Werther nights. How I envy Miss Eames her self-possession, her quiet consciousness of being founded on a rock, her good looks (oh, those calmly regular eyebrows!), and, above all, that splendid middle to her voice, enabling her to fill the huge theatre without an effort!

Werther is a more congenial subject for Massenet than even Manon was. When he gets away from the artificial and rhetorical into the regions of candid sentiment and the childlike sincerities of love and grief he is charming. Des Grieux, a hero whom we forgive even for cheating at cards, suited him well: Werther suits him still better. The surroundings suit him too. The constant hum and murmur of the country evening, and the pleasant noisiness of the children when they are not rehearsing their carol or munching the bread-and-butter, make the first act quite delightful to a jaded critic sitting in a well-situated and comfortable stall.

In the rococo of the following scenes the modishness is made interesting by a certain frank naturalness which never deserts Massenet as long as he is treating subjects that give it a chance—that is, as long as he steers clear of the traditions of Parisian grand opera. On his own ground he has an engaging force and charm of expression; and though he is not exactly a creator in harmony or orchestration, yet in both he has a lively individual style. At all events, he has succeeded in keeping up the interest of a libretto consisting of four acts of a lovelorn tenor who has only two active moments, one when he tries to ravish a kiss from the fair as aforesaid, and the other when he shoots himself behind the scenes.

Naturally, the success of the work in performance depends a great deal on the artist who plays Werther; and Massenet is certainly fortunate in Jean de Reszke, whose performances as Werther and Romeo last week were masterly. His grip of these two parts is now extraordinarily firm and intimate: he is in the heart of them from the first note to the last. Not a tone nor gesture has a touch of anything common or cheap in it: the parts are elaborately studied and the execution sensitively beautiful throughout, the result, aided by his natural grace and distinction, being in both operas an impersonation not only unflaggingly interesting, but exquisitely attractive. His voice leaves nothing to be desired: at the beginning of the evening there is the slightest possible fur on the first two or three notes; but it wears off at once, and leaves him in the most confident possession of all his forces.

In Werther there are several formidable declamatory

passages, accompanied by the full power of the orchestra. He attacks these with triumphant force, and next moment is singing quietly with his voice as unstrained, as responsive, as rich in quality as if it had been wrapped in cotton wool for a week, instead of clashing against Massenet's most strenuous orchestration with a vehemence that would put most tenors practically *hors de combat* for several minutes. He seems to me to be at the height of his physical powers, and at the same time to have perfected his artistic integrity, if I may so express myself, my meaning being that he is now magnificently in earnest about his work and undivided in his attention to it.

The effect of this on his colleagues is excellent: Melba especially surpasses herself when playing with him. I must admit reluctantly that these performances of Werther and Romeo seem sure of a place in the front rank of my operatic recollections. I say reluctantly, because, after all, Romeo is *vieux jeu* and Werther is hardly to be counted a great part; therefore it still rankles in me that we have to send for Herr Alvary to play Tristan and Siegfried.

Edouard de Reszke made his re-entry for the season as Frère Laurent. In that matter of artistic integrity he lags behind his brother. The old Adam is strong within him, and tempts him to bawl occasionally. When he yields, he invariably adds an apologetic attempt at a piano passage, which gets out of tune from the after-effects of the bawling, and leaves him abashed. When he sings with a dignified reticence, content with the normal strength of his abnormally powerful voice, he is hugely satisfying from the musical, if not from the severely intellectual, point of view. Bonnard was not precisely the man for Tybalt, a part which requires before all things a swordsman.

If Jean de Reszke had gone for him as he used to go for the condescending Montariol, he would infallibly have stained the Covent Garden boards with his gore. On the whole, the duels were made failures by the extreme caution needed to prevent their becoming mortally realistic successes. Miss Lucile Hill, who ought to have played Romeo's page very well, missed her chance, apparently for want of a few hours' scale practice. Her voice was in very indifferent order; her French diction was hardly presentable after De Reszke's; and the effect of certain passages—for instance, the skip of an octave in Que fais-tu—was quite unworthy of her former performances. She got through the part on the strength of her appearance and reputation, instead of doing justice to it. I invite her to retrieve this shortcoming: she can do it easily enough if she likes. Of Albers as Mercutio I cannot speak, as I was prevented by a concert from hearing the first act.

In Rigoletto the final duet was restored. As far as I know, it has never been done on the stage since its excision immediately after the opera was first produced. Its orchestration is celestially pretty, so much so, that as I have not a full score within my reach, I will not undertake to swear that it has not been touched up by Mancinelli, or someone with all the latest discoveries at his fingers' ends.

Ancona's Rigoletto was a disappointment. Considering that he has shewn considerable dramatic feeling, and that he has exactly the voice for which the part was written—that is, a rich baritone of such range as to enable him not only to sing with ease up to G, but to keep singing for pages together above the bass stave, as if that were the middle of his voice—great things were expected of him; and I am almost compelled to admire the ingenuity with which he avoided doing them.

In all the less important moments he was tremendous, or looked as if he was going to be; but when the crises arrived, and one expected those terrible explosions of ferocity or paroxysms of abasement which are the great opportunities of the part, he somehow slipped round them with an entirely gentlemanlike aversion to anything like making a scene.

He sang the music with consummate ease, always excepting his consistent failure from beginning to end to seize and strike the right dramatic accent; but after Maurel, who only gets through the music by an occasionally almost painful exercise of vocal ingenuity, he made no mark; and the honors of the performance went to Giulia Ravogli for a very clever piece of playing as Maddalena; to De Lucia, who, over-parted as he was, got through with the Duke's music adroitly and pluckily; and, of course, to Melba, whose acting, if conventional, was earnest and careful, and whose long shake at her exit after Caro nome was as beautiful as ever.

Monterone was impersonated by that versatile artist De Vaschetti, who has played, since the season commenced, more parts than most of the leading artists have ventured upon in all their lives. Innkeeper, nobleman, courtier, ghost, bandit, soldier, statesman, chemist, buffoon: nothing comes amiss to De Vaschetti, whose brazen voice rings throughout all operas, and whose old weakness for singing the most unexpected and startling wrong notes—he once, as the statue in Don Giovanni, planted one of these unearthly intervals on me with such deadly effect that, before I could think, I had bounded out of my stall with a shriek, to the great terror of my neighbors—has now yielded to experience and, presumably, study. He has gained a firm hold on the affection of the subscribers, and will, I doubt not, flourish usefully at the Royal Italian Opera for the next thirty or forty years, outliving as many reputations as that veteran tenor Rinaldini.

I am glad that Mr Leonard Borwick's recital on Tuesday last week gave me an opportunity of renewing the regard for him as a pianist which has of late been almost destroyed by the frequency with which I have come upon him when he has been dealing with Beethoven. He cannot play Beethoven: his attempts to sentimentalize and prettify that virile master's work are quite beyond my patience. But his playing of Chopin's sonata in B flat minor is really worth hearing, and was deservedly received with enthusiasm. In Mendelssohn's fine prelude and foolish fugue in E minor,

Saint-Saëns' Alceste caprice, and some pieces by Schumann, he gave the concourse of young ladies who filled St James's Hall further excellent value for their money. The Don Juan fantasia he had better, perhaps, have let alone.

At Mr Isidor Cohn's recital a trio by Dvořák in E minor, called Dumky for some reason, was played for the first time by Mr Cohn, Mr Whitehouse, and Lady Hallé. What I heard of it—I missed the first movement—was mere rhapsody, with more or less pretence of sonata form about it, pretty enough, but not getting much higher than that. Miss Lydia Müller sang some German songs very competently.

THEATRE

THE REJECTED STATEMENT

(From the Preface to The Shewing-up of Blanco Posnet)

THE WITNESS'S QUALIFICATIONS

I AM by profession a playwright. I have been in practice since 1892. I am a member of the Managing Committee of the Society of Authors and of the Dramatic Sub-Committee of that body. I have written nineteen plays, some of which have been translated and performed in all European countries except Turkey, Greece, and Portugal. They have been performed extensively in America. Three of them have been refused licences by the Lord Chamberlain. In one case a licence has since been granted. The other two are still unlicensed. I have suffered both in pocket and reputation by the action of the Lord Chamberlain. In other countries I have not come into conflict with the censorship except in Austria, where the production of a comedy of mine was postponed for a year because it alluded to the part taken by Austria in the Servo-Bulgarian war. This comedy was not one of the plays suppressed in England by the Lord Chamberlain. One of the plays so suppressed was prosecuted in America by the police in consequence of an immense crowd of disorderly persons having been attracted to the first performance by the Lord Chamberlain's condemnation of it; but on appeal to a higher court it was decided that the representation was lawful and the intention innocent, since when it has been repeatedly performed.

I am not an ordinary playwright in general practice. I am a specialist in immoral and heretical plays. My reputation has been gained by my persistent struggle to force the public to reconsider its morals. In particular, I regard much current morality as to economic and sexual relations as disastrously wrong; and I regard certain doctrines of the Christian religion as understood in England today with abhorrence. I write plays with the deliberate object of converting the nation to my opinions in these matters. I have no other effectual incentive to write plays, as I am not dependent on the theatre for my livelihood. If I were prevented from producing immoral and heretical plays, I should cease to write for the theatre, and propagate my views from the platform and through books. I mention these facts to shew that I have a special interest in the achievement by my profession of those rights of liberty of speech and conscience which are matters of course in other professions. I object to censorship not merely because the existing form of it grievously injures and hinders me individually, but on public grounds.

THE DEFINITION OF IMMORALITY

In dealing with the question of the censorship, everything depends on the correct use of the word immorality, and a careful discrimination between the powers of a magistrate or judge to administer a code, and those of a censor to please himself.

Whatever is contrary to established manners and customs is immoral. An immoral act or doctrine is not necessarily a sinful one: on the contrary, every advance in thought and conduct is by definition immoral until it has converted the majority. For this reason it is of the most enormous importance that immorality should be protected jealously against the attacks of those who have no standard except the standard of custom, and who regard any attack on custom—that is, on morals—as an attack on society, on religion, and on virtue.

A censor is never intentionally a protector of immorality. He always aims at the protection of morality. Now morality is extremely valuable to society. It imposes conventional conduct on the great mass of persons who are incapable of original ethical judgment, and who would be quite lost if they were not in leading-strings devised by lawgivers, philosophers, prophets, and poets for their guidance. But morality is not dependent on censorship for protection. It is already powerfully fortified by the magistracy and the whole body of law. Blasphemy, indecency, libel, treason, sedition, obscenity, profanity, and all the other evils which a censorship is supposed to avert, are punishable by the civil magistrate with all the severity of vehement prejudice. Morality has not only every engine that lawgivers can devise in full operation for its protection, but also that enormous weight of public opinion enforced by social ostracism which is stronger than all the statutes. A censor pretending to protect morality is like a child pushing the cushions of a railway carriage to give itself the sensation of making the train travel at sixty miles an hour. It is immorality, not morality, that needs protection: it is morality, not immorality, that needs restraint; for morality, with all the dead weight of human inertia and superstition to hang on the back of the pioneer, and all the malice of vulgarity and prejudice to threaten him, is responsible for many persecutions and many martyrdoms.

Persecutions and martyrdoms, however, are trifles compared to the mischief done by censorships in delaying the general march of enlightenment. This can be brought home to us by imagining what would have been the effect of applying to all literature the censorship we still apply to the stage. The works of Linnaeus and the evolutionists of 1790–1830, of Darwin, Wallace, Huxley, Helmholtz, Tyndall, Spencer, Carlyle, Ruskin, and Samuel Butler, would not have been published, as they were all immoral and heretical in the very highest degree, and gave pain to many worthy and pious people. They are at present condemned by the Greek and Roman Catholic censorships as unfit for general reading. A censorship of conduct would have been equally disastrous. The disloyalty of Hampden and of Washington; the revolting immorality of Luther in not only marrying when he was a priest, but actually marrying a nun; the heterodoxy of Galileo; the shocking blasphemies and sacrileges of Mahomet against the idols whom he dethroned to make way for his conception of one god; the still more startling blasphemy of Jesus when He declared God to be the son of man and Himself to be the son of God, are all examples of shocking immoralities (every immorality shocks somebody), the suppression and extinction of which would have been more disastrous than the utmost mischief that can be conceived as ensuing from the toleration of vice.

These facts, glaring as they are, are disguised by the promotion of immoralities into moralities which is constantly going on. Christianity and Mahometanism, once thought of and dealt with exactly as Anarchism is thought of and dealt with today, have become established religions; and fresh immoralities are persecuted in their name. The truth is that the vast majority of persons professing these religions have never been anything but simple moralists. The respectable Englishman who is a Christian because he was born in Clapham would be a Mahometan for the cognate reason if he had been born in Constantinople. He has never willingly tolerated immorality. He did not adopt any innovation until it had become moral; and then he adopted it, not on its merits, but solely because it had become moral. In doing so he never realized that it had ever been immoral: consequently its early struggles taught him no lesson; and he has opposed the next step in human progress as indignantly as if neither manners, customs, nor thought had ever changed since the beginning of the world. Toleration must be imposed on him as a mystic and painful duty by his spiritual and political leaders, or he will condemn the world to stagnation, which is the penalty of an inflexible morality.

WHAT TOLERATION MEANS

This must be done all the more arbitrarily because it is not possible to make the ordinary moral man understand what toleration and liberty really mean. He will accept them verbally with alacrity, even with enthusiasm, because the word toleration has been moralized by eminent Whigs; but what he means by toleration is toleration of doctrines that he considers enlightened, and, by liberty, liberty to do what he considers right: that is, he does not mean toleration or liberty at all; for there is no need to tolerate what appears enlightened or to claim liberty to do what most people consider right. Toleration and liberty have no sense or use except as toleration of opinions that are considered damnable, and liberty to do what seems wrong. Setting Englishmen free to marry their deceased wife's sisters is not tolerated by the people who approve of it, but by the people who regard it as incestuous. Catholic Emancipation and the admission of Jews to parliament needed no toleration from Catholics and Jews: the toleration they needed was that of the people who regarded the one measure as a facilitation of idolatry, and the other as a condonation of the crucifixion. Clearly such toleration is not clamored for by the multitude or by the press which reflects its prejudices. It is essentially one of those abnegations of passion and prejudice which the common man submits to because uncommon men whom he respects as wiser than himself assure him that it must be so, or the higher affairs of human destiny will suffer.

Such submission is the more difficult because the arguments against tolerating immorality are the same as the arguments against tolerating murder and theft; and this is why the Censor seems to the inconsiderate as obviously desirable a functionary as the police magistrate. But there is this simple and tremendous difference between the cases: that whereas no evil can conceivably result from the total suppression of murder and theft, and all communities prosper in direct proportion to such suppression, the total suppression of immorality, especially in matters of religion and sex, would stop enlightenment, and produce what used to be called a Chinese civilization until the Chinese lately took to immoral courses by permitting railway contractors to desecrate the graves of their ancestors, and their soldiers to wear clothes which indecently revealed the fact that they had legs and waists and even posteriors. At about the same moment a few bold Englishwomen ventured on the immorality of riding astride their horses, a practice that has since established itself so successfully that before another generation has passed away there may not be a new side-saddle in England, or a woman who could use it if there was.

THE CASE FOR TOLERATION

Accordingly, there has risen among wise and far-sighted men a perception of the need for setting certain departments of human activity entirely free from legal interference. This has nothing to do with any sympathy these liberators may themselves have with immoral views. A man with the strongest conviction of the Divine ordering of the universe and of the superiority of monarchy to all forms of government may nevertheless quite consistently and conscientiously be ready to lay down his life for the right of every man to advocate Atheism or Republicanism if he believes in them. An attack on morals may turn out to be the salvation of the race. A hundred years ago nobody foresaw that Tom Paine's centenary would be the subject of a laudatory special article in The Times; and only a few understood that the persecution of his works and the transportation of men for the felony of reading them was a mischievous mistake. Even less, perhaps, could they have guessed that Proudhon, who became notorious by his essay entitled "What is Property? It is Theft," would have received, on the like occasion and in the same paper, a respectful consideration which nobody would now dream of according to Lord Liverpool or Lord Brougham. Nevertheless there was a mass of evidence to shew that such a development was not only possible but fairly probable, and that the risks of suppressing liberty of propaganda were far graver than the risk of Paine's or Proudhon's writings wrecking civilization. Now there was no such evidence in favor of tolerating the cutting of throats and the robbing of tills. No case whatever can be made out for the statement that a nation cannot do without common thieves and homicidal ruffians. But an overwhelming case can be made out for the statement that no nation can prosper or even continue to exist without heretics and advocates of shockingly immoral doctrines. The Inquisition and the Star Chamber, which were nothing but censorships, made ruthless war on impiety and immorality. The result was once familiar to Englishmen, though of late years it seems to have been forgotten. It cost England a revolution to get rid of the Star Chamber. Spain did not get rid of the Inquisition, and paid for that omission by becoming a barely third-rate power politically, and intellectually no power at all, in the

Europe she had once dominated as the mightiest of the Christian empires.

THE LIMITS TO TOLERATION

But the large toleration these considerations dictate has limits. For example, though we tolerate, and rightly tolerate, the propaganda of Anarchism as a political theory which embraces all that is valuable in the doctrine of Laisser-Faire and the method of Free Trade as well as all that is shocking in the views of Bakounine, we clearly cannot, or at all events will not, tolerate assassination of rulers on the ground that it is "propaganda by deed" or sociological experiment. A play inciting to such an assassination cannot claim the privileges of heresy or immorality, because no case can be made out in support of assassination as an indispensable instrument of progress. Now it happens that we have in the Julius Cæsar of Shakespear a play which the Tsar of Russia or the Governor-General of India would hardly care to see performed in their capitals just now. It is an artistic treasure; but it glorifies a murder which Goethe described as the silliest crime ever committed. It may quite possibly have helped the regicides of 1649 to see themselves, as it certainly helped generations of Whig statesmen to see them, in a heroic light; and it unquestionably vindicates and ennobles a conspirator who assassinated the head of the Roman State not because he abused his position but solely because he occupied it, thus affirming the extreme republican principle that all kings, good or bad, should be killed because kingship and freedom cannot live together. Under certain circumstances this vindication and ennoblement might act as an incitement to an actual assassination as well as to Plutarchian republicanism; for it is one thing to advocate republicanism or royalism: it is quite another to make a hero of Brutus or Ravaillac, or a heroine of Charlotte Corday. Assassination is the extreme form of censorship; and it seems hard to justify an incitement to it on anti-censorial principles. The very people who would have scouted the notion of prohibiting the performances of Julius Cæsar at His Majesty's

Theatre in London last year, might now entertain very seriously a proposal to exclude Indians from them, and to suppress the play completely in Calcutta and Dublin; for if the assassin of Cæsar was a hero, why not the assassins of Lord Frederick Cavendish, Presidents Lincoln and McKinley, and Sir Curzon Wyllie? Here is a strong case for some constitutional means of preventing the performance of a play. True, it is an equally strong case for preventing the circulation of the Bible, which was always in the hands of our regicides; but as the Roman Catholic Church does not hesitate to accept that consequence of the censorial principle, it does not invalidate the argument.

Take another actual case. A modern comedy, Arms and The Man, though not a comedy of politics, is nevertheless so far historical that it reveals the unacknowledged fact that as the Servo-Bulgarian War of 1885 was much more than a struggle between the Servians and Bulgarians, the troops engaged were officered by two European Powers of the first magnitude. In consequence, the performance of the play was for some time forbidden in Vienna, and more recently it gave offence in Rome at a moment when popular feeling was excited as to the relations of Austria with the Balkan States. Now if a comedy so remote from political passion as Arms and The Man can, merely because it refers to political facts, become so inconvenient and inopportune that Foreign Offices take the trouble to have its production postponed, what may not be the effect of what is called a patriotic drama produced at a moment when the balance is quivering between peace and war? Is there not something to be said for a political censorship, if not for a moral one? May not those continental governments who leave the stage practically free in every other respect, but muzzle it politically, be justified by the practical exigencies of the situation?

THE DIFFERENCE BETWEEN LAW AND CENSORSHIP

The answer is that a pamphlet, a newspaper article, or a resolution moved at a political meeting can do all the mischief that a play can, and often more; yet we do not set up a permanent censorship of the press or of political meetings. Any journalist may publish an article, any demagogue may deliver a speech without giving notice to the government or obtaining its licence. The risk of such freedom is great; but as it is the price of our political liberty, we think it worth paying. We may abrogate it in emergencies by a Coercion Act, a suspension of the Habeas Corpus Act, or a proclamation of martial law, just as we stop the traffic in a street during a fire, or shoot thieves at sight if they loot after an earthquake. But when the emergency is past, liberty is restored everywhere except in the theatre. The Act of 1843 is a permanent Coercion Act for the theatre, a permanent suspension of the Habeas Corpus Act as far as plays are concerned, a permanent proclamation of martial law with a single official substituted for a court martial. It is, in fact, assumed that actors, playwrights, and theatre managers are dangerous and dissolute characters whose existence creates a chronic state of emergency, and who must be treated as earthquake looters are treated. It is not necessary now to discredit this assumption. It was broken down by the late Sir Henry Irving when he finally shamed the Government into extending to his profession the official recognition enjoyed by the other branches of fine art. To-day we have on the roll of knighthood actors, authors, and managers. The rogue and vagabond theory of the depravity of the theatre is as dead officially as it is in general society; and with it has perished the sole excuse for the Act of 1843 and for the denial to the theatre of the liberties secured, at far greater social risk, to the press and the platform.

There is no question here of giving the theatre any larger liberties than the press and the platform, or of claiming larger powers for Shakespear to eulogize Brutus than Lord Rosebery has to eulogize Cromwell. The abolition of the censorship does not involve the abolition of the magistrate and of the whole civil and criminal code. On the contrary, it would make the theatre more effectually subject to them than it is at present; for once a play now runs the gauntlet of the censorship, it is practically placed above the law. It is almost humiliating to have to demonstrate the essential difference between a censor and a magistrate or a sanitary inspector; but it is impossible to ignore the carelessness with which even distinguished critics of the theatre assume that all the arguments proper to the support of a magistracy and body of jurisprudence apply equally to a censorship.

A magistrate has laws to administer: a censor has nothing but his own opinion. A judge leaves the question of guilt to the jury: the Censor is jury and judge as well as lawgiver. A magistrate may be strongly prejudiced against an atheist or an anti-vaccinator, just as a sanitary inspector may have formed a careful opinion that drains are less healthy than cesspools; but the magistrate must allow the atheist to affirm instead of to swear, and must grant the anti-vaccinator an exemption certificate, when their demands are lawfully made; and in cities the inspector must compel the builder to make drains and must prosecute him if he makes cesspools. The law may be only the intolerance of the community; but it is a defined and limited intolerance. The limitation is sometimes carried so far that a judge cannot inflict the penalty for housebreaking on a burglar who can prove that he found the door open and therefore made only an unlawful entry. On the other hand, it is sometimes so vague, as for example in the case of the American law against obscenity, that it makes the magistrate virtually a censor. But in the main a citizen can ascertain what he may do and what he may not do; and, though no one knows better than a magistrate that a single ill-conducted family may demoralize a whole street, no magistrate can imprison or otherwise restrain its members on the ground that their immorality may corrupt their neighbors. He can prevent any citizen from carrying certain specified weapons, but not from handling pokers, table-knives, bricks or bottles of corrosive fluid, on the ground that he might use them to commit murder or inflict malicious injury. He has no general power to prevent citizens from selling unhealthy or poisonous substances, or judging for themselves what substances are unhealthy and what wholesome, what poisonous and what innocuous: what he *can* do is to prevent anybody who has not a specific qualification from selling certain specified poisons of which a schedule is kept. Nobody is forbidden to sell minerals without a licence; but everybody is forbidden to sell silver without a licence. When the law has forgotten some atrocious sin—for instance, contracting marriage whilst suffering from contagious disease—the magistrate cannot arrest or punish the wrongdoer, however he may abhor his wickedness. In short, no man is lawfully at the mercy of the magistrate's personal caprice, prejudice, ignorance, superstition, temper, stupidity, resentment, timidity, ambition, or private conviction. But a playwright's livelihood, his reputation, and his inspiration and mission are at the personal mercy of the Censor. The two do not stand, as the criminal and the judge stand, in the presence of a law that binds them both equally, and was made by neither of them, but by the deliberate collective wisdom of the community. The only law that affects them is the Act of 1843, which empowers one of them to do absolutely and finally what he likes with the other's work. And when it is remembered that the slave in this case is the man whose profession is that of Eschylus and Euripides, of Shakespear and Goethe, of Tolstoy and Ibsen, and the master the holder of a party appointment which by the nature of its duties practically excludes the possibility of its acceptance by a serious statesman or great lawyer, it will be seen that the playwrights are justified in reproaching the framers of that Act for having failed not only to appreciate the immense importance of the theatre as a most powerful instrument for teaching the nation how and what to think and feel, but even to conceive that those who make their living by the theatre are normal human beings with the common rights of English citizens. In this extremity of inconsiderateness it is not surprising that they also did not trouble themselves to study the difference between a censor and a magistrate. And it will be found that almost all the people who disinterestedly defend the censorship today are defending him on the assumption that there is no constitutional difference between him and any other functionary whose duty it is to restrain crime and disorder.

One further difference remains to be noted. As a magistrate grows old his mind may change or decay; but the law remains the same. The censorship of the theatre fluctuates with every change in the views and character of the man who exercises it. And what this implies can only be appreciated by those who can imagine what the effect on the mind must be of the duty of reading through every play that is produced in the kingdom year in, year out.

WHY THE LORD CHAMBERLAIN?

What may be called the high political case against censorship as a principle is now complete. The pleadings are those which have already freed books and pulpits and political platforms in England from censorship, if not from occasional legal persecution. The stage alone remains under a censorship of a grotesquely unsuitable kind. No play can be performed if the Lord Chamberlain happens to disapprove of it. And the Lord Chamberlain's functions have no sort of relationship to dramatic literature. A great judge of literature, a far-seeing statesman, a born champion of liberty of conscience and intellectual integrity—say a Milton, a Chesterfield, a Bentham—would be a very bad Lord Chamberlain: so bad, in fact, that his exclusion from such a post may be regarded as decreed by natural law. On the other hand, a good Lord Chamberlain would be a stickler for morals in the narrowest sense, a busy-body, a man to whom a matter of two inches in the length of a gentleman's sword or the absence of a feather from a lady's head-dress would be a graver matter than the Habeas Corpus Act. The Lord Chancellor, as Censor of the theatre, is a direct descendant of the King's Master of the Revels, appointed in 1544 by Henry VIII. to keep order among the players and musicians of that day when they performed at Court. This first appearance of the theatrical censor in politics as the whipper-in of the player, with its conception of the player as a rich man's servant hired to amuse him, and, outside his professional duties, as a gay, disorderly, anarchic spoilt child, half privileged, half outlawed, probably as much vagabond as actor, is the real foundation of the subjection of the whole profession, actors, managers, authors and all, to the despotic authority of an officer whose business it is to preserve decorum among menials. It must be remembered that it was not until a hundred years later, in the reaction against the Puritans, that a woman could appear on the English stage without being pelted off as the Italian actresses were. The theatrical profession was regarded as a shameless one; and it is only of late years that actresses have at last succeeded in living down the assumption that actress and prostitute are synonymous terms, and made good their position in respectable society. This makes the survival of the old ostracism in the Act of 1843 intolerably galling; and though it explains the apparently unaccountable absurdity of choosing as Censor of dramatic literature an official whose functions and qualifications have nothing whatever to do with literature, it also explains why the present arrangement is not only criticized as an institution, but resented as an insult.

THE DIPLOMATIC OBJECTION TO THE LORD CHAMBERLAIN

There is another reason, quite unconnected with the susceptibilities of authors, which makes it undesirable that a member of the King's Household should be responsible for the character and tendency of plays. The drama, dealing with all departments of human life, is necessarily political. Recent events have shewn—what indeed needed no demonstration—that it is impossible to prevent inferences being made, both at home and abroad, from the action of the Lord Chamberlain. The most talked-about play of the present year (1909), An Englishman's Home, has for its main interest an invasion of England by a fictitious power which is understood, as it is meant to be understood, to represent

Germany. The lesson taught by the play is the danger of invasion and the need for every English citizen to be a soldier. The Lord Chamberlain licensed this play, but refused to license a parody of it. Shortly afterwards he refused to license another play in which the fear of a German invasion was ridiculed. The German press drew the inevitable inference that the Lord Chamberlain was an anti-German alarmist, and that his opinions were a reflection of those prevailing in St. James's Palace. Immediately after this, the Lord Chamberlain licensed the play. Whether the inference, as far as the Lord Chamberlain was concerned, was justified is of no consequence. What is important is that it was sure to be made, justly or unjustly, and extended from the Lord Chamberlain to the Throne.

THE OBJECTION OF COURT ETIQUET

There is another objection to the Lord Chamberlain's censorship which affects the author's choice of subject. Formerly very little heed was given in England to the susceptibilities of foreign courts. For instance, the notion that the Mikado of Japan should be as sacred to the English playwright as he is to the Japanese Lord Chamberlain would have seemed grotesque a generation ago. Now that the maintenance of *entente cordiale* between nations is one of the most prominent and most useful functions of the crown, the freedom of authors to deal with political subjects, even historically, is seriously threatened by the way in which the censorship makes the King responsible for the contents of every play. One author—the writer of these lines, in fact—has long desired to dramatize the life of Mahomet. But the possibility of a protest from the Turkish Ambassador—or the fear of it—causing the Lord Chamberlain to refuse to license such a play has prevented the play from being written. Now, if the censorship were abolished, nobody but the author could be held responsible for the play. The Turkish Ambassador does not now protest against the publication of Carlyle's essay on the prophet, or of the English translations of the Koran in the prefaces to which Mahomet is criticized as an impostor, or of the older books in which he is reviled as Mahound and classed with the devil himself. But if these publications had to be licensed by the Lord Chamberlain it would be impossible for the King to allow the licence to be issued, as he would thereby be made responsible for the opinions expressed. This restriction of the historical drama is an unmixed evil. Great religious leaders are more interesting and more important subjects for the dramatist than great conquerors. It is a misfortune that public opinion would not tolerate a dramatization of Mahomet in Constantinople. But to prohibit it here, where public opinion would tolerate it, is an absurdity which, if applied in all directions, would make it impossible for the Queen to receive a Turkish ambassador without veiling herself, or the Dean and Chapter of St. Paul's to display a cross on the summit of their Cathedral in a city occupied largely and influentially by Jews. Court etiquet is no doubt an excellent thing for court ceremonies; but to attempt to impose it on the drama is about as sensible as an attempt to make everybody in London wear court dress.

WHY NOT AN ENLIGHTENED CENSORSHIP

In the above cases the general question of censorship is separable from the question of the present form of it. Everyone who condemns the principle of censorship must also condemn the Lord Chamberlain's control of the drama; but those who approve of the principle do not necessarily approve of the Lord Chamberlain being the Censor *ex officio*. They may, however, be entirely opposed to popular liberties, and may conclude from what has been said, not that the stage should be made as free as the church, press, or platform, but that these institutions should be censored as strictly as the stage. It will seem obvious to them that nothing is needed to remove all objections to a censorship except the placing of its powers in better hands.

Now though the transfer of the censorship to, say, the Lord Chancellor, or the Primate, or a Cabinet Minister, would be much less humiliating to the persons immediately concerned, the inherent vices of the institution would not be appreciably less disastrous. They would even be aggravated, for reasons which do not appear on the surface, and therefore need to be followed with some attention.

It is often said that the public is the real censor. That this is to some extent true is proved by the fact that plays which are licensed and produced in London have to be expurgated for the provinces. This does not mean that the provinces are more strait-laced, but simply that in many provincial towns there is only one theatre for all classes and all tastes, whereas in London there are separate theatres for separate sections of playgoers: so that, for example, Sir Herbert Beerbohm Tree can conduct His Majesty's Theatre without the slightest regard to the tastes of the frequenters of the Gaiety Theatre; and Mr. George Edwardes can conduct the Gaiety Theatre without catering in any way for lovers of Shakespear. Thus the farcical comedy which has scandalized the critics in London by the libertinage of its jests is played to the respectable dress circle of Northampton with these same jests slurred over so as to be imperceptible by even the most prurient spectator. The public, in short, takes care that nobody shall outrage it.

But the public also takes care that nobody shall starve it, or regulate its dramatic diet as a schoolmistress regulates the reading of her pupils. Even when it wishes to be debauched, no censor can—or at least no censor does—stand out against it. If a play is irresistibly amusing, it gets licensed no matter what its moral aspect may be. A brilliant instance is the Divorçons of the late Victorien Sardou, which may not have been the naughtiest play of the 19th century, but was certainly the very naughtiest that any English manager in his senses would have ventured to produce. Nevertheless, being a very amusing play, it passed the licenser with the exception of a reference to impotence as a ground for divorce which no English actress would have ventured on in any case. Within the last few months a very amusing comedy with a strongly polygamous moral was found irresistible by the Lord Chamberlain. Plenty of fun and a happy ending will get anything licensed, because the public will have it so, and the Examiner of Plays, as the holder of the office testified before the Commission of 1892 (Report, page 330), feels with the public, and knows that his office could not survive a widespread unpopularity. In short, the support of the mob—that is, of the unreasoning, unorganized, uninstructed mass of popular sentiment—is indispensable to the censorship as it exists today in England. This is the explanation of the toleration by the Lord Chamberlain of coarse and vicious plays. It is not long since a judge before whom a licensed play came in the course of a lawsuit expressed his scandalized astonishment at the licensing of such a work. Eminent churchmen have made similar protests. In some plays the simulation of criminal assaults on the stage has been carried to a point at which a step further would have involved the interference of the police. Provided the treatment of the theme is gaily or hypocritically popular, and the ending happy, the indulgence of the Lord Chamberlain can be counted on. On the other hand, anything unpleasing and unpopular is rigorously censored. Adultery and prostitution are tolerated and even encouraged to such an extent that plays which do not deal with them are commonly said not to be plays at all. But if any of the unpleasing consequences of adultery and prostitution—for instance, an *unsuccessful* illegal operation (successful ones are tolerated) or venereal disease—are mentioned, the play is prohibited. This principle of shielding the playgoer from unpleasant reflections is carried so far that when a play was submitted for licence in which the relations of a prostitute with all the male characters in the piece was described as "immoral," the Examiner of Plays objected to that passage, though he made no objection to the relations themselves. The Lord Chamberlain dare not, in short, attempt to exclude from the stage the tragedies of murder and lust, or the farces of mendacity, adultery, and dissolute gaiety in which vulgar people delight. But when these same vulgar people are threatened with an unpopular play in which dissoluteness is shewn to be no laughing matter, it is prohibited at once amid the vulgar applause, the net result being that vice is made delightful and virtue banned by the very institution which is supported on the understanding that it produces exactly the opposite result.

THE WEAKNESS OF THE LORD CHAMBERLAIN'S DEPARTMENT

Now comes the question, Why is our censorship, armed as it is with apparently autocratic powers, so scandalously timid in the face of the mob? Why is it not as autocratic in dealing with playwrights below the average as with those above it? The answer is that its position is really a very weak one. It has no direct coercive forces, no funds to institute prosecutions and recover the legal penalties of defying it, no powers of arrest or imprisonment, in short, none of the guarantees of autocracy. What it can do is to refuse to renew the licence of a theatre at which its orders are disobeyed. When it happens that a theatre is about to be demolished, as was the case recently with the Imperial Theatre after it had passed into the hands of the Wesleyan Methodists, unlicensed plays can be performed, technically in private, but really in full publicity, without risk. The prohibited plays of Brieux and Ibsen have been performed in London in this way with complete impunity. But the impunity is not confined to condemned theatres. Not long ago a West End manager allowed a prohibited play to be performed at his theatre, taking his chance of losing his licence in consequence. The event proved that the manager was justified in regarding the risk as negligible; for the Lord Chamberlain's remedy—the closing of a popular and well-conducted theatre—was far too extreme to be practicable. Unless the play had so outraged public opinion as to make the manager odious and provoke a clamor for his exemplary punishment, the Lord Chamberlain could only have had his revenge at the risk of having his powers abolished as unsupportably tyrannical.

The Lord Chamberlain then has his powers so adjusted

that he is tyrannical just where it is important that he should be tolerant, and tolerant just where he could screw up the standard a little by being tyrannical. His plea that there are unmentionable depths to which managers and authors would descend if he did not prevent them is disproved by the plain fact that his indulgence goes as far as the police, and sometimes further than the public, will let it. If our judges had so little power there would be no law in England. If our churches had so much, there would be no theatre, no literature, no science, no art, possibly no England. The institution is at once absurdly despotic and abjectly weak.

AN ENLIGHTENED CENSORSHIP STILL WORSE THAN THE LORD CHAMBERLAIN'S

Clearly a censorship of judges, bishops, or statesmen would not be in this abject condition. It would no doubt make short work of the coarse and vicious pieces which now enjoy the protection of the Lord Chamberlain, or at least of those of them in which the vulgarity and vice are discoverable by merely reading the prompt copy. But it would certainly disappoint the main hope of its advocates: the hope that it would protect and foster the higher drama. It would do nothing of the sort. On the contrary, it would inevitably suppress it more completely than the Lord Chamberlain does, because it would understand it better. The one play of Ibsen's which is prohibited on the English stage, Ghosts, is far less subversive than A Doll's House. But the Lord Chamberlain does not meddle with such far-reaching matters as the tendency of a play. He refuses to license Ghosts exactly as he would refuse to license Hamlet if it were submitted to him as a new play. He would license even Hamlet if certain alterations were made in it. He would disallow the incestuous relationship between the King and Queen. He would probably insist on the susbtitution of some fictitious country for Denmark in deference to the near relations of our reigning house with that realm. He would certainly make it an absolute condition that the closet scene, in which a son, in an agony of shame and revulsion, reproaches his mother for her relations with his uncle, should be struck out as unbearably horrifying and improper. But compliance with these conditions would satisfy him. He would raise no speculative objections to the tendency of the play.

This indifference to the larger issues of a theatrical performance could not be safely predicated of an enlightened censorship. Such a censorship might be more liberal in its toleration of matters which are only objected to on the ground that they are not usually discussed in general social conversation or in the presence of children; but it would presumably have a far deeper insight to and concern for the real ethical tendency of the play. For instance, had it been in existence during the last quarter of a century, it would have perceived that those plays of Ibsen's which have been licensed without question are fundamentally immoral to an altogether extraordinary degree. Every one of them is a deliberate act of war on society as at present constituted. Religion, marriage, ordinary respectability, are subjected to a destructive exposure and criticism which seems to mere moralists—that is, to persons of no more than average depth of mind—to be diabolical. It is no exaggeration to say that Ibsen gained his overwhelming reputation by undertaking a task of no less magnitude than changing the mind of Europe with the view of changing its morals. Now you can not license work of that sort without making yourself responsible for it. The Lord Chamberlain accepted the responsibility because he did not understand it or concern himself about it. But what really enlightened and conscientious official dare take such a responsibility? The strength of character and range of vision which made Ibsen capable of it are not to be expected from any official, however eminent. It is true that an enlightened censor might, whilst shrinking even with horror from Ibsen's views, perceive that any nation which suppressed Ibsen would presently find itself falling behind the nations which tolerated him just as Spain fell behind England; but the proper action to take on such a conviction is the abdication of censorship, not the practice of it. As long as a censor is a censor, he cannot endorse by his licence opinions which seem to him dangerously heretical.

We may, therefore, conclude that the more enlightened a censorship is, the worse it would serve us. The Lord Chamberlain, an obviously unenlightened Censor, prohibits Ghosts and licenses all the rest of Ibsen's plays. An enlightened censorship would possibly license Ghosts; but it would certainly suppress many of the other plays. It would suppress subversiveness as well as what is called bad taste. The Lord Chamberlain prohibits one play by Sophocles because, like Hamlet, it mentions the subject of incest; but an enlightened censorship might suppress all the plays of Euripides because Euripides, like Ibsen, was a revolutionary Freethinker. Under the Lord Chamberlain, we can smuggle a good deal of immoral drama and almost as much coarsely vulgar and furtively lascivious drama as we like. Under a college of cardinals, or bishops, or judges, or any other conceivable form of experts in morals, philosophy, religion, or politics, we should get little except stagnant mediocrity.

THE PRACTICAL IMPOSSIBILITIES OF CENSORSHIP

There is, besides, a crushing material difficulty in the way of an enlightened censorship. It is not too much to say that the work involved would drive a man of any intellectual rank mad. Consider, for example, the Christmas pantomimes. Imagine a judge of the High Court, or an archbishop, or a Cabinet Minister, or an eminent man of letters, earning his living by reading through the mass of trivial doggerel represented by all the pantomimes which are put into rehearsal simultaneously at the end of every year. The proposal to put such mind-destroying drudgery upon an official of the class implied by the demand for an enlightened censorship falls through the moment we realize what it implies in practice.

Another material difficulty is that no play can be judged by merely reading the dialogue. To be fully effective a censor should witness the performance. The *mise-en-scène* of a play is as much a part of it as the words spoken on the stage. No censor could possibly object to such a speech as "Might I speak to you for a moment, miss?" yet that apparently innocent phrase has often been made offensively improper on the stage by popular low comedians, with the effect of changing the whole character and meaning of the play as understood by the official Examiner. In one of the plays of the present season, the dialogue was that of a crude melodrama dealing in the most conventionally correct manner with the fortunes of a good-hearted and virtuous girl. Its morality was that of the Sunday school. But the principal actress, between two speeches which contained no reference to her action, changed her underclothing on the stage! It is true that in this case the actress was so much better than her part that she succeeded in turning what was meant as an impropriety into an inoffensive stroke of realism; yet it is none the less clear that stage business of this character, on which there can be no check except the actual presence of a censor in the theatre, might convert any dialogue, however innocent, into just the sort of entertainment against which the Censor is supposed to protect the public.

It was this practical impossibility that prevented the London County Council from attempting to apply a censorship of the Lord Chamberlain's pattern to the London music halls. A proposal to examine all entertainments before permitting their performance was actually made; and it was abandoned, not in the least as contrary to the liberty of the stage, but because the executive problem of how to do it at once reduced the proposal to absurdity. Even if the Council devoted all its time to witnessing rehearsals of variety performances, and putting each item to the vote, possibly after a prolonged discussion followed by a division, the work would still fall into arrear. No committee could be induced to undertake such a task. The attachment of an inspector of morals to each music hall would have meant an appreciable addition to the ratepayers' burden. In the face of such difficulties the proposal melted away. Had it been pushed through, and the inspectors appointed, each of them would have become a censor, and the whole body of inspectors would have become a *police des mœurs*. Those who know the history of such police forces on the Continent will understand how impossible it would be to procure inspectors whose characters would stand the strain of their opportunities of corruption, both pecuniary and personal, at such salaries as a local authority could be persuaded to offer.

It has been suggested that the present censorship should be supplemented by a board of experts, who should deal, not with the whole mass of plays sent up for licence, but only those which the Examiner of Plays refuses to pass. As the number of plays which the Examiner refuses to pass is never great enough to occupy a Board in permanent session with regular salaries, and as casual employment is not compatible with public responsibility, this proposal would work out in practice as an addition to the duties of some existing functionary. A Secretary of State would be objectionable as likely to be biased politically. An ecclesiastical referee might be biased against the theatre altogether. A judge in chambers would be the proper authority. This plan would combine the inevitable intolerance of an enlightened censorship with the popular laxity of the Lord Chamberlain. The judge would suppress the pioneers, whilst the Examiner of Plays issued two guinea certificates for the vulgar and vicious plays. For this reason the plan would no doubt be popular; but it would be very much as a relaxation of the administration of the Public Health Acts accompanied by the cheapening of gin would be popular.

THE ARBITRATION PROPOSAL

On the occasion of a recent deputation of playwrights to the Prime Minister it was suggested that if a censorship be inevitable, provision should be made for an appeal from the Lord Chamberlain in cases of refusal of licence. The authors of this suggestion propose that the Lord Chamberlain shall choose one umpire and the author another. The two umpires shall then elect a referee, whose decision shall be final.

This proposal is not likely to be entertained by constitutional lawyers. It is a naïve offer to accept the method of arbitration in what is essentially a matter, not between one private individual or body and another, but between a public offender and the State. It will presumably be ruled out as a proposal to refer a case of manslaughter to arbitration would be ruled out. But even if it were constitutionally sound, it bears all the marks of that practical inexperience which leads men to believe that arbitration either costs nothing or is at least cheaper than law. Who is to pay for the time of the three arbitrators, presumably men of high professional standing? The author may not be able: the manager may not be willing: neither of them should be called upon to pay for a public service otherwise than by their contributions to the revenue. Clearly the State should pay. But even so, the difficulties are only beginning. A licence is seldom refused except on grounds which are controversial. The two arbitrators selected by the opposed parties to the controversy are to agree to leave the decision to a third party unanimously chosen by themselves. That is very far from being a simple solution. An attempt to shorten and simplify the passing of the Finance Bill by referring it to an arbitrator chosen unanimously by Mr Asquith and Mr Balfour might not improbably cost more and last longer than a civil war. And why should the chosen referee—if he ever succeeded in getting chosen—be assumed to be a safer authority than the Examiner of Plays? He would certainly be a less responsible one: in fact, being (however eminent) a casual person called in to settle a single case, he would be virtually irresponsible. Worse still, he would take all responsibility away from the Lord Chamberlain, who is at least an official of the King's Household and a nominee of the Government. The Lord Chamberlain, with all his shortcomings, thinks twice before he refuses a licence, knowing that his refusal is final and may promptly be made public. But if he could transfer his responsibility to an arbitrator, he would naturally do so whenever he felt the slightest misgiving, or whenever, for diplomatic reasons, the licence would come more gracefully from an authority unconnected with the court. These considerations, added to the general objection to the principle of censorship, seem sufficient to put the arbitration expedient quite out of the question.

END OF THE FIRST PART OF THE REJECTED STATEMENT

Editor's note: The second part of *The Rejected Statement* has to do with the technical problems concerned in licensing theatres.

Selections from
OUR THEATRES IN THE NINETIES

WHY NOT SIR HENRY IRVING?

[*9 February* 1895]

IN an old-fashioned play revived the other day by Mr Terry, a kitchen discussion of literature leads to the question, "Who wrote Shakespear?" Let me put a cognate question. Who writes Mr Irving's lectures? Of course, I must not altogether exclude the hypothesis that he writes them himself; but I had rather flatter him by assuming that he contents himself with jotting down a scenario, and orders some literary retainer to write the dialogue, enjoining him especially to put in plenty of art and learning, and not to forget some good declamatory passages, in the manner of the late Mr Wills, for elocutionary display. At all events, this is what is suggested by the report of his recent discourse at the Royal Institution. Dr Johnson—"Punch, sir, has no feelings"—Homer—"poetry, music, sculpture, painting" —Hamlet—Shakespear—"the poor player of Wittenberg" —Hogarth—Edmund Kean—Raphael and Michael Angelo—Praxiteles and Phidias—the Colosseum and the Parthenon—"Roscius a name that lives in history": who could not deliver the lecture verbatim from these notes as easily as Mr Percy Fitzgerald could write a book from them? And would we stand it from anybody but Henry Irving? Some years ago Mr William Archer lectured on the drama at the Royal Institution. What would the directors have said to Mr Archer had he put them off with stuff which any sufficiently old-fashioned auctioneer could improvise at a sale of theatrical prints? No: let us deal faithfully with Mr Irving in this matter, and not treat him like a spoiled child. The other evening, after King Arthur, he wished us all a happy new year. He wished it heartily, respectfully, and so on; and then, with a friendly impulse to get on more intimate terms with us, he asked whether he might wish it to us "affectionately." Naturally, the house immediately shook hands with him, so to speak—I among the rest. Consequently I hold myself privileged now to drop all insincere ceremony, and tell Mr Irving bluntly what every competent person thinks of his lecture. Their opinion may not seem consistent with their applause; but Mr Irving must remember that we now applaud him, not critically, but affectionately, and that we allow him to play like a child at being a learned lecturer, just as we indulge him, every evening at the Lyceum, with a broadsword combat the solemn absurdity of which quite baffles my powers of description. If we treat his orations as lectures, do we not also treat Mr Gladstone's tree-felling exploits as acts of statesmanship? No one can say that we are not indulgent to our favorites.

Mr Irving, however, began his lecture seriously and well, by putting forward "a formal claim to have acting classified *officially* among the fine arts." We all know what official recognition of a fine art means; but for the benefit of the millions of persons who never know anything, and therefore are not included in such general expressions as "we all," Mr Irving explicitly said, "Official recognition of anything worthy is a good, or at least a useful thing. It is a part, and an important part, of the economy of the State: if it is not, of what use are titles and distinctions, names, badges, offices, in fact all the titular and sumptuary ways of distinction?" Here the "formal claim" is put as precisely as Mr Irving himself feels he can decorously put it. I, who am not an actor, and am therefore not hampered by any personal interest in the claim, can put it much more definitely. What Mr Irving means us to answer is this question: "The artist who composed the music for King Arthur is Sir Arthur Sullivan; the artist who composed the poem which made King Arthur known to this generation died Lord Tennyson; the artist who designed the suit of armour worn by King Arthur is Sir Edward Burne-Jones: why should the artist who plays King Arthur be only Mister Henry Irving?" That is clearly

Mr Irving's meaning, since his art lacks no other sort of recognition or advancement than this.

Here let me plead against any envious and base-minded view of this claim. Mr Irving is entitled to an entirely honorable construction: we owe him an unhesitating assumption that his jealousy is for the dignity of his art and not of himself, and that it would never have been advanced if the friend of Sir Joshua Reynolds had been Sir David Garrick, and if every successive P.R.A. had had for his officially recognized peer the leading actor of his day. The theatre at present only boasts one title, that of Sir Augustus Harris, who was knighted, not on the excellent ground of his public services as opera impresario, but through the perfectly irrelevant accident of his having been sheriff when the Emperor of Germany visited the City. Who can deny that the actor is regarded as less worthy of official honors than the musician, the painter, or the poet? We have Sir Arthur Sullivan, Sir A. M. Mackenzie, and Sir Charles Hallé (a purely "executive" artist); and we have Sir Edward Burne-Jones, Sir John Millais, and Sir Frederick Leighton. No one questions the social position of these gentlemen; and an expression of any doubt as to whether it was right to go to a concert or to the Royal Academy Exhibition would be considered an unheard-of eccentricity. But numbers of respectable English people still regard a visit to the theatre as a sin; and numbers more, including most of those who have become accustomed to meeting even rank-and-file actors and actresses in society where thirty years ago they would as soon have expected to meet an acrobat, would receive a proposal from an actor for the hand of their daughter with a sense of *mésalliance* which they would certainly not have if the suitor were a lawyer, a doctor, a clergyman, or a painter. Such people, being intellectually and socially mere sheep, are very much influenced by titles—indeed, that influence is the *raison d'être* of titles; and there can be no doubt that if the next list of birthday honors were to include the names of Sir Henry Irving, Sir John Hare, and Sir Charles Wyndham, the boycott would lose half its force and all its credit at one stroke. On this account it is tenable, not only that Mr Irving might with perfect propriety and dignity accept an official honor which we should expect a great poet, for instance, to refuse just as a great commoner is expected to refuse a peerage, but that he is quite right, on behalf of his profession, to claim it as his due before it is offered. His lecture is such a claim; and in advancing it, he has done worthily and courageously—worthily, because a title can add nothing to his personal eminence, and courageously, because many unworthy persons will wound him by seeing nothing in the act but a vain man grasping at a handle for his name.

But since this was Mr Irving's meaning, why was he too shy to say so in plain words, with the i's dotted and the t's crossed? Why observe that "the philologists define the word Art, as we have it, as coming through the Latin from the Greek. In this language the root-word means etc. etc. etc."? In the Royal Institution an actor should not meddle with philology, for precisely the same reason as a philologist should not meddle with acting. And even when an actor exercises his right as an artist to talk about art, he should be careful to speak from his knowledge and not from his imagination, lest he unknowingly fall into the style of a Cabinet Minister proposing the health of the President of the Royal Academy, and be received by irreverent Slade scholars with the thumb to the nose. For example:

"What is there in works of genius, howsoever they may be represented, which touches the heart with emotion? We feel it as we gaze on the beauty which Canova wrought in marble, which Raphael and Velasquez and Vandyke and Reynolds and Gainsborough depicted on canvas, which Michael Angelo piled up to the dome of St Peter's, or as we listen to the tender strains of Mozart, the sad witchery of Mendelssohn, or the tempestuous force of Wagner."

I have no doubt Mr Irving, reading this over, and not for the life of him being able to see what I have to complain of in it, will think me nothing short of a wizard when I tell him that I have discovered from it that he does not know Arnolfo from Brunelleschi in architecture, nor Carpaccio from Guido in painting, nor Rossini from Rubinstein in music. One does not illustrate Michael Angelo's genius from the dome of St Peter's, which was another man's affair; nor do you lump Canova with Velasquez or Raphael with Gainsborough, any more than you lump Blondin and the late Mr Spurgeon with Henry Irving. As to the "sad witchery" put forward as Mendelssohn's general characteristic, I can only wish Mr Irving better luck next time. Never did man make a worse shot in the dark. And yet Mr Irving has a fine ear; for he hears the music of Mozart, Mendelssohn, and Wagner, as aforesaid, "in Nature's choral forces—that mighty gamut of creation which rises from the tiniest whisper of whirring wings in the insect world, through the sighing of the night wind, the crackle of swaying corn, the roar of falling water, and the mighty voice of the sounding sea, up to the hiss of the lightning flash and the crash of the thunderbolt."

This quotation, by the way, also proves that Mr Irving does not know fine literature from penny-a-liner's fustian—though that, alas! we have known ever since we heard him, a Mephistopheles, threatening to do all manner of horrible things to Faust in a passage not at all unlike the above.

Here I can imagine some good-natured reader asking me why I go on like this at our favorite actor—whether I deliberately wish to be disagreeable. My answer is, yes. I do deliberately want to make it impossible for Mr Irving, or any other member of his profession, ever hereafter to get on the Royal Institution or any other platform, and, with stores of first-hand experience to draw on for a sincere and authoritative, and consequently enormously interesting and valuable lecture on his art, to put us off with two columns of stereo concerning which I can tell Mr Irving with the utmost exactitude, and without fear of contradiction, that if he wrote it himself he wasted his time, and that if—as I prefer to believe—he got it written for him, he need not have paid the writer a farthing more than one-and-sixpence an hour, at which rate I will undertake to procure him, in the reading-room of the British Museum and at the shortest notice, as much literary matter to match his sample as he wants. And of all the critics who paid Mr Irving flowery little compliments on his exhibition next day, there is not one who does not know this as well as I know it. Some day, no doubt, I, too, shall succumb to Mr Irving's charm and prestige. But for the present I prefer to say what I think. I can well understand that it is natural for an actor to resort to his art on the platform, and to *act* the lecturer from a written part rather than venture, without experience, to be the lecturer. But surely, if Mr Irving could so happily come before the curtain at the Lyceum, and wish an audience of friends that affectionate happy new year, he could equally come before a still more select circle of friends in Albemarle Street, and, having told them frankly what he knew about his own art, plead that whether it be ranked as a creative art, like Sir Frederick Leighton's (or like Liszt's playing of Beethoven's sonatas, according to a memorable and luminous criticism of Wagner's), or an executive art like Sir Charles Hallé's, it is no less worthy than theirs of a recognition which, though it could make no personal difference to him, would make all the difference in the world to the status of his profession. Of course, that would not be acting; but then acting is the one thing that is intolerable in a lecturer. Even on the stage it is a habit that only the finest actors get rid of completely.

THE LIVING PICTURES

[6 *April* 1895]

I HAVE been to see the Living Pictures at the Palace Theatre. The moment Lady Henry Somerset called public attention to the fact that they were obnoxious to the National Vigilance Association, I resolved to try whether they would offend me. But this, like many other good resolutions of mine, remained unfulfilled until I was reminded of it by the address recently delivered by Mr William Alexander Coote, the secretary of the Association, to the Church and Stage Guild, as reported verbatim in that excellent little paper the Church Reformer. In this address, Mr Coote said that he considered the Living Pictures "the ideal form of indecency." I at first supposed this to mean an ideally desirable form of indecency; but later on I found Mr Coote denouncing the pictures as "shameful productions, deserving the condemnation of all right-thinking people." That cured my procrastination, and incidentally brought five shillings into the till of the Palace Theatre. For I hurried off to see the Living Pictures at once, not because I wanted to wallow in indecency—no man in his senses would go to a public theatre with that object even in the most abandoned condition of public taste, privacy being a necessary condition of thorough-going indecency—but because, as a critic, I at once perceived that Mr Coote had placed before the public an issue of considerable moment: namely, whether Mr Coote's opinion is worth anything or not. For Mr Coote is a person of real importance, active, useful, convinced, thoroughly respectable, able to point to achievements which we must all admit honorable to him, and backed by an Association strong enough to enable him to bring his convictions to bear effectively on our licensing authorities. But all this is quite compatible with Mr Coote being in artistic matters a most intensely stupid man, and on sexual questions something of a monomaniac.

I sat out the entire list of sixteen Living Pictures. Half a dozen represented naiads, mountain sprites, peris, and

Lady Godiva, all practically undraped, and all, except perhaps Lady Godiva, who was posed after a well-known picture by Van Lerius (who should have read Landor's imaginary conversation between Lady Godiva and her husband), very pretty. I need hardly say that the ladies who impersonated the figures in these pictures were not actually braving our climate without any protection. It was only too obvious to a practised art critic's eye that what was presented as flesh was really spun silk. But the illusion produced on the ordinary music-hall frequenter was that of the undraped human figure, exquisitely clean, graceful, and, in striking contrast to many of the completely draped and elaborately dressed ladies who were looking at them, perfectly modest. Many of the younger and poorer girls in the audience must have gone away with a greater respect for their own persons, a greater regard for the virtues of the bath, and a quickened sense of the repulsiveness of that personal slovenliness and gluttony which are the real indecencies of popular life, in addition to the valuable recreation of an escape for a moment into the enchanted land to which naiads and peris belong. In short, the living pictures are not only works of art: they are excellent practical sermons; and I urge every father of a family who cannot afford to send his daughters the round of the picture galleries in the Haymarket and Bond Street, to take them all (with their brothers) to the Palace Theatre.

This is how they struck me. Now let Mr Coote explain how they struck him.

"What cant to talk about 'Art' in connection with these living picture exhibitions! They are so obviously 'living.' Human nature is so very much in evidence. The nude as represented by the true artist on canvas never has the slightest tendency to demoralize. The artist's soul so consciously pervades the work that the beauty of form and pose hides that which would mar or vulgarize the picture. The subject is spiritualized, and becomes an inspiration for good and lovely thoughts. It is very different with the 'living picture.'

There is no art in it. Paradoxical as it may seem, there is no life in the living picture: it is even posed as a lifeless mass. There is a marked difference between the canvas or marble and the living picture, much to the disadvantage of the latter."

In discussing the above utterance, I do not want to take an unfair advantage of the fact that in writing about art I am a trained expert, and Mr Coote a novice. Mr Coote's object in undertaking a task so far beyond my powers as an explanation of the operation of the artist's soul is clearly to persuade us that he sees a distinction between an art that is false and an art that is true, and that it is his passionate devotion to the former that makes him so wroth with the latter. Let us see.

First, Mr Coote tells us that there is no art in the Palace pictures. Well, I can quite believe that Mr Coote conceives that the posing and lighting of the figures so as to throw the figure into the required light and shadow is pure accident. Let me therefore make a suggestion. Let Mr Morton, the manager of the Palace, request Mr Dando, the arranger of the pictures, to stand aside and entrust his functions for one night (on which a stall may be reserved for me at any price the management chooses to exact) to Mr William Alexander Coote. Let the entire resources of the establishment be placed absolutely under his direction; and let us then see whether he can take advantage of there being "no art in it" to produce a single tableau that will not be ludicrously and outrageously deficient in the artist qualities without which Mr Dando's compositions would be hooted off the stage.

Now as to Mr Coote's assertion that the artist's soul spiritualizes his subject, and finds in it an inspiration for good and lovely thoughts. I can assure Mr Coote that he never made a greater mistake in his life. There are artists, and very able artists too, whose souls exactly resemble those of some members of the National Vigilance Association in debauching every subject, and finding in it an inspiration for obscene and unlovely thoughts. If Mr Coote, in the course of his next holiday, will travel from Padua to Mantua and compare Giotto's pictorial decoration of the arena chapel with Giulio Romano's decoration of the Palazzo Té, he will learn that the artist's soul can commune with the satyrs as well as with the saints. He need go no further than our own National Gallery to see the work of great artists who, like Paul Veronese, or Rubens, materialize all their subjects and appeal to our love of physical splendor and vitality, exhibited under the same roof with those of the pre-Raphaelites (the real ones), whose works of art were also works of devotion. What is more, he will find the same artist expressing his devotional mood in one picture and his voluptuous mood in another; and if he will go as far as Venice—and the journey will be well worth his while—he can see there, in Titian's Virgin of the Assumption, a union of the flesh and the spirit so triumphantly beautiful, that he will return abashed to the Church and Stage Guild, and apologize to them very humbly for having mixed up his account of his Vigilance stewardship with a sham lecture on a subject of which he does not know enough to be even conscious of his own ignorance.

Let me now help Mr Coote out of his difficulty. He admits by implication that works of art are above the law, and should be tolerated at all hazards. He then attempts to show that the works he objects to are not "true art," and that therefore his hostility to them does not imply any hostility to Phidias and Raphael and the Royal Academy and so on. No person who really understands Art would make any such admission. A work of art is no more above the law than anything else. An old bridge may be a beautiful work of mediaeval art; but if it obstructs navigation, causes the river to silt up, or becomes insufficient for the traffic, it must come down. A palace may be a gem of the builder's art; but if its site is imperatively required for a better lighted and drained modern building, however ugly, or for a new thoroughfare, down it must come too. And if the living pictures, or M. Jules Garnier's illustrations to Rabelais, can be proved to be doing more harm than good, then Mr Coote is quite right to demand their suppression, works of art or no works of art. Mr Coote is quite entitled to carry out all his aims, to forbid the circulation of cheap unexpurgated Shakespears; to make it a punishable offense for an artist to paint from a nude model; and to send the manager of the Palace Theatre to prison, if he can convince us that it is for the public interest that these things should be done. No plea as to the sacredness of art could in that case be admitted for a moment. If Mr Coote feels modest about claiming so much, let him consult the gentleman whom he describes as "that strange, peculiar, yet splendid man, Mr. Stead." Mr Stead will, I think, as a matter of common sense, at once assure him that I am right.

Having now got rid of the Art question, and pulled Mr Coote out of that morass on to solid ground, I am almost tempted to begin by exhorting him to go to his Bible, and ponder the saying, "He which is filthy, let him be filthy still." But no public man in these islands ever believes that the Bible means what it says: he is always convinced that it says what he means; and I have no reason to hope that Mr Coote may be an exception to the rule. What, then, does Mr Coote found himself on? Apparently on this position, which I state in his own words: "Nothing in the management of our public entertainments can justify the exhibition of nude and semi-nude women as a means of amusement for a mixed audience." But why not, if the audience thinks the woman prettier and no less decent in that state than when fully draped, and she agrees with them; or if nudity or semi-nudity is appropriate to the character she is impersonating; or if she is performing athletic feats which skirts would hinder? Here is an instance which fulfils all three conditions. When Sir Augustus Harris first introduced at Covent Garden the Walpurgis ballet, which is one of the features of Gounod's Faust as performed at the Paris Grand Opéra, the dancer who impersonated Phryne dispensed with skirts altogether, and danced to the one exquisite tune that the ballet contains, in a costume which produced the illusion of nudity (I presume Mr Coote knows that it is only an illusion). She wore certain decorative ribbons, but no dress. She looked very graceful and quite modest; nobody in that huge theatre, which was crowded from floor to ceiling, objected in the least; it did not occur to us for a moment to complain of the absence of the ballet skirts and petticoats which make a woman look like an ostrich or a teetotum.

I will not pretend to misunderstand Mr Coote's objection to this. There are in the world a certain number of persons who, owing to morbid irritability in certain directions, are greatly incommoded by circumstances which are indifferent, or even agreeable, to the normal man. For instance, London is rather an ill-smelling place; and people with exceptionally acute noses suffer agonies on stagnant days when ordinary people notice nothing. Carlyle, even in the comparative quietude of Chelsea, had to take special measures to keep the noises of the streets from his irritable ears; people with tender eyes have to resort to blue spectacles; humane people are made miserable by the treatment of our beasts of burden; and we find people oppressed by a special susceptibility to the dread inspired by hydrophobia, cholera, the Jesuits, the possibility of being damned, and many other contingencies which only occur to normal persons when they are out of health. On the other hand, we find people who are deficient in certain faculties—blind people, deaf people, color-blind people, people with no musical faculty, callous people, unsocial people, and so on. And we also find people in whom a deficiency in one respect is associated with an excess of sensitiveness in others. Now, it is quite impossible to legislate and administer with a view to the comfort of these abnormal people, even though there may, in so large a population as ours, be enough of any one variety of them to form an association and make a vigorous agitation. For instance, the Church will not modify the rite of communion because certain deplorable cases are on record in which the taste of the sacramental wine has brought on a ruinous attack of drink craze in the communicant. We do not suppress public meetings and abolish the right of free speech because people who are peculiarly susceptible to political excitement and the stimulus of platform oratory are led to behave foolishly and misuse their votes on such occasions. We do not prohibit "revivalist" prayer meetings because of the mischievously hysterical condition into which weak people are thrown by them, a condition which the ignorant preacher glories in producing. We shall not stop the performances of The Notorious Mrs Ebbsmith because it has produced a case of suicide. In short, we shall not lead the life of invalids for the sake of a handful of unfortunate people to whom such a life is the only safe one.

The application of all this to Mr Coote's position is obvious. We have among us a certain number of people who are morbidly sensitive to sexual impressions, and quite insensible to artistic ones. We have certain sects in which such a condition is artificially induced as a matter of religious duty. Children have their affections repressed, and their susceptibility to emotional excitement nursed on sin, wrath, terror, and vengeance, whilst they are forbidden to go to the theatre or to amuse themselves with stories or "profane" pictures. Naturally, when such people grow up, life becomes to them a prolonged temptation of St Anthony. You try to please them by a picture which appeals to their delight in graceful form and bright warm color, to their share in the romance which peoples the woods and streams with sylphs and water maidens, to the innocent and highly recreative love of personal beauty, which is one of the great advantages of having a sex at all. To your horror and discomposure, you are met by a shriek of "Nude woman: nude woman: police!" The one thing that the normal spectator overlooks in the picture is the one thing that St Anthony sees in it. Let me again put his protest in Mr Coote's own words: "Nothing can justify the exhibition of nude and semi-nude women as a means of amusement for a mixed audience. They are shameful productions, and deserve the condemnation of all right-thinking people. The manager deserves, and should have, the immediate attention of the County Council." You remonstrate, perhaps, from the point of view of the artist. Mr Coote at once pleads: "They are so very obviously *living*. Human nature is so very much in evidence." And there you have the whole of Mr Coote's pessimistic, misanthropic philosophy in two sentences. Human nature and the human body are to him nasty things. Sex is a scourge. Woman is a walking temptation which should be covered up as much as possible. Well, let us be charitable to Mr Coote's infirmity, and ask him, as kindly as may be, what good covering women up will do. Carmencita is covered up; our skirt dancers are all petticoats; each of our serpentine dancers carries drapery enough to make skirts for a whole dozen schoolgirls. And yet they appeal far more to the sex instinct and far less to the artistic instinct than the Naiads and Phryne. There is only one solution of the difficulty; and that is for Mr Coote and those that sympathize with him to keep away from the Palace Theatre. Of course that will not protect them altogether. Every low-necked dress, every gust of wind that catches a skirt and reveals an ankle, perhaps every child in whom "human nature is in evidence" to the extent of a pair of sturdy little legs, may be a torment to the victims of this most pitiable of all obsessions. A quarrel with human nature admits of no fundamental remedy except the knife; and I should be sorry to see the members of the Vigilance Association cutting their own throats; they are useful and even necessary in keeping order among the people who suffer from morbid attractions instead of morbid repulsions. For it must not be forgotten that Mr Coote's error does not lie in his claim that the community shall suppress indecent exhibitions, but in his attempt to make nudity or semi-nudity the criterion of indecency. Perhaps I should qualify this statement of his position by limiting nudity to the female sex; for I notice that the semi-nudity which is quite a common spectacle in the case of male athletes is not complained of, though, if there were anything in the Vigilance Association's view of such exhibitions as demoralizing, our women ought by this time to be much more demoralized than our men.

SARDOODLEDOM

FEDORA (Herman Merivale's English version). By Victorien Sardou. Haymarket Theatre, 25 May 1895.

GISMONDA. By Victorien Sardou. Daly's Theatre, 27 May 1895.

THE PRUDE'S PROGRESS. A Comedy in three acts. By Jerome K. Jerome and Eden Phillpotts. Comedy Theatre, 22 May 1895. [1 *June* 1895]

UP to this day week I had preserved my innocence as a playgoer sufficiently never to have seen Fedora. Of course I was not altogether new to it, since I had seen Diplomacy Dora, and Theodora, and La Toscadora, and other machine dolls from the same firm. And yet the thing took me aback. To see that curtain go up again and again only to disclose a bewildering profusion of everything that has no business in a play, was an experience for which nothing could quite prepare me. The postal arrangements, the telegraphic arrangements, the police arrangements, the names and addresses, the hours and seasons, the tables of consanguinity, the railway and shipping time-tables, the arrivals and departures, the whole welter of Bradshaw and Baedeker, Court Guide and Post Office Directory, whirling round one incredible little stage murder and finally vanishing in a gulp of impossible stage poison, made up an entertainment too Bedlamite for any man with settled wits to preconceive. Even the murder was arranged, in pure wantonness, flatly contrary to common sense. The hero is suspected by the heroine of having been a Nihilist at a period when matters were so bad in Russia that refugees who made no secret of their sympathy with the Terrorists were sympathetically welcomed by the strictest Constitutionalists in every other country in Europe. He completely regains her sympathy by proving to her that he is no Nihilist at all but a common assassin who has deliberately murdered a man out of jealousy. Surely, if dramatists are bent on the fundamentally impossible task of inventing pardonable assassinations, they should recognize that the man who, for no reward or satisfaction to his direct personal instincts, but at the risk of his own life, kills for the sake of an idea, believing that he is striking in the cause of the general weal, is at any rate more respectable than the dehumanized creature who stabs or shoots to slake a passion which he has in common with a stag. I strongly object to heroic criminals, whether political or personal; but if the stage cannot yet get on without its illustrated police news, let us at least shun the most repulsive motives for the stage crimes we are expected to condone. This Loris Ipanoff is a vulgar scoundrel as far as he is credibly human at all; and Fedora, who has at first the excuse of being the avenger of blood, sinks to his level when, on learning that her husband preferred another woman to her, she gloats over his murder, and is disappointed because Loris did not kill his wife on the spot too. Why need plays be so brutally, callously, barbarously immoral as this? I wish Sir Henry Irving would give us at least a matinée of The Lady from the Sea to show the playgoing public how a humane gentleman acts when he finds he has had the misfortune to lose the affection of his wife. Miss Terry as Ellida would be quite as worthy of the Lyceum Theatre as Nance Oldfield as Miss Terry.

It is greatly to Mrs Patrick Campbell's credit that, bad as the play was, her acting was worse. It was a masterpiece of failure. Not, pray observe, that Mrs Campbell herself did not succeed. The moment she was seen, our reason collapsed and our judgment fled. Every time the curtain fell there was a delirious roar. If the play was not tragic, our infatuation was. I solemnly warn all and sundry that no common man's opinion of the artistic merits of that performance was worth a farthing after the first flash of the heroine's eyes. It was not Fedora; but it was Circe; and I, as sworn critic, must make the best attempt I can to be Ulysses.

It cannot, I think, be disputed now that Mrs Campbell's force, which is intense enough, has only one mode, and that one the vituperative. This was proved at one stroke in the first act, when Fedora goes to her husband's bedside and discovers him dead. Mr Campbell uttered a shriek, as any actress would; but it was a shriek that suggested nothing of grief, or mortally wounded tenderness, or even horror. What it did suggest very strongly was that Fedora had surprised the secret which Loris reveals to her in the third act. In short, it was a scream of rage. Again, in the second act, when Loris admitted the killing of Vladimir, her cry of "Murderer, assassin," might have been any abusive term hurled at a man, appropriately or not, under an impulse of violent anger. Last week I politely attributed to Mrs Campbell's sense of character her catching, as Mrs Ebbsmith, what Miss Nethersole misses: namely, the tone of invective in "Trafalgar Squaring" the Duke of St Olpherts. But it now appears that her emotion declines to take any other form than that of invective. When she is not abusing somebody, she sits visibly concentrating her forces to restrain the vituperative pressure which is struggling to expand in reckless aggression, the general effect being that of a magnificent woman with a magnificent temper, which she holds in or lets loose with exciting uncertainty. This of course means that Mrs Campbell is not yet mistress of her art, though she has a rare equipment for it. Even her diction is technically defective. In order to secure refinement of tone, she articulates with the tip of her tongue against her front teeth as much as possible. This enters for what it is worth and no more into the method of every fine speaker; but it should not suggest the snobbish Irishman who uses it as a cheap recipe for speaking genteel English; and once or twice Mrs Campbell came dangerously near to producing this mincing effect. For instance, "One absorbing thought which meeks a sleeve of me," is clearly not the excess of a genuine refinement of diction, like Sir Henry Irving's pure vowel method, which would lead him to say "One ap-sorbing thot which m*è*ks a sl*è*v of me" (the p in absorbing being a German b, and the italic letters pronounced as in the French *fidèle*). I am only moderately pedantic in this matter, and do not object at all to Mrs Campbell's saying "Forgimme" for "Forgive me," or the traditional and ugly "Be't so" for the correct and pretty "Be it so"; but I protest against "hatrid" and "disseived," which are pure inaccuracies produced by that Irish recipe. I make no apology for going into these details; for stage usage is one of our few standards of diction; and it is rather alarming to hear the extent to which our younger actresses are left to pick up the stage trick of speech without in the least understanding the phonetic part of it.

The death scene begins like a feeble drawing room plagiarism of the murder of Nancy by Bill Sykes, and ends with the Gilbertian absurdity of the woman, as she realizes with disgust that her husband actually proposes to commit the vulgarity of strangling her, rising with a dignity which paralyzes him, and saying, "Oh, if you are determined to behave in that way, I will poison myself like a lady; and you, I hope, will look on quietly like a gentleman," or words to that effect. Here Mrs Campbell did for a moment produce the effect which Sardou has so tediously and laboriously lath-and-plastered up, and produce it in a way which showed unmistakeably that she is quite capable of the modern equivalents of the whole Bernhardtian range of sensational effects—effects so enormously popular and lucrative that, though their production is hardly more of a fine art than lion-taming, few women who are able for them can resist the temptation to devote their lives to them. At every other point, Mrs Campbell threw Sardou out of the window and substituted her own personal magnetism for the stale mechanical tragedy of Fedora. It was irrelevant; but it was effective.

Sardou's latest edition of the Kiralfian entertainment which Madame Bernhardt has for years past dragged from sea to sea in her Armada of transports, is called Gismonda, and is surpassingly dreary, although it is happily relieved four times by very long waits between the acts. The scene being laid in the Middle Ages, there are no newspapers, letters, or telegrams; but this is far from being an advantage as the characters tell each other the news all through except when a child is dropped into a tiger's cage as a cue for Madame Bernhardt's popular scream; or when the inevitable stale, puerile love scene is turned on to show off that "voix celeste" stop which Madame Bernhardt, like a sentimental New England villager with an American organ, keeps always pulled out; or when, in a paroxysm of the basest sensationalism, we are treated to the spectacle of Gismonda chopping a man to death with a hatchet as a preliminary to appearing as a mediæval saint with a palm in her hand at the head of a religious procession. What does it matter whether such an entertainment is called Gismonda, or Theodora, or Venice, or Constantinople, or The Orient, or Captain Boyton's water show? Personally, I prefer the water show, because the sixty-foot header interested me, which Madame Bernhardt has long ceased to do; and the sensation of shooting the chute thrilled me, which Gismonda does not. As a pageant the affair may pass very well with people who, never having been touched by the peculiar spiritual beauty of the art of the Middle Ages, compare the scene-painter's titivated imitations with the Lord Mayor's Show and the architecture of Regent Street instead of with the originals; but it is no more to be compared to the pageantry of King Arthur at the Lyceum than the clever but thoroughly shoppy stage business of Madame Bernhardt is to be compared to the acting of Miss Ellen Terry. I confess I regard with a certain jealousy the extent to which this ex-artist, having deliberately exercised her unquestioned right to step down from the national theatre in which she became famous to posture in a travelling show, is still permitted the privileges and courtesies proper to her former rank. It is open to all actresses to say either, "Give me a dignified living wage and let me work at my art," or, "Give me as much money and applause as can possibly be got out of me, and let my art go hang." Only, when the choice is made, it is the business of the critic to see that the chooser of the lower level does not take precedence of the devoted artist who takes the higher one. Madame Bernhardt has elected to go round the world pretending to kill people with hatchets and hairpins, and making, I presume, heaps of money. I wish her every success; but I shall certainly not treat her as a dramatic artist of the first rank unless she pays me well for it. As a self-respecting critic I decline to be bought for nothing.

It seems a strange thing to me that we should still be so little awake to the fact that in these plays which depend wholly on poignant intensity of expression for the simple emotions the sceptre has passed to the operatic artist. What surprises me is not that this exhibition of Madame Bernhardt's should be flagrantly vulgar and commercial, or that it should be hackneyed and old-fashioned, but that we should dream of going to see it now that we have seen Calvé as Carmen and La Navarraise. In the front ranks of art there is a place for the methods of Duse, and for the drama in which emotion exists only to make thought live and move us, but none for Sarah Bernhardt and the claptraps which Sardou contrives for her. To me, at least, the whole affair seems antiquated and ridiculous, except when I regard it as a high modern development of the circus and the waxworks. I have seen it, just as I have seen, in my time, Madame Celeste in Green Bushes and The Red Woman. Though I always preferred Buckstone to Sardou as a tragic dramatist, and still do, I used to think Madame Bernhardt a greater actress than Celeste. But I almost believe now that this must have been a delusion of the departed days when Madame Bernhardt was so slim that when she went for a trip in a captive balloon, it was said that her stepping into the car had the same effect as throwing out ballast. At all events, I am quite sure that if I had to choose between seeing Miami and Gismonda again, I should vote eagerly for Miami, who was at least amusing.

To revert for a moment to Fedora, I hope Mrs Campbell will note that Sarah Bernhardt's career cannot be repeated now—that her art is out of date and her dramas dead. The proof is that Mrs Campbell cannot act Fedora, although to any actress over forty-five Fedora is more natural than Mrs Tanqueray. By the way, I have forgotten to say that Mrs Bancroft is in the cast, and is as amusing and skilful as ever. Mr Tree, confronted with the impossible Loris Ipanoff, was forced to take the part seriously, and, with the help of a Polish make-up, try to pull it through by a creditably awkward attempt at conventional melodramatic acting. Besides, Mrs Campbell ruined his clothes. Wherever her beautiful white arms touched him they left their mark. She knelt at his feet and made a perfect zebra of his left leg with bars across it. Then she flung her arms convulsively right round him; and the next time he turned his back to the footlights there was little to choose between his coat-back and his shirtfront. Before the act was over a gallon of benzine would hardly have set him right again. Mr Tree had his revenge at the end of the play, when, in falling on Fedora's body, he managed to transfer a large black patch to her check, which was strikingly in evidence when she bowed her acknowledgment of the frantic applause with which the evening ended; but he was still so unhinged by the futility of Loris and the ill-treatment of his garments, that when the audience called for Mr Bancroft he informed them that Mr Bancroft was prevented from coming forward by modesty, but that Mrs Bancroft—and here Mrs Bancroft came forward smiling; and the audience naturally chuckled hugely.

May I suggest that soap and water is an excellent cosmetic for the arms, and that it does not mark coats? Also that this whitewashing malpractice has become an intolerable absurdity, and that there is at least one critic who means to try whether ridicule can kill it.

It is an unspeakable relief to get away from Sardou to Mr Jerome K. Jerome, whose Prude's Progress is much better than its name. Happy is the nation that has no history, and happy the play that has no criticism in this column. The Prude's Progress is a shrewd, goodnatured, clever cockney play (Mr Jerome will not think me foolish enough to use cockney as a term of disparagement), interesting and amusing all through, with pleasantly credible characters and pleasantly incredible incidents, ending happily but not fatuously; so that there is no sense of facts shirked on the one hand nor of problems stage-solved on the other. The play, from which, thanks to its unattractive name, not much was expected, won its way and was very favorably received. It is capitally acted, Miss Lena Ashwell being much better fitted than she was in King Arthur as Elaine, and Mr Cyril Maude having at last got a real part to act, instead of being condemned to paint wrinkles on his face, take snuff, and say "damn." Miss Brough and Mr Righton, who does a clever piece of acting by himself in the third act, keep the piece going with their accustomed comic vigor and geniality.

DUSE

La Femme de Claude. By Alexandre Dumas *fils*. Drury Lane Theatre, 5 June 1895. [8 *June* 1895]

The appearance of Duse at Drury Lane on Wednesday

in La Femme de Claude, is too recent for my judgment to have recovered from the emotional disturbance produced by such an appeal as she made to my passion for very fine acting. The furthest extremes of Duse's range as an artist must always, even in this greatest art centre in the world, remain a secret between herself and a few fine observers. I should say without qualification that it is the best modern acting I have ever seen, were it not that the phrase suggests a larger experience of first-rate acting in this department than I possess. I have only seen Salvini and Ristori in their historic-heroic parts, or in Shakespear; and my experience of Coquelin is limited to Molière and such plays of our own day as Les Surprises de Divorce. The work of these three great artists seemed to me (humanly speaking) quite thorough and perfect in its application to their conception of the parts they played; and their conception was, for the most part, adequate, and more than adequate, to the culture of their generation. But their incubatory period was the period before the theatre had advanced to the point at which Wagner and Ibsen became its master spirits. Duse is the first actress whom we have seen applying the method of the great school to characteristically modern parts or to characteristically modern conceptions of old parts. Her style is not, to the attentive observer of the stage, entirely new: nothing arrives at such perfection without many tentative approaches to it. I remember years ago, when The Lady of Lyons was first produced at the Lyceum, being struck with two things about it: first, the fact that Henry Irving, after much striving and, if I may be allowed the expression, not a little floundering, had at last discovered the method of heroic acting; and, second, that in the scene where Claude brings Pauline home after their wedding, Miss Ellen Terry, by a number of delicate touches, slipped into the scene a play of subtle emotion quite foreign to its traditions, with such effect that I can conjure up those moments perfectly to this day, though my utmost effort of memory cannot bring back the very faintest adumbration of any other scene in Pauline's part, which was as useless as material for Miss Terry's peculiar genius as most of those twenty-three Lyceum heroines—Catherine Duval in A Dead Heart, and so forth—of which Mr Clement Scott has made a list for my benefit, evidently to make me cry afresh over the wicked waste of so rare a talent. Of course the twenty-three parts are not all bad parts as parts are reckoned conventionally; and equally of course Miss Terry has not exactly played any of them badly. But neither is Shakespear's Cleopatra a bad part; and neither did Duse exactly play it badly. Yet who on earth would know that Duse was a great actress if he had never seen her play anything but Cleopatra? And who on earth will ever know what Miss Terry can do if we are never to see her except in plays that date, in feeling if not in actual composition, from the dark ages before the Married Women's Property Act? I can only guess at her powers myself from my recollections of the old Court Theatre, and the little interpolations in the Lyceum parts by which her genius so often instinctively thrusts through the old play to the new style, only, of course, to be beaten back by the giving out of the material. Still, just in these thrustings you could see Duse's style coming. Long after the Lady of Lyons came Miss Janet Achurch, whose playing as Alexandra, in Voss's play, came nearer to Duse's work in subtlety, continuity and variety of detail, and in beauty of execution, than anything I have seen on the English stage. But Duse has been helped to her supremacy by the fortunate sternness of Nature in giving her nothing but her genius. Miss Ellen Terry is a woman of quite peculiar and irresistible personal charm. Miss Achurch has been kept in constant danger of missing the highest distinction in her art by having, as an extra and cheaper string to her bow, an endowment of conventional good looks, and a large share of that power of expressing all the common emotions with extraordinary intensity which makes the vulgar great actress of the Bernhardt school. Consequently you have two Miss Achurches: the Miss Achurch of Nora and Alexandra, and the Miss Achurch of Adrienne and Forget-me-not; and there are moments when the two get mixed. But in Duse you necessarily get the great school in its perfect integrity, because Duse without her genius would be a plain little woman of no use to any manager, whereas Miss Terry or Miss Achurch, if they had no more skill than can be acquired by any person of ordinary capacity in the course of a few years' experience, would always find a certain degree of favor as pretty leading ladies. Duse, *with* her genius, is so fascinating that it is positively difficult to attend to the play instead of attending wholly to her. The extraordinary richness of her art can only be understood by those who have studied the process by which an actress is built up. You offer a part to a young lady who is an enthusiastic beginner. She reads it devoutly, and forms, say, half a dozen great ideas as to points which she will make. The difficulty then is to induce her to do nothing between these points; so that the play may be allowed at such moments to play itself. Probably when it comes to the point, these intervals will prove the only effective periods during her performance, the points being ill chosen or awkwardly executed. The majority of actresses never get beyond learning not to invent new points for themselves, but rather to pick out in their parts the passages which admit of certain well worn and tried old points being reapplied. When they have learnt to make these points smoothly and to keep quiet between whiles with a graceful air of having good reasons for doing nothing, they are finished actresses. The great actress has a harder struggle. She goes on inventing her points and her business determinedly, constantly increasing the original half-dozen, and constantly executing them with greater force and smoothness. A time comes when she is always making points, and making them well; and this is the finishing point with some actresses. But with the greatest artists there soon commences an integration of the points into a continuous whole, at which stage the actress appears to make no points at all, and to proceed in the most unstudied and "natural" way. This rare consummation Duse has reached. An attentive study of her

Marguerite Gauthier, for instance, by a highly trained observer of such things, will bring to light how its apparently simple strokes are combinations of a whole series of strokes, separately conceived originally, and added one by one to the part, until finally, after many years of evolution, they have integrated into one single highly complex stroke. Take, as a very simple illustration, the business of Camille's tying up the flowers in the third act. It seems the most natural thing in the world; but it is really the final development of a highly evolved dance with the arms—even, when you watch it consciously, a rather prolonged and elaborate one. The strokes of character have grown up in just the same way. And this is the secret of the extraordinary interest of such acting. There are years of work, bodily and mental, behind every instant of it—work, mind, not mere practice and habit, which is quite a different thing. It is the rarity of the gigantic energy needed to sustain this work which makes Duse so exceptional; for the work is in her case highly intellectual work, and so requires energy of a quality altogether superior to the mere head of steam needed to produce Bernhardtian explosions with the requisite regularity. With such high energy, mere personal fascination becomes a thing which the actress can put off and on like a garment. Sarah Bernhardt has nothing but her own charm, for the exhibition of which Sardou contrives love scenes—save the mark. Duse's own private charm has not yet been given to the public. She gives you Césarine's charm, Marguerite Gauthier's charm, the charm of La Locandiera, the charm, in short, belonging to the character she impersonates; and you are enthralled by its reality and delighted by the magical skill of the artist without for a moment feeling any complicity either on your own part or hers in the passion represented. And with that clue to the consistency of supreme admiration for the artist with perfect respect for the woman—a combination so rare that some people doubt its possibility—I must leave discussion of the plays she has appeared in this week to my next article.

DUSE AND BERNHARDT

[15 *June* 1895]

MR WILLIAM ARCHER'S defence of the dramatic critics against Mr Street's indictment of them for their indifference to acting appears to be falling through. Mr Archer pleads that whereas Hazlitt and Leigh Hunt had frequent opportunities of comparing ambitious actors in famous parts, the modern dramatic critic spends his life in contemplating "good acting plays" without any real people in them, and performers who do not create or interpret characters, but simply lend their pretty or popular persons, for a consideration, to fill up the parts. Mr Archer might have added another reason which applies to nearly all modern works: to wit, the operation of our copyright laws, whereby actors and actresses acquire the right not only to perform new plays but to prevent anyone else from performing them. Nevertheless we critics can now at last outdo Hazlitt and Leight Hunt if we have a mind to; for we have just had two Mrs Ebbsmiths to compare, besides a fourth Fedora, and Duse and Sarah Bernhardt playing La Dame aux Camellias and Sudermann's Heimat against one another at Daly's Theatre and at Drury Lane. Clearly now or never is the time for a triumphant refutation of the grievance of the English actor against the English Press: namely, that hardly any critic knows enough about acting to be able to distinguish between an effective part and a well played one, or between the bag of tricks which every old hand carries and the stock of ideas and sense of character which distinguish the master-actor from the mere handy man.

This week began with the relapse of Sarah Bernhardt into her old profession of serious actress. She played Magda in Sudermann's Heimat, and was promptly challenged by Duse in the same part at Drury Lane on Wednesday. The contrast between the two Magdas is as extreme as any contrast could possibly be between artists who have finished their twenty years apprenticeship to the same profession under closely similar conditions. Madame Bernhardt has the charm of a jolly maturity, rather spoilt and petulant, perhaps, but always ready with a sunshine-through-the-clouds smile if only she is made much of. Her dresses and diamonds, if not exactly splendid, are at least splendacious; her figure, far too scantily upholstered in the old days, is at its best; and her complexion shows that she has not studied modern art in vain. Those charming roseate effects which French painters produce by giving flesh the pretty colour of strawberries and cream, and painting the shadows pink and crimson, are cunningly reproduced by Madame Bernhardt in the living picture. She paints her ears crimson and allows them to peep enchantingly through a few loose braids of her auburn hair. Every dimple has its dab of pink; and her finger-tips are so delicately incarnadined that you fancy they are transparent like her ears, and that the light is shining through their delicate blood-vessels. Her lips are like a newly painted pillar box; her cheeks, right up to the languid lashes, have the bloom and surface of a peach; she is beautiful with the beauty of her school, and entirely inhuman and incredible. But the incredibility is pardonable, because, though it is all the greatest nonsense, nobody believing in it, the actress herself least of all, it is so artful, so clever, so well recognized a part of the business, and carried off with such a genial air, that it is impossible not to accept it with good-humour. One feels, when the heroine bursts on the scene, a dazzling vision of beauty, that instead of imposing on you, she adds to her own piquancy by looking you straight in the face, and saying, in effect: "Now who would ever suppose that I am a grandmother?" That, of course, is irresistible; and one is not sorry to have been coaxed to relax one's notions of the dignity of art when she gets to serious business and shows how ably she does her work. The coaxing suits well with the childishly egotistical character of her acting, which is not the art of making you think more highly or feel more deeply, but the art of making you admire her, pity her, champion her, weep with her, laugh at her jokes, follow her fortunes breathlessly, and applaud her wildly when the curtain falls. It is the art of finding out all your weaknesses and practizing on them—cajoling you, harrowing you, exciting you—on the whole, fooling you. And it is always Sarah Bernhardt in her own capacity who does this to you. The dress, the title of the play, the order of the words may vary; but the woman is always the same. She does not enter into the leading character: she substitutes herself for it.

All this is precisely what does not happen in the case of Duse, whose every part is a separate creation. When she comes on the stage, you are quite welcome to take your opera-glass and count whatever lines time and care have so far traced on her. They are the credentials of her humanity; and she knows better than to obliterate that significant handwriting beneath a layer of peach-bloom from the chemist's. The shadows on her face are grey, not crimson; her lips are sometimes nearly grey also; there are neither dabs nor dimples; her charm could never be imitated by a barmaid with unlimited pin money and a row of footlights before her instead of the handles of a beer-engine. The result is not so discouraging as the patrons of the bar might suppose. Wilkes, who squinted atrociously, boasted that he was only quarter of an hour behind the handsomest man in Europe: Duse is not in action five minutes before she is quarter of a century ahead of the handsomest woman in the world. I grant that Sarah's elaborate Monna Lisa smile, with the conscious droop of the eyelashes and the long carmined lips coyly disclosing the brilliant row of teeth, is effective of its kind—that it not only appeals to your susceptibilities, but positively jogs them. And it lasts quite a minute, sometimes longer. But Duse, with a tremor of the lip which you feel rather than see, and which lasts half an instant, touches you straight on the very heart; and there is not a line in the face, or a cold tone in the grey shadow that does not give poignancy to that tremor. As to youth and age, who can associate purity and delicacy of emotion, and simplicity of expression, with the sordid craft that repels us in age; or voluptuous appeal and egotistical self-insistence with the candor and generosity that attract us in youth? Who ever thinks of Potiphar's wife as a young woman, or St Elizabeth of Hungary as an old one? These associations are horribly unjust to age, and undeserved by youth: they belong of right to differences of character, not of years; but they rule our imaginations; and the great artist profits by them to appear eternally young. However, it would be a critical blunder as well as a personal folly on my part to suggest that Duse, any more than Sarah Bernhardt, neglects any art that could heighten the effect of her acting when she is impersonating young and pretty women. The truth is that in the art of being beautiful, Madame Bernhardt is a child beside her. The French artist's stock of attitudes and facial effects could be catalogued as easily as her stock of dramatic ideas: the counting would hardly go beyond the fingers of both hands. Duse produces the illusion of being infinite in variety of beautiful pose and motion. Every idea, every shade of thought and mood, expresses itself delicately but vividly to the eye; and yet, in an apparent million of changes and inflexions, it is impossible to catch any line at an awkward angle, or any strain interfering with the perfect abandonment of all the limbs to what appears to be their natural gravitation towards the finest grace. She is ambidextrous and supple, like a gymnast or a panther; only the multitude of ideas which find physical expression in her movements are all of that high quality which marks off humanity from the animals, and, I fear I must add, from a good many gymnasts. When it is remembered that the majority of tragic actors excel only in explosions of those passions which are common to man and brute, there will be no difficulty in understanding the indescribable distinction which Duse's acting acquires from the fact that behind every stroke of it is a distinctively human idea. In nothing is this more apparent than in the vigilance in her of that high human instinct which seeks to awaken the deepest responsive feeling without giving pain. In La Dame aux Camellias, for instance, it is easy for an intense actress to harrow us with her sorrows and paroxysms of phthisis, leaving us with a liberal pennyworth of sensation, not fundamentally distinguishable from that offered by a public execution, or any other evil in which we still take a hideous delight. As different from this as light from darkness is the method of the actress who shows us how human sorrow can express itself only in its appeal for the sympathy it needs, whilst striving by strong endurance to shield others from the infection of its torment. That is the charm of Duse's interpretation of the stage poem of Marguerite Gauthier. It is unspeakably touching because it is exquisitely considerate: that is, exquisitely sympathetic. No physical charm is noble as well as beautiful unless it is the expression of a moral charm; and it is because Duse's range includes these moral high notes, if I may so express myself, that her compass, extending from the depths of a mere predatory creature like Claude's wife up to Marguerite Gauthier at her kindest or Magda at her bravest, so immeasurably dwarfs the poor little octave and a half on which Sarah Bernhardt plays such pretty canzonets and stirring marches.

Obvious as the disparity of the two famous artists has been to many of us since we first saw Duse, I doubt whether any of us realized, after Madame Bernhardt's very clever performance as Magda on Monday night, that there was room in the nature of things for its annihilation within forty-eight hours by so comparatively quiet a talent as Duse's. And yet annihilation is the only word for it. Sarah was very charming, very jolly when the sun shone, very petulant when the clouds covered it, and positively angry when they wanted to take her child away from her. And she did not trouble us with any fuss about the main theme of Sudermann's play, the revolt of the modern woman against that ideal of home which exacts the sacrifice of her whole life to its care, not by her grace, and as its own sole help and refuge, but as a right which it has to the services of all females as abject slaves. In fact, there is not the slightest reason to suspect Madame Bernhardt of having discovered any such theme in the play; though Duse, with one look at Schwartze, the father, nailed it to the stage as the subject of the impending dramatic struggle before she had been five minutes on the scene. Before long, there came a stroke of acting which will probably never be forgotten by those who saw it, and which explained at once why those artifices of the dressing-table which help Madame Bernhardt would hinder Duse almost as much as a screen placed in front of her. I should explain, first, that the real name of the play is not Magda but Home. Magda is a daughter who has been turned out of doors for defying her father, one of those outrageous persons who mistake their desire to have everything their own way in the house for a sacred principle of home life. She has a hard time of it, but at last makes a success as an opera singer, though not until her lonely struggles have thrown her for sympathy on a fellow student, who in due time goes his way, and leaves her to face motherhood as best she can. In the fullness of her fame she returns to her native town, and in an attack of homesickness makes advances to her father, who consents to receive her again. No sooner is she installed in the house than she finds that one of the most intimate friends of the family is the father of her child. In the third act of the play she is on the stage when he is announced as a visitor. It must be admitted that Sarah Bernhardt played this scene very lightly and pleasantly: there was genuine good fellowship in the way in which she reassured the embarrassed gallant and made him understand that she was not going to play off the sorrows of Gretchen on him after all those years, and that she felt that she owed him the priceless experience of maternity, even if she did not particularly respect him for it. Her self possession at this point was immense: the peach-bloom never altered by a shade. Not so with Duse. The moment she read the card handed her by the servant, you realized what it was to have to face a meeting with the man. It was interesting to watch how she got through it when he came in, and how, on the whole, she got through it pretty well. He paid his compliments and offered his flowers; they sat down; and she evidently felt that she had got it safely over and might allow herself to think at her ease, and to look at him to see how much he had altered. Then a terrible thing happened to her. She began to blush; and in another moment she was conscious of it, and the blush was slowly spreading and deepening until, after a few vain efforts to avert her face or to obstruct his view of it without seeming to do so, she gave up and hid the blush in her hands. After that feat of acting I did not need to be told why Duse does not paint an inch thick. I could detect no trick in it: it seemed to me a perfectly genuine effect of the dramatic imagination. In the third act of La Dame aux Camellias, where she produces a touching effect by throwing herself down, and presently rises with her face changed and flushed with weeping, the flush is secured by the preliminary plunge to a stooping attitude, imagination or no imagination; but Magda's blush did not admit of that explanation; and I must confess to an intense professional curiosity as to whether it always comes spontaneously.

I shall make no attempt to describe the rest of that unforgettable act. To say that it left the house not only frantically applauding, but actually roaring, is to say nothing; for had we not applauded Sarah as Gismonda and roared at Mrs Patrick Campbell as Fedora? But there really was something to roar at this time. There was a real play, and an actress who understood the author and was a greater artist than he. And for me, at least, there was a confirmation of my sometimes flagging faith that a dramatic critic is really the servant of a high art, and not a mere advertiser of entertainments of questionable respectability of motive.

THE CASE FOR THE CRITIC-DRAMATIST

MERRIFIELD'S GHOST. An original comedietta in one act. By H. M. Paull. Vaudeville Theatre, 13 November 1895. [16 *November* 1895]

A DISCUSSION has arisen recently as to whether a dramatic critic can also be a dramatic author without injury to his integrity and impartiality. The feebleness with which the point has been debated may be guessed from the fact that the favorite opinion seems to be that a critic is either an honest man or he is not. If honest, then dramatic authorship can make no difference to him. If not, he will be dishonest whether he write plays or not. This childish evasion cannot, for the honor of the craft, be allowed to stand. If I wanted to ascertain the melting-point of a certain metal, and how far it would be altered by an alloy of some other metal, and an expert were to tell me that a metal is either fusible or it is not—that if not, no temperature will melt it; and if so, it will melt anyhow—I am afraid I should ask that expert whether he was a fool himself or took me for one. Absolute honesty is as absurd an abstraction as absolute temperature or absolute value. A dramatic critic who would die rather than read an American pirated edition of a copyright English book might be considered an absolutely honest man for all practical purposes on that particular subject—I say on that one, because very few men have more than one point of honor; but as far as I am aware, no such dramatic critic exists. If he did, I should regard him as a highly dangerous monomaniac. That honesty varies inversely with temptation is proved by the fact that every additional penny on the income-tax yields a less return than the penny before it, showing that men state their incomes less honestly for the purposes of taxation at sevenpence in the pound than sixpence. The matter may be tested by a simple experiment. Go to one of the gentlemen whose theory is that a man is either honest or he is not, and obtain from him the loan of half a crown on some plausible pretext of a lost purse or some such petty emergency. He will not ask you for a written acknowledgment of the debt. Return next day and ask for a loan of £500 without a promissory note, on the ground that you are either honest or not honest, and that a man who will pay back half a crown without compulsion will also pay back £500. You will find that the theory of absolute honesty will collapse at once.

Are we then to believe that the critic-dramatist who stands to make anything from five hundred to ten thousand pounds by persuading a manager to produce his plays, will be prevented by his honesty from writing about that manager otherwise than he would if he had never written a play and were quite certain that he never should write one? I can only say that people who believe such a thing would believe anything. I am myself a particularly flagrant example of the critic-dramatist. It is not with me a mere case of an adaptation or two raked up against me as incidents in my past. I have written half a dozen "original" plays, four of which have never been performed; and I shall presently write half a dozen more. The production of one of them, even if it attained the merest success of esteem, would be more remunerative to me than a couple of years of criticism. Clearly, since I am no honester than other people, I should be the most corrupt flatterer in London if there were nothing but honesty to restrain me. How is it, then, that the most severe criticisms of managers come from me and from my fellow critic-dramatists, and that the most servile puffery comes from writers whose every sentence proves that they have nothing to hope or fear from any manager? There are a good many answers to this question, one of the most obvious being that as the respect inspired by a good criticism is permanent whilst the irritation it causes is temporary, and as, on the other hand, the pleasure given by a venal criticism is temporary and the contempt it inspires permanent, no man really secures his advancement as a dramatist by making himself despised as a critic. The thing has been tried extensively during the last twenty years; and it has failed. For example, the late Frank Marshall, a dramatist and an extravagantly enthusiastic admirer of Sir Henry Irving's genius, followed a fashion which at one time made the Lyceum Theatre a sort of court formed by a retinue of literary gentlemen. I need not question either their sincerity or the superiority of Canute to their idolatry; for Canute never produced their plays: Robert Emmett and the rest of their masterpieces remain unacted to this day. It may be said that this brings us back to honesty as the best policy; but honesty has nothing to do with it: plenty of the men who know that they can get along faster fighting than crawling, are no more honest than the first Napoleon was. No virtue, least of all courage, implies any other virtue. The cardinal guarantee for a critic's integrity is simply the force of the critical instinct itself. To try to prevent me from criticizing by pointing out to me the superior pecuniary advantages of puffing is like trying to keep a young Irving from going on the stage by pointing out the superior pecuniary advantages of stockbroking. If my own father were an actor-manager, and his life depended on his getting favorable notices of his performance, I should orphan myself without an instant's hesitation if he acted badly. I am by no means the willing victim of this instinct. I am keenly susceptible to contrary influences—to flattery, which I swallow greedily if the quality is sufficiently good; to the need of money, to private friendship or even acquaintanceship, to the pleasure of giving pleasure and the pain of giving pain, to consideration for people's circumstances and prospects, to personal likes and dislikes, to sentimentality, pity, chivalry, pugnacity and mischief, laziness and cowardice, and a dozen other human conditions which make the critic vulnerable; but the critical instinct gets the better of them all. I spare no efforts to mitigate its inhumanity, trying to detect and strike out of my articles anything that would give pain without doing any good. Those who think the things I say severe, or even malicious, should just see the things I do *not* say. I do my best to be partial, to hit out at remediable abuses rather than at accidental shortcomings, and at strong and responsible people rather than weak and helpless ones. And yet all my efforts do not alter the result very much. So stubborn is the critic within me, that with every disposition to be as goodnatured and as popular an authority as the worst enemy of art could desire, I am to all intents and purposes incorruptible. And that is how the dramatist-critic, if only he is critic enough, "slates" the actor-manager in defiance of the interest he has in conciliating him. He cannot help himself, any more than the ancient mariner could help telling his story. And the actor-manager can no more help listening than the wedding guest could. In short, the better formula would have been, that a man is either a critic or not a critic; that to the extent to which he is one he will criticize the managers in spite of heaven or earth; and that to the extent to which he is not, he will flatter them anyhow, to save himself trouble.

The advantage of having a play criticized by a critic who is also a playwright is as obvious as the advantage of having a ship criticized by a critic who is also a master shipwright. Pray observe that I do not speak of the criticism of dramas and ships by dramatists and shipwrights who are not also critics; for that would be no more convincing than the criticism of acting by actors. Dramatic authorship no more constitutes a man a critic than actorship constitutes him a dramatic author; but a dramatic critic learns as much from having been a dramatic author as Shakespear or Mr Pinero from having been actors. The average London critic, for want of practical experience, has no real confidence in himself: he is always searching for an imaginary "right" opinion, with which he never dares to identify his own. Consequently every public man finds that as far as the press is concerned his career divides itself into two parts: the first, during which the critics are afraid to praise him; and the second, during which they are afraid to do anything else.

In the first, the critic is uncomfortably trying to find faults enough to make out a case for his timid coldness: in the second, he is eagerly picking out excellences to justify his eulogies. And of course he blunders equally in both phases. The faults he finds are either inessential or are positive reforms, or he blames the wrong people for them: the triumphs of acting which he announces are stage tricks that any old hand could play. In criticizing actresses he is an open and shameless voluptuary. If a woman is pretty, well dressed, and self-satisfied enough to be at her ease on the stage, he is delighted; and if she is a walking monument of handsome incompetence, so much the better, as your voluptuary rarely likes a woman to be cleverer than himself, or to force him to feel deeply and think energetically when he only wants to wallow in her good looks. Confront him with an actress who will not condescend to attack him on this side—who takes her work with thorough seriousness and self-respect—and his resentment, his humiliation, his sense of being snubbed, break out ludicrously in his writing, even when he dare not write otherwise than favorably. A great deal of this nonsense would be taken out of him if he could only write a play and have it produced. No dramatist begins by writing plays merely as excuses for the exhibition of pretty women on the stage. He comes to that ultimately perhaps; but at first he does his best to create real characters and make them pass through three acts of real experiences. Bring a critic who has done this face to face with the practical question of selecting an actress for his heroine, and he suddenly realizes for the first time that there is not such a galaxy of talent on the London stage as he thought, and that the handsome walking ladies whom he always thought good enough for other people's plays are not good enough for his own. That is already an immense step in his education. There are other steps, too, which he will have taken before the curtain falls on the first public representation of his play; but they may be summed up in the fact that the author of a play is the only person who really wants to have it well done in every respect, and who therefore has every drawback brought fully home to him. The man who has had that awakening about one play will thenceforth have his eyes open at all other plays; and there you have at once the first moral with the first technical qualification of the critic—the determination to have every play as well done as possible, and the knowledge of what is standing in the way of that consummation. Those of our critics who, either as original dramatists or adapters and translators, have superintended the production of plays with paternal anxiety, are never guilty of the wittily disguised indifference of clever critics who have never seen a drama through from its first beginnings behind the scenes. Compare the genuine excitement of Mr Clement Scott, or the almost Calvinistic seriousness of Mr William Archer, with the gaily easy what-does-it-matterness of Mr Walkley, and you see at once how the two critic-dramatists influence the drama, whilst the critic-playgoer only makes it a pretext for entertaining his readers. On the whole there is only as much validity in the theory that a critic should not be a dramatist, as in the theory that a judge should not be a lawyer nor a general a soldier. You cannot have qualifications without experience; and you cannot have experience without personal interest and bias. That may not be an ideal arrangement; but it is the way the world is built; and we must make the best of it.

Poor Mr Potton, at the Vaudeville, is now preceded by a little play by Mr H. V. Paull, entitled Merrifield's Ghost, which I cannot honestly pretend to have enjoyed. Mere custom has inured me to the stage hero who is impossibly virtuous; but the modern gentleman who appeals for my sympathy solely on the ground that he has forged or stolen just as any ordinary criminal does, gets beyond my patience. Merrifield's ghost had not the ghost of an excuse for forging his friend's name or inflicting his confession on me. He does not interest me; and I do not see why I should be put to a great deal of trouble simply to form a low opinion of him.

The revival of Liberty Hall at the St James's was

chiefly remarkable for the happy termination of an absurd incident by Mr Alexander's reception, which attained the proportions of a public demonstration, and was so tremendously enthusiastic that he must have felt almost glad that the occasion of it, intensely disagreeable as it must have been, had happened to him. Liberty Hall is too long; and the scene in which the heroine overhears the hero saying to her sister "Nobody need ever know," and misunderstands it, is unpardonable; but otherwise it is a goodnatured and amusing play. Miss Furtado Clarke played the part of the sister seriously and well; but probably the audience regretted Miss Maude Millet, because she is more interesting than the part, and would have taken care not to sacrifice herself to it. Serious acting is all very well for Ibsen and people of that kind; but with popular west end authors it is a most dangerous habit for a young actress to indulge.

THE OLD ACTING AND THE NEW

THE COMEDY OF ERRORS. Performance by the Elizabethan Stage Society in Gray's Inn Hall, 7 December 1895.

[14 *December* 1895]

FOR a delightful, as distinguished from a commercially promising first night, the palm must be given this season to the Elizabethan Stage Society's performance of The Comedy of Errors in Gray's Inn Hall this day week. Usually I enjoy a first night as a surgeon enjoys an operation: this time I enjoyed it as a playgoer enjoys a pleasant performance. I have never, I hope, underrated the importance of the amateur; but I am now beginning to cling to him as the savior of theatrical art. He alone among the younger generation seems to have any experience of acting. Nothing is more appalling to the dramatic author than the discovery that professional actors of ten years standing have acquired nothing but a habit of brazening out their own incompetence. What is an actor nowadays, or an actress? In nine case out of ten, simply a person who has been "on tour" with half a dozen "London successes," playing parts that involve nothing but a little business thoughtlessly copied from the performances of their London "creators," with long intervals spent between each tour in the ranks of the unemployed. At the end of a lifetime so spent, the "actor" will no doubt be a genuine expert at railway travelling, at taking lodgings, and at cajoling and bullying landladies; but a decent amateur of two years standing, and of the true irrepressible sort, will beat him hopelessly at his art. What a fate is that of these unhappy young professionals, sick to desperation of a provincial routine compared to which that of a commercial traveller is a dream of romance, longing for a chance which they have not skill enough to turn to account even if some accident thrust it upon them, and becoming less interesting and attractive year by year at a profession in which the steady increase of personal fascination should have no limit but positive senility and decrepitude! I remember, years ago, when the Playgoers' Club was in its infancy, hearing Mr Pinero, in the course of an address to that body, break into an enthusiastic eulogium on the actor of the past, produced by the old stock-company system, versatile, a singer, a dancer, a fencer, an elocutionist, ready to play any part at a day's notice, and equally expert in comedy, drama, melodrama, Christmas pantomime, and the "legitimate." There is some German novel in which a crowd of medieval warriors, fired by the eloquence of Peter the Hermit, burns with a Christian longing to rush to the Holy Land and charge in serried ranks on the Paynim hosts—all except one man, who is obviously not impressed. Indignant at his coldness, they demand what he means by it. "Ive been there," is his sufficient explanation. That is how I felt when I was listening to Mr Pinero. Having been brought up on the old stock-company actor, I knew that he was the least versatile of beings—that he was nailed helplessly to his own line of heavy or light, young or old and played all the parts that fell to him as the representative of that line in exactly the same way. I knew that his power of hastily "swallowing" the words of a part and disgorging them at short notice more or less inaccurately and quite unimprovably (three months rehearsal would have left him more at sea than three hours) was incompatible with his ever knowing his part in any serious sense at all. I remembered his one absurd "combat" that passed for fencing, the paltry stepdance between the verses of his song in the pantomime that constituted him a dancer, the obnoxiousness of utterance which he called elocution and would impart to pupils for a consideration, the universal readiness which only meant that in his incorrigible remoteness from nature and art it mattered nothing what he did. Mr Pinero madly cited Sir Henry Irving as an example of the product of the stock-company training; but the fact is, when Sir Henry first attempted classical acting at the Lyceum, he did not know the A B C of it, and only succeeded by his original and sympathetic notions of the X Y Z. Nobody who is familiar with the best technical work of the Irving of today, its finish, dignity, and grace, and the exactitude of its expression of his thought and feeling, can (unless he remembers) form any idea of what our chief actor had to teach himself before he could carry veteran playgoers with him in his breach with the tradition of superhuman acting of which Barry Sullivan was, as far as I know, the last English exponent (need I say that the great Irish actor was born in Birmingham?). Barry Sullivan was a splendidly monstrous performer in his prime: there was hardly any part sufficiently heroic for him to be natural in it. He had deficiencies in his nature, or rather blanks, but no weaknesses, because he had what people call no heart. Being a fine man, as proud as Lucifer, and gifted with an intense energy which had enabled him to cultivate himself physically to a superb degree, he was the very incarnation of the old individualistic, tyrannical conception of a great actor. By magnifying that conception to sublimity, he reduced it to absurdity. There were just two serious parts which he could play—Hamlet and Richelieu—the two loveless parts in the grand repertory. I know that some people do not like to think of Hamlet as loveless, and that the Irving Hamlet has his heart in the right place, and almost breaks it in the scene with Ophelia; but this I take to be the actor's rebuke to Shakespear rather than an attempt to fulfil his intentions. Sir Henry Irving has never thought much of the immortal William, and has given him more than one notable lesson—for instance, in The Merchant of Venice, where he gave us, not "the Jew that Shakespear drew," but the one he ought to have drawn if he had been up to the Lyceum mark. Barry Sullivan, with his gift of lovelessness, *was* Hamlet, and consequently used to put his Ophelias out of countenance more than it is easy to describe. In Hamlet, as in Richelieu, it was right to create a figure whose utter aloofness from his fellows gave him an almost supernatural distinction, and cut him off from all such trifling intimacy with them as love implies. And it was his success in producing this very curious and very imposing effect that made for Barry Sullivan, in his best days (I am not now speaking of the period after 1870 or thereabout), a unique provincial and Australian reputation which carried him over parts he could not play at all, such as Othello, through which he walked as if the only line in the play that conveyed any idea to him was the description of Othello as "perplexed in the extreme," or Macbeth, who was simply Cibber's Richard (a favorite part of his) in mutton-chop whiskers. No doubt his temperament, with its exceptional combination of imaginative energy with coldness and proud timidity of the sympathetic passions, accentuated the superhuman pretension in the style of acting which he practised; but his predecessor, Macready (if I may judge from that extremely depressing document, his diary), must have been much more like him than like Sir Henry Irving. At all events, both Macready and Sullivan had abominable tempers, and relied for their stage climaxes on effects of violence and impetuosity, and for their ordinary impressiveness on grandiose assumption of style. Once, when my father mentioned to me that he had seen Macready play Coriolanus, and I asked him what it was like, he replied that it was like a mad bull. I do not offer this as evidence that my critical faculty is an inherited one—clearly there must have been some artistic method in the bull's madness to have gained such a reputation—but I feel quite sure that when Sir Henry Irving fulfils his promise to appear as Coriolanus, no father will describe him to his son as my father described Macready to me. Barry Sullivan, then, represented the grandiose and the violent on its last legs, and could do nothing for the young Irving but mislead him. Irving's mission was to re-establish on the stage the touching, appealing nobility of sentiment and affection—the dignity which only asserts itself when it is wounded; and his early attempts to express these by the traditional methods of the old domineering, self-assertive, ambitious, thundering, superb school led him for a time into a grotesque confusion of style. In playing villains, too, his vein of callous, humorous impishness, with its occasional glimpses of a latent bestial dangerousness, utterly defied the methods of expression proper to the heaven-defying, man-quelling tyrant, usurper, and murderer, who was the typical villain of the old school, and whose flavorless quintessence will be found by the curious distilled into that instructive Shakespearean forgery, Ireland's Vortigern. In short, Irving had to find the right expression for a perfectly new dignity and a perfectly new indignity; and it was not until he had done this that he really accomplished his destiny, broke the old tradition, and left Barry Sullivan and Macready half a century behind. I will not say that he also left Shakespear behind: there is too much of the "not for an age but for all time" about our bard for that; but it is a pity that the new acting was not applied to a new author. For though Sir Henry Irving's acting is no longer a falsification of the old style, his acting versions are falsifications of the old plays. His Hamlet, his Shylock, his Lear, though interesting in their own way, are spurious as representations of Shakespear. His Othello I have never seen: his Macbeth I thought fine and genuine, indicating that his business is with Shakespear's later plays and not with his earlier ones. But he owes it to literature to connect his name with some greater modern dramatist than the late Wills, or Tennyson, who was not really a dramatist at all. There is a nice bishop's part in Ibsen's——but I digress.

My point is that Sir Henry Irving's so-called training under the old stock-company system not only did not give him the individuality of his style—for to that it did not pretend—but that it failed to give him even those generalities of stage deportment which are common to all styles. The stock actor, when the first travelling companies came along, vanished before them, unwept, unhonored, and unsung, because the only sentiment he had inspired in the public was an intense desire for some means of doing without him. He was such an unpresentable imposter that the smart London person, well dressed and well spoken, figuring in plays ingeniously contrived so as to dispense with any greater powers of acting than every adroit man of the world picks up, came as an inexpressible relief. Dare I now confess that I am beginning to have moments of regret for him. The smart nullity of the London person is becoming intolerably tedious; and the exhaustion of the novelty of the plays constructed for him has stripped them of their illusion and left their jingling, rickety mechanism patent to a disgusted public. The latest generation of "leading ladies" and their heroes simply terrify me: Mr Bourchier, who had the good fortune to learn his business as an amateur, towers above them as an actor. And the latest crop of plays has been for the most part deliberately selected for production because of the very abjectness and venality which withered them, harvestless, almost as soon as they were above ground.

And yet there is more talent now than ever—more skill now than ever—more artistic culture—better taste, better acting, better theatres, better dramatic literature. Mr Tree, Mr Alexander, Mr Hare, have made honorable experiments; Mr Forbes Robertson's enterprise at the Lyceum is not a sordid one; Mr Henry Arthur Jones and Mr Pinero are doing better work than ever before, and doing it without any craven concession to the follies of "the British public." But it is still necessary, if you want to feel quite reassured, to turn your back on the ordinary commercial west end theatre, with its ignoble gambling for "a catch-on," and its eagerly envious whisperings of how much Mr Penley has made by Charley's Aunt, to watch the forlorn hopes that are led from time to time by artists and amateurs driven into action by the starvation of their artistic instincts. The latest of these is the Elizabethan Stage Society; and I am delighted to be able to taunt those who missed the performance in Gray's Inn Hall with being most pitiably out of the movement. The Lyceum itself could not have drawn a more distinguished audience; and the pleasant effect of the play, as performed on the floor of the hall without proscenium or fittings of any kind, and played straight through in less than an hour and a half without any division into acts, cannot be as much as imagined by any frequenter of our ordinary theatres. The illusion, which generally lapses during performances in our style whenever the principal performers are off the stage, was maintained throughout: neither the torchbearers on the stage nor the very effective oddity of the Dromio costumes interfering with it in the least. Only, the modern dresses of the audience, the gasaliers, and the portrait of Manisty next that of Bacon, were anachronisms which one had to ignore. The stage management was good as regards the exits, entrances, and groupings—not so good in the business of the speeches, which might have been made more helpful to the actors, especially to Adriana, whose best speeches were underdone. On the whole the acting was fair—much better than it would have been at an average professional performance. Egeon, one of the Dromios, and the courtezan distinguished themselves most. The evening wound up with a Dometsch concert of lute and viol, virginal and voice, a delectable entertainment which defies all description by the pen.

DE MORTUIS

[4 *July* 1896]

THOSE lazy spectators of the pageant of life who love to reflect on the instability of human greatness have by this time yawned and gone to bed after reading the last of the subsiding rush of paragraphs about the late Sir Augustus Harris. The day after his death one of the greetings addressed to me was, "And so your old enemy is gone." This shocked me at the moment; for, though I had no illusions whatever about his imaginary greatness as an operatic reformer, I did not dislike him personally; and I was naturally in a softer mood after the news of his premature death than I used to be at the time when, as a musical critic, I was making onslaught after onslaught on the spurious artistic prestige of Covent Garden. In those days the relations between us were certainly somewhat strained. There were seasons when I always sat down in my stall at Covent Garden with the virtuous consciousness of having paid hard money for it, instead of being the invited guest of the manager whose scalp it was my business to take. There were times, too, when I was warned that my criticisms were being collated by legal experts for the purpose of proving "prejudice" against me, and crushing me by mulcting my editor in fabulous damages. And, as sure as fate, if that editor had been a skinflint and a coward; if he had corruptly regarded his paper, in its critical relation to the fine arts, solely as a convenient instrument for unlimited sponging on managers, publishers, and picture-dealers for gratuitous boxes, stalls, books, prints, and private-view invitations; if he had been willing to sell his critic for an advertisement or for an invitation to the dinner or garden parties of the smartest partizans of the fashionable tenor or prima donna of the season; or if he had been a hired editor at the mercy of a proprietor of that stamp, then I should have been silenced, as many other critics were silenced. But the late Edmund Yates was not that sort of editor. He had his faults; but he did not run away from his own sword for fear of cutting his fingers with it; he did not beg the tribute he could compel; and he had a strong and loyal *esprit de corps*. The World proved equal to the occasion in the conflict with Covent Garden; and finally my invitations to the Opera were renewed; the impresario made my personal acquaintance, and maintained the pleasantest personal relations with me from that time onward; and so, as I have said, when his death was announced, I was quite taken aback by the reference to our ancient warfare.

I refer to it myself now because it is well that the public should know the truth as to the perils of the relation between the Press, the theatre, and the law. I have sometimes been asked whether the attempt to suppress my criticism was made with a Napoleonic dispassionateness, as part of the routine of a huge commercial enterprise fighting for its monopoly as a matter of life or death, and bent on bringing the Press to heel at any cost, or whether the impresario regarded me as a sort of critical cobra, unable to contain my venom, and subject to fits of blind, purposeless, altogether brutish fits of malicious rage against his splendid and beloved Opera. I reply that even if he had entertained the latter opinion of me—and no doubt, being only human, he may have done so once or twice for a day or so after reading some particularly exasperating sally of mine—yet the practical steps he took to silence or intimidate me were taken in legitimate self-defence, and were as much a part of his business as his advertisements were. All managers do the same —why should they not?—and that is why so few critics say what they think. Personal motives do not count for much in any theatre, even in the case of actor-managers who angrily profess them, simply because the commercial pressure under which a manager works, with his money flying away at the rate of from five hundred to a thousand a week, and no sort of certainty of the receipts amounting to fifty, will nail the touchiest actor to strict business if he is capable of management at all. But if this is true of the theatre, what must be the state of mind of the Covent Garden impresario, whose expenses for one performance would keep a theatre going for a fortnight? Such conditions bring the most wilful and thin-skinned man back to his business interests every time he lapses into petulance or sentimental generosity. Besides, there was one gigantic business obligation which was peculiar to Sir Augustus Harris. In ordinary theatrical management nobody proposes a policy of monopoly. It is quite understood that Mr Alexander must count on the competition of Mr Tree, Mr Hare, Sir Henry Irving, and, in fact, as many competitors as there are suitable theatres in London. But the Augustan policy at Covent Garden was one of monopoly at all costs. The impresario well knew what the old system of two competing operas, one at Her Majesty's and the other at Covent Garden, was like behind the scenes. To issue flashy lying prospectuses; to slip into your theatre by back ways so as to avoid the ambuscades of the unpaid chorus; to hold your artists spellbound with flattering conversations until after bank hour lest they should present their cheques before money could be scraped together to meet them: all these shifts and dodges of the bankrupt two-opera system were no part of the Harris *régime*, under which the credit of the Covent Garden treasury became as that of the Bank of England. Sir Augustus Harris paid more money every year to prevent artists from working for anybody else than some of his predecessors paid for work actually done on their stages. The grievance at Covent Garden was, not that you could not get your money, but that you were not allowed to earn it. He not only held Drury Lane and Covent Garden against all comers, but took Her Majesty's and locked it up until it was demolished. Even in smaller theatres tenants found clauses in their agreements barring Italian Opera. Just as he forestalled possible rivals as a pantomime manager by engaging all the stars of the music-hall, whether he had work for them or not, so, as an impresario, he engaged every operatic artist who shewed the slightest promise of becoming a source of strength to a competitor.

When Signor Lago discovered Cavaleria, the Ravoglis, and Ancona, they were bought over his head immediately. There was no malice in the matter. The alternative to monopoly was bankruptcy. Sir Augustus Harris's triumph as a business impresario was his acceptance of that big condition and his achievement of the feat of finance and organization involved by it.

As an artistic impresario, he applied his Drury Lane experience of the stage management of crowds with great effect to a few simple melodramatic operas, notably to William Tell, and afterwards to La Navarraise and L'Attaque du Moulin. But the current notion that he could handle the masterpieces of dramatic music is a ludicrous delusion. I notice that The World, forgetting its back numbers, says, "Sir Augustus Harris's most excellent work was his resuscitation of Grand Opera in England. Hitherto opera had spelt ruin, for it had been slipshod, inartistic, absurd. Sir Augustus Harris labored to cast aside the fatuous conventions of the Italian school, and to adopt all that was best in the German stage." *Sancta simplicitas!* The truth is that he fought obstinately for the Italian fatuities against the German reforms. He was saturated with the obsolete operatic traditions of the days of Tietjens, whose Semiramide and Lucrezia he admired as great tragic impersonations. He described Das Rheingold as "a damned pantomime"; he persisted for years in putting Tannhäuser on the stage with Venusberg effects that would have disgraced a Whitechapel Road gaff, with the twelve horns on the stage replaced by a military band behind the scenes, and with Rotten Row trappings on the horses; he introduced *opéra-bouffe* warriors—girls with flaxen wigs and Greek helmets—into the Elysian Fields in Gluck's Orfeo; he could not be persuaded to engage a first-rate or even a second-rate conductor, or to make his stage manager at least ask somebody to tell him enough of the stories of the operas to prevent Meyerbeer's Huguenot soldiers from joining in the prayers of the Catholics, or to provide something more plausible for Gilda to die upon than a comfortable sofa placed in the middle of a street in a thunderstorm; he wasted the talents of dramatic singers like Maurel and Giulia Ravogli, who required intelligent management and casting to make the most of them; he could provide unlimited luxury and limelight, but not artistic incentive, for the wonderful bevy of singers, the de Reszkes, Melba, Eames, Calvé, and Plançon, who were the real winners of his success; in short, he did and undid and left undone such things as I dare not set down here at this moment lest I should jog the memory of the Recording Angel to his peril. It was only in the last few years that he began to learn something from Calvé and the young Italian school, from Wagner, from Massenet and Bruneau, and from Verdi's latest works. Had he been merely an ignorant man, it would have been much better for him; for then he might have had that advantage over his predecessors which Mr Archer lays his finger on in speaking of his start as manager of Drury Lane—"he was too young and practical to be in the least degree hampered by tradition." In opera, unfortunately, he was soaked in tradition, and kept London a quarter of a century behind New York and Berlin—down almost to the level of Paris—in dramatic music.

As to his making opera pay, he did not succeed in doing that until he was in business on an enormous scale, and was making one enterprise pay for another, besides raising the price of the stalls on the best nights to twenty-five shillings. Then he at last declared the usual privately subscribed subvention more trouble than it was worth, and did without it. The Opera had by that time grown to dimensions of which his predecessors never dreamt. It overflowed from Covent Garden into Drury Lane; the superfluous artists, engaged only to secure them from capture by Signor Lago or Mr Mapleson, were turned to account at a second series of performances; the chorus was engaged for the year instead of the season; spring seasons and winter seasons were added; cheap performances of Faust, Cavalleria, The Bohemian Girl, Lohengrin, I Pagliacci, and Hansel and Gretel were kept going like Madame Tussaud's or the Crystal Palace; companies were sent into the provinces; and finally, when the non-musical side of the huge business was brought in as well—the Drury Lane pantomime, the melodramas, and all their offshoots—the fact that this or that summer night at Covent Garden, taken by itself, might not pay, was of no more account than the fact that the billposting, taken by itself, did not pay. I have always said that to criticize Sir Augustus Harris it was not enough to be a musician: one had to be an economist as well; and the columns of elaborate error emptied on his grave abundantly prove how right I was. Quite the most enthralling memorial of him would be the publication of his accounts, if he kept any. Copies should be appended of the contracts imposed by him on the more dependent classes of artists engaged. The extent to which he succeeded in inducing such people to place themselves at his disposal when wanted without exacting any reciprocal obligation would considerably astonish those innocent persons who think of the operatic stage as a specially free and irresponsible profession. You can drive a second-class prima donna to sign an agreement that a mason, a carpenter, or an engine-fitter, backed by their Trade-Unions, would tear up and throw in your face.

To discuss the operations of a commercial organization of this extent as if they were the outcome of the private character of the entrepreneur is idle. It is like discussing whether the battle of Waterloo was a humane proceeding on Wellington's part, or a personally courageous one on Napoleon's. The Reverend Dr Ker Gray, we are told, gave an impressive address at the funeral on the work of the dead man, "honest, honorable, straightforward." But one feels a want of real life in this description—after all, the reverend gentleman may say as much for the next bookmaker he buries, or for Prince Bismarck. Big games are played with the cards on the table; and in businesses where there is no trust all payments are prompt. What the orator meant was, I suspect, that Sir Augustus Harris was impatient of humbug; that he was proud of promising the public nothing, and giving them gorgeous value for their money as a matter of course; and that he pursued his business simply and with integrity, simplicity and integrity being possible in everything, from burglary to martyrdom. But we have not yet heard the devil's advocate on his case. Was he, for instance, a good employer as well as a punctual paymaster—I do not mean to Messieurs de Reszke and Mesdames Melba and Eames, but to "extra" ladies and gentlemen (formerly called "supers"), to the rank and file of his orchestras, and to the multitude of poor people who are needed in the business of a great showman, and who are helplessly at the mercy of their master? Did he, in feasting the public with the annual melodramatic display of stage sport, stage "high life," and jingo stage war, ever sacrifice a farthing to any consideration for the sincerity or morality of the sentiments he was appealing to? Did he produce or encourage the production of any great work of art, new or old, for its own sake? Did the advance that was visible in his later enterprises spring from anything deeper than a famous man's desire to live up to his reputation, and an ambitious plutocrat's pride in having the dearest of everything? I really do not know; and neither do the writers who have been cheapening public applause by writing of him in terms which would flatter a great prime minister.

For my own part I confess to liking the man better than I had any reason to like him. There was a certain pathos about him, with a touch of humor; and I do not doubt the assurances of his friends that he was very sensitive to stories of distress. But I know that he was not a great manager; and I am not convinced that he was even a very clever one. Attentive observers of great "captains of industry" know that their success often comes to them in spite of themselves—that instead of planning and guiding complicated enterprises with a master-hand, they are simply following the slot of the market with a sort of doglike instinct into the center of all sorts of enterprises which are too big to be upset by their misunderstandings. I am perfectly certain that if Sir Augustus Harris had managed the Opera according to his own ideas, he would have destroyed it quite as effectually as Mr Mapleson did. It seems hardly credible now that I once exhausted myself, in the columns of The World, in apparently hopeless attempts to shame the de Reszkes out of their perpetual Faust and Mephistopheles, Romeo and Laurent, and in poohpoohed declarations that there were such works in existence as Die Walküre and Tristan. It was not Sir Augustus Harris that roused Jean de Reszke from his long lethargy, but his own artistic conscience and the shock of Vandyk's brilliant success in Massenet's Manon. Today I am told that Jean de Reszke is playing Tristan with unspeakable glory to Edouard's King Mark; and my World successor is telling his readers—*my* readers—that the performance is "a passion flower on Sir Augustus Harris's grave," and of "the happy expression on his face two years ago, when he told us of the delight he had in preparation for us." My dear Mr Hichens, you should have seen the happy expression on his face five or six years ago, when I used to urge that Tristan, having been composed in 1859, was perhaps a little overdue. I do not grudge the grave its passion flowers; but I do suggest that the next great impresario who takes thirty-seven years to realize the value of a masterpiece must not be surprised if he finds that not even his premature death on the eve of its production will persuade an "old enemy" that he died of artistic enthusiasm.

In short, on this subject, I am, like the gentleman in The Corsican Brothers, "still implacable." I said it all when he was alive; I say it now that he is dead; and I shall say it again whenever I see the Press bowing a little too low before commercial success, and offering it the wreaths that belong to genius and devotion alone.

BLAMING THE BARD

CYMBELINE. By Shakespear. Lyceum Theatre, 22 September 1896. [26 *September* 1896]

I CONFESS to a difficulty in feeling civilized just at present. Flying from the country, where the gentlemen of England are in an ecstasy of chicken-butchering, I return to town to find the higher wits assembled at a play three hundred years old, in which the sensation scene exhibits a woman waking up to find her husband reposing gorily in her arms with his head cut off.

Pray understand, therefore, that I do not defend Cymbeline. It is for the most part stagey trash of the lowest melodramatic order, in parts abominably written, throughout intellectually vulgar, and, judged in point of thought by modern intellectual standards, vulgar, foolish, offensive, indecent, and exasperating beyond all tolerance. There are moments when one asks despairingly why our stage should ever have been cursed with this "immortal" pilferer of other men's stories and ideas, with his monstrous rhetorical fustian, his unbearable platitudes, his pretentious reduction of the subtlest problems of life to commonplaces against which a Polytechnic debating club would revolt, his incredible unsuggestiveness, his sententious combination of ready reflection with complete intellectual sterility, and his consequent incapacity for getting out of the depth of even the most ignorant audience, except when he solemnly says something so transcendently platitudinous that his more humble-minded hearers cannot bring themselves to believe that so great a man really meant to talk like their grandmothers. With the single exception of Homer, there is no eminent writer, not even Sir Walter Scott, whom I can despise so entirely as I despise Shakespear when I measure my mind against his. The intensity of my impatience with him occasionally reaches such a pitch, that it would positively be a relief to me to dig him up and throw stones at him, knowing as I do how incapable he and his worshippers are of understanding any less obvious form of indignity. To read Cymbeline and to think of Goethe, of Wagner, of Ibsen, is, for me, to imperil the habit of studied moderation of statement which years of public responsibility as a journalist have made almost second nature in me.

But I am bound to add that I pity the man who cannot enjoy Shakespear. He has outlasted thousands of abler thinkers, and will outlast a thousand more. His gift of telling a story (provided some one else told it to him first); his enormous power over language, as conspicuous in his senseless and silly abuse of it as in his miracles of expression; his humor; his sense of idiosyncratic character; and his prodigious fund of that vital energy which is, it seems, the true differentiating property behind the faculties, good, bad, or indifferent, of the man of genius, enable him to entertain us so effectively that the imaginary scenes and people he has created become more real to us than our actual life—at least, until our knowledge and grip of actual life begins to deepen and glow beyond the common. When I was twenty I knew everybody in Shakespear, from Hamlet to Abhorson, much more intimately than I knew my living contemporaries; and to this day, if the name of Pistol or Polonius catches my eye in a newspaper, I turn to the passage with more curiosity than if the name were that of—but perhaps I had better not mention any one in particular.

How many new acquaintances, then, do you make in reading Cymbeline, provided you have the patience to break your way into it through all the fustian, and are old enough to be free from the modern idea that Cymbeline must be the name of a cosmetic and Imogen of the latest scientific discovery in the nature of a hitherto unknown gas? Cymbeline is nothing; his queen nothing, though some attempt is made to justify her description as "a woman that bears all down with her brain"; Posthumus, nothing—most fortunately, as otherwise he would be an unendurably contemptible hound; Belarius, nothing—at least, not after Kent in King Lear (just as the Queen is nothing after Lady Macbeth);

Iachimo, not much—only a *diabolus ex machinâ* made plausible; and Pisanio, less than Iachimo. On the other hand, we have Cloten, the prince of numbskulls, whose part, indecencies and all, is a literary masterpiece from the first line to the last; the two princes—fine presentments of that impressive and generous myth, the noble savage; Caius Lucius, the Roman general, urbane among the barbarians; and, above all, Imogen. But do, please, remember that there are two Imogens. One is a solemn and elaborate example of what, in Shakespear's opinion, a real lady ought to be. With this unspeakable person virtuous indignation is chronic. Her object in life is to vindicate her own propriety and to suspect everybody else's, especially her husband's. Like Lothaw in the jeweller's shop in Bret Harte's burlesque novel, she cannot be left alone with unconsidered trifles of portable silver without officiously assuring the proprietors that she has stolen naught, nor would not, though she had found gold strewed i' the floor. Her fertility and spontaneity in nasty ideas is not to be described: there is hardly a speech in her part that you can read without wincing. But this Imogen has another one tied to her with ropes of blank verse (which can fortunately be cut)—the Imogen of Shakespear's genius, an enchanting person of the most delicate sensitiveness, full of sudden transitions from ecstasies of tenderness to transports of childish rage, and reckless of consequences in both, instantly hurt and instantly appeased, and of the highest breeding and courage. But for this Imogen, Cymbeline would stand about as much chance of being revived now as Titus Andronicus.

The instinctive Imogen, like the real live part of the rest of the play, has to be disentangled from a mass of stuff which, though it might be recited with effect and appropriateness by young amateurs at a performance by the Elizabethan Stage Society, is absolutely unactable and unutterable in the modern theatre, where a direct illusion of reality is aimed at, and where the repugnance of the best actors to play false passages is practically insuperable. For the purposes of the Lyceum, therefore, Cymbeline had to be cut, and cut liberally. Not that there was any reason to apprehend that the manager would flinch from the operation: quite the contrary. In a true republic of art Sir Henry Irving would ere this have expiated his acting versions on the scaffold. He does not merely cut plays: he disembowels them. In Cymbeline he has quite surpassed himself by extirpating the antiphonal third verse of the famous dirge. A man who would do that would do anything—cut the coda out of the first movement of Beethoven's Ninth Symphony, or shorten one of Velasquez's Philips into a kitcat to make it fit over his drawing room mantelpiece. The grotesque character tracery of Cloten's lines, which is surely not beyond the appreciation of an age educated by Stevenson, is defaced with Cromwellian ruthlessness; and the patriotic scene, with the Queen's great speech about the natural bravery of our isle, magnificent in its Walkürenritt swing, is shorn away, though it might easily have been introduced in the Garden scene. And yet, long screeds of rubbish about "slander, whose edge is sharper than the sword," and so on, are preserved with superstitious veneration.

This curious want of connoisseurship in literature would disable Sir Henry Irving seriously if he were an interpretative actor. But it is, happily, the fault of a great quality—the creative quality. A prodigious deal of nonsense has been written about Sir Henry Irving's conception of this, that, and the other Shakespearean character. The truth is that he has never in his life conceived or interpreted the characters of any author except himself. He is really as incapable of acting another man's play as Wagner was of setting another man's libretto; and he should, like Wagner, have written his plays for himself. But as he did not find himself out until it was too late for him to learn that supplementary trade, he was compelled to use other men's plays as the framework for his own creations. His first great success in this sort of adaptation was with the Merchant of Venice. There was no question then of a bad Shylock or a good Shylock: he was simply not Shylock at all; and when his own creation came into conflict with Shakespear's, as it did quite openly in the Trial scene, he simply played in flat contradiction of the lines, and positively acted Shakespear off the stage. This was an original policy, and an intensely interesting one from the critical point of view; but it was obvious that its difficulty must increase with the vividness and force of the dramatist's creation. Shakespear at his highest pitch cannot be set aside by any mortal actor, however gifted; and when Sir Henry Irving tried to interpolate a most singular and fantastic notion of an old man between the lines of a fearfully mutilated acting version of King Lear, he was smashed. On the other hand, in plays by persons of no importance, where the dramatist's part of the business is the merest trash, his creative activity is unhampered and uncontradicted; and the author's futility is the opportunity for the actor's masterpiece. Now I have already described Shakespear's Iachimo as little better than any of the lay figures in Cymbeline—a mere *diabolus ex machinâ*. But Irving's Iachimo is a very different affair. It is a new and independent creation. I knew Shakespear's play inside and out before last Tuesday; but this Iachimo was quite fresh and novel to me. I witnessed it with unqualified delight: it was no vulgar bagful of "points," but a true impersonation, unbroken in its life-current from end to end, varied on the surface with the finest comedy, and without a single lapse in the sustained beauty of its execution. It is only after such work that an artist can with perfect naturalness and dignity address himself to his audience as "their faithful and loving servant"; and I wish I could add that the audience had an equal right to offer him their applause as a worthy acknowledgment of his merit. But when a house distributes its officious first-night plaudits impartially between the fine artist and the blunderer who roars a few lines violently and rushes off the stage after compressing the entire art of How Not to Act into five intolerable minutes, it had better be told to reserve its impertinent and obstreperous demonstrations until it has learnt to bestow them with some sort of discrimination. Our first-night people mean well, and will, no doubt, accept my assurance that they are donkeys with all possible good humor; but they should remember that to applaud for the sake of applauding, as schoolboys will cheer for the sake of cheering, is to destroy our own power of complimenting those who, as the greatest among us, are the servants of all the rest.

Over the performances of the other gentlemen in the cast let me skate as lightly as possible. Mr Norman Forbes's Cloten, though a fatuous idiot rather than the brawny "beef-witted" fool whom Shakespear took from his own Ajax in Troilus and Cressida, is effective and amusing, so that one feels acutely the mangling of his part, especially the cutting of that immortal musical criticism of his upon the serenade. Mr Gordon Craig and Mr Webster are desperate failures as the two noble savages. They are as spirited and picturesque as possible; but every pose, every flirt of their elfin locks, proclaims the wild freedom of Bedford Park. They recite the poor maimed dirge admirably, Mr Craig being the more musical of the twain; and Mr Webster's sword-and-cudgel fight with Cloten is very lively; but their utter deficiency in the grave, rather sombre, uncivilized primeval strength and Mohican dignity so finely suggested by Shakespear, takes all the ballast out of the fourth act, and combines with the inappropriate prettiness and sunniness of the landscape scenery to handicap Miss Ellen Terry most cruelly in the trying scene of her awakening by the side of the flower-decked corpse: a scene which, without every accessory to heighten its mystery, terror, and pathos, is utterly and heart-breakingly impossible for any actress, even if she were Duse, Ristori, Mrs Siddons, and Miss Terry rolled into one. When I saw this gross and palpable oversight, and heard people talking about the Lyceum stage management as superb, I with difficulty restrained myself from tearing out my hair in handfuls and scattering it with imprecations to the four winds. That cave of the three mountaineers wants nothing but a trellised porch, a bamboo bicycle, and a nice little bed of standard roses, to complete its absurdity.

With Mr Frederic Robinson as Belarius, and Mr Tyars as Pisanio, there is no reasonable fault to find, except that they might, perhaps, be a little brighter with advantage; and of the rest of their male colleagues I think I shall ask to be allowed to say nothing at all, even at the cost of omitting a tribute to Mr Fuller Mellish's discreet impersonation of the harmless necessary Philario. There remains Miss Geneviève Ward, whose part, with the Neptune's park speech lopped off, was not worth her playing, and Miss Ellen Terry, who invariably fascinates me so much that I have not the smallest confidence in my own judgment respecting her. There was no Bedford Park about the effect she made as she stepped into the King's garden; still less any of the atmosphere of ancient Britain. At the first glance, we were in the Italian fifteenth century; and the house, unversed in the cinquecento, but dazzled all the same, proceeded to roar until it stopped from exhaustion. There is one scene in Cymbeline, the one in which Imogen receives the summons to "that same blessed Milford," which might have been written for Miss Terry, so perfectly does its innocent rapture and frank gladness fit into her hand. Her repulse of Iachimo brought down the house as a matter of course, though I am convinced that the older Shakespeareans present had a vague impression that it could not be properly done except by a stout, turnip-headed matron, with her black hair folded smoothly over her ears and secured in a classic bun. Miss Terry had evidently cut her own part; at all events the odious Mrs Grundyish Imogen had been dissected out of it so skilfully that it went without a single jar. The circumstances under which she was asked to play the fourth act were, as I have explained, impossible. To wake up in the gloom amid the wolf and robber-haunted mountain gorges which formed the Welsh mountains of Shakespear's imagination in the days before the Great Western existed is one thing: to wake up at about three on a nice Bank-holiday afternoon in a charming spot near the valley of the Wye is quite another. With all her force, Miss Terry gave us faithfully the whole process which Shakespear has presented with such dramatic cunning—Imogen's bewilderment, between dreaming and waking, as to where she is; the vague discerning of some strange bedfellow there; the wondering examination of the flowers with which he is so oddly covered; the frightful discovery of blood on the flowers, with the hideous climax that the man is headless and that his clothes are her husband's; and it was all ruined by that blazing, idiotic, prosaic sunlight in which everything leapt to the eye at once, rendering the mystery and the slowly growing clearness of perception incredible and unintelligible, and spoiling a scene which, properly stage-managed, would have been a triumph of histrionic intelligence. Cannot somebody be hanged for this?—men perish every week for lesser crimes. What consolation is it to me that Miss Terry, playing with infinite charm and delicacy of appeal, made up her lost ground in other directions, and had more than as much success as the roaring gallery could feel the want of?

A musical accompaniment to the drama has been specially composed; and its numbers are set forth in the bill of the play, with the words "LOST PROPERTY" in conspicuous red capitals in the margin. Perhaps I can be of some use in restoring at least some of the articles to their rightful owner. The prelude to the fourth act belongs to Beethoven—first movement of the Seventh Symphony. The theme played by "the ingenious instrument" in the cave is Handel's, and is familiar to lovers of Judas Maccabeus as O never bow we down to the rude stock or sculptured stone. J. F. R. will, I feel sure, be happy to carry the work of identification further if necessary.

Sir Henry Irving's next appearance will be on Bosworth Field. He was obviously astonished by the startling shout of approbation with which the announcement was received. We all have an old weakness for Richard. After that, Madame Sans-Gêne, with Sardou's Napoleon.

LITTLE EYOLF

LITTLE EYOLF. A play in three acts, by Henrik Ibsen. Avenue Theatre, 23 November 1896. [28 *November* 1896]

THE happiest and truest epithet that has yet been applied to the Ibsen drama in this country came from Mr Clement Scott when he said that Ibsen was "suburban." That is the whole secret of it. If Mr Scott had only embraced his discovery instead of quarrelling with it, what a splendid Ibsen critic he would have made! Suburbanity at present means modern civilization. The active, germinating life in the households of today cannot be typified by an aristocratic hero, an ingenuous heroine, a gentleman-forger abetted by an Artful Dodger, and a parlormaid who takes half-sovereigns and kisses from the male visitors. Such interiors exist on the stage, and nowhere else: therefore the only people who are accustomed to them and at home in them are the dramatic critics. But if you ask me where you can find the Helmer household, the Allmers household, the Solness household, the Rosmer household, and all the other Ibsen households, I reply, "Jump out of a train anywhere between Wimbledon and Haslemere; walk into the first villa you come to; and there you are." Indeed you need not go so far: Hampstead, Maida Vale, or West Kensington will serve your turn; but it is as well to remind people that the true suburbs are now the forty-mile radius, and that Camberwell and Brixton are no longer the suburbs, but the overflow of Gower Street—the genteel slums, in short. And this suburban life, except in so far as it is totally vegetable and undramatic, is the life depicted by Ibsen. Doubtless some of our critics are quite sincere in thinking it a vulgar life, in considering the conversations which men hold with their wives in it improper, in finding its psychology puzzling and unfamiliar, and in forgetting that its bookshelves and its music cabinets are laden with works which did not exist for them, and which are the daily bread of young women educated very differently from the sisters and wives of their day. No wonder they are not at ease in an atmosphere of ideas and assumptions and attitudes which seem to them bewildering, morbid, affected, extravagant, and altogether incredible as the common currency of suburban life. But Ibsen knows better. His suburban drama is the inevitable outcome of a suburban civilization (meaning a civilization that appreciates fresh air); and the true explanation of Hedda Gabler's vogue is that given by Mr Grant Allen—"I take her in to dinner twice a week."

Another change that the critics have failed to reckon with is the change in fiction. Byron remarked that

> Romances paint at full length people's wooings,
> But only give a bust of marriages.

That was true enough in the days of Sir Walter Scott, when a betrothed heroine with the slightest knowledge of what marriage meant would have shocked the public as much as the same ignorance today would strike it as tragic if real, and indecent if simulated. The result was that the romancer, when he came to a love scene, had frankly to ask his "gentle reader" to allow him to omit the conversation as being necessarily too idiotic to interest anyone. We have fortunately long passed out of that stage in novels. By the time we had reached Vanity Fair and Middlemarch—both pretty old and prim stories now—marriage had become the starting point of our romances. Love is as much the romancer's theme as ever; but married love and the courtships of young people who are appalled by the problems of life and motherhood have left the governesses and curates, the Amandas and Tom Joneses of other days, far out of sight. Ten years ago the stage was as far behind Sir Walter Scott as he is behind Madame Sarah Grand. But when Ibsen took it by the scruff of the neck just as Wagner took the Opera, then, willy nilly, it had to come along. And now what are the critics going to do? The Ibsen drama is pre-eminently the drama of marriage. If dramatic criticism receives it in the spirit of the nurse's husband in Romeo and Juliet, if it grins and makes remarks about "the secrets of the alcove," if it pours forth columns which are half pornographic pleasantry and the other half sham propriety, then the end will be, not in the least that Ibsen will be banned, but that dramatic criticism will cease to be read. And what a frightful blow that would be to English culture!

Little Eyolf is an extraordinarily powerful play, although none of the characters are as fascinatingly individualized as Solness or Rosmer, Hedda or Nora. The theme is a marriage—an ideal marriage from the suburban point of view. A young gentleman, a student and an idealist, is compelled to drudge at teaching to support himself. He meets a beautiful young woman. They fall in love with one another; and by the greatest piece of luck in the world (suburbanly considered) she has plenty of money. Thus is he set free by his marriage to live his own life in his own way. That is just where an ordinary play leaves off, and just where an Ibsen play begins. The husband begins to make those discoveries which everybody makes, except, apparently, the dramatic critics. First, that love, instead of being a perfectly homogeneous, unchanging, unending passion, is of all things the most mutable. It will pass through several well-marked stages in a single evening, and, whilst seeming to slip back to the old starting point the next evening, will yet not slip quite back; so that in the course of years it will appear that the moods of an evening were the anticipation of the evolution of a lifetime. But the evolution does not occur in different people at the same time or in the same order. Consequently the hero of Little Eyolf, being an imaginative, nervous, thoughtful person, finds that he has had enough of caresses, and wants to dream alone among the mountain peaks and solitudes, whilst his wife, a warm-blooded creature, has only found her love intensified to a fiercely jealous covetousness of him. His main refuge from this devouring passion is in his peacefully affectionate relations with his sister, and in certain suburban dreams very common among literary amateurs living on their wives' incomes: to wit, forming the mind and character of his child, and writing a great book (on Human Responsibility if you please). Of course the wife, in her jealousy, hates the sister, hates the child, hates the book, hates her husband for making her jealous of them, and hates herself for her hatreds with the frightful logic of greedy, insatiable love. Enter then our old friend, Ibsen's divine messenger. The Ratwife, alias the Strange Passenger, alias the Button Moulder, alias Ulrik Brendel, comes in to ask whether there are any little gnawing things there of which she can rid the house. They do not understand—the divine messenger in Ibsen is never understood, especially by the critics. So the little gnawing thing in the house—the child—follows the Ratwife and is drowned, leaving the pair awakened by the blow to a frightful consciousness of themselves, the woman as a mere animal, the man as a moonstruck nincompoop, keeping up appearances as a suburban lady and gentleman with nothing to do but enjoy themselves. Even the sister has discovered now that she is not really a sister—also a not unprecedented suburban possibility—and sees that the passionate stage is ahead of her too; so, though she loves the husband, she has to get out of his way by the pre-eminently suburban expedient of marrying a man whom she does not love, and who, like Rita, is warm-blooded and bent on the undivided, unshared possession of the object of his passion. At last the love of the woman passes out of the passionate stage; and immediately, with the practical sense of her sex, she proposes, not to go up into the mountains or to write amateur treatises, but to occupy herself with her duties as landed proprietress, instead of merely spending the revenues of her property in keeping a monogamic harem. The gentleman asks to be allowed to lend a hand; and immediately the storm subsides, easily enough, leaving the couple on solid ground. This is the play, as actual and near to us as the Brighton and South Coast Railway—this is the mercilessly heart-searching sermon, touching all of us somewhere, and some of us everywhere, which we, the critics, have summed up as "secrets of the alcove." Our cheeks, whose whiteness Mr Arthur Roberts has assailed in vain, have mantled at "the coarseness and vulgarity which are noted characteristics of the author" (I am quoting, with awe, my fastidiously high-toned colleague of the Standard). And yet the divine messenger only meant to make us ashamed of ourselves. That is the way divine messengers always do muddle their business.

The performance was of course a very remarkable one. When, in a cast of five, you have the three best yet discovered actresses of their generation, you naturally look for something extraordinary. Miss Achurch was the only one who ran any risk of failure. The Ratwife and Asta are excellent parts; but they are not arduous ones. Rita, on the other hand, is one of the heaviest ever written: any single act of it would exhaust an actress of no more than ordinary resources. But Miss Achurch was more than equal to the occasion. Her power seemed to grow with its own expenditure. The terrible outburst at the end of the first act did not leave a scrape on her voice (which appears to have the compass of a military band) and threw her into victorious action in that tearing second act instead of wrecking her. She played with all her old originality and success, and with more than her old authority over her audience. She had to speak some dangerous lines—lines of a kind that usually find out the vulgar spots in an audience and give an excuse for a laugh—but nobody laughed or wanted to laugh at Miss Achurch. "There stood your champagne; but you tasted it not," neither shirked nor slurred, but driven home to the last syllable, did not elicit an audible breath from a completely dominated audience. Later on I confess I lost sight of Rita a little in studying the surprising capacity Miss Achurch shewed as a dramatic instrument. For the first time one clearly saw the superfluity of power and the vehemence of intelligence which make her often so reckless as to the beauty of her methods of expression. As Rita she produced almost every sound that a big human voice can, from a creak like the opening of a rusty canal lock to a melodious tenor note that the most robust Siegfried might have envied. She looked at one moment like a young, well-dressed, very pretty woman: at another she was like a desperate creature just fished dripping out of the river by the Thames Police. Yet another moment, and she was the incarnation of impetuous, ungovernable strength. Her face was sometimes winsome, sometimes listlessly wretched, sometimes like the head of a statue of Victory, sometimes suffused, horrible, threatening, like Bellona or Medusa. She would cross from left to right like a queen, and from right to left with, so to speak, her toes turned in, her hair coming down, and her slippers coming off. A more utter recklessness, not only of fashion, but of beauty, could hardly be imagined: beauty to Miss Achurch is only one effect among others to be produced, not a condition of all effects. But then she can do what our beautiful actresses cannot do: attain the force and terror of Sarah Bernhardt's most vehement explosions without Sarah's violence and abandonment, and with every appearance of having reserves of power still held in restraint. With all her cleverness as a realistic actress she must be classed technically as a heroic actress; and I very much doubt whether we shall see her often until she comes into the field with a repertory as highly specialized as that of Sir Henry Irving or Duse. For it is so clear that she would act an average London success to pieces and play an average actor-manager off the stage, that we need not expect to see much of her as that useful and pretty auxiliary, a leading lady.

Being myself a devotee of the beautiful school, I like being enchanted by Mrs Patrick Campbell better than being frightened, harrowed, astonished, conscience-stricken, devastated, and dreadfully delighted in general by Miss Achurch's untamed genius. I have seen Mrs Campbell play the Ratwife twice, once quite enchantingly, and once most disappointingly. On the first occasion Mrs Campbell divined that she was no village harridan, but the messenger of heaven. She played supernaturally, beautifully: the first notes of her voice came as from the spheres into all that suburban prose: she played to the child with a witchery that might have drawn him not only into the sea, but into her very bosom. Nothing jarred except her obedience to Ibsen's stage direction in saying "Down where all the rats are" harshly, instead of getting the effect, in harmony with her own inspired reading, by the most magical tenderness. The next time, to my unspeakable fury, she amused herself by playing like any melodramatic old woman, a profanation for which, whilst my critical life lasts, never will I forgive her. Of Miss Robins's Asta it is difficult to say much, since the part, played as she plays it, does not exhibit anything like the full extent of her powers. Asta is a study of a temperament—the quiet, affectionate, enduring, reassuring, faithful, domestic temperament. That is not in the least Miss Robins's temperament: she is nervous, restless, intensely self-conscious, eagerly energetic. In parts which do not enable her to let herself loose in this, her natural way, she falls back on pathos, on mute misery, on a certain delicate plaintive note in her voice and grace in her bearing which appeal to our sympathy and pity without realizing any individuality for us. She gave us, with instinctive tact and refinement, the "niceness," the consideratcness, the ladylikeness, which differentiate Asta from the wilful, passionate, somewhat brutal Rita. Perhaps only an American playing against an Englishwoman could have done it so discriminately; but beyond this and the pathos there was nothing: Asta was only a picture, and, like a picture, did not develop. The picture, being sympathetic and pretty, has been much admired; but those who have not seen Miss Robins play Hilda Wangel have no idea of what she is like when she really acts her part instead of merely giving an urbanely pictorial recommendation of it. As to Allmers, how could he recommend himself to spectators who saw in him everything that they are ashamed of in themselves? Mr Courtenay Thorpe played very intelligently, which, for such a part, and in such a play, is saying a good deal; but he was hampered a little by the change from the small and intimate auditorium in which he has been accustomed to play Ibsen, to the Avenue, which ingeniously combines the acoustic difficulties of a large theatre with the pecuniary capacity of a small one. Master Stewart Dawson, as Eyolf, was one of the best actors in the company. Mr Lowne, as Borgheim, was as much out of tone as a Leader sunset in a Rembrandt picture—no fault of his, of course (the audience evidently liked him), but still a blemish on the play.

And this brings me to a final criticism. The moment I put myself into my old attitude as musical critic, I at once perceive that the performance, as a whole, was an unsatisfactory one. You may remonstrate, and ask me how I can say so after admitting that the performers shewed such extraordinary talent—even genius. It is very simple, nevertheless. Suppose you take Isaye, Sarasate, Joachim, and Hollmann, and tumble them all together to give a scratch performance of one of Beethoven's posthumous quartets at some benefit concert. Suppose you also take the two De Reszkes, Calvé, and Miss Eames, and set them to sing a glee under the same circumstances. They will all shew prodigious individual talent; but the resultant performances of the quartet and glee will be inferior, as wholes, to that of an ordinary glee club or group of musicians who have practised for years together. The Avenue performance was a parallel case. There was nothing like the atmosphere which Lugné Poë got in Rosmersholm. Miss Achurch managed to play the second act as if she had played it every week for twenty years; but otherwise the performance, interesting as it was, was none the less a scratch one. If only the company could keep together for a while! But perhaps that is too much to hope for at present, though it is encouraging to see that the performances are to be continued next week, the five matinees—all crowded, by the way—having by no means exhausted the demand for places.

Several performances during the past fortnight remain to be chronicled; but Ibsen will have his due; and he has not left me room enough to do justice to any one else this week.

IBSEN WITHOUT TEARS

[12 *December* 1896]

LITTLE EYOLF, which began at the Avenue Theatre only the other day as an artistic forlorn hope led by Miss Elizabeth Robins, has been promoted into a full-blown fashionable theatrical speculation, with a Morocco Bound syndicate in the background, unlimited starring and bill-posting, and everything complete. The syndicate promptly set to work to shew us how Ibsen should really be done. They found the whole thing wrong from the root up. The silly Ibsen people had put Miss Achurch, an Ibsenite actress, into the leading part, and Mrs Patrick Campbell, a fashionable actress, into a minor one. This was soon set right. Miss Achurch was got rid of altogether, and her part transferred to Mrs Campbell. Miss Robins, though tainted with Ibsenism, was retained, but only, I presume, because, having command of the stage-right in the play, she could not be replaced—say by Miss Maude Millet—without her own consent. The rest of the arrangements are economical rather than fashionable, the syndicate, to all appearance, being, like most syndicates, an association for the purpose of getting money rather than supplying it.

Mrs Patrick Campbell has entered thoroughly into the spirit of the alterations. She has seen how unladylike, how disturbing, how full of horror even, the part of Rita Allmers is, acted as Miss Achurch acted it. And she has remedied this with a completeness that leaves nothing to be desired—or perhaps only one thing. Was there not a Mr Arcedeckne who, when Thackeray took to lecturing, said, "Have a piano, Thack"? Well, Rita Allmers wants a piano. Mrs Tanqueray had one, and played it so beautifully that I have been her infatuated slave ever since. There need be no difficulty about the matter: the breezy Borgheim has only to say, "Now that Alfred is back, Mrs Allmers, wont you give us that study for the left hand we are all so fond of?" and there you are. However, even without the piano, Mrs Campbell succeeded wonderfully in eliminating all unpleasantness from the play. She looked charming; and her dresses were beyond reproach: she carried a mortgage on the "gold and green forests" on her back. Her performance was infinitely reassuring and pretty: its note was, "You silly people: what are you making all this fuss about? The secret of life is charm and self-possession, and not tantrums about drowned children." The famous line "There stood your champagne; but you tasted it not," was no longer a "secret of the alcove," but a good-humored, mock petulant remonstrance with a man whom there was no pleasing in the matter of wine. There was not a taste of nasty jealousy: this Rita tolerated her dear old stupid's preoccupation with Asta and Eyolf and his books as any sensible (or insensible) woman would. Goodness gracious, I thought, what things that evil-minded Miss Achurch did read into this harmless play! And how nicely Mrs Campbell took the drowning of the child! Just a pretty waving of the fingers, a moderate scream as if she had very nearly walked on a tin tack, and it was all over, without tears, without pain, without more fuss than if she had broken the glass of her watch.

At this rate, it was not long before Rita thoroughly gained the sympathy of the audience. We felt that if she could only get rid of that ridiculous, sentimental Asta (Miss Robins, blind to the object lesson before her, persisted in acting Ibsenitically), and induce her fussing, self-conscious, probably underbred husband not to cry for spilt milk, she would be as happy as any lady in the land. Unfortunately, the behavior of Mr Allmers became more and more intolerable as the second act progressed, though he could not exhaust Rita's patience, slily humorous tolerance. As usual, he wanted to know whether she would like to go and drown herself; and the sweet, cool way in which she answered, "Oh, I dont know, Alfred. No: I think I should have to stay here with *you*—a *litt*-le while" was a lesson to all wives. What a contrast to Miss Achurch, who so unnecessarily filled the stage with the terror of death in this passage! This is what comes of exaggeration, of over-acting, of forgetting that people go to the theatre to be amused, and not to be upset! When Allmers shook his fist at his beautiful wife—O unworthy the name of Briton!—and shouted "*You* are the guilty one in this," her silent dignity overwhelmed him. Nothing could have been in better taste than her description of the pretty way in which her child had lain in the water when he was drowned—his mother's son all over. All the pain was taken out of it by the way it was approached. "I got Borgheim to go down to the pier with me [so nice of Borgheim, dear fellow!]." "And what," interrupts the stupid Allmers, "did you want there?" Rita gave a little laugh at his obtuseness, a laugh which meant "Why, you dear silly," before she replied, "To question the boys as to how it happened." After all, it is these Ibsenite people that create the objections to Ibsen. If Mrs Campbell had played Rita from the first, not a word would have been said against the play; and the whole business would have been quietly over and the theatre closed by this time. But nothing would serve them but their Miss Achurch; and so, instead of a pretty arrangement of the "Eyolf" theme for boudoir pianette, we had it flung to the "Götterdämmerung" orchestra, and blared right into our shrinking souls.

In the third act, the smoothness of the proceedings was somewhat marred by the fact that Mrs Campbell, not knowing her words, had to stop acting and frankly bring the book on the stage and read from it. Now Mrs Campbell reads very clearly and nicely; and the result of course was that the Ibsenite atmosphere began to assert itself, just as it would if the play were read aloud in a private room. However, that has been remedied, no doubt, by this time; and the public may rely on an uninterruptedly quiet evening.

The main drawback is that it is impossible not to feel that Mrs Campbell's Rita, with all her charm, is terribly hampered by the unsuitability of the words Ibsen and Mr Archer have put into her mouth. They were all very well for

Miss Achurch, who perhaps, if the truth were known, arranged her acting to suit them; but they are forced, strained, out of tune in all sorts of ways in the mouth of Mrs Campbell's latest creation. Why cannot the dialogue be adapted to her requirements and harmonized with her playing, say by Mr William Black? Ibsen is of no use when anything really ladylike is wanted: you might as well put Beethoven to compose Chaminades. It is true that no man can look at the new Rita without wishing that Heaven had sent him just such a wife, whereas the boldest man would hardly have envied Allmers the other Rita if Miss Achurch had allowed him a moment's leisure for such impertinent speculations; but all the same, the evenings at the Avenue Theatre are likely to be a little languid. I had rather look at a beautiful picture than be flogged, as a general thing; but if I were offered my choice between looking at the most beautiful picture in the world continuously for a fortnight and submitting to, say, a dozen, I think I should choose the flogging. For just the same reason, if I had to choose between seeing Miss Achurch's Rita again, with all its turns of beauty and flashes of grandeur obliterated, and nothing left but its insane jealousy, its agonizing horror, its lacerating remorse, and its maddening unrest, the alternative being another two hours' contemplation of uneventful feminine fascination as personified by Mrs Patrick Campbell, I should go like a lamb to the slaughter. I prefer Mrs Campbell's Rita to her photograph, because it moves and talks; but otherwise there is not so much difference as I expected. Mrs Campbell, as Magda, could do nothing with a public spoiled by Duse. I greatly fear she will do even less, as Rita, with a public spoiled by Miss Achurch.

The representation generally is considerably affected in its scale and effect by the change of Ritas. Mr Courtenay Thorpe, who, though playing *con tutta la forza*, could hardly avoid seeming to underact with Miss Achurch, has now considerable difficulty in avoiding overacting, since he cannot be even earnest and anxious without producing an effect of being good-humoredly laughed at by Mrs Campbell. Miss Robins, as Asta, has improved greatly on the genteel misery of the first night. She has got complete hold of the part; and although her old fault of resorting to the lachrymose for all sorts of pathetic expression produces something of its old monotony, and the voice clings to one delicate register until the effect verges on affectation, yet Asta comes out as a distinct person about whose history the audience has learnt something, and not as an actress delivering a string of lines and making a number of points more or less effectively. The difficulty is that in this cheap edition of Little Eyolf Asta, instead of being the tranquillizing element, becomes the centre of disturbance; so that the conduct of Allmers in turning for the sake of peace and quietness from his pretty, coaxing, soothing wife to his agitated high-strung sister becomes nonsensical. I pointed out after the first performance that Miss Robins had not really succeeded in making Asta a peacemaker; but beside Miss Achurch she easily seemed gentle, whereas beside Mrs Campbell she seems a volcano. It is only necessary to recall her playing of the frightful ending to the first act of Alan's Wife, and compare it with Mrs Campbell's finish to the first act of Little Eyolf, to realize the preposterousness of their relative positions in the cast. Mrs Campbell's old part of the Ratwife is now played by Miss Florence Farr. Miss Farr deserves more public sympathy than any of the other Ibsenite actresses; for they have only damaged themselves professionally by appearing in Ibsen's plays, whereas Miss Farr has complicated her difficulties by appearing in mine as well. Further, instead of either devoting herself to the most personally exacting of all the arts or else letting it alone, Miss Farr has written clever novels and erudite works on Babylonish lore; has managed a theatre capably for a season; and has only occasionally acted. For an occasional actress she has been rather successful once or twice in producing singular effects in singular parts—her Rebecca in Rosmersholm was remarkable and promising—but she has not pursued her art with sufficient constancy to attain any authoritative power of carrying out her conceptions, which are, besides, only skin deep. Her Ratwife is a favorable example of her power of producing a certain strangeness of effect; but it is somewhat discounted by want of sustained grip in the execution. Miss Farr will perhaps remedy this if she can find time enough to spare from her other interests to attend to it. The rest of the cast is as before. One has no longer any real belief in the drowning of Master Stewart Dawson, thanks to the gentle method of Mrs Campbell. Mr Lowne's sensible, healthy superiority to all this morbid Ibsen stuff is greatly reinforced now that Rita takes things nicely and easily.

I cannot help thinking it a great pity that the Avenue enterprise, just as it seemed to be capturing that afternoon classical concert public to which I have always looked for the regeneration of the classical drama, should have paid the penalty of its success by the usual evolution into what is evidently half a timid speculation in a "catch-on," and half an attempt to slacken the rate at which the Avenue Theatre is eating its head off in rent. That evolution of course at once found out the utter incoherence of the enterprise. The original production, undertaken largely at Miss Robins's individual risk, was for the benefit of a vaguely announced Fund, as to the constitution and purpose of which no information was forthcoming, except that it proposed to produce Echegaray's Mariana, with Miss Robins in the title-part. But neither Miss Robins's nor anyone else's interests in this fund seem to have been secured in any way. The considerable profit of the first week of Little Eyolf may, for all that is guaranteed to the contrary, be devoted to the production of an opera, a shadow play from Paris, or a drama in which neither Miss Robins nor any of those who have worked with her may be offered any part or share whatever. There is already just such a fund in existence in the treasury of the Independent Theatre, which strove hard to obtain Little Eyolf for production, and which actually guaranteed part of the booking at the Avenue. But here the same difficulty arose. Miss Achurch would no doubt have trusted the Independent, for the excellent reason that her husband is one of the directors; but no other artist playing for it would have had the smallest security that, had its fortunes been established through their efforts, they would ever have been cast for a part in its future productions. On the other hand, Miss Achurch had no hold on the new fund, which had specially declared its intention of supporting Miss Robins. This has not prevented the production of Little Eyolf, though it has greatly delayed it; for everybody finally threw security to the winds, and played by friendly arrangement on such terms as were possible. As it happened, there was a substantial profit, and it all went to the Fund. Naturally, however, when the enterprise entered upon a purely commercial phase, the artists at once refused to work for the profit of a syndicate on the enthusiastic terms (or no terms) on which they had worked for Ibsen and for one another. The syndicate, on the other hand, had no idea of wasting so expensive a star as Mrs Patrick Campbell on a small part that could be filled for a few pounds, when they could transfer her to the leading part and save Miss Achurch's salary. If they could have substituted an inferior artist for Miss Robins, they could have effected a still further saving, relying on Mrs Pat to draw full houses; but that was made impossible by Miss Robin's power over the stage-right. Consequently, the only sufferer was Miss Achurch; but it is impossible for Miss Robins and Mrs Campbell not to feel that the same thing might have happened to them if there had been no stage-right, and if the syndicate had realized that, when it comes to Ibsen, Miss Achurch is a surer card to play than Mrs Campbell.

Under these circumstances, what likelihood is there of the experiment being resumed or repeated on its old basis? Miss Robins will probably think twice before she creates Mariana without some security that, if she succeeds, the part will not immediately be handed over to Miss Winifred Emery or Miss Julia Neilson. Miss Achurch, triumphantly as she has come out of the comparison with her successor, is not likely to forget her lesson. Mrs Campbell's willingness to enlist in forlorn hopes in the humblest capacity may not improbably be received in future as Laocoon received the offer of the wooden horse. I do not presume to meddle in the affairs of all these actors and authors, patrons and enthusiasts, subscribers and guarantors, though this is quite as much my business as theirs; but after some years' intimate experience of the results of unorganized Ibsenism, I venture to suggest that it would be well to have some equitable form of theatrical organization ready to deal with Ibsen's new play, on the translation of which Mr Archer is already at work.

BETTER THAN SHAKESPEAR

THE PILGRIM'S PROGRESS. A mystery play, with music, in four acts, by G. G. Collingham; founded on John Bunyan's immortal allegory. Olympic Theatre, 24 December 1896.

BLACK-EY'D SUSAN; OR, ALL IN THE DOWNS. Douglas Jerrold's famous nautical drama, in two acts. Preceded by J. Maddison Morton's domestic comedy, in two acts, ALL THAT GLITTERS IS NOT GOLD. Adelphi Theatre, 23 December 1896.

THE EIDER DOWN QUILT. Farcical comedy, in three acts, by Tom S. Wotton. Terry's Theatre, 21 December 1896.

BETSY. The celebrated comedy, in three acts, by F. C. Burnand. Revival. Criterion Theatre, 29 December 1896.

HOLLY TREE INN. Adapted by Mrs Oscar Beringer from Charles Dickens's story. In one act. Terry's Theatre, 28 December 1896 [2 *January* 1897]

WHEN I saw a stage version of The Pilgrim's Progress announced for production, I shook my head, knowing that Bunyan is far too great a dramatist for our theatre, which has never been resolute enough even in its lewdness and venality to win the respect and interest which positive, powerful wickedness always engages, much less the services of men of heroic conviction. Its greatest catch, Shakespear, wrote for the theatre because, with extraordinary artistic powers, he understood nothing and believed nothing. Thirty-six big plays in five blank verse acts, and (as Mr Ruskin, I think, once pointed out) not a single hero! Only one man in them all who believes in life, enjoys life, thinks life worth living, and has a sincere, unrhetorical tear dropped over his death-bed; and that man—Falstaff! What a crew they are—these Saturday to Monday athletic stockbroker Orlandos, these villains, fools, clowns, drunkards, cowards, intriguers, fighters, lovers, patriots, hypochondriacs who mistake themselves (and are mistaken by the author) for philosophers, princes without any sense of public duty, futile pessimists who imagine they are confronting a barren and unmeaning world when they are only contemplating their own worthlessness, self-seekers of all kinds, keenly observed and masterfully drawn from the romantic-commercial point of view. Once or twice we scent among them an anticipation of the crudest side of Ibsen's polemics on the Woman Question, as in All's Well that Ends Well, where the man cuts as meanly selfish a figure beside his enlightened lady doctor wife as Helmer beside Nora; or in Cymbeline, where Posthumus, having, as he believes, killed his wife for inconstancy, speculates for a moment on what his life would have been worth if the same standard of continence had been applied to himself. And certainly no modern study of the voluptuous temperament, and the spurious heroism and heroinism which its ecstasies produce, can add much to Antony and Cleopatra, unless it were some sense of the spuriousness on the author's part. But search for statesmanship, or even citizenship, or any sense of the commonwealth, material or spiritual, and you will not find the making of a decent vestryman or curate in the whole horde. As to faith, hope, courage, conviction, or any of the true heroic qualities, you find nothing but death made sensational, despair made stage-sublime, sex made romantic, and barrenness covered up by sentimentality and the mechanical lilt of blank verse.

All that you miss in Shakespear you find in Bunyan, to whom the true heroic came quite obviously and naturally. The world was to him a more terrible place than it was to Shakespear; but he saw through it a path at the end of which a man might look not only forward to the Celestial City, but back on his life and say:—"Tho' with great difficulty I am got hither, yet now I do not repent me of all the trouble I have been at to arrive where I am. My sword I give to him that shall succeed me in my pilgrimage, and my courage and skill to him that can get them." The heart vibrates like a bell to such an utterance as this: to turn from it to "Out, out, brief candle," and "The rest is silence," and "We are such stuff as dreams are made of; and our little life is rounded by a sleep" is to turn from life, strength, resolution, morning air and eternal youth, to the terrors of a drunken nightmare.

Let us descend now to the lower ground where Shakespear is not disabled by his inferiority in energy and elevation of spirit. Take one of his big fighting scenes, and compare its blank verse, in point of mere rhetorical strenuousness, with Bunyan's prose. Macbeth's famous cue for the fight with Macduff runs thus:—

> Yet I will try the last: before my body
> I throw my warlike shield. Lay on, Macduff,
> And damned be him that first cries Hold, enough!

Turn from this jingle, dramatically right in feeling, but silly and resourceless in thought and expression, to Apollyon's cue for the fight in the Valley of Humiliation: "I am void of fear in this matter. Prepare thyself to die; for I swear by my infernal den that thou shalt go no farther: here will I spill thy soul." This is the same thing done masterly. Apart from its superior grandeur, force, and appropriateness, it is better claptrap and infinitely better word-music.

Shakespear, fond as he is of describing fights, has hardly ever sufficient energy or reality of imagination to finish without betraying the paper origin of his fancies by dragging in something classical in the style of the Cyclops' hammer falling "on Mars's armor, forged for proof eterne." Hear how Bunyan does it: "I fought till my sword did cleave to my hand; and when they were joined together as if the sword grew out of my arm; and when the blood run thorow my fingers, then I fought with most courage." Nowhere in all Shakespear is there a touch like that of the blood running down through the man's fingers, and his courage rising to passion at it. Even in mere technical adaptation to the art of the actor, Bunyan's dramatic speeches are as good as Shakespear's tirades. Only a trained dramatic speaker can appreciate the terse manageableness and effectiveness of such a speech as this, with its grandiose exordium, followed up by its pointed question and its stern threat: "By this I perceive thou art one of my subjects; for all that country is mine, and I am the Prince and the God of it. How is it then that thou hast ran away from thy King? Were it not that I hope thou mayst do me more service, I would strike thee now at one blow to the ground." Here there is no raving and swearing and rhyming and classical allusion. The sentences go straight to their mark; and their concluding phrases soar like the sunrise, or swing and drop like a hammer, just as the actor wants them.

I might multiply these instances by the dozen; but I had rather leave dramatic students to compare the two authors at first-hand. In an article on Bunyan lately published in the Contemporary Review—the only article worth reading on the subject I ever saw (yes, thank you: I am quite familiar with Macaulay's patronizing prattle about The Pilgrim's Progress)—Mr Richard Heath, the historian of the Anabaptists, shows how Bunyan learnt his lesson, not only from his own rough pilgrimage through life, but from the tradition of many an actual journey from real Cities of Destruction (under Alva), with Interpreters' houses and convoy of Greathearts all complete. Against such a man what chance had our poor immortal William, with his "little Latin" (would it had been less, like his Greek), his heathen mythology, his Plutarch, his Boccaccio, his Holinshed, his circle of London literary wits, soddening their minds with books and their nerves with alcohol (quite like us), and all the rest of his Strand and Fleet Street surroundings, activities, and interests, social and professional, mentionable and unmentionable? Let us applaud him, in due measure, in that he came out of it no blackguardly Bohemian, but a thoroughly respectable snob; raised the desperation and cynicism of its outlook to something like sublimity in his tragedies; dramatized its morbid, self-centred passions and its feeble and shallow speculations with all the force that was in them; disinfected it by copious doses of romantic poetry, fun, and common sense; and gave to its perpetual sex-obsession the relief of individual character and feminine winsomeness. Also—if you are a sufficiently good Whig—that after incarnating the spirit of the whole epoch which began with the sixteenth century and is ending (I hope) with the nineteenth, he is still the idol of all well-read children. But as he never thought a noble life worth living or a great work worth doing, because the commercial profit-and-loss sheet shewed that the one did not bring happiness nor the other money, he never struck the great vein—the vein in which Bunyan told of that "man of a very stout countenance" who went up to the keeper of the book of life and said, not "Out, out, brief candle," but "Set down my name, sir," and immediately fell on the armed men and cut his way into heaven after receiving and giving many wounds.

Let me not, however, be misunderstood by the Anglo-American Theatrical Syndicate, Limited, which has introduced the entertainment at the Olympic described as The Pilgrim's Progress, a mystery play, by G. G. Collingham, founded on John Bunyan's Immortal Allegory. That syndicate has listened to the voice of Demas; and I wish it joy of the silver mines to which he has led it. As to Mr Collingham, he does not take my view of the excellence of Bunyan's language or ideas. It is true that his hero is called Christian, and the villain Apollion, on the analogy of Rapscallion, Scullion, and the like, instead of Appol Lyon, which is what Bunyan called him. Also, three of the scenes are called Vanity Fair, The Valley of the Shadow of Death, and Doubting Castle, from which Christian escapes with the key called Promise. I fancied, too, I detected a paraphrase of a Bunyan passage in the following couplet:

> Heed not this king: he never gives reward,
> But always leaves his followers in the lurch.

But, these points apart, it would not have occurred to me that Mr Collingham or anyone else connected with the Olympic production had ever read or heard of Bunyan. It has been stated publicly that "Mr Collingham" is a lady who has been encouraged to venture a good deal of her private means on the production of a work which is perilously deficient in the stage qualities needed to justify such encouragement. If this is true, I need not say what I think of the enterprise. If not, I desire to treat it with respect because it has attracted capital; for the other day, when subscriptions were invited to produce Little Eyolf, several of those colleagues of mine who still devotedly keep knocking their heads against the Norwegian stone wall laid great stress on this failure on Ibsen's part to attract capital from the ordinary theatrical sources. I sardonically invite them to go and revel in The Pilgrim's Progress as a play which has attracted capital enough to produce Little Eyolf six times over.

The new bill at the Adelphi should not be missed by anyone who wishes to qualify as an experienced playgoer. All that Glitters is not Gold is a most fearful specimen of obsolete pinchbeck, in spite of the pleasant qualities of the author of Box and Cox. But, of course, what one goes for is Black-Ey'd Susan, not Wills's genteel edition, with which Mrs Kendal made us cry so at the St James's, but the real original with San Domingo Billy, hornpipe, song about My sweet Willy-yum, and nautical lingo all complete. Mr Terriss makes brilliant play with his diamond shoebuckles in the hornpipe, justifies his ear in his song, and delivers the jargon of the first two scenes like a conjurer producing miles of ribbon from his mouth. Miss Millward, when rudely accosted by Mr Fulton as Captain Crosstree, says, "He is intoxicated. I must hence," as if that were the most natural observation possible for the wife of an able seaman. But Black-Ey'd Susan, when it once gets to business, is an excellent play. It is the second act that tries the actor; and here Mr Terriss plays with perfect judgment, producing just the right effect of humble but manly sincerity and naturalness in great distress by the most straightforward methods. Is it not odd that the Adelphi is the only theatre in London devoted to sentimental modern drama where the acting is not vulgar? In other houses the actors' subordination of drama to "good taste," their consciousness of the stalls, their restrained drawing room voices, made resonant enough for the theatre by clarionet effects from the nose, their perpetual thinking of their manners and appearance when they ought to be thinking of their work, all produce a detestable atmosphere of candidature for social promotion which makes me wish sometimes that the stage were closed to all classes except only those accustomed to take their position for granted and their own ways as the standard ways, or those who frankly make no social pretension at all. At the Adelphi the actors provide for their appearance in their dressing rooms, and when they come on the stage go straight for the play with all their force, as if their point of honor lay in their skill, and not in persuading smart parties in the boxes that it would be quite safe to send them cards for an "At Home" in spite of their profession. The result is that they look better, dress better, and behave better than their competitors at the intentionally fashionable theatres. Instead of having caught the "form" of South Kensington (and what an appalling complaint that is for anyone to catch!), they have universal good manners, the proof being that Mr Terriss, without the lightest self-disguise or "character-acting" trickery of any sort, is equally engaging and equally natural as the officer in One of the Best and as the common sailor in Black-Ey'd Susan. Miss Millward, though she is, I am told, always so scrupulously in fashion that women's hearts sink if they see her sleeves vary by an inch from their latest frocks, is always in her part, and always fits it if there is any sort of possible humanity and charm in it. Mr Fulton, too, is a courageous and self-respecting actor who is at home everywhere on the stage. Even Mr Harry Nicholls, badly spoiled funny man as he is, has serious qualities as an actor, and can make real bricks when the author provides any straw. In short, the secret of the Adelphi is not, as is generally assumed, bad drama, but simply good acting and plenty of it. And, unlike most critics, I am fond of acting.

The Eider Down Quilt, at Terry's, a somewhat artlessly amusing piece, owes a good deal to the genius of Miss Fanny Brough as a lady who has, as she believes, sat on a man and smothered him, and to Mr de Lange, who tries the very dangerous experiment of taking a purely farcical figure (an Italian waiter disguised as a prince), and making a realistic character study of him. However, the result justifies the attempt; and Alberto da Bologna is another of Mr de Lange's successes.

Betsy has been revived at the Criterion to give Mr Wyndham a holiday. I hope he will enjoy it at least as much as I enjoyed Betsy, which, though funny, is somewhat too pre-Ibsenite for my taste.

The afternoon performances of Love in Idleness at Terry's now begin with Mrs Oscar Beringer's adaptation of Boots at the Holly Tree Inn, in which Master Stewart Dawson, late of Little Eyolf, and Miss Valli Valli play the tiny elopers. It is very prettily done, and just the sort of piece that old people like.

HAMLET

[2 *October* 1897]

THE Forbes Robertson Hamlet at the Lyceum is, very unexpectedly at that address, really not at all unlike Shakespear's play of the same name. I am quite certain I saw Reynaldo in it for a moment; and possibly I may have seen Voltimand and Cornelius; but just as the time for their scene arrived, my eye fell on the word "Fortinbras" in the program, which so amazed me that I hardly know what I saw for the next ten minutes. Ophelia, instead of being a strenuously earnest and self-possessed young lady giving a concert and recitation for all she was worth, was mad—actually mad. The story of the play was perfectly intelligible, and quite took the attention of the audience off the principal actor at moments. What is the Lyceum coming to? Is it for this that Sir Henry Irving has invented a whole series of original romantic dramas, and given the credit of them without a murmur to the immortal bard whose profundity (as exemplified in the remark that good and evil are mingled in our natures) he has just been pointing out to the inhabitants of Cardiff, and whose works have been no more to him than the word-quarry from which he has hewn and blasted the lines and titles of masterpieces which are really all his own? And now, when he has created by these means a reputation for Shakespear, he no sooner turns his back for a moment on London than Mr Forbes Robertson competes with him on the boards of his own theatre by actually playing off against him the authentic Swan of Avon. Now if the result had been the utter exposure and collapse of that imposter, poetic justice must have proclaimed that it served Mr Forbes Robertson right. But alas! the wily William, by literary tricks which our simple Sir Henry has never quite understood, has played into Mr Forbes Robertson's hands so artfully that the scheme is a prodigious success. The effect of this success, coming after that of Mr Alexander's experiment with a Shakespearean version of As You Like It, makes it almost probable that we shall presently find managers vying with each other in offering the public as much of the original Shakespearean stuff as possible, instead of, as heretofore, doing their utmost to reassure us that everything that the most modern resources can do to relieve the irreducible minimum of tedium inseparable from even the most heavily cut acting version will be lavished on their revivals. It is true that Mr Beerbohm Tree still holds to the old scepticism, and calmly proposes to insult us by offering us Garrick's puerile and horribly caddish knockabout farce of Katherine and Petruchio for Shakespear's Taming of the Shrew; but Mr Tree, like all romantic actors, is incorrigible on the subject of Shakespear.

Mr Forbes Robertson is essentially a classical actor, the only one, with the exception of Mr Alexander, now established in London management. What I mean by classical is that he can present a dramatic hero as a man whose passions are those which have produced the philosophy, the poetry, the art, and the statecraft of the world, and not merely those which have produced its weddings, coroners' inquests, and executions. And that is just the sort of actor that Hamlet requires. A Hamlet who only understands his love for Ophelia, his grief for his father, his vindictive hatred of his uncle, his fear of ghosts, his impulse to snub Rosencrantz and Guildenstern, and the sportsman's excitement with which he lays the "mousetrap" for Claudius, can, with sufficient force or virtuosity of execution, get a great reputation in the part, even though the very intensity of his obsession by these sentiments (which are common not only to all men but to many animals) shews that the characteristic side of Hamlet, the side that differentiates him from Fortinbras, is absolutely outside the actor's consciousness. Such a reputation is the actor's, not Hamlet's. Hamlet is not a man in whom "common humanity" is raised by great vital energy to a heroic pitch, like Coriolanus or Othello. On the contrary, he is a man in whom the common personal passions are so superseded by wider and rarer interests, and so discouraged by a degree of critical self-consciousness which makes the practical efficiency of the instinctive man on the lower plane impossible to him, that he finds the duties dictated by conventional revenge and ambition as disagreeable a burden as commerce is to a poet. Even his instinctive sexual impulses offend his intellect; so that when he meets the woman who excites them he invites her to join him in a bitter and scornful criticism of their joint absurdity, demanding "What should such fellows as I do crawling between heaven and earth?" "Why wouldst thou be a breeder of sinners?" and so forth, all of which is so completely beyond the poor girl that she naturally thinks him mad. And, indeed, there is a sense in which Hamlet is insane; for he trips over the mistake which lies on the threshold of intellectual self-consciousness: that of bringing life to utilitarian or Hedonistic tests, thus treating it as a means instead of an end. Because Polonius is "a foolish prating knave," because Rosencrantz and Guildenstern are snobs, he kills them as remorselessly as he might kill a flea, shewing that he has no real belief in the superstitious reason which he gives for not killing himself, and in fact anticipating exactly the whole course of the intellectual history of Western Europe until Schopenhauer found the clue that Shakespear missed. But to call Hamlet mad because he did not anticipate Schopenhauer is like calling Marcellus mad because he did not refer the Ghost to the Psychical Society. It is in fact not possible for any actor to represent Hamlet as mad. He may (and generally does) combine some notion of his own of a man who is the creature of affectionate sentiment with the figure drawn by the lines of Shakespear; but the result is not a madman, but simply one of those monsters produced by the imaginary combination of two normal species, such as sphinxes, mermaids, or centaurs. And this is the invariable resource of the instinctive, imaginative, romantic actor. You will see him weeping bucketsful of tears over Ophelia, and treating the players, the gravedigger, Horatio, Rosencrantz, and Guildenstern as if they were mutes at his own funeral. But go and watch Mr Forbes Robertson's Hamlet seizing delightedly on every opportunity for a bit of philosophic discussion or artistic recreation to escape from the "cursed spite" of revenge and love and other common troubles; see how he brightens up when the players come; how he tries to talk philosophy with Rosencrantz and Guildenstern the moment they come into the room; how he stops on his country walk with Horatio to lean over the churchyard wall and draw out the gravedigger whom he sees singing at his trade; how even his fits of excitement find expression in declaiming scraps of poetry; how the shock of Ophelia's death relieves itself in the fiercest intellectual contempt for Laertes's ranting, whilst an hour afterwards, when Laertes stabs him, he bears no malice for that at all, but embraces him gallantly and comradely; and how he dies as we forgive everything to Charles II for dying, and makes "the rest is silence" a touchingly humorous apology for not being able to finish his business. See all that; and you have seen a true classical Hamlet. Nothing half so charming has been seen by this generation. It will bear seeing again and again.

And please observe that this is not a cold Hamlet. He is none of your logicians who reason their way through the world because they cannot feel their way through it: his intellect is the organ of his passion: his eternal self-criticism is as alive and thrilling as it can possibly be. The great soliloquy—no: I do NOT mean "To be or not to be": I mean the dramatic one, "O what a rogue and peasant slave am I!"—is as passionate in its scorn of brute passion as the most bull-necked affirmation or sentimental dilution of it could be. It comes out so without violence: Mr Forbes Robertson takes the part quite easily and spontaneously. There is none of that strange Lyceum intensity which comes from the perpetual struggle between Sir Henry Irving and Shakespear. The lines help Mr Forbes Robertson instead of getting in his way at every turn, because he wants to play Hamlet, and not to slip into his inky cloak a changeling of quite another race. We may miss the craft, the skill double-distilled by constant peril, the sublety, the dark rays of heat generated by intense friction, the relentless parental tenacity and cunning with which Sir Henry nurses his own pet creations on Shakespearean food like a fox rearing its litter in the den of a lioness; but we get light, freedom, naturalness, credibility, and Shakespear. It is wonderful how easily everything comes right when you have the right man with the right mind for it—how the story tells itself, how the characters come to life, how even the failures in the cast cannot confuse you, though they may disappoint you. And Mr Forbes Robertson has certainly not escaped such failures, even in his own family. I strongly urge him to take a hint from Claudius and make a real ghost of Mr Ian Robertson at once; for there is no sort of use in going through that scene night after night with a Ghost so solidly, comfortably, and dogmatically alive as his brother. The voice is not a bad voice; but it is the voice of a man who does not believe in ghosts. Moreover, it is a hungry voice, not that of one who is past eating. There is an indescribable little complacent drop at the end of every line which no sooner calls up the image of purgatory by its words than by its smug elocution it convinces us that this particular penitent is cosily warming his shins and toasting his muffin at the flames instead of expiating his bad acting in the midst of them. His aspect and bearing are worse than his recitations. He beckons Hamlet away like a beadle summoning a timid candidate for the post of junior footman to the presence of the Lord Mayor. If I were Mr Forbes Robertson I would not stand that from any brother: I would cleave the general ear with horrid speech at him first. It is a pity; for the Ghost's part is one of the wonders of the play. And yet, until Mr Courtenay Thorpe divined it the other day, nobody seems to have had a glimpse of the reason why Shakespear would not trust anyone else with it, and played it himself. The weird music of that long speech which should be the spectral wail of a soul's bitter wrong crying from one world to another in the extremity of its torment, is invariably handed over to the most squaretoed member of the company, who makes it sound, not like Rossetti's Sister Helen, or even, to suggest a possible heavy treatment, like Mozart's statue-ghost, but like Chambers's Information for the People.

Still, I can understand Mr Ian Robertson, by sheer force of a certain quality of sententiousness in him, overbearing the management into casting him for the Ghost. What I cannot understand is why Miss Granville was cast for the Queen. It is like setting a fashionable modern mandolinist to play Hadyn's sonatas. She does her best under the circumstances; but she would have been more fortunate had she been in a position to refuse the part.

On the other hand, several of the impersonations are conspicuously successful. Mrs Patrick Campbell's Ophelia is a surprise. The part is one which has hitherto seemed incapable of progress. From generation to generation actresses have, in the mad scene, exhausted their musical skill, their ingenuity in devising fantasias in the language of flowers, and their intensest powers of portraying anxiously earnest sanity. Mrs Patrick Campbell, with that complacent audacity of hers which is so exasperating when she is doing the wrong thing, this time does the right thing by making Ophelia really mad. The resentment of the audience at this outrage is hardly to be described. They long for the strenuous mental grasp and attentive coherence of Miss Lily Hanbury's conception of maiden lunacy; and this wandering, silly, vague Ophelia, who no sooner catches an emotional impulse than it drifts away from her again, emptying her voice of its tone in a way that makes one shiver, makes them horribly uncomfortable. But the effect on the play is conclusive. The shrinking discomfort of the King and Queen, the rankling grief of Laertes, are created by it at once; and the scene, instead of being a pretty interlude coming in just when a little relief from the inky cloak is welcome, touches us with a chill of the blood that gives it its right tragic power and dramatic significance. Playgoers naturally murmur when something that has always been pretty becomes painful; but the pain is good for them, good for the theatre, and good for the play. I doubt whether Mrs Patrick Campbell fully appreciates the dramatic value of her quite simple and original sketch—it is only a sketch—of the part; but in spite of the occasional triviality of its execution and the petulance with which it has been received, it seems to me to settle finally in her favor the question of her right to the very important place which Mr Forbes Robertson has assigned to her in his enterprises.

I did not see Mr Bernard Gould play Laertes: he was indisposed when I returned to town and hastened to the Lyceum; but he was replaced very creditably by Mr Frank Dyall. Mr Martin Harvey is the best Osric I have seen: he plays Osric from Osric's own point of view, which is, that Osric is a gallant and distinguished courtier, and not, as usual, from Hamlet's, which is that Osric is "a waterfly." Mr Harrison Hunter hits off the modest, honest Horatio capitally; and Mr Willes is so good a Gravedigger that I venture to suggest to him that he should carry his work a little further, and not virtually cease to concern himself with the play when he has spoken his last line and handed Hamlet the skull. Mr Cooper Cliffe is not exactly a subtle Claudius; but he looks as if he had stepped out of a picture by Madox Brown, and plays straightforwardly on his very successful appearance. Mr Barnes makes Polonius robust and elderly instead of aged and garrulous. He is good in the scenes where Polonius appears as a man of character and experience; but the senile exhibitions of courtierly tact do not match these, and so seem forced and farcical.

Mr Forbes Robertson's own performance has a continuous charm, interest, and variety which are the result not only of his well-known grace and accomplishment as an actor, but of a genuine delight—the rarest thing on our stage—in Shakespear's art, and a natural familiarity with the plane of his imagination. He does not superstitiously worship William: he enjoys him and understands his methods of expression. Instead of cutting every line that can possibly be spared, he retains every gem, in his own part or anyone else's, that he can make time for in a spiritedly brisk performance lasting three hours and a half with very short intervals. He does not utter half a line; then stop to act; then go on with another half line; and then stop to act again, with the clock running away with Shakespear's chances all the time. He plays as Shakespear should be played, on the line and to the line, with the utterance and acting simultaneous, inseparable and in fact identical. Not for a moment is he solemnly conscious of Shakespear's reputation, or of Hamlet's momentousness in literary history: on the contrary, he delivers us from all these boredoms instead of heaping them on us. We forgive him the platitudes, so engagingly are they delivered. His novel and astonishingly effective and touching treatment of the final scene is an inspiration, from the fencing match onward. If only Fortinbras could also be inspired with sufficient force and brilliancy to rise to the warlike splendor of his helmet, and make straight for that throne like a man who intended to keep it against all comers, he would leave nothing to be desired. How many generations of Hamlets, all thirsting to outshine their competitors in effect and originality, have regarded Fortinbras, and the clue he gives to this kingly death for Hamlet, as a wildly unpresentable blunder of the poor foolish old Swan, than whom they all knew so much better! How sweetly they have died in that faith to slow music, like Little Nell in The

Old Curiosity Shop! And now how completely Mr Forbes Robertson has bowled them all out by being clever enough to be simple.

By the way, talking of slow music, the sooner Mr Hamilton Clarke's romantic Irving music is stopped, the better. Its effect in this Shakespearean version of the play is absurd. The four Offenbachian young women in tights should also be abolished, and the part of the player-queen given to a man. The courtiers should be taught how flatteringly courtiers listen when a king shews off his wisdom in wise speeches to his nephew. And that nice wooden beach on which the ghost walks would be the better for a seaweedy looking cloth on it, with a handful of shrimps and a pennorth of silver sand.

AT SEVERAL THEATRES

Francillon. From the French of Alexandre Dumas *fils*. A comedy in three acts. Duke of York's Theatre.

Triple Bill at the Avenue Theatre, 2 October 1897.

As You Like It. Grand Theatre, Islington, 4 October 1897.

Oh, Susannah! Farcical comedy in three acts. By Messrs Ambient, Atwood, and Vaun. Royalty Theatre, 5 October 1897.

The Liars. A new and original comedy. By Henry Arthur Jones. Criterion Theatre, 6 October 1897.

[9 *October* 1897]

I NEVER see Miss Ada Rehan act without burning to present Mr Augustin Daly with a delightful villa in St Helena, and a commission from an influential committee of his admirers to produce at his leisure a complete set of Shakespear's plays, entirely rewritten, reformed, rearranged, and brought up to the most advanced requirements of the year 1850. He was in full force at the Islington Theatre on Monday evening last with his version of As You Like It just as I dont like it. There I saw Amiens under the greenwood tree, braving winter and rough weather in a pair of crimson plush breeches, a spectacle to benumb the mind and obscure the passions. There was Orlando with the harmony of his brown boots and tunic torn asunder by a piercing discord of dark volcanic green, a walking tribute to Mr Daly's taste in tights. There did I hear slow music stealing up from the band at all the well-known recitations of Adam, Jacques, and Rosalind, lest we should for a moment forget that we were in a theatre and not in the forest of Arden. There did I look through practicable doors in the walls of sunny orchards into an abyss of pitchy darkness. There saw I in the attitudes, grace, and deportment of the forest dwellers the plastique of an Arcadian past. And the music synchronized with it all to perfection, from La Grande Duchesse and Dichter und Bauer, conducted by the leader of the band, to the inevitable old English airs conducted by the haughty musician who is Mr Daly's special property. And to think that Mr Daly will die in his bed, whilst innocent presidents of republics, who never harmed an immortal bard, are falling on all sides under the knives of well-intentioned reformers whose only crime is that they assassinate the wrong people! And yet let me be magnanimous. I confess I would not like to see Mr Daly assassinated: St Helena would satisfy me. For Mr Daly was in his prime an advanced man relatively to his own time and place, and was a real manager, with definite artistic aims which he trained his company to accomplish. His Irish-American Yanko-German comedies, as played under his management by Ada Rehan and Mrs Gilbert, John Drew, Otis Skinner and the late John Lewis, turned a page in theatrical history here, and secured him a position in London which was never questioned until it became apparent that he was throwing away Miss Rehan's genius. When, after the complete discovery of her gifts by the London public, Mr Daly could find no better employment for her than in a revival of Dollars and Cents, his annihilation and Miss Rehan's rescue became the critic's first duty. Shakespear saved the situation for a time, and got severely damaged in the process; but The Countess Gucki convinced me that in Mr Daly's hands Miss Rehan's talent was likely to be lost not only to the modern drama, but to the modern Shakespearean stage: that is to say, to the indispensable conditions of its own fullest development. No doubt starring in Daly Shakespear is as lucrative and secure as the greatest of Duse's achievements are thankless and precarious; but surely it must be better fun making money enough by La Dame aux Camélias to pay for Heimat and La Femme de Claude, and win the position of the greatest actress in the world with all three, than to astonish provincials with versions of Shakespear which are no longer up even to metropolitan literary and dramatic standards.

However, since I cannot convert Miss Rehan to my view of the position, I must live in hope that some day she will come to the West End of London for a week or two, just as Réjane and Sarah Bernhardt do, with some work of sufficient novelty and importance to make good the provincial wear and tear of her artistic prestige. Just now she is at the height of her powers. The plumpness that threatened the Countess Gucki has vanished: Rosalind is as slim as a girl. The third and fourth acts are as wonderful as ever — miracles of vocal expression. If As You Like It were a typical Shakespearean play, I should unhesitatingly declare Miss Rehan the most perfect Shakespearean executant in the world. But when I think of those plays in which our William anticipated modern dramatic art by making serious attempts to hold the mirror up to nature—All's Well, Measure for Measure, Troilus and Cressida, and so on—I must limit the tribute to Shakespear's popular style. Rosalind is not a complete human being: she is simply an extension into five acts of the most affectionate, fortunate, delightful five minutes in the life of a charming woman. And all the other figures in the play are cognate impostures. Orlando, Adam, Jacques, Touchstone, the banished Duke, and the rest play each the same tune all through. This is not human nature or dramatic character; it is juvenile lead, first old man, heavy lead, heavy father, principal comedian, and leading lady, transfigured by magical word-music. The Shakespearolators who are taken in by it do not know drama in the classical sense from "drama" in the technical Adelphi sense. You have only to compare Orlando and Rosalind with Bertram and Helena, the Duke and Touchstone with Leontes and Autolycus, to learn the difference from Shakespear himself. Therefore I cannot judge from Miss Rehan's enchanting Rosalind whether she is a great Shakespearean actress or not: there is even a sense in which I cannot tell whether she can act at all or not. So far, I have never seen her create a character: she has always practised the same adorable arts on me, by whatever name the playbill has called her—Nancy Brasher (ugh!), Viola, or Rosalind. I have never complained: the drama with all its heroines levelled up to a universal Ada Rehan has seemed no such dreary prospect to me; and her voice, compared to Sarah Bernhardt's *voix d'or*, has been as all the sounds of the woodland to the chinking of twenty-franc pieces. In Shakespear (what Mr Daly leaves of him) she was and is irresistible: at Islington on Monday she made me cry faster than Mr Daly could make me swear. But the critic in me is bound to insist that Ada Rehan has as yet created nothing but Ada Rehan. She will probably never excel that masterpiece; but why should she not superimpose a character study or two on it! Duse's greatest work is Duse; but that does not prevent Césarine, Santuzza, and Camille from being three totally different women, none of them Duses, though Duse is all of them. Miss Rehan would charm everybody as Mirandolina as effectually as Duse does. But how about Magda? It is because nobody in England knows the answer to that question that nobody in England as yet knows whether Ada Rehan is a creative artist or a mere virtuosa.

The Liars, Mr Henry Arthur Jones's new comedy, is one of his lighter works, written with due indulgence to the Criterion company and the playgoing public. Its subject is a common enough social episode—a married lady sailing too close to the wind in a flirtation, and her friends and relatives interposing to half hustle, half coax the husband and wife into a reconciliation, and the gallant off to Africa. Mr Jones has extracted from this all the drama that can be got from it without sacrificing verisimilitude, or spoiling the reassuring common sense of the conclusion. Its interest, apart from its wealth of comedy, lies in its very keen and accurate picture of smart society. Smart society will probably demur, as it always does to views of it obtained from any standpoint outside itself. Mr Jones's detachment is absolute: he describes Mayfair as an English traveller describes the pygmies or the Zulus, caring very little about the common human perversities of which (believing them, of course, to be the caste-mark of their class) they are so self-importantly conscious, and being much tickled by the morally significant peculiarities of which they are not conscious at all. "Society" is intensely parochial, intensely conceited, and, outside that art of fashionable life for which it has specialized itself, and in which it has acquired a fairly artistic technique, trivial, vulgar, and horribly tiresome. Its conceit, however, is not of the personally self-complacent kind. Within its own limits it does not flatter itself: on the contrary, being chronically bored with itself, it positively delights in the most savage and embittered satire at its own expense from its own point of view. For example, Thackeray, who belonged to it and hated it, is admired and endorsed by it, because, with all his rancor against its failings, he took Hyde Park Corner as the cosmic headquarters, a Ptolemaic mistake which saved his gentility throughout all his Thersites railings at it. Charles Dickens, on the other hand, could never be a gentleman, because it never occurred to him to look at fashionable society otherwise than from the moral and industrial centres of the community, in which position he was necessarily "an outsider" from the point of view of the parishioners of St James of Piccadilly and St George of Hanover Square. That this outside position could be a position of advantage, even to a literary lion flatteringly petted and freely fed at the parish tables, is a conception impossible to the insider, since if he thought so, he would at once, by that thought, be placed outside. All fiction which deals with fashionable society as a class exhibits this division into Thackeray and Dickens—into the insider and the outsider. For my own part I recommend the outside, because it is possible for the outsider to comprehend and enjoy the works of the insiders, whereas they can never comprehend his. From Dickens's point of view Thackeray and Trollope are fully available, whilst from their point of view Dickens is deplorable. Just so with Mr Jones and Mr Pinero. Mr Jones's pictures of society never seem truthful to those who see ladies and gentlemen as they see themselves. They are restricted to Mr Pinero's plays, recognizing in them alone poetic justice to the charm of good society. But those who appreciate Mr Jones accommodate themselves without difficulty to Mr Pinero's range, and so enjoy both. In the latest plays of these two authors the difference is very marked. The pictures of fashionable life in The Princess and the Butterfly, containing, if we except the mere kodaking, not one stroke that is objectively lifelike or even plausible, is yet made subjectively appropriate in a most acceptable degree by the veil of sentimental romance which it casts over Mayfair. In The Liars, the "smart" group which carries on the action of the piece is hit off to the life, with the result that the originals will probably feel brutally misrepresented.

And now comes in the oddity of the situation. Mr Jones, with a wide and clear vision of society, is content with theories of it that have really no relation to his observation. The comedic sentiment of The Liars is from beginning to end one of affectionate contempt for women and friendly contempt for men, applied to their affairs with shrewd worldly common sense and much mollifying humor; whilst its essentially pious theology and its absolute conceptions of duty belong to a passionately anti-comedic conception of them as temples of the Holy Ghost. Its observations could only have been made today; its idealism might have been made yesterday; its reflections might have been made a long time ago. Against this I am inclined to protest. It is surely immoral for an Englishman to keep two establishments, much more three.

The incongruities arising from the different dates of Mr Jones's brain compartments have, happily, the effect of keeping his sense of humor continually stirring. I am sure The Liars must be an extremely diverting play on the stage. But I have not seen it there. Mr Wyndham's acting-manager wrote to ask whether I would come if I were invited. I said Yes. Accordingly I was *not* invited. The shock to my self-esteem was severe and unexpected. I desire it to be distinctly understood, however, that I forgive everybody.

The conscientious transliteration (for the most part) of the Francillon of Dumas *fils* at the Duke of York's Theatre makes a very tolerable evening's amusement. It is, of course, only here to get hallmarked as a London success, and is planned to impress unsophisticated audiences as an exceedingly dashing and classy representation of high life. Mrs Brown Potter is unsparing of the beauties of her wardrobe, and indeed of her own person. She seems, as far as I can judge, congenitally incapable of genuine impersonation; but she has coached herself into a capital imitation of a real French actress playing the part, which she thoroughly understands. Saving one or two lapses into clowning for provincial laughs, her performance is not a bad specimen of manufactured acting. The best manufactured acting I ever saw was Modjeska's. It was much stricter, adroiter, finer, cleverer, more elaborate and erudite than Mrs Brown Potter's; but Modjeska was not genial. Mrs Brown Potter is genial. Her good looks are unimpaired; and only the very hard-hearted will feel much ill used by her shortcomings, especially as she is well supported in a good play, carefully managed and staged up to the point of making several prolonged passages of pure pantomime quite successful. Mr Bellew should stay in London a while, to brush away a few trifling stage habits which, like the comedy itself, begin to date a little. He plays with his old grace and much more than his old skill and ease, in the quiet style of the eighties, which is also revived with success by Messrs Elwood, Thursby, and Beauchamp. Mr J. L. Mackay keeps to his own somewhat later date, not unwisely, as Stanislas.

Oh, Susannah! at the Royalty, by Messrs Mark Ambient, A. Atwood, and R. Vaun, would be an extremely ingenious farce if its authors had contrived to make the incidents credible or even possible. It is nevertheless made positively thrilling by the genius of a Miss Louie Freear, who flings down a weedy glove on the stage and exclaims, "Aw chucks dahn me gimlet" (I throw down my gauntlet), and makes the audience scream—made *me* scream—frantically with laughter at this simple-minded pleasantry. She has sense of character, enormous comic force of the rare *pathetic* kind, wonderful powers of mimicry, instinctive good judgment as an executant, and unrivalled artistic command of all the humors of the slum and back kitchen. The popular history of the English stage for the next ten years will be the history of Miss Freear and Mr Dan Leno.

The triple bill at the Avenue begins with a trivial comedietta in eighteenth-century costume which any well-trained footman and lady's-maid could move through with credit. If actors would only learn their business as footmen do, such trifles would be more popular. My Lady's Orchard, by Mrs Oscar Beringer, is a little tale of chivalry of the naïve Waverley school—a play for children. Miss Esme Beringer, by some desperate and very clever and striking overplaying as the troubadour, undertakes to force it up to concert pitch, a heroic but impossible task. Mr Brookfield's part misfits him amusingly. In The Mermaid there is some bearable music, especially a new version of that charming old song I've been roaming. With Miss Lottie Venne and Mr Wyatt to act, and an agreeably grave young lady named Miss Davenport to provide serious relief as prima donna, the piece, which is of just the right length for its kind, serves its turn better than the usual overdose.

HAMLET REVISITED

[18 *December* 1897]

PUBLIC feeling has been much harrowed this week by the accounts from America of the 144 hours' bicycle race; but what are the horrors of such an exhibition compared to those of the hundred-nights run of Hamlet! On Monday last I went, in my private capacity, to witness the last lap but five of the Lyceum trial of endurance. The performers had passed through the stage of acute mania, and were for the most part sleep-walking in a sort of dazed blank-verse dream. Mr Barnes raved of some New England maiden named Affection Poo; the subtle distinctions made by Mrs Patrick Campbell between madness and sanity had blurred off into a placid idiocy turned to favor and to prettiness; Mr Forbes Robertson, his lightness of heart all gone, wandered into another play at the words "Sleep? No more!" which he delivered as, "Sleep no more." Fortunately, before he could add "Macbeth does murder sleep," he relapsed into Hamlet and saved the situation. And yet some of the company seemed all the better for their unnatural exercise. The King was in uproarious spirits; and the Ghost, always comfortable, was now positively pampered, his indifference to the inconveniences of purgatory having developed into a bean-fed enjoyment of them. Fortinbras, as I judged, had sought consolation in religion: he was anxious concerning Hamlet's eternal welfare; but his general health seemed excellent. As Mr Gould did not play on the occasion of my first visit, I could not compare him with his former self; but his condition was sufficiently grave. His attitude was that of a castaway mariner who has no longer hope enough to scan the horizon for a sail; yet even in this extremity his unconquerable generosity of temperament had not deserted him. When his cue came, he would jump up and lend a hand with all his old alacrity and resolution. Naturally the players of the shorter parts had suffered least: Rosencrantz and Guildenstern were only beginning to enjoy themselves; and Bernardo (or was it Marcellus?) was still eagerly working up his part to concert pitch. But there could be no mistake as to the general effect. Mr Forbes Robertson's exhausting part had been growing longer and heavier on his hands; whilst the support of the others had been falling off; so that he was keeping up the charm of the representation almost single-handed just when the torturing fatigue and monotony of nightly repetition had made the task most difficult. To the public, no doubt, the justification of the effort is its success. There was no act which did not contain at least one scene finely and movingly played; indeed some of the troubled passages gained in verisimilitude by the tormented condition of the actor. But Hamlet is a very long play; and it only seems a short one when the high-mettled comedy with which it is interpenetrated from beginning to end leaps out with all the lightness and spring of its wonderful loftiness of temper. This was the secret of the delighted surprise with which the public, when the run began, found that Hamlet, far from being a funereally classical bore, was full of a celestial gaiety and fascination. It is this rare vein that gives out first when the exigencies of theatrical commerce force an actor to abuse it. A sentimental Hamlet can go on for two years, or ten for the matter of that, without much essential depreciation of the performance; but the actor who sounds Hamlet from the lowest note to the top of his compass very soon finds that compass contracting at the top. On Monday night the first act, the third act, and the fifth act from the entrance of Laertes onward, had lost little more than they had gained as far as Mr Forbes Robertson was concerned; but the second act, and the colloquy with the grave-digger, which were the triumphs of the representation in its fresher stages, were pathetically dulled, with the result that it could no longer be said that the length of the play was forgotten.

The worst of the application of the long-run system to

heroic plays is that, instead of killing the actor, it drives him to limit himself to such effects as he can repeat to infinity without committing suicide. The opposite system, in its extreme form of the old stock company playing two or three different pieces every night, led to the same evasion in a more offensive form. The recent correspondence in the Morning Post on The Stage as a Profession, to which I have myself luminously contributed, has produced the usual fallacious eulogies of the old stock company as a school of acting. You can no more prevent contributors to public correspondences falling into this twenty-times-exploded error than from declaring that duelling was a school of good manners, that the lash suppressed garotting, or any other of the gratuitous ignorances of the amateur sociologist. The truth is, it is just as impossible for a human being to study and perform a new part of any magnitude every day as to play Hamlet for a hundred consecutive nights. Nevertheless, if an actor is required to do these things, he will find some way out of the difficulty without refusing. The stock actor solved the problem by adopting a "line": for example, if his "line" was old age, he acquired a trick of doddering and speaking in a cracked voice: if juvenility, he swaggered and effervesced. With these accomplishments, eked out by a few rules of thumb as to wigs and face-painting, one deplorable step dance, and one still more deplorable "combat," he "swallowed" every part given to him in a couple of hours, and regurgitated it in the evening over the footlights, always in the same manner, however finely the dramatist might have individualized it. His infamous incompetence at last swept him from the reputable theatres into the barns and booths; and it was then that he became canonized, in the imagination of a posterity that had never suffered from him, as the incarnation of the one quality in which he was quite damnably deficient: to wit, versatility. His great contribution to dramatic art was the knack of earning a living for fifty years on the stage without ever really acting, or either knowing or caring for the difference between the Comedy of Errors and Box and Cox.

A moment's consideration will shew that the results of the long-run system at its worst are more bearable than the horrors of the past. Also, that even in point of giving the actor some chance of varying his work, the long-run system is superior, since the modern actor may at all events exhaust the possibilities of his part before it exhausts him, whereas the stock actor, having barely time to apply his bag of tricks to his daily task, never varies his treatment by a hair's breadth from one half century to another. The best system, of course, lies between these extremes. Take the case of the great Italian actors who have visited us, and whose acting is of an excellence apparently quite beyond the reach of our best English performers. We find them extremely chary of playing every night. They have a repertory containing plays which count as resting places for them. For example, Duse relieves Magda with Mirandolina just as our own Shakespearean star actors used to relieve Richard the Third and Othello with Charles Surface and Don Felix. But even with this mitigation no actor can possibly play leading parts of the first order six nights a week all the year round unless he underplays them, or routines them mechanically in the old stock manner, or faces a terrible risk of disablement by paralysis, or, finally, resorts to alcohol or morphia, with the usual penalties. What we want in order to get the best work is a repertory theatre with alternative casts. If, for instance, we could have Hamlet running at the Lyceum with Sir Henry Irving and Miss Ellen Terry on Thursdays and Saturdays. Mr Forbes Robertson and Mrs Patrick Campbell on Wednesdays and Fridays, and the other two days devoted to comedies in which all four could occasionally appear, with such comedians as Mr Charles Wyndham, Mr Weedon Grossmith, Mr Bourchier, Mr Cyril Maude, and Mr Hawtrey, then we should have a theatre which we could invite serious people to attend without positively insulting them. I am aware that the precise combination which I have named is not altogether a probable one at present; but there is no reason why we should not at least turn our faces in that direction. The actor-manager system, which has hitherto meant the star system carried to its utmost possible extreme, has made the theatre so insufferable that, now that its monopoly has been broken up by the rise of the suburban theatres, there is a distinct weakening of the jealous and shameless individualism of the last twenty years, and a movement towards combination and co-operation.

By the way, is it quite prudent to start a public correspondence on the Stage as a Profession? Suppose someone were to tell the truth about it!

HENRY IRVING AND ELLEN TERRY

[*Henry Irving died on the* 14*th October* 1905. *I was asked by the Neue Freie Presse of Vienna to contribute an obituary notice, as I was then somewhat prominently in practice in London as a critic of plays and players. Unfortunately the translator* *made a slip or two in his haste, and gave a malicious turn to some of my comments. These were retranslated by the London papers; and the malicious turn lost less than nothing in the process. And when the retranslation was paraphrased by scandalized admirers of Irving, or by enemies of his who did not dare to disparage him at first hand, there arose a nine days fuss, including a heated correspondence in The Times, in which I was pilloried as a heartless slanderer of the dead. All I could do finally was to circulate the original text of my article to all the newspapers in the kingdom and place it freely at their disposal for literal reproduction. Only one of them, and that not a London one, availed themselves of my offer; for there is no getting over the hard journalistic fact that as quarrels and vituperations make thrilling reading whilst vindications are dull and disappointing, it is much easier to get a calumny published than its refutation, unless, as in France, the paper is legally obliged to give equal space to the attack and the defence.*

Those who are curious about the affair will find it more intimately dealt with in my published correspondence with Ellen Terry.

The Neue Freie Presse promptly demanded an article on Ellen Terry to supplement the one on Irving. Accordingly I republish the two together here. But they do not by themselves reveal the subjective relations of the three parties to them. For that I must refer readers not only to the correspondence aforesaid, but to the criticisms of Irving's enterprises and Ellen Terry's part in them contained in my volumes entitled Our Theatres in the Nineties.]

SIR HENRY IRVING, who has just died suddenly after an evening spent in the only way he cared to spend an evening: that is, on the stage, was 68 years old, and had been for thirty years the foremost actor in London. His death, like his life and his art, is an event of personal interest only. He was an extraordinarily interesting actor, enthusiastically admired by some, violently disliked by others, but never ignored, never insignificant, always able to force the world to accept him as a public dignitary standing quite alone in his eminence. The crowning event of his life was his admission to the order of knighthood. He was the first English actor whose social status was ever officially confirmed in this way; and, what is still more remarkable, he actually compelled the Court to knight him by publicly and explicitly demanding that he, as the head of the London stage, should be treated as the peer of the President of the Royal Academy of Arts, who is always knighted in England as a matter of course. The demand was made at a lecture which Irving delivered at the Royal Institution on the 1st February 1895, ostensibly on some dramatic subject, but really on the claims of his profession and of himself to official recognition. Any other actor would have been laughed at. Irving was knighted with apologies for the delay, and with gratitude for his condescension in accepting a title which he never afterwards deigned to print on a playbill.

There is nothing more to be said about him. When I was asked, the day after his death, to pay a tribute to his memory, I wrote: "He did nothing for the living drama; and he mutilated the remains of the dying Shakespear; but he won his lifelong fight to have the actor recognized as the peer of all other artists; and this was enough for one man to accomplish. *Requiescat in pace*." The truth is that Irving took no interest in anything except himself; and he was not interested even in himself except as an imaginary figure in an imaginary setting. He lived in a dream which he was so loth to have disturbed that when an actor told him once that he was being scandalously robbed, he thanked him and begged him not to tell him anything of the kind again. His scholarship and his connoisseurship in art and literature were equally imaginary. He was willing to have a retinue of writers, with Lord Tennyson, the Poet Laureate, at the head, and the journalists who helped him to write his lectures and speeches at the tail; but he had no literary sense, and was quite outside the intellectual life of his time. He was ignorant even of the theatre, having seen nothing of it since about thirty years ago, when he became master in his own playhouse, and shut the world out. He murdered Shakespear's Lear so horribly in cutting it down that he made it unintelligible; and he allowed one of his retainers to turn Goethe's Faust into so cheap a spectacular melodrama that it was repeated every night for a year. He played Macaire, the Corsican Brothers, Richelieu, Claude Melnotte, and all the old repertory of Charles Kean without a thought that they could be in the least old-fashioned. In the case of Macaire the new version by Robert Louis Stevenson, a masterpiece of literature, lay ready to his hand; but he used the old traditional version which is still played in booths and barns. Many persons were indignant at his supposed pretensions to be a thinker, a scholar, a connoisseur; but though such pretensions were undoubtedly made for him, he never made them himself. The truth is, his bearing was so dignified that the world made all possible pretences for him. When they saw him as Becket, they could not doubt that he was a great statesman and churchman; when they saw him as the Vicar of Wakefield, they recognized the scholar and the divine in every silver hair in his wig; when they saw him as Charles I, they felt that the patron of Van Dyck could not be ignorant of painting.

And yet this artist, who could produce every illusion about himself off the stage by the mere force and singularity of his personality, was prevented by just this force and singularity from producing any great range of illusion on it. He had really only one part; and that part was the part of Irving. His Hamlet was not Shakespear's Hamlet, nor his Lear Shakespear's Lear: they were both avatars of the imaginary Irving in whom he was so absorbingly interested. His huge and enduring success as Shylock was due to his absolutely refusing to allow Shylock to be the discomfited villain of the piece. The Merchant of Venice became the Martyrdom of Irving, which was, it must be confessed, far finer than the Tricking of Shylock. His Iachimo, a very fine performance, was better than Shakespear's Iachimo, and not a bit like him. On the other hand, his Lear was an impertinent intrusion of a quite silly conceit of his own into a great play. His Romeo, though a very clever piece of acting, wonderfully stage-managed in the scene where Romeo dragged the body of Paris down a horrible staircase into the tomb of the Capulets, was an absurdity, because it was impossible to accept Irving as Romeo, and he had no power of adapting himself to an author's conception: his creations were all his own; and they were all Irvings.

Technically he became very skilful. He was too much interested in himself not to cultivate himself to the utmost possible degree; and he was both imaginative and industrious in devising and executing stage effects, and what is called on the English stage "business." His Vanderdecken was a stage effect from first to last, and a most weirdly and beautifully effective one. His Mathias in The Bells and his Charles I were elaborated to the most extreme degree. They were such miracles of finished execution that they raised a melodrama of no importance and a surpassingly bad historical play into dramatic masterpieces. Just as Paganini fascinated the world with trumpery music by his own skill and strangeness, so Irving fascinated London with trumpery plays. But he had some serious physical defects and peculiarities; and though he succeeded in making the peculiarities interesting and characteristic, the defects limited him to the last. His voice was so poor that it would have prevented him from attaining any success at all had he not had a large and cavernous nose. By throwing his voice forward into it he gave it an impressive resonance which sometimes produced a strikingly beautiful effect in spite of its nasal tone. But this was only practicable when he could deliver a speech slowly. In rapid, violent, energetic passages, his nasal method produced a hysterical whinnying which was ridiculous; and for many years after he began playing heavy tragic parts he was the butt of every mimic and the object of continual ridicule from vulgar people who could see his obvious physical defects but could not appreciate his artistic qualities. It was not until he abandoned all pretence of robust acting that the laughter stopped. He was thus driven into a very slow method; and the more subtly he elaborated it, the worse became the performances at his theatre; for though he himself was always effective, those who were on the stage with him had to wait so long for his replies, and were so hurried in the vain attempt to make up for the time he was losing (if they had all played as slowly as he the play would never have ended), that they soon gave up all attempt to act, and simply gave him his cues as he wanted them. Under our English actor-manager system they could not remonstrate. They were his employees, completely in his power, and he simply could not get his effects in any other way.

In judging Irving, Austrians must remember that he had to assume a very high position without having had the training and culture that can be given only by a great national theatre with a highly trained audience and an established artistic tradition. There is nothing of the sort in England. Imagine a lad with his head full of nothing but romances, pitchforked into a city office, and leaving it to go on the stage as a member of the stock company in provincial cities where the theatre was abhorred as the gate of hell, and playing a piano on Sunday considered an unpardonable crime, by many of the most respectable citizens! Imagine him, after picking up his profession technically in this way, being enabled, by a private subvention from a charitable lady, to lease a metropolitan theatre and become its absolute and sole director, and you will get some idea of Irving's position in London. It would carry me too far to go into the whole question of the deplorable intellectual and artistic condition of the English theatre in Irving's time. Suffice it to say that the environment and tradition which an actor can obtain in Vienna cannot be obtained in England, and that Irving had to do his best to supply them out of his own romantic imagination, without much schooling and virtually without any general artistic culture. His success under such disadvantages was extraordinary; but in the end he had to give up his theatre and take to the provinces to live on his reputation. A theatre without a living drama is in the long run impossible; and when Irving had exhausted the old plays in which his personality was effective, he was—to be quite frank—too ignorant and old-fashioned to know how to choose fresh material. His greatest achievement was his social achievement, the redemption of his profession from Bohemianism, the imposing himself on the nation as one of the most eminent men in it, and the official acknowledgment of that estimate by the accolade.

Contributed to the Neue Freie Presse (Vienna) of the 24th December 1905 by request after the death of Henry Irving.

ELLEN TERRY, apart from her professional accomplishments as an actress, is so remarkable a woman that it is very difficult to describe her to the Austrian public without writing her private rather than her public history.

The part she has played in the life of her time will never be known until some day—perhaps fifty years hence—when her correspondence will be collected and published in twenty or thirty volumes. It will then, I believe, be discovered that every famous man of the last quarter of the nineteenth century—provided he were a playgoer—has been in love with Ellen Terry, and that many of them have found in her friendship the utmost consolation one can hope for from a wise, witty, and beautiful woman whose love is already engaged elsewhere, and whose heart has withstood a thousand attempts to capture it. To me—for I am one of the unsuccessful lovers—Ellen Terry's skill as an actress is the least interesting thing about her. Unlike Irving, to whom his art was everything and his life nothing, she found life more interesting than art; and when she became associated with him in his long and famous management of the Lyceum Theatre, she—the most modern of modern women, the most vital of modern personalities—set to work, more in the spirit of a thrifty intelligent housekeeper than of a self-obsessed artist, to fill up the leading feminine rôles in the old-fashioned plays he delighted in. Fortunately these plays included the handful of Shakespearean comedies and tragedies which still keep the stage in England as stalking horses for ambitious actors. We therefore had at the Lyceum Theatre Ellen Terry as Portia, as Beatrice, as Juliet, as Imogen, as Ophelia, though never as Rosalind in As You Like It, which she would certainly have insisted on playing if she had cared as much for her own professional renown as for helping Irving.

Probably there were never two eminent members of the same profession so unlike one another as Ellen Terry and Henry Irving. They both had beautiful and interesting faces; but faces like Irving's have looked at the world for hundreds of years past from portraits of churchmen, statesmen, princes, and saints, whilst Ellen's face had never been seen in the world before. She actually invented her own beauty; for her portraits as a girl have hardly anything in them of the wonderful woman who, after leaving the stage for seven years, reappeared in 1875 and took London by storm. The much abused word "unique" was literally true of Ellen Terry. If Shakespear had met Irving in the street, he would have recognized a distinguished but familiar type. Had he met Ellen Terry, he would have stared as at a new and irresistibly attractive species of womankind. Her portrait as Lady Macbeth, by Sargent, will stand out among all the portraits of famous women as that of a woman who was like nobody else. Again, Irving was simple, reserved, and slow. Ellen Terry is quick, restless, clever, and can get on the most unembarrassed and familiar terms in an instant with even the shyest strangers. Irving did not like writing: his correspondence was carried on by the late L. F. Austin, Bram Stoker, and perhaps others of his retinue: the few letters he really wrote himself owing their charm to their unaffected and unskilled lack of literary pretence and the handwriting not remarkable. Ellen Terry, on the other hand, is one of the greatest letter writers that ever lived. She can flash her thought down on paper in a handwriting that is as characteristic and as unforgettable as her face. When you find a letter from her among your morning's correspondence, you see the woman as vividly as you see the handwriting; and you open that letter first and feel that the day is a fortunate one. Her few published writings give no idea of her real literary power. All her letters are too intimate, too direct, too penetrating to be given to anyone but those to whom they are addressed. And here we come to another difference from Irving. Irving was sentimental and affectionate, and like most sentimental and affectionate people was limited and concentrated in his interests. He never understood others, and indeed never understood himself. Ellen Terry is not sentimental and not affectionate; but she is easily interested in anybody or anything remarkable or attractive: she is intelligent: she understands: she sympathizes because she understands and is naturally benevolent; but she has been interested oftener than deeply touched, and has pitied and helped oftener than loved. With all her ready sacrifice of her stage talent and skill, first to domestic ties, and then, on her return to the stage, to the Lyceum enterprise, she has never really sacrificed her inner self. In sacrificing her art she only sacrificed a part of herself. Irving's art was the whole of himself; and that was why he sacrificed himself—and everybody and everything else—to his art. It is a curious piece of artistic psychology, this, and will be misunderstood by stupid people and Philistines; but one does not write about artists of genius for people who know nothing about genius.

I have never, either in public or private, made any secret of my opinion that the Lyceum enterprise, famous as it became, was on the purely dramatic side of theatrical art a deplorable waste of two of the most remarkable talents of the last quarter of a century. In a former article I described how Irving used the plays of Shakespear as settings for figures which were the creations of his own fancy—how his

Shylock was not Shakespear's Shylock, his Iachimo not Shakespear's Iachimo, his Lear not Shakespear's Lear. I may now add that if circumstances had forced Irving into the living drama of his own time—if he had gone forward from his early successes as Digby Grant in Albery's Two Roses to Ibsen's Master Builder and John Gabriel Borkman—if he had played Bishop Nicolas instead of Shakespear's Wolsey and Tennyson's Becket and Sardou's Dante—he would have carried the English theatre forward into line with the Scandinavian and German-speaking theatre instead of being, as he actually was, the most conspicuous obstacle to its development. Now in precisely the same way as he wasted his own talent on obsolete reactionary or Shakespearean drama, so also he wasted Ellen Terry's. He did so, of course, quite unconsciously: if anyone had accused him of it, he would have pointed to The Lady of Lyons, The Amber Heart, Wills's Faust, Olivia (an adaptation of Goldsmith's Vicar of Wakefield), the Shakespearean repertory, and finally, as a daring concession to the ultra-modern spirit made expressly for Ellen Terry's sake, Madame Sans Gêne. He would have asked whether anyone but a madman could say that a talent which had triumphed in all these masterpieces had been wasted. What more could any actress desire? Was not Shakespear the greatest of all dramatic poets, past, present, or future? Was not Goethe, though a foreigner, at least worthy to be "adapted" by Wills? Was not Lord Tennyson the Poet Laureate? Were obscure, eccentric, and immoral Norwegians and Germans—Ibsens, Hauptmanns, Sudermanns, and their English imitators—to be accepted at the Lyceum Theatre merely because literary cliques talked about them, and because Duse, Réjane, and English actresses poor enough to play for such private subscription enterprises as the Independent Theatre and the State Society occasionally played a new and objectionable sort of stage heroine like Nora Helmer, Magda, Hedda Gabler, etc., etc.?

All this seemed, and even still seems, sound common

sense to the bulk of our English playgoers and their critical bellwethers. In Germany and Austria the position of Ellen Terry at the Lyceum Theatre will be more intelligible. It meant that she was completely cut off from the modern drama and all its intensely interesting heroines. And her opportunities in the older drama were much less satisfying than Irving's, because she understood Shakespear and played Beatrice, Juliet, Portia, Imogen, etc., intelligently and charmingly just as Shakespear planned them, whereas Irving, as Benedick, Romeo, Shylock, or Iachimo, was embodying some fancy of his own, the irrelevance of which only made it more enigmatic and consequently more Irvingesque and fascinating. It was inevitable that she should at last break loose from the Lyceum and practise her art under her own management.

But the question remains, why did she stay so long? The answer to that is that the Lyceum, whilst it starved her dramatically, gave great scope to her wonderful sense of pictorial art. Ellen Terry has always been adored by painters. She was married almost in her childhood to one of the greatest painters of her time.

Now whatever the Lyceum productions may have lacked in intellectual modernity, they never failed as stage pictures. If Ellen could not collaborate with Ibsen to explain the revolt of Nora Helmer, she could collaborate with Burne-Jones and Alma Tadema to make living pictures of Guinevere and Imogen. I quite forget what Tennyson's first play at the Lyceum Theatre was about; but I shall never forget Ellen Terry as Camma. I can recall picture after picture in which she and Irving posed as no other artists of that time could pose. Her incomparable beauty and his incomparable distinction: there lay the Lyceum magic: that was the spell that blinded everyone to the fact that the converts of the grim old gentleman in Norway were biding their time, and that when the enchantment of youth was no longer added to the enchantment of beauty, the Lyceum would come down like the walls of Jericho.

I escaped the illusion solely because I was a dramatist, and wanted Ellen Terry for my own plays. When her son, Mr Gordon Craig, became a father she said that nobody would write plays for a grandmother. I immediately wrote Captain Brassbound's Conversion to prove the contrary. I had already tried to tempt her by writing into my play called The Man of Destiny a description of the heroine which is simply a description of Ellen Terry: a very faint one, by the way; for who can describe the indescribable? But Irving checkmated me on that occasion by announcing his desire to perform the play; and it was impossible for me to evade the compliment, though, of course, nothing came of it. In the case of Captain Brassbound's Conversion, it was impossible for Irving to persuade himself even momentarily that he could produce it. Yet it was clear that it was in plays of this modern kind, with parts for women which were intellectually interesting and of commanding importance, that Ellen Terry's future business lay. Of this she said nothing; but she could not be restrained from telling the world that she was born in 1848 and that her apparent youthfulness was an illusion: in short, that the day had gone by for the Lady of Lyons, Gretchen, and Juliet. Her withdrawal from Sir Henry Irving's company at last became inevitable, though she postponed it long after it had become urgently advisable in her own interest if not in his.

Even then her first step shewed all her old indifference to her own career. She produced Ibsen's Vikings in Helgeland solely to enable Mr Gordon Craig to make an expensive experiment in his peculiar methods of stage presentation. It was a most unnecessary maternal extravagance; for Mr Gordon Craig's new development of the art of the theatre had already been convincingly demonstrated in London. No doubt his processions of Vikings coming up the cliffs from the sea in the moonlight, with their spears used as cunningly for decorative purposes as the spears in Velasquez's Surrender at Breda, or in the pictures of Paolo di Uccello, were very striking, and very instructive as to the possibility of doing away with the eternal flat wooden floor and footlight illumination which are so destructive of stage illusion; but they could not enable Ellen Terry to contradict her own nature by playing the fierce Hiordis of Ibsen convincingly. The public wanted Ellen Terry in an Ellen Terry part, and was too Philistine to see the beauty or care about the importance of Mr Gordon Craig's art. So Mr Gordon Craig shook the dust of London off his feet, and went to Germany. And Ellen Terry at last did what she should have done many years before—devoted herself to a modern play written for her by a modern playwright. She made a decisive success in creating Sir James Barrie's Alice Sit by the Fire; and she will follow that up next March [1905] by at last appearing as Lady Cicely in Captain Brassbound's Conversion, which has waited seven years for her. And here for the present I must leave her; for her saga is not yet ended.

P.S. 1930. Her saga as an actress ended with her impersonation of Lady Cicely, which she played on her final tour through America as her farewell to the stage. But she lived to be eighty and Dame Grand Cross of The British Empire. To the generation that grew up with the Great War, to which horror she never deigned to hold a candle, she had become a legend. She was born in 1848 and died in 1928.

BEERBOHM TREE

Contributed to Max Beerbohm's collection of memoirs of his brother

A TRIBUTE to Tree from the playwright's point of view is a duty of such delicacy that it is quite impossible to be delicate about it at all: one must confess bluntly at the outset that Tree was the despair of authors. His attitude towards a play was one of wholehearted anxiety to solve the problem of how to make it please and interest the audience.

Now this is the author's business, not the actor's. The function of the actor is to make the audience imagine for the moment that real things are happening to real people. It is for the author to make the result interesting. If he fails, the actor cannot save the play unless it is so flimsy a thing that the actor can force upon it some figure of his own fancy and play the author off the stage. This has been done successfully in several well-known, though very uncommon cases. Robert Macaire and Lord Dundreary were imposed by their actors on plays which did not really contain them. Grimaldi's clown was his own invention. These figures died with their creators, though their ghosts still linger on the stage. Irving's Shylock was a creation which he thrust successfully upon Shakespear's play; indeed, all Irving's impersonations were changelings. His Hamlet and his Lear were to many people more interesting than Shakespear's Hamlet and Lear; but the two pairs were hardly even related. To the author, Irving was not an actor: he was either a rival or a collaborator who did all the real work. Therefore, he was anathema to master authors, and a godsend to journeymen authors, with the result that he had to confine himself to the works of dead authors who could not interfere with him, and, very occasionally, live authors who were under his thumb because they were unable to command production of their works in other quarters.

Into this tradition of creative acting came Tree as Irving's rival and successor; and he also, with his restless imagination, felt that he needed nothing from an author but a literary scaffold on which to exhibit his own creations. He, too, turned to Shakespear as to a forest out of which such scaffolding could be hewn without remonstrance from the landlord, and to foreign authors who could not interfere with him, their interests being in the hands of adapters who could not stand up against his supremacy in his own theatre. As far as I could discover, the notion that a play could succeed without any further help from the actor than a simple impersonation of his part never occurred to Tree. The author, whether Shakespear or Shaw, was a lame dog to be helped over the stile by the ingenuity and inventiveness of the actor-producer. How to add and subtract, to interpolate and prune, until an effective result was arrived at, was the problem of production as he saw it. Of living authors of eminence the two he came into personal contact with were Brieux and Henry Arthur Jones; and I have reason to believe that their experience of him in no way contradicts my own. With contemporary masters of the stage like Pinero and Carton, in whose works the stage business is an integral part of the play, and the producer, when he is not the author in person, is an executant and not an inventor, Tree had never worked; and when he at last came upon the species in me, and found that, instead of having to discover how to make an effective histrionic entertainment on the basis of such scraps of my dialogue as might prove useful, he had only to fit himself into a jig-saw puzzle cut out by me, and just to act his part as well as he could, he could neither grasp the situation nor resist the impersonal compulsion of arrangements which he had not made, and was driven to accept only by the fact that they were the only ones which would work. But to the very end they bewildered him; and he had to go to the box office to assure himself that the omission of his customary care had not produced disastrous results.

Just before the production of my play we lunched together at the Royal Automobile Club. I said to him: "Have you noticed during the rehearsals that though you and I are no longer young, and have achieved all the success possible in our respective professions, we have been treating one another throughout as beginners?" To this, on reflection, he had to assent, because we actually were, relatively to one another, beginners. I had never had to deal with him professionally before, nor he with me; and he was quite unaccustomed to double harness, whilst I was so accustomed to every extremity of multiple harness, both in politics and in the theatre, that I had been trained to foresee everything and consider everybody. Now if I were to say that Tree foresaw nothing and considered nobody, I should suggest that he was a much less amiable man than he was. Let me therefore say that he never foresaw anything or considered anybody in cold blood. Of the foresight which foresees and faces entirely uninteresting facts, and the consideration which considers entirely uninteresting persons, he had as little as a man can have without being run over in the street. When his feelings were engaged, he was human and even shrewd and tenacious. But you really could not lodge an indifferent fact in his mind. This disability of his was carried to such a degree that he could not remember the passages in a play which did not belong to or bear directly upon his own conception of his own part: even the longest run did not mitigate his surprise when they recurred. Thus he never fell into that commonest fault of the actor: the betrayal to the audience that he knows what his interlocutor is going to say, and is waiting wearily for his cue instead of conversing with him. Tree always seemed to have heard the lines of the other performers for the first time, and even to be a little taken aback by them.

Let me give an extreme instance of this. In Pygmalion the heroine, in a rage, throws the hero's slippers in his face.

When we rehearsed this for the first time, I had taken care to have a very soft pair of velvet slippers provided; for I knew that Mrs Patrick Campbell was very dexterous, very strong, and a dead shot. And, sure enough, when we reached this passage, Tree got the slippers well and truly delivered with unerring aim bang in his face. The effect was appalling. He had totally forgotten that there was any such incident in the play; and it seemed to him that Mrs Campbell, suddenly giving way to an impulse of diabolical wrath and hatred, had committed an unprovoked and brutal assault on him. The physical impact was nothing; but the wound to his feelings was terrible. He collapsed on the nearest chair, and left me staring in amazement, whilst the entire personnel of the theatre crowded solicitously round him, explaining that the incident was part of the play, and even exhibiting the prompt-book to prove their words. But his *moral* was so shattered that it took quite a long time, and a good deal of skilful rallying and coaxing from Mrs Campbell, before he was in a condition to resume the rehearsal. The worst of it was that as it was quite evident that he would be just as surprised and wounded next time, Mrs Campbell took care that the slippers should never hit him again, and the incident was consequently one of the least convincing in the performance.

This, and many similar scenes that are told of Tree, will not be believed by experienced men of business. They will say curtly that it is no use trying to stuff them with stories like that: that running a theatre like His Majesty's must have been a big business, and that no man could possibly have done it for so long without being too capable and wide-awake to forget everything that did not amuse or interest him. But they will be quite wrong. Theatrical business is not like other business. A man may enter on the management of a theatre without business habits or knowledge, and at the end of forty years of it know less about business than when he began. The explanation is that a London West End theatre is always either making such an enormous profit that the utmost waste caused by unbusinesslike management is not worth considering, or else losing so much that the strictest economy cannot arrest the process by a halfpenny in the pound. In an industrial concern the addition of a penny to the piecework rate or the hourly time rate of wages, the slowing of a steam engine by a few revolutions, the retention of a machine two years out-of-date, or the loss of fifteen minutes' work in the day by unpunctuality, may make all the difference between profit and bankruptcy. The employer is held to rigid conditions by a stringent factory code enforced by a Government inspector on the one hand and by a jealous trade union on the other. He is the creature of circumstance and the slave of law, with so little liberty for sentiment and caprice that he very soon loses not only the habit of indulging them but even the sense of possessing them. Not so the manager of a theatre. Tree was accustomed to make two hundred per cent profit every day when he was in luck. With such a margin to play with, it was no more worth his while to economize or remember uninteresting things than it was to walk when there was a taxi at his beck. When his theatre was built for him, the equipment of its stage, apart from the electric lighting instalment, was exactly what it would have been a hundred years before, except that there were no grooves for side wings. If every employee on the premises had come an hour late every day and had received double wages, the difference in profit would have been hardly worth noticing. A theatre is a maddening place to a thrifty man of business, and an economic paradise to an artist, because there is practically no limit to the waste of time and money that may go on, provided the doors are open every night and the curtain up half an hour later. But for this necessity, and a few County Council by-laws, an actor-manager would be as unbridled as Nero, without even the Neronian check of a Prætorian Guard to kill him if he went beyond all bearing.

There is no denying that such conditions put a strain on human character that it can seldom sustain without injury.

If Tree's caprices, and his likes and dislikes, had not been on the whole amiable, the irresponsibility and power of his position would have made a fiend of him. As it was, they produced the oddest results. He was always attended in the theatre by a retinue of persons with no defined business there, who were yet on the salary list. There was one capable gentleman who could get things done; and I decided to treat him as the stage manager; but until I saw his name in the bill under that heading I never felt sure that he was not some casual acquaintance whom Tree had met in the club or in the street and invited to come in and make himself at home. Tree did not know what a stage manager was, just as he did not know what an author was. He had not even made up his mind any too definitely what an actor was. One moment he would surprise and delight his courtiers (for that is the nearest word I can find for his staff and entourage) by some stroke of kindness and friendliness. The next he would commit some appalling breach of etiquette by utterly ignoring their functions and privileges, when they had any. It was amiable and modest in him not to know his own place, since it was the highest in the theatre; but it was exasperating in him not to know anyone else's. I very soon gave up all expectation of being treated otherwise than as a friend who had dropped in; so, finding myself as free to interfere in the proceedings as anyone else who dropped in would apparently have been, I interfered not only in my proper department but in every other as well; and nobody gainsaid me. One day I interfered to such an extent that Tree was moved to a mildly sarcastic remonstrance. "I seem to have heard or read somewhere," he said, "that plays have actually been produced, and performances given, in this theatre, under its present management, before you came. According to you, that couldnt have happened. How do you account for it?" "I cant account for it," I replied, with the blunt good faith of a desperate man. "I suppose you put a notice in the papers that a performance will take place at half-past eight, and take the money at the doors. Then you *have* to do the play somehow. There is no other way of accounting for it." On two such occasions it seemed so brutal to worry him, and so hopeless to advance matters beyond the preliminary arrangement of the stage business (which I had already done), that I told him quite cordially to put the play through in his own way, and shook the dust of the theatre from my feet. On both occasions I had to yield to urgent appeals from other members of the cast to return and extricate them from a hopeless mess; and on both occasions Tree took leave of me as if it had been very kind of me to look in as I was passing to see his rehearsals, and received me on my return as if it were still more friendly of me to come back and see how he was getting on. I tried once or twice to believe that he was only pulling my leg; but that was incredible: his sincerity and insensibility were only too obvious. Finally, I had to fight my way through to a sort of production in the face of an unresisting, amusing, friendly, but heart-breakingly obstructive principal.

We finally agreed that I should have been an actor and he an author; and he always sent me his books afterwards. As a matter of fact, he had a very marked literary talent, and, even as an amateur, achieved a finish of style and sureness of execution that was not always evident in his acting, especially when, as in the case of Pygmalion, he had to impersonate a sort of man he had never met and of whom he had no conception. He tried hard to induce me to let him play the dustman instead of the Miltonic professor of phonetics; and when he resigned himself to his unnatural task, he set to work to make this disagreeable and incredible person sympathetic in the character of a lover, for which I had left so little room that he was quite baffled until he lit on the happy thought of throwing flowers to Eliza in the very brief interval between the end of the play and the fall of the curtain. If he had not been so amusing, so ingenious, and so entirely well-intentioned he would have driven me crazy. As it was, he made me feel like his grandfather. I should add that he never bore the slightest malice for my air of making the best of a bad job. A few days before his death, when he was incredibly young and sanguine, and made me feel hopelessly old and grumpy, he was discussing a revival of Pygmalion as if it promised to be a renewal of the most delightful experience of our lives. The only reproach he ever addressed to me was for not coming to Pygmalion every night, which he thought the natural duty of an author. I promised to come on the hundredth night, adding rather unkindly that this was equivalent to not coming at all. The hundredth night, however, was reached and survived; and I redeemed my promise, only to find that he had contributed to my second act a stroke of comic business so outrageously irrelevant that I solemnly cursed the whole enterprise, and bade the delinquents farewell for ever.

The fact that Tree could do and be done by thus without bloodshed, although he had all the sensitiveness of his profession, and all the unrestrained impulsiveness of a man who had succeeded in placing himself above discipline from the beginning of his adult life, shews that he was never quite unpardonable; and though this, to the world that knows nothing of the theatre, may seem more of an apology than a tribute, those who know the theatre best will understand its value. It has to be considered, too, that the statement that he did nothing unpardonable does not imply that he did nothing irreparable. Almost all the wrongs and errors of the West End London theatre are like the wrongs and errors of the battlefield: they cannot be undone. If an actor's or an author's chance is spoilt, it is spoilt for years and perhaps for ever: neither play nor part gets a second chance. I doubt whether there is an actor-manager living who has not done both these wrongs more than once. Tree was no exception; but as the result, like that of the elephant sitting on the hen's eggs, was never intended, it was impossible to bear malice for long. I have seen him try to help a very able Shakespearean actor, and, incidentally, to help Shakespear, through what he thought a tedious scene, by pretending to catch flies, with ruinous consequences to both player and Bard. He put a new complexion on Brieux's La Foi, with effects on the feelings of that illustrious author which I shall not attempt to describe. He meant equally well on both occasions.

And here I come to a source of friction between authors and actor-managers which is worth explaining with some care, as it bears on the general need in England for a school of physical training for the arts of public life as distinguished from the sports. An author who understands acting, and writes for the actor as a composer writes for an instrument, giving it the material suitable to its range, tone, character, agility and mechanism, necessarily assumes a certain technical accomplishment common to all actors; and this requires the existence of a school of acting, or at least a tradition. Now we had no such provision in the days of Tree's novitiate. He had not inherited the tradition handed down at rehearsal by Phelps to Forbes Robertson; nor was there any academic institution with authority enough to impress a novice of his calibre. To save others from this disadvantage he later on founded the Academy of Dramatic Art in Gower Street, which now supplies the want as far as an unendowed institution can. But he had to do without teaching himself. Like Irving, he had to make a style and technique out of his own personality: that is, out of his peculiar weaknesses as well as his peculiar powers. And here he sowed dragons' teeth between himself and the authors. For no uncommissioned author can write for an idiosyncratic style and technique: he knows only the classical one. He must, like Shakespear, assume an executant who can perform and sustain certain physical feats of deportment, and build up vocal climaxes with his voice through a long crescendo of rhetoric. Further, he assumes the possession of an English voice and an English feeling for splendor of language and rhythm of verse. Such professional skill and national gift are not accidents of personality: they are more or less within every Englishman's capacity. By themselves they will no more make an actor than grammar and spelling will make an author, or fingering and blowing a bandsman; but one expects every actor to possess them, just as one expects every author to parse and spell correctly and every bandsman to finger and blow properly.

Tree, like so many of our actors who have picked up their profession on the stage without systematic training, found that he could not produce these stock effects. When they were demanded by the author, he had to find a way round them, and, if possible, an interesting way. Thus he had not only to struggle against his handicap, but to triumph over it by turning it into an advantage. And his handicap was not a light one. Instead of that neutral figure which an actor can turn into anything he pleases, he was tall, and built like nobody else on earth. His Dutch extraction gave him an un-English voice, which, again, was like nobody else's voice and could not be disguised. His feeling for verbal music was entirely non-Miltonic: he had a music of his own; but it was not the music characteristic of English rhetoric; and blank verse, as such, had no charm for him; nor, I suspect, did he credit it with charm for anyone else.

The results were most marked in his Shakespearean work, and would certainly have produced curious scenes at rehearsal had the author been present. No doubt it is an exaggeration to say that the only unforgettable passages in his Shakespearean acting are those of which Tree and not Shakespear was the author. His Wolsey, which was a "straight" performance of high merit and dignity, could be cited to the contrary. But take, for examples, his Richard II and his Malvolio. One of the most moving points in his Richard was made with the assistance of a dog who does not appear among Shakespear's *dramatis personae*. When the dog—Richard's pet dog—turned to Bolingbroke and licked his hand, Richard's heart broke; and he left the stage with a sob. Next to this came his treatment of the entry of Bolingbroke and the deposed Richard into London. Shakespear makes the Duke of York describe it. Nothing could be easier with a well-trained actor at hand. And nothing could be more difficult and inconvenient than to bring horses on the stage and represent it in action. But this is just what Tree did. One still remembers that great white horse, and the look of hunted terror with which Richard turned his head as the crowd hooted him. It passed in a moment; and it flatly contradicted Shakespear's description of the saint-like patience of Richard; but the effect was intense: no one but Chaliapine has since done so much by a single look and an appearance for an instant on horseback. Again, one remembers how Richard walked out of Westminster Hall after his abdication.

Turn now to the scenes in which Shakespear has given the actor a profusion of rhetoric to declaim. Take the famous "For God's sake let us sit upon the ground, and tell sad stories of the death of kings." My sole recollection of that scene is that when I was sitting in the stalls listening to it, a paper was passed to me. I opened it and read: "If you will rise and move a resolution, I will second it.—Murray Carson." The late Murray Carson was, above all things, an elocutionist; and the scene was going for nothing. Tree was giving Shakespear, at immense trouble and expense, and with extraordinary executive cunning, a great deal that Shakespear had not asked for, and denying him something much simpler that he did ask for, and set great store by.

As Malvolio, Tree was inspired to provide himself with four smaller Malvolios, who aped the great chamberlain in dress, in manners, in deportment. He had a magnificent flight of stairs on the stage; and when he was descending it majestically, he slipped and fell with a crash sitting. Mere clowning, you will say; but no: the fall was not the point. Tree, without betraying the smallest discomfiture, raised his eyeglass and surveyed the landscape as if he had sat down on purpose. This, like the four satellite Malvolios, was not only funny but subtle. But when he came to speak those lines with which any old Shakespearean hand can draw a laugh by a simple trick of the voice, Tree made nothing of them, not knowing a game which he had never studied.

Even if our actors came to the stage with complete executive mastery of all the traditions and all the conventions, there would still be a conflict between the actor's tendency to adapt the play to his own personality and the author's desire to adapt the actor's personality to the play. But this would not make any serious trouble between them; for a good part can be played a dozen different ways by a dozen different actors and be none the worse: no author worth his salt attaches a definite and invariable physiognomy to each variety of human character. Every actor must be allowed to apply his own methods to his own playing. But if, as under our system, an actor, instead of laying the foundation of a general technique of speech and action, is driven, by the absence of any school in which he can acquire such a technique, to develop his own personality, and acquire a technique of exploiting that personality which is not applicable to any other purpose, then there will be friction at rehearsals if the author produces his own play, as all authors should. For the actor will inevitably try to force a changeling on the author. He will say, in effect: "I will not play this part that you have written; but I will substitute one of my own which is ever so much better." And it will be useless for the author to assert himself, and say: "You *shall* play the part as I have written it." If he knows his business, he will see that the "will not" of the actor really means "cannot," because the author has written for a classical technique which the actor does not possess and cannot learn in three weeks, or even three years. It is better to let the actor do what he can: indeed, there is no alternative.

What Tree could do was always entertaining in some way or other. But, for better for worse, it was hardly ever what the author meant him to do. His parts were his avatars; and the play had to stand the descent of the deity into it as best it could. Sometimes, as in my case, the author understood the situation and made the best of it. Sometimes, no doubt, the author either did not understand the situation or would not make the best of it. But Tree could not act otherwise than as he did; and his productions represented an output of invention on his part that may have supplied many deficiencies in the plays.

One of his ambitions was to create a Tree Don Quixote. He used to discuss this with me eagerly as a project we might carry out together. "What I see," he said, "is a room full of men in evening dress smoking. Somebody mentions the Don. They begin talking about him. They wonder what he would make of our modern civilization. The back wall vanishes; and there is Piccadilly, with all the buses and cabs coming towards you in a stream of traffic; and with them, in the middle, the long tall figure in armor on the lean horse, amazing, foreign, incongruous, and yet impressive, right in the centre of the picture." "That is really a very good idea," I would say. "I must certainly carry it out. But how could we manage the buses and things?" "Yes," he would go on, not listening to me after my first words of approval: "there you see him going down the mountain-side in Spain just after dawn, through the mist, you know, on the horse, and—" "And Calvert as Sancho Panza on the ass," I would say. That always surprised him. "Yes," he would say slowly. "Yes. Sancho, of course. Oh, yes." Though he had quite forgotten Sancho, yet, switching instantly over to his Falstaff line, he would begin to consider whether he could not double the two parts, as he doubled Micawber and Peggotty. For your true actor is still what he was in the days of Bottom: he wants to play every part in the comedy.

But the heart of the matter (which I have been coming to slowly all this time) is that the cure for the disease of actor-managership (every author must take that pathological view of it) is actor-author-managership: the cure of Molière, who acted his plays as well as wrote them, and managed his theatre into the bargain. And yet he lasted fifty-one years. Richard Wagner was author-composer-conductor-manager at Bayreuth: a much more arduous combination. Tree should have written his own plays. He could have done so. He had actually begun to do it as Shakespear and Molière began, by tinkering other men's plays. The conflict that raged between him and me at the rehearsals in his theatre would then have taken place in his own bosom. He would have taken a parental pride in other parts beside his own. He would have come to care for a play as a play, and to understand that it has powers over the audience even when it is read by people sitting round a table or performed by wooden marionettes. It would have developed that talent of his that wasted itself in *jeux d'esprit* and epigrams. And it would have given him what he was always craving from authors, and in the nature of the case could never get from them: a perfect projection of the great Tree personality. What did he care for Higgins or Hamlet? His real objective was his amazing self. That also was Shakespear's objective in Hamlet; but Shakespear was not Tree, and therefore Hamlet could never be to Tree what Hamlet was to Shakespear. For with all his cleverness in the disguises of the actor's dressing room, Tree was no mere character actor. The character actor never dares to appear frankly in his own person: he is the victim of a mortal shyness that agonizes and paralyzes him when his mask is stripped off and his cothurnus snatched from beneath his feet. Tree, on the contrary, broke through all his stage disguises: they were his robes of state; and he was never happier than when he stepped in front of the curtain and spoke in his own immensity to the audience, if not as deep calling unto deep (for the audience could not play up to him as splendidly as that), at least as a monarch to his courtiers.

I trust that in the volume of memoirs collected by his equally famous brother Max, who has asked me to contribute this pen-and-ink sketch, he may find his bard, as Elliston found Charles Lamb. It is my misfortune that I cannot do him justice, because, as author and actor, we two were rivals who regarded one another as usurpers. Happily, no bones were broken in the encounter; and if there is any malice in my description of it, I hope I have explained sufficiently to enable the reader to make the necessary allowance and correction.

THE QUINTESSENCE OF IBSENISM

(*Preface to the third edition*)

SINCE the last edition of this book was printed, war, pestilence and famine have wrecked civilization and killed a number of people of whom the first batch is calculated as not less than fifteen millions. Had the gospel of Ibsen been understood and heeded, these fifteen millions might have been alive now; for the war was a war of ideals. Liberal ideals, Feudal ideals, National ideals, Dynastic ideals, Republican ideals, Church ideals, State ideals, and Class ideals, bourgeois and proletarian, all heaped up into a gigantic pile of spiritual high explosive, and then shovelled daily into every house with the morning milk by the newspapers, needed only a bomb thrown at Serajevo by a handful of regicide idealists to blow the centre out of Europe. Men with empty phrases in their mouths and foolish fables in their heads have seen each other, not as fellow-creatures, but as dragons and devils, and have slaughtered each other accordingly. Now that our frenzies are forgotten, our commissariats disbanded, and the soldiers they fed demobilized to starve when they cannot get employment in mending what we broke, even the iron-mouthed Ibsen, were he still alive, would perhaps spare us, disillusioned wretches as we are, the well-deserved "I told you so."

Not that there is any sign of the lesson being taken to heart. Our reactions from Militarist idealism into Pacifist idealism will not put an end to war: they are only a practical form of the *reculer pour mieux sauter*. We still cannot bring ourselves to criticize our ideals, because that would be a form of self-criticism. The vital force that drives men to throw away their lives and those of others in the pursuit of an imaginative impulse, reckless of its apparent effect on human welfare, is, like all natural forces, given to us in enormous excess to provide against an enormous waste. Therefore men, instead of economizing it by consecrating it to the service of their highest impulses, grasp at a phrase in a newspaper article, or in the speech of a politician on a vote-catching expedition, as an excuse for exercising it violently, just as a horse turned out to grass will gallop and kick merely to let off steam. The shallowness of the ideals of men ignorant of history is their destruction.

But I cannot spend the rest of my life drawing the moral of the war. It must suffice to say here that as war throws back civilization inevitably, leaving everything worse than it was, from razors and scissors to the characters of the men that make and sell and buy them, old abuses revive eagerly in a world that dreamed it had got rid of them for ever; old books on morals become new and topical again; and old prophets stir in their graves and are read with a new sense of the importance of their message. That is perhaps why a new edition of this book is demanded.

In spite of the temptation to illustrate it afresh by the moral collapse of the last ten years, I have left the book untouched. To change a pre-war book into a post-war book would in this case mean interpreting Ibsen in the light of a catastrophe of which he was unaware. Nobody can pretend to say what view he would have taken of it. He might have thought the demolition of three monstrous idealist empires cheap at the cost of fifteen million idealists' lives. Or he might have seen in the bourgeois republics which have superseded them a more deeply entrenched fortification of idealism at its suburban worst. So I have refrained from tampering with what I wrote when I, too, was as pre-war as Isben.

G.B.S.

1922.

PREFACE: 1913

IN the pages which follow I have made no attempt to tamper with the work of the bygone man of thirty-five who wrote them. I have never admitted the right of an elderly author to alter the work of a young author, even when the young author happens to be his former self. In the case of a work which is a mere exhibition of skill in conventional art, there may be some excuse for the delusion that the longer the artist works on it the nearer he will bring it to perfection. Yet even the victims of this delusion must see that there is an age limit to the process, and that though a man of forty-five may improve the workmanship of a man of thirty-five, it does not follow that a man of fifty-five can do the same.

When we come to creative art, to the living word of a man delivering a message to his own time, it is clear that any attempt to alter this later on is simply fraud and forgery. As I read the old Quintessence of Ibsenism I may find things that I see now at a different angle, or correlate with so many things then unnoted by me that they take on a different aspect. But though this may be a reason for writing another book, it is not a reason for altering an existing one. What I have written I have written, said Pilate, thinking (rightly, as it turned out) that his blunder might prove truer than its revision by the elders; and what he said after a lapse of twenty-one seconds I may very well say after a lapse of twenty-one years.

However, I should not hesitate to criticize my earlier work if I thought it likely to do any mischief that criticism can avert. But on reading it through I have no doubt that it is as much needed in its old form as ever it was. Now that Ibsen is no longer frantically abused, and is safe in the Pantheon, his message is in worse danger of being forgotten or ignored than when he was in the pillory. Nobody now dreams of calling me a "muck ferretting dog" because I think Ibsen a great teacher. I will not go so far as to say I wish they did; but I do say that the most effective way of shutting our minds against a great man's ideas is to take them for granted and admit he was great and have done with him. It really matters very little whether Ibsen was a great man or not: what does matter is his message and the need of it.

That people are still interested in the message is proved by the history of this book. It has long been out of print in England; but it has never been out of demand. In spite of the smuggling of unauthorized American editions, which I have winked at because the absence of an English reprint was my own fault (if it be a fault not to be able to do more than a dozen things at a time), the average price of copies of the original edition stood at twenty-four shillings some years ago, and is no doubt higher now. But it was not possible to reprint it without additions. When it was issued in 1891 Ibsen was still alive, and had not yet produced The Master Builder, or Little Eyolf, or John Gabriel Borkman, or When We Dead Awaken. Without an account of these four final masterpieces, a book entitled The Quintessence of Ibsenism would have been a fraud on its purchasers; and it was the difficulty of finding time to write the additional chapters on these plays and review Ibsen's position from the point of view reached when his work ended with his death and his canonization as an admitted grand master of European literature, that has prevented me for twenty years from complying with the demand for a second edition. Also, perhaps, some relics of my old, or rather my young conscience, which revolted against hasty work. Now that my own stream is nearer the sea, I am more inclined to encourage myself in haste and recklessness by reminding myself that *le mieux est l'ennemi du bien*, and that I had better cobble up a new edition as best I can than not supply it at all.

I have taken all possible precautions to keep the reader's mind free from verbal confusion in following Ibsen's attack on ideals and idealism, a confusion that might have been avoided could his plays, without losing the naturalness of their dialogue, have been translated into the language of the English Bible. It is not too much to say that the works of

Ibsen furnish one of the best modern keys to the prophecies of Scripture. Read the prophets, major and minor, from Isaiah to Malachi, without such a key; and you will be puzzled and bored by the almost continuous protest against and denunciation of idolatry and prostitution. Simpletons read all this passionate invective with sleepy unconcern, concluding thoughtlessly that idolatry means praying to stocks and stones instead of to brass lectern eagles and the new reredos presented by the local distiller in search of a title; and as to prostitution, they think of it as "the social evil," and regret that the translators of the Bible used a much blunter word. But nobody who has ever heard real live men talking about graven images and traders in sex can for a moment suppose them to be the things the prophets denounced so earnestly. For idols and idolatry read ideals and idealism; for the prostitution of Piccadilly Circus read not only the prostitution of the journalist, the political lawyer, the parson selling his soul to the squire, the ambitious politician selling his soul for office, but the much more intimate and widespread idolatries and prostitutions of the private snob, the domestic tyrant and voluptuary, and the industrial adventurer. At once the prophetic warnings and curses take on meaning and proportion, and lose that air of exaggerated righteousness and tiresome conventional rant which repels readers who do not possess Ibsen's clue. I have sometimes thought of reversing the operation, and substituting in this book the words idol and idolatry for ideal and idealism; but it would be impossible without spoiling the actuality of Ibsen's criticism of society. If you call a man a rascally idealist, he is not only shocked and indignant but puzzled: in which condition you can rely on his attention. If you call him a rascally idolater, he concludes calmly that you do not know that he is a member of the Church of England. I have therefore left the old wording. Save for certain adaptations made necessary by the lapse of time and the hand of death, the book stands as it did, with a few elucidations which I might have made in 1891 had I given the text a couple of extra revisions. Also, of course, the section dealing with the last four plays. The two concluding chapters are new. There is no fundamental change: above all, no dilution.

Whether this edition will change people's minds to the extent to which the first did (to my own great astonishment) I do not know. In the eighteen-nineties one jested about the revolt of the daughters, and of the wives who slammed the front door like Nora. At present the revolt has become so general that even the feeblest and oldest after-dinner jesters dare no longer keep Votes for Women on their list of stale pleasantries about mothers-in-law, rational dress, and mixed bathing. Men are waking up to the perception that in killing women's souls they have killed their own. Mr. Granville-Barker's worthy father of six unmarriageable daughters in The Madras House, ruefully exclaiming, "It seems to me Ive been made a convenience of all my life," has taken away the excited attention that Nora once commanded when she said, "I have been living all these years with a strange man." When she meets Helmer's "No man sacrifices his honor for a woman" with her "Thousands of women have done that for men," there is no longer the old impressed assent: men fiercely protest that it is not true; that, on the contrary, for every woman who has sacrificed her honor for a man's sake, ten men have sacrificed their honor for a woman's. In the plays of Gorki and Tchekov, against which all the imbecilities and outrages of the old anti-Ibsen campaign are being revived (for the Press never learns anything by experience), the men appear as more tragically sacrificed by evil social conditions and their romantic and idealistic disguises than the women. Now it may be that into this new atmosphere my book will come with quite an old-fashioned air. As I write these lines the terrible play with which Strindberg wreaked the revenge of the male for A Doll's House has just been performed for the first time in London under the title of Creditors. In that, as in Brieux's Les Hannetons, it is the man who is the victim of domesticity, and the woman who is the tyrant and soul destroyer. Thus A Doll's House did not dispose of the question: it only brought on the stage the endless recriminations of idealistic marriage. And how has Strindberg, Ibsen's twin giant, been received? With an even idler stupidity than Ibsen himself, because Ibsen appealed to the rising energy of the revolt of women against idealism; but Strindberg attacks women ruthlessly, trying to rouse men from the sloth and sensuality of their idealized addiction to them; and as the men, unlike the women, do not want to be roused, whilst the women do not like to be attacked, there is no conscious Strindberg movement to relieve the indifference, the dull belittlement, the spiteful hostility against which the devotees of Ibsen fought so slashingly in the nineties. But the unconscious movement is violent enough. As I write, it is only two days since an eminent bacteriologist filled three columns of The Times with a wild Strindbergian letter in which he declared that women must be politically and professionally secluded and indeed excluded, because their presence and influence inflict on men an obsession so disabling and dangerous that men and women can work together or legislate together only on the same conditions as horses and mares: that is, by the surgical destruction of the male's sex. The Times and The Pall Mall Gazette gravely accept this outburst as "scientific," and heartily endorse it; though only a few weeks have elapsed since The Times dismissed Strindberg's play and Strindberg himself with curt superciliousness as uninteresting and negligible. Not many years ago, a performance of a play by myself, the action of which was placed in an imaginary Ibsen Club, in which the comedy of the bewilderment of conventional people when brought suddenly into contact with the Ibsenist movement (both understood and misunderstood) formed the atmosphere of the piece, was criticized in terms which shewed that our critics are just as hopelessly in the rear of Ibsen as they were in 1891. The only difference was that whereas in 1891 they would have insulted Ibsen, they now accept him as a classic. But understanding of the change of mind produced by Ibsen, or notion that they live in a world which is seething with the reaction of Ibsen's ideas against the ideas of Sardou and Tom Taylor, they have none. They stare with equal unintelligence at the sieges and stormings of separate homesteads by Ibsen or Strindberg, and at the attack all along the front of refined society into which these sieges and stormings have now developed. Whether the attack is exquisite, touching, delicate, as in Tchekov's Cherry Orchard, Galsworthy's Silver Box, and Granville-Barker's Anne Leete, or ruthless, with every trick of intellectual ruffianism and ribaldry, and every engine of dramatic controversy, there is the same pettish disappointment at the absence of the old conventions, the same gaping unconsciousness of the meaning and purpose of the warfare in which each play is a battle, as in the days when this book was new.

Our political journalists are even blinder than our artistic ones in this matter. The credit of our domestic ideals having been shaken to their foundations, as through a couple of earthquake shocks, by Ibsen and Strindberg (the Arch Individualists of the nineteenth century) whilst the Socialists have been idealizing, sentimentalizing, denouncing Capitalism for sacrificing Love and Home and Domestic Happiness and Children and Duty to money greed and ambition, yet it remains a commonplace of political journalism to assume that Socialism is the deadliest enemy of the domestic ideals and Unsocialism their only hope and refuge. In the same breath the world-grasping commercial synthesis we call Capitalism, built up by generations of Scotch Rational ists and English Utilitarians, Atheists, Agnostics and Natural-Selectionists, with Malthus as the one churchman among all its prophets, is proclaimed the bulwark of the Christian Churches. We used to be told that the people that walked in darkness have seen a great light. When our people see the heavens blazing with suns, they simply keep their eyes shut, and walk on in darkness until they have led us into the pit. No matter: I am not a domestic idealist; and it pleases me to think that the Life Force may have providential aims in thus keeping my opponents off the trail.

But for all that I must not darken counsel. I therefore, without further apology, launch my old torpedo with the old charge in it, leaving to the new chapters at the end what I have to say about the change in the theatre since Ibsen set his potent leaven to work there.

Ayot St Lawrence, 1912–13.

PREFACE TO THE FIRST EDITION

IN the spring of 1890, the Fabian Society, finding itself at a loss for a course of lectures to occupy its summer meetings, was compelled to make shift with a series of papers put forward under the general heading of Socialism in Contemporary Literature. The Fabian Essayists, strongly pressed to do "something or other," for the most part shook their heads; but in the end Sydney Olivier consented to "take Zola"; I consented to "take Ibsen"; and Hubert Bland undertook to read all the Socialist novels of the day, an enterprise the desperate failure of which resulted in the most amusing paper of the series. William Morris, asked to read a paper on himself, flatly declined, but gave us one on Gothic Architecture. Stepniak also came to the rescue with a lecture on modern Russian fiction; and so the Society tided over the summer without having to close its doors, but also without having added anything whatever to the general stock of information on Socialism in Contemporary Literature. After this I cannot claim that my paper on Ibsen, which was duly read at the St James's Restaurant on the 18th July 1890, under the presidency of Mrs Annie Besant, and which was the first form of this little book, is an original work in the sense of being the result of a spontaneous internal impulse on my part. Having purposely couched it in the most provocative terms (of which traces may be found by the curious in its present state), I did not attach much importance to the somewhat lively debate that arose upon it; and I had laid it aside as a *pièce d'occasion* which had served its turn, when the production of Rosmersholm at the Vaudeville Theatre by Florence Farr, the inauguration of the Independent Theatre by Mr J. T. Grein with a performance of Ghosts, and the sensation created by the experiment of Elizabeth Robins and Marion Lea with Hedda Gabler, started a frantic newspaper controversy, in which I could see no sign of any of the disputants having ever been forced by circumstances, as I had, to make up his mind definitely as to what Ibsen's plays meant, and to defend his view face to face with some of the keenest debaters in London. I allow due weight to the fact that Ibsen himself has not enjoyed this Fabian advantage; but I have also shewn that the existence of a discoverable and perfectly definite thesis in a poet's work by no means depends on the completeness of his own intellectual consciousness of it. At any rate, the controversialists, whether in the abusive stage, or the apologetic stage, or the hero-worshipping stage, by no means made clear what they were abusing, or apologizing for, or going into ecstasies about; and I came to the conclusion that my explanation might as well be placed in the field until a better could be found.

With this account of the origin of the book, and a reminder that it is not a critical essay on the poetic beauties of Ibsen, but simply an exposition of Ibsenism, I offer it to my readers to make what they can of.

LONDON, June 1891.

THE TWO PIONEERS

THAT is, pioneers of the march to the plains of heaven (so to speak).

The second, whose eyes are in the back of his head, is the man who declares that it is wrong to do something that no one has hitherto seen any harm in.

The first, whose eyes are very longsighted and in the usual place, is the man who declares that it is right to do something hitherto regarded as infamous.

The second is treated with great respect by the army. They give him testimonials; name him the Good Man; and hate him like the devil.

The first is stoned and shrieked at by the whole army. They call him all manner of opprobrious names; grudge him his bare bread and water; and secretly adore him as their saviour from utter despair.

Let me take an example from life of my pioneers. Shelley was a pioneer and nothing else: he did both first and second pioneer's work.

Now compare the effect produced by Shelley as abstinence preacher or second pioneer with that which he produced as indulgence preacher or first pioneer. For example:

Second Pioneer Proposition: It is wrong to kill animals and eat them.

First Pioneer Proposition: It is not wrong to take your sister as your wife.[1]

[1] The curious persistence of this proposition in the higher poetry of the nineteenth century is not easy to account for now that it sounds both unimportant and old-fashioned. It is as if one said "It is not wrong to stand on one's head." The reply is "You may be very right; but as nobody wants to, why bother about it?" Yet I think this sensible way of treating the matter—obviously more healthy than the old morbid horror—has been produced largely by the refusal of poets like Shelley and Wagner to accept the theory of natural antipathy as the basis of the tables of Consanguinity, and by the subsequent publication of masses of evidence by soci-

Here the second pioneer appears as a gentle humanitarian, and the first as an unnatural corrupter of public morals and family life. So much easier is it to declare the right wrong than the wrong right in a society with a guilty conscience, to which, as to Dickens's detective, "Any possible move is a probable move provided it's in a wrong direction." Just as the liar's punishment is, not in the least that he is not believed, but that he cannot believe any one else; so a guilty society can more easily be persuaded that any apparently innocent act is guilty than that any apparently guilty act is innocent.

The English newspaper which best represented the guilty conscience of the middle class, was, when Ibsen's plays reached England, The Daily Telegraph. If we can find that The Daily Telegraph attacked Ibsen as The Quarterly Review used to attack Shelley, it will occur to us at once that there must be something of the first pioneer about Ibsen.

The late Clement Scott, at that time dramatic critic to The Daily Telegraph, was a sentimentally goodnatured gentleman, not then a pioneer, though he had in his time fought hard for the advance in British drama represented by

---

ologists, from Herbert Spencer to Westermarck, shewing that such tables are entirely conventional, and that all our prohibitions have been either ignored or actually turned into positive obligations at one time or another without any shock to human instincts. The consequence is that our eyes are now opened to the practical social reasons for barring marriage between Laon and Cythna, Siegmund and Sieglinda; and the preaching of incest as something poetic in itself has lost all its morbid interest and ceased. Also we are beginning to recognize the important fact that the absence of romantic illusion as between persons brought up together, which undoubtedly exists, and which used to be mistaken for natural antipathy, cannot be depended on as between strangers, however close their consanguinity, and that any domestic or educational system which segregates the sexes produces romantic illusion, no matter how undesirable it may be. It will be seen later on in the chapter dealing with the play called Ghosts, that Ibsen took this modern view that consanguinity does not count between strangers. I have accepted it myself in my play Mrs Warren's Profession. (1912).

the plays of Robertson. He was also an emotional, impressionable, zealous, and sincere Roman Catholic. He accused Ibsen of dramatic impotence, ludicrous amateurishness, nastiness, vulgarity, egotism, coarseness, absurdity, uninteresting verbosity, and "suburbanity," declaring that he has taken ideas that would have inspired a great tragic poet, and vulgarized and debased them in dull, hateful, loathsome, horrible plays. This criticism, which occurs in a notice of the first performance of Ghosts in England, is to be found in The Daily Telegraph for the 14th March 1891, and is supplemented by a leading article which compares the play to an open drain, a loathsome sore unbandaged, a dirty act done publicly, or a lazar house with all its doors and windows open. Bestial, cynical, disgusting, poisonous, sickly, delirious, indecent, loathsome, fetid, literary carrion, crapulous stuff, clinical confessions: all these epithets are used in the article as descriptive of Ibsen's work. "Realism," said the writer, "is one thing; but the nostrils of the audience must not be visibly held before a play can be stamped as true to nature. It is difficult to expose in decorous words the gross and almost putrid indecorum of this play." As the performance of Ghosts took place on the evening of the 13th March, and the criticism appeared next morning, it is evident that Clement Scott must have gone straight from the theatre to the newspaper office, and there, in an almost hysterical condition, penned his share of this extraordinary protest. The literary workmanship bears marks of haste and disorder, which, however, only heighten the expression of the passionate horror produced in the writer by seeing Ghosts on the stage. He calls on the authorities to cancel the license of the theatre, and declares that he has been exhorted to laugh at honor, to disbelieve in love, to mock at virtue, to distrust friendship, and to deride fidelity.

If this document were at all singular, it would rank as one of the curiosities of criticism, exhibiting, as it does, the most seasoned playgoer in London thrown into convulsions by a performance which was witnessed with approval, and even with enthusiasm, by many persons of approved moral and artistic conscientiousness. But Clement Scott's criticism was hardly distinguishable in tone from dozens of others which appeared simultaneously. His opinion was the vulgar opinion. Mr Alfred Watson, critic to The Standard, the leading Tory daily paper, proposed that proceedings should be taken against the theatre under Lord Campbell's Act for the suppression of disorderly houses. Clearly Clement Scott and his editor Sir Edwin Arnold, with whom rested the final responsibility for the article which accompanied the criticism, represented a considerable party.

How then is it that Ibsen, a Norwegian playwright of European celebrity, attracted one section of the English people so strongly that they hailed him as the greatest living dramatic poet and moral teacher, whilst another section was so revolted by his works that they described him in terms which they themselves admitted to be, by the necessities of the case, all but obscene? This phenomenon, which has occurred throughout Europe whenever Ibsen's plays have been acted, as well as in America and Australia, must be exhaustively explained before the plays can be described without danger of reproducing the same confusion in the reader's own mind. Such an explanation, therefore, must be my first business.

Understand, at the outset, that the explanation will not be an explaining away. Clement Scott's judgment did not mislead him in the least as to Ibsen's meaning. Ibsen means all that most revolted his critic. For example, in Ghosts, the play in question, a clergyman and a married woman fall in love with one another. The woman proposes to abandon her husband and live with the clergyman. He recalls her to her duty, and makes her behave as a virtuous woman. She afterwards tells him that this was a crime on his part. Ibsen agrees with her, and has written the play to bring you round to his opinion. Clement Scott did not agree with her, and believed that when you are brought round to her opinion you have been morally corrupted. By this conviction he was impelled to denounce Ibsen as he did, Ibsen being equally impelled to propagate the convictions which provoked the attack. Which of the two is right cannot be decided until it is ascertained whether a society of persons holding Ibsen's opinions would be higher or lower than a society holding Clement Scott's.

There are many people who cannot conceive this as an open question. To them a denunciation of any recognized practices is an incitement to unsocial conduct; and every utterance in which an assumption of the eternal validity of these practices is not implicit is a paradox. Yet all progress involves the beating of them from that position. By way of illustration, one may rake up the case of Proudhon, who in the year 1840 carefully defined property as theft. This was thought the very maddest paradox that ever man hazarded: it seemed obvious that a society which countenanced such a proposition must speedily be reduced to the condition of a sacked city. Today schemes for the confiscation by taxation and supertaxation of mining royalties and ground rents are commonplaces of social reform; and the honesty of the relation of our big property holders to the rest of the community is challenged on all hands. It would be easy to multiply instances, though the most complete are now ineffective through the triumph of the original paradox having obliterated all memory of the opposition it first had to encounter. The point to seize is that social progress takes effect through the replacement of old institutions by new ones; and since every institution involves the recognition of the duty of conforming to it, progress must involve the repudiation of an established duty at every step. If the Englishman had not repudiated the duty of absolute obedience to his king, his political progress would have been impossible. If women had not repudiated the duty of absolute submission to their husbands, and defied public opinion as to the limits set by modesty to their education, they would never have gained the protection of the Married Women's Property Act, the municipal vote, or the power to qualify themselves as medical practitioners. If Luther had not trampled on his duty to the head of his Church and on his vow of chastity, our clergy would still have to choose between celibacy and profligacy. There is nothing new, then, in the defiance of duty by the reformer: every step of progress means a duty repudiated, and a scripture torn up. And every reformer is denounced accordingly: Luther as an apostate, Cromwell as a traitor, Mary Wollstonecraft as an unwomanly virago, Shelley as a libertine, and Ibsen as all the things enumerated in The Daily Telegraph.

This crablike progress of social evolution, in which the individual advances by seeming to go backward, continues to illude us in spite of all the lessons of history. To the pious man the newly made freethinker, suddenly renouncing supernatural revelation, and denying all obligation to believe the Bible and obey the commandments as such, appears to be claiming the right to rob and murder at large. But the freethinker soon finds reasons for not doing what he does not want to do; and these reasons seem to him to be far more binding on our conscience than the precepts of a book of which the infallibility cannot be rationally proved. The pious man is at last forced to admit—as he was in the case of the late Charles Bradlaugh, for instance—that the disciples of Voltaire and Tom Paine do not pick pockets or cut throats oftener than your even Christian: he actually is driven to doubt whether Voltaire himself (poor Voltaire, who built a church, and was the greatest philanthropist of his time!) really screamed and saw the devil on his deathbed.

This experience by no means saves the rationalist[1] from falling into the same conservatism when the time comes for his own belief to be questioned. No sooner has he triumphed over the theologian than he forthwith sets up as binding on all men the duty of acting logically with the object of securing the greatest good of the greatest number, with the re-

[1] I had better here warn students of philosophy that I am speaking of rationalism, not as classified in the books, but as apparent in men.

sult that he is presently landed in vivisection, Contagious Diseases Acts, dynamite conspiracies, and other grotesque but strictly reasonable abominations. Reason becomes Dagon, Moloch, and Jehovah rolled into one. Its devotees exult in having freed themselves from the old slavery to a collection of books written by Jewish men of letters. To worship such books was, they can prove, as absurd as to worship sonatas composed by German musicians, as was done by the hero of Wagner's novelette, who sat up on his deathbed to say his creed, beginning, "I believe in God, Mozart, and Beethoven." The Voltairian freethinker despises such a piece of sentiment; but is it not much more sensible to worship a sonata constructed by a musician than to worship a syllogism constructed by a logician, since the sonata may encourage heroism, or at least inspire feelings of awe and devotion? This does not occur to the votary of reason; and the rationalist's freethinking soon comes to mean syllogism worship with rites of human sacrifice; for just as the rationalist's pious predecessor thought that the man who scoffed at baptism and the Bible must infallibly yield without resistance to all his criminal propensities, so the rationalist in turn becomes convinced that when a man once loses his faith in vaccination and in Herbert Spencer's Data of Ethics, he is no longer to be trusted to keep his hands off his neighbor's person, purse, or wife.

In process of time the age of reason had to go its way after the age of faith. In actual experience, the first shock to rationalism comes from the observation that though nothing can persuade women to adopt it, their impatience of reasoning no more prevents them from arriving at right conclusions than the masculine belief in it (never a very deeply rooted faith in England, by the way, whatever it may have been in France or Greece) saves men from arriving at wrong ones. When this generalization has to be modified in view of the fact that some women are beginning to try their skill at ratiocination, reason is not re-established on the throne; because the result of Woman's reasoning is that she begins to fall into all the errors which men are just learning to mistrust. The moment she sets about doing things for reasons instead of merely finding reasons for what she wants to do, there is no saying what mischief she will be at next: there being just as good reasons for burning a heretic at the stake as for rescuing a shipwrecked crew from drowning: in fact, there are better.

One of the first and most famous utterances of rationalism would have condemned it without further hearing had its full significance been seen at the time. Voltaire, taking exception to the trash of some poetaster, was met with the plea "One must live." "I dont see the necessity," replied Voltaire. The evasion was worthy of the Father of Lies himself; for Voltaire was face to face with the very necessity he was denying; must have known, consciously or not, that it is the universal postulate; would have understood, if he had lived today, that since all valid human institutions are constructed to fulfil man's will, and his will is to live even when his reason teaches him to die, logical necessity, which was the sort Voltaire meant (the other sort being visible enough) can never be a motor in human action, and is, in short, not necessity at all. But that was not brought to light in Voltaire's time; and he died impenitent, bequeathing to his disciples that most logical of agents, the guillotine, which also "did not see the necessity."

In our own century the recognition of the will as distinct from the reasoning machinery began to spread. Schopenhauer was the first among the moderns[1] to appreciate the

[1] I say the moderns, because the will is our old friend the soul or spirit of man; and the doctrine of justification, not by works, but by faith, clearly derives its validity from the consideration that no action, taken apart from the will behind it, has any moral character: for example, the acts which make the murderer and incendiary infamous are exactly similar to those which make the patriotic hero famous. "Original sin" is the will doing mischief. "Divine grace" is the will doing good. Our fathers, unversed in the Hegelian dialectic, could not conceive that these two, each the negation of the other, were the same. Schopenhauer's philosophy, like that of

enormous practical importance of the distinction, and to make it clear to amateur metaphysicians by concrete instances. Out of his teaching came the formulation of the dilemma Voltaire had shut his eyes to. Here it is. Rationally considered, life is only worth living when its pleasures are greater than its pains. Now to a generation which has ceased to believe in heaven, and has not yet learned that the degradation by poverty of four out of every five of its number is artificial and remediable, the fact that life is not rationally worth living is obvious. It is useless to pretend that the pessimism of Koheleth, Shakespear, Dryden, and Swift can be refuted if the world progresses solely by the destruction of the unfit, and yet can only maintain its civilization by manufacturing the unfit in swarms of which that appalling proportion of four to one represents but the comparatively fit survivors. Plainly then, the reasonable thing for the rationalists to do is to refuse to live. But as none of them will commit suicide in obedience to this demonstration of "the necessity" for it, there is an end of the notion that we live for reasons instead of in fulfilment of our will to live. Thus we are landed afresh in mystery; for positive science gives no account whatever of this will to live. Positive science has dazzled us for nearly a century with its analyses of the machinery of sensation. Its researches into the nature of sound and the construction of the ear, the nature of light and the construction of the eye, its measurement of the speed of sensation, its localization of the functions of the brain, and its hints as to the possibility of producing a homunculus presently as the fruit of its chemical investigation of protoplasm have satisfied the souls of our atheists as completely as belief in divine omniscience and scriptural revelation satisfied the souls of their pious fathers. The fact remains that when

all pessimists, is really based on the old view of the will as original sin, and on the 1750–1850 view that the intellect is the divine grace that is to save us from it. It is as well to warn those who fancy that Schopenhauerism is one and indivisible, that acceptance of its metaphysics by no means involves endorsement of its philosophy.

Young, Helmholtz, Darwin, Haeckel, and the rest, popularized here among the literate classes by Tyndall and Huxley, and among the proletariat by the lectures of the National Secular Society, have taught you all they know, you are still as utterly at a loss to explain the fact of consciousness as you would have been in the days when you were instructed from The Child's Guide to Knowledge. Materialism, in short, only isolated the great mystery of consciousness by clearing away several petty mysteries with which we had confused it; just as Rationalism isolated the great mystery of the will to live. The isolation made both more conspicuous than before. We thought we had escaped for ever from the cloudy region of metaphysics; and we were only carried further into the heart of them.[1]

We have not yet worn off the strangeness of the position to which we have now been led. Only the other day our highest boast was that we were reasonable human beings. Today we laugh at that conceit, and see ourselves as wilful creatures. Ability to reason accurately is as desirable as ever; for by accurate reasoning only can we calculate our actions so as to do what we intend to do: that is, to fulfil our will; but faith in reason as a prime motor is no longer the criterion of the sound mind, any more than faith in the Bible is the criterion of righteous intention.

At this point, accordingly, the illusion as to the retrogressive movement of progress recurs as strongly as ever. Just as the beneficent step from theology to rationalism seems to the theologist a growth of impiety, does the step from rationalism to the recognition of the will as the prime

[1] The correlation between Rationalism and Materialism in this process has some immediate practical importance. Those who give up Materialism whilst clinging to Rationalism generally either relapse into abject submission to the most paternal of the Churches, or are caught by the attempts, constantly renewed, of mystics to found a new faith by rationalizing on the hollowness of materialism. The hollowness has nothing in it; and if you have come to grief as a materialist by reasoning about something, you are not likely, as a mystic, to improve matters by reasoning about nothing.

motor strike the rationalist as a lapse of common sanity; so that to both theologist and rationalist progress at last appears alarming, threatening, hideous, because it seems to tend towards chaos. The deists Voltaire and Tom Paine were, to the divines of their day, predestined devils, tempting mankind hellward.[1] To deists and divines alike Ferdinand Lassalle, the godless self-worshipper and man-worshipper, would have been a monster. Yet many who today echo Lassalle's demand that economic and political institutions should be adapted to the poor man's will to eat and drink his fill out of the product of the labor he shares, are revolted by Ibsen's acceptance of the impulse towards greater freedom as sufficient ground for the repudiation of any customary duty, however sacred, that conflicts with it. Society, were it even as free as Lassalle's Social-Democratic republic, *must*, it seems to them, go to pieces when conduct is no longer regulated by inviolable covenants.

For what, during all these overthrowings of things sacred and things infallible, has been happening to that preeminently sanctified thing, Duty? Evidently it cannot have come off scatheless. First there was man's duty to God, with the priest as assessor. That was repudiated; and then came Man's duty to his neighbor, with Society as the assessor. Will this too be repudiated, and be succeeded by Man's duty to himself, assessed by himself? And if so, what will be the effect on the conception of Duty in the abstract? Let us see.

I have just called Lassalle a self-worshipper. In doing so I cast no reproach on him; for this is the last step in the evolution of the conception of duty. Duty arises at first, a

[1] This is not precisely true. Voltaire was what we should now call an advanced Congregationalist: in fact, modern Dissent, on its educated side, is sound Voltaireanism. Voltaire was for some time on very friendly terms with the Genevese pastors. But what with his jests at the expense of Bible worship, and the fact that he could not formally cut himself off from the Established Church of France without placing himself in its power, the pastors had finally to conceal their agreement with him. (1912).

gloomy tyranny, out of man's helplessness, his self-mistrust, in a word, his abstract fear. He personifies all that he abstractly fears as God, and straightway becomes the slave of his duty to God. He imposes that slavery fiercely on his children, threatening them with hell, and punishing them for their attempts to be happy. When, becoming bolder, he ceases to fear everything, and dares to love something, this duty of his to what he fears evolves into a sense of duty to what he loves. Sometimes he again personifies what he loves as God; and the God of Wrath becomes the God of Love: sometimes he at once becomes a humanitarian, an altruist, acknowledging only his duty to his neighbor. This stage is correlative to the rationalist stage in the evolution of philosophy and the capitalist phase in the evolution of industry. But in it the emancipated slave of God falls under the dominion of Society, which, having just reached a phase in which all the love is ground out of it by the competitive struggle for money, remorselessly crushes him until, in due course of the further growth of his courage, a sense at last arises in him of his duty to himself. And when this sense is fully grown the tyranny of duty perishes; for now the man's God is his own humanity; and he, self-satisfied at last, ceases to be selfish. The evangelist of this last step must therefore preach the repudiation of duty. This, to the unprepared of his generation, is indeed the wanton masterpiece of paradox. What! after all that has been said by men of noble life as to the secret of all right conduct being only Duty, Duty, Duty, is he to be told now that duty is the primal curse from which we must redeem ourselves before we can advance another step on the road along which, as we imagine (having forgotten the repudiations made by our fathers) duty and duty alone has brought us thus far? But why not? God Almighty was once the most sacred of our conceptions; and he had to be denied. Then Reason became the Infallible Pope, only to be deposed in turn. Is Duty more sacred than God or Reason?

Having now arrived at the prospect of the repudiation of duty by Man, I shall make a digression on the subject of ideals and idealists, as treated by Ibsen. I shall go round in a loop, and come back to the same point by way of the repudiation of duty by Woman; and then at last I shall be in a position to describe Ibsen's plays without risk of misunderstanding.

IDEALS AND IDEALISTS

WE have seen that as Man grows through the ages, he finds himself bolder by the growth of his courage: that is, of his spirit (for so the common people name it), and dares more and more to love and trust instead of to fear and fight. But his courage has other effects: he also raises himself from mere consciousness to knowledge by daring more and more to face facts and tell himself the truth. For in his infancy of helplessness and terror he could not face the inexorable; and facts being of all things the most inexorable, he masked all the threatening ones as fast as he discovered them; so that now every mask requires a hero to tear it off. The king of terrors, Death, was the Arch-Inexorable: Man could not bear the dread of that. He must persuade himself that Death can be propitiated, circumvented, abolished. How he fixed the mask of personal immortality on the face of Death for this purpose we all know. And he did the like with all disagreeables as long as they remained inevitable. Otherwise he must have gone mad with terror of the grim shapes around him, headed by the skeleton with the scythe and hourglass. The masks were his ideals, as he called them; and what, he would ask, would life be without ideals? Thus he became an idealist, and remained so until he dared to begin pulling the masks off and looking the spectres in the face—dared, that is, to be more and more a realist. But all men are not equally brave; and the greatest terror prevailed whenever some realist bolder than the rest laid hands on a mask which they did not yet dare to do without.

We have plenty of these masks around us still: some of them more fantastic than any of the Sandwich islanders' masks in the British Museum. In our novels and romances especially we see the most beautiful of all the masks: those devised to disguise the brutalities of the sexual instinct in the earlier stages of its development, and to soften the rigorous aspect of the iron laws by which Society regulates its gratification. When the social organism becomes bent on civilization, it has to force marriage and family life on the individual, because it can perpetuate itself in no other way whilst love is still known only by fitful glimpses, the basis of sexual relationship being in the main mere physical appetite. Under these circumstances men try to graft pleasure on necessity by desperately pretending that the institution forced upon them is a congenial one, making it a point of public decency to assume always that men spontaneously love their kindred better than their chance acquaintances, and that the woman once desired is always desired: also that the family is woman's proper sphere, and that no really womanly woman ever forms an attachment, or even knows what it means, until she is requested to do so by a man. Now if anyone's childhood has been embittered by the dislike of his mother and the ill-temper of his father; if his wife has ceased to care for him and he is heartily tired of his wife; if his brother is going to law with him over the division of the family property, and his son acting in studied defiance of his plans and wishes, it is hard for him to persuade himself that passion is eternal and that blood is thicker than water. Yet if he tells himself the truth, all his life seems a waste and a failure by the light of it. It comes then to this, that his neighbors must either agree with him that the whole system is a mistake, and discard it for a new one, which cannot possibly happen until social organization so far outgrows the institution that Society can perpetuate itself without it; or else they must keep him in countenance by resolutely making believe that all the illusions with which it has been masked are realities.

For the sake of precision, let us imagine a community of a thousand persons, organized for the perpetuation of the species on the basis of the British family as we know it at present. Seven hundred of them, we will suppose, find the British family arrangement quite good enough for them. Two hundred and ninety-nine find it a failure, but must put up with it since they are in a minority. The remaining person occupies a position to be explained presently. The 299 failures will not have the courage to face the fact that they are irremediable failures, since they cannot prevent the 700 satisfied ones from coercing them into conformity with the marriage law. They will accordingly try to persuade themselves that, whatever their own particular domestic arrangements may be, the family is a beautiful and holy natural institution. For the fox not only declares that the grapes he cannot get are sour: he also insists that the sloes he *can* get are sweet. Now observe what has happened. The family as it really is is a conventional arrangement, legally enforced, which the majority, because it happens to suit them, think good enough for the minority, whom it happens not to suit at all. The family as a beautiful and holy natural institution is only a fancy picture of what every family would have to be if everybody was to be suited, invented by the minority as a mask for the reality, which in its nakedness is intolerable to them. We call this sort of fancy picture an Ideal; and the policy of forcing individuals to act on the assumption that all ideals are real, and to recognize and accept such action as standard moral conduct, absolutely valid under all circumstances, contrary conduct or any advocacy of it being discountenanced and punished as immoral, may therefore be described as the policy of Idealism. Our 299 domestic failures are therefore become idealists as to marriage; and in proclaiming the ideal in fiction, poetry, pulpit and platform oratory, and serious private conversation, they will far outdo the 700 who comfortably accept marriage as a matter of course, never dreaming of calling it an "institution," much less a holy and beautiful one, and being pretty plainly of opinion that Idealism is a crackbrained fuss about nothing. The idealists, hurt by this, will retort by calling them Philistines. We then have our society classified as 700 Philistines and 299 idealists, leaving one man unclassified: the man strong enough to face the truth the idealists are shirking.

Such a man says of marriage, "This thing is a failure for many of us. It is insufferable that two human beings, having entered into relations which only warm affection can render tolerable, should be forced to maintain them after such affections have ceased to exist, or in spite of the fact that they have never arisen. The alleged natural attractions and repulsions upon which the family ideal is based do not exist; and it is historically false that the family was founded for the purpose of satisfying them. Let us provide otherwise for the social ends which the family subserves, and then abolish its compulsory character altogether." What will be the attitude of the rest to this outspoken man? The Philistines will simply think him mad. But the idealists will be terrified beyond measure at the proclamation of their hidden thought—at the presence of the traitor among the conspirators of silence—at the rending of the beautiful veil they and their poets have woven to hide the unbearable face of the truth. They will crucify him, burn him, violate their own ideals of family affection by taking his children away from him, ostracize him, brand him as immoral, profligate, filthy, and appeal against him to the despised Philistines, specially idealized for the occasion as Society. How far they will proceed against him depends on how far his courage exceeds theirs. At his worst, they call him cynic and paradoxer: at his best they do their utmost to ruin him if not to take his life. Thus, purblindly courageous moralists like Mandeville and Laroche foucauld, who merely state unpleasant facts without denying the validity of current ideals, and who indeed depend on those ideals to make their statements piquant, get off with nothing worse than this name of cynic, the free use of which is a familiar mark of the zealous idealist. But take the case of the man who has already served us as an example: Shelley. The idealists did not call Shelley a cynic: they called him a fiend until they invented a new illusion to enable them to enjoy the beauty of his lyrics, this illusion being nothing less than the pretence that since he was at bottom an idealist himself, his ideals must be identical with those of Tennyson and Longfellow, neither of whom ever wrote a line in which some highly respectable ideal was not implicit.[1]

[1] The following are examples of the two stages of Shelley criticism:
"We feel as if one of the darkest of the fiends had been clothed

Here the admission that Shelley, the realist, was an idealist too, seems to spoil the whole argument. And it certainly spoils its verbal consistency. For we unfortunately use this word ideal indifferently to denote both the institution which the ideal masks and the mask itself, thereby producing desperate confusion of thought, since the institution may be an effete and poisonous one, whilst the mask may be, and indeed generally is, an image of what we would fain have in its place. If the existing facts, with their masks on, are to be called ideals, and the future possibilities which the masks depict are also to be called ideals—if, again, the man who is defending existing institutions by maintaining their identity with their masks is to be confounded under one name with the man who is striving to realize the future possibilities by tearing the mask and the thing masked asunder, then the position cannot be intelligibly described by mortal pen: you and I, reader, will be at cross purposes at every sentence unless you allow me to distinguish pioneers like Shelley and Ibsen as realists from the idealists of my imaginary community of one thousand. If you ask why I have not allotted the terms the other way, and called Shelley and Ibsen idealists and the conventionalists realists, I reply that Ibsen himself, though he has not formally made the distinction, has so

---

with a human body to enable him to gratify his enmity against the human race, and as if the supernatural atrocity of his hate were only heightened by his power to do injury. So strongly has this impression dwelt upon our minds that we absolutely asked a friend, who had seen this individual, to describe him to us—as if a cloven hoof, or horn, or flames from the mouth, must have marked the external appearance of so bitter an enemy of mankind." (Literary Gazette, 19th May 1821.)

"A beautiful and ineffectual angel, beating in the void his luminous wings in vain." (MATTHEW ARNOLD, in the preface to his selection of poems by Byron, dated 1881.)

The 1881 opinion is much sillier than the 1821 opinion. Further samples will be found in the articles of Henry Salt, one of the few writers on Shelley who understand his true position as a social pioneer.

repeatedly harped on conventions and conventionalists as ideals and idealists that if I were now perversely to call them realities and realists, I should confuse readers of The Wild Duck and Rosmersholm more than I should help them. Doubtless I shall be reproached for puzzling people by thus limiting the meaning of the term ideal. But what, I ask, is that inevitable passing perplexity compared to the inextricable tangle I must produce if I follow the custom, and use the word indiscriminately in its two violently incompatible senses? If the term realist is objected to on account of some of its modern associations, I can only recommend you, if you must associate it with something else than my own description of its meaning (I do not deal in definitions), to associate it, not with Zola and Maupassant, but with Plato.

Now let us return to our community of 700 Philistines, 299 idealists, and 1 realist. The mere verbal ambiguity against which I have just provided is as nothing beside that which comes of any attempt to express the relations of these three sections, simple as they are, in terms of the ordinary systems of reason and duty. The idealist, higher in the ascent of evolution than the Philistine, yet hates the highest and strikes at him with a dread and rancor of which the easy-going Philistine is guiltless. The man who has risen above the danger and the fear that his acquisitiveness will lead him to theft, his temper to murder, and his affections to debauchery: this is he who is denounced as an arch-scoundrel and libertine, and thus confounded with the lowest because he is the highest. And it is not the ignorant and stupid who maintain this error, but the literate and the cultured. When the true prophet speaks, he is proved to be both rascal and idiot, not by those who have never read of how foolishly such learned demonstrations have come off in the past, but by those who have themselves written volumes on the crucifixions, the burnings, the stonings, the headings and hangings, the Siberia transportations, the calumny and ostracism which have been the lot of the pioneer as well as of the camp follower. It is from men of established literary reputation that we learn that William Blake was mad, that Shelley was spoiled by living in a low set, that Robert Owen was a man who did not know the world, that Ruskin was incapable of comprehending political economy, that Zola was a mere blackguard, and that Ibsen was "a Zola with a wooden leg." The great musician, accepted by the unskilled listener, is vilified by his fellow-musicians: it was the musical culture of Europe that pronounced Wagner the inferior of Mendelssohn and Meyerbeer. The great artist finds his foes among the painters, and not among the men in the street: it was the Royal Academy which placed forgotten nobodies above Burne Jones. It is not rational that it should be so; but it is so, for all that.

The realist at last loses patience with ideals altogether, and sees in them only something to blind us, something to numb us, something to murder self in us, something whereby, instead of resisting death, we can disarm it by committing suicide. The idealist, who has taken refuge with the ideals because he hates himself and is ashamed of himself, thinks that all this is so much the better. The realist, who has come to have a deep respect for himself and faith in the validity of his own will, thinks it so much the worse. To the one, human nature, naturally corrupt, is held back from ruinous excesses only by self-denying conformity to the ideals. To the other these ideals are only swaddling clothes which man has outgrown, and which insufferably impede his movements. No wonder the two cannot agree. The idealist says, "Realism means egotism; and egotism means depravity." The realist declares that when a man abnegates the will to live and be free in a world of the living and free, seeking only to conform to ideals for the sake of being, not himself, but "a good man," then he is morally dead and rotten, and must be left unheeded to abide his resurrection, if that by good luck arrive before his bodily death.[1] Unfortunately, this is the

[1] The above was written in 1890, ten years before Ibsen, in When We Dead Awaken, fully adopted its metaphor without, as far as I know, having any knowledge of my essay. Such an antici-

sort of speech that nobody but a realist understands. It will be more amusing as well as more convincing to take an actual example of an idealist criticizing a realist.

---

pation is a better proof than any mere argument that I found the right track of Ibsen's thought. (1912).

IN 1890 the literary sensation of the day was the Diary of Marie Bashkirtseff. An outline of it, with a running commentary, was given in The Review of Reviews (June 1890) by the editor, the late William Stead, who, having gained an immense following by a public service in rendering which he had to simulate a felony and suffer imprisonment for it in order to prove that it was possible, was engaged in a campaign with the object of establishing the ideal of sexual "purity" as a condition of public life. He had certain Ibsenist qualities: faith in himself, wilfulness, conscientious unscrupulousness, and could always make himself heard. Prominent among his ideals was an ideal of womanliness. In support of that ideal he would, like all idealists, make and believe any statement, however obviously and grotesquely unreal. When he found Marie Bashkirtseff's account of herself utterly incompatible with the picture of a woman's mind presented to him by his ideal, he was confronted with the dilemma that either Marie was not a woman or else his ideal was false to nature. He actually accepted the former alternative. "Of the distinctively womanly," he says, "there is in her but little trace. She was the very antithesis of a true woman." William's next difficulty was, that self-control, being a leading quality in his ideal, could not have been possessed by Marie: otherwise she would have been more like his ideal. Nevertheless he had to record that she, without any compulsion from circumstances, made herself a highly skilled artist by working ten hours a day for six years. Let anyone who thinks that this is no evidence of self-control just try it for six months. William's verdict nevertheless was "No self-control." However, his fundamental quarrel with Marie came out in the following lines. "Marie," he said, "was artist, musician, wit, philosopher, student, anything you like but a natural woman with a heart to love, and a soul to find its supreme satisfaction in sacrifice for lover or for child." Now of all the idealist abominations that make society pestiferous, I doubt if there be any so mean as that of forcing self-sacrifice on a woman under pretence that she likes it; and, if she ventures to contradict the pretence, declaring her no true woman. In India they carried this piece of idealism to the length of declaring that a wife could not bear to survive her husband, but would be prompted by her own faithful, loving, beautiful nature to offer up her life on the pyre which consumed his dead body. The astonishing thing is that women, sooner than be branded as unsexed wretches, allowed themselves to be stupefied with drink, and in that unwomanly condition burnt alive. British Philistinism put down widow idealizing with the strong hand; and suttee is abolished in India. The English form of it still flourishes; and Stead, the rescuer of the children,[1] was one of its high priests. Imagine his feelings on coming across this entry in a woman's diary: "I love myself." Or this, "I swear solemnly —by the Gospels, by the passion of Christ, by MYSELF—that in four years I will be famous." The young woman was positively proposing to exercise for her own sake all the powers that were given to her, in Stead's opinion, solely that she might sacrifice them for her lover or child! No wonder he was driven to exclaim again, "She was very clever, no doubt; but woman she was not."

Now observe this notable result. Marie Bashkirtseff, instead of being a less agreeable person than the ordinary female conformer to the ideal of womanliness, was most conspicuously the reverse. Stead himself wrote as one infatuated with her mere diary, and pleased himself by representing her as a person who fascinated everybody, and was a source of delight to all about her by the mere exhilaration and hope-giving atmosphere of her wilfulness. The truth is, that in real life a self-sacrificing woman, or, as Stead would have put it, a womanly woman, is not only taken advantage of, but disliked as well for her pains. No man pretends that his soul finds its supreme satisfaction in self-sacrifice: such an

[1] It was to force the Government to take steps to suppress child prostitution that Stead resorted to the desperate expedient already alluded to. He succeeded.

affectation would stamp him as coward and weakling: the manly man is he who takes the Bashkirtseff view of himself. But men are not the less loved on this account. No one ever feels helpless by the side of the self-helper; whilst the self-sacrificer is always a drag, a responsibility, a reproach, an everlasting and unnatural trouble with whom no really strong soul can live. Only those who have helped themselves know how to help others, and to respect their right to help themselves.[1]

Although romantic idealists generally insist on self-surrender as an indispensable element in true womanly love, its repulsive effect is well known and feared in practice by both sexes. The extreme instance is the reckless self-abandonment seen in the infatuation of passionate sexual desire. Everyone who becomes the object of that infatuation shrinks from it instinctively. Love loses its charm when it is not free; and whether the compulsion is that of custom and law, or of infatuation, the effect is the same: it becomes valueless and even abhorrent, like the caresses of a maniac. The desire to give inspires no affection unless there is also the power to withhold; and the successful wooer, in both sexes alike, is the one who can stand out for honorable conditions, and, failing them, go without. Such conditions are evidently not offered to either sex by the legal marriage of today; for it is

[1] Shortly after the publication of this passage, a German lady told me that she knew "where I had got it from," evidently not meaning from Ibsen. She added "You have been reading Nietzsche's Through Good and Evil and Out at the other Side." That was the first I ever heard of Nietzsche. I mention this fact, not with the ridiculous object of vindicating my "originality" in nineteenth century fashion, but because I attach great importance to the evidence that the movement voiced by Schopenhauer, Wagner, Ibsen, Nietzsche, and Strindberg, was a world movement, and would have found expression if every one of these writers had perished in his cradle. I have dealt with this question in the preface to my play Major Barbara. The movement is alive today in the philosophy of Bergson and the plays of Gorki, Tchekoff, and the post-Ibsen English drama. (1912.)

the intense repugnance inspired by the compulsory character of the legalized conjugal relation that leads, first to the idealization of marriage whilst it remains indispensable as a means of perpetuating society; then to its modification by divorce and by the abolition of penalties for refusal to comply with judicial orders for restitution of conjugal rights; and finally to its disuse and disappearance as the responsibility for the maintenance and education of the rising generation is shifted from the parent to the community.[1]

Although the growing repugnance to face the Church of England marriage service has led many celebrants to omit those passages which frankly explain the object of the institution, we are not likely to dispense with legal ties and obligations, and trust wholly to the permanence of love, until the continuity of society no longer depends on the private

[1] A dissertation on the anomalies and impossibilities of the marriage law at its present stage would be too far out of the main course of my argument to be introduced in the text above; but it may be well to point out in passing to those who regard marriage as an inviolable and inviolate institution, that necessity has already forced us to tamper with it to such an extent that at this moment (1891) the highest court in the kingdom is face to face with a husband and wife, the one demanding whether a woman may saddle him with all the responsibilities of a husband and then refuse to live with him, and the other asking whether the law allows her husband to commit abduction, imprisonment, and rape upon her. If the court says Yes to the husband, indissoluble marriage is made intolerable for men; if it says Yes to the wife, the position is made intolerable for women; and as this exhausts the possible alternatives, it is clear that provision must be made for the dissolution of such marriages if the institution is to be maintained at all, which it must be until its social function is otherwise provided for. Marriage is thus, by force of circumstances, compelled to buy extension of life by extension of divorce, much as if a fugitive should try to delay a pursuing wolf by throwing portions of his own heart to it. [The court decided against the man; but England still lags behind the rest of Protestant Europe in the necessary readjustment of the law of divorce. See the preface to my play Getting Married, which supplies the dissertation crowded out of the foregoing note. (1912).]

nursery. Love, as a practical factor in society, is still a mere appetite. That higher development of it which Ibsen shews us occurring in the case of Rebecca West in Rosmersholm is only known to most of us by the descriptions of great poets, who themselves, as their biographies prove, have known it, not by sustained experience, but only by brief glimpses. Dante loved Beatrice with the higher love; but neither during her life nor after her death was he "faithful" to her or to the woman he actually married. And he would be a bold bourgeois who would pretend to a higher mind than Dante. Tannhäuser may die in the conviction that one moment of the emotion he felt with St Elizabeth was fuller and happier than all the hours of passion he spent with Venus; but that does not alter the fact that love began for him with Venus, and that its earlier tentatives towards the final goal were attended with relapses. Now Tannhäuser's passion for Venus is a development of the humdrum fondness of the bourgeois Jack for his Jill, a development at once higher and more dangerous, just as idealism is at once higher and more dangerous than Philistinism. The fondness is the germ of the passion: the passion is the germ of the more perfect love. When Blake told men that through excess they would learn moderation, he knew that the way for the present lay through the Venusberg, and that the race would assuredly not perish there as some individuals have, and as the Puritan fears we all shall unless we find a way round. Also he no doubt foresaw the time when our children would be born on the other side of it, and so be spared that fiery purgation.

But the very facts that Blake is still commonly regarded as a crazy visionary, and that the current criticism of Rosmersholm entirely fails even to notice the evolution of Rebecca's passion for Rosmer into her love for him, much more to credit the moral transfiguration which accompanies it, shew how absurd it would be to pretend, for the sake of edification, that the ordinary marriage of today is a union between a William Blake and a Rebecca West, or that it would be possible, even if it were enlightened policy, to deny the satisfaction of the sexual appetite to persons who have not reached that stage. An overwhelming majority of such marriages as are not purely *de convenance* are entered into for the gratification of that appetite either in its crudest form or veiled only by those idealistic illusions which the youthful imagination weaves so wonderfully under the stimulus of desire, and which older people indulgently laugh at.

This being so, it is not surprising that our society, being directly dominated by men, comes to regard Woman, not as an end in herself like Man, but solely as a means of ministering to his appetite. The ideal wife is one who does everything that the ideal husband likes, and nothing else. Now to treat a person as a means instead of an end is to deny that person's right to live. And to be treated as a means to such an end as sexual intercourse with those who deny one's right to live is insufferable to any human being. Woman, if she dares face the fact that she is being so treated, must either loathe herself or else rebel. As a rule, when circumstances enable her to rebel successfully—for instance, when the accident of genius enables her to "lose her character" without losing her employment or cutting herself off from the society she values—she does rebel; but circumstances seldom do. Does she then loathe herself? By no means: she deceives herself in the idealist fashion by denying that the love which her suitor offers her is tainted with sexual appetite at all. It is, she declares, a beautiful, disinterested, pure, sublime devotion to another by which a man's life is exalted and purified, and a woman's rendered blest. And of all the cynics, the filthiest to her mind is the one who sees, in the man making honorable proposals to his future wife, nothing but the human male seeking his female. The man himself keeps her confirmed in her illusion; for the truth is unbearable to him too: he wants to form an affectionate tie, and not to drive a degrading bargain. After all, the germ of the highest love is in them both; though as yet it is no more than the appetite they are disguising so carefully from themselves. Consequently every stockbroker who has just brought his business up to marrying point woos in terms of the romantic illusion; and it is agreed between the two that their marriage shall realize the romantic ideal. Then comes the breakdown of the plan. The young wife finds that her husband is neglecting her for his business; that his interests, his activities, his whole life except that one part of it to which only a cynic ever referred before her marriage, lies away from home; and that her business is to sit there and mope until she is wanted. Then what can she do? If she complains, he, the self-helper, can do without her; whilst she is dependent on him for her position, her livelihood, her place in society, her home, her name, her very bread.[1] All this is brought home to her by the first burst of displeasure her complaints provoke. Fortunately, things do not remain for ever at this point: perhaps the most wretched in a woman's life. The self-respect she has lost as a wife she regains as a mother, in which capacity her use and importance to the community compare favorably with those of most men of business. She is wanted in the house, wanted in the market, wanted by the children; and now, instead of weeping because her husband is away in the city, thinking of stocks and shares instead of his ideal woman, she would regard his presence in the house all day as an intolerable nuisance. And so, though she is completely disillusioned on the subject of ideal love, yet, since it has not turned out so badly after all, she countenances the illusion still from the point of view that it is a useful and harmless means of getting boys and girls to marry and settle down. And this conviction is the stronger in her because she feels that if she had known as much about marriage the day before

[1] I should have warned my male readers to be very careful how they presume on this position. In actual practice marriage reduces the man to a greater dependence on the woman than is good for either party. But the woman can tyrannize only by misconduct or threats of misconduct, whilst the man can tyrannize legally, though it must be added that a good deal of the makeshift law that has been set up to restrain this tyranny is very unfair to the man. The writings of Belfort Bax are instructive on this point. (1912).

her wedding as she did six months after, it would have been extremely hard to induce her to get married at all.

This prosaic solution is satisfactory only within certain limits. It depends altogether upon the accident of the woman having some natural vocation for domestic management and the care of children, as well as on the husband being fairly good-natured and livable-with. Hence arises the idealist illusion that a vocation for domestic management and the care of children is natural to women, and that women who lack them are not women at all, but members of the third, or Bashkirtseff sex. Even if this were true, it is obvious that if the Bashkirtseffs are to be allowed to live, they have a right to suitable institutions just as much as men and women. But it is not true. The domestic career is no more natural to all women than the military career is natural to all men; and although in a population emergency it might become necessary for every ablebodied woman to risk her life in childbed just as it might become necessary in a military emergency for every man to risk his life in the battlefield, yet even then it would by no means follow that the child-bearing would endow the mother with domestic aptitudes and capacities as it would endow her with milk. It is of course quite true that the majority of women are kind to children and prefer their own to other people's. But exactly the same thing is true of the majority of men, who nevertheless do not consider that their proper sphere is the nursery. The case may be illustrated more grotesquely by the fact that the majority of women who have dogs are kind to them, and prefer their own dogs to other people's; yet it is not proposed that women should restrict their activities to the rearing of puppies. If we have come to think that the nursery and the kitchen are the natural sphere of a woman, we have done so exactly as English children come to think that a cage is the natural sphere of a parrot: because they have never seen one anywhere else. No doubt there are Philistine parrots who agree with their owners that it is better to be in a cage than out, so long as there is plenty of hempseed and Indian corn there.

There may even be idealist parrots who persuade themselves that the mission of a parrot is to minister to the happiness of a private family by whistling and saying Pretty Polly, and that it is in the sacrifice of its liberty to this altruistic pursuit that a true parrot finds the supreme satisfaction of its soul. I will not go so far as to affirm that there are theological parrots who are convinced that imprisonment is the will of God because it is unpleasant; but I am confident that there are rationalist parrots who can demonstrate that it would be a cruel kindness to let a parrot out to fall a prey to cats, or at least to forget its accomplishments and coarsen its naturally delicate fibres in an unprotected struggle for existence. Still, the only parrot a free-souled person can sympathize with is the one that insists on being let out as the first condition of making itself agreeable. A selfish bird, you may say: one that puts its own gratification before that of the family which is so fond of it—before even the greatest happiness of the greatest number: one that, in aping the independent spirit of a man, has unparroted itself and become a creature that has neither the home-loving nature of a bird nor the strength and enterprise of a mastiff. All the same, you respect that parrot in spite of your conclusive reasoning; and if it persists, you will have either to let it out or kill it.

The sum of the matter is that unless Woman repudiates her womanliness, her duty to her husband, to her children, to society, to the law, and to everyone but herself, she cannot emancipate herself. But her duty to herself is no duty at all, since a debt is cancelled when the debtor and creditor are the same person. Its payment is simply a fulfilment of the individual will, upon which all duty is a restriction, founded on the conception of the will as naturally malign and devilish. Therefore Woman has to repudiate duty altogether. In that repudiation lies her freedom; for it is false to say that Woman is now directly the slave of Man: she is the immediate slave of duty; and as man's path to freedom is strewn with the wreckage of the duties and ideals he has trampled on, so must hers be. She may indeed mask her iconoclasm by proving in rationalist fashion, as Man has often done for the sake of a quiet life, that all these discarded idealist conceptions will be fortified instead of shattered by her emancipation. To a person with a turn for logic, such proofs are as easy as playing the piano is to Paderewski. But it will not be true. A whole basketful of ideals of the most sacred quality will be smashed by the achievement of equality for women and men. Those who shrink from such a clatter and breakage may comfort themselves with the reflection that the replacement of the broken goods will be prompt and certain. It is always a case of "The ideal is dead: long live the ideal!" And the advantage of the work of destruction is that every new ideal is less of an illusion than the one it has supplanted; so that the destroyer of ideals, though denounced as an enemy of society, is in fact sweeping the world clear of lies.

My digression is now over. Having traversed my loop as I promised, and come back to Man's repudiation of duty by way of Woman's, I may at last proceed to give some more particular account of Ibsen's work without further preoccupation with Clement Scott's protest, or the many others of which it is the type. For we now see that the pioneer must necessarily provoke such outcry as he repudiates duties, tramples on ideals, profanes what was sacred, sanctifies what was infamous, always driving his plough through gardens of pretty weeds in spite of the laws made against trespassers for the protection of the worms which feed on the roots, always letting in light and air to hasten the putrefaction of decaying matter, and everywhere proclaiming that "the old beauty is no longer beautiful, the new truth no longer true." He can do no less; and what more and what else he does it is not given to all of his generation to understand. And if any man does not understand, and cannot foresee the harvest, what can he do but cry out in all sincerity against such destruction, until at last we come to know the cry of the blind like any other street cry, and to bear with it as an honest cry, albeit a false alarm?

BRAND 1866

WE are now prepared to learn without misgiving that a typical Ibsen play is one in which the leading lady is an unwomanly woman, and the villain an idealist. It follows that the leading lady is not a heroine of the Drury Lane type; nor does the villain forge or assassinate, since he is a villain by virtue of his determination to do nothing wrong. Therefore readers of Ibsen—not playgoers—have sometimes so far misconceived him as to suppose that his villains are examples rather than warnings, and that the mischief and ruin which attend their actions are but the tribulations from which the soul comes out purified as gold from the furnace. In fact, the beginning of Ibsen's European reputation was the edification with which the pious received his great dramatic poem Brand. Brand is not his first play: indeed it is his seventh; and of its six forerunners all are notable and some splendid; but it is in Brand that he definitely, if not yet quite consciously, takes the field against idealism and, like another Luther, nails his thesis to the door of the Temple of Morality. With Brand therefore we must begin, lest we should be swept into an eddy of mere literary criticism, a matter altogether beside the purpose of this book, which is to distil the quintessence of Ibsen's message to his age.

Brand the priest is an idealist of heroic earnestness, strength, and courage. Conventional, comfortable, sentimental churchgoing withers into selfish snobbery and cowardly weakness before his terrible word. "Your God," he cries, "is an old man: mine is young"; and all Europe, hearing him, suddenly realizes that it has so far forgotten God as to worship an image of an elderly gentleman with a well-trimmed beard, an imposing forehead, and the expression of a headmaster. Brand, turning from such idolatrous follies with fierce scorn, declares himself the champion, not of things as they are, nor of things as they can be made, but of things as they ought to be. Things as they ought to be mean for him things as ordered by men conformed to his ideal of the perfect Adam, who, again, is not man as he is or can be, but man conformed to all the ideals: man as it is his duty to be. In insisting on this conformity, Brand spares neither himself nor anyone else. Life is nothing: self is nothing: the perfect Adam is everything. The imperfect Adam does not fall in with these views. A peasant whom he urges to cross a glacier in a fog because it is his duty to visit his dying daughter, not only flatly declines, but endeavors forcibly to prevent Brand from risking his own life. Brand knocks him down, and sermonizes him with fierce earnestness and scorn. Presently Brand has to cross a fiord in a storm to reach a dying man who, having committed a series of murders, wants "consolation" from a priest. Brand cannot go alone: someone must hold the rudder of his boat whilst he manages the sail. The fisher folk, in whom the old Adam is strong, do not adopt his estimate of the gravity of the situation, and refuse to go. A woman, fascinated by his heroism and idealism, goes. That ends in their marriage, and in the birth of a child to which they become deeply attached. Then Brand, aspiring from height to height of devotion to his ideal, plunges from depth to depth of murderous cruelty. First the child must die from the severity of the climate because Brand must not flinch from the post of duty and leave his congregation exposed to the peril of getting an inferior preacher in his place. Then he forces his wife to give the clothes of the dead child to a gipsy whose baby needs them. The bereaved mother does not grudge the gift; but she wants to hold back only one little garment as a relic of her darling. But Brand sees in this reservation the imperfection of the imperfect Eve. He forces her to regard the situation as a choice between the relic and his ideal. She sacrifices the relic to the ideal, and then dies, broken-hearted. Having killed her, and thereby placed himself beyond ever daring to doubt the idealism upon whose altar he has immolated her; having also refused to go to his mother's death-bed because she compromises with his principles in disposing of her property, he is hailed by the people as a saint, and finds his newly built church too small for his congregation. So he calls upon them to follow him to worship God in His own temple, the mountains. After a brief practical experience of this arrangement, they change their minds, and stone him. The very mountains themselves stone him, indeed; for he is killed by an avalanche.

PEER GYNT 1867

Brand dies a saint, having caused more intense suffering by his saintliness than the most talented sinner could possibly have done with twice his opportunities. Ibsen does not leave this to be inferred. In another dramatic poem he gives us a rapscallion named Peer Gynt, an idealist who avoids Brand's errors by setting up as his ideal the realization of himself through the utter satisfaction of his own will. In this he would seem to be on the path to which Ibsen himself points; and indeed all who know the two plays will agree that whether or no it was better to be Peer Gynt than Brand, it was beyond all question better to be the mother or the sweetheart of Peer, scapegrace and liar as he was, than mother or wife to the saintly Brand. Brand would force his ideal on all men and women: Peer Gynt keeps his ideal for himself alone: it is indeed implicit in the ideal itself that it should be unique—that he alone should have the force to realize it. For Peer's first boyish notion of the self-realized man is not the saint, but the demigod whose indomitable will is stronger than destiny, the fighter, the master, the man whom no woman can resist, the mighty hunter, the knight of a thousand adventures, the model, in short, of the lover in a lady's novel, or the hero in a boy's romance. Now, no such person exists, or ever did exist, or ever can exist. The man who cultivates an indomitable will and refuses to make way for anything or anybody, soon finds that he cannot hold a street crossing against a tram car, much less a world against the whole human race. Only by plunging into illusions to which every fact gives the lie can he persuade himself that his will is a force that can overcome all other forces, or that it is less conditioned by circumstances than a wheelbarrow is. However, Peer Gynt, being imaginative enough to conceive his ideal, is also imaginative enough to find illusions to hide its unreality, and to persuade himself that Peer Gynt, the shabby countryside loafer, is Peer Gynt, Emperor of Himself, as he writes over the door of his hut in the mountains. His hunting feats are invented; his military genius has no solider foundation than a street fight with a smith; and his reputation as an adventurous daredevil he has to gain by the bravado of carrying off the bride from a wedding at which the guests snub him. Only in the mountains can he enjoy his illusions undisturbed by ridicule; yet even in the mountains he finds obstacles he cannot force his way through, obstacles which withstand him as spirits with voices, telling him that he must go round. But he will not: he will go forward: he will cut his path sword in hand, in spite of fate. All the same, he has to go round; for the world-will is outside Peer Gynt as well as inside him.

Then he tries the supernatural, only to find that it means nothing more than the transmogrifying of squalid realities by lies and pretences. Still, like our amateurs of thaumaturgy, he is willing to enter into a conspiracy of make believe up to a certain point. When the Trold king's daughter appears as a repulsive ragged creature riding on a pig, he is ready to accept her as a beautiful princess on a noble steed, on condition that she accepts his mother's tumble-down farmhouse, with the broken window panes stopped up with old clouts, as a splendid castle. He will go with her among the Trolds, and pretend that the gruesome ravine in which they hold their orgies is a glorious palace; he will partake of their filthy food and declare it nectar and ambrosia; he will applaud their obscene antics as exquisite dancing, and their discordant din as divine music; but when they finally propose to slit his eyes so that he may see and hear these things, not as they are, but as he has been pretending to see and hear them, he draws back, resolved to be himself even in self-deception. He leaves the mountains and becomes a prosperous man of business in

America, highly respectable and ready for any profitable speculation: slave trade, Bible trade, whisky trade, missionary trade, anything! His commercial success in this phase persuades him that he is under the special care of God; but he is shaken in his opinion by an adventure in which he is marooned on the African coast, and does not recover his faith until the treacherous friends who marooned him are destroyed before his eyes by the blowing-up of the steam yacht they have just stolen from him, when he utters his celebrated exclamation, "Ah, God is a Father to me after all; but economical he certainly is not." He finds a white horse in the desert, and is accepted on its account as the Messiah by an Arab tribe, a success which moves him to declare that now at last he is really worshipped for himself, whereas in America people only respected his breast-pin, the symbol of his money. In commerce, too, he reflects, his eminence was a mere matter of chance, whilst as a prophet he is eminent by pure natural fitness for the post. This is ended by his falling in love with a dancing-girl, who, after leading him into every sort of undignified and ludicrous extravagance, ranging from his hailing her as the Eternal-Feminine of Goethe to the more practical folly of giving her his white horse and all his prophetic finery, runs away with the spoil, and leaves him once more helpless and alone in the desert. He wanders until he comes to the Great Sphinx, beside which he finds a German gentleman in great perplexity as to who the Sphinx is. Peer Gynt, seeing in that impassive, immovable, majestic figure, a symbol of his own ideal, is able to tell the German gentleman at once that the Sphinx is itself. This explanation dazzles the German, who, after some further discussion of the philosophy of self-realization, invites Peer Gynt to accompany him to a club of learned men in Cairo, who are ripe for enlightenment on this very question. Peer, delighted, accompanies the German to the club, which turns out to be a madhouse in which the lunatics have broken loose and locked up their keepers. It is in this madhouse, and by these madmen, that Peer Gynt is at last crowned Emperor of Himself.

He receives their homage as he lies in the dust fainting with terror.

As an old man, Peer Gynt, returning to the scenes of his early adventures, is troubled with the prospect of meeting a certain button moulder who threatens to make short work of his realized self by melting it down in his crucible with a heap of other button-material. Immediately the old exaltation of the self realizer is changed into an unspeakable dread of the button moulder Death, to avoid whom Peer Gynt has already pushed a drowning man from the spar he is clinging to in a shipwreck lest it should not suffice to support two. At last he finds a deserted sweetheart of his youth still waiting for him and still believing in him. In the imagination of this old woman he finds the ideal Peer Gynt; whilst in himself, the loafer, the braggart, the confederate of sham magicians, the Charleston speculator, the false prophet, the dancing-girl's dupe, the bedlam emperor, the thruster of the drowning man into the waves, there is nothing heroic: nothing but commonplace self-seeking and shirking, cowardice and sensuality, veiled only by the romantic fancies of the born liar. With this crowningly unreal realization he is left to face the button moulder as best he can.[1]

[1] Miss Pagan, who has produced scenes from Peer Gynt in Edinburgh and London (which, to its shame, has not yet seen a complete public performance of Peer Gynt), regards the death of Peer as occurring in the scene where all the wasted possibilities of his life drift about him as withered leaves and fluffs of bog-cotton. He picks up an onion, and, playing with the idea that it is himself, and that its skins are the phases of his own career wrapped round the kernel of his real self, strips them off one after another, only to discover that there is no kernel. "Nature is ironical," says Peer bitterly; and that discovery of his own nothingness is taken by Miss Pagan as his death, the subsequent adventures being those of his soul. It is impossible to demur to so poetic an interpretation; though it assumes, in spite of the onion, that Peer had not wholly destroyed his soul. Still, as the button moulder (who might be Brand's ghost) does respite Peer "until the next cross roads," it cannot be said that Ibsen leaves Peer definitely scrapped. (1912).

Peer Gynt has puzzled a good many people by Ibsen's fantastic and subtle treatment of its metaphysical thesis. It is so far a difficult play, that the ideal of unconditional self-realization, however familiar its suggestions may be to the ambitious reader, is not understood by him. When it is stated to him by some one who does understand it, he unhesitatingly dismisses it as idiotic; and because he is perfectly right in doing so—because it is idiotic in the most accurate sense of the term—he does not easily recognize it as the common ideal of his own prototype, the pushing, competitive, success-craving man who is the hero of the modern world.

There is nothing novel in Ibsen's dramatic method of reducing these ideals to absurdity. Exactly as Cervantes took the old ideal of chivalry, and shewed what came of a man attempting to act as if it were real, so Ibsen takes the ideals of Brand and Peer Gynt, and subjects them to the same test. Don Quixote acts as if he were a perfect knight in a world of giants and distressed damsels instead of a country gentleman in a land of innkeepers and farm wenches; Brand acts as if he were the perfect Adam in a world where, by resolute rejection of all compromise with imperfection, it was immediately possible to change the rainbow "bridge between flesh and spirit" into as enduring a structure as the tower of Babel was intended to be, thereby restoring man to the condition in which he walked with God in the garden; and Peer Gynt tries to act as if he had in him a special force that could be concentrated so as to prevail over all other forces. They ignore the real—ignore what they are and where they are, not only, like Nelson, shutting their eyes to the signals a brave man may disregard, but insanely steering straight on rocks no man's resolution can move or resist. Observe that neither Cervantes nor Ibsen is incredulous, in the Philistine way, as to the power of ideals over men. Don Quixote, Brand, and Peer Gynt are, all three, men of action seeking to realize their ideals in deeds. However ridiculous Don Quixote makes himself, you cannot dislike or despise him, much less think that it would have been better for him to have been a Philistine like Sancho; and Peer Gynt, selfish rascal as he is, is not unlovable. Brand, made terrible by the consequences of his idealism to others, is heroic. Their castles in the air are more beautiful than castles of brick and mortar; but one cannot live in them; and they seduce men into pretending that every hovel is such a castle, just as Peer Gynt pretended that the Trold king's den was a palace.

EMPEROR AND GALILEAN 1873

When Ibsen, by merely giving the rein to the creative impulse of his poetic nature, had produced Brand and Peer Gynt, he was nearly forty. His will, in setting his imagination to work, had produced a tough puzzle for his intellect. In no case does the difference between the will and the intellect come out more clearly than in that of the poet, save only that of the lover. Had Ibsen died in 1867, he, like many another great poet, would have gone to his grave without having ever rationally understood his own meaning. Nay, if in that year an intellectual expert—a commentator, as we call him—having read Brand, had put forward the explanation which Ibsen himself must have arrived at before he constructed Ghosts and The Wild Duck, he would perhaps have repudiated it with as much disgust as a maiden would feel if anyone were prosaic enough to give her the physiological explanation of her dreams of meeting a fairy prince. Only simpletons go to the creative artist presuming that he must be able to answer their "What does this obscure passage mean?" That is the very question the poet's own intellect, which had no part in the conception of the poem, may be asking him. And this curiosity of the intellect, this restless life in it which differentiates it from dead machinery, and troubles our lesser artists but little, is one of the marks of the greater sort. Shakespear, in Hamlet, made a drama of the self-questioning that came upon him when his intellect rose up in alarm, as well it might, against the vulgar optimism of his Henry V, and yet could mend it to no better purpose than by the equally vulgar pessimism of

Troilus and Cressida. Dante took pains to understand himself: so did Goethe. Richard Wagner, one of the greatest poets of our own day, has left us as many volumes of criticism of art and life as he has left musical scores; and he has expressly described how the keen intellectual activity he brought to the analysis of his music dramas was in abeyance during their creation. Just so do we find Ibsen, after composing his two great dramatic poems, entering on a struggle to become intellectually conscious of what he had done.

We have seen that with Shakespear such an effort became itself creative and produced a drama of questioning. With Ibsen the same thing occurred: he harked back to an abandoned project of his, and wrote two huge dramas on the subject of the apostasy of the Emperor Julian. In this work we find him at first preoccupied with a piece of old-fashioned freethinking: the dilemma that moral responsibility presupposes free-will, and that free-will sets man above God. Cain, who slew because he willed, willed because he must, and must have willed to slay because he was himself, comes upon the stage to claim that murder is fertile, and death the ground of life, though, not having read Weismann on death as a method of evolution, he cannot say what is the ground of death. Judas asks whether, when the Master chose him, he chose foreknowingly. This part of the drama has no very deep significance. It is easy to invent conundrums which dogmatic evangelicalism cannot answer; and no doubt, whilst it was still a nine days' wonder that evangelicalism could not solve all enigmas, such invention seemed something much deeper than the mere intellectual chess-play which it is seen to be now that the nine days are past. In his occasional weakness for such conundrums, and later on in his harping on the hereditary transmission of disease, we see Ibsen's active intellect busy, not only with the problems peculiar to his own plays, but with the fatalism and pessimism of the middle of the nineteenth century, when the typical advanced culture was attainable by reading Strauss's Leben Jesu, the popularizations of Helmholtz and Darwin by Tyndall and Huxley, and George Eliot's novels, vainly protested against by Ruskin as peopled with "the sweepings of a Pentonville omnibus." The traces of this period in Ibsen's writings shew how well he knew the crushing weight with which the sordid cares of the ordinary struggle for money and respectability fell on the world when the romance of the creeds was discredited, and progress seemed for the moment to mean, not the growth of the spirit of man, but an effect of the survival of the fittest brought about by the destruction of the unfit, all the most frightful examples of this systematic destruction being thrust into the utmost prominence by those who were fighting the Church with Mill's favorite dialectical weapon, the incompatibility of divine omnipotence with divine benevolence. His plays are full of an overwhelming sense of the necessity for rousing ourselves into self-assertion against this numbing fatalism; and yet he certainly had not at this time freed his intellect from an acceptance of its scientific validity as our Samuel Butler did, though Butler was more like Ibsen than any man in Europe, having the same grim hoaxing humor, the same grip of spiritual realities behind material facts, the same toughness of character holding him unshaken against the world.

Butler revelled in Darwinism for six weeks, and then grasping the whole scope and the whole horror of it, warned us (we did not listen until we had revelled for half a century) that Darwin had "banished mind from the universe," meaning from Evolution. Ibsen, belonging to an earlier generation, and intellectually nursed on northern romance and mysticism rather than on the merely industrious and prosaic science of the interval between the discovery of Evolution at the end of the eighteenth century and the discovery and overrating of Natural Selection as a method of evolution in the middle of the nineteenth, was, when Darwin arrived, past the age at which Natural Selection could have swept him away as it swept Butler and his contemporaries. But, like them, he seems to have welcomed it for the mortal blow it dealt to the current travesties of Christianity, which were really only reductions of the relations between man and God to the basis of the prevalent Commercialism, shewing how God may be cheated, and how salvation can be got for nothing through the blood of Christ by sweaters, adulterators, quacks, sharks, and hypocrites; also how God, though the most dangerously capricious and short-tempered of Anarchists, is also the most sentimental of dupes. It is against this conception of God as a sentimental dupe that Brand rages. Ibsen evidently regarded the brimstone conception, "the Almighty Fiend" of Shelley, as not worth his powder and shot, partly, no doubt, because he knew that the Almighty Fiend's votaries would never read or understand his works, and partly because the class he addressed, the cultured class, had thrown off that superstition, and were busy with the sentimental religion of love in which we are still wallowing, and which only substitutes twaddle for terror.

At first sight this may seem an improvement; but it is no defence against that fear of man which is so much more mischievous than the fear of God. The cruelty of Natural Selection was a powerful antidote to such sentimentalism; and Ibsen, who was perhaps no expert in recent theories of evolution, was quite ready to rub it in uncritically for the sake of its value as a tonic. Indeed, as a fearless observer of the cruelty of Nature, he was quite independent of Darwin: what we find in his works is an unmistakable Darwinian atmosphere, but not the actual Darwinian discoveries and technical theory. If Natural Selection, the gloomiest and most formidable of the castles of Giant Despair, had stopped him, he would no doubt, like Butler, have set himself deliberately to play Greatheart and reduce it; but his genius pushed him past it and left it to be demolished philosophically by Butler, and practically by the mere march of the working class, which, by its freedom from the economic bias of the middle classes, has escaped their characteristic illusions, and solved many of the enigmas they found insoluble because they did not wish to have them solved. For instance, according to the theory of Natural Selection, progress can take place only through an increase in the severity of the material conditions of existence; and as the working classes were quite determined that progress should consist of just the opposite, they had no difficulty in seeing that it generally does occur in that way, whereas the middle class wished, on the contrary, to be convinced that the poverty of the working classes and all the hideous evils attending it were inevitable conditions of progress, and that every penny in the pound on the rates spent in social amelioration, and every attempt on the part of the workers to raise their wages by Trade Unionism or otherwise, were vain defiances of biologic and economic science.

How far Ibsen was definitely conscious of all this is doubtful; but one of his most famous utterances pointed to the working class and the women as the great emancipators. His prophetic belief in the spontaneous growth of the will made him a meliorist without reference to the operation of Natural Selection; but his impression of the light thrown by physical and biological science on the facts of life seems to have been the gloomy one of the middle of the nineteenth century. External nature often plays her most ruthless and destructive part in his works, which have an extraordinary fascination for the pessimists of that period, in spite of the incompatibility of his individualism with that mechanical utilitarian ethic of theirs which treats Man as the sport of every circumstance, and ignores his will altogether.

Another inessential but very prominent feature in Ibsen's dramas will be understood easily by anyone who has observed how a change of religious faith intensifies our concern about our own salvation. An ideal, pious or secular, is practically used as a standard of conduct; and whilst it remains unquestioned, the simple rule of right is to conform to it. In the theological stage, when the Bible is accepted as the revelation of God's will, the pious man, when in doubt as to whether he is acting rightly or wrongly, quiets his misgivings by searching the Scripture until he finds a text which endorses his action.[1] The rationalist, for whom the Bible has no authority, brings his conduct to such tests as asking himself, after Kant, how it would be if everyone did as he proposes to do; or by calculating the effect of his action on the greatest happiness of the greatest number; or by judging whether the liberty of action he is claiming infringes the equal liberty of others, etc. etc. Most men are ingenious enough to pass examinations of this kind successfully in respect to everything they really want to do. But in periods of transition, as, for instance, when faith in the infallibility of the Bible is shattered, and faith in that of reason not yet perfected, men's uncertainty as to the rightness and wrongness of their actions keeps them in a continual perplexity, amid which casuistry seems the most important branch of intellectual activity. Life, as depicted by Ibsen, is very full of it. We find the great double drama of Emperor and Galilean occupied at first with Julian's case regarded as a case of conscience. It is compared, in the manner already described, with the cases of Cain and Judas, the three men being introduced as "corner stones under the wrath of necessity," "great freedmen under necessity," and so forth. The qualms of Julian are theatrically effective in producing the most exciting suspense as to whether he will dare to choose between Christ and the imperial purple; but the mere exhibition of a man struggling between his ambition and his creed belongs to a phase of intellectual interest which Ibsen had passed even before the production of Brand, when he wrote his Kongs Emnerne (The Pretenders). Emperor and Galilean might have been appropriately, if prosaically, named The Mistake of Maximus the Mystic. It is Maximus who forces the choice on Julian, not as between ambition and principle; between Paganism and Christianity; between "the old beauty that is no longer beautiful and the new truth that

[1] As such misgivings seldom arise except when the conscience revolts against the contemplated action, an appeal to Scripture to justify a point of conduct is generally found in practice to be an attempt to excuse a crime.

is no longer true," but between Christ and Julian himself. Maximus knows that there is no going back to "the first empire" of pagan sensualism. "The second empire," Christian or self-abnegatory idealism, is already rotten at heart. "The third empire" is what he looks for: the empire of Man asserting the eternal validity of his own will. He who can see that not on Olympus, not nailed to the cross, but in himself is God: he is the man to build Brand's bridge between the flesh and the spirit, establishing this third empire in which the spirit shall not be unknown, nor the flesh starved, nor the will tortured and baffled. Thus throughout the first part of the double drama we have Julian prompted step by step to the stupendous conviction that he no less than the Galilean is God. His final resolution to seize the throne is expressed in his interruption of the Lord's prayer, which he hears intoned by worshippers in church as he wrestles in the gloom of the catacombs with his own fears and the entreaties and threats of his soldiers urging him to take the final decisive step. At the cue "Lead us not into temptation; but deliver us from evil" he rushes to the church with his soldiers, exclaiming "For mine is the kingdom." Yet he halts on the threshold, dazzled by the light, as his follower Sallust points the declaration by adding, "and the power, and the glory."

Once on the throne Julian becomes a mere pedant-tyrant, trying to revive Paganism mechanically by cruel enforcement of external conformity to its rites. In his moments of exaltation he half grasps the meaning of Maximus, only to relapse presently and pervert it into a grotesque mixture of superstition and monstrous vanity. We have him making such speeches as this, worthy of Peer Gynt at his most ludicrous: "Has not Plato long ago enunciated the truth that only a god can rule over men? What did he mean by that saying? Answer me: what did he mean? Far be it from me to assert that Plato, incomparable sage though he was, had any individual, even the greatest, in his prophetic eye," etc. In this frame of mind Christ appears to him, not as the prototype of himself, as Maximus would have him feel, but as a rival god over whom he must prevail at all costs. It galls him to think that the Galilean still reigns in the hearts of men whilst the emperor can only extort lip honor from them by brute force; for in his wildest excesses of egotism he never so loses his saving sense of the realities of things as to mistake the trophies of persecution for the fruits of faith. "Tell me who shall conquer," he demands of Maximus: "the emperor or the Galilean?"

"Both the emperor and the Galilean shall succumb," says Maximus. "Whether in our time or in hundreds of years I know not; but so it shall be when the right man comes."

"Who is the right man?" says Julian.

"He who shall swallow up both emperor and Galilean,"[1] replies the seer. "Both shall succumb; but you shall not therefore perish. Does not the child succumb in the youth and the youth in the man: yet neither child nor youth perishes. You know I have never approved of your policy as emperor. You have tried to make the youth a child again. The empire of the flesh is fallen a prey to the empire of the spirit. But the empire of the spirit is not final, any more than the youth is. You have tried to hinder the youth from growing: from becoming a man. Oh fool, who have drawn your sword against that which is to be: against the third empire, in which the twin-natured shall reign. For him the Jews have a name. They call him Messiah, and are waiting for him."

Still Julian stumbles on the threshold of the idea without entering into it. He is galled out of all comprehension by the rivalry of the Galilean, and asks despairingly who shall break his power. Then Maximus drives the lesson home.

MAXIMUS. Is it not written, "Thou shalt have none other gods but me"?

JULIAN. Yes—yes—yes.

MAXIMUS. The seer of Nazareth did not preach this god or that: he said "God is I: I am God."

JULIAN. And that is what makes the emperor powerless? The third empire? The Messiah? Not the Jews' Messiah,

[1] Or, as we should now say, the Superman. (1912).

but the Messiah of the two empires, the spirit and the world?

MAXIMUS. The God-Emperor.

JULIAN. The Emperor-God.

MAXIMUS. Logos in Pan, Pan in Logos.

JULIAN. How is he begotten?

MAXIMUS. He is self-begotten in the man who wills.

But it is of no use. Maximus's idea is a synthesis of relations in which not only is Christ God in exactly the same sense as that in which Julian is God, but Julian is Christ as well. The persistence of Julian's jealousy of the Galilean shews that he has not comprehended the synthesis at all, but only seized on that part of it which flatters his own egotism. And since this part is only valid as a constituent of the synthesis, and has no reality when isolated from it, it cannot by itself convince Julian. In vain does Maximus repeat his lesson in every sort of parable, and in such pregnant questions as "How do you know, Julian, that you were not in him whom you now persecute?" He can only wreak him to utter commands to the winds, and to exclaim, in the excitement of burning his fleet on the borders of Persia, "The third empire is here, Maximus. I feel that the Messiah of the earth lives within me. The spirit has become flesh and the flesh spirit. All creation lies within my will and power. More than the fleet is burning. In that glowing, swirling pyre the crucified Galilean is burning to ashes; and the earthly emperor is burning with the Galilean. But from the ashes shall arise, phœnix-like, the God of earth and the Emperor of the spirit in one, in one, in one." At which point he is informed that a Persian refugee, whose information has emboldened him to burn his ships, has fled from the camp and is a manifest spy. From that moment he is a broken man. In his next and last emergency, when the Persians fall upon his camp, his first desperate exclamation is a vow to sacrifice to the gods. "To what gods, oh fool?" cries Maximus. "Where are they; and what are they?" "I will sacrifice to this god and that god: I will sacrifice to many," he answers desperately.

"One or other must surely hear me. *I must call on something without me and above me*." A flash of lightning seems to him a response from above; and with this encouragement he throws himself into the fight, clinging, like Macbeth, to an ambiguous oracle which leads him to suppose that only in the Phrygian regions need he fear defeat. He imagines he sees the Nazarene in the ranks of the enemy; and in fighting madly to reach him he is struck down, in the name of Christ, by one of his own soldiers. Then his one Christian General, Jovian, calls on his "believing brethren" to give Cæsar what is Cæsar's. Declaring that the heavens are open and the angels coming to the rescue with their swords of fire, he rallies the Galileans of whom Julian has made slave-soldiers. The pagan free legions, crying out that the god of the Galileans is on the Roman side, and that he is the strongest, follow Jovian as he charges the enemy, who fly in all directions whilst Julian, sinking back from a vain effort to rise, exclaims, "Thou hast conquered, O Galilean."

Julian dies quietly in his tent, averring, in reply to a Christian friend's inquiry, that he has nothing to repent of. "The power which circumstances placed in my hands," he says, "and which is an emanation of divinity, I am conscious of having used to the best of my skill. I have never wittingly wronged anyone. If some should think that I have not fulfilled all expectations, they should in justice reflect that there is a mysterious power outside us, which in a great measure governs the issue of human undertakings." He still does not see eye to eye with Maximus, though there is a flash of insight in his remark to him, when he learns that the village where he fell is called the Phrygian region, that "the world-will has laid an ambush for him." It was something for Julian to have seen that the power which he found stronger than his individual will was itself will; but inasmuch as he conceived it, not as the whole of which his will was but a part, but as a rival will, he was not the man to found the third empire. He had felt the godhead in himself, but not in others. Being only able to say, with half conviction, "The kingdom of heaven is within ME," he had been utterly vanquished by the Galilean who had been able to say, "The kingdom of heaven is within YOU." But he was on the way to that full truth. A man cannot believe in others until he believes in himself; for his conviction of the equal worth of his fellows must be filled by the overflow of his conviction of his own worth. Against the spurious Christianity of asceticism, starving that indispensable prior conviction, Julian rightly rebelled; and Maximus rightly incited him to rebel. But Maximus could not fill the prior conviction even to fulness, much less to overflowing; for the third empire was not yet, and is not yet.

However, the tyrant dies with a peaceful conscience; and Maximus is able to tell the priest at the bedside that the world-will will answer for Julian's soul. What troubles the mystic is his having misled Julian by encouraging him to bring upon himself the fate of Cain and Judas. As water can be boiled by fire, man can be prompted and stimulated from without to assert his individuality; but just as no boiling can fill a half-empty well, no external stimulus can enlarge the spirit of man to the point at which he can self-beget the Emperor-God in himself by willing. At that point "to will is to have to will"; and it is with these words on his lips that Maximus leaves the stage, still sure that the third empire is to come.

It is not necessary to translate the scheme of Emperor and Galilean into terms of the antithesis between idealism and realism. Julian, in this respect, is a reincarnation of Peer Gynt. All the difference is that the subject which was instinctively projected in the earlier poem, is intellectually constructed in the later history, Julian plus Maximus the Mystic being Peer plus one who understands him better than Ibsen did when he created him.

The interest for us of Ibsen's interpretation of original Christianity is obvious. The deepest sayings recorded in the gospels are now nothing but eccentric paradoxes to most of those who reject the supernatural view of Christ's divinity.

Those who accept that view often consider that such acceptance absolves them from attaching any sensible meaning to his words at all, and so might as well pin their faith to a stock or stone. Of these attitudes the first is superficial, and the second stupid. Ibsen's interpretation, whatever may be its validity, will certainly hold the field long after the current "Crosstianity," as it has been aptly called, becomes unthinkable.

THE OBJECTIVE ANTI-IDEALIST PLAYS

IBSEN had now written three immense dramas, all dealing with the effect of idealism on individual egotists of exceptional imaginative excitability. This he was able to do whilst his intellectual consciousness of his theme was yet incomplete, by simply portraying sides of himself. He has put himself into the skin of Brand and Peer Gynt. He has divided himself between Maximus and Julian. These figures have accordingly a certain direct vitality which we shall find in none of his later male figures until it reappears under the shadow of death, less as vitality than as mortality putting on immortality, in the four great plays with which he closed and crowned his life's work. There are flashes of it in Relling, in Lövborg, in Ellida's stranger from the sea; but they are only flashes: henceforth for many years, indeed until his warfare against vulgar idealism is accomplished and a new phase entered upon in The Master Builder, all his really vivid and solar figures are women. For, having at last completed his intellectual analysis of idealism, he could now construct methodical illustrations of its social working, instead of, as before, blindly projecting imaginary personal experiences which he himself had not yet succeeded in interpreting. Further, now that he understood the matter, he could see plainly the effect of idealism as a social force on people quite unlike himself: that is to say, on everyday people in everyday life: on shipbuilders, bank managers, parsons, and doctors, as well as on saints, romantic adventurers, and emperors.

With his eyes thus opened, instances of the mischief of idealism crowded upon him so rapidly that he began deliberately to inculcate their lesson by writing realistic prose plays of modern life, abandoning all production of art for art's sake His skill as a playwright and his genius as an artist were thenceforth used only to secure attention and effectiveness for his detailed attack on idealism. No more verse, no more tragedy for the sake of tears or comedy for the sake of laughter, no more seeking to produce specimens of art forms in order that literary critics might fill the public belly with the east wind. The critics, it is true, soon declared that he had ceased to be an artist; but he, having something else to do with his talent than to fulfil critics' definitions, took no notice of them, not thinking their ideal sufficiently important to write a play about.

THE LEAGUE OF YOUTH 1869

The first of the series of realistic prose plays is called Pillars of Society; but before describing this, a word must be said about a previous work which seems to have determined the form the later series took. Between Peer Gynt and Emperor and Galilean, Ibsen had let fall an amusing comedy called The League of Youth (*De Unges Forbund*) in which the imaginative egotist reappears farcically as an ambitious young lawyer-politician who, smarting under a snub from a local landowner and county magnate, relieves his feelings with such a passionate explosion of Radical eloquence that he is cheered to the echo by the progressive party. Intoxicated with this success, he imagines himself a great leader of the people and a wielder of the mighty engine of democracy. He narrates to a friend a dream in which he saw kings swept helplessly over the surface of the earth by a mighty wind. He has hardly achieved this impromptu when he receives an invitation to dine with the local magnate, whose friends, to spare his feelings, have misled him as to the person aimed at in the new demagogue's speech. The invitation sets the egotist's imagination on the opposite tack: he is presently pouring forth his soul in the magnate's drawing-room to the very friend to whom he related the great dream.

"My goal is this: in the course of time I shall get into Parliament, perhaps into the Ministry, and marry happily into a rich and honorable family. I intend to reach it by my own exertions. I must and shall reach it without help from anyone. Meanwhile I shall enjoy life here, drinking in beauty and sunshine. Here there are fine manners: life moves gracefully here: the very floors seem laid to be trodden only by lacquered shoes: the arm chairs are deep; and the ladies sink exquisitely into them. Here the conversation goes lightly and elegantly, like a game at battledore; and no blunders come plumping in to make an awkward silence. Here I feel for the first time what distinction means. Yes: we have indeed an aristocracy of culture; and to it I will belong. Dont you yourself feel the refining influence of the place," etc., etc.

For the rest, the play is an ingenious comedy of intrigue, clever enough in its mechanical construction to entitle the French to claim that Ibsen owes something to his technical education as a playwright in the school of Scribe. One or two episodes are germs of later plays; and the suitability of the realistic prose comedy form to these episodes no doubt confirmed Ibsen in his choice of it.

PILLARS OF SOCIETY 1877

Pillars of Society is the history of one Karsten Bernick, a "pillar of society" who, in pursuance of the duty of maintaining the respectability of his father's firm of shipbuilders, has averted a disgraceful exposure by allowing another man to bear the discredit not only of a love affair in which he himself had been the sinner, but of a theft which was never committed at all, having been merely alleged as an excuse for the firm being out of funds at a critical period. Bernick is an abject slave to the idealizings of one Rörlund, a schoolmaster, about respectability, duty to society, good example, social influence, health of the community, and so on. When Bernick falls in love with a married actress, he feels that no man has a right to shock the feelings of Rörlund and the community for his own selfish gratification. However, a clandestine intrigue will shock nobody, since nobody need know of it. He accordingly adopts this method of satisfying himself and preserving the moral tone of the community at the same time. Unluckily, the intrigue is all but discovered; and Bernick has either to see the moral security of the community shaken to its foundations by the terrible scandal of his exposure, or else to deny what he did and put it on another man. As the other man happens to be going to America, where he can easily conceal his imputed shame, Bernick's conscience tells him that it would be little short of a crime against society to neglect such an opportunity; and he accordingly lies his way back into the good opinion of Rörlund and Company at the emigrant's expense.

There are three women in the play for whom the schoolmaster's ideals have no attractions. First, there is the actress's daughter, who wants to get to America because she hears that people there are not good; for she is heartily tired of good people, since it is part of their goodness to look down on her because of her mother's disgrace. The schoolmaster, to whom she is engaged, condescends to her for the same reason. The second has already sacrificed her happiness and wasted her life in conforming to the Rörlund ideal of womanliness; and she earnestly advises the younger woman not to commit that folly, but to break her engagement with the schoolmaster, and elope promptly with the man she loves. The third is a naturally free woman who has snapped her fingers at the current ideals all her life; and it is her presence that at last encourages the liar to break with the ideals by publicly telling the truth about himself.

The comic personage of the piece is a useless hypochondriac whose function in life, as described by himself, is "to hold up the banner of the ideal." This he does by sneering at everything and everybody for not resembling the heroic incidents and characters he reads about in novels and tales of adventure. But his obvious peevishness and folly make him much less dangerous than the pious idealist, the earnest and respectable Rörlund. The play concludes with Bernick's admission that the spirits of Truth and Freedom are the true pillars of society, a phrase which sounds so like an idealistic commonplace that it is necessary to add that Truth in this passage does not mean the nursery convention of truth-telling satirized by Ibsen himself in a later play, as well as by Labiche and other comic dramatists. It means the unflinching recognition of facts, and the abandonment of the conspiracy to ignore such of them as do not bolster up the ideals. The idealist rule as to truth dictates the recognition only of those facts or idealistic masks of facts which have a respectable air, and the mentioning of these on all occasions and at all hazards. Ibsen urges the recognition of all facts; but as to mentioning them, he wrote a whole play, as we shall see presently, to shew that you must do that at your own peril, and that a truth-teller who cannot hold his tongue on occasion may do as much mischief as a whole universityful of trained liars. The word Freedom means freedom from the tyranny of the Rörlund ideals.

A DOLL'S HOUSE 1879

Unfortunately, Pillars of Society, as a propagandist play, is disabled by the circumstance that the hero, being a fraudulent hypocrite in the ordinary police-court sense of the phrase, would hardly be accepted as a typical pillar of society by the class he represents. Accordingly, Ibsen took care next time to make his idealist irreproachable from the standpoint of the ordinary idealist morality. In the famous Doll's House, the pillar of society who owns the doll is a model husband, father, and citizen. In his little household, with the three darling children and the affectionate little wife, all on the most loving terms with one another, we have the sweet home, the womanly woman, the happy family life of the idealist's dream. Mrs Nora Helmer is happy in the belief that she has attained a valid realization of all these illusions; that she is an ideal wife and mother; and that Helmer is an ideal husband who would, if the necessity arose, give his life to save her reputation. A few simply contrived incidents disabuse her effectually on all these points. One of her earliest acts of devotion to her husband has been the secret raising of a sum of money to enable him to make a tour which was necessary to restore his health. As he would have broken down sooner than go into debt, she has had to persuade him that the money was a gift from her father. It was really obtained from a moneylender, who refused to make her the loan unless she induced her father to endorse the promissory note. This being impossible, as her father was dying at the time, she took the shortest way out of the difficulty by writing the name herself, to the entire satisfaction of the moneylender, who, though not at all duped, knew that forged bills are often the surest to be paid. Since then she has slaved in secret at scrivener's work until she has nearly paid off the debt.

At this point Helmer is made manager of the bank in which he is employed; and the moneylender, wishing to obtain a post there, uses the forged bill to force Nora to exert her influence with Helmer on his behalf. But she, having a hearty contempt for the man, cannot be persuaded by him that there was any harm in putting her father's name on the bill, and ridicules the suggestion that the law would not recognize that she was right under the circumstances. It is her husband's own contemptuous denunciation of a forgery formerly committed by the moneylender himself that destroys her self-satisfaction and opens her eyes to her ignorance of the serious business of the world to which her husband belongs: the world outside the home he shares with her. When he goes on to tell her that commercial dishonesty is generally to be traced to the influence of bad mothers, she begins to perceive that the happy way in which she plays with the children, and the care she takes to dress them nicely, are not sufficient to constitute her a fit person to train them. To redeem the forged bill, she resolves to borrow the balance due upon it from an intimate friend of the family. She has learnt to coax her husband into giving her what she asks by appealing to his affection for her: that is, by playing all sorts of pretty tricks until he is wheedled into an amorous humor. This plan she has adopted without thinking about it, instinctively taking the line of least resistance with him. And now she naturally takes the same line with her husband's friend. An unexpected declaration of love from him is the result; and it at once explains to her the real nature of the domestic influence she has been so proud of.

All her illusions about herself are now shattered. She sees herself as an ignorant and silly woman, a dangerous mother, and a wife kept for her husband's pleasure merely; but she clings all the harder to her illusion about him: he is still the ideal husband who would make any sacrifice to rescue her from ruin. She resolves to kill herself rather than allow him to destroy his own career by taking the forgery on himself to save her reputation. The final disillusion comes when he, instead of at once proposing to pursue this ideal line of conduct when he hears of the forgery, naturally enough flies into a vulgar rage and heaps invective on her for disgracing him. Then she sees that their whole family life has been a fiction: their home a mere doll's house in which they have been playing at ideal husband and father, wife and mother. So she leaves him then and there and goes out into the real world to find out its reality for herself, and to gain some position not fundamentally false, refusing to see her children again until she is fit to be in charge of them, or to live with him until she and he become capable of a more honorable relation to one another. He at first cannot understand what has happened, and flourishes the shattered ideals over her as if they were as potent as ever. He presents the course most agreeable to him —that of her staying at home and avoiding a scandal—as her duty to her husband, to her children, and to her religion; but the magic of these disguises is gone; and at last even he understands what has really happened, and sits down alone to wonder whether that more honorable relation can ever come to pass between them.

GHOSTS 1881

In his next play, Ibsen returned to the charge with such an uncompromising and outspoken attack on marriage as a useless sacrifice of human beings to an ideal, that his meaning was obscured by its very obviousness. Ghosts, as it is called, is the story of a woman who has faithfully acted as a model wife and mother, sacrificing herself at every point with selfless thoroughness. Her husband is a man with a huge capacity and appetite for sensuous enjoyment. Society, prescribing ideal duties and not enjoyment for him, drives him to enjoy himself in underhand and illicit ways. When he marries his model wife, her devotion to duty only makes life harder for him; and he at last takes refuge in the caresses of an undutiful but pleasure-loving housemaid, and leaves his wife to satisfy her conscience by managing his business affairs whilst he satisfies his cravings as best he can by reading novels, drinking, and flirting, as aforesaid, with the servants. At this point even those who are most indignant with Nora Helmer for walking out of the doll's house must admit that Mrs Alving would be justified in walking out of *her* house. But Ibsen is determined to shew you what comes of the scrupulous line of conduct you were so angry with Nora for not pursuing. Mrs Alving feels that her place is by her husband for better for worse, and by her child. Now the ideal of wifely and womanly duty which demands this from her also demands that she shall regard herself as an outraged wife, and her husband as a scoundrel. And the family ideal calls upon her to suffer in silence lest she shatter her innocent son's faith in the purity of home life by letting him know the disreputable truth about his father. It is her duty to conceal that truth from the world and from him. In this she falters for one moment only. Her marriage has not been a love match: she has, in pursuance of her duty as a daughter, contracted it for the sake of her family, although her heart inclined to a highly respectable clergyman, a professor of her own idealism, named Manders. In the humiliation of her first discovery of her husband's infidelity, she leaves the house and takes refuge with Manders; but he at once leads her back to the path of duty, from which she does not again swerve. With the utmost devotion she now carries out an elaborate scheme of lying and imposture. She so manages her husband's affairs and so shields his good name that everybody believes him to be a public-spirited citizen of the strictest conformity to current ideals of respectability and family life. She sits up of nights listening to his lewd and silly conversation, and even drinking with him, to keep him from going into the streets and being detected by the neighbors in what she considers his vices. She provides for the servant he has seduced, and brings up his illegitimate daughter as a maid in her own household. And, as a crowning sacrifice, she sends her son away to Paris to be educated there, knowing that if he stays at home the shattering of his ideals must come sooner or later.

Her work is crowned with success. She gains the esteem of her old love the clergyman, who is never tired of holding up her household as a beautiful realization of the Christian ideal of marriage. Her own martyrdom is brought to an end at last by the death of her husband in the odor of a most sanctified reputation, leaving her free to recall her son from Paris and enjoy his society, and his love and gratitude, in the flower of his early manhood.

But when her son comes home, the facts refuse as obstinately as ever to correspond to her ideals. Oswald has inherited his father's love of enjoyment; and when, in dull rainy weather, he returns from Paris to the solemn strictly ordered house where virtue and duty have had their temple for so many years, his mother sees him shew the unmistakable signs of boredom with which she is so miserably familiar from of old; then sit after dinner killing time over the bottle; and finally—the climax of anguish—begin to flirt with the maid who, as his mother alone knows, is his own father's daughter. But there is this worldwide difference in her insight to the cases of the father and the son. She did not love the father: she loves the son with the intensity of a heart-starved woman who has nothing else left to love. Instead of recoiling from him with pious disgust and Pharisaical consciousness of moral superiority, she sees at once that he has a right to be happy in his own way, and that she has no right to force him to be dutiful and wretched in hers. She sees, too, her injustice to the unfortunate father, and the cowardice of the monstrous fabric of lies and false appearances she has wasted her life in manufacturing. She resolves that the son's life shall not be sacrificed to ideals which are to him joyless and unnatural. But she finds that the work of the ideals is not to be undone quite so easily. In driving the father to steal his pleasures in secrecy and squalor, they had brought upon him the diseases bred by such conditions; and her son now tells her that those diseases have left their mark on him, and that he carries poison in his pocket against the time, foretold to him by a Parisian surgeon, when general paralysis of the insane may destroy his faculties. In desperation she undertakes to rescue him from this horrible apprehension by making his life happy. The house shall be made as bright as Paris for him: he shall have as much champagne as he wishes until he is no longer driven to that dangerous resource by the dulness of his life with her: if he loves the girl he shall marry her if she were fifty times his half-sister. But the half-sister, on learning the state of his health, leaves the house; for she, too, is her father's daughter, and is not going to sacrifice her life in devotion to an invalid. When the mother and son are left alone in their dreary home, with the rain still falling outside, all she can do for him is to promise that if his doom overtakes him before he can poison himself, she will make a final sacrifice of her natural feelings by performing that dreadful duty, the first of all her duties that has any real basis. Then the weather clears up at last; and the sun, which the young man has so longed to see, appears. He asks her to give it to him to play with; and a glance at him shews her that the ideals have claimed their victim, and that the time has come for her to save him from a real horror by sending him from her out of the world, just as she saved him from an imaginary one years before by sending him out of Norway.

This last scene of Ghosts is so appallingly tragic that the emotions it excites prevent the meaning of the play from being seized and discussed like that of A Doll's House. In England nobody, as far as I know, seems to have perceived that Ghosts is to A Doll's House what the late Sir Walter

Besant intended his own sequel[1] to that play to be. Besant attempted to shew what might come of Nora's repudiation of that idealism of which he was one of the most popular professors. But the effect made on Besant by A Doll's House was very faint compared to that produced on the English critics by the first performance of Ghosts in this country. In the earlier part of this essay I have shewn that since Mrs Alving's early conceptions of duty are as valid to ordinary critics as to Pastor Manders, who must appear to them as an admirable man, endowed with Helmer's good sense without Helmer's selfishness, a pretty general disapproval of the moral of the play was inevitable. Fortunately, the newspaper press went to such bedlamite lengths on this occasion that Mr William Archer, the well-known dramatic critic and translator of Ibsen, was able to put the whole body of hostile criticism out of court by simply quoting its excesses in an article entitled Ghosts and Gibberings, which appeared in The Pall Mall Gazette of the 8th of April 1891. Mr Archer's extracts, which he offers as a nucleus for a Dictionary of Abuse modelled upon the Wagner *Schimpf-Lexicon*, are worth reprinting here as samples of contemporary idealist

[1] A forgotten production, published in the English Illustrated Magazine for January 1890. Besant makes the moneylender, as a reformed man, and a pattern of all the virtues, hold a forged bill *in terrorem* over Nora's grown-up daughter, engaged to his son. The bill has been forged by her brother, who has inherited a tendency to forge from his mother. Helmer having taken to drink after the departure of his wife, and forfeited his social position, the moneylender tells the girl that if she persists in disgracing him by marrying his son, he will send her brother to gaol. She evades the dilemma by drowning herself. The moral is that if Nora had never run away from her husband her daughter would never have drowned herself. Note that the moneylender does over again what he did in Ibsen's play, with the difference that, having become eminently respectable, he has also become a remorseless scoundrel. Ibsen shews him as a good-natured fellow at bottom. I wrote a sequel to this sequel. Another sequel was written by Eleanor, the youngest daughter of Karl Marx. I forget where they appeared.

criticism of the drama.

DESCRIPTIONS OF THE PLAY

"Ibsen's positively abominable play entitled Ghosts... This disgusting representation... Reprobation due to such as aim at infecting the modern theatre with poison after desperately inoculating themselves and others... An open drain; a loathsome sore unbandaged; a dirty act done publicly; a lazar-house with all its doors and windows open... Candid foulness. . . Kotzebue turned bestial and cynical. Offensive cynicism... Ibsen's melancholy and malodorous world... Absolutely loathsome and fetid... Gross, almost putrid indecorum... Literary carrion. . . Crapulous stuff. . . Novel and perilous nuisance." *Daily Telegraph* [leading article]. "This mass of vulgarity, egotism, coarseness, and absurdity." *Daily Telegraph* [criticism]. "Unutterably offensive. . . Prosecution under Lord Campbell's Act. . . Abominable piece... Scandalous." *Standard*. "Naked loathsomeness... Most dismal and repulsive production." *Daily News*. "Revoltingly suggestive and blasphemous... Characters either contradictory in themselves, uninteresting or abhorrent." *Daily Chronicle*. "A repulsive and degrading work." *Queen*. "Morbid, unhealthy, unwholesome and disgusting story. . . A piece to bring the stage into disrepute and dishonour with every right-thinking man and woman." *Lloyd's*. "Merely dull dirt long drawn out." *Hawk*. "Morbid horrors of the hideous tale. . . Ponderous dulness of the didactic talk... If any repetition of this outrage be attempted, the authorities will doubtless wake from their lethargy." *Sporting and Dramatic News*. "Just a wicked nightmare." *The Gentlewoman*. "Lugubrious diagnosis of sordid impropriety... Characters are prigs, pedants, and profligates. . . Morbid caricatures. . . Maunderings of nookshotten Norwegians... It is no more of a play than an average Gaiety burlesque." *Black and White*. "Most loathsome of all Ibsen's plays. . . Garbage and offal." *Truth*. "Ibsen's putrid play called Ghosts. . . So loathsome an enterprise." *Academy*. "As foul and filthy a concoction as has ever been allowed to disgrace the boards of an English theatre... Dull and disgusting... Nastiness and malodorousness laid on thickly as with a trowel." *Era*. "Noisome corruption." *Stage*.

DESCRIPTIONS OF IBSEN

"An egotist and a bungler." *Daily Telegraph*. "A crazy fanatic... A crazy, cranky being... Not only consistently dirty but deplorably dull." *Truth*. "The Norwegian pessimist *in petto*" [*sic*]. *Black and White*. "Ugly, nasty, discordant, and downright dull... A gloomy sort of ghoul, bent on groping for horrors by night, and blinking like a stupid old owl when the warm sunlight of the best of life dances into his wrinkled eyes." *Gentlewoman*. "A teacher of the æstheticism of the Lock Hospital." *Saturday Review*.

DESCRIPTIONS OF IBSEN'S ADMIRERS

"Lovers of prurience and dabblers in impropriety who are eager to gratify their illicit tastes under the pretence of art." *Evening Standard*. "Ninety-seven per cent. of the people who go to see Ghosts are nasty-minded people who find the discussion of nasty subjects to their taste in exact proportion to their nastiness." *Sporting and Dramatic News*. "The sexless... The unwomanly woman, the unsexed females, the whole army of unprepossessing cranks in petticoats... Educated and muck-ferreting dogs... Effeminate men and male women... They all of them—men and women alike—know that they are doing not only a nasty but an illegal thing... The Lord Chamberlain left them alone to wallow in Ghosts... Outside a silly clique, there is not the slightest interest in the Scandinavian humbug or all his works... A wave of human folly." *Truth*.[1]

[1] Outrageous as the above extracts now seem, I could make them appear quite moderate by setting beside them the hue and cry raised in New York in 1905 against a play of my own entitled Mrs Warren's Profession. But there was a commercial reason for that. My play exposed what has since become known as the White Slave Traffic: that is, the organization of prostitution as a regular commercial industry yielding huge profits to capital invested in it,

AN ENEMY OF THE PEOPLE 1882

After this, the reader will understand the temper in which Ibsen set about his next play, An Enemy of the People, in which, having done sufficient execution among the ordinary middle-class domestic and social ideals, he puts his finger for a moment on commercial political ideals. The play deals with a local majority of middle-class people who are pecuniarily interested in concealing the fact that the famous baths which attract visitors to their town and customers to their shops and hotels are contaminated by sewage. When an honest doctor insists on exposing this danger, the townspeople immediately disguise themselves ideally. Feeling the disadvantage of appearing in their true character as a conspiracy of interested rogues against an honest man, they pose as Society, as The People, as Democracy, as the solid Liberal Majority, and other imposing abstractions, the doctor, in attacking them, of course being thereby made an

---

directly or indirectly, by "pillars of society." The attack on the play was so corrupt that the newspaper that took the lead in it was heavily fined shortly afterwards for trading in advertisements of the traffic. But the attack on Ghosts was, I believe, really disinterested and sincere on its moral side. No doubt Ibsen was virulently hated by some of the writers quoted, as all great and original artists are hated by contemporary mediocrity, which needs must hate the highest when it sees it. Our own mediocrities would abuse Ibsen as heartily as their fathers did if they were not young enough to have started with an entirely inculcated and unintelligent assumption that he is a classic, like Shakespear and Goethe, and therefore must not be abused and need not be understood. But we have only to compare the frantic and indecent vituperation quoted above with the mere disparagement and dislike expressed towards Ibsen's other plays at the same period to perceive that here Ibsen struck at something much deeper than the fancies of critics as to the proper way to write plays. An ordinary farcical comedy ridiculing Pastor Manders and making Alving out to be a good fellow would have enlisted their sympathy at once, as their tradition was distinctly "Bohemian." Their horror at Ghosts is a striking proof of the worthlessness of mere Bohemianism, which has all the idle sentimentality and idolatry of conventionality without any of its backbone of contract and law. (1912).

enemy of The People, a danger to Society, a traitor to Democracy, an apostate from the great Liberal party, and so on. Only those who take an active part in politics can appreciate the grim fun of the situation, which, though it has an intensely local Norwegian air, will be at once recognized as typical in England, not, perhaps, by the professional literary critics, who are for the most part *fainéants* as far as political life is concerned, but certainly by everyone who has got as far as a seat on the committee of the most obscure Ratepayers' Association.

As An Enemy of the People contains one or two references to Democracy which are anything but respectful, it is necessary to examine Ibsen's criticism of it with precision. Democracy is really only an arrangement by which the governed are allowed to choose (as far as any choice is possible, which in capitalistic society is not saying much) the members of the representative bodies which control the executive. It has never been proved that this is the best arrangement; and it has been made effective only to the very limited extent short of which the dissatisfaction which it appeases might take the form of actual violence. Now when men had to submit to kings, they consoled themselves by making it an article of faith that the king was always right, idealizing him as a Pope, in fact. In the same way we who have to submit to majorities set up Voltaire's pope, *Monsieur Tout-le-monde*, and make it blasphemy against Democracy to deny that the majority is always right, although that, as Ibsen says, is a lie. It is a scientific fact that the majority, however eager it may be for the reform of old abuses, is always wrong in its opinion of new developments, or rather is always unfit for them (for it can hardly be said to be wrong in opposing developments for which it is not yet fit). The pioneer is a tiny minority of the force he heads; and so, though it is easy to be in a minority and yet be wrong, it is absolutely impossible to be in the majority and yet be right as to the newest social prospects. We should never progress at all if it were possible for each of us to stand still on democratic principles until we saw whither all the rest were moving, as our statesmen declare themselves bound to do when they are called upon to lead. Whatever clatter we may make for a time with our filing through feudal serf collars and kicking off old mercantilist fetters, we shall never march a step forward except at the heels of "the strongest man, he who is able to stand alone" and to turn his back on "the damned compact Liberal majority." All of which is no disparagement of parliaments and adult suffrage, but simply a wholesome reduction of them to their real place in the social economy as pure machinery: machinery which has absolutely no principles except the principles of mechanics, and no motive power in itself whatsoever. The idealization of public organizations is as dangerous as that of kings or priests. We need to be reminded that though there is in the world a vast number of buildings in which a certain ritual is conducted before crowds called congregations by a functionary called a priest, who is subject to a central council controlling all such functionaries on a few points, there is not therefore any such thing in the concrete as the ideal Catholic Church, nor ever was, nor ever will be. There may, too, be a highly elaborate organization of public affairs; but there is no such thing as the ideal State. There may be a combination of persons living by the practice of medicine, surgery, or physical or biological research; or by drawing up wills and leases, and preparing, pleading, or judging cases at law; or by painting pictures, writing books, and acting plays; or by serving in regiments and battle ships; or by manual labor or industrial service. But when any of these combinations, through its organizers or leaders, claims to deliver the Verdict of Science, or to act with the Authority of the Law, or to be as sacred as the Mission of Art, or to revenge criticisms of themselves as outrages on the Honor of His Majesty's Services, or to utter the Voice of Labor, there is urgent need for the guillotine, or whatever may be the mode in vogue of putting presumptuous persons in their proper place. All abstractions invested with collective consciousness or collective authority, set above the individual, and exacting duty from him on pretence of acting or thinking with greater validity than he, are man-eating idols red with human sacrifices.

This position must not be confounded with Anarchism, or the idealization of the repudiation of Governments. Ibsen did not refuse to pay the tax collector, but may be supposed to have regarded him, not as the vicar of an abstraction called THE STATE, but simply as the man sent round by a committee of citizens (mostly fools as far as Maximus the Mystic's Third Empire is concerned) to collect the money for the police or the paving and lighting of the streets.

THE WILD DUCK 1884

After An Enemy of the People, Ibsen, as I have said, left the vulgar ideals for dead, and set about the exposure of those of the choicer spirits, beginning with the incorrigible idealists who had idealized his very self, and were becoming known as Ibsenites. His first move in this direction was such a tragi-comic slaughtering of sham Ibsenism that his astonished victims plaintively declared that The Wild Duck, as the new play was called, was a satire on his former works; whilst the pious, whom he had disappointed so severely by his interpretation of Brand, began to hope that he was coming back repentant to the fold. The household to which we are introduced in The Wild Duck is not, like Mrs Alving's, a handsome one made miserable by superstitious illusions, but a shabby one made happy by romantic illusions. The only member of it who sees it as it really is is the wife, a good-natured Philistine who desires nothing better. The husband, a vain, petted, spoilt dawdler, believes that he is a delicate and high-souled man, devoting his life to redeeming his old father's name from the disgrace brought on it by imprisonment for breach of the forest laws. This redemption he proposes to effect by making himself famous as a great inventor some day when he has the necessary inspiration. Their daughter, a girl in her teens, believes intensely in her father and in the promised invention. The disgraced grandfather cheers himself by drink whenever he can get it; but his chief resource is a wonderful garret full of rabbits and pigeons. The old man has procured a number of second-hand Christmas trees; and with these he has turned the garret into a sort of toy forest, in which he can play at bear hunting, which was one of the sports of his youth and prosperity. The weapons employed in the hunting expeditions are a gun which will not go off, and a pistol which occasionally brings down a rabbit or a pigeon. A crowning touch is given to the illusion by a wild duck, which, however, must not be shot, as it is the special property of the girl, who reads and dreams whilst her mother cooks, washes, sweeps and carries on the photographic work which is supposed to be the business of her husband. Mrs Ekdal does not appreciate Hjalmar's highly strung sensitiveness of character, which is constantly suffering agonizing jars from her vulgarity; but then she does not appreciate that other fact that he is a lazy and idle impostor. Downstairs there is a disgraceful clergyman named Molvik, a hopeless drunkard; but even he respects himself and is tolerated because of a special illusion invented for him by another lodger, Dr Relling, upon whom the lesson of the household above has not been thrown away. Molvik, says the doctor, must break out into drinking fits because he is daimonic, an imposing explanation which completely relieves the reverend gentleman from the imputation of vulgar tippling.

Into this domestic circle there comes a new lodger, an idealist of the most advanced type. He greedily swallows the daimonic theory of the clergyman's drunkenness, and enthusiastically accepts the photographer as the high-souled hero he supposes himself to be; but he is troubled because the relations of the man and his wife do not constitute an ideal marriage. He happens to know that the woman, before her marriage, was the cast-off mistress of his own father; and because she has not told her husband this, he conceives her life as founded on a lie, like that of Bernick in Pillars of Society. He accordingly sets himself to work out the woman's salvation for her, and establish ideally frank relations between the pair, by simply blurting out the truth, and then asking them, with fatuous self-satisfaction, whether they do not feel much the better for it. This wanton piece of mischief has more serious results than a mere domestic scene. The husband is too weak to act on his bluster about outraged honor and the impossibility of his ever living with his wife again; and the woman is merely annoyed with the idealist for telling on her; but the girl takes the matter to heart and shoots herself. The doubt cast on her parentage, with her father's theatrical repudiation of her, destroy her ideal place in the home, and make her a source of discord there; so she sacrifices herself, thereby carrying out the teaching of the idealist mischief-maker, who has talked a good deal to her about the duty and beauty of self-sacrifice, without foreseeing that he might be taken in mortal earnest. The busybody thus finds that people cannot be freed from their failings from without. They must free themselves. When Nora is strong enough to live out of the doll's house, she will go out of it of her own accord if the door stands open; but if before that period you take her by the scruff of the neck and thrust her out, she will only take refuge in the next establishment of the kind that offers to receive her. Woman has thus two enemies to deal with: the old-fashioned one who wants to keep the door locked, and the new-fashioned one who wants to thrust her into the street before she is ready to go. In the cognate case of a hypocrite and liar like Bernick, exposing him is a mere police measure: he is none the less a liar and hypocrite when you have exposed him. If you want to make a sincere and truthful man of him, all you can wisely do is to remove what you can of the external obstacles to his exposing himself, and then wait for the operation of his internal impulse to confess. If he has no such impulse, then you must put up with him as he is. It is useless to make claims on him which he is not yet prepared to meet. Whether, like Brand, we make such claims because to refrain would be to compromise with evil, or, like Gregers Werle, because we think their moral beauty must recommend them at sight to every one, we shall alike incur Relling's impatient assurance that "life would be quite tolerable if we could only get rid of the confounded duns that keep on pestering us in our poverty with the claims of the ideal."

ROSMERSHOLM 1886

Ibsen did not in The Wild Duck exhaust the subject of the danger of forming ideals for other people, and interfering in their lives with a view to enabling them to realize those ideals. Cases far more typical than that of the meddlesome lodger are those of the priest who regards the ennobling of mankind as a sort of trade process of which his cloth gives him a monopoly, and the clever woman who pictures a noble career for the man she loves, and devotes herself to helping him to achieve it. In Rosmersholm, the play with which Ibsen followed up The Wild Duck, there is an unpractical country parson, a gentleman of ancient stock, whose family has been for many years a centre of social influence. The tradition of that influence reinforces his priestly tendency to regard the ennoblement of the world as an external operation to be performed by himself; and the need of such ennoblement is very evident to him; for his nature is a fine one: he looks at the world with some dim prevision of "the third empire." He is married to a woman of passionately affectionate nature, who is very fond of him, but does not regard him as a regenerator of the human race. Indeed she does not share any of his dreams, and only acts as an extinguisher on the sacred fire of his idealism. He, she, her brother Kroll the headmaster, Kroll's wife, and their set, form a select circle of the best people in the place, comfortably orbited in our social system, and quite planetary in ascertained position and unimpeachable respectability. Into the orbit comes presently a wandering star, one Rebecca Gamvik, an unpropertied orphan, who has been allowed to read advanced books, and is a Freethinker and a Radical: things that disqualify a poor woman for admission to the Rosmer world. However, one must live somewhere; and as the Rosmer world is the only one in which an ambitious and cultivated woman can find powerful allies and educated companions, Rebecca, being both ambitious and cultivated, makes herself agreeable to the Rosmer circle with such success that the affectionate and impulsive but unintelligent Mrs Rosmer becomes wildly fond of her, and is not content until she has persuaded her to come and live with them. Rebecca, then a mere adventuress fighting for a foothold in polite society (which has hitherto shewn itself highly indignant at her thrusting herself in where nobody has thought of providing room for her), accepts the offer all the more readily because she has taken the measure of Parson Rosmer, and formed the idea of playing upon his aspirations, and making herself a leader in politics and society by using him as a figurehead.

But now two difficulties arise. First, there is Mrs Rosmer's extinguishing effect on her husband: an effect which convinces Rebecca that nothing can be done with him whilst his wife is in the way. Second—a contingency quite unallowed for in her provident calculations—she finds herself passionately enamored of him. The poor parson, too, falls in love with her; but he does not know it. He turns to the woman who understands him like a sunflower to the sun, and makes her his real friend and companion. The wife feels this soon enough; and he, quite unconscious of it, begins to think that her mind must be affected, since she has become so intensely miserable and hysterical about nothing—nothing that he can see. The truth is that she has come under the curse of Rebecca's ideal: she sees herself standing, a useless obstacle, between her husband and the woman he really loves, the woman who can help him to a glorious career. She cannot even be the mother in the household; for she is childless. Then comes Rebecca, fortified with a finely reasoned theory that Rosmer's future is staked against his wife's life, and says that it is better for all their sakes that she should quit Rosmersholm. She even hints that she must go at once if a grave scandal is to be avoided. Mrs Rosmer, regarding a scandal in Rosmersholm as the most terrible thing that can happen, and seeing that it could be averted by the marriage of Rebecca and Rosmer if she were out of the way, writes a letter secretly to Rosmer's bitterest enemy, the editor of the local Radical paper, a man who has forfeited his moral reputation by an intrigue which Rosmer has pitilessly denounced. In this letter she implores him not to believe or publish any stories that he may hear about Rosmer, to the effect that he is in any way to blame for anything that may happen to her. Then she sets Rosmer free to marry Rebecca, and to realize his ideals, by going out into the garden and throwing herself into the millstream that runs there.

Now follows a period of quiet mourning at Rosmersholm. Everybody except Rosmer suspects that Mrs Rosmer was not mad, and guesses why she committed suicide. Only it would not do to compromise the aristocratic party by treating Rosmer as the Radical editor was treated. So the neighbors shut their eyes and condole with the bereaved clergyman; and the Radical editor holds his tongue because Radicalism is growing respectable, and he hopes, with Rebecca's help, to get Rosmer over to his side presently. Meanwhile the unexpected has again happened to Rebecca. Her passion is worn out; but in the long days of mourning she has found the higher love; and it is now for Rosmer's own sake that she urges him to become a man of action, and brood no more over the dead. When his friends start a Conservative paper and ask him to become editor, she induces him to reply by declaring himself a Radical and Freethinker. To his utter amazement, the result is, not an animated discussion of his views, but just such an attack on his home life and private conduct as he had formerly made on those of the Radical editor. His friends tell him plainly that the compact of silence is broken by his defection, and that there will be no mercy for the traitor to the party. Even the Radical editor not only refuses to publish the fact that his new ally is a Freethinker (which would destroy all his social weight as a Radical recruit), but brings up the dead woman's letter as a proof that the attack is sufficiently well-founded to make it unwise to go too far. Rosmer, who at first had been simply shocked that men whom he had always honored as gentlemen should descend to such hideous calumny, now sees that he really did love Rebecca, and is indeed guilty of his wife's death. His first impulse is to shake off the spectre of the dead woman by marrying Rebecca; but she, knowing that the guilt is hers, puts that temptation behind her and refuses. Then, as he thinks it all over, his dream of ennobling the world slips away from him: such work can only be done by a man conscious of his own innocence. To save him from despair, Rebecca makes a great sacrifice. She "gives him back his innocence" by confessing how she drove his wife to kill herself; and, as the confession is made in the presence of Kroll, she ascribes the whole plot to her ambition, and says not a word of her passion. Rosmer, confounded as he realizes what helpless puppets they have all been in the hands of this clever woman, for the moment misses the point that unscrupulous ambition, though it explains her crime, does not account for her confession. He turns his back on her and leaves the house with Kroll. She quietly packs up her trunk, and is about to vanish from Rosmersholm without another word when he comes back alone to ask why she confessed. She tells him why, offering him her self-sacrifice as a proof that his power of ennobling others was no vain dream, since it is his companionship that has changed her from the selfish adventuress she was to the devoted woman she has just proved herself to be. But he has lost his faith in himself, and cannot believe her. The proof seems to him subtle, artful: he cannot forget that she duped him by flattering this very weakness of his before. Besides, he knows now that it is not true: people are not ennobled from without. She has no more to say; for she can think of no further proof. But he has thought of an unanswerable one. Dare she make all doubt impossible by sacrificing her share in his future in the only absolutely final way: that is, by doing for his sake what his wife did? She asks what would happen if she had the heart and the will to do it. "Then," he replies, "I should have to believe in you. I should recover my faith in my mission. Faith in my power to ennoble human souls. Faith in the human soul's power to attain nobility." "You shall have your faith again," she answers. At this pass the inner truth of the situation comes out; and the thin veil of a demand for proof, with its monstrous sequel of asking the woman to kill herself in order to restore the man's good opinion of himself, falls away. What is really driving Rosmer is the superstition of expiation by sacrifice. He sees that when Rebecca goes into the millstream he must go too. And he speaks his real mind in the words, "There is no judge over us: therefore we must do justice upon ourselves." But the woman's soul is free of this to the end; for when she says, "I am under the power of the Rosmersholm view of life *now*. What I have sinned it is fit I should expiate," we feel in that speech a protest against the Rosmersholm view of life: the view that denied her right to live and be happy from the first, and now at the end, even in denying its God, exacts her life as a vain blood-offering for its own blindness. The woman has the higher light: she goes to her death out of fellowship with the man who is driven thither by the superstition which has destroyed his will. The story ends with his taking her solemnly as his wife, and casting himself with her into the millstream.

It is unnecessary to repeat here what is said on page 28 as to the vital part played in this drama by the evolution of the lower into the higher love. Peer Gynt, during the prophetic episode in his career, shocks the dancing girl Anitra into a remonstrance by comparing himself to a cat. He replies, with his wisest air, that from the standpoint of love there is perhaps not so much difference between a tomcat and a prophet as she may imagine. The number of critics who have entirely missed the point of Rebecca's transfiguration seems to indicate that the majority of men, even among critics of dramatic poetry, have not got beyond Peer Gynt's opinion in this matter. No doubt they would not endorse it as a definitely stated proposition, aware, as they are, that there is a poetic convention to the contrary. But if they fail to recognize the only possible alternative proposition when it is not only stated in so many words by Rebecca West, but when without it her conduct dramatically contradicts her character—when they even complain of the contradiction as a blemish on the play, I am afraid there can be no further doubt that the extreme perplexity into which the first performance of Rosmersholm in England plunged the Press was due entirely to the prevalence of Peer Gynt's view of love among the dramatic critics.

THE LADY FROM THE SEA 1888

Ibsen's next play, though it deals with the old theme, does not insist on the power of ideals to kill, as the two previous plays do. It rather deals with the origin of ideals in unhappiness, in dissatisfaction with the real. The subject of The Lady from the Sea is the most poetic fancy imaginable. A young woman, brought up on the sea-coast, marries a respectable doctor, a widower, who idolizes her and places her in his household with nothing to do but dream and be made much of by everybody. Even the housekeeping is done by her stepdaughter: she has no responsibility, no care, and no trouble. In other words, she is an idle, helpless, utterly dependent article of luxury. A man turns red at the thought of being such a thing; but he thoughtlessly accepts a pretty and fragile-looking woman in the same position as a charming natural picture. The lady from the sea feels an indefinite want in her life. She reads her want into all other lives, and comes to the conclusion that man once had to choose whether he would be a land animal or a creature of the sea; and that having chosen the land, he has carried about with him ever since a secret sorrow for the element he has forsaken. The dissatisfaction that gnaws her is, as she interprets it, this desperate longing for the sea. When her only child dies and leaves her without the work of a mother to give her a valid place in the world, she yields wholly to her longing, and no longer cares for her husband, who, like Rosmer, begins to fear that she is going mad.

At last a seaman appears and claims her as his wife on the ground that they went years before through a rite which consisted of their marrying the sea by throwing their rings into it. This man, who had to fly from her in the old time because he killed his captain, and who fills her with a sense of dread and mystery, seems to her to embody the mystic attraction the sea has for her. She tells her husband that she must go away with the seaman. Naturally the doctor expostulates—declares that he cannot for her own sake let her do so mad a thing. She replies that he can only prevent her by locking her up, and asks him what satisfaction it will be to him to have her body under lock and key whilst her heart is with the other man. In vain he urges that he will only keep her under restraint until the seaman goes—that he must not, dare not, allow her to ruin herself. Her argument remains unanswerable. The seaman openly declares that she will come; so that the distracted husband asks him does he suppose he can force her from her home. To this the seaman replies that, on the contrary, unless she comes of her own free will there is no satisfaction to him in her coming at all: the unanswerable argument again. She echoes it by demanding her freedom to choose. Her husband must cry off his law-made and Church-made bargain; renounce his claim to the fulfilment of her vows; and leave her free to go back to the sea with her old lover. Then the doctor, with a heavy heart, drops his prate about his heavy responsibility for her actions, and throws the responsibility on her by crying off as she demands. The moment she feels herself a free and responsible woman, all her childish fancies vanish: the seaman becomes simply an old acquaintance whom she no longer cares for; and the doctor's affection produces its natural effect. In short, she says No to the seaman, and takes over the housekeeping keys from her stepdaughter without any further maunderings over that secret sorrow for the abandoned sea.

It should be noted here that Ellida [call her Eleeda], the

Lady from the Sea, seems more fantastic to English readers than to Norwegian ones. The same thing is true of many other characters drawn by Ibsen, notably Peer Gynt, who, if born in England, would certainly not have been a poet and metaphysician as well as a blackguard and a speculator. The extreme type of Norwegian, as depicted by Ibsen, imagines himself doing wonderful things, but does nothing. He dreams as no Englishman dreams, and drinks to make himself dream the more, until his effective will is destroyed, and he becomes a broken-down, disreputable sot, carrying about the tradition that he is a hero, and discussing himself on that assumption. Although the number of persons who dawdle their life away over fiction in England must be frightful, and is probably increasing, yet their talk is not the talk of Ulric Brendel, Rosmer, Ellida, or Peer Gynt; and it is for this reason that Rosmersholm and the Lady from the Sea strike English audiences as more fantastic and less literal than A Doll's House and the plays in which the leading figures are men and women of action, though to a Norwegian there is probably no difference in this respect.

HEDDA GABLER 1890

Hedda Gabler has no ethical ideals at all, only romantic ones. She is a typical nineteenth-century figure, falling into the abyss between the ideals which do not impose on her and the realities she has not yet discovered. The result is that though she has imagination, and an intense appetite for beauty, she has no conscience, no conviction: with plenty of cleverness, energy, and personal fascination she remains mean, envious, insolent, cruel in protest against others' happiness, fiendish in her dislike of inartistic people and things, a bully in reaction from her own cowardice. Hedda's father, a general, is a widower. She has the traditions of the military caste about her; and these narrow her activities to the customary hunt for a socially and pecuniarily eligible husband. She makes the acquaintance of a young man of genius who, prohibited by an ideal-ridden society from taking his pleasures except where there is nothing to restrain him from excess, is going to the bad in search of his good, with the usual consequences. Hedda is intensely curious about the side of life which is forbidden to her, and in which powerful instincts, absolutely ignored and condemned in her circle, steal their satisfaction. An odd intimacy springs up between the inquisitive girl and the rake. Whilst the general reads the paper in the afternoon, Lövborg and Hedda have long conversations in which he describes to her all his disreputable adventures. Although she is the questioner, she never dares to trust him: all the questions are indirect; and the responsibility for his interpretations rests on him alone. Hedda has no conviction whatever that these conversations are disgraceful; but she will not risk a fight with society on the point: it is easier to practise hypocrisy, the homage that truth pays to falsehood, than to endure ostracism. When he proceeds to make advances to her, Hedda has again no conviction that it would be wrong for her to gratify his instinct and her own; so that she is confronted with the alternative of sinning against herself and him, or sinning against social ideals in which she has no faith. Making the coward's choice, she carries it out with the utmost bravado, threatening Lövborg with one of her father's pistols, and driving him out of the house with all that ostentation of outraged purity which is the instinctive defence of women to whom chastity is not natural, much as libel actions are mostly brought by persons concerning whom libels are virtually, if not technically, justifiable.

Hedda, deprived of her lover, now finds that a life of conformity without faith involves something more terrible than the utmost ostracism: to wit, boredom. This scourge, unknown among revolutionists, is the curse which makes the security of respectability as dust in the balance against the unflagging interest of rebellion, and which forces society to eke out its harmless resources for killing time by licensing gambling, gluttony, hunting, shooting, coursing, and other vicious distractions for which even idealism has no disguise. These licenses, being expensive, are available only for people who have more than enough money to keep up appearances; and as Hedda's father, being in the army instead of in commerce, is too poor to leave her much more than the pistols, her boredom is only mitigated by dancing, at which she gains much admiration, but no substantial offers of marriage.

At last she has to find somebody to support her. A good-natured mediocrity of a professor is the best that is to be had; and though she regards him as a member of an inferior class, and despises almost to loathing his family circle of two affectionate old aunts and the inevitable general servant who has helped to bring him up, she marries him *faute de mieux*, and immediately proceeds to wreck this prudent provision for her livelihood by accommodating his income to her expenditure instead of accommodating her expenditure to his income. Her nature so rebels against the whole sordid transaction that the prospect of bearing a child to her husband drives her almost frantic, since it will not only expose her to the intimate solicitude of his aunts in the course of a derangement of her health in which she can see nothing that is not repulsive and humiliating, but will make her one of his family in earnest.

To amuse herself in these galling circumstances, she forms an underhand alliance with a visitor who belongs to her old set, an elderly gallant who quite understands how little she cares for her husband, and proposes a *ménage à trois* to her. She consents to his coming there and talking to her as he pleases behind her husband's back; but she keeps her pistols in reserve in case he becomes seriously importunate. He, on the other hand, tries to get some hold over her by placing her husband under pecuniary obligations, as far as he can do it without being out of pocket.

Meanwhile Lövborg is drifting to disgrace by the nearest way: drink. In due time he descends from lecturing at the university on the history of civilization to taking a job in an out-of-the-way place as tutor to the little children of Sheriff

Elvsted. This functionary, on being left a widower with a number of children, marries their governess, finding that she will cost him less and be bound to do more for him as his wife. As for her, she is too poor to dream of refusing such a settlement in life. When Lövborg comes, his society is heaven to her. He does not dare to tell her about his dissipations; but he tells her about his unwritten books, which he never discussed with Hedda. She does not dare to remonstrate with him for drinking; but he gives it up as soon as he sees that it shocks her. Just as Mr Fearing, in Bunyan's story, was in a way the bravest of the pilgrims, so this timid and unfortunate Mrs Elvsted trembles her way to a point at which Lövborg, quite reformed, publishes one book which makes him celebrated for the moment, and completes another, fair-copied in her handwriting, to which he looks for a solid position as an original thinker. But he cannot now stay tutoring Elvsted's children; so off he goes to town with his pockets full of the money the published book has brought him. Left once more in her old lonely plight, knowing that without her Lövborg will probably relapse into dissipation, and that without him her life will not be worth living, Mrs Elvsted must either sin against herself and him or against the institution of marriage under which Elvsted purchased his housekeeper. It never occurs to her that she has any choice. She knows that her action will count as "a dreadful thing"; but she sees that she must go; and accordingly Elvsted finds himself without a wife and his children without a governess, and so disappears unpitied from the story.

Now it happens that Hedda's husband, Jörgen Tesman, is an old friend and competitor (for academic honors) of Lövborg, and also that Hedda was a schoolfellow of Mrs Elvsted, or Thea, as she had better now be called. Thea's first business is to find out where Lövborg is; for hers is no preconcerted elopement: she has hurried to town to keep Lövborg away from the bottle, a design she dare not hint at to himself. Accordingly, the first thing she does in town is to call on the Tesmans, who have just returned from their honeymoon, to beg them to invite Lövborg to their house so as to keep him in good company. They consent, with the result that the two pairs are brought together under the same roof, and the tragedy begins to work itself out.

Hedda's attitude now demands a careful analysis. Lövborg's experience with Thea has enlightened his judgment of Hedda; and as he is, in his gifted way, an arrant *poseur* and male coquet, he immediately tries to get on romantic terms with her (for have they not "a past"?) by impressing her with the penetrating criticism that she is and always was a coward. She admits that the virtuous heroics with the pistol were pure cowardice; but she is still so void of any other standard of conduct than conformity to the conventional ideals, that she thinks her cowardice consisted in not daring to be wicked. That is, she thinks that what she actually did was the right thing; and since she despises herself for doing it, and feels that he also rightly despises her for doing it, she gets a passionate feeling that what is wanted is the courage to do wrong. This unlooked-for reaction of idealism, this monstrous but very common setting-up of wrong-doing as an ideal, and of the wrongdoer as hero or heroine *qua* wrongdoer, leads Hedda to conceive that when Lövborg tried to seduce her he was a hero, and that in allowing Thea to reform him he has played the recreant. In acting on this misconception she is restrained by no consideration for any of the rest. Like all people whose lives are valueless, she has no more sense of the value of Lövborg's or Tesman's or Thea's lives than a railway shareholder has of the value of a shunter's. She gratifies her intense jealousy of Thea by deliberately taunting Lövborg into breaking loose from her influence by joining a carouse at which he not only loses his manuscript, but finally gets into the hands of the police through behaving outrageously in the house of a disreputable woman whom he accuses of stealing it, not knowing that it has been picked up by Tesman and handed to Hedda for safe keeping. Now Hedda's jealousy of Thea is not jealousy of her bodily fascination: at that Hedda can beat her. It is jealousy of her power of making a man of Lövborg, of her part in his life as a man of genius. The manuscript which Tesman gives to Hedda to lock up safely is in Thea's handwriting. It is the fruit of Lövborg's union with Thea: he himself speaks of it as "their child." So when he turns his despair to romantic account by coming to the two women and making a tragic scene, telling Thea that he has cast the manuscript, torn into a thousand pieces, out upon the fiord; and then, when she is gone, telling Hedda that he has brought "the child" to a house of ill-fame and lost it there, she, deceived by his posing, and thirsting to gain faith in the beauty of her own influence over him from a heroic deed of some sort, makes him a present of one of her pistols, only begging him to "do it beautifully," by which she means that he is to kill himself in some manner that will make his suicide a romantic memory and an imaginative luxury to her for ever. He takes it unblushingly, and leaves her with the air of a man who is looking his last on earth. But the moment he is out of sight of his audience, he goes back to the house where he still supposes the manuscript to lie stolen, and there renews the wrangle of the night before, using the pistol to threaten the woman, with the result that he gets shot in the abdomen, leaving the weapon to fall into the hands of the police. Meanwhile Hedda deliberately burns "the child." Then comes her elderly gallant to disgust her with the unromantically ugly details of the deed which Lövborg promised her to do so beautifully, and to make her understand that he himself has now got her into his power by his ability to identify the pistol. She must either be the slave of this man, or else face the scandal of the connection of her name at the inquest with a squalid debauch ending in a murder. Thea, too, is not crushed by Lövborg's death. Ten minutes after she has received the news with a cry of heartfelt loss, she sits down with Tesman to reconstruct "the child" from the old notes she has piously preserved. Over the congenial task of collecting and arranging another man's ideas Tesman is perfectly happy, and forgets his beautiful Hedda for the first time. Thea the trembler is still mistress of the situation, holding the dead Lövborg, gaining Tesman, and leaving Hedda to her elderly admirer, who smoothly remarks that he will answer for Mrs Tesman not being bored whilst her husband is occupied with Thea in putting the pieces of the book together. However, he has again reckoned without General Gabler's second pistol. She shoots herself then and there; and so the story ends.

THE LAST FOUR PLAYS

DOWN AMONG THE DEAD MEN

IBSEN now lays down the completed task of warning the world against its idols and anti-idols, and passes into the shadow of death, or rather into the splendor of his sunset glory; for his magic is extraordinarily potent in these four plays, and his purpose more powerful. And yet the shadow of death is here; for all four, except Little Eyolf, are tragedies of the dead, deserted and mocked by the young who are still full of life. The Master Builder is a dead man before the curtain rises: the breaking of his body to pieces in the last act by its fall from the tower is rather the impatient destruction of a ghost of whose delirious whisperings Nature is tired than of one who still counts among the living. Borkman and the two women, his wife and her sister, are not merely dead: they are buried; and the creatures we hear and see are only their spirits in torment. "Never dream of life again," says Mrs Borkman to her husband: "lie quiet where you are." And the last play of all is frankly called When We Dead Awaken. Here the quintessence of Ibsenism reaches its final distillation; morality and reformation give place to mortality and resurrection; and the next event is the death of Ibsen himself: he, too, creeping ghost-like through the blackening mental darkness until he reaches his actual grave, and can no longer make Europe cry with pity by sitting at a copybook, like a child, trying to learn again how to write, only to find that divine power gone for ever from his dead hand. He, the crustiest, grimmest hero since Beethoven, could not die like him, shaking his fist at the thunder and alive to the last: he must follow the path he had traced for Solness and Borkman, and survive himself. But as these two were dreamers to the last, and never so luminous in their dreams as when they could no longer put the least of them into action; so we may believe that when Ibsen could no longer remember the alphabet, or use a dictionary, his soul may have been fuller than ever before of the unspeakable. Do not snivel, reader, over the contrast he himself drew between the man who was once the greatest writer in the world, and the child of seventy-six trying to begin again at pothooks and hangers. Depend on it, whilst there was anything left of him at all there was enough of his iron humor to grin as widely as the skeleton with the hour-glass who was touching him on the shoulder.

THE MASTER BUILDER 1892

Halvard Solness is a dead man who has been a brilliantly successful builder, and, like the greatest builders, his own architect. He is sometimes in the sublime delirium that precedes bodily death, and sometimes in the horror that varies the splendors of delirium. He is mortally afraid of young rivals; of the younger generation knocking at the door. He has built churches with high towers (much as Ibsen built great historical dramas in verse). He has come to the end of that and built "homes for human beings" (much as Ibsen took to writing prose plays of modern life). He has come to the end of that too, as men do at the end of their lives; and now he must take to dead men's architecture, the building of castles in the air. Castles in the air are the residences not only of those who have finished their lives, but of those who have not yet begun them. Another peculiarity of castles in the air is that they are so beautiful and so wonderful that human beings are not good enough to live in them: therefore when you look round you for somebody to live with you in your castle in the air, you find nobody glorious enough for that sanctuary. So you resort to the most dangerous of all the varieties of idolization: the idolization of the person you are most in love with; and you take him or her to live with you in your castle. And as imaginative young people, because they are young, have no illusions about youth, whilst old people, because they are old, have no illusions about age, elderly gentlemen very often idolize adolescent girls, and adolescent girls idolize elderly gentlemen. When the idolization is not reciprocal, the idolizer runs terrible risks if the idol is selfish and unscrupulous. Cases of girls enslaved by elderly gentlemen whose scrupulous respect for their maiden purity is nothing but an excuse for getting a quantity of secretarial or domestic service out of them that is limited only by their physical endurance, without giving them anything in return, are not at all so rare as they would be if the theft of a woman's youth and devotion were as severely condemned by public opinion as the comparatively amiable and negligible theft of a few silver spoons and forks. On the other hand doting old gentlemen are duped and ruined by designing young women who care no more for them than a Cornish fisherman cares for a conger eel. But sometimes, when the two natures are poetic, we have scenes of Bettina and Goethe, which are perhaps wholesome as well as pleasant for both parties when they are good enough and sensible enough to face the inexorable on the side of age and to recognize the impossible on the side of youth. On these conditions, old gentlemen are indulged in fancies for poetic little girls; and the poetic little girls have their emotions and imaginations satisfied harmlessly until they find a suitable mate.

But the master builder, though he gets into just such a situation, does not get out of it so cheaply, because he is not outwardly an old, or even a very elderly gentleman. "He is a man no longer young, but healthy and vigorous, with closely cut curly hair, dark moustache, and dark thick eyebrows." Also he is daimonic, not sham daimonic like Molvik in The Wild Duck, but really daimonic, with luck, a star, and mystic "helpers and servers" who find the way through the maze of life for him. In short, a very fascinating man, whom nobody, himself least of all, could suspect of having shot his bolt and being already dead. Therefore a man for whom a girl's castle in the air is a very dangerous place, as she may easily thrust upon him adventures that would tax the prime of an unexhausted man, and are mere delirious madness for a spent one.

Grasp this situation and you will be able to follow a performance of The Master Builder without being puzzled; though to the unprepared theatregoer it is a bewildering business. You see Solness in his office, ruthlessly exploiting the devotion of the girl secretary Kaia, who idolizes him, and giving her nothing in return but a mesmerizing word occasionally. You see him with equal ruthlessness apparently, but really with the secret terror of "the priest who slew the slayer and shall himself be slain," trying to suppress a young rival who is as yet only a draughtsman in his employment. To keep the door shut against the younger generation already knocking at it: that is all he can do now, except build castles in the air; for, as I have said, the effective part of the man is dead. Then there is his wife, who, knowing that he is failing in body and mind, can do nothing but look on in helpless terror. She cannot make a happy home for Solness, because her own happiness has been sacrificed to his genius. Or rather, her own genius, which is for "building up the souls of little children," has been sacrificed to his. For they began their family life in an old house that was part of her property: the sort of house that may be hallowed by old family associations and memories of childhood, but that it pays the speculative builder to pull down and replace by rows of villas. Now the ambitious Solness knows this but dares not propose such a thing to his wife, who cherishes all the hallowing associations, and even keeps her dolls: nine lovely dolls, feeling them "under her heart, like little unborn children." Everything in the house is precious to her: the old silk dresses, the lace, the portraits. Solness knows that to touch these would be tearing her heart up by the roots. So he says nothing; does nothing; only notes a crack in the old chimney which should be repaired if the house is to be safe against fire, and does not repair it. Instead, he pictures to himself a fire, with his wife out in the sledge with his two children, and nothing but charred ruins facing her when she returns; but what matter, since the children have escaped and are still with her? He even calls upon his helpers and servers to consider whether this vision might not become a reality. And it does. The house is burnt; the villas rise on its site and cover the park; and Halvard Solness becomes rich and successful.

But the helpers and servers have not stuck to the program for all that. The fire did not come from the crack in the chimney when all the domestic fires were blazing. It came at night when the fires were low, and began in a cupboard quite away from the chimney. It came when Mrs Solness and the children were in bed. It shattered the mother's health; it killed the children she was nursing; it devoured the portraits and the silk dresses and the old lace; it burnt the nine lovely dolls; and it broke the heart under which the dolls had lain like little unborn children. That was the price of the master builder's success. He is married to a dead woman; and he is trying to atone by building her a new villa: a new tomb to replace the old home; for he is gnawed with remorse.

But the fire was not only a good building speculation: it also led to his obtaining commissions to build churches. And one triumphant day, when he was celebrating the completion of the giant tower he had added to the old church at Lysanger, it suddenly flashed on him that his house had been burnt, his wife's life laid waste, and his own happiness destroyed, so that he might become a builder of churches. Now it happens that one of his difficulties as a builder is that he has a bad head for heights, and cannot venture even on a second floor balcony. Yet in the fury of that thought he mounts to the pinnacle of his tower, and there, face to face with God, who has, he feels, wasted the wife's gift of building up the souls of little children to make the husband a builder of steeples, he declares that he will never set hand to church-building again, and will henceforth build nothing but homes for happier men than he. Which vow he keeps, only to find that the home, too, is a devouring idol, and that men and women have no longer any use for it.

In spite of his excitement, he very nearly breaks his neck after all; for among the crowd below there is a little devil of a girl who waves a white scarf and makes his head swim. This tiny animal is no other than the younger stepdaughter of Ellida, The Lady from the Sea, Hilda Wangel, of whose taste for "thrilling" sensations we had a glimpse in that play. On the same evening Solness is entertained at a club banquet, in consequence of which he is not in the most responsible condition when he returns to sup at the house of Dr Wangel, who is putting him up for the night. He meets the imp there; thinks her like a little princess in her white dress; kisses her; and promises her to come back in ten years and carry her off to the kingdom of Orangia. Perhaps it is only just to mention that he stoutly denies these indiscretions afterwards; though he admits that when he wishes something to happen between himself and somebody else, the somebody else always imagines it actually has happened.

The play begins ten years after the climbing of the tower. The younger generation knocks at the door with a vengeance. Hilda, now a vigorous young woman, and a great builder of castles in the air, bursts in on him and demands her kingdom; and very soon she sends him up a tower again (the tower of the new house) and waves her scarf to him as madly as ever. This time he really does break his neck; and so the story ends.

LITTLE EYOLF 1894

Though the most mischievous ideals are social ideals which have become institutions, laws, and creeds, yet their evil must come to a personal point before they can strike down the individual. Jones is not struck down by an ideal in the abstract, but by Smith making monstrous claims or inflicting monstrous injuries on him in the name of an ideal. And it is fair to add that the ideals are sometimes beneficent, and their repudiation sometimes cruel. For ideals are in practice not so much matters of conscience as excuses for doing what we like; and thus it happens that of two people worshipping the same ideals, one will be a detestable tyrant and the other a kindly and helpful friend of mankind. What makes the bad side of idealism so dangerous is that wicked people are allowed to commit crimes in the name of the ideal that would not be tolerated for a moment as open devilment. Perhaps the worst, because the commonest and most intimate cases, are to be found in family life. Even during the Reign of Terror, the chances of any particular Frenchman or Frenchwoman being guillotined were so small as to be negligible. Under Nero a Christian was far safer from being smeared with pitch and set on fire than he was from domestic trouble. If the private lives that have been wasted by idealistic persecution could be recorded and set against the public martyrdoms and slaughterings and torturings and imprisonments, our millions of private Neros and Torquemadas and Calvins, Bloody Maries and Cleopatras and Semiramises, would eclipse the few who have come to the surface of history by the accident of political or ecclesiastical conspicuousness.

Thus Ibsen, at the beginning of his greatness, shewed us Brand sacrificing his wife; and this was only the first of a series of similar exhibitions, ending, so far, in Solness sacrificing his wife and being himself sacrificed to a girl's enthusiasm. And he brings Solness to the point of rebelling furiously against the tyranny of his wife's ideal of home, and declaring that "building homes for happy human beings is not worth a rap: men are not happy in these homes: I should not have been happy in such a home if I had had one." It is not surprising to find that Little Eyolf is about such a home.

This home clearly cannot be a working-class home. And here let it be said that the comparative indifference of the working class to Ibsen's plays is neither Ibsen's fault nor that of the working class. To the man who works for his living in modern society home is not the place where he lives, nor his wife the woman he lives with. Home is the roof under which he sleeps and eats; and his wife is the woman who makes his bed, cooks his meals, and looks after their children when they are neither in school nor in the streets, or who at least sees that the servants do these things. The man's work keeps him from home from eight to twelve hours a day. He is unconscious through sleep for another eight hours. Then there is the public house and the club. There is eating, washing, dressing, playing with the children or the dog, entertaining or visiting friends, reading, and pursuing hobbies such as gardening and the like. Obviously the home ideal cannot be tested fully under these conditions, which enable a married pair to see less and know less of one another than they do of those who work side by side with them. It is in the propertied class only that two people can really live together and devote themselves to one another if they want to. There are certain businesses which men and women can conduct jointly, and certain professions which men can pursue at home; and in these the strain of idealism on marriage is more severe than when the two work separately. But the full strain comes on with the modern unearned income from investments, which does not involve even the management of an estate. And it is under this full strain that Ibsen tests it in Little Eyolf.

Shakespear, in a flash of insight which has puzzled many commentators, and even set them proposing alterations of a passage which they found unthinkable, has described one of his characters as "a fellow almost damned in a fair wife." There is no difficulty or obscurity about this phrase at all: you have only to look round at the men who have ventured to marry very fascinating women to see that most of them are not merely "almost damned" but wholly damned. Allmers, in Little Eyolf, is a fellow almost damned in a fair wife. She, Rita Allmers, has brought him "gold and green forests" (a reminiscence from an early play called The Feast at Solhoug), and not only troubles and uncentres him as only a woman can trouble and uncentre a man who is susceptible to her bodily attraction, but is herself furiously and jealously in love with him. In short, they form the ideal home of romance; and it would be hard to find a compacter or more effective formula for a small private hell. The "almost damned" are commonly saved by the fact that the devotion is usually on one side only, and that the lovely lady (or gentleman; for a woman almost damned in a fair husband is also a common object in domestic civilization), if she has only one husband, relieves the boredom of his devotion by having fifty courtiers. But Rita will neither share Allmers with anyone else nor be shared. He must be wholly and exclusively hers; and she must be wholly and exclusively his. By her gold and green forests she snatches him from his work as a schoolmaster and imprisons him in their house, where the poor wretch pretends to occupy himself by writing a book on Human Responsibility, and forming the character of their son, little Eyolf. For your male sultana takes himself very seriously indeed, as do most sultanas and others who are so closely shut up with their own vanities and appetites that they think the world a little thing to be moulded and arranged at their silly pleasure like a lump of plasticine. Rita is jealous of the book, and hates it not only because Allmers occupies himself with it instead of with her, but talks about it to his half-sister Asta, of whom she is of course also jealous. She is jealous of little Eyolf, and hates him too, because he comes between her and her prey.

One day, when the baby child is lying on the table, they have an amorous fit and forget all about him. He falls off the table and is crippled for life. He and his crutch become thenceforth a standing reproach to them. They hate themselves; they hate each other; they hate him; their atmosphere of ideal conjugal love breeds hate at every turn: hatred masquerading as a loving bond that has been drawn closer and sanctified by their common misfortune. After ten years of this hideous slavery the man breaks loose: actually insists on going for a short trip into the mountains by himself. It is true that he reassures Rita by coming back before his time; but her conclusion that this was because he could not abstain from her society is rudely shattered by his conduct on his return. She dresses herself beautifully to receive him, and makes the seraglio as delightful as possible for their reunion; but he purposely arrives tired out, and takes refuge in the sleep of exhaustion, without a caress. As she says, quoting a popular poem when reproaching him for this afterwards, "There stood your champagne and you tasted it not." It soon appears that he has come to loathe his champagne, and that the escape into the mountains has helped him to loathe his situation to some extent, even to discovering the absurdity of his book on Human Responsibility, and the cruelty of his educational experiments on Eyolf. In future he is going to make Eyolf "an open air little boy," which of course involves being a good deal in the open air with him, and out of the seraglio. Then the woman's hatred of the child unveils itself; and she openly declares what she really feels as to this little creature, with its "evil eyes," that has come between them.

At this point, very opportunely, comes the Rat Wife, who, like the Pied Piper, clears away rats for a consideration. Has Rita any little gnawing things she wants to get rid of? Here, it seems, is a helper and server for Rita. The Rat Wife's method is to bewitch the rats so that when she rows out to sea they follow her and are drowned. She describes this with a heart-breaking poetry that frightens Rita, who makes Allmers send her away. But a helper and server is not so easily exorcized. Rita's little gnawing thing, Eyolf, has come under the spell; and when the Rat Wife rows out to sea, he follows her and is drowned.

The family takes the event in a very proper spirit. Horror, lamentation, shrieks and tears, and all the customary homages to death and attestations of bereavement are duly and even sincerely gone through; for the shock of such an accident makes us all human for a moment. But next morning Allmers finds some difficulty in keeping it up, miserable as he is. He finds himself forgetting about Eyolf for several minutes, and thinking about other things, even about his breakfast; and in his idealistic self-devotion to artificial attitudes he reproaches himself and tries to force himself to keep thinking of Eyolf and being overwhelmed with grief about him. Besides, it is an excuse for avoiding his wife. The revulsion against his slavery to her has made her presence unbearable to him. He can bear nobody but his half-sister Asta, whose relation to him is a most blessed comfort and relief because their blood kinship excludes from it all the torment and slavery of his relation to Rita. But this consolation is presently withdrawn; for Asta has just discovered, in some old correspondence, convincing proofs that she is not related to him at all; and the effect of the discovery has been to remove the inhibition which has hitherto limited her strong affection for him; so that she now perceives that she must leave him. Hitherto, she has refused, for his sake, the offers of Borgheim, an engineer who wants to marry her, but who, like Rita, wants to take her away and make her exclusively his own; for he, too, cannot share with anyone. And though both Allmers and Rita implore her to stay, dreading now nothing so much as being left alone with one another, she knows that she cannot stay innocently, and accepts the engineer and banishes lest a worse thing should befall.

And now Rita has her man all to herself. Eyolf dead, Asta gone, the Book on Human Responsibility thrown into the waste paper basket: there are no more rivals now, no more distractions: the field is clear for the ideal union of "two souls with but a single thought, two hearts that beat as one." The result may be imagined.

The situation is insufferable from the beginning. Allmers' attempts to avoid seeing or speaking to Rita are of course impracticable. Equally impracticable are their efforts to behave kindly to one another. They are presently at it hammer and tongs, each tearing the mask from the other's grief for the child, and leaving it exposed as their remorse: hers for having jealously hated Eyolf: his for having sacrificed him to his passion for Rita, and to the schoolmasterly vanity and folly which sees in the child nothing more than the vivisector sees in a guinea-pig: something to experiment on with a view to rearranging the world to suit his own little ideas. If ever two cultivated souls of the propertied middle class were stripped naked and left bankrupt, these two are. They cannot bear to live; and yet they are forced to confess that they dare not kill themselves.

The solution of their problem, as far as it is solved, is, as coming from Ibsen, very remarkable. It is not, as might have been expected after his long propaganda of Individualism, that they should break up the seraglio and go out into the world until they have learnt to stand alone, and through that to accept companionship on honorable conditions only. Ibsen here explicitly insists for the first time that "we are members one of another," and that though the strongest man is he who stands alone, the man who is standing alone for his own sake solely is literally an idiot. It is indeed a staring fact in history and contemporary life that nothing is so gregarious as selfishness, and nothing so solitary as the selflessness that loathes the word Altruism because to it there are no "others": it sees and feels in every man's case the image of its own. "Inasmuch as ye have done it unto one of the least of these my brethren ye have done it unto me" is not Altruism or Othersism. It is an explicit repudiation of the patronizing notion that "the least of these" is *another* to whom you are invited to be very nice and kind: in short, it accepts entire identification of "me" with "the least of these." The fashionably sentimental version, which runs, in effect, "If you subscribe eighteenpence to give this little dear a day in the country I shall regard it as a loan of one-and-sixpence to myself" is really more conceitedly remote from the spirit of the famous Christian saying than even the sham political economy that took in Mr Gradgrind. Accordingly, if you would see industrial sweating at its vilest, you must go, not to the sempstresses who work for commercial firms, but to the victims of pious Altruistic Ladies' Work Guilds and the like, in which ladies with gold and green forests offer to "others" their blouses to be stitched at prices that the most sordid East End slave-driver would recoil from offering.

Thus we see that in Ibsen's mind, as in the actual history of the nineteenth century, the way to Communism lies through the most resolute and uncompromising Individualism. James Mill, with an inhuman conceit and pedantry which leaves the fable of Allmers and Eyolf far behind, educated John Stuart Mill to be the arch Individualist of his time, with the result that John Stuart Mill became a Socialist quarter of a century before the rest of his set moved in that direction. Herbert Spencer lived to write despairing pamphlets against the Socialism of his ablest pupils. There is no hope in Individualism for egotism. When a man is at last brought face to face with himself by a brave Individualism, he finds himself face to face, not with an individual, but with a species, and knows that to save himself, he must save the race. He can have no life except a share in the life of the community; and if that life is unhappy and squalid, nothing that he can do to paint and paper and upholster and shut off his little corner of it can really rescue him from it.

It happens so to that bold Individualist Mrs Rita Allmers. The Allmers are, of course, snobs, and have always been very determined that the common little children down at the pier should be taught their place as Eyolf's inferiors. They even go the length of discussing whether these dirty little wretches should not be punished for their cowardice in not rescuing Eyolf. Thereby they raise the terrible question whether they themselves, who are afraid to commit suicide in their misery, would have been any braver. There is nobody to comfort them; for the income from the gold and green forests, by enabling them to cut themselves off from all industry of the place, has led them into something like total isolation. They hate their neighbors as themselves. They are alone together with nothing to do but wear each other out and drive each other mad to an extent impossible under any other conditions. And Rita's plight is the more desperate of the two, because as she has been the more unscrupulous, the more exacting, she has left him something to look forward to: freedom from her. He is bent on that, at least: he will not live with her on any terms, not stay anywhere within reach of her: the one thing he craves is that he may never see her or speak to her again. That is the end of the "two souls with but a single thought," &c. But to her his release is only a supreme privation, the end of everything that gave life any meaning for her. She has not even egotism to fall back on.

At this pass, an annoyance of which she has often complained occurs again. The children down at the pier make a noise, playing and yelling as if Eyolf had never existed. It suddenly occurs to her that these are children too, just like Eyolf, and that they are suffering a good deal from neglect. After all, they too are little Eyolfs. Inasmuch as she can do it unto one of the least of these his brethren she can do it unto him. She determines to take the dirty little wretches in hand and look after them. It is at all events a more respectable plan than that of the day before, which was to throw herself away on the first man she met if Allmers dared to think of anybody but her. And it has the domestic advantage that Allmers has nothing to fear from a woman who has something else to do than torment him with passions that devour and jealousies that enslave him. The world and the home suddenly take on their natural aspect. Allmers offers to stay and help her. And so they are delivered from their evil dream, and, let us hope, live happily ever after.

JOHN GABRIEL BORKMAN 1896

In Little Eyolf the shadow of death lifted for a moment; but now we enter it again. Here the persons of the drama are not only dead but buried. Borkman is a Napoleon of finance. He has the root of finance in him in a born love of money in its final reality: a love, that is, of precious metals. He does not dream of beautiful ladies calling to him for knightly rescue from dragons and tyrants, but of metals imprisoned in undiscovered mines, calling to him to release them and send them out into all lands fertilizing, encouraging, creating. Music to him means the ring of the miner's pick and hammer: the eternal night underground is as magical to him as the moonlit starlit night of the upper air to the romantic poet. This love of metal is common enough: no man feels towards a cheque for £20 as he does towards twenty gold sovereigns: he will part from the paper with less of a pang than from the coins. There are misers whose fingers tremble when they touch gold, but close steadily on banknotes. True love of money is, in fact, a passion based on a physical appetite for precious metals. It is not greed: you cannot call a man who starves himself sooner than part with one sovereign from his sack of sovereigns, greedy. If he did the same for the love of God, you would call him a saint: if for the love of a woman, a perfect gentle knight. Men grow rich according to the strength of their obsession by this passion: its great libertines become Napoleons of finance: its narrow debauchees become misers, petty moneylenders, and the like. It must not be looked for in all our millionaires, because most of these are rich by pure accident (our abandonment of industry to the haphazard scrambles of private adventurers necessarily produces occasional windfalls which enrich the man who happens to be on the spot), as may be seen when the lucky ones are invited to display their supposed Napoleonic powers in spending their windfalls, when they reveal themselves as quite ordinary mortals, if not indeed sometimes as exceptionally resourceless ones. Besides, finance is one business, and industrial organization another: the man with a passion for altering the map by digging isthmuses never thinks of money save as a means to his end. But those who as financiers have passionately "made" money instead of merely holding their hats under an accidental shower of it will be found to have a genuine disinterested love of it. It is not easy to say how common this passion is. Poverty is general, which would seem to indicate a general lack of it; but poverty is mainly the result of organized robbery and oppression (politely called Capitalism) starving the passion for gold as it starves all the passions. The evidence is further confused by the decorative instinct: some men will load their fingers and shirt-fronts with rings and studs, whilst others of equal means are ringless and fasten their shirts with sixpennorth of mother-of-pearl. But it is significant that Plato, and, following him, Sir Thomas More, saw with Ibsen, and made complete indifference to the precious metals, minted or not, a necessary qualification for aristocracy. This indifference is, as a matter of fact, so characteristic of our greatest non-industrial men that when they do not happen to inherit property they are generally poor and in difficulties.

Therefore we who have never cared for money enough to do more than keep our heads above water, and are therefore tempted to regard ourselves as others regard us (that is, as failures, or, at best, as persons of no account) may console ourselves with the reflection that money-hunger is no more respectable than gluttony, and that unless its absence or feebleness is only a symptom of a general want of power to care for anything at all, it usually means that the soul has risen above it to higher concerns.

All this is necessary to the appreciation of Ibsen's presentment of the Napoleon of finance. Ibsen does not take him superficially: he goes to the poetic basis of the type: the love of gold—actual metallic gold—and the idealization of gold through that love.

Borkman meets the Misses Rentheim: two sisters: the elder richer than the younger. He falls in love with the younger; and she falls in love with him; but the love of gold is the master passion: he marries the elder. Yet he respects his secondary passion in the younger. When he speculates with other people's securities he spares hers. On the point of bringing off a great stroke of finance, the other securities are missed; and he is imprisoned for embezzlement. That is the end of him. He comes out of prison a ruined man and a dead man, and would not have even a tomb to sleep in but for the charity of Ella Rentheim, whose securities he spared when he broke her heart. She maintains his old home for him.

He now enters on the grimmest lying in state ever exposed to public view by mortal dramatist. His wife, a proud woman, must live in the same house with the convicted thief who has disgraced her, because she has nowhere else to lay her head; but she will not see him nor speak to him. She sits downstairs in the drawing-room eating the bitter bread of her sister's charity, and listening with loathing to her husband's steps as he paces to and fro in the long gallery upstairs "like a sick wolf." She listens not for days but for years. And her one hope is that her son Erhart will rehabilitate the family name; repay the embezzled money; and lead her from her tomb up again into honor and prosperity. To this task she has devoted *his* life.

Borkman has quite another plan. He is still Napoleon, and will return from his Elba to scatter his enemies and complete the stroke that ill-luck and the meddlesomeness of the law frustrated. But he is proud: prouder than Napoleon. He will not come back to the financial world until it finds out that it cannot do without him and comes to ask him to resume his place at the head of the board. He keeps himself in readiness for that deputation. He is always dressed for it; and when he hears steps on the threshold he stands up by the table; puts one hand into the breast of his coat; and assumes the attitude of a conqueror receiving suppliants. And this also goes on not for days but for years, long after the world has forgotten him, and there is nobody likely to come for him except Peer Gynt's button moulder.

Borkman, like all madmen, cannot nourish his delusion without some response from without. One of the victims of his downfall is a clerk who once wrote a tragedy, and has lived ever since in his own imagination as a poet. His family ridicules his tragedy and his pretensions; and as he is a poor ineffectual little creature who has never lived enough to feel dignified among the dead, like Borkman, he too finds it hard to keep his illusion alive without help. Fortunately he has admired Borkman, the great financier; and Borkman, when he has ruined him and ruined himself, is quite willing to be admired by this humble victim, and even to reward him by a pretence of believing in his poetic genius. Thus the two form one of those Mutual Admiration Societies on which the world so largely subsists, and make the years in the long gallery tolerable by flattering each other. There are even moments when Borkman is nerved to the point of starting for his second advent as a great financial redeemer. On such occasions the woman downstairs hears the footsteps of the sick wolf on the stairs approaching the hatstand where his hat and stick have waited unused all the years of his entombment; but they never reach that first stage of the journey. They always turn back into the gallery again.

This melancholy household of the dead crumbles to dust at the knock of the younger generation at the door. Erhart, dedicated by his mother to the task of paying his father's debts and retrieving his ruin, and by his aunt to the task of sweetening her last days with his grateful love, has dedicated himself to his own affairs—for the moment mostly love affairs—and has not the faintest intention of concerning himself with the bygone career of the crazy ex-felon upstairs or the sentimentalities of the old maid downstairs. He detests the house and the atmosphere, and associates his aunt's broken heart with nothing more important than the scent of stale lavender, which he dislikes. He spends his time happily in the house of a pretty lady in the neighborhood, who has been married and divorced, and knows how to form an adolescent youth. And as to the unpardonable enemy of the family, one Hinkel, who betrayed Borkman to the police and rose on his ruins, Erhart cares so little for that old story that he goes to Hinkel's parties and enjoys himself there very much. And when at last the pretty lady raises his standard of happiness to a point at which the old house and the old people become impossible, unthinkable, unbearable, he goes off with her to Italy and leaves the dead to bury their dead.

The details of this catastrophe make the play. The fresh air and the light of day break into the tomb; and its inhabitants crumble into dust. Foldal, the poet clerk, lets slip the fact that he has not the slightest belief in Borkman's triumphant return to the world; and Borkman retorts by telling him he is no poet. After this comedy comes the tragedy of the son's defection; and amid the recriminations of the broken heart, the baffled pride, and the shattered dreams, the castles in the air vanish and reveal the open grave they have hidden. Poor Foldal, limping home after being run over by a sledge in which his daughter is running away to act as "second string" and chaperone for Erhart and the pretty lady, is the only one who is wanted in the world, since he must still work for his derisive family. But Borkman returns to his dream, and ventures out of doors at last, not this time to resume his place as governor of the bank, but to release the imprisoned metal that rings and sings to him from the earth. In other words, to die in the open, mad but happy, whilst the two sisters, "we two shadows," end their strife over his body.

WHEN WE DEAD AWAKEN 1900

This play, the last work of Ibsen, and at first the least esteemed, has had its prophecy so startlingly fulfilled in England that nobody will now question the intensity of its inspiration. With us the dead have awakened in the very manner prefigured in the play. The simplicity and brevity of the story is so obvious, and the enormous scope of the conception so difficult to comprehend, that many of Ibsen's most devoted admirers failed to do it justice. They knew that he was a man of seventy, and were prepossessed with the belief that at such an age his powers must be falling off. It certainly was easier at that time to give the play up as a bad job than to explain it. Now that the great awakening of women which we call the Militant Suffrage Movement is upon us, and you may hear our women publicly and passionately paraphrasing Ibsen's heroine without having read a word of the play, the matter is simpler. There is no falling-off here in Ibsen. It may be said that this is physically impossible; but those who say so forget that the natural decay of a writer's powers may shew itself in two ways. The inferiority of the work produced is only one way. The other is the production of equally good or even better work with much greater effort than it would have cost its author ten years earlier. Ibsen produced this play with great difficulty in twice as long a period as had before sufficed; and even at that the struggle left his mind a wreck; for he not only never wrote another play, but, like an overstrained athlete, lost even the normal mental capacity of an ordinary man. Yet it would be hard to say that the play was not worth the sacrifice. It shews no decay of Ibsen's highest qualities: his magic is nowhere more potent. It is shorter than usual: that is all. The extraordinarily elaborate private history, family and individual, of the personages, which lies behind the action of the other plays, is replaced by a much simpler history of a few people in their general human relations without any family history at all. And the characteristically conscientious fitting of the play to the mechanical conditions of old-fashioned stages has given way to demands that even the best equipped and largest modern stages cannot easily comply with; for the second act takes place in a valley; and though it is easy to represent a valley by a painted scene when the action is confined to one spot in the foreground, it is a different matter when the whole valley has to be practicable, and the movements of the figures cover distances which do not exist on the stage, and cannot, as far as my experience goes, be satisfactorily simulated by the stage carpenter, though they are easy enough for the painter. I should attach no importance at all to this in a writer less mindful of technical limitations and less ingenious in circumventing them than Ibsen, who was for some years a professional stage manager; but in his case it is clear that in calling on the theatre to expand to his requirements instead of, as his custom was, limiting his scene of action to the possibilities of a modest provincial theatre, he knew quite well what he was doing. Here, then, we have three differences from the earlier plays. None of them are inferiorities. They are proper to the difference of subject, and in fact increased the difficulty of the playwright's task by throwing him back on sheer dramatic power, unaided by the cheaper interest that can be gained on the stage by mere ingenuity of construction. Ibsen, who has always before played on the spectator by a most elaborate gradual development which would have satisfied Dumas, here throws all his cards on the table as rapidly as possible, and proceeds to deal intensively with a situation that never alters.

This situation is simple enough in its general statement,

though it is so complex in its content that it raises the whole question of domestic civilization. Take a man and a woman at the highest pitch of natural ability and charm yet attained, and enjoying all the culture that modern art and literature can offer them; and what does it all come to? Contrast them with an essentially uncivilized pair, with a man who lives for hunting and eating and ravishing, and whose morals are those of the bully with the strong hand: in short, a man from the stone age as we conceive it (such men are still common enough in the classes that can afford the huntsman's life); and couple him with a woman who has no interest or ambition in life except to be captured by such a man (and of these we have certainly no lack). Then face this question. What is there to choose between these two pairs? Is the cultured gifted man less hardened, less selfish towards the women, than the paleolithic man? Is the woman less sacrificed, less enslaved, less dead spiritually in the one case than in the other? Modern culture, except when it has rotted into mere cynicism, shrieks that the question is an insult. The stone age, anticipating Ibsen's reply, guffaws heartily and says, "Bravo, Ibsen!" Ibsen's reply is that the sacrifice of the woman of the stone age to fruitful passions which she herself shares is as nothing compared to the wasting of the modern woman's soul to gratify the imagination and stimulate the genius of the modern artist, poet, and philosopher. He shews us that no degradation ever devized or permitted is as disastrous as this degradation; that through it women die into luxuries for men, and yet can kill them; that men and women are becoming conscious of this; and that what remains to be seen as perhaps the most interesting of all imminent social developments is what will happen "when we dead awaken."

Ibsen's greatest contemporary outside his own art was Rodin the French sculptor. Whether Ibsen knew this, or whether he was inspired to make his hero a sculptor just as Dickens was inspired to make Pecksniff an architect, is not known. At all events, having to take a type of the highest and ablest masculine genius, he made him a sculptor, and called his name, not Rodin, but Rubeck: a curious assonance, if it was not intentional. Rubeck is as able an individual as our civilization can produce. The difficulty of presenting such an individual in fiction is that it can be done only by a writer who occupies that position himself; for a dramatist cannot conceive anything higher than himself. No doubt he can invest an imaginary figure with all sorts of imaginary gifts. A drunken author may make his hero sober; an ugly, weak, puny, timid one may make him a Hyperion or a Hercules; a deaf mute may write novels in which the lover is an orator and his mistress a prima donna; but whatever ornaments and accomplishments he may pile up on his personages, he cannot give them greater souls than his own. Defoe could invent wilder adventures for Robinson Crusoe than Shakespear for Hamlet; but he could not make that mean adventurer, with his dull eulogies of the virtues of "the middle station of life," anything even remotely like Shakespear's prince.

For Ibsen this difficulty did not exist. He knew quite well that he was one of the greatest men living; so he simply said "Suppose ME to be a sculptor instead of a playwright," and the thing was done. Thus he came forward himself to plead to his own worst indictment of modern culture. One of the touches by which he identifies himself has all the irony of his earliest work. Rubeck has to make money out of human vanity, as all sculptors must nowadays, by portrait busts; but he revenges himself by studying and bringing out in his sitters "the respectable pompous horse faces, and self-opinionated donkey-muzzles, and lop-eared low-browed dog-skulls, and fatted swine-snouts, and dull brutal bull fronts" that lurk in so many human faces. All artists who deal with humanity do this, more or less. Leonardo da Vinci ruled his notebook in columns headed fox, wolf, etc., and made notes of faces by ticking them off in these columns, finding this, apparently, as satisfactory a memorandum as a drawing. Domestic animals, terriers, pugs, poultry, parrots, and cockatoos, are specially valuable to the caricaturist, as giving the original types which explain many faces. Ibsen must have classified his acquaintances a good deal in this way, not without an occasional chuckle; and his attribution of the practice to Rubeck is a confession of it.

Rubeck makes his reputation, as sculptors often do, by a statue of a woman. Not, be it observed, of a dress and a pair of boots, with a head protruding from them, but of a woman from the hand of Nature. It is worth noting here that we have hardly any portraits, either painted or carved, of our famous men and women or even of our nearest and dearest friends. Charles Dickens is known to us as a guy with a human head and face on top. Shakespear is a laundry advertisement of a huge starched collar with his head sticking out of it. Dr Johnson is a face looking through a wig perched on a snuffy suit of old clothes. All the great women of history are fashion plates of their period. Bereaved parents, orphans, and widows weep fondly over photographs of uniforms, frock coats, gowns, and hats, for the sake of the little scrap of humanity that is allowed to peep through these trappings. Women with noble figures and plain or elderly faces are outdressed and outfaced by rivals who, if revealed as they really are, would be hardly human. Carlyle staggers humanity by inviting the House of Commons to sit unclothed, so that we, and they themselves, shall know them for what they really are.

Hence it is that the artist who adores mankind as his highest subject always comes back to the reality beneath the clothes. His claim to be allowed to do this is so irresistible that in every considerable city in England you will find, supported by the rates of prudish chapel goers, and even managed and inspected by committees of them, an art school where, in the "life class" (significant term!) young women posed in ridiculous and painful attitudes by a drawing master, and mostly under the ugliest circumstances of light, color, and surroundings, earn a laborious wage by allowing a crowd of art students to draw their undraped figures. It is a joylessly grotesque spectacle: one wonders whether anything can really be learnt from it; for never have I seen one of these school models in an attitude which any human being would, unless the alternative were starvation, voluntarily sustain for thirty seconds, or assume on any natural occasion or provocation whatever. Male models are somewhat less slavish; and the stalwart laborer or olive-skinned young Italian who poses before a crowd of easels with ludicrously earnest young ladies in blue or vermilion gowns and embroidered pinafores drawing away at him for dear life is usually much more comfortably and possibly posed. But Life will not yield up her more intimate secrets for eighteenpence an hour; and these earnest young ladies and artsome young men, when they have filled portfolios with such sordid life studies, know less about living humanity than they did before, and very much less about even the mechanism of the body and the shape of its muscles than they could learn less inhumanly from a series of modern kinematographs of figures in motion.

Rubeck does not make his statues in a class at a municipal art school by looking at a weary girl in a tortured attitude with a background of match-boarding, under a roof of girders, and with the ghastly light of a foggy, smoky manufacturing town making the light side of her flesh dirty yellow and the shadowed side putrid purple. He knows better than that. He finds a beautiful woman, and tells her his vision of a statue of The Resurrection Day in the form of a woman "filled with a sacred joy at finding herself unchanged in the higher, freer, happier region after the long dreamless sleep of death." And the woman, immediately seizing his inspiration and sharing it, devotes herself to the work, not merely as his model, but as his friend, his helper, fellow worker, comrade, all things, save one, that may be humanly natural and necessary between them for an unreserved co-operation in the great work. The one exception is that they are not lovers; for the sculptor's ideal is a virgin, or, as he calls it, a pure woman.

And her reward is that when the work is finished and the statue achieved, he says "Thank you for a priceless EPISODE," at which significant word, revealing as it does that she has, after all, been nothing to him but a means to his end, she leaves him and drops out of his life. To earn her living she must then pose, not to him, but before crowds in Variety Theatres in living pictures, gaining much money by her beauty, winning rich husbands, and driving them all to madness or to death by "a fine sharp dagger which she always has with her in bed," much as Rita Allmers nearly killed her husband. And she calls the statue her child and Rubeck's, as the book in Hedda Gabler was the child of Thea and Eilert Lövberg. But finally she too goes mad under the strain.

Rubeck presently meets a pretty Stone Age woman, and marries her. And as he is not a Stone Age man, and she is bored to distraction by his cultured interests, he disappoints her as thoroughly as she disgusts and wearies him: the symptoms being that though he builds her a splendid villa, full of works of art and so forth, neither he nor she can settle down quietly; and they take trips here, trips there, trips anywhere to escape being alone and at home together.

But the retribution for his egotism takes a much subtler form, and strikes at a much more vital place in him: namely, his artistic inspiration. Working with Irene, the lost model, he had achieved a perfect work of art; and, having achieved it, had supposed that he was done with her. But art is not so simple as that. The moment she forsakes him and leaves him to the Stone Age woman and to his egotism, he no longer sees the perfection of his work. He becomes dissatisfied with it. He sees that it can be improved: for instance, why should it consist of a figure of Irene alone? Why should he not be in it himself? Is he not a far more important factor in the conception? He changes the single figure design to a group. He adds a figure of himself. He finds that the woman's figure, with its wonderful expression of gladness, puts his own image out of countenance. He rearranges the group so as to give himself more prominence. Even so the gladness outshines him; and at last he "tones it down," striking the gladness out with his chisel, and making his own expression the main interest of the group. But he cannot stop there. Having destroyed the thing that was superior to him, he now wants to introduce things that are inferior. He carves clefts in the earth at the feet of his figure, and from these clefts he makes emerge the folk with the horse faces and the swine snouts that are nearer the beast than his own fine face. Then he is satisfied with his work; and it is in this form that it makes him famous and is finally placed in a public museum. In his days with Irene, they used to call these museums the prisons of works of art. Precisely what the Italian Futurist painters of today are calling them.

And now the play begins. Irene comes from her madhouse to a "health resort." Thither also comes Rubeck, wandering about with the Stone Age woman to avoid being left at home with her. Thither also comes the man of the Stone Age with his dogs and guns, and carries off the Stone Age woman, to her husband's great relief. Rubeck and Irene meet; and as they talk over old times, she learns, bit by bit, what has happened to the statue, and is about to kill him when she realizes, also bit by bit, that the history of its destruction is the history of his own, and that as he used her up and left her dead, so with her death the life went out of him. But, like Nora in A Doll's House, she sees the possibility of a miracle. The dead may awaken if only they can find an honest and natural relation in which they shall no longer sacrifice and slay one another. She asks him to climb to the top of a mountain with her and see that promised land. Half way up, they meet the Stone Age pair hunting. There is a storm coming. It is death to go up and danger to climb down. The Stone Age man faces the danger and carries his willing prey down. The others are beyond the fear of death, and go up. And that is the end of them and of the plays of Henrik Ibsen.

The end, too, let us hope, of the idols, domestic, moral, religious and political, in whose name we have been twaddled into misery and confusion and hypocrisy unspeakable. For

Ibsen's dead hand still keeps the grip he laid on their masks when he first tore them off; and whilst that grip holds, all the King's horses and all the King's men will find it hard to set those Humpty-Dumpties up again.

THE LESSON OF THE PLAYS

IN following this sketch of the plays written by Ibsen to illustrate his thesis that the real slavery of today is slavery to ideals of goodness, it may be that readers who have conned Ibsen through idealist spectacles have wondered that I could so pervert the utterances of a great poet. Indeed I know already that many of those who are most fascinated by the poetry of the plays will plead for any explanation of them rather than that given by Ibsen himself in the plainest terms through the mouths of Mrs Alving, Relling, and the rest. No great writer uses his skill to conceal his meaning. There is a tale by a famous Scotch story-teller which would have suited Ibsen exactly if he had hit on it first. Jeanie Deans sacrificing her sister's life on the scaffold to ideal truthfulness is far more horrible than the sacrifice in Rosmersholm; and the *deus ex machina* expedient by which Scott makes the end of his story agreeable is no solution of the ethical problem raised, but only a puerile evasion of it. He dared not, when it came to the point, allow Effie to be hanged for the sake of Jeanie's ideals.[1] Nevertheless, if I were to pretend that Scott wrote The Heart of Midlothian to shew that people are led to do as mischievous, as unnatural, as murderous things by their religious and moral ideals as by their envy and ambition, it would be easy to confute me from the pages of the book itself. And Ibsen, like Scott, has made his opinion plain. If any one attempts to maintain that Ghosts is a polemic in favor of indissoluble monogamic marriage, or that The Wild Duck was written to inculcate that truth

[1] The common-sense solution of the ethical problem has often been delivered by acclamation in the theatre. Many years ago I witnessed a performance of a melodrama founded on this story. After the painful trial scene, in which Jeanie Deans condemns her sister to death by refusing to swear to a perfectly innocent fiction, came a scene in the prison. "If it had been me," said the jailor, "I wad ha sworn a hole through an iron pot." The roar of applause which burst from the pit and gallery was thoroughly Ibsenist in sentiment. The speech, by the way, must have been a gag of the actor's: at all events I cannot find it in the acting edition of the play.

should be told for its own sake, they must burn the text of the plays if their contention is to stand. The reason that Scott's story is tolerated by those who shrink from Ghosts is not that it is less terrible, but that Scott's views are familiar to all well-brought-up ladies and gentlemen, whereas Ibsen's are for the moment so strange to them as to be unthinkable. He is so great a poet that the idealist finds himself in the dilemma of being unable to conceive that such a genius should have an ignoble meaning, and yet equally unable to conceive his real meaning otherwise than as ignoble. Consequently he misses the meaning altogether in spite of Ibsen's explicit and circumstantial insistence on it, and proceeds to substitute a meaning congenial to his own ideal of nobility.

Ibsen's deep sympathy with his idealist figures seems to countenance this confusion. Since it is on the weaknesses of the higher types of character that idealism seizes, his most tragic examples of vanity, selfishness, folly, and failure are not vulgar villains, but men who in an ordinary novel or melodrama would be heroes. Brand and Rosmer, who drive those they love to death, do so with all the fine airs of the Sophoclean or Shakespearean good man persecuted by Destiny. Hilda Wangel, who kills the Master Builder literally to amuse herself, is the most fascinating of sympathetic girl-heroines. The ordinary Philistine commits no such atrocities: he marries the woman he likes and lives with her more or less happily ever after; but that is not because he is greater than Brand or Rosmer: he is less. The idealist is a more dangerous animal than the Philistine just as a man is a more dangerous animal than a sheep. Though Brand virtually murdered his wife, I can understand many a woman, comfortably married to an amiable Philistine, reading the play and envying the victim her husband. For when Brand's wife, having made the sacrifice he has exacted, tells him that he was right; that she is happy now; that she sees God face to face; and then reminds him that "whoso sees Jehovah dies," he instinctively clasps his hands over her eyes; and that action raises him at once far above the criticism that sneers at idealism from beneath, instead of surveying it from the clear ether above, which can only be reached through its mists.

If, in my account of the plays, I have myself suggested false judgments by describing the errors of the idealists in the terms of the life they have risen above rather than in those of the life they fall short of, I can only plead, with but moderate disrespect for the general reader, that if I had done otherwise I should have failed wholly to make my exposition intelligible. Indeed accurate terms for realist morality, though they are to be found in the Bible, are so out of fashion and forgotten that in this very distinction between idealism and realism, I am forced to insist on a sense of the words which, had not Ibsen forced my hand, I should perhaps have conveyed otherwise, to avoid the conflict of many of its applications with the vernacular use of the words.

This, however, was a trifle compared to the difficulty which arose from our inveterate habit of labelling men with the abstract names of their qualities without the slightest reference to the underlying will which sets these qualities in action. At an anniversary celebration of the Paris Commune of 1871, I was struck by the fact that no speaker could find a eulogy for the Federals which would not have been equally appropriate to the peasants of La Vendée who fought for their tyrants against the French revolutionists, or to the Irishmen and Highlanders who fought for the Stuarts at the Boyne or Culloden. The statements that the slain members of the Commune were heroes who died for a noble ideal would have left a stranger quite as much in the dark about them as the counter statements, once common enough in our newspapers, that they were incendiaries and assassins. Our obituary notices are examples of the same ambiguity. Of all the public men lately deceased when Ibsenism was first discussed in England, none was made more interesting by strongly marked personal characteristics than the famous atheist orator Charles Bradlaugh. He was not in the least like any other notable member of the House of Commons.

Yet when the obituary notices appeared, with the usual string of qualities: eloquence, determination, integrity, strong common-sense, and so on, it would have been possible, by merely expunging all names and other external details from these notices, to leave the reader entirely unable to say whether the subject of them was Gladstone, Lord Morley, William Stead, or any one else no more like Bradlaugh than Garibaldi or the late Cardinal Newman, whose obituary certificates of morality might nevertheless have been reprinted almost verbatim for the occasion without any gross incongruity. Bradlaugh had been the subject of many sorts of newspaper notices in his time. Thirty years ago, when the middle classes supposed him to be a revolutionist, the string of qualities which the press hung upon him were all evil ones, great stress being laid on the fact that as he was an atheist it would be an insult to God to admit him to Parliament. When it became apparent that he was an anti-socialist force in politics, he, without any recantation of his atheism, at once had the string of evil qualities exchanged for a rosary of good ones; but it is hardly necessary to add that neither the old badge nor the new could ever give any inquirer the least clue to the sort of man he actually was: he might have been Oliver Cromwell or Wat Tyler or Jack Cade, Penn or Wilberforce or Wellington, the late Mr Hampden of flat-earth-theory notoriety or Proudhon or the Archbishop of Canterbury, for all the distinction such labels could give him one way or the other. The worthlessness of these abstract descriptions is recognized in practice every day. Tax a stranger before a crowd with being a thief, a coward, and a liar; and the crowd will suspend its judgment until you answer the question, "What's he done?" Attempt to take up a collection for him on the ground that he is an upright, fearless, high-principled hero; and the same question must be answered before a penny goes into the hat.

The reader must therefore discount those partialities which I have permitted myself to express in telling the stories of the plays. They are as much beside the mark as any other example of the sort of criticism which seeks to create an impression favorable or otherwise to Ibsen by simply pasting his characters all over with good or bad conduct marks. If any person cares to describe Hedda Gabler as a modern Lucretia who preferred death to dishonor, and Thea Elvsted as an abandoned, perjured strumpet who deserted the man she had sworn before her God to love, honor, and obey until her death, the play contains conclusive evidence establishing both points. If the critic goes on to argue that as Ibsen manifestly means to recommend Thea's conduct above Hedda's by making the end happier for her, the moral of the play is a vicious one, that, again, cannot be gainsaid. If, on the other hand, Ghosts be defended, as the dramatic critic of Piccadilly did defend it, because it throws into divine relief the beautiful figure of the simple and pious Pastor Manders, the fatal compliment cannot be parried. When you have called Mrs Alving an emancipated woman or an unprincipled one, Alving a debauchee or a victim of society, Nora a fearless and noble-hearted woman or a shocking little liar and an unnatural mother, Helmer a selfish hound or a model husband and father, according to your bias, you have said something which is at once true and false, and in both cases perfectly idle.

The statement that Ibsen's plays have an immoral tendency, is, in the sense in which it is used, quite true. Immorality does not necessarily imply mischievous conduct: it implies conduct, mischievous or not, which does not conform to current ideals. All religions begin with a revolt against morality, and perish when morality conquers them and stamps out such words as grace and sin, substituting for them morality and immorality. Bunyan places the town of Morality, with its respectable leading citizens Mr Legality and Mr Civility, close to the City of Destruction. In the United States today he would be imprisoned for this. Born as I was in the seventeenth century atmosphere of mid-nineteenth century Ireland, I can remember when men who talked about morality were suspected of reading Tom Paine, if not of being downright atheists. Ibsen's attack on morality is a symptom of the revival of religion, not of its extinction. He is on the side of the prophets in having devoted himself to shewing that the spirit or will of Man is constantly outgrowing the ideals, and that therefore thoughtless conformity to them is constantly producing results no less tragic than those which follow thoughtless violation of them. Thus the main effect of his plays is to keep before the public the importance of being always prepared to act immorally. He reminds men that they ought to be as careful how they yield to a temptation to tell the truth as to a temptation to hold their tongues, and he urges upon women who either cannot or will not marry that the inducements held out to them by society to preserve their virginity and refrain from motherhood may be called temptations as logically as the inducements to the contrary held out by individuals and by their own temperaments, the practical decision depending on circumstances just as much as a decision between walking and taking a cab, however less trivial both the action and the circumstances may be. He protests against the ordinary assumption that there are certain moral institutions which justify all means used to maintain them, and insists that the supreme end shall be the inspired, eternal, ever growing one, not the external unchanging, artificial one; not the letter but the spirit; not the contract but the object of the contract; not the abstract law but the living will. And because the will to change our habits and thus defy morality arises before the intellect can reason out any racially beneficent purpose in the change, there is always an interval during which the individual can say no more than that he wants to behave immorally because he likes, and because he will feel constrained and unhappy if he acts otherwise. For this reason it is enormously important that we should "mind our own business" and let other people do as they like unless we can prove some damage beyond the shock to our feelings and prejudices. It is easy to put revolutionary cases in which it is so impossible to draw the line that they will always be decided in practice more or less by physical force; but for all ordinary purposes of government and social conduct the distinction is a commonsense one. The plain working truth is that it is not only good for people to be shocked occasionally, but absolutely necessary to the progress of society that they should be shocked pretty often. But it is not good for people to be garotted occasionally, or at all. That is why it is a mistake to treat an atheist as you treat a garotter, or to put "bad taste" on the footing of theft and murder. The need for freedom of evolution is the sole basis of toleration, the sole valid argument against Inquisitions and Censorships, the sole reason for not burning heretics and sending every eccentric person to the madhouse.

In short, our ideals, like the gods of old, are constantly demanding human sacrifices. Let none of them, says Ibsen, be placed above the obligation to prove itself worth the sacrifices it demands; and let everyone religiously refuse to sacrifice himself and others from the moment he loses his faith in the validity of the ideal. Of course it will be said here by incorrigibly slipshod readers that this, far from being immoral, is the highest morality; but I really will not waste further definition on those who will neither mean one thing or another by a word nor allow me to do so. Suffice it that among those who are not ridden by current ideals no question as to the ethical soundness of Ibsen's plays will ever arise; and among those who are so ridden his plays will be denounced as immoral, and cannot be defended against the accusation.

There can be no question as to the effect likely to be produced on an individual by his conversion from the ordinary acceptance of current ideals as safe standards of conduct, to the vigilant open-mindedness of Ibsen. It must at once greatly deepen the sense of moral responsibility. Before conversion the individual anticipates nothing worse in the way of examination at the judgment bar of his conscience than such questions as, Have you kept the commandments? Have you obeyed the law? Have you attended church regularly?

paid your rates and taxes to Cæsar? and contributed, in reason, to charitable institutions? It may be hard to do all these things; but it is still harder not to do them, as our ninety-nine moral cowards in the hundred well know. And even a scoundrel can do them all and yet live a worse life than the smuggler or prostitute who must answer No all through the catechism. Substitute for such a technical examination one in which the whole point to be settled is, Guilty or Not Guilty? one in which there is no more and no less respect for virginity than for incontinence, for subordination than for rebellion, for legality than for illegality, for piety than for blasphemy: in short, for the standard qualities than for the standard faults, and immediately, instead of lowering the ethical standard by relaxing the tests of worth, you raise it by increasing their stringency to a point at which no mere Pharisaism or moral cowardice can pass them.

Naturally this does not please the Pharisee. The respectable lady of the strictest Church principles, who has brought up her children with such relentless regard to their ideal morality that if they have any spirit left in them by the time they arrive at years of independence they use their liberty to rush deliriously to the devil: this unimpeachable woman has always felt it unjust that the respect she wins should be accompanied by deep-seated detestation, whilst the latest spiritual heiress of Nell Gwynne, whom no respectable person dare bow to in the street, is a popular idol. The reason is—though the idealist lady does not know it—that Nell Gwynne is a better woman than she; and the abolition of the idealist test which brings her out a worse one, and its replacement by the realist test which would shew the true relation between them, would be a most desirable step forward in public morals, especially as it would act impartially, and set the good side of the Pharisee above the bad side of the Bohemian as ruthlessly as it would set the good side of the Bohemian above the bad side of the Pharisee.[1] For as long as conven-

[1] The warning implied in this sentence is less needed now than it was twenty years ago. The association of Bohemianism with the

tion goes counter to reality in these matters, people will be led into Hedda Gabler's error of making an ideal of vice. If we maintain the convention that the distinction between Catherine of Russia and Queen Victoria, between Nell Gwynne and Mrs Proudie, is the distinction between a bad woman and a good woman, we need not be surprised when those who sympathize with Catherine and Nell conclude that it is better to be a loose woman than a strict one, and go on recklessly to conceive a prejudice against teetotalism and monogamy, and a prepossession in favour of alcoholic excitement and promiscuous amours. Ibsen himself is kinder to the man who has gone his own way as a rake and a drunkard than to the man who is respectable because he dare not be otherwise. We find that the franker and healthier a boy is, the more certain is he to prefer pirates and highwaymen, or Dumas musketeers, to "pillars of society" as his favorite heroes of romance. We have already seen both Ibsenites and anti-Ibsenites who seem to think that the cases of Nora and Mrs Elvsted are meant to establish a golden rule for women who wish to be 'emancipated': the said golden rule being simply, Run away from your husband. But in Ibsen's view of life, that would come under the same condemnation as the ecclesiastical rule, Cleave to your husband until death do you part. Most people know of a case or two in which it would be wise for a wife to follow the example of Nora or even of Mrs Elvsted. But they must also know cases in which the results of such a course would be as tragi-comic as those of Gregers Werle's attempt in The Wild Duck to do for the Ekdal household what Lona Hessel did for the Bernick houschold. What Ibsen insists on is that there is no golden rule; that conduct must justify itself by its effect

---

artistic professions and with revolutionary political views has been weakened by the revolt of the children of the Bohemians against its domestic squalor and social outlawry. Bohemianism is now rather one of the stigmata of the highly conservative "smart sets" of the idle rich than of the studio, the stage, and the Socialist organizations. (1912).

upon life and not by its conformity to any rule or ideal. And since life consists in the fulfilment of the will, which is constantly growing, and cannot be fulfilled today under the conditions which secured its fulfilment yesterday, he claims afresh the old Protestant right of private judgment in questions of conduct as against all institutions, the so-called Protestant Churches themselves included.

Here I must leave the matter, merely reminding those who may think that I have forgotten to reduce Ibsenism to a formula for them, that its quintessence is that there is no formula.

WHAT IS THE NEW ELEMENT IN THE NORWEGIAN SCHOOL?

I NOW come to the question: Why, since neither human nature nor the specific talent of the playwright has changed since the days of Charles Dickens and Dumas *père*, are the works of Ibsen, of Strindberg, of Tolstoy, of Gorki, of Tchekov, of Brieux, so different from those of the great fictionists of the first half of the nineteenth century? Tolstoy actually imitated Dickens. Ibsen was not Dickens's superior as an observer, nor is Strindberg, nor Gorki, nor Tchekov, nor Brieux. Tolstoy and Ibsen together, gifted as they were, were not otherwise gifted or more gifted than Shakespear and Molière. Yet a generation which could read all Shakespear and Molière, Dickens and Dumas, from end to end without the smallest intellectual or ethical perturbation, was unable to get through a play by Ibsen or a novel by Tolstoy without having its intellectual and moral complacency upset, its religious faith shattered, and its notions of right and wrong conduct thrown into confusion and sometimes even reversed. It is as if these modern men had a spiritual force that was lacking in even the greatest of their forerunners. And yet, what evidence is there in the lives of Wagner, Ibsen, Tolstoy, Strindberg, Gorki, Tchekov, and Brieux, that they were or are better men in any sense than Shakespear, Molière, Dickens and Dumas?

I myself have been told by people that the reading of a single book of mine or the witnessing of a single play has changed their whole lives; and among these are some who tell me that they cannot read Dickens at all, whilst all of them have read books and seen plays by authors obviously quite as gifted as I am, without finding anything more in them than pastime.

The explanation is to be found in what I believe to be a general law of the evolution of ideas. "Every jest is an earnest in the womb of time" says Peter Keegan in John Bull's Other Island. "There's many a true word spoken in jest" says the first villager you engage in philosophic discussion.

All very serious revolutionary propositions begin as huge jokes. Otherwise they would be stamped out by the lynching of their first exponents. Even these exponents themselves have their revelations broken to them mysteriously through their sense of humor. Two friends of mine, travelling in remote parts of Spain, were asked by the shepherds what their religion was. "Our religion," replied one of them, a very highly cultivated author and traveller, with a sardonic turn, "is that there is no God." This reckless remark, taken seriously, might have provided nineteenth century scepticism with a martyr. As it was, the countryside rang with laughter for days afterwards as the stupendous joke was handed round. But it was just by tolerating the blasphemy as a joke that the shepherds began to build it into the fabric of their minds. Being now safely lodged there, it will in due time develop its earnestness; and at last travellers will come who will be taken quite seriously when they say that the imaginary hidalgo in the sky whom the shepherds call God does indeed not exist. And they will remain godless, and call their streets Avenue Paul Bert and so forth, until in due time another joker will arrive with sidesplitting intimations that Shakespear's "There's a divinity that shapes our ends, rough hew them how we will" was a strictly scientific statement of fact, and that "neo-Darwinism" consists for the most part of grossly unscientific statements of superstitious nonsense. Which jest will in its due time come to its own as very solid earnest.

The same phenomenon may be noticed in our attitude towards matters of fact so obvious that no dispute can arise as to their existence. And here the power of laughter is astonishing. It is not enough to say merely that men enable themselves to endure the unbearablest nuisances and the deadliest scourges by setting up a merry convention that they are amusing. We must go further and face the fact that they actually are amused by them—that they are not laughing with the wrong side of the mouth. If you doubt it, read the popular fiction of the pre-Dickensian age, from the novels of

Smollett to Tom Cringle's Log. Poverty in rags is a joke, yellow fever is a joke, drunkenness is a joke, dysentery is a joke, kickings, floggings, falls, frights, humiliations and painful accidents of all sorts are jokes. Henpecked husbands and termagant mothers-in-law are prime jokes. The infirmities of age and the inexperience and shyness of youth are jokes; and it is first-rate fun to insult and torment those that suffer from them.

We take some of these jokes seriously enough now. Humphrey Clinker may not have become absolutely unreadable (I have not tried him for more than forty years); but there is certainly a good deal in the book that is now simply disgusting to the class of reader that in its own day found it uproariously amusing. Much of Tom Cringle has become mere savagery: its humors are those of a donkey race. Also, the fun is forced: one sees beneath the determination of the old sea dog to put a hearty smiling English face on pain and discomfort, that he has not merely looked on at it, and that he did not really like it. The mask of laughter wears slowly off the shames and the evils; but men finally see them as they really are.

Sometimes the change occurs, not between two generations, but actually in the course of a single work by one author. Don Quixote and Mr Pickwick are recognized examples of characters introduced in pure ridicule, and presently gaining the affection and finally the respect of their authors. To them may be added Shakespear's Falstaff. Falstaff is introduced as a subordinate stage figure with no other function than to be robbed by the Prince and Poins, who was originally meant to be the *raisonneur* of the piece, and the chief figure among the prince's dissolute associates. But Poins soon fades into nothing, like several characters in Dickens's early works; whilst Falstaff develops into an enormous joke and an exquisitely mimicked human type. Only in the end the joke withers. The question comes to Shakespear: *Is* this really a laughing matter? Of course there can be only one answer; and Shakespear gives it as best he can by the mouth of the prince become king, who might, one thinks, have the decency to wait until he has redeemed his own character before assuming the right to lecture his boon companion. Falstaff, rebuked and humiliated, dies miserably. His followers are hanged, except Pistol, whose exclamation "Old do I wax; and from my weary limbs honor is cudgelled" is a melancholy exordium to an old age of beggary and imposture.

But suppose Shakespear had begun where he left off! Suppose he had been born at a time when, as the result of a long propaganda of health and temperance, sack had come to be called alcohol, alcohol had come to be called poison, corpulence had come to be regarded as either a disease or a breach of good manners, and a conviction had spread throughout society that the practice of consuming "a half-pennyworth of bread to an intolerable deal of sack" was the cause of so much misery, crime, and racial degeneration that whole States prohibited the sale of potable spirits altogether, and even moderate drinking was more and more regarded as a regrettable weakness! Suppose (to drive the change well home) the women in the great theatrical centres had completely lost that amused indulgence for the drunken man which still exists in some out-of-the-way places, and felt nothing but disgust and anger at the conduct and habits of Falstaff and Sir Toby Belch! Instead of Henry IV and The Merry Wives of Windsor, we should have had something like Zola's L'Assommoir. Indeed, we actually have Cassio, the last of Shakespear's gentleman-drunkards, talking like a temperance reformer, a fact which suggests that Shakespear had been roundly lectured for the offensive vulgarity of Sir Toby by some woman of refinement who refused to see the smallest fun in giving a knight such a name as Belch, with characteristics to correspond to it. Suppose, again, that the first performance of The Taming of the Shrew had led to a modern Feminist demonstration in the theatre, and forced upon Shakespear's consideration a whole century of agitatresses, from Mary Wollstonecraft to Mrs

Fawcett and Mrs Pankhurst, is it not likely that the jest of Katharine and Petruchio would have become the earnest of Nora and Torvald Helmer?

In this light the difference between Dickens and Strindberg becomes intelligible. Strindberg simply refuses to regard the cases of Mrs Raddle and Mrs Macstinger and Mrs Jo Gargery as laughing matters. He insists on taking them seriously as cases of a tyranny which effects more degradation and causes more misery than all the political and sectarian oppressions known to history. Yet it cannot be said that Strindberg, even at his fiercest, is harder on women than Dickens. No doubt his case against them is far more complete, because he does not shirk the specifically sexual factors in it. But this really softens it. If Dickens had allowed us, were it but for an instant, to see Jo Gargery and Mrs Jo as husband and wife, he would perhaps have been accused by fools of immodesty; but we should have at least some more human impression than the one left by an unredeemed shrew married to a grown-up terrified child. It was George Gissing, a modern realist, who first pointed out the power and truth to nature of Dickens's women, and the fact that, funny as they are, they are mostly detestable. Even the amiable ones are silly and sometimes disastrous. When the few good ones are agreeable they are not specifically feminine: they are the Dickensian good man in petticoats; yet they lack that strength which they would have had if Dickens had seen clearly that there is no such species in creation as "Woman, lovely woman," the woman being simply the female of the human species, and that to have one conception of humanity for the woman and another for the man, or one law for the woman and another for the man, or one artistic convention for woman and another for man, or, for the matter of that, a skirt for the woman and a pair of breeches for the man, is as unnatural, and in the long run as unworkable, as one law for the mare and another for the horse. Roughly it may be said that all Dickens's studies from life of the differentiated creatures our artificial sex institutions have made of women are, for all their truth, either vile or ridiculous or both. Betsy Trotwood is a dear because she is an old bachelor in petticoats: a manly woman, like all good women: good men being equally all womanly men. Miss Havisham, an insanely womanly woman, is a horror, a monster, though a Chinese monster: that is, not a natural one, but one produced by deliberate perversion of her humanity. In comparison, Strindberg's women are positively amiable and attractive. The general impression that Strindberg's women are the revenge of a furious woman-hater for his domestic failures, whilst Dickens is a genial idealist (he had little better luck domestically, by the way), is produced solely by Dickens either making fun of the affair or believing that women are born so and must be admitted to the fellowship of the Holy Ghost on a feminine instead of a human basis; whilst Strindberg takes womanliness with deadly seriousness as an evil not to be submitted to for a moment without vehement protest and demand for quite practicable reform. The nurse in his play who wheedles her old nursling and then slips a strait waistcoat on him revolts us; but she is really ten times more lovable and sympathetic than Sairey Gamp, an abominable creature whose very soul is putrid, and who is yet true to life. It is very noteworthy that none of the modern writers who take life as seriously as Ibsen have ever been able to bring themselves to depict depraved people so pitilessly as Dickens and Thackeray and even the genial Dumas *père*. Ibsen was grim enough in all conscience: no man has said more terrible things both privately and publicly; and yet there is not one of Ibsen's characters who is not, in the old phrase, the temple of the Holy Ghost, and who does not move you at moments by the sense of that mystery. The Dickens-Thackeray spirit is, in comparison, that of a Punch and Judy showman, who is never restrained from whacking his little figures unmercifully by the sense that they, too, are images of God, and, "but for the grace of God," very like himself. Dickens does deepen very markedly towards this as he grows older, though it is impossible to pretend that Mrs Wilfer is treated with less levity than Mrs Nickleby; but to Ibsen, from beginning to end, every human being is a sacrifice, whilst to Dickens he is a farce. And there you have the whole difference. No character drawn by Dickens is more ridiculous than Hjalmar Ekdal in The Wild Duck, or more eccentric than old Ekdal, whose toy game-preserve in the garret is more fantastic than the house of Miss Havisham; and yet these Ekdals wring the heart whilst Micawber and Chivery (who sits between the lines of clothes hung out to dry because "it reminds him of groves" as Hjalmar's garret reminds old Ekdal of bear forests) only shake the sides.

It may be that if Dickens could read these lines he would say that the defect was not in him but in his readers; and that if we will return to his books now that Ibsen has opened our eyes we will have to admit that he also saw more in the soul of Micawber than mere laughing gas. And indeed one cannot forget the touches of kindliness and gallantry which ennoble his mirth. Still, between the man who occasionally remembered and the man who never forgot, between Dick Swiveller and Ulrik Brendel, there is a mighty difference. The most that can be said to minimize it is that some of the difference is certainly due to the difference in the attitude of the reader. When an author's works produce violent controversy, and are new, people are apt to read them with that sort of seriousness which is very appropriately called deadly: that is, with a sort of solemn paralysis of every sense except a quite abstract and baseless momentousness which has no more to do with the contents of the author's works than the horrors of a man in delirium tremens have to do with real rats and snakes. The Bible is a sealed literature to most of us because we cannot read it naturally and unsophisticatedly: we are like the old lady who was edified by the word Mesopotamia, or Samuel Butler's Chowbok, who was converted to Christianity by the effect on his imagination of the prayer for Queen Adelaide. Many years elapsed before those who were impressed with Beethoven's music ventured to enjoy it sufficiently to discover what a large part of it is a riot of whimsical fun. As to Ibsen, I remember a performance of The Wild Duck, at which the late Clement Scott pointed out triumphantly that the play was so absurd that even the champions of Ibsen could not help laughing at it. It had not occurred to him that Ibsen could laugh like other men. Not until an author has become so familiar that we are quite at our ease with him, and are up to his tricks of manner, do we cease to imagine that he is, relatively to older writers, terribly serious.

Still, the utmost allowance we can make for this difference does not persuade us that Dickens took the improvidence and futility of Micawber as Ibsen took the improvidence and futility of Hjalmar Ekdal. The difference is plain in the works of Dickens himself; for the Dickens of the second half of the nineteenth century (the Ibsen half) is a different man from the Dickens of the first half. From Hard Times and Little Dorrit to Our Mutual Friend every one of Dickens's books lays a heavy burden on our conscience without flattering us with any hopes of a happy ending. But from The Pickwick Papers to Bleak House you can read and laugh and cry and go happy to bed after forgetting yourself in a jolly book. I have pointed out elsewhere how Charles Lever, after producing a series of books in which the old manner of rollicking through life as if all its follies and failures were splendid jokes, and all its conventional enjoyments and attachments delightful and sincere, suddenly supplied the highly appreciative Dickens (as editor of All the Year Round) with a quite new sort of novel, called A Day's Ride: A Life's Romance, which affected both Dickens and the public very unpleasantly by the bitter but tonic flavor we now know as Ibsenism; for the hero began as that uproarious old joke, the boaster who, being a coward, is led into all sorts of dangerous situations, like Bob Acres and Mr Winkle, and then unexpectedly made them laugh very much on the wrong side of their mouths, exactly as if he were a hero by Ibsen, Strindberg, Turgenieff, Tolstoy, Gorki, Tchekov, or

Brieux. And here there was no question of the author being taken too gloomily. His readers, full of Charles O'Malley and Mickey Free, were approaching the work with the most unsuspicious confidence in its entire jollity. The shock to the security of their senseless laughter caught them utterly unprepared; and they resented it accordingly.

Now that a reaction against realism has set in, and the old jolly ways are coming into fashion again, it is perhaps not so easy as it once was to conceive the extraordinary fascination of this mirthless comedy, this tragedy that stripped the soul naked instead of bedizening it in heroic trappings. But if you have not experienced this fascination yourself, and cannot conceive it, you may take my word for it that it exists, and operates with such power that it puts Shakespear himself out of countenance. And even for those who are in full reaction against it, it can hardly be possible to go back from the death of Hedwig Ekdal to the death of Little Nell otherwise than as a grown man goes down on all fours and pretends to be a bear for the amusement of his children. Nor need we regret this: there are noble compensations for our increase of wisdom and sorrow. After Hedwig you may not be able to cry over Little Nell, but at least you can read Little Dorrit without calling it twaddle, as some of its first critics did. The jests do not become poorer as they mature into earnest. It was not through joyless poverty of soul that Shelley never laughed, but through an enormous apprehension and realization of the gravity of things that seemed mere fun to other men. If there is no Swiveller and no Trabbs's boy in The Pilgrim's Progress, and if Mr Badman is drawn as Ibsen would have drawn him and not as Sheridan would have seen him, it does not follow that there is less strength (and joy is a quality of strength) in Bunyan than in Sheridan and Dickens. After all, the salvation of the world depends on the men who will not take evil good-humoredly, and whose laughter destroys the fool instead of encouraging him. "Rightly to be great," said Shakespear when he had come to the end of mere buffoonery, "is greatly to find quarrel in a straw." The English cry of "Amuse us: take things easily: dress up the world prettily for us" seems mere cowardice to the strong souls that dare look facts in the face; and just so far as people cast off levity and idolatry they find themselves able to bear the company of Bunyan and Shelley, of Ibsen and Strindberg and the great Russian realists, and unable to tolerate the sort of laughter that African tribes cannot restrain when a man is flogged or an animal trapped and wounded. They are gaining strength and wisdom: gaining, in short, that sort of life which we call the life everlasting, a sense of which is worth, for pure well-being alone, all the brutish jollities of Tom Cringle and Humphrey Clinker, and even of Falstaff, Pecksniff, and Micawber.

THE TECHNICAL NOVELTY IN IBSEN'S PLAYS

IT is a striking and melancholy example of the preoccupation of critics with phrases and formulas to which they have given life by taking them into the tissue of their own living minds, and which therefore seem and feel vital and important to them whilst they are to everybody else the deadest and dreariest rubbish (this is the great secret of academic dryasdust), that to this day they remain blind to a new technical factor in the art of popular stage-play making which every considerable playwright has been thrusting under their noses night after night for a whole generation. This technical factor in the play is the discussion. Formerly you had in what was called a well made play an exposition in the first act, a situation in the second, an unravelling in the third. Now you have exposition, situation, and discussion; and the discussion is the test of the playwright. The critics protest in vain. They declare that discussions are not dramatic, and that art should not be didactic. Neither the playwrights nor the public take the smallest notice of them. The discussion conquered Europe in Ibsen's Doll's House; and now the serious playwright recognizes in the discussion not only the main test of his highest powers, but also the real centre of his play's interest. Sometimes he even takes every possible step to assure the public beforehand that his play will be fitted with that newest improvement.

This was inevitable if the drama was ever again to be raised above the childish demand for fables without morals. Children have a settled arbitrary morality: therefore to them moralizing is nothing but an intolerable platitudinizing. The morality of the grown-up is also very largely a settled morality, either purely conventional and of no ethical significance, like the rule of the road or the rule that when you ask for a yard of ribbon the shopkeeper shall give you thirty six inches and not interpret the word yard as he pleases, or else too obvious in its ethics to leave any room for discussion: for instance, that if the boots keeps you waiting too long for your shaving water you must not plunge your razor into his throat in your irritation, no matter how great an effort of self-control your forbearance may cost you.

Now when a play is only a story of how a villain tries to separate an honest young pair of betrothed lovers; to gain the hand of the woman by calumny; and to ruin the man by forgery, murder, false witness, and other commonplaces of the Newgate Calendar, the introduction of a discussion would clearly be ridiculous. There is nothing for sane people to discuss; and any attempt to Chadbandize on the wickedness of such crimes is at once resented as, in Milton's phrase, "moral babble."

But this sort of drama is soon exhausted by people who go often to the theatre. In twenty visits one can see every possible change rung on all the available plots and incidents out of which plays of this kind can be manufactured. The illusion of reality is soon lost: in fact it may be doubted whether any adult ever entertains it: it is only to very young children that the fairy queen is anything but an actress. But at the age when we cease to mistake the figures on the stage for *dramatis personae*, and know that they are actors and actresses, the charm of the performer begins to assert itself; and the child who would have been cruelly hurt by being told that the Fairy Queen was only Miss Smith dressed up to look like one, becomes the man who goes to the theatre expressly to see Miss Smith, and is fascinated by her skill or beauty to the point of delighting in plays which would be unendurable to him without her. Thus we get plays "written round" popular performers, and popular performers who give value to otherwise useless plays by investing them with their own attractiveness. But all these enterprises are, commercially speaking, desperately precarious. To begin with, the supply of performers whose attraction is so far independent of the play that their inclusion in the cast sometimes makes the difference between success and failure is too small to enable all our theatres, or even many of them, to depend on their actors rather than on their plays. And to finish with, no actor can make bricks entirely without straw. From Grimaldi to Sothern, Jefferson, and Henry Irving (not to mention living actors) we have had players succeeding once in a lifetime in grafting on to a play which would have perished without them some figure imagined wholly by themselves; but none of them has been able to repeat the feat, nor to save many of the plays in which he has appeared from failure. In the long run nothing can retain the interest of the playgoer after the theatre has lost its illusion for his childhood, and its glamor for his adolescence, but a constant supply of interesting plays; and this is specially true in London, where the expense and trouble of theatregoing have been raised to a point at which it is surprising that sensible people of middle age go to the theatre at all. As a matter of fact, they mostly stay at home.

Now an interesting play cannot in the nature of things mean anything but a play in which problems of conduct and character of personal importance to the audience are raised and suggestively discussed. People have a thrifty sense of taking away something from such plays: they not only have had something for their money, but they retain that something as a permanent possession. Consequently none of the commonplaces of the box office hold good of such plays. In vain does the experienced acting manager declare that people want to be amused and not preached at in the theatre; that they will not stand long speeches; that a play must not contain more than 18,000 words; that it must not begin before nine nor last beyond eleven; that there must be no politics and no religion in it; that breach of these golden rules will drive people to the variety theatres; that there must be a woman of bad character, played by a very attractive actress, in the piece; and so on and so forth. All these counsels are valid for plays in which there is nothing to discuss. They may be disregarded by the playwright who is a moralist and a debater as well as a dramatist. From him, within the inevitable limits set by the clock and by the physical endurance of the human frame, people will stand anything as soon as they are matured enough and cultivated enough to be susceptible to the appeal of his particular form of art. The difficulty at present is that mature and cultivated people do not go to the theatre, just as they do not read penny novelets; and when an attempt is made to cater for them they do not respond to it in time, partly because they have not the habit of playgoing, and partly because it takes too long for them to find out that the new theatre is not like all the other theatres. But when they do at last find their way there, the attraction is not the firing of blank cartridges at one another by actors, nor the pretence of falling down dead that ends the stage combat, nor the simulation of erotic thrills by a pair of stage lovers, nor any of the other tomfooleries called action, but the exhibition and discussion of the character and conduct of stage figures who are made to appear real by the art of the playwright and the performers.

This, then, is the extension of the old dramatic form effected by Ibsen. Up to a certain point in the last act, A Doll's House is a play that might be turned into a very ordinary French drama by the excision of a few lines, and the substitution of a sentimental happy ending for the famous last scene: indeed the very first thing the theatrical wiseacres did with it was to effect exactly this transformation, with the result that the play thus pithed had no success and attracted no notice worth mentioning. But at just that point in the last act, the heroine very unexpectedly (by the wiseacres) stops her emotional acting and says: "We must sit down and discuss all this that has been happening between us." And it was by this new technical feature: this addition of a new movement, as musicians would say, to the dramatic form, that A Doll's House conquered Europe and founded a new school of dramatic art.

Since that time the discussion has expanded far beyond the limits of the last ten minutes of an otherwise "well made" play. The disadvantage of putting the discussion at the end was not only that it came when the audience was fatigued, but that it was necessary to see the play over again, so as to follow the earlier acts in the light of the final discussion, before it became fully intelligible. The practical utility of this book is due to the fact that unless the spectator at an Ibsen play has read the pages referring to it beforehand, it is hardly possible for him to get its bearings at a first hearing if he approaches it, as most spectators still do, with conventional idealist prepossessions. Accordingly, we now have plays, including some of my own, which begin with discussion and end with action, and others in which the discussion interpenetrates the action from beginning to end. When Ibsen invaded England discussion had vanished from the stage; and women could not write plays. Within twenty years women were writing better plays than men; and these plays were passionate arguments from beginning to end. The action of such plays consists of a case to be argued. If the case is uninteresting or stale or badly conducted or obviously trumped up, the play is a bad one. If it is important and novel and convincing, or at least disturbing, the play is a good one. But anyhow the play in which there is no argument and no case no longer counts as serious drama. It may still please the child in us as Punch and Judy does; but nobody nowadays pretends to regard the well made play as anything more than a commercial product which is not in question when modern schools of serious drama are under discussion. Indeed within ten years of the production of A Doll's House in London, audiences had become so derisive of the more obvious and hackneyed features of the methods of Sardou that it became dangerous to resort to them; and playwrights who persisted in "constructing" plays in the old French manner lost ground not for lack of ideas, but because their technique was unbearably out of fashion.

In the new plays, the drama arises through a conflict of unsettled ideals rather than through vulgar attachments, rapacities, generosities, resentments, ambitions, misunderstandings, oddities and so forth as to which no moral question is raised. The conflict is not between clear right and wrong: the villain is as conscientious as the hero, if not more so: in fact, the question which makes the play interesting (when it *is* interesting) is which is the villain and which the hero. Or, to put it another way, there are no villains and no heroes. This strikes the critics mainly as a departure from dramatic art; but it is really the inevitable return to nature which ends all the merely technical fashions. Now the natural is mainly the everyday; and its climaxes must be, if not everyday, at least everylife, if they are to have any importance for the spectator. Crimes, fights, big legacies, fires, shipwrecks, battles, and thunderbolts are mistakes in a play, even when they can be effectively simulated. No doubt they may acquire dramatic interest by putting a character through the test of an emergency; but the test is likely to be too obviously theatrical, because, as the playwright cannot in the nature of things have much experience of such catastrophes, he is forced to substitute a set of conventions or conjectures for the feelings they really produce.

In short, pure accidents are not dramatic: they are only anecdotic. They may be sensational, impressive, provocative, ruinous, curious, or a dozen other things; but they have no specifically dramatic interest. There is no drama in being knocked down or run over. The catastrophe in Hamlet would not be in the least dramatic had Polonius fallen downstairs and broken his neck, Claudius succumbed to delirium tremens, Hamlet forgotten to breathe in the intensity of his philosophic speculation, Ophelia died of Danish measles, Laertes been shot by the palace sentry, and Rosencrantz and Guildenstern drowned in the North Sea. Even as it is, the Queen, who poisons herself by accident, has an air of being polished off to get her out of the way: her death is the one dramatic failure of the piece. Bushels of good paper have been inked in vain by writers who imagined they could produce a tragedy by killing everyone in the last act accidentally. As a matter of fact no accident, however sanguinary, can produce a moment of real drama, though a difference of opinion between husband and wife as to living in town or country might be the beginning of an appalling tragedy or a capital comedy.

It may be said that everything is an accident: that Othello's character is an accident, Iago's character another accident, and the fact that they happened to come together in the Venetian service an even more accidental accident. Also that Torvald Helmer might just as likely have married Mrs Nickleby as Nora. Granting this trifling for what it is worth, the fact remains that marriage is no more an accident than birth or death: that is, it is expected to happen to everybody. And if every man has a good deal of Torvald Helmer in him, and every woman a good deal of Nora, neither their characters nor their meeting and marrying are accidents. Othello, though entertaining, pitiful, and resonant with the thrills a master of language can produce by mere artistic sonority, is certainly much more accidental than A Doll's House; but it is correspondingly less important and interesting to us. It has been kept alive, not by its manufactured misunderstandings and stolen handkerchiefs and the like, nor even by its orchestral verse, but by its exhibition and discussion of human nature, marriage, and jealousy; and it would be a prodigiously better play if it were a serious discussion of the highly interesting problem of how a simple Moorish soldier would get on with a "supersubtle" Venetian lady of fashion if he married her. As it is, the play turns on a mistake; and though a mistake can produce a murder, which is the vulgar substitute for a tragedy, it cannot produce a real tragedy in the modern sense. Reflective people are not more interested in the Chamber of Horrors than in their own homes, nor in murderers, victims, and villains than in themselves; and the moment a man has acquired sufficient reflective power to cease gaping at waxworks, he is on his way to losing interest in Othello, Desdemona, and Iago exactly to the extent to which they become interesting to the police. Cassio's weakness for drink comes much nearer home to most of us than Othello's strangling and throat cutting, or Iago's theatrical confidence trick. The proof is that Shakespear's professional colleagues, who exploited all his sensational devices, and piled up torture on murder and incest on adultery until they had far out-Heroded Herod, are now unmemorable and unplayable. Shakespear survives because he coolly treated the sensational horrors of his borrowed plots as inorganic theatrical accessories, using them simply as pretexts for dramatizing human character as it exists in the normal world. In enjoying and discussing his plays we unconsciously discount the combats and murders: commentators are never so astray (and consequently so ingenious) as when they take Hamlet seriously as a madman, Macbeth as a homicidal Highlander, and impish humorists like Richard and Iago as lurid villains of the Renascence. The plays in which these figures appear could be changed into comedies without altering a hair of their beards. Shakespear, had anyone been intelligent enough to tax him with this, would perhaps have said that most crimes are accidents that happen to people exactly like ourselves, and that Macbeth, under propitious circumstances, would have made an exemplary rector of Stratford, a real criminal being a defective monster, a human accident, useful on the stage only for minor parts such as Don Johns, second murderers, and the like. Anyhow, the fact remains that Shakespear survives by what he has in common with Ibsen, and not by what he has in common with Webster and the rest. Hamlet's surprise at finding that he "lacks gall" to behave in the idealistically conventional manner, and that no extremity of rhetoric about the duty of revenging "a dear father slain" and exterminating the "bloody bawdy villain" who murdered him seems to make any difference in their domestic relations in the palace in Elsinore, still keeps us talking about him and going to the theatre to listen to him, whilst the older Hamlets, who never had any Ibsenist hesitations, and shammed madness, and entangled the courtiers in the arras and burnt them, and stuck hard to the theatrical school of the fat boy in Pickwick ("I wants to make your flesh creep"), are as dead as John Shakespear's mutton.

We have progressed so rapidly on this point under the

impulse given to the drama by Ibsen that it seems strange now to contrast him favorably with Shakespear on the ground that he avoided the old catastrophes which left the stage strewn with the dead at the end of an Elizabethan tragedy. For perhaps the most plausible reproach levelled at Ibsen by modern critics of his own school is just that survival of the old school in him which makes the death rate so high in his last acts. Do Oswald Alving, Hedvig Ekdal, Rosmer and Rebecca, Hedda Gabler, Solness, Eyolf, Borkman, Rubeck and Irene die dramatically natural deaths, or are they slaughtered in the classic and Shakespearean manner, partly because the audience expects blood for its money, partly because it is difficult to make people attend seriously to anything except by startling them with some violent calamity? It is so easy to make out a case for either view that I shall not argue the point. The post-Ibsen playwrights apparently think that Ibsen's homicides and suicides were forced. In Tchekov's Cherry Orchard, for example, where the sentimental ideals of our amiable, cultured, Schumann playing propertied class are reduced to dust and ashes by a hand not less deadly than Ibsen's because it is so much more caressing, nothing more violent happens than that the family cannot afford to keep up its old house. In Granville Barker's plays, the campaign against our society is carried on with all Ibsen's implacability; but the one suicide (in Waste) is unhistorical; for neither Parnell nor Dilke, who were the actual cases in point of the waste which was the subject of the play, killed himself. I myself have been reproached because the characters in my plays "talk but do nothing", meaning that they do not commit felonies. As a matter of fact we have come to see that it is no true *dénouement* to cut the Gordian knot as Alexander did with a stroke of the sword. If people's souls are tied up by law and public opinion it is much more tragic to leave them to wither in these bonds than to end their misery and relieve the salutary compunction of the audience by outbreaks of violence. Judge Brack was, on the whole, right when he said that people dont do such things.

If they did, the idealists would be brought to their senses very quickly indeed.

But in Ibsen's plays the catastrophe, even when it seems forced, and when the ending of the play would be more tragic without it, is never an accident; and the play never exists for its sake. His nearest to an accident is the death of little Eyolf, who falls off a pier and is drowned. But this instance only reminds us that there is one good dramatic use for an accident: it can awaken people. When England wept over the deaths of little Nell and Paul Dombey, the strong soul of Ruskin was moved to scorn: to novelists who were at a loss to make their books sell he offered the formula: When at a loss, kill a child. But Ibsen did not kill little Eyolf to manufacture pathos. The surest way to achieve a thoroughly bad performance of Little Eyolf is to conceive it as a sentimental tale of a drowned darling. Its drama lies in the awakening of Allmers and his wife to the despicable quality and detestable rancors of the life they have been idealizing as blissful and poetic. They are so sunk in their dream that the awakening can be effected only by a violent shock. And that is just the one dramatically useful thing an accident can do. It can shock. Hence the accident that befalls Eyolf.

As to the deaths in Ibsen's last acts, they are a sweeping up of the remains of dramatically finished people. Solness's fall from the tower is as obviously symbolic as Phaeton's fall from the chariot of the sun. Ibsen's dead bodies are those of the exhausted or destroyed: he does not kill Hilda, for instance, as Shakespear killed Juliet. He is ruthless enough with Hedvig and Eyolf because he wants to use their deaths to expose their parents; but if he had written Hamlet nobody would have been killed in the last act except perhaps Horatio, whose correct nullity might have provoked Fortinbras to let some of the moral sawdust out of him with his sword. For Shakespearean deaths in Ibsen you must go back to Lady Inger and the plays of his nonage, with which this book is not concerned.

The drama was born of old from the union of two desires:

the desire to have a dance and the desire to hear a story. The dance became a rant: the story became a situation. When Ibsen began to make plays, the art of the dramatist had shrunk into the art of contriving a situation. And it was held that the stranger the situation, the better the play. Ibsen saw that, on the contrary, the more familiar the situation, the more interesting the play. Shakespear had put ourselves on the stage but not our situations. Our uncles seldom murder our fathers, and cannot legally marry our mothers; we do not meet witches; our kings are not as a rule stabbed and succeeded by their stabbers; and when we raise money by bills we do not promise to pay pounds of our flesh. Ibsen supplies the want left by Shakespear. He gives us not only ourselves, but ourselves in our own situations. The things that happen to his stage figures are things that happen to us. One consequence is that his plays are much more important to us than Shakespear's. Another is that they are capable both of hurting us cruelly and of filling us with excited hopes of escape from idealistic tyrannies, and with visions of intenser life in the future.

Changes in technique follow inevitably from these changes in the subject matter of the play. When a dramatic poet can give you hopes and visions, such old maxims as that stage-craft is the art of preparation become boyish, and may be left to those unfortunate playwrights who, being unable to make anything really interesting happen on the stage, have to acquire the art of continually persuading the audience that it is going to happen presently. When he can stab people to the heart by shewing them the meanness or cruelty of something they did yesterday and intend to do tomorrow, all the old tricks to catch and hold their attention become the silliest of superfluities. The play called The Murder of Gonzago, which Hamlet makes the players act before his uncle, is artlessly constructed; but it produces a greater effect on Claudius than the Œdipus of Sophocles, because it is about himself. The writer who practises the art of Ibsen therefore discards all the old tricks of preparation, catastrophe, *dénouement*, and so forth without thinking about it, just as a modern rifleman never dreams of providing himself with powder horns, percussion caps, and wads: indeed he does not know the use of them. Ibsen substituted a terrible art of sharpshooting at the audience, trapping them, fencing with them, aiming always at the sorest spot in their consciences. Never mislead an audience, was an old rule. But the new school will trick the spectator into forming a meanly false judgment, and then convict him of it in the next act, often to his grievous mortification. When you despise something you ought to take off your hat to, or admire and imitate something you ought to loathe, you cannot resist the dramatist who knows how to touch these morbid spots in you and make you see that they are morbid. The dramatist knows that as long as he is teaching and saving his audience, he is as sure of their strained attention as a dentist is, or the Angel of the Annunciation. And though he may use all the magic of art to make you forget the pain he causes you or to enhance the joy of the hope and courage he awakens, he is never occupied in the old work of manufacturing interest and expectation with materials that have neither novelty, significance, nor relevance to the experience or prospects of the spectators.

Hence a cry has arisen that the post-Ibsen play is not a play, and that its technique, not being the technique described by Aristotle, is not a technique at all. I will not enlarge on this: the fun poked at my friend Mr A. B. Walkley in the prologue of Fanny's First Play need not be repeated here. But I may remind him that the new technique is new only on the modern stage. It has been used by preachers and orators ever since speech was invented. It is the technique of playing upon the human conscience; and it has been practised by the playwright whenever the playwright has been capable of it. Rhetoric, irony, argument, paradox, epigram, parable, the rearrangement of haphazard facts into orderly and intelligent situations: these are both the oldest and the newest arts of the drama; and your plot construction and art of preparation are only the tricks of theatrical talent and the shifts of moral sterility, not the weapons of dramatic genius. In the theatre of Ibsen we are not flattered spectators killing an idle hour with an ingenious and amusing entertainment: we are "guilty creatures sitting at a play"; and the technique of pastime is no more applicable than at a murder trial.

The technical novelties of the Ibsen and post-Ibsen plays are, then: first, the introduction of the discussion and its development until it so overspreads and interpenetrates the action that it finally assimilates it, making play and discussion practically identical; and, second, as a consequence of making the spectators themselves the persons of the drama, and the incidents of their own lives its incidents, the disuse of the old stage tricks by which audiences had to be induced to take an interest in unreal people and improbable circumstances, and the substitution of a forensic technique of recrimination, disillusion, and penetration through ideals to the truth, with a free use of all the rhetorical and lyrical arts of the orator, the preacher, the pleader, and the rhapsodist.

It must now be plain to my readers that the doctrine taught by Ibsen can never be driven home from the stage whilst his plays are presented to us in haphazard order at the commercial theatres. Indeed our commercial theatres are so well aware of this that they have from the first regarded Ibsen as hopelessly uncommercial: he might as well never have lived as far as they are concerned. Even the new advanced theatres which now deal freely with what I have called post-Ibsenist plays hardly meddle with him. Had it not been for the great national service disinterestedly rendered by Mr William Archer in giving us a complete translation of Ibsen's plays (a virtually unremunerated public service which I hope the State will recognize fitly), Ibsen would be less known in England than Swedenborg. By losing his vital contribution to modern thought we are losing ground relatively to the countries which, like Germany, have made his works familiar to their playgoers. But even in Germany Ibsen's meaning is seen only by glimpses. What we need is a theatre devoted primarily to Ibsen as the Bayreuth Festspielhaus is devoted to Wagner. I have shewn how the plays, as they succeed one another, are parts of a continuous discussion; how the difficulty left by one is dealt with in the next; how Mrs Alving is a reply to your hasty remark that Nora Helmer ought to be ashamed of herself for leaving her husband; how Gregers Werle warns you not to be as great a fool in your admiration of Lona Hessel as of Patient Grisel. The plays should, like Wagner's Ring, be performed in cycles; so that Ibsen may hunt you down from position to position until you are finally cornered.

The larger truth of the matter is that modern European literature and music now form a Bible far surpassing in importance to us the ancient Hebrew Bible that has served us so long. The notion that inspiration is something that happened thousands of years ago, and was then finished and done with, never to occur again: in other words, the theory that God retired from business at that period and has not since been heard from, is as silly as it is blasphemous. He who does not believe that revelation is continuous does not believe in revelation at all, however familiar his parrot's tongue and pewsleepy ear may be with the word. There comes a time when the formula "Also sprach Zarathustra" succeeds to the formula "Thus saith the Lord", and when the parable of the doll's house is more to our purpose than the parable of the prodigal son. When Bunyan published The Pilgrim's Progress, his first difficulty was with the literal people who said, "There is no such individual in the directory as Christian, and no such place in the gazetteer as the City of Destruction: therefore you are a liar". Bunyan replied by citing the parables: asking, in effect, whether the story of the wise and foolish virgins is also a lie. A couple of centuries or so later, when I myself wrote a play for the Salvation Army to shew them that the dramatic method might be used for their gospel as effectively as the lyric or orchestral method, I was told that unless I could guarantee that the persons in my play actually existed, and the incidents had actually occurred, I, like Bunyan, would be regarded by the elderly soldiers in the army as no better than Ananias. As it was useless for me to try to make these simple souls understand that in real life truth is revealed by parables and falsehood supported by facts, I had to leave the army to its oratorical metaphors and to its popular songs about heartbroken women waiting for the footsteps of their drunken husbands, and hearing instead the joyous step of the converted man whose newly found salvation will dry all their tears. I had not the heart to suggest that these happy pairs were as little authentic as The Second Mrs Tanqueray; for I spied behind the army's confusion of truth with mere fact the old doubt whether anything good can come out of the theatre, a doubt as inveterate and neither more nor less justifiable than the doubt of our Secularists whether anything good can come out of the gospels.

But I think Ibsen has proved the right of the drama to take scriptural rank, and his own right to canonical rank as one of the major prophets of the modern Bible. The sooner we recognize that rank and give up the idea of trying to make a fashionable entertainment of his plays the better. It ends in our not performing them at all, and remaining in barbarous and dangerous ignorance of the case against idealism. We want a frankly doctrinal theatre. There is no more reason for making a doctrinal theatre inartistic than for putting a cathedral organ out of tune: indeed all experience shews that doctrine alone nerves us to the effort called for by the greatest art. I therefore suggest that even the sciolists and voluptuaries who care for nothing in art but its luxuries and its executive feats are as strongly interested in the establishment of such a theatre as those for whom the What is always more important than the How, if only because the How cannot become really magical until such magic is indispensable to the revelation of an all-important What.

I do not suggest that the Ibsen theatre should confine itself to Ibsen any more than the Established Church confines itself to Jeremiah. The post-Ibsenists could also be expounded there; and Strindberg should have his place, were it only as Devil's Advocate. But performances should be in the order of academic courses, designed so as to take audiences over the whole ground as Ibsen and his successors took them; so that the exposition may be consecutive. Otherwise the doctrine will not be interesting, and the audiences will not come regularly. The efforts now being made to regenerate the drama are often wasted through lack of doctrinal conviction and consequent want of system, the net result being an irresolute halting between the doctrinal and the merely entertaining.

For this sort of enterprise an endowment is necessary, because commercial capital is not content in a theatre with reasonable interest: it demands great gains even at the cost of great hazards. Besides, nobody will endow mere pleasure, whereas doctrine can always command endowment. It is the foolish disclaiming of doctrine that keeps dramatic art unendowed. When we ask for an endowed theatre we always take the greatest pains to assure everybody that we do not mean anything unpleasantly serious, and that our endowed theatre will be as bright and cheery (meaning as low and common) as the commercial theatres. As a result of which we get no endowment. When we have the sense to profit by this lesson and promise that our endowed theatre will be an important place, and that it will make people of low tastes and tribal or commercial ideas horribly uncomfortable by its efforts to bring conviction of sin to them, we shall get endowment as easily as the religious people who are not foolishly ashamed to ask for what they want.

SOCIALISM

THE ECONOMIC BASIS OF SOCIALISM

(*From Fabian Essays*, 1889)

ALL economic analyses begin with the cultivation of the earth. To the mind's eye of the astronomer the earth is a ball spinning in space without ulterior motives. To the bodily eye of the primitive cultivator it is a vast green plain, from which, by sticking a spade into it, wheat and other edible matters can be made to spring. To the eye of the sophisticated city man this vast green plain appears rather as a great gaming table, your chances in the game depending chiefly on the place where you deposit your stakes. To the economist, again, the green plain is a sort of burial place of hidden treasure, where all the forethought and industry of man are set at naught by the caprice of the power which hid the treasure. The wise and patient workman strikes his spade in here, and with heavy toil can discover nothing but a poor quality of barley, some potatoes, and plentiful nettles, with a few dock leaves to cure his stings. The foolish spendthrift on the other side of the hedge, gazing idly at the sand glittering in the sun, suddenly realizes that the earth is offering him gold—is dancing it before his listless eyes lest it should escape him. Another man, searching for some more of this tempting gold, comes upon a great hoard of coal, or taps a jet of petroleum. Thus is Man mocked by Earth his stepmother, and never knows as he tugs at her closed hand whether it contains diamonds or flints, good red wheat or a few clayey and blighted cabbages. Thus too he becomes a gambler, and scoffs at the theorists who prate of industry and honesty and equality. Yet against this fate he eternally rebels. For since in gambling the many must lose in order that the few may win; since dishonesty is mere shadow-grasping where everyone is dishonest; and since inequality is bitter to all except the highest, and miserably lonely for him, men come greatly to desire that these capricious gifts of Nature might be intercepted by some agency having the power and the goodwill to distribute them justly according to the labor done by each in the collective search for them. This desire is Socialism; and, as a means to its fulfilment, Socialists have devised communes, kingdoms, principalities, churches, manors, and finally, when all these had succumbed to the old gambling spirit, the Social Democratic State, which yet remains to be tried. As against Socialism, the gambling spirit urges man to allow no rival to come between his private individual powers and Stepmother Earth, but rather to secure some acres of her and take his chance of getting diamonds instead of cabbages. This is Private Property or Unsocialism. Our own choice is shewn by our continual aspiration to possess property, our common hailing of it as sacred, our setting apart of the word Respectable for those who have attained it, our ascription of pre-eminent religiousness to commandments forbidding its violation, and our identification of law and order among men with its protection. Therefore is it vital to a living knowledge of our society that Private Property should be known in every step of its progress from its source in cupidity to its end in confusion.

Let us, in the manner of the Political Economist, trace the effects of settling a country by private property with undisturbed law and order. Figure to yourself the vast green plain of a country virgin to the spade, awaiting the advent of man. Imagine then the arrival of the first colonist, the original Adam, developed by centuries of civilization into an Adam Smith, prospecting for a suitable patch of Private Property. Adam is, as Political Economy fundamentally assumes him to be, "on the make": therefore he drives his spade into, and sets up his stockade around, the most fertile and favorably situated patch he can find. When he has tilled it, Political Economy, inspired to prophecy by the spectacle, metaphorically exhibits Adam's little patch of cultivation as a pool that will yet rise and submerge the whole land. Let us not forget this trope: it is the key to the ever-recurring phrase "margin of cultivation," in which, as may now be perceived, there lurks a little unsuspected poetry. And truly the pool soon spreads. Other Adams come, all on the make, and therefore all sure to pre-empt patches as near as may be to the first Adam's, partly because he has chosen the best situation, partly for the pleasure of his society and conversation, and partly because where two men are assembled together there is a two-man power that is far more than double one-man power, being indeed in some instances a quite new force, totally destructive of the idiotic general hypothesis that society is no more than the sum of the units which compose it. These Adams, too, bring their Cains and Abels, who do not murder one another, but merely pre-empt adjacent patches. And so the pool rises, and the margin spreads more and more remote from the centre, until the pool becomes a lake, and the lake an inland sea.

RENT

But in the course of this inundation the caprices of Nature begin to operate. That specially fertile region upon which Adam pitched is sooner or later all pre-empted; and there is nothing for the newcomer to pre-empt save soil of the second quality. Again, division of labor sets in among Adam's neighbors; and with it, of course, comes the establishment of a market for the exchange of the products of their divided labor. Now it is not well to be far afield from that market, because distance from it involves extra cost for roads, beasts of burden, time consumed in travelling thither and back again. All this will be saved to Adam at the centre of cultivation, and incurred by the newcomer at the margin of cultivation. Let us estimate the annual value of Adam's produce at £1000, and the annual produce of the newcomer's land on the margin of cultivation at £500, assuming that Adam and the newcomer are equally industrious. Here is a clear advantage of £500 a year to the first comer. This £500 is economic rent. It matters not at all that it is merely a difference of income and not an overt payment from a tenant to a landlord. The two men labor equally; and yet one gets £500 a year more than the other through the superior fertility of his land and convenience of its situation. The excess due to that fertility is rent; and before long we shall find it recognized as such and paid in the fashion with which we are familiar. For why should not Adam let his patch to the newcomer at a rent of £500 a year? Since the produce will be £1000, the newcomer will have £500 left for himself, or as much as he could obtain by cultivating a patch of his own at the margin; and it is pleasanter, besides, to be in the centre of society than on the outskirts of it. The newcomer will himself propose the arrangement; and Adam may retire as an idle landlord with a perpetual pension of £500 rent. The excess of fertility in Adam's land is thenceforth recognized as rent and paid, as it is today, regularly by a worker to a drone. A few samples of the way in which this simple and intelligible transaction is stated by our economists may now, I hope, be quoted without any danger of their proving so difficult as they appear in the textbooks from which I have copied them.

Stuart Mill[1] says that "the rent of land consists of the excess of its return above the return to the worst land in cultivation." Fawcett[2] says that "the rent of land represents the pecuniary value of the advantages which such land possesses over the worst land in cultivation." Professor Marshall[3] says that "the rent of a piece of land is the excess of its produce over the produce of an adjacent piece of land which would not be cultivated at all if rent were paid for it." Professor Sidgwick[4] cautiously puts it that "the normal rent *per acre* of any piece [of land] is the surplus of the value of its produce over the value of the net produce per acre of the least advantageous land that it is profitable to cultivate." General Walker[5] declares that "specifically, the rent of any

[1] Principles of Political Economy, vol. i. Index to chap. xvi. (1865).

[2] Manual of Political Economy, Book II. chap. iii. p. 116 (1876).

[3] Economics of Industry, Book II. chap. iii. sec. 3, p. 84 (1870).

[4] Principles of Political Economy, Book II. chap. vii. p. 301 (1883).

[5] Brief Text Book of Political Economy, chap. ii. sec. 216, p. 173 (1885).

piece of land is determined by the difference between its annual yield and that of the least productive land actually cultivated for the supply of the same market, it being assumed that the quality of the land as a productive agent is, in neither case, impaired or improved by such cultivation." All these definitions are offered by the authors as elaborations of that given by their master Ricardo,[1] who says, "Rent is that portion of the produce of the earth which is paid to the landlord for the use of the original and indestructible powers of the soil."

THE COUNTY FAMILY

Let us return to our ideal country. Adam is retiring from productive industry on £500 a year; and his neighbors are hastening to imitate him as fresh tenants present themselves. The first result is the beginning of a tradition that the oldest families in the country enjoy a superior position to the rest, and that the main advantage of their superior position is that they enjoy incomes without working. Nevertheless, since they still depend on their tenants' labor for their subsistence, they continue to pay Labor, with a capital L, a certain meed of mouth honor; and the resultant association of prosperity with idleness, and praise with industry, practically destroys morality by setting up that incompatibility between conduct and principle which is the secret of the ingrained cynicism of our own time, and which produces the curious Ricardian phenomenon of the man of business who goes on Sunday to the church with the regularity of the village blacksmith, there to renounce and abjure before his God the line of conduct which he intends to pursue with all his might during the following week.

According to our hypothesis, the inland sea of cultivation has now spread into the wilderness so far that at its margin the return to a man's labor for a year is only £500. But as there is always a flood tide in that sea, caused by the incessant increase of population, the margin will not stop

[1] Principles of Political Economy and Taxation, chap. ii. p. 34 (1817).

there: it will at last encroach upon every acre of cultivable land, rising to the snow line on the mountains and falling to the coast of the actual salt water sea, but always reaching the barrenest places last of all, because the cultivators are still, as ever, on the make, and will not break bad land when better is to be had. But suppose that now, at last, the uttermost belt of free land is reached, and that upon it the yield to a man's year's labor is only £100. Clearly now the rent of Adam's primeval patch has risen to £900, since that is the excess of its produce over what is by this time all that is to be had rent free. But Adam has yielded up his land for £500 a year to a tenant. It is this tenant accordingly who now lets Adam's patch for £900 a year to the newcomer, who of course loses nothing by the bargain, since it leaves him the £100 a year with which he must be content anyhow. Accordingly he labors on Adam's land; raises £1000 a year from it; keeps £100 and pays £900 to Adam's tenant, who pays £500 to Adam, keeping £400 for himself, and thus also becoming an idle gentleman, though with a somewhat smaller income than the man of older family. It has, in fact, come to this, that the private property in Adam's land is divided between three men, the first doing none of the work and getting half the produce; the second doing none of the work and getting two-fifths of the produce; and the third doing all the work and getting only one-tenth of the produce. Incidentally also, the moralist who is sure to have been prating somewhere about private property leading to the encouragement of industry, the establishment of a healthy incentive, and the distribution of wealth according to exertion, is exposed as a futile purblind person, starting *a priori* from blank ignorance, and proceeding deductively to mere contradiction and patent folly.

All this, however, is a mere trifle compared to the sequel. When the inland sea has risen to its confines—when there is nothing but a strip of sand round the coast between the furrow and the wave—when the very waves themselves are cultivated by fisherfolk—when the pastures and timber forests have touched the snow line—when, in short, the land is all private property, yet every man is a proprietor, though it may be only of a tenant right—he enjoys fixity of tenure at what is called a fair rent: that is, he fares as well as he could on land wholly his own. All the rent is economic rent: the landlord cannot raise it nor the tenant lower it: it is fixed naturally by the difference between the fertility of the land for which it is paid and that of the worst land in the country. Compared with the world as we know it, such a state of things is freedom and happiness.

THE PROLETARIAT

But at this point there appears in the land a man in a strange plight—one who wanders from snow line to sea coast in search of land, and finds none that is not the property of someone else. Private property had forgotten this man. On the roads he is a vagrant: off them he is a trespasser: he is the first disinherited son of Adam, the first Proletarian, one in whose seed all the generations of the earth shall yet be blest, but who is himself for the present foodless, homeless, shiftless, superfluous, and everything that turns a man into a tramp or a thrall. Yet he is still a man with brain and muscle, able to devise and execute, able to deal puissantly with land if only he could get access to it. But how to get that access! Necessity is the mother of Invention. It may be that this second Adam, the first father of the great Proletariat, has one of those scarce brains which are not the least of Nature's capricious gifts. If the fertile field yields rent, why not the fertile brain? Here is the first Adam's patch still yielding its £1000 a year to the labor of the tenant who, as we have seen, has to pay £900 away in rent. How if the Proletarian were boldly to bid £1000 a year to that man for the property? Apparently the result would be the starvation of the Proletarian, since he would have to part with all the produce. But what if the Proletarian can contrive—invent—anticipate a new want—turn the land to some hitherto undreamt-of use—wrest £1500 a year from the soil and site that only yielded £1000 before? If he can do this, he can pay the full £1000 rent, and have an income of £500 left for himself. This is his profit—the rent of his ability—the excess of its produce over that of ordinary stupidity. Here then is the opportunity of the cunning Proletarian, the hero of that modern Plutarch, Mr Samuel Smiles. Truly, as Napoleon said, the career is open to the talented. But alas! the social question is no more a question of the fate of the talented than of the idiotic. In due replenishment of the earth there comes another Proletarian who is no cleverer than other men, and can do as much, but not more than they. For him there is no rent of ability. How then is he to get a tenant right? Let us see. It is certain that by this time not only will the new devices of the renter of ability have been copied by people incapable of inventing them; but division of labor, the use of tools and money, and the economies of civilization will have greatly increased man's power of extracting wealth from Nature. All this increase will be so much gain to the holder of a tenant right, since his rent is a fixed payment out of the produce of his holding, and the balance is his own. Therefore an addition to the produce not foreseen by the landlord enriches the tenant. So that it may well be that the produce of land on the margin of cultivation, which, as we have seen, fixes the produce left to the cultivators throughout the whole area, may rise considerably. Suppose the yield to have doubled; then our old friends who paid £900 rent and kept £100 for themselves, have now, though they still pay £900 rent, £1100 for themselves, the total produce having risen to £2000. Now here is an opportunity for our Proletarian who is not clever. He can very well offer to cultivate the land subject to a payment of, for instance, £1600 a year, leaving himself £400 a year. This will enable the last holder of the tenant right to retire as an idle gentleman receiving a net income of £700 a year, and a gross income of £1600, out of which he pays £900 a year rent to a landlord who again pays to the head landlord £500. But it is to be marked that this £700 a year net is not economic rent. It is not the difference between the best and the worst land. It has nothing to do with the margin of cultivation. It is a payment for the privilege of using land at all—for access to that which is now a close monopoly; and its amount is regulated, not by what the purchaser could do for himself on land of his own at the margin, but simply by the landholder's eagerness to be idle on the one hand, and the proletarian's need of subsistence on the other. In current economic terms the price is regulated by supply and demand. As the demand for land intensifies by the advent of fresh proletarians, the price goes up; and the bargains are made more stringent. Tenant rights, instead of being granted in perpetuity, and so securing for ever to the tenant the increase due to unforeseen improvements in production, are granted on leases for finite terms, at the expiration of which the landlord can revise the terms or eject the tenant. The payments rise until the original head rents and quit rents appear insignificant in comparison with the incomes reaped by the intermediate tenant right holders or middlemen. Sooner or later the price of tenant right will rise so high that the actual cultivator will get no more of the produce than suffices him for subsistence. At that point there is an end of sub-letting tenant rights. The land's absorption of the proletarians as tenants paying more than the economic rent stops.

And now, what is the next proletarian to do? For all his forerunners we have found a way of escape: for him there seems none. The board is at the door, inscribed "Only standing room left"; and it might well bear the more poetic legend, *Lasciate ogni speranza, voi ch' entrate*. This man, born a proletarian, must die a proletarian, and leave his destitution as an only inheritance to his son. It is not yet clear that there is ten days' life in him; for whence is his subsistence to come if he cannot get at the land? Food he must have, and clothing; and both promptly. There is food in the market, and clothing also; but not for nothing: hard money must be paid for it, and paid on the nail too; for he who has no property gets no credit. Money then is a necessity of life; and money can only be procured by selling commodities. This presents no difficulty to the cultivators of the land, who can raise commodities by their labor; but the proletarian being landless, has neither commodities nor means of producing them. Sell something he must. Yet he has nothing to sell—except himself. The idea seems a desperate one; but it proves quite easy to carry out. The tenant cultivators of the land have not strength enough or time enough to exhaust the productive capacity of their holdings. If they could buy men in the market for less than these men's labor would add to the produce, then the purchase of such men would be a sheer gain. It would indeed be only a purchase in form: the men would literally cost nothing, since they would produce their own price, with a surplus for the buyer. Never in the history of buying and selling was there so splendid a bargain for buyers as this. Aladdin's uncle's offer of new lamps for old ones was in comparison a catchpenny. Accordingly, the proletarian no sooner offers himself for sale than he finds a rush of bidders for him, each striving to get the better of the others by offering to give him more and more of the produce of his labor, and to content themselves with less and less surplus. But even the highest bidder must have some surplus, or he will not buy. The proletarian, in accepting the highest bid, sells himself openly into bondage. He is not the first man who has done so; for it is evident that his forerunners, the purchasers of tenant right, had been enslaved by the proprietors who lived on the rents paid by them. But now all the disguise falls off: the proletarian renounces not only the fruit of his labor, but also his right to think for himself and to direct his industry as he pleases. The economic change is merely formal: the moral change is enormous. Soon the new direct traffic in men overspreads the whole market, and takes the place formerly held by the traffic in tenant rights. In order to understand the consequences, it is necessary to undertake an analysis of the exchange of commodities in general, since labor power is now in the market on the same footing as any other ware exposed there for sale.

EXCHANGE VALUE

It is evident that the custom of exchange will arise in the first instance as soon as men give up providing each for his own needs by his own labor. A man who makes his own tables and chairs, his own poker and kettle, his own bread and butter, and his own house and clothes, is jack of all trades and master of none. He finds that he would get on much faster if he stuck to making tables and chairs, and exchanged them with the smith for a poker and kettle, with bakers and dairymen for bread and butter, and with builders and tailors for a house and clothes. In doing this, he finds that his tables and chairs are worth so much—that they have an exchange value, as it is called. As a matter of general convenience, some suitable commodity is set up to measure this value. We set up gold, which, in this particular use of it, is called money. The chairmaker finds how much money his chairs are worth, and exchanges them for it. The blacksmith finds out how much money his pokers are worth, and exchanges them for it. Thus, by employing money as a go-between, chairmakers can get pokers in exchange for their chairs, and blacksmiths chairs for their pokers. This is the mechanism of exchange; and once the values of the commodities are ascertained it works simply enough. But it is a mere mechanism, and does not fix the values or explain them. And the attempt to discover what does fix them is beset with apparent contradictions which block up the right path, and with seductive coincidences which make the wrong seem the more promising.

The apparent contradictions soon shew themselves. It is evident that the exchange value of anything depends on its utility, since no mortal exertion can make a useless thing exchangeable. And yet fresh air and sunlight, which are so useful as to be quite indispensable, have no exchange value; whilst a meteoric stone, shot free of charge from the firmament into the back garden, has a considerable exchange value, although it is an eminently dispensable curiosity. We soon find that this somehow depends on the fact that fresh air is plenty and meteoric stones scarce. If by any means the supply of fresh air could be steadily diminished, and the supply of meteoric stones, by celestial cannonade or otherwise, steadily increased, the fresh air would presently acquire an exchange value which would gradually rise, whilst the exchange value of meteoric stones would gradually fall, until at last fresh air would be supplied through a meter and charged for like gas, and meteoric stones would be as unsaleable as ordinary pebbles. The exchange value, in fact, decreases with the supply. This is due to the fact that the supply decreases in utility as it goes on, because when people have had some of a commodity, they are partly satisfied, and do not value the rest so much. The usefulness of a pound of bread to a man depends on whether he has already eaten some. Every man wants a certain number of pounds of bread per week: no man wants much more; and if more is offered he will not give much for it—perhaps not anything. One umbrella is very useful: a second umbrella is a luxury: a third is mere lumber. Similarly, the curators of our museums want a moderate collection of meteoric stones; but they do not want a cartload apiece of them. Now the exchange value is fixed by the utility, not of the most useful, but of the least useful part of the stock. Why this is so can readily be made obvious by an illustration. If the stock of umbrellas in the market were sufficiently large to provide two for each umbrella carrier in the community, then, since a second umbrella is not so useful as the first, the doctrinaire course would be to ticket half the umbrellas at, say, fifteen shillings and the other half at eight and sixpence. Unfortunately, no man will give fifteen shillings for an article which he can get for eight and sixpence; and when the public came to buy, they would buy up all the eight and sixpenny umbrellas. Each person being thus supplied with an umbrella, the remainder of the stock, though marked fifteen shillings, would be in the position of second umbrellas, only worth eight and sixpence. This is how the exchange value of the least useful part of the supply fixes the exchange value of all the rest.

Technically, it occurs by "the law of indifference." And since the least useful unit of the supply is generally that which is last produced, its utility is called the final utility of the commodity. The utility of the first or most useful unit is called the total utility of the commodity. If there were but one umbrella in the world, the exchange value of its total utility would be what the most delicate person would pay for it on a very wet day sooner than go without it. But practically, thanks to the law of indifference, the most delicate person pays no more than the most robust: that is, both pay alike the exchange value of the utility of the last umbrella produced—or of the final utility of the whole stock of umbrellas. These terms—law of indifference, total utility, and final utility—though admirably expressive and intelligible when you know beforehand exactly what they mean, are, taken by themselves, failures in point of lucidity and suggestiveness. Some economists, transferring from cultivation to utility our old metaphor of the spreading pool, call final utility "marginal utility." Either will serve our present purpose, as I do not intend to use the terms again. The main point to be grasped is, that however useful any commodity may be, its exchange value can be run down to nothing by increasing the supply until there is more of it than is wanted. The excess being useless and valueless, is to be had for nothing; and nobody will pay anything for a commodity as long as plenty of it is to be had for nothing. This is why air and other indispensable things have no exchange value, whilst scarce gewgaws fetch immense prices.

These, then, are the conditions which confront man as a producer and exchanger. If he produces a useless thing, his labor will be wholly in vain: he will get nothing for it. If he produces a useful thing, the price he will get for it will depend on how much of it there is for sale already. If he increases the supply by producing more than is sufficient to replace the current consumption, he inevitably lowers the value of the whole. It therefore behoves him to be wary in choosing his occupation as well as industrious in pursuing it. His choice will naturally fall on the production of those commodities whose value stands highest relatively to the labor required to produce them—which fetch the highest price in proportion to their cost, in fact. Suppose, for example, that a maker of musical instruments found that it cost him exactly as much to make a harp as to make a pianoforte, but that harps were going out of fashion and pianofortes coming in. Soon there would be more harps than were wanted, and fewer pianofortes: consequently the value of harps would fall, and that of pianofortes rise. Since the labor cost of both would be the same, he would immediately devote all his labor to pianoforte making; and other manufacturers would do the same, until the increase of supply brought down the value of pianofortes to the value of harps. Possibly fashion then might veer from pianofortes to American organs, in which case he would make less pianofortes and more American organs. When these, too, had increased sufficiently, the exertions of the Salvation Army might create such a demand for tambourines as to make them worth four times their cost of production, whereupon there would instantly be a furious concentration of the instrument-making energy on the manufacture of tambourines; and this concentration would last until the supply had brought down the profit[1] to less than might be gained by gratifying the public craving for trombones. At last, as pianofortes were cheapened until they were no more profitable than harps; then American organs until they were no more profitable than pianos; and then tambourines until they were level with American organs; so eventually trombones will pay no better than tambourines; and a general level of profit will be attained, indicating the proportion in which the instruments are wanted by the public. But to skim off even this level of profit, more of the instruments may be produced in the ascertained proportion until their prices fall to their costs of production, when there will be no profit. Here the

[1] Profit is here used colloquially to denote the excess of the value of an article over its cost.

production will be decisively checked, since a further supply would cause only a loss; and men can lose money, without the trouble of producing commodities, by the simple process of throwing it out of the window.

What occurred with the musical instruments in this illustration occurs in practice with the whole mass of manufactured commodities. Those which are scarce, and therefore relatively high in value, tempt us to produce them until the increase of the supply reduces their value to a point at which there is no more profit to be made out of them than out of other commodities. The general level of profit thus attained is further exploited until the general increase brings down the price of all commodities to their cost of production, the equivalent of which is sometimes called their normal value. And here a glance back to our analysis of the spread of cultivation, and its result in the phenomenon of rent, suggests the question: What does the cost of production of a commodity mean? We have seen that, owing to the differences in fertility and advantage of situation between one piece of land and another, cost of production varies from district to district, being highest at the margin of cultivation. But we have also seen how the landlord skims off as economic rent all the advantage gained by the cultivators of superior soils and sites. Consequently, the addition of the landlord's rent to the expenses of production brings them up even on the best land to the level of those incurred on the worst. Cost of production, then, means cost of production on the margin of cultivation, and is equalized to all producers, since what they may save in labor per commodity is counterbalanced by the greater mass of commodities they must produce in order to bring in the rent. It is only by a thorough grasp of this levelling-down action that we can detect the trick by which the ordinary economist tries to cheat us into accepting the private property system as practically just. He first shews that economic rent does not enter into cost of production on the margin of cultivation. Then he shews that the cost of production on the margin of cultivation determines the price of a commodity. Therefore, he argues, first, that rent does not enter into price; and second, that the value of commodities is fixed by their cost of production, the implication being that the landlords cost the community nothing, and that commodities exchange in exact proportion to the labor they cost. This trivially ingenious way of being disingenuous is officially taught as political economy in our schools to this day. It will be seen at once that it is mere thimblerig. So far from commodities exchanging, or tending to exchange, according to the labor expended in their production, commodities produced well within the margin of cultivation will fetch as high a price as commodities produced at the margin with much greater labor. So far from the landlord costing nothing, he costs all the difference between the two.

This, however, is not the goal of our analysis of value. We now see how Man's control over the value of commodities consists solely in his power of regulating their supply. Individuals are constantly trying to decrease supply for their own advantage. Gigantic conspiracies have been entered into to forestall the world's wheat and cotton harvests, so as to force their value to the highest possible point. Cargoes of East Indian spices have been destroyed by the Dutch, as cargoes of fish are now destroyed in the Thames, to maintain prices by limiting supply. All rings, trusts, corners, combinations, monopolies, and trade secrets have the same object. Production and the development of the social instincts are alike hindered by each man's consciousness that the more he stints the community the more he benefits himself, the justification, of course, being that when every man has benefited himself at the expense of the community, the community will benefit by every man in it being benefited. From one thing the community is safe. There will be no permanent conspiracies to reduce values by increasing supply. All men will cease producing when the value of their product falls below its cost of production, whether in labor or in labor *plus* rent. No man will keep on producing bread until it will fetch nothing, like the sunlight, or until it becomes a nuisance, like the rain in the summer of 1888. So far, our minds are at ease as to the excessive increase of commodities voluntarily produced by the labor of man.

WAGES

I now ask you to pick up the dropped subject of the spread of cultivation. We had got as far as the appearance in the market of a new commodity—of the proletarian man compelled to live by the sale of himself! In order to realize at once the latent horror of this, you have only to apply our investigation of value, with its inevitable law that only by restricting the supply of a commodity can its value be kept from descending finally to zero. The commodity which the proletarian sells is one over the production of which he has practically no control. He is himself driven to produce it by an irresistible impulse. It was the increase of population that spread cultivation and civilization from the centre to the snowline, and at last forced men to sell themselves to the lords of the soil: it is the same force that continues to multiply men so that their exchange value falls slowly and surely until it disappears altogether—until even black chattel slaves are released as not worth keeping in a land where men of all colors are to be had for nothing. This is the condition of our English laborers today: they are no longer even dirt cheap: they are valueless, and can be had for nothing. The proof is the existence of the unemployed, who can find no purchasers. By the law of indifference, nobody will buy men at a price when he can obtain equally serviceable men for nothing. What then is the explanation of the wages given to those who are in employment, and who certainly do not work for nothing? The matter is deplorably simple. Suppose that horses multiplied in England in such quantities that they were to be had for the asking, like kittens condemned to the bucket. You would still have to feed your horse—feed him and lodge him well if you used him as a smart hunter—feed him and lodge him wretchedly if you used him only as a drudge. But the cost of keeping would not mean that the horse had an exchange value. If you got him for nothing in the first instance—if no one would give you anything for him when you were done with him, he would be worth nothing, in spite of the cost of his keep. That is just the case of every member of the proletariat who could be replaced by one of the unemployed today. Their wage is not the price of themselves; for they are worth nothing: it is only their keep. For bare subsistence wages you can get as much common labor as you want, and do what you please with it within the limits of a criminal code which is sure to be interpreted by a proprietary-class judge in your favor. If you have to give your footman a better allowance than your wretched hewer of match-wood, it is for the same reason that you have to give your hunter beans and a clean stall instead of chopped straw and a sty.[1]

CAPITALISM

At this stage the acquisition of labor becomes a mere question of provender. If a railway is required, all that is necessary is to provide subsistence for a sufficient number of laborers to construct it. If, for example, the railway requires the labor of a thousand men for five years, the cost to the proprietors of the site is the subsistence of a thousand men for five years. This subsistence is technically called capital. It is provided for by the proprietors not consuming the whole excess over wages of the produce of the labor of their other wage workers, but setting aside enough for the subsistence of the railway makers. In this way capital can claim to be the result of saving, or, as one ingenious apologist neatly put it, the reward of abstinence, a gleam of humor which still enlivens treatises on capital. The savers, it need hardly be said, are those who have more money than they want to spend: the abstainers are those who have less. At the

[1] When one of the conditions of earning a wage is the keeping up of a certain state, subsistence wages may reach a figure to which the term seems ludicrously inappropriate. For example, a fashionable physician in London cannot save out of £1000 a year; and the post of Lord-Lieutenant of Ireland can only be filled by a man who brings considerable private means to the aid of his official salary of £20,000.

end of the five years, the completed railway is the property of the capitalists; and the railway makers fall back into the labor market as helpless as they were before. Sometimes the proprietors call the completed railway their capital; but, strictly, this is only a figure of speech. Capital is simply spare subsistence. Its market value, indicated by the current rate of interest, falls with the increase of population, whereas the market value of established stock rises with it.[1] If Mr Goschen, encouraged by his success in reducing Consols, were to ask the proprietors of the London and North-Western Railway to accept as full compensation for their complete expropriation capital just sufficient to make the railway anew, their amazement at his audacity would at once make him feel the difference between a railway and capital. Colloquially, one property with a farm on it is said to be land yielding rent; whilst another, with a railway on it, is called capital yielding interest. But economically there is no distinction between them when they once become sources of revenue. This would be quite clearly seen if costly enterprises like railways could be undertaken by a single landlord on his own land out of his own surplus wealth. It is the necessity of combining a number of possessors of surplus wealth, and devising a financial machinery for apportioning their shares in the produce to their shares in the capital contributed, that modifies the terminology and external aspect of the exploitation. But the modification is not an alteration: shareholder and landlord live alike on the produce extracted from their property by the labor of the proletariat.

"OVERPOPULATION"

The introduction of the capitalistic system is a sign that the exploitation of the laborer toiling for a bare subsistence

[1] The current rate must, under present conditions, eventually fall to zero, and even become "negative." By that time shares which now bring in a dividend of 100 per cent may very possibly bring in 200 or more. Yet the fall of the rate has been mistaken for a tendency of interest to disappear. It really indicates a tendency of interest to increase.

wage has become one of the chief arts of life among the holders of tenant rights. It also produces a delusive promise of endless employment which blinds the proletariat to those disastrous consequences of rapid multiplication which are obvious to the small cultivator and peasant proprietor. But indeed the more you degrade the workers, robbing them of all artistic enjoyment, and all chance of respect and admiration from their fellows, the more you throw them back, reckless, on the one pleasure and the one human tie left to them —the gratification of their instinct for producing fresh supplies of men. You will applaud this instinct as divine until at last the excessive supply becomes a nuisance: there comes a plague of men; and you suddenly discover that the instinct is diabolic, and set up a cry of "overpopulation." But your slaves are beyond caring for your cries: they breed like rabbits; and their poverty breeds filth, ugliness, dishonesty, disease, obscenity, drunkenness, and murder. In the midst of the riches which their labor piles up for you, their misery rises up too and stifles you. You withdraw in disgust to the other end of the town from them; you appoint special carriages on your railways and special seats in your churches and theatres for them; you set your life apart from theirs by every class barrier you can devise; and yet they swarm about you still: your face gets stamped with your habitual loathing and suspicion of them: your ears get so filled with the language of the vilest of them that you break into it when you lose your self-control: they poison your life as remorselessly as you have sacrificed theirs heartlessly. You begin to believe intensely in the devil. Then comes the terror of their revolting; the drilling and arming of bodies of them to keep down the rest; the prison, the hospital, paroxysms of frantic coercion, followed by paroxysms of frantic charity. And in the meantime, the population continues to increase!

"ILLTH"

It is sometimes said that during this grotesquely hideous march of civilization from bad to worse, wealth is increasing side by side with misery. Such a thing is eternally impossible: wealth is steadily decreasing with the spread of poverty. But riches are increasing, which is quite another thing. The total of the exchange values produced in the country annually is mounting perhaps by leaps and bounds. But the accumulation of riches, and consequently of an excessive purchasing power, in the hands of a class, soon satiates that class with socially useful wealth, and sets them offering a price for luxuries. The moment a price is to be had for a luxury, it acquires exchange value, and labor is employed to produce it. A New York lady, for instance, having a nature of exquisite sensibility, orders an elegant rosewood and silver coffin, upholstered in pink satin, for her dead dog. It is made; and meanwhile a live child is prowling barefooted and hunger-stunted in the frozen gutter outside. The exchange value of the coffin is counted as part of the national wealth; but a nation which cannot afford food and clothing for its children cannot be allowed to pass as wealthy because it has provided a pretty coffin for a dead dog. Exchange value itself, in fact, has become bedevilled like everything else, and represents, no longer utility, but the cravings of lust, folly, vanity, gluttony, and madness, technically described by genteel economists as "effective demand." Luxuries are not social wealth: the machinery for producing them is not social wealth: labor skilled only to manufacture them is not socially useful labor: the men, women, and children who make a living by producing them are no more self-supporting than the idle rich for whose amusement they are kept at work. It is the habit of counting as wealth the exchange values involved in these transactions that makes us fancy that the poor are starving in the midst of plenty. They are starving in the midst of plenty of jewels, velvets, laces, equipages, and racehorses; but not in the midst of plenty of food. In the things that are wanted for the welfare of the people we are abjectly poor; and England's social policy today may be likened to the domestic policy of those adventuresses who leave their children half-clothed and half-fed in order to keep a carriage and deal with a fashionable dressmaker. But it is quite true that whilst wealth and welfare are decreasing, productive power is increasing; and nothing but the perversion of this power to the production of socially useless commodities prevents the apparent wealth from becoming real. The purchasing power that commands luxuries in the hands of the rich would command true wealth in the hands of all. Yet private property must still heap the purchasing power upon the few rich and withdraw it from the many poor. So that, in the end, the subject of the one boast that private property can make—the great accumulation of so-called "wealth" which it points so proudly to as the result of its power to scourge men and women daily to prolonged and intense toil—turns out to be a simulacrum. With all its energy, its Smilesian "self-help," its merchant-princely enterprise, its ferocious sweating and slave-driving, its prodigality of blood, sweat and tears, what has it heaped up, over and above the pittance of its slaves? Only a monstrous pile of frippery, some tainted class literature and class art, and not a little poison and mischief.

This, then, is the economic analysis which convicts Private Property of being unjust even from the beginning, and utterly impossible as a final solution of even the individualist aspect of the problem of adjusting the share of the worker in the distribution of wealth to the labor incurred by him in its production. All attempts yet made to construct true societies upon it have failed: the nearest things to societies so achieved have been civilizations, which have rotted into centres of vice and luxury, and eventually been swept away by uncivilized races. That our own civilization is already in an advanced stage of rottenness may be taken as statistically proved. That further decay instead of improvement must ensue if the institution of private property be maintained, is economically certain. Fortunately, private property in its integrity is not now practicable. Although the safety valve of emigration has been furiously at work during this century, yet the pressure of population has forced us to begin the restitution to the people of the sums taken from them for the ground landlords, holders of tenant right, and capitalists, by the imposition of an income tax, and by compelling them to establish out of their revenues a national system of education, besides imposing restrictions—as yet only of the forcible-feeble sort—on their terrible power of abusing the wage contract. These, however, are dealt with by Mr Sidney Webb in the historic essay which follows. I should not touch upon them at all, were it not that experience has lately convinced all economists that no exercise in abstract economics, however closely deduced, is to be trusted unless it can be experimentally verified by tracing its expression in history. It is true that the process which I have presented as a direct development of private property between free exchangers had to work itself out in the Old World indirectly and tortuously through a struggle with political and religious institutions and survivals quite antagonistic to it. It is true that cultivation did not begin in Western Europe with the solitary emigrant pre-empting his private property, but with the tribal communes in which arose subsequently the assertion of the right of the individual to private judgment and private action against the tyranny of primitive society. It is true that cultivation has not proceeded by logical steps from good land to less good; from less good to bad; and from bad to worse: the exploration of new countries and new regions, and the discovery of new uses for old products, has often made the margin of cultivation more fruitful than the centre, and, for the moment (whilst the centre was shifting to the margin), turned the whole movement of rent and wages directly counter to the economic theory. Nor is it true that, taking the world as one country, cultivation has yet spread from the snowline to the water's edge. There is free land still for the poorest East End match-box maker if she could get there, reclaim the wilderness there, speak the language there, stand the climate there, and be fed, clothed, and housed there whilst she cleared her farm; learned how to cultivate it; and waited for the harvest. Economists have been ingenious enough to prove that this alternative really secures her independence; but I shall not waste time in dealing with that. Practically, if there is no free land in England, the economic analysis holds good of England, in spite of Siberia, Central Africa, and the Wild West. Again, it is not immediately true that men are governed in production solely by a determination to realize the maximum of exchange value. The impulse to production often takes specific direction in the first instance; and a man will insist on producing pictures or plays although he might gain more money by producing boots or bonnets. But, his specific impulse once gratified, he will make as much money as he can. He will sell his picture or play for a hundred pounds rather than for fifty. In short, though there is no such person as the celebrated "economic man," man being wilful rather than rational, yet when the wilful man has had his way he will take what else he can get; and so he always does appear, finally if not primarily, as the economic man. On the whole, history, even in the Old World, goes the way traced by the economist. In the New World the correspondence is exact. The United States and the Colonies have been peopled by fugitives from the full-blown individualism of Western Europe, pre-empting private property precisely as assumed in this investigation of the conditions of cultivation. The economic relations of these cultivators have not since put on any of the old political disguises. Yet among them, in confirmation of the validity of our analysis, we see all the evils of our old civilizations growing up; and though with them the end is not yet, still it is from them to us that the great recent revival of the cry for nationalization of the land has come, articulated by a man who had seen the whole tragedy of private property hurried through its acts with unprecedented speed in the mushroom cities of America.

On Socialism the analysis of the economic action of Individualism bears as a discovery, in the private appropriation of land, of the source of those unjust privileges against which Socialism is aimed. It is practically a demonstration that public property in land is the basic economic condition of Socialism. But this does not involve at present a literal restoration of the land to the people. The land is at present in the hands of the people: its proprietors are for the most part absentees. The modern form of private property is simply a legal claim to take a share of the produce of the national industry year by year without working for it. It refers to no special part or form of that produce; and in process of consumption its revenue cannot be distinguished from earnings, so that the majority of persons, accustomed to call the commodities which form the income of the proprietor his private property, and seeing no difference between them and the commodities which form the income of a worker, extend the term private property to the worker's subsistence also, and can only conceive an attack on private property as an attempt to empower everybody to rob everybody else all round. But the income of a private proprietor can be distinguished by the fact that he obtains it unconditionally and gratuitously by private right against the public weal, which is incompatible with the existence of consumers who do not produce. Socialism involves discontinuance of the payment of these incomes, and addition of the wealth so saved to incomes derived from labor. As we have seen, incomes derived from private property consist partly of economic rent; partly of pensions, also called rent, obtained by the subletting of tenant rights; and partly of a form of rent called interest, obtained by special adaptations of land to production by the application of capital: all these being finally paid out of the difference between the produce of the worker's labor and the price of that labor sold in the open market for wages, salary, fees, or profits.[1] The whole, except economic rent, can be added directly to the incomes of the workers by simply discontinuing its exaction from them. Economic rent, arising as it does from variations of fertility or advan-

[1] This excess of the product of labor over its price is treated as a single category with impressive effect by Karl Marx, who called it "surplus value" (*mehrwerth*).

tages of situation, must always be held as common or social wealth, and used, as the revenues raised by taxation are now used, for public purposes, among which Socialism would make national insurance and the provision of capital matters of the first importance.

The economic problem of Socialism is thus solved; and the political question of how the economic solution is to be practically applied does not come within the scope of this essay. But if we have got as far as an intellectual conviction that the source of our social misery is no eternal well-spring of confusion and evil, but only an artificial system susceptible of almost infinite modification and readjustment—nay, of practical demolition and substitution at the will of Man—then a terrible weight will be lifted from the minds of all except those who are, whether avowedly to themselves or not, clinging to the present state of things from base motives. We have had in this century a stern series of lessons on the folly of believing anything for no better reason than that it is pleasant to believe it. It was pleasant to look round with a consciousness of possessing a thousand a year, and say, with Browning's David, "All's love; and all's law." It was pleasant to believe that the chance we were too lazy to take in this world would come back to us in another. It was pleasant to believe that a benevolent hand was guiding the steps of society; overruling all evil appearances for good; and making poverty here the earnest of a great blessedness and reward hereafter. It was pleasant to lose the sense of worldly inequality in the contemplation of our equality before God. But utilitarian questioning and scientific answering turned all this tranquil optimism into the blackest pessimism. Nature was shewn to us as "red in tooth and claw": if the guiding hand were indeed benevolent, then it could not be omnipotent; so that our trust in it was broken: if it were omnipotent, it could not be benevolent; so that our love of it turned to fear and hatred. We had never admitted that the other world, which was to compensate for the sorrows of this, was open to horses and apes (though we had not on that account been any the more merciful to our horses); and now came Science to shew us the corner of the pointed ear of the horse on our own heads, and present the ape to us as our blood relation. No proof came of the existence of that other world and that benevolent power to which we had left the remedy of the atrocious wrongs of the poor; proof after proof came that what we called Nature knew and cared no more about our pains and pleasures than we know or care about the tiny creatures we crush underfoot as we walk through the fields. Instead of at once perceiving that this meant no more than that Nature was unmoral and indifferent, we relapsed into a gross form of devil worship, and conceived Nature as a remorselessly malignant power. This was no better than the old optimism, and infinitely gloomier. It kept our eyes still shut to the truth that there is no cruelty and selfishness outside Man himself; and that his own active benevolence can combat and vanquish both. When the Socialist came forward as a meliorist on these lines, the old school of political economists, who could see no alternative to private property, put forward in proof of the powerlessness of benevolent action to arrest the deadly automatic production of poverty by the increase of population, the very analysis I have just presented. Their conclusions exactly fitted in with the new ideas. It was Nature at it again—the struggle for existence—the remorseless extirpation of the weak—the survival of the fittest—in short, natural selection at work. Socialism seemed too good to be true: it was passed by as merely the old optimism foolishly running its head against the stone wall of modern science. But Socialism now challenges individualism, scepticism, pessimism, worship of Nature personified as a devil, on their own ground of science. The science of the production and distribution of wealth is Political Economy. Socialism appeals to that science, and, turning on Individualism its own guns, routs it in incurable disaster. Henceforth the bitter cynic who still finds the world an eternal and unimprovable doghole, with the placid person of means who repeats the familiar misquotation, "the poor ye shall have always with you," lose their usurped place among the cultured, and pass over to the ranks of the ignorant, the shallow, and the superstitious. As for the rest of us, since we were taught to revere proprietary respectability in our unfortunate childhood, and since we found our childish hearts so hard and unregenerate that they secretly hated and rebelled against respectability in spite of that teaching, it is impossible to express the relief with which we discover that our hearts were all along right, and that the current respectability of today is nothing but a huge inversion of righteous and scientific social order weltering in dishonesty, uselessness, selfishness, wanton misery, and idiotic waste of magnificent opportunities for noble and happy living. It was terrible to feel this, and yet to fear that it could not be helped—that the poor must starve and make you ashamed of your dinner—that they must shiver and make you ashamed of your warm overcoat. It is to economic science—once the Dismal, now the Hopeful—that we are indebted for the discovery that though the evil is enormously worse than we knew, yet it is not eternal—not even very long lived, if we only bestir ourselves to make an end of it.

THE COMMON SENSE OF MUNICIPAL TRADING

(Preface to the Fabian edition)

WHEN I handed over this work to the Fabian Society to be distributed at a price low enough to make it easy for those most concerned to buy a copy, I did not find it necessary to add any new matter or withdraw any old. The ordinary electioneering opponents of municipal trading had for the most part left my book alone, having neither the economic knowledge, the practical experience of municipal work, nor the literary skill to cope with me. But they still persuade the public that trading municipalities are staggering towards bankruptcy under a burden of ever-increasing debt. The trick is simple: instead of calling the funds of the municipality its capital, you call it "municipal debt," and go on to contend that the success of the municipalities in serving the public at cost price and eliminating idle shareholders, means that they are less capable and businesslike than the commercial concerns which measure their soundness by the excess of their charges over their expenses, and by the resultant magnitude of their dividends.

But the opponents of municipal trading could not, when this book was first published, get over the unanswerable fact that in spite of all their denunciations of our municipalities as bankrupt and mismanaged concerns—denunciations which would have ruined even the soundest private businesses, but against which private businesses have a remedy (witness the enormous damages obtained by "the Soap Trust" against a popular newspaper which can slander municipal trading with complete impunity)—municipal credit, as shewn by the prices of its stock, remained unshaken; and the very people who were declaring it to be worthless were glad to invest their own money in municipal stock at gilt-edged prices. They did, however, point out triumphantly that the price of municipal stock had fallen, and that the London County Council could no longer get as much money as it wanted at 3 per cent. In reply, I could only say that a controversialist desperate enough to claim that this is the result of a loss of confidence in municipal security is desperate enough for anything. The credit of our municipalities stood as high as ever. What really happened was that the value of money had risen after the South African War. Consols had fallen from above par to nearly eighty. The bank rate had touched seven. The Anti-Municipalizers forget that if they wish to claim a fall in the price of municipal stock as evidence that their campaign against English civic activity is producing some effect, they must point, not to a general fall in prices which has hit private enterprises much harder than public enterprises, but to a fall confined to municipal stocks and unaccompanied by a rise in the price of money. It is no use triumphing over the difficulties of the Borough Treasurer when the Chancellor of the Exchequer and the Rothschilds are in the same straits. The argument would not be worth mentioning but that it illustrates the amazing ineptitude and ignorance with which the question is discussed in the daily press.

Perhaps the stupidest cry raised in the Anti-Municipal agitation—which is really an agitation to reserve all public services for the profit of private individuals—is the cry for "a commercial audit." I venture to believe that no honorable and sensible man who will take the trouble to read these pages will ever again disgrace himself by echoing that cry, or by casting a vote for any person capable of such an elementary blunder. Those who did so at the last municipal elections are now sufficiently ashamed of themselves; and we hear nothing more of the gentlemen who think a reduction of the death-rate a commercial mistake because it does not shew a profit of 10 per cent in cash, as it would have to do before a contractor would undertake it. But we must face the fact that honorable, sensible, and ordinarily intelligent people, from thoughtlessness, ignorance, and the tyranny of commercial habit, do make these blunders, and, as voters, become the tools of the moneyed interests which see in every extension of municipal activity the closing to them of some field which has been to them a veritable Tom Tiddler's ground on which they have been picking up gold and silver at the expense of the ratepayers for years past.

It is generally assumed that the result of the municipal elections of 1907 was a severe set-back for municipal trading. The causes of that set-back, in so far as they had produced a genuine revolt of the ratepayer against municipal activity, are explained in this book. Before the revolt occurred I pointed out that our system of rating, and the success with which the cost of our social ameliorations was being evaded by the property owners and by the working classes, and thrown on the struggling mass of middle-class ratepayers, was producing intolerable injustice. The remedy proposed—that of putting back the clock—was impracticable. I knew, and everybody who had ever served on a public body knew, that the first hour spent on a committee would knock out of the new representatives most of the nonsense they had been talking at their election meetings, and that the most intelligent and disinterested of them would presently become ardent municipalizers. But it is still true that until municipal finance is radically reformed, and constitutional machinery provided for public enterprises extending over much larger areas than those marked out by our present obsolete and obstructive municipal boundaries, we shall continue to have ratepayers' revolts, and crippled public enterprise.

In London the issue was so confused with the usual political party considerations that hardly anyone noticed that the clean sweep which was supposed to have been made of Municipal Socialists was really a clean sweep of those Liberals who had been the most determined opponents of the Municipal Socialists in the previous Council. It was these Anti-Socialists who were swept away, whilst the professed Fabian Socialists held their seats in the midst of the *débâcle*. I mention this for the sake of its lesson, which is, that the ratepayers must not put their trust in electioneering literature which proceeds on the wildly erroneous assumption that every Liberal is a Socialist and every Conservative an opponent of State or Municipal activity. There is no salvation for the voter except in understanding exactly what the municipalities are doing; and this book is intended to put him in that position as far as a book can supply the need of that actual first-hand experience of the working of municipalities which only very few of us can obtain, and without which I certainly should not have been able, merely as a man of letters, to make my book of any value.

In conclusion, I again warn the ratepayer who is gasping for breath under the pressure of the propertied class squeezing rents from him from above, and the working class squeezing education, housing, medical attendance, poor relief, and old age pensions from him from below, that his condition will become more and more precarious, no matter whether he votes Moderate or Progressive, until he takes his public business as seriously and unromantically as his private business, and resorts to the simple and obvious means of relieving and protecting himself that may be gathered from these pages.

Two new developments of the opposition to civic enterprise have occurred lately. One is the practice of circulating to the ratepayers statements implying that municipal trading and taxation of unearned incomes involve irreligion and licentiousness. This I need not deal with: it is only too obvious that the irreligion and licentiousness in which we are already steeped are the result of abandoning our people to the unscrupulous rapacity of commercial enterprise, which makes huge profits out of the evils our municipalities strive constantly to suppress. No municipality has yet taken or proposed to take a single step against religion or morals, whereas private enterprise openly and shamelessly exploits poverty, vice, and irreligion for its own profit to the despair of the ratepayer, who has to pay for dealing with all the disease, the crime, and the depravation of character that enriches the sweater, the distiller, and the brothel-keeper.

The other development is the offer of Tariff Reform as a means of relieving the ratepayer without recourse to Municipal Socialism. On this I have only to say that if Tariff Reform succeeds in suppressing manufactured imports and substituting home production (its original object), it will not be a source of revenue at all. If, however, importation continues, and a revenue is derived from taxing imports, the ratepayer has no security that this revenue will be applied to his relief by increasing our present Grants in Aid by the central government to the local authority rather than to reducing the income-tax on unearned incomes, in which case he would be paying more for imported goods only to see the excess pocketed by the very people who already exact so large a share of his earnings as rent. So, as municipal trading is not an evil to be staved off by any possible means, but a highly desirable and beneficial extension of civilization, equally good for Free Trade and Protectionist countries, there is no reason whatever why the most ardent Tariff Reformer should not also be an ardent Municipal Socialist.

Perhaps the most impudent of the recent complaints of municipal trading is that it drives capital out of the country. It is almost the only sure means of keeping it at home. The present system, which sends English capital to develop Bahia Blanca whilst leaving Birmingham to wallow in its own death-rate, is driving capital abroad as fast as it will go. Municipal trading, if it had nothing more to recommend it than its effect in making home investment compulsory, would be justified by that alone from the patriotic point of view.

G. B. S.

Ayot St Lawrence,
15th January 1908.

I
THE COMMERCIAL SUCCESSES OF MUNICIPAL TRADING

MUNICIPAL Trading seems a very simple matter of business. Yet it is conceivable by a sensible man that the political struggle over it may come nearer to a civil war than any issue raised in England since the Reform Bill of 1832. It will certainly not be decided by argument alone. Private property will not yield its most fertile provinces to the logic of Socialism; nor will the sweated laborer or the rackrented and rackrated city shopkeeper or professional man refrain, on abstract Individualist grounds, from an obvious way of lightening his burden. The situation is as yet so little developed that until the other day few quarter columns in the newspaper attracted less attention than the occasional one headed Municipal Trading; but the heading has lately changed in The Times to Municipal Socialism; and this, in fact, is what is really on foot among us under the name of Progressivism.

At first sight the case in favor of Municipal Trading seems overwhelming. Take the case of a shopkeeper consuming a great deal of gas or electric light for the attractive display of his wares, or a factory owner with hundreds of work benches to illuminate. For all this light he has to pay the cost of production plus interest on capital at the rate necessary to induce private investors to form ordinary commercial gas or electric light companies, which are managed with the object of keeping the rate of interest up instead of down: all improvement in the service and reductions in price (if any) being introduced with the sole aim of making the excess of revenue over cost as large as possible.

Now the shopkeeper in his corporate capacity as citizen-constituent of the local governing body can raise as much capital as he likes at less than four per cent. It is much easier to stagger Consols than to discredit municipal stock. Take the case of the London County Council. For ten years past the whole weight of the Government and the newspapers which support it has been thrown against the credit of the

Council. A late prime minister denounced it in such terms that, to save his face, his party was forced to turn all the vestries into rival councils on the "divide and govern" principle. The name of the London County Council has been made a hissing among all who take their politics from the Court and the Conservative papers. To such a torrent of denunciation a private company would have succumbed helplessly: the results of an attempt to issue fresh stock would not have paid the printer's bill. But the County Council has only to hold up its finger to have millions heaped on it at less than four per cent. It has to make special arrangements to allow small investors a chance. The very people who have been denouncing its capital as "municipal indebtedness" struggle for the stock without the slightest regard to their paper demonstrations of the approaching collapse of all our municipal corporations under a mountain of debt, and of the inevitable bankruptcy of New Zealand and the Australasian colonies generally through industrial democracy. The investor prefers the corporation with the largest municipal debt exactly as he prefers the insurance company with the largest capital. And he is quite right. Municipal expenditure in trading is productive expenditure: its debts are only the capital with which it operates. And that is why it never has any difficulty in raising that capital. Sultans and South American Republics may beg round the world in vain; chancellors may have to issue national stock at a discount; but a Borough Treasurer simply names a figure and gets it at par.

This is the central commercial fact of the whole question. The shopkeeper, by municipal trading, can get his light for the current cost of production plus a rate of interest which includes no insurance against risk of loss, because the security, in spite of all theoretical demonstrations to the contrary, is treated by the investing public and by the law of trusteeship as practically perfect. Any profit that may arise through accidental overcharge returns to the ratepayer in relief of rates or in public service of some kind.

The moment this economic situation is grasped, the

successes of municipal trading become intelligible; and the entreaties of commercial joint stock organization to be protected against the competition of municipal joint stock organization become as negligible as the plea of the small shopkeeper to be protected against the competition of the Civil Service or Army and Navy Stores. Shew the most bitterly Moderate ratepayer a municipal lighting bill at sixpence a thousand feet or a penny a unit cheaper than the private company charges him, and he is a converted man as far as gas or electric light is concerned. And until commercial companies can raise capital at lower rates than the City Accountant or the Borough Treasurer, and can find shareholders either offering their dividends to relieve the rates or jealously determining to reduce the price of light to a minimum lest they should be paying a share of their neighbors' rates in their lighting bills, it will always be possible for a municipality of average capacity to underbid a commercial company.

Here, then, is the explanation of the popularity and antiquity of municipal trading. As far as their legal powers have gone, municipalities have always traded, and will always trade, to the utmost limits of the business capacity and public spirit of their members.

No doubt a body of timid and incapable councillors will leave as many public services as possible to commercial enterprise, just as, in their private concerns, they keep small shops in a small way instead of becoming Whiteleys and Wanamakers, Morgans, and Carnegies. And a body of rich and commercially able councillors may pursue exactly the same policy because they hold shares in the commercial enterprises which municipal enterprise would supplant, and have in fact deliberately taken the trouble to get elected for the purpose of protecting their private enterprises against the "unfair" (meaning the irresistible) competition of the municipality. Further, a body of amateur doctrinaires who rush into municipal trading on principle without enough business training and experience either to manage the business themselves or allow their staff to do it for them, will make a mess of it at first, precisely as that much commoner object the amateur joint stock company makes a mess of it. There is no magic in the ordeal of popular election to change narrow minds into wide ones, cowards into commanders, private ambition into civic patriotism, or crankiness into common sense. But still less is there any tendency to reverse the operation; for the narrowest fool, the vulgarest adventurer, the most impossible fanatic, gets socially educated by public life and committee work to a degree never reached in private life, or even in private commerce. The moment public spirit and business capacity meet on a municipality you get an irresistible development of municipal activity. Operations in land like those effected by the Corporation of Birmingham in Mr Chamberlain's time, and by the London County Council in our own, are taken in hand; and the town supplies of water, of light, of tramways, and even of dwellings, are conquered from competitive commerce by civic co-operation. And there is no arguing with the practical results. You take a man who has just paid a halfpenny for a ride in a municipal tramcar which under commercial management would have cost him a penny or twopence; and you undertake to go into the corporation accounts with him and prove that under a "fair" system of book-keeping he should have paid fourpence. You explain to the workingman voter how true economy demands that his relative who is employed as a driver and conductor in the municipal service for ten hours a day, and six days a week, with standard wages and a uniform, should go back to competition wages, seventeen hours, seven days, and his own seedy overcoat and muffler. You buttonhole the shopkeeper who has just paid two and threepence per thousand cubic feet for his gas, with the public lighting rate and a bonus thrown in; and you assure him that unless he votes for a return to the supremacy of the commercial company at three shillings per thousand and a reimposition of the Lighting Rate, the city will be bankrupt and the Mayor replaced by a Man in Possession. You unfold a Union Jack in London, and tell the careworn cockney, who pays for his water to a private company more than double what his neighbor across the border pays to the Croydon Corporation, that the Empire stands or falls with the practice of buying water at a price which varies inversely with the quantity consumed, with the right of a water shareholder to a vote in every constituency through which one of his pipes runs, and with the maintenance, free of Probate Duty, of a monopoly granted by James I, and by this time appreciated by 1000 per cent in value. It is all pathetically useless. The municipal trader does not contradict you: he laughs at you. So long as the municipal market is the cheapest market, the public will buy in it; and the protests of the companies are as futile as the protest of the stationer and the apothecary against the stores.

It is not necessary to overload these pages by quoting, from the Municipal Year Book, examples of successful municipal trading in verification of the above. Progressive electioneering literature teems with such examples. The tracts of the Fabian Society and of the London Reform Union, the columns of the Progressive papers, the protests against "municipal indebtedness" in the Anti-Progressive papers, the annual reports of the local authorities, the weekly papers devoted to municipal matters with their endless photographs and figures, the handbooks of municipal socialism compiled by such papers as the Clarion from its own columns, and the County Council returns and parliamentary reports on municipal trading, have so surfeited the public with the facts that a recapitulation here would be beyond human endurance. It is waste of time to force an open door; and in all public services in which the determining commercial factor is practically unlimited command of cheap capital combined with indifference to dividend, the door is more than wide open: it has been carried clean off its hinges by the victorious rush of municipal socialism under the reassuring name of Progressivism.

II
MUNICIPAL MANAGEMENT

THE importance of management as a factor in industrial success cannot easily be exaggerated; but management is nowadays as completely dissociated from ownership, and as easy to buy in the market, as machinery. Nobody now suggests that a railway company is an impossibility because railways cannot be managed by a mob of shareholders, even when they act through committees of directors who do not know the difference between a piston rod and a sun-and-planets gear. The directors simply prescribe the results they wish to obtain, and engage a staff of skilled administrators and railway engineers to tell them how to obtain it. Thus the London and North-Western Railway Company manufactures everything it wants, from locomotives to wooden legs, without the intervention of a contractor. A mob of ratepayers acting through a municipal authority is in precisely the same position. The ratepayers are just as stupid and short-sighted as ordinary joint stock shareholders; and the worst of their representatives on the municipalities are as incapable as the worst ordinary guinea-pig directors. But the ratepayers and councillors light their towns with electricity; run tramway services; build dwellings; dredge harbors; erect dust destructors and crematoria; construct roads and manage cemeteries, as easily as a body of clergymen's widows can lay an Atlantic cable if they have money enough, or an illiterate millionaire start a newspaper. The labor market now includes an ability market in which a manager worth £10,000 a year can be hired as certainly as a navvy.

In the ability market, the municipalities have a decisive advantage in the superior attraction of public appointments for prudent and capable organizers and administrators. A municipality can always get an official more cheaply than a company can. A municipality never becomes bankrupt, is never superseded by a new discovery, and never dismisses an official without giving his case prolonged consideration in committee, from which he has practically an appeal to the whole body. A man who behaves himself and does his work has nothing to fear in public employment: his income and position are permanently assured. Besides, he enjoys his salary to the full: he has no appearances to keep up beyond the ordinary decencies of life: he need not entertain; need not keep equipages or servants for purposes of ostentation; may travel third class if he likes, live in the most unfashionable neighborhood, belong to what sect he pleases or to no sect, and dispose of his time and gratify his tastes out of office hours with a personal independence unknown to commercial employees. It is no exaggeration to say that these considerations make a municipal post of £350 a year more desirable than some commercial posts and professional practices that bring in £1000 a year; and this is why the ratepayers, in spite of their stinginess in the matter of salaries on the professional scale, get so much better served than they deserve.

All that can be said on the other side is that if the municipal officer has no fears, he has also strictly limited hopes. The Town Clerk and the Borough Engineer, the County Surveyor and the Medical Officer of Health, all know that they will never get £15,000 a year, nor even £5000, in the municipal service. The dreams of vulgar ambition, and the excitements of financial speculation, of party politics, and of fashionable life, are not for them. But these very disabilities have their value as selective conditions. The vulgarly ambitious commercial and social adventurer is very far from representing a desirable type of municipal officer; and ambitions that are not vulgar have full scope in municipal life, where a departmental chief can attain a position of enviable consideration and real public usefulness. Promotion is not only from step to step in the same municipality, but from municipality to municipality; so that if the clerkship to the London County Council, worth £2000 a year with the chance of a knighthood, becomes vacant, every provincial Town Clerk can present himself as a candidate for the post without forfeiting or risking his already secured position in any way. He can also, of course, resign his post and engage in commercial enterprise at any moment; but the fact that he practically never does so shews that there is nothing to be gained by such a step.

On the whole, then, when the directors of a joint stock company on the one hand, and the representatives of the ratepayers on the other, both being alike "amateurs carrying on business with other people's money," come into the market to engage an executive staff, the municipality has the advantage of its competitor. It can get its management cheaper as certainly as it can get its capital cheaper.

III
WHEN MUNICIPAL TRADING DOES NOT PAY

IF the Medical Officer of Health wants a microscope or the County Surveyor a theodolite, it will not pay the municipality to set up a scientific instrument factory to produce that single article, possibly of a kind which can be produced by half a dozen firms in sufficient quantity to supply the whole of Europe. Even the London County Council, with all its bands, has not yet proposed to manufacture its own trombones. The demand of the authority must be sufficiently extensive and constant to keep the necessary plant fully employed. The moment this limitation is grasped, the current vague terrors of a Socialism that will destroy all private enterprise laugh themselves into air. The more work the municipality does, the more custom it will bring to private enterprise; for every extension of its activity involves the purchase of innumerable articles which can, in the fullest social sense, be produced much more economically by private enterprise, provided it is genuinely self-supporting, and does not spunge on the poor rates or on other private enterprises for part of the subsistence of its employees: in short, provided it works under a "fair wages" clause.

There is another way in which private enterprise will hold its own even in pieces of work sufficiently vast to use up the necessary plant. Personal talent in all its gradations, from smartness and push up to positive genius, plays as important a part in industry as it does in the fine arts. It is perfectly possible for a born captain of industry to be in a position to say to a municipality: "Here is such and such a big undertaking to be carried through. Although I may have to raise at 10 per cent the capital that you can raise at $3\frac{1}{2}$; although I pay and treat my employees so well that they would not exchange my employment for yours; although I have to pay my sub-chiefs double the salaries you can get men of the same quality for; yet I will so organize the work, and so command and inspire my industrial troops that I will do the work for less than it will cost you to do it yourselves, and do it better, and have a satisfactory profit for myself into the bargain. Here is my tender, which is lower than the estimate of your Works Department!" Under such circumstances—assuming, of course, that there were sufficient reason to believe that the contractor could make his boast good—the tender should and would be accepted. Nobody who has any experience of opening tenders for important and difficult engineering work will consider this instance far-fetched. Even when the total figure is under £20,000, the difference between the lowest and highest tender is often more than 100 per cent. Although the specification may be so minutely detailed as to leave very little room for variation in the nature or quality of the product, one contractor will undertake work for £6000 which another will ask £14,000 for, without any discoverable ulterior motives. One is driven to conclude that it is the personal factor that makes the difference. Fertility and promptitude in device, boldness and swiftness in execution, power of making other men work enthusiastically: all these may give a contractor as decisive an advantage over a borough engineer as over a rival contractor. Sometimes the advantage is on the other side: it is the municipal official or the committee chairman who suggests improvements and economies to the contractor, upon whose mechanical routine the fresh minds even of a committee of amateurs (which practically always includes somebody who is not an amateur) often play very beneficially. In fact there are many matters in which municipal experience is so necessary that even the ablest contractor, when he first touches public work, can learn a good deal from the most ordinary municipality. But as municipal experience is always at the contractor's service, there is nothing in municipal trading to deprive an able enterpriser of the legitimate advantage of his talent. On the contrary, it protects him against the sort of competition that he really dreads: the competition of scamping and sweating, of underbidding by the apparent cheapness that is really the worst sort of extravagance. It narrows the competition to competition in ability of management and excellence of product, which is just the sort of competition in which he can win.

It follows that a joint stock company, if it is clever or lucky enough to secure a manager of exceptional talent, may compete successfully with a municipality of only ordinary managerial resources. Or, to put the facts in the order in which they usually occur, an industrial genius, by forming a joint stock company to provide him with capital, may do so.

But the business of the world is mainly ordinary work carried on by ordinary men and women. And all such public business of sufficient magnitude to keep the necessary plant working full time until it has paid for itself, can, when it is purely local, be done more cheaply by municipal than by private enterprise.

IV
THE ANTI-SOCIAL REACTIONS OF COMMERCIAL ENTERPRISE

IN many public services, labor plays a larger part than machinery. In them, consequently, the cost depends much more on wages and vigor of superintendence than on the rate of interest. Take for example the collection of dust from house to house, where the plant required consists of horses and carts, shovels and baskets. Not only is the cost of this plant negligible compared to the cost of the labor, but the labor is the motive power: the man drives the horse, not the horse the man: the man plies the shovel, not the shovel the man. It is quite otherwise in, for example, an electric lighting station. There the cost of the plant is higher relatively to the cost of labor; and the plant drives the man instead of the man driving the plant; for the steam engine and the dynamo do not stop and pull out a pipe when the foreman goes round the corner. There is another difference: the labor in the electric lighting station is skilled and organized: its price is standardized by Trade Unionism; so that municipalities and commercial companies have to pay the same price for it, and therefore cannot enter into a competition in sweating. The dustman, on the other hand, is an unskilled, unorganized, casual laborer, obtainable by private employers at a wage which no Progressive municipality, committed to a "moral minimum" subsistence wage, can offer. Furthermore, the private contractor, who, in the dust business, is seldom very delicate in handling his employees, can slavedrive his men in a way that may be very necessary to get the greatest result from their labor at a job in which they have no interest, but which in municipal employment is as impracticable as it is undesirable.

Now it is clear that precisely the same argument that converts even the Moderate ratepayer to municipal electric lighting (its comparative cheapness) converts even the Progressive ratepayer to private enterprise in dust collecting; for no municipality with the smallest sense of decency or social duty can bring out its bill for dust collecting at so low a figure as the sweating contractor. Consequently, as long as the question is settled, as it too often is at present, by the ratepayer's thoughtless preference for the lowest tender, municipal trading will be stopped just at the points where it is most needed. For a moment's reflection will convince any intelligent person that whereas the private electric lighting companies do their work as well, if not so cheaply, as the municipalities, the most disastrous inefficiency and unscrupulous recklessness are possible in dust collecting and such cognate work as the stripping or cleansing of rooms after cases of infectious disease. What is more, this inefficiency and recklessness will not only put the ratepayers to heavy private expense for medical attendance, disablement, and so forth, but recoil directly on the rates themselves in sanitary expenditure; whereas the extinction of the electric light for an hour occasionally, though it provokes loud complaints and is undeniably exasperating, costs nothing but the inconvenience of the moment and a little candle grease and lamp oil. We must therefore conclude, not merely that the commercial test is a misleading one, but that the desirability of municipal trading is actually in inverse ratio to its commercial profitableness. A few illustrations will make this clear.

Take the most popular branch of commercial enterprise: the drink traffic. It yields high profits. Take the most obvious and unchallenged branch of public enterprise: the making of roads. It is not commercially profitable at all. But suppose the drink trade were debited with what it costs in disablement, inefficiency, illness, and crime, with all their depressing effects on industrial productivity, and with their direct cost in doctors, policemen, prisons, &c. &c. &c.! Suppose at the same time the municipal highways and bridges account were credited with the value of the time and wear and tear saved by them! It would at once appear that the roads and bridges pay for themselves many times over, whilst the pleasures of drunkenness are costly beyond all reason. Consequently a municipalized drink traffic which should check drinking at the point of excess would be a much better bargain for the ratepayers than our present system, even if the profits made at present by brewers and publicans were changed to losses made up by subsidies from the rates.

But the drink traffic is not the best illustration of the fallacy of the commercial test. The main factor to be taken into account in comparing private with public enterprise is neither the Drink Question nor any of the other Questions which occupy so many sectional bodies of reformers, but the Poverty Question, of which all the others are only facets. Give a man a comfortable income and you solve all the Questions for him, except perhaps the Servant Question. Now the all-important difference between the position of the commercial investor and the ratepayer is that whilst the commercial investor has no responsibility for the laborers whom he employs beyond paying them their wages whilst they are working for him, the ratepayer is responsible for their subsistence from the cradle to the grave. Consequently private companies can and do make large profits out of sweated and demoralized labor at the expense of the ratepayers; and these very profits are often cited as proofs of the superior efficiency of private enterprise, especially when they are set in sensational contrast to the inability of municipalities to make any commercial profits at all in the same business.

For example, consider the case of a great dock company. Near the docks three institutions are sure to be found: a workhouse, an infirmary, and a police court. The loading and unloading of ships is dangerous labor, and to a great extent casual labor, because the ships do not arrive in regular numbers of regular tonnage at regular intervals, nor does the work average itself sufficiently to keep a complete staff regularly employed as porters are at a railway station. Numbers of men are taken on and discharged just as they are wanted, at sixpence an hour (in London) or less. This is convenient for the dock company; but it surrounds the dock with a demoralized, reckless, and desperately poor population. No human being, however solid his character and careful his training, can loaf at the street corner waiting to be picked up for a chance job without becoming more or less a vagabond: one sees this even in the artistic professions, where the same evil exists under politer conditions, as unmistakeably as in the ranks of casual labor. The shareholders and directors do not live near the docks; so this does not affect them personally. But the ratepayers who do live near the dock are affected very seriously both in person and pocket. A visit to the workhouse and a chat with one of the Poor Law Guardians will help to explain matters.

Into that workhouse every dock laborer can walk at any moment, and, by announcing himself as a destitute person, compel the guardians to house and feed and clothe him at the expense of the ratepayers. When he begins to tire of the monotony of "the able bodied ward" and its futile labor, he can wait until a ship comes in; demand his discharge; do a day's work at the docks; spend the proceeds in a carouse and a debauch; and return to the workhouse next morning, again a destitute person. This is systematically done at present by numbers of men who are by no means the least intelligent or capable of their class. Occasionally the carouse ends in their being taken to the police station instead of returning immediately to the workhouse. And if they are unlucky at their work, they may be carried for surgical treatment to the infirmary; for in large docks accidents that require hospital treatment occur in busy times at intervals of about fifteen minutes. Finally, when they are worn out, they subside into the workhouse permanently as aged paupers until they are buried by the guardians.

Now workhouses, infirmaries, and police courts cannot be maintained for nothing. Of late years workhouses have become much more expensive: in fact the outcry against the increase of the rates, which is being so vigorously used to discredit municipal trading, is due primarily and overwhelmingly to Poor Law, and only secondarily to educational and police expenditure, and has actually forced forward those branches of municipal trading which promise contributions out of their profits in relief of the general rate. This expenditure out of the rates on the workhouse is part of the cost of poverty and demoralization; and if these are caused in any district by the employment of casual labor, and its remuneration at less than subsistence rates, then it is clear that a large part of the cost of the casual labor is borne by the ratepayer and not by the dock company. The dividends, in fact, come straight out of the ratepayers' pockets, and are not in any real sense profits at all. Thus is it one of the many ironies of the situation that the sacrifices the ratepayer makes to relieve the poor really go largely to subsidize the rich.

A municipality cannot pick the ratepayer's pocket in this fashion. Transfer the docks to the municipality, and it will not be able to justify a loss at the workhouse and police station by a profit at the docks. The ratepayer does not go into the accounts: all he knows is whether the total number of pence in the pound has risen or fallen. Consequently the municipality, on taking over the docks, would be forced to aim in the first instance at organizing its work so as to provide steady permanent employment for its laborers at a living wage, even at the cost of being overstaffed on slack days, until the difficulty had been solved by new organization and machinery, as such difficulties always are when they can no longer be shirked. Under these conditions it is quite possible that the profits made formerly by the dock company might disappear; but if a considerable part of the pauperism and crime of the neighborhood disappeared simultaneously, the bargain would be a very profitable one indeed for the ratepayers, though The Times would abound with letters contrasting the former commercial prosperity of the dock company with the present "indebtedness" of the municipality.

If we now turn back from the grand scale of commercial

enterprise as represented by the dock company to the petty scale represented by the parish dust contractor, we find the same danger of false economy. When a municipality does its own dust collecting for a year, it is usually quite easy for those members whose only conception of economy is to reduce every item of expenditure separately to the lowest possible figure, to obtain estimates from contractors offering to do the work for less than it has cost the municipal Works Department. The contractor's secret is a simple one: casual labor at very low wages eked out by tips from the householders. And here the consequences reach further than in the case of the docks. The collection of dust, unlike the unloading of ships, has a direct relation to the health, comfort, and energy of the inhabitants. The individual ratepayer who fancies he has saved a few pence by the employment of a contractor may lose anything from a shilling to several pounds through illness, and suffer a constant depreciation of his own energy and that of his employees, if the dust is not punctually, frequently, and efficiently collected. The annoyance and the increase of domestic labor caused by the visits of a casually employed underpaid dustman, even when he is conciliated by tips, is known only to the woman at home, whose worries have an important reaction on the national energy, as married men well know. During smallpox epidemics, which are very costly, rates may be heavily increased by the results of cheap contracting. The ratepayer is always paying for the notifiable infectious diseases, especially scarlet fever, diphtheria, and measles; and if the disinfection after these and after smallpox is done by casual labor, so that the man who disinfects a scarlet fever room today may be discharged by the contractor in the evening, and go straight to an ordinary job tomorrow, the disinfector may himself spread more infection than he prevents. In sanitary work, then, the cost of poverty in poor law relief, and the cost of the demoralization of the casual laborer in drunkenness and crime, is increased by the cost of inefficiency and hygienic unscrupulousness in disease, with its expensive public routine of inspection, disinfection, cleansing, and stripping, in addition to its privately borne cost in medical attendance, nursing, and disablement.

But it is not yet clear that the remedy is for the municipality to do the work. It may be argued that under a proper system of inspection and an effective scale of resolutely enforced penalties, a contractor could be induced to do it as thoroughly as the municipality itself, without resorting to casual or underfed labor. Let us suppose, then, that a contractor offers to do municipal work at a figure which works out lower than the estimate of the Works Department even when the cost of sufficient inspection and enforcement of penalties to secure efficiency is added to the sum named in the contract; and that he also undertakes that everyone in his employment shall, judged by the standard of the laboring class, be in comfortable circumstances. Satisfactory as this seems, there will still be a heavy loss to the ratepayer in accepting the contract unless everyone employed by the contractor actually receives a full living wage, as the following analysis will shew.

The payment of less than a living wage is possible in two ways. There is the direct form in which the underpaid, underfed, underhoused, underclothed, underrespected, undercomforted employee draws on his or her vital capital for a few years and is then discharged and replaced by younger and less exhausted travellers on the same road to ruin. Contractors can make profits on relays of this kind just as publicans in seaports or in the Australian bush can make profits by relays of sailors and shepherds who come to them with the earnings of several months' work, and are thrown out by the potman as soon as all their money is spent in drink. On this form of sweating, common as it is, nothing need be said. To everyone intelligent enough to read a book on municipal trading it must be clear without argument that the employment of a contractor of this type would be ruinously dear to the ratepayer even if the contractor did the work for nothing and paid a bonus in aid of rates into the bargain.

But sweating is not in actual practice so obvious and simple a matter. The commonest and most dangerous form is not the direct and sensationally cruel sweating of a scandalously wretched victim by a sordidly brutal employer, but the unsensational and quite popular sweating of one industry by another, with the result that the actual starvation of the worker often takes place in neither industry, though it occurs elsewhere in consequence of their relation. This economic phenomenon, which was first analysed by Mr and Mrs Sidney Webb,[1] and is only beginning to be appreciated even by professional economists, is quite compatible with normal goodnature on the part of the employer and normal cheerfulness and decency on that of the employee.

Take a familiar example. A married laborer, or a shop assistant or clerk of the grade that makes no pretension to gentility, earns, say, from eighteen to twenty-four shillings a week. An additional six shillings a week will make a difference in the comfort and social standing of the family enormously greater than could be produced by raising an income of a thousand a year to five thousand. It is difficult for the readers of, say, the Spectator and The Times, to form any conception of the magnitude of a promotion from eighteen shillings a week to twenty-four, or from twenty-four to thirty. Such well-to-do persons are often scandalized when their attention is called to the apparent ferocity with which the very poor resist Factory Legislation when it protects their children from being withdrawn from school and sent out to earn a few shillings at an early age; but the truth is that if five shillings a week made as much difference to a duke as it does to many laborers, he would send his son out into the streets to earn it at ten years old if the law allowed him. And if he had a couple of sturdy daughters, he would not allow them to eat their heads off at home, so to speak, when they

[1] Industrial Democracy. By Sidney and Beatrice Webb (London, Longmans, 1897).

might go into a factory, or dust yard, or shop, and bring home five, ten, twelve, or perhaps even fifteen shillings apiece. If he had no children, or not enough to require a woman's whole time for the housekeeping, his duchess would give half her day as a charwoman in a lower middle-class house for five shillings a week or as much more as she could get for it. Such family circumstances seldom occur in the peerage except after revolutions; but millions of English laborers' homes are in that position. The consequence is that there is a huge mass of the labor of women and minors always in the market at less than subsistence rates; and whole industries can be carried on by such labor with plenty of profit to their organizers. But they are carried on at a loss to the ratepayer, who has finally to make up much more than the whole difference between the wage paid and the cost of subsistence, except where the debt is cancelled by premature death.

Let us follow the process in the instance most favorable to it. A laborer is working for twenty-four shillings a week (the present London "moral minimum" subsistence wage) for the London County Council. If he and his wife can get a boarder at six shillings a week (for which a separate apartment and much more food than would otherwise be wasted can hardly be expected) the twenty-four shillings become thirty: an immense difference. Economically, it does not matter to the laborer whether the boarder is his own son or daughter or somebody else's. The London factory girl can always find a family to board with if she has none of her own; but the evil is so far exaggerated by family affection that a girl who could bring home only five shillings would probably have to board with an eighteen shilling laborer instead of a twenty-four shilling one unless the latter were her father.

Now it is clear that though the girl (or lad) takes five shillings home, and thereby eases the family circumstances very appreciably; so that both the parents and the daughter are benefited and pleased, the father is partly supporting the girl out of the wage paid him by the County Council. That means that her employer is spunging on the ratepayer for part of the cost of the labor he uses. With this advantage he tenders to the Government for a clothing contract, or to one of the Borough Councils for a dusting contract. These bodies, being now mostly bound by resolution to pay full living wages to their own direct employees, find that they cannot do the work themselves so cheaply. It is therefore given to the contractor in the name of economy; so that though the ratepayers pay full subsistence wages to their own adult male laborers, yet by employing a contractor to sweat the laborer's daughter, who brings her wage up to subsistence point by indirectly sweating him, they get the labor of two persons for less than a subsistence wage and a half, even if they pay the contractor ten shillings for the labor he pays five for. No doubt many ratepayers will regard this as a clever stroke of business; but it would have been still cleverer for the ratepayer to have paid the laborer twenty-nine shillings a week for the services of himself and his daughter in direct employment and so saved the contractor's profit. Yet even from this point of view the system of allowing one industry to flourish as a parasite on another is a penny-wise and pound-foolish one, as we shall see when we pursue the process to its end—for we are by no means done with it yet. Meanwhile it must be remembered that our hypothetic laborer need not be in the employment of the County Council. He may be in the employment of a commercial company or firm at a living wage, in which case both the contractor and the public body accepting his contract are making the company pay for the difference between what the contractor pays his employees and what it costs them to live.

Let us now follow the career of the laborer's daughter. In course of time her parents die, or else get past working and become dependent on their children instead of helping to support them. Five shillings a week will not meet this emergency. If the daughter marries a man earning a subsistence wage, she provides for herself and either puts her parents on her husband's back (he having parents of his own, probably) or else lets them go into the workhouse. But this solution of the difficulty does not always occur. She may not marry; and if she does her husband may die, or desert her, or be disabled, or be out of employment in times of bad trade. These things occur sufficiently often to produce at all times a considerable number of women struggling to live and to bring up their children by their own unaided exertions.

Imagine the fate of such a woman. She seeks employment in a factory, and is offered five shillings a week. If she refuses it on the ground that she cannot feed herself and her children on it, plenty of younger, jollier, better looking laborers' daughters, with their fathers' wages to fall back on, will take her place willingly. She tries to earn something as a charwoman, and finds that plenty of laborers' wives are willing to "come in for an hour a day" for the same five shilling wage, though in this case the hour may mean half the day, a midday meal, and certain stray perquisites of washing and the like which may, at best, perhaps double the nominal value of the job. Permanent domestic service is barred by the children; and so is boarding with a family. Rent may be anything up to six and sixpence a room. At every turn the competition of the subsidized laborer's boarder, whether wife, daughter, or stranger, has reduced wages below subsistence point; and there is seldom any prospect of an improvement, because most of these sweated industries would, if they were compelled to pay a living wage, either disappear altogether or else save themselves by reorganizing their system, introducing machinery, and employing labor of quite a different class. The situation is a desperate one; and though nearly every middle-class family knows (and has perhaps helped to sweat) some respectable widow who has weathered it, no middle-class family knows or tolerates the many widows, deserted wives, and single women of the prevalent "middling" character, who give up the struggle, and drudge and drink and pilfer their way along as best they can, qualifying themselves and their children for poor relief, sick relief, and police coercion, and forming a centre of infection for that disease of hopeless inefficiency and unconscientiousness in daily work which costs the ratepayers more than the whole budget, imperial and local, civil and military.

Thus we find that even when a contractor can guarantee that the labor he employs is not casual labor; that it is efficient, regular, respectable, cheerful, healthy, and untouched directly by pauperism, prostitution, or crime; and that he pays the full wage customary in his industry, it will still not pay the ratepayer to accept his tender unless he can shew that every person he proposes to employ on the work will get a self-supporting adult's living wage for it. Not until this fundamental condition is insisted on can a simple comparison of the contractor's tender with the Borough Engineer's estimate be accepted as a test of the relative merits of commercial and municipal enterprise.

This is the common sense of the modern innovation of a Fair Wages clause in all industrial contracts made by municipalities, and of the payment of a full living wage to all municipal employees.

V
THE BENEFICIAL REACTIONS OF COMMERCIAL ENTERPRISE

IN reading the last chapter, the intelligent advocate of commercial enterprise must have been oppressed with a sense of unfairness, because it says nothing of the employers who are not sweaters, nor of the great social benefits which commercial enterprise has conferred on the community. If commerce has its anti-social reactions, represented by the prison, the workhouse, and the poor rate, what about its beneficial social reactions? It feeds us, clothes us, provides our system of transport. In a word, our subsistence and our civilization are its daily work, done at its own risk.

Unfortunately, though it does, if not all this, at least enough of it to establish high claims to our consideration, it does so at the commercial disadvantage of being unable to appropriate the total benefit resulting from its operations. If on the one hand the dock company is able, as we have seen, to spunge on the ratepayer for the maintenance of its labor, and to throw on his shoulders the social wreckage its methods involve, it is, on the other hand, quite unable to reap for itself the whole value of the docks to the seaport. It may be scraping together a very paltry dividend with the utmost anxiety, whilst trade to the value of many millions is coming to the town through its gates. Indeed it may pay no dividend at all, and yet see commercial companies all round it making handsome profits which would instantly disappear if the docks were swallowed up by an earthquake. And the dust contractor, with all his opportunities of sweating, has to quote such low figures lest his competitors should send in the lowest tender, that he sometimes becomes a bankrupt in consequence of operations which have reduced the death-rate of the parish and saved many doctor's bills.

Now it is the chief and overwhelming advantage of public enterprise that it can and does reap the total benefit of its operations when there is a benefit, just as it suffers and is warned by the total damage of them when there is damage.

In the technical language of the political economists, public enterprise goes into business to gain the value in use or total utility of industrial activity, whilst commercial enterprise can count only on the value in exchange or marginal utility. An illustration or two will make the meaning clear.

It is commonly enough understood that there are certain highly beneficial industrial operations which cannot be left to commercial enterprise, because their profits are necessarily communized from the beginning; so that a company undertaking the work could not get paid for it. The provision of thoroughfares in a city is a case in point. It has never been possible to put a toll-bar at the end of every city street and compel each passenger to pay for using it. Commercially, therefore, city street-making "does not pay"; so it is left to the municipality, with the result that the ratepayers gain enormously by their expenditure. What is not so generally recognized is that this power of the ratepayers to realize profits inaccessible to private speculators, applies to a greater or less extent over the whole field of public industry. Streets and highways are only a part of the industry of locomotion: commercial enterprise, which cannot touch them, can and does undertake toll bridges, tramways, railways, cab services, and, in short, every means of locomotion which can be charged for per passenger. But though commercial companies can make a dividend in this way, they cannot charge for, and consequently cannot reap for themselves, more than a fraction of the value of the service they render, even when they have the closest monopoly of the traffic. The reason is that the actual passengers are not the only people benefited by facility of communication. Take an extreme case: that of a rich invalid in the country whose life depends on the arrival of a London surgeon to operate within, say, two hours. He will pay anything, "skin for skin, yea, all that a man hath will he give for his life"—much less the necessary hundred guineas or so—to bring the surgeon to his bedside; and the railway company will do it for him; but the railway company will not get the hundred guineas. It will get no more than if the surgeon were starting on a pleasure trip, and were paying for the fun of the journey instead of being heavily paid to endure its fatigues. In the same way everybody who buys a pound of tea or a ton of coal derives from the commercial enterprise which has established communication between China and Newcastle a benefit which is out of all proportion to the charge for freight and for commercial travellers' tickets which is all that the railway and steamship company get. Suppose these charges were abolished! Suppose, even, that people became so sensitive to the discomforts of railway travelling and of seasickness that they had to be paid so much per mile at the ticket office to induce them to travel. Private enterprise in locomotion, as at present organized, would be ruined at once; but it would still pay the ratepayer and the taxpayer handsomely to keep the railways and shipping lines—in other words, to maintain civilization—on these terms.

This difference is fundamental. It quite disables all commercial comparisons between commercial and communal industry. When a joint stock company spends more than it takes, it is carrying on business at a loss. When a public authority does so, it may be carrying on business at a huge profit. And there is no question here of the shopkeeper's trick of selling canary seed under cost price in order to induce bird fanciers to buy their flour and fodder from him. A municipality might trade in this manner too, if it saw fit: for instance, it might wire houses for electric light under cost price in order to stimulate a commercially profitable consumption of current. But it is quite possible that a municipality might engage in a hundred departments of trade; might shew a commercial loss on every one of them at the end of every half year; and yet continue in that course with the full approval and congratulation of the very ratepayers who would have to make up the loss. Its total gains are immeasurable; and its success can only be estimated by constant reference to the statistics of public welfare. For instance, if the statistics of health, and of crime, had been applied a century ago to test the alleged prosperity of Manchester under unrestricted private enterprise, nobody would have boasted of a factory system that "used up nine generations of men in one generation" as profitable because it produced a commercial peerage of cotton lords. If the new education authorities adopt the recommendation of Dr J. F. J. Sykes, and have the children in the schools periodically weighed and measured, the vital statistics thus obtained will provide an important test of the social value of the industrial order under which the children live. Thus, let us imagine a city in which the poor rates, police rates, and sanitary rates are very low, and the children in the schools flourishing and of full weight, whilst all the public services of the city are municipalized and conducted without a farthing of profit, or even with occasional deficits made up out of the rates. Suppose another city in which all the public services are in the hands of flourishing joint stock companies paying from 7 to 21 per cent, and in which the workhouses, the prisons, the hospitals, the sanitary inspectors, the disinfectors and strippers and cleansers, are all as busy as the joint stock companies, whilst the schools are full of rickety children. According to the commercial test, the second town would be a triumphant proof of the prosperity brought by private enterprise, and the first a dreadful example of the bankruptcy of municipal trade. But which town would a wise man rather pay rates in? The very shareholders of the companies in the second town would take care to live in the first. And what chance would a European State consisting of towns of the second type have in a struggle for survival with a State of the first?

This demonstration of the irrelevance of the ordinary comparisons of commercial profits and expenses with municipal profits and expenses leads to a comparison of the very important factor of incentive. The commercial incentive stops where its profit stops. The municipal incentive extends to the total social utility, direct and indirect, of the enterprise. What is more, the incentive of commercial profit is often actually stronger on the side of socially harmful enterprises than of beneficial ones. Vicious entertainments and exhibitions, unscrupulous newspapers and books, liquor licenses in neighborhoods already overstocked with drink-shops, are only the obvious instances, just as our commercially unprofitable cathedrals, national galleries, and blue books are conspicuous at the opposite extreme.

But it may be contended that an efficient censorship would bar the downward path to commercial enterprise, very much as the London County Council has forced the London music halls into the comparatively decent courses which have produced their present enormous prosperity. The fact remains that the music halls did not see their own interest until they were forced to look at it through the public eye; and this goes to shew that the limitation of the gains of commercial enterprise to its commercial dividend, also limits its mind, and, by making it habitually blind to public considerations, prevents it from grasping even the commercial opportunities which large public needs offer.

Take a simple instance. London is at present helplessly at the mercy of a cab service which caricatures all the worst weaknesses of commercial enterprise. It costs a shilling to go ten yards in a cab: consequently the stands are always full of idle cabs, and the most energetic policing cannot clear the streets of crawling ones. Yet if you want to take a cab for an hour, which hardly anybody does, you get it for a halfpenny a minute. What is wanted is the penny-a-minute cab, which would, for hundreds of thousands of Londoners who now never take a cab except when they are travelling with luggage, abolish walking for all purposes except constitutional ones. The penny bus, still a comparative novelty, has shewn that even twopence is a prohibitive fare in London; for the increase of passengers produced by the reduction to a penny has been so lucrative that the main thoroughfares will not accommodate all the omnibuses that seek to ply in them. The London cabmen could introduce a penny-a-minute fare if they had sufficient business capacity; but if they had they would not be cabmen. It is easy to say that the cab proprietors would do it if it would pay. It is equally easy and equally absurd to say that a tube railway from the Mansion House to Uxbridge Road would have existed ten years ago if it would have paid ten years ago, or that the grime of the underground railway was a wise economy of its directors. The truth about private enterprise is that it is not enterprising enough for modern public needs. It will not start a new system until it is forced to scrap the old one. And the reason—one that no profusion of technical education will wholly remove—is that only a fraction of the public benefit of industrial enterprise is commercially appropriable by it. It will not risk colossal capitals with the certainty that it must do enormous service to the public, and create a prodigious unearned increment for the ground landlords, before it can touch a farthing of dividend; and therefore, however crying the public need may be, if the municipalities will not move in the matter nothing is done until millionaires begin to loathe their superfluity and become reckless as to its investment; until railways are promoted merely to buy tubes from Steel Trusts, and monster hotels floated, after the usual three liquidations, to buy tables and carpets from furniture companies. And even then what is done is only enough to shew that it should have been done fifty years sooner, and might even have been done commercially but for the fatal, though inevitable, commercial habit of mind which must consider only the dividend which it can grasp and not the social benefit that it must share with its neighbors.

VI
COMMERCIAL AND MUNICIPAL PRICES

THE effect of municipal enterprise on prices is an important factor in the situation. The rough and ready conclusion as to market prices is that sellers will compete for custom by underbidding one another, and that thus free competition will secure the utmost possible cheapness to the consumer. The simple reply to this optimistic receipt for a self-acting millennium is that as soon as sellers find this out they stop competing; and competition is replaced by conspiracy. The far-seeing and capable heads of the trade combine, and finally get the whole trade into their own hands, even if they have to sell at less than cost for long enough to ruin all the small manufacturers who are too poor or too stupid to join the combination. A monopoly being thus established, a market price is fixed, and retailers are supplied only on condition of their selling at that price.

Now it does not follow that this price will be higher than the old competition price it has superseded. On the contrary, the cost of production is so much reduced by the concentration of the trade in the hands of the most intelligent masters, manufacturing on a large scale with the best machinery and the largest capitals, and public consumption is so much increased by every reduction in price, that a frequent result of the substitution of combination for competition, and of relative monopoly for complete freedom of trade, is the appearance in the market of a better and cheaper article.

But there are limits to this beneficial process. The Trust, after all, is not a philanthropic enterprise, which is exactly what the municipality is. The Trust aims at the maximum of profit; and its prices will always be fixed so as to carry that profit. The municipality, on the other hand, must aim at the suppression of profit, because municipal profit, as we shall see presently, has the effect of making the consumer pay more than his fair share of the rates. But no matter what result is aimed at, whether profit or no profit, that result can be produced, not by one price and one price only, but by any one of several different prices.

To make this clear, take a case: a fantastic one to begin with. Let the problem be to fix the price of a newly invented patent flying machine for a single passenger. As the patent excludes competition, the patentee may fix its price at anything from its bare cost to a completely prohibitive figure. Our experience of the automobile shows us what he would do. He would offer the aeroplane first at £500,000. It is quite possible, in view of the insane distribution of riches at the present time, that he would sell half a dozen through Europe and America at that figure; for ridiculously rich people do spend such sums on much less attractive whims. That is, he would receive three millions. When there were no more buyers at half a million, he would introduce the Popular Aeroplane at £100,000. Probably there would be no buyers: everybody would wait confidently for a further reduction. He would then come down to £1000, and make a stand at that, probably, for some years, meanwhile paying artizans £2 a week to fly about in aeroplanes and familiarize the public with their existence and practicability, just as until quite recently the most expensive autocars were seen running on our main roads, crowded, not with dukes and millionaires, but with people whose average family income was clearly not much above thirty shillings.

If he sold 3000 aeroplanes at £1000 apiece, the takings would be the same as that from the sale of six at £500,000. A sale of 6000 at £500, of 30,000 at £100, or of 150,000 at £20, would all produce the same sum, and a slight modification of the larger numbers to allow for varying cost of production would make them all return the same profit; for the labor of organizing the production and distribution of a million and a half aeroplanes would be enormously greater than of half a dozen, whilst, per contra, the market would be much more stable, and the manufacture of the million and a half would be a matter for machines turning out aeroplanes by the gross like pins, whilst six only would have to be built as primitively as a village carpenter builds a wheelbarrow.

All these changes would enter into the calculations of the seller; but the main factor in his choice would be the sliding scale by which the number of buyers goes up as the price comes down. And it is clear that neither the lowest price, nor any single price whatever, would have a decisive advantage from the purely commercial point of view. There might be hundreds of equally convenient prices all yielding the same commercial result; and when, after a long series of trials, something like a stable customary price was reached as the most satisfactory to the seller, all experience is against the hope that it would, in a community stratified as ours is in purchasing power, be the price at which the most socially beneficial use of the invention would be possible. It would either be too cheap, like gin, or too dear, like house room. As in the case of the motor car, the whole industry of the world might be deprived of its benefit for years whilst producers were competing for the custom of plutocratic young sportsmen with racing machines of extravagantly superfluous horse power.

Let us take a more prosaic case. Let the problem be to fix the price per word of a cable message, say to the United States. Here there is clearly no single most profitable price. The difference between the cost of sending one message a day and twenty is negligible: consequently the profit on one message a day at a pound and twenty messages at a shilling apiece is the same. Still, it saves trouble to send one message instead of twenty; so the commercial tendency will be to charge a pound. At present, accordingly, cabling to the United States is an expensive luxury. The charge is a shilling a word; and a couple of tiny offices in Northumberland Avenue, in which one never finds as many as two customers at the same time, suffice for all the people in that populous centre who wish to avoid the crowding in the postal telegraph offices. It is difficult to believe that a sweeping reduction in this heavy charge would reduce profits, however much it might multiply cables, offices, plant, and staff. But it is not certain that it would increase profits; and if it did not, the company would have reduced their charges and magnified their operations for nothing. The huge benefit to both nations from the development of their intercourse would not go into the company's pocket.

But it would go into the nation's pocket. It would probably pay the nation to make telegraphic communication with the American continent quite free of direct charges except possibly for the purpose of checking a frivolous use of the cables. At all events the nation's interest in keeping charges down is as clear as the company's interest in keeping them up to the highest point at which the loss by restricting the use of the cable will be less than the gain by high rates.

A municipality does not meddle with transatlantic cables; but it does with telephones. Its advantage over local commercial enterprise is of the same nature. There is not one price only available, and that the most profitable, but several prices all yielding the same total profit. It is the interest of the private company to select the highest of these, and the interest of the public and of the municipality to select the lowest. There is, however, one very important difference between a telegraph and a telephone service. Competition between telegraph companies may duplicate cables unnecessarily; but it may nevertheless keep down charges. But competing telephone exchanges are intolerable: the nature of the service compels monopoly. At Tunbridge Wells, where the municipality established an exchange in competition with a private company, all the arguments in favor of municipal enterprise, and all its promises of a cheaper service, broke down before the nuisance of ringing up your butcher or baker, your doctor or solicitor, and finding that he was on the rival exchange. It was perhaps natural for the ratepayers of Tunbridge Wells to sell their own baby exchange rather than buy the grown-up one of the commercial company; but it was not the final solution of the difficulty; and the victory was not really one of private enterprise over municipal socialism, but of national over local organization of an essentially national service. The private company was not tied by the municipal boundary of Tunbridge Wells; and this advantage made it irresistible when the question arose which competitor should swallow the other.

Take a third case of the simplest oilshop order. Let the problem be to fix the retail price per gallon of the petroleum of, say, the Standard Oil Trust. A practical monopoly of the petroleum supply may be assumed; but a monopoly of petroleum is not a monopoly of light. Petroleum could be put out of use altogether by too high a price. On the other hand, every reduction of price means an increase of consumption. Lamps are lighted earlier and extinguished later; duplex lamps are substituted for single wicks; the poor man puts a light in the passage as well as in the room; oil stoves come into use; oil is used lavishly in cleaning bicycles and sewing machines; and though the difference may not amount to more than a spoonful a day per house, yet a spoonful multiplied by millions has to be reckoned with by a Trust. Under these circumstances petroleum is likely to be very cheap. The cost of production and distribution will be economized to the utmost by the monopoly because one monopoly factory will do the work of ten competing ones with much less than ten times the land and plant; and a Trust can control railways and manipulate freights; whilst the fact that a low price means an enormous demand, and that every attempt to put on an extra penny a gallon cuts off that demand so seriously as to reduce the gross profit instead of increasing it, acts as a far better guarantee of cheapness than the old-fashioned competitive system. The Trust, in fact, has a larger appetite for customers than the scattered competitors it has extinguished; and so, from the social point of view, the Trust is a very welcome industrial development, and the present outcry against it is but a straw fire compared to the blaze of indignation which would break out if the old system were miraculously reimposed on the consumer.

A municipality could not compete with the Oil Trust because, as we shall see later, it is disabled by its boundaries. It may be argued that a public body could undersell a Trust because it does not aim at profit. But in practice, as there is a good deal of commercial human nature in public bodies, it would be found that without the incentive of a little profit to boast of at elections the public body would aim rather at the minimum of trouble to itself than at the maximum demand for oil. Municipalities as a matter of fact do always make as much profit as they dare; and though this is beyond all question unfair to the consumer, who is made to contribute more than his share to the rates, yet the incidence of rating is already so unfair—indeed, so absurd—that to object to a small profit on this ground would be to strain at a gnat whilst swallowing a camel, especially as without the incentive of this profit the tendency would be to a high price and a restricted supply rather than to a low price and an extended supply. The real advantage of public enterprise would therefore be, not the complete reduction of price to cost, but the application of the profits to the public good instead of their private appropriation by idle shareholders. The United States, by owning the Standard Oil Trust, could avoid such horrible absurdities as the annual export of millions of dollars in dividends to be wasted in parasitic fashionable life in European capitals and Mediterranean pleasure cities, whilst large sections of the American population are miserably poor. But even on this point the Trust is better than the mob of small competitors; for if profits are not socialized it is better to concentrate them on a few millionaires, who are forced by the mere weight of their superfluities to throw whole masses of money back on the public in the manner of Mr Carnegie, than to scatter them on a crowd of "successful tradesmen" whose children become unprofitable pensioners on the nation, and cannot afford to give anything back except an occasional subscription to maintain the evil of irresponsibly managed begging hospitals.

The tendency of private enterprise, with its preference for "a high class connection," and its natural desire to make the rate of profit as high as possible, is to keep up prices to the point beyond which the contraction of the market would make the trade unstable. The sudden reintroduction of competition by a new departure—for example, the tube railway suddenly upsetting the monopoly of the old underground in London—always brings down prices, a fact which proves that private enterprise maintains the highest price that will pay instead of the lowest. This tendency is clearly an anti-social one. Through its operation the various inventions which are the sole real assets of modern civilization, instead of raising the standard of life of the whole population, may remain for a long time the toys of the rich, who themselves cannot escape from an overwhelming environment of primitive poverty, to which more civilization means only less air, less house room, less decency, less health, and less freedom.

The pressure on a municipality is in the opposite direction. Once its inertia is overcome, all its inducements and obligations tend to cheapness and the widest possible diffusion of its products. Instead of the large number of prices that are equally remunerative commercially, it has to consider only one ideal price: that is, cost price on the basis of the greatest attainable number of customers; and any modification it makes in this price can be dictated only by its desire to raise its revenue as conveniently and popularly as possible, or by considerations of social welfare, such as those which make Bibles artificially cheap and brandy artificially dear. In short, the radical antagonism between enterprise that has for its object the making of the largest possible profit at the expense of the community, and that which aims simply at supplying public needs as cheaply and effectively as possible, inevitably tells heavily in favor of municipal trading. The incidental public benefit of private enterprise has been very great, *faute de mieux*, in the anarchic period of transition from medievalism to modern collectivism, during which we should have had no industry at all without private enterprise. But the benefit has been at best incidental, and has stopped short, by the laws of its own nature, of the attainable maximum. The benefits of public enterprise are not incidental: they are the sole reason for its existence; and there is nothing to limit them but remediable defects of political machinery and those human infirmities which are common to private and public interest alike.

The one drawback is municipal inertia. It is as possible for a local authority as for an imperial government to do nothing over and above the work that cannot be left undone without obvious and immediate disaster. Private enterprise, on the other hand, must discover and supply public wants or else starve. Unfortunately, this incentive, instead of being strongest where the public need is most vital, and weakest where it is most frivolous, is graduated in just the opposite way. The public need is greatest where the purchasing power is least: the commercial incentive is strongest where purchasing power is heaped up in ridiculous superfluity. Private enterprise begins with 100 horse-power racing automobiles, and reluctantly filters down to cheap and useful locomotion: public enterprise begins at the other end and helps those who cannot individually help themselves. Thus, even if we grant that the desire to make money is a stronger incentive than public spirit and public need, we must admit that it is strongest at the wrong end, and dwindles to nothing at the right end, whereas public spirit and public need are strongest at the right end and are not wanted at the other except for repressive purposes. It may be said that the remedy is a redistribution of purchasing power and not more municipal trading. This proposition is quite unquestionable from the extreme Socialist point of view; but as the present opponents of municipal trading would certainly reject this remedy as more fatal to their hopes than the disease, it need not be dealt with here further than by an emphatic reminder that poverty is at the root of most of our social difficulties; that it is incompatible with liberty and variety; and that it has put the opponents of municipal trading so far in a cleft stick that they cannot abolish poverty except by public enterprise, and cannot escape public enterprise except by the abolition of poverty.

VII
DIFFICULTIES OF MUNICIPAL TRADING
ELECTRICAL ENTERPRISE

SO far, the case for Municipal Trading seems clear enough. Indeed, on all the issues raised by its opponents, it comes out of the controversy triumphantly. But if a simple verdict of Go Ahead be delivered, the real difficulties, which are seldom mentioned and never appreciated in popular controversy, will soon assert themselves.

To begin with, Private Enterprise enjoys a degree of licence which may be described as almost anarchic. It has for its area the heaven above, the earth beneath, and the minerals under the earth. National frontiers and local boundaries do not exist for it. In the matter of advertizing it is exempt from all moral obligations: the most respectable newspapers give up the greater part of their space every day to statements which every well-instructed person knows to be false, and dangerously false, since they lead people to trust to imaginary cures in serious illnesses, and to ride bicycles through greasy mud in heavy traffic on tires advertized as "non-slipping": in short, to purchase all sorts of articles and invest in all sorts of enterprises on the strength of shameless lies, perfectly well known to be lies by the newspaper proprietor, who would at once dismiss the editor if a falsehood of the same character appeared in a leading article. Its operations are practically untrammelled by restrictive legislation; the accepted principle of the State towards it is *laisser-faire*; it has an overwhelming direct representation in Parliament; and in private life there are ten thousand people engaged in it for every one who knows anything of the municipality of which he is a constituent except that it periodically extorts money from him by the hands of the detested rate collector. Political ignorance, individual selfishness, the habit of regarding every piece of public work as a job for somebody, the narrowness that makes the Englishman's house a castle to be defended *contra mundum*, the poverty and long hours of work that leave the toiler no energy to spare for public work or public interest, the vague association of public aid with pauperism and of private enterprise with independence, the intense sense of caste which resents municipal activity as the meddling of pretentious tradesmen and seditious labor agitators: all these symptoms of the appalling poverty of public spirit, and the virulence and prevalence of private spirit in our commercial civilization, are on the side of private enterprise, and have hitherto secured for it a monopoly, as far as a monopoly was practicable, of the national industry: a monopoly that is only slowly giving way before the manifest private advantages of municipal employment to the employee class, and of municipal gas and water to the employer class.

Municipal enterprise, on the other hand, is handicapped from the outset not only by all the influences just cited, but by the national presumption against State action of all kinds inherited from the long struggle for individual liberty which followed the break-up of the medieval system. That struggle led men to assume that corruption is inherent in public offices; that a trading municipality is the same thing as a seventeenth-century monopoly; and that the remedy for all such evils is free competition between private enterprisers rigidly protected from public competition. Nominally this view is obsolete; but in practice it is still assumed that whereas private men and private companies may do anything they are not expressly forbidden to do, a municipality may do nothing that it is not expressly authorized to do; and as every authorization has to come from a Parliament in which private enterprise is powerfully represented, the municipalities so far can get little more than the refuse of private enterprise. The municipality, in fact, does not enjoy freedom of trade, and the private capitalist does, the natural result being that whilst municipal enterprise is struggling to get trading Bills through hostile parliaments, and agitating for larger powers, private enterprise is forming gigantic industrial conspiracies which ruthlessly stamp out the old-fashioned huckstering competition on which the nation foolishly relied for protection against monopoly, and establishing a predatory capitalistic collectivism which has knocked more anti-Socialist nonsense out of the English people in the last five years than the arguments and pamphlets of the Socialists have done in the last fifty. Nevertheless the race between municipal and national Collectivism, and the frankly plutocratic Collectivism of the Trusts, is one in which, under existing circumstances, the municipalities have no chance except in the industries which the Trusts will not touch because they do not pay in the commercial sense.

To illustrate this, let us take the leading instance to the contrary: the provision of electric light and locomotion. A moment's consideration will shew that the successes of municipal electricity belong to the early stages of the industry, and can only be maintained if the municipalities deliberately check its inevitable development by suppressing private competitors. So long as private enterprise can range over the whole country, whilst municipal enterprise cannot cross its own little boundary, so long will the attainment of the maximum of economy and efficiency by the municipality be impossible. In London the absurdity of the separate electric lighting concerns of the Borough Councils can be got over by their consolidation in the hands of the County Council, which would then have an area at its disposal which no single private enterprise seems yet prepared to handle as a whole. But the administrative county of London is not England; and even London's boundaries do not form the most economical terminuses for her electric trams. In the country, municipal enterprise is reduced to absurdity by the smallness of the areas and their openly nonsensical boundaries. Mr H. G. Wells's description of his residence on the boundary between Sandgate and Folkestone [1] (two places as continuous as Mayfair and St James's), a boundary which no municipal tramcar or drain-pipe can cross, shews the hopelessness of substituting public for private

[1] Mankind in the Making, by H. G. Wells (London: Chapman and Hall, 1903), Appendix, p. 410.

Collectivism there. A shipping firm whose vessels were forbidden to cross any degree of latitude or longitude might as easily compete with the Peninsular and Oriental as the Folkestone municipality with a Trust which could (and would) operate over a whole province.

Abroad, this difficulty is emphasized by the use of water power as a source of electricity. If Niagara happened to be one of the falls of the Regent's Canal, the fact that St Pancras and Marylebone may not light Shoreditch with electricity would be an unbearable folly. In England we look to our coal for power; and we are coming to the end of our easily accessible coal, whilst other countries are as yet coming only to the beginning of theirs. The loss of our relative advantage in power will sooner or later force us to look to our water power. We have not, like the Swiss and the Italians, an abundance of waterfalls. But we have the tides; and what hardly any of us yet seem to realize, in spite of the fascinating lectures of Mr H. J. Mackinder on political geography,[1] is that tides such as ours, instead of being universal, occur only in a very few places on the globe; so that if we could harness to our industries the stupendous daily rush of millions of tons of tidal water through the Pentland Firth, not only need no Englishman ever go underground again for fuel, but the advantage would not be shared directly by other nations who have no such tides at their disposal. I mention this grossly insular consideration to those whose social sympathies stop at the frontier.

The alternative to water power is the generation of electric current from coal at the pit's mouth, and its distribution therefrom without regard to administrative boundaries over areas which include several municipal districts.

In neither case can the electrical industry be handled adequately by local authorities whilst their activity is limited to existing areas. The boundaries of these areas correspond to no contemporary reality in distribution of population or

[1] Britain and the British Seas, by H. J. Mackinder (London: Heinemann, 1902), p. 339, etc.

natural configuration. Many of them are imaginary lines drawn along the middle of busy streets and closely inhabited roads: others cut across country like the scent of a hunted fox. In London at present, neither the London County Council nor the commercial electric traction companies can run an electric tram through a London borough without the consent of the Borough Council, which, being too small to provide London with tramways itself, can, and often does, prevent other people from doing it, mostly on grounds which are beyond human patience—for instance, that Tottenham Court Road rivals Bond Street as a fashionable shopping centre, and that if tram-lines were laid along it the aristocracy would desert it. Even when the London County Council is given power to override this sort of opposition, it will be unable to touch railways, though it is clear enough that the problems of London housing will never be solved as long as Surrey and Kent remain for the most part less accessible to men who have daily business in London than Yorkshire and Lancashire.[1]

Here, then, we find how impossible is the situation set up by the growth, within the last quarter century, of a vast machinery of modern industrial collectivism on the lines of a parochial system of localization which belongs to the time when it was possible for a famine to rage in one English county whilst there was a glut in the adjoining one. The Industrial Freedom League is an inevitable product of that situation. It is true that the Industrial Freedom League does not put the situation frankly before the public, because the moral of such an elucidation would not be the suppression of public enterprise in the interest of private enterprise, but the further reform, co-ordination, and extension of local government with a view to enabling it to deal with large districts. This is the last thing the League desires, because

[1] I have myself had to leave a house situated on the main road from London to Portsmouth, with the fortieth milestone at my gate, because I could not keep appointments in London in less than three hours from door to door. The case of the more remote residents may be imagined.

its one valid plea against the municipalities is the inadequacy of their areas.

Suppose, for instance, Mr Emil Garcké were to say, "The Industrial Freedom League does not claim Industrial Freedom; it protests against Industrial Bondage. It is practically a committee of the commercial electrical enterprises of the country to protest against an intolerable state of things in which the municipalities, without having the power to develop the electrical industry fully itself, has the power—and uses it—to prevent our doing it. We are ready to effect a revolution in English industry by establishing, throughout whole provinces, a house-to-house distribution of electrical power which will enable the intelligent individual craftsman to compete once more with the brute force of the factory. We are ready to link up entire manufacturing districts with networks of electric trams which will enable Englishmen to work in towns whilst their children grow up in the country instead of in slums. But we are stopped by the municipalities. This one has an Electric Lighting Order which gives it a virtual monopoly within its own ridiculous limits: that one will not allow a tramway to pass down its main street because the shopkeepers consider tramways vulgar. We represent capital, intelligence, education, technical knowledge, scope of enterprise and breadth of view; and we are stopped at every turn by the narrowness, the ignorance, the timidity, the jealousy, the poverty of a series of little gangs of small shopkeepers, led by the local solicitor, the local auctioneer, the local publican, and the local builder, who flourish their little monopolies and vetoes in our faces, and are determined that what was good enough for their great-grandfathers shall be good enough for the modern British Empire."

All this would be quite true enough and fair enough for all purposes of commercial controversy; but the remedy is, not to make our petty local authorities still more petty, but to develop our system of local government so that there shall be machinery for provincial and national collectivism as well as for parochial collectivism. Such a conclusion would not suit the anti-municipal agitators: consequently they are driven to obscure the issue by attempting to revive the obsolete doctrines of the *laisser-faire* school, and to disparage municipal enterprise by those comparisons of private with public balance-sheets which, as we have seen, are worthless as a measure of advantage to the ratepayer.

None the less, as things now stand, the ratepayer has a real grievance. If he tries to establish electric tramways from county to county, or to reduce the cost of electric power (still ridiculously expensive in its application to domestic heating, for example) by making the generating centre supply a whole province, he can do so only through the local authority or through a commercial joint stock company. If, for the sake of cheap service and public control, he tries the local authority, he finds that its power, like that of the witch who cannot cross running water, stops at a boundary which dates, probably, from the Heptarchy. If he submits to the prices and the power of the joint stock company, he finds that the local authority vetoes the tramway, or has a virtual monopoly of power distribution within its own area. So it ends in his going without.

The reason why the League, which would be very powerful in Parliament but for the tight hand kept by the great provincial municipalities on their borough members, does not get any serious grip of the electorate, is that its case is strong only where the interest of the ordinary private citizen is weak. The grievance of being hampered in the exploitation of a whole province, is the grievance of a millionaire or of a Trust controlled by a group of millionaires, who are generally assumed to be Americans. The hostility of the average municipal councillor to these combinations, though it is a thoroughly unenlightened one, reflects that of the public at large. The municipal areas are still large enough for ordinary trading capitals of six or seven figures; and, as we have seen, the case for municipal trading within these limits is overwhelming.

VIII
DIFFICULTIES OF MUNICIPAL TRADING (*continued*)

HOUSING

A LEADING case in which commercial enterprise has such decisive artificial, legal, and political advantages over municipal enterprise that the municipality cannot compete with it, is the great building industry of housing the population. Compare, for example, a municipal housing scheme with a municipal electric lighting scheme. In the latter the municipality has as much scope within its own area as any joint stock company. It can light the palace of an ambassador, the show rooms of a universal provider, the benches of a factory, the dining room of the business or professional man, and the kitchen of a laborer. In short, it can supply everybody in the constituency. But in housing it is restricted by law to insanitary areas and to workmen's dwellings. The London County Council may accept as a tenant an artizan earning from thirty shillings a week to several pounds; but a struggling journalist scraping together a precarious pound a week is turned from its doors. A private builder is under no such restriction. He can take an order for a cathedral and for a potting shed, for a millionaire's house in Park Lane and for the cottage of the millionaire's gamekeeper. In the intervals between large contracts he can keep his staff and plant employed on small ones. If he decides to go into the business of the housing of the working classes, he can proceed much more cheaply than the municipality. Instead of erecting huge blocks of dwellings with fireproof floors and all the solidities and sanitary appliances of what may be called parliamentary building, he may "run up" rows of small private houses which will presently become lodging houses; or he may adapt the family mansions of a neighborhood deserted by fashion for occupation by working-class families. Under these conditions there can be no question of a commercial or any other test: comparison is impossible. The municipality is compelled to take the refuse of a trade and to carry it on in the most expensive way: the private builder has the pick of the trade, and can adapt his expenditure to the pecuniary resources of the tenant. The result is that municipal trading cannot justify itself by its results in this direction as it can in others, especially in great cities. The buildings may seem palatial in comparison with the slums they replace; and they are better appointed and not more barrack-like than many of the piles of flats used by middle-class people; but a visit to even the best of them will reveal the fact that the rents are too high for the wages of the occupiers. A flat let at nine shillings a week to a man earning twenty-four, married and with a family, solves the housing problem for him in a highly questionable manner. It makes parasitic labor practically compulsory for his wife and children. In fact it is the value of the County Council flat as a testimonial of respectability to the woman seeking parasitic labor that makes it worth the man's while to pay so high a rent, exactly as an address in Park Lane may be worth a huge rent to a man whose personal requirements would be equally satisfied by a house in Holloway or Peckham.

In passing, it may be said here that the views of the poor as to how to make the most of the family income vary more strikingly than the views of the rich. The laborer or humble shop assistant who pays nine shillings a week for a flat of two or three rooms out of a wage of twenty-four, contrasts with the skilled workman who earns from thirty to fifty shillings a week, and sometimes more, and who nevertheless lives in one room, never troubles himself about respectability, and spends his money on "good living," by which he means a gluttonous Falstaffian jollity. He and his family are hearty eaters, hearty drinkers, loud laughers, indefatigable excursionists, noisy neighbors, and prompt strikers. And it is not easy to declare with any conviction that they have chosen worse than the people who sacrifice everything to a craze for respectability, which is sometimes almost as ruinous as a craze for drink. For the twenty-four shilling votary of respectability is a very mild case. Every house-to-house student of poverty tells us of single women or widows with wages that fluctuate from four to ten shillings, or, in momentary crises of prosperity, to twelve or thirteen, who nevertheless keep their rooms spotlessly neat, and shiver through the winter, fireless, without underclothing, in dresses that are superficially decent, while in the same house slatterns live disgracefully on four times their income, or Bardolph and Mrs Quickly set an example of roaring, jovial blackguardism. Then there is the poor person with a "fancy," who cannot live without a horse, or a dog, or a bird, or flowers, or pigeons, or some musical instrument, things apparently as wildly beyond their means as steam yachts and motor cars, which they yet manage to procure by simply sacrificing every other consideration to them, as beggar-misers get and keep bags of sovereigns even if they have to eat carrion to do it. We are apt to forget that the fancy for respectability is often as unintelligent and thriftless as any of the other fancies. We are revolted at the heartlessness of the man who starves his wife to provide cutlets for his pet dog; but we applaud the widow who starves her children, physically and morally, in order to bring them up respectably and be respectable herself. In the poor middle-class this is a crying evil: boys who have the making of strong artizans in them degenerate into underfed clerks; numbers of wretched little private-venture schools for young gentlemen and ladies, which ought to be suppressed more ruthlessly than gambling hells, keep children out of the Board schools and Polytechnics; and girls grow up into shabby-genteel "ladies," whose ignorance, incompetence, and unsociability defy description. But this mania for respectability does not disappear at the boundary of the middle class. It goes down to the very basement of society; and this fact has an important bearing on the housing problem, because your respectability is judged by the street, house, or room you live in just as much in the slums as in the squares. And the tendency in all classes is to spend too much in keeping up appearances. However honorable any ambition may be when it is taken in the economic order of its real importance, it may become disastrous when it is taken out of that order. If you have to choose between underfeeding your boy and patching his knickers, patch his knickers. If you have to choose between underclothing your daughter comfortably and overclothing her presentably, underclothe her comfortably. But unfortunately underfeeding and underclothing can be concealed; and patching and overclothing cannot. And so the order in which they are taken is too often the opposite of the economic order. In the same way the obvious respectability and order of the County Council flat at three shillings a room, however great an advance they may be on the poisonous squalor of the sewage saturated cellars at four and sixpence which figure in the report of the Royal Commission as samples of the results of private enterprise, are nevertheless too dear in a city where twenty-four shillings is the standard municipal wage for laborers, and where the Imperial Treasury, to its disgrace, refuses to pay even that modest figure.

The special difficulty in housing finance is the extraordinary manner in which the question of cost price is complicated by the phenomenon of economic rent, that rock on which all civilizations ultimately split and founder. In a municipal electric supply there is no difficulty about cost price, because a unit in Piccadilly costs no more than a unit in Putney. But the freehold of an acre of space for dwelling purposes costs from nothing to a million according to its situation. To convert the Mansion House into a block of workmen's dwellings would cost the price of a small frontier war; but the Richmond Corporation finds it within its resources to devote a whole road to workmen's cottages with gardens; and the Richmond Corporation itself envies the still greater facility with which municipal cottages are multiplied in Ireland. If a municipality owned all the land within its jurisdiction, it would still have to make the occupiers, including its own departments, pay rent in proportion to the commercial or residential desirability of their holdings; but it could pool the total rent and establish a "moral minimum" of house accommodation at a "fair rent" on a perfectly sound economic basis. At present it has to throw economics to the winds by buying land at its real market value, and charging it to its housing schemes at its value for working class dwellings (a pure figment), the ratepayer making up the difference between this and the real market value. Having performed this conjuring trick, the municipality generally proceeds to pass a resolution that the dwellings shall be let at rents sufficient to prevent any loss coming upon the ratepayers, without mentioning that they have already borne a loss which does not appear in the housing accounts. Even then, the effect of the resolution, when it is strictly carried out, is to put the rents too high for the sake of enabling the Borough Treasurer to make a delusive demonstration that the dwellings are paying their way commercially.

Socially, of course, they may pay their way with a handsome profit. It is true that they are seldom occupied to any extent worth reckoning by the occupants of the slums which have been demolished to make room for them. They are taken by people who are on the verge of the middle class, and by the respectable-at-any-price poor. But these people are shifted up from private lodgings of the highest working class grade, which, being left vacant, have to be relet to second grade tenants, who leave their rooms vacant for the third, and so on to the lowest grade, all being shifted a step up. But the transaction is very slow and very costly. Each scheme is entered upon to meet a particular local emergency; and long before the years of preliminary red tape are worried through, the emergency has been settled by the brute force of necessity; and though new emergencies have arisen, the old scheme is more or less a misfit for them: indeed it may have become apparent that the right cure is not a local housing scheme but a locomotion and country housing scheme.

On the whole, though municipal housing is popular because "there is something to shew for the money," and because it deals with a notorious and frightful evil, its opponents can always easily demonstrate that in city centres at least the schemes are commercially hopeless, and that though the rents are too high for the incomes of the tenants they are yet so low relatively to the real site value that the tenants are virtually receiving a grant in aid of their wages at the expense of their fellow citizens, which grant is exploited by the parasitic trades in the manner explained in Chapter IV.

It should not be forgotten that the housing question is not one of building only: it is also one of demolition. Houses do not last for ever; and we have not yet settled the best lifetime for the builder to aim at. Building "great bases for eternity" may be the work of a cathedral builder; but as far as ordinary dwelling houses are concerned, there is a growing opinion that living in the same house all your life and then leaving it to your children is as unwholesome as wearing the same sheepskin and handing it also on to posterity. It may be that the municipal by-laws of the future will include a prohibition of the use of a dwelling house for longer than twenty years. In any case it is clear that a good deal of XIX century building will prove very shortlived, and that the rows of cheap houses built for clerks and artizans on the sites of the suburban parks and country houses of fifty years ago will presently begin to figure as "condemned areas" on our municipal agenda papers. Besides the decay of the jerry-built brick box, we shall have to face the obsolescence of the solidly built "model" or municipal tenement block. These places seem at first so enormously superior to the filthy rookeries they replace that their revolting ugliness, their asphalted yards with the sunlight shut out by giant cliffs of brick and mortar, their flights upon flights of stony steps between the street and the unfortunate women and children on the upper floors, their quaint plan of relieving a crowd on the floor by stacking the people on shelves, are overlooked for the moment; but long before they become uninhabitable from decay they will become as repugnant as the warrens they have supplanted. In short, the municipalities of the future will be almost as active in knocking our towns down as in building them up.

At present the demolition problem has been so little thought out that the law gravely enacts that the municipality must rehouse all the people it displaces by demolishing a rookery. As a rookery is always so outrageously overcrowded that not even by replacing two-storey houses by dwellings built up to the extreme limit allowed by the Building Acts is it possible to rehouse the tenants on the same site, the municipality has either to let the rookery alone or acquire extra land for rehousing. Now this is not always possible without fresh displacements. The whole district may be overcrowded; and in that case the only remedy is for the excessive people to go elsewhere; and this, of course, raises the insoluble question as to which persons are excessive. In practice what happens is that the letter of the law is admitted to be impracticable; and the municipality bargains with the Local Government Board as to how many people it must rehouse. It offers to rehouse a third; the Board demands two thirds; and after much chaffering what is possible under all the circumstances is done.

If the obligation to rehouse were imposed on private and municipal enterprise alike, municipal housing would be at no disadvantage on this point. But commercial enterprise is practically exempt from such social obligations. Within recent years Chelsea has been transfigured by the building operations of Lord Cadogan. Hundreds of acres of poor dwellings have been demolished and replaced by fashionable streets and "gardens." The politics of Chelsea, once turbulently Radical, are now effusively Conservative. The sites voluntarily set aside by Lord Cadogan for working class dwellings on uncommercial principles of public spirit and personal honor have not undone the inevitable effects of the transfiguration of the whole neighborhood. The displaced have solved the rehousing problem by crossing the river into Battersea. Thus Lord Cadogan is more powerful than the Chelsea Borough Council. He can drive the poorer inhabitants out of the borough: the Council cannot. He can replace them with rich inhabitants: the Council cannot. He can build what kind of house pays him best, mansion, shop, stable, or pile of flats: the Council cannot. Under such circumstances comparison between the results of his enterprise and the Council's is idle. The remedy is either to curtail Lord Cadogan's freedom until it is no greater than the Council's, or else make the Council as free as Lord Cadogan. As the former alternative would end in nothing being done at all, and rendering impossible such great improvements as have been made both in Chelsea and Battersea by Lord Cadogan's enterprise, the second alternative—that of untying the hands of the ratepayer—is obviously the sensible one.

The obligation to rehouse is imposed on railway companies and other enterprises which have to obtain parliamentary powers. But they evade the obligation to a great extent by privately acquiring the house property they need, and evicting the tenants before they clear the area; so that when the hour for demolition comes there is nobody to be rehoused. This is the explanation of the furious intensity of local feeling against the railway companies. The people driven off the areas cleared by them overcrowd the surrounding neighborhood; and many small shopkeepers who are not themselves disturbed are ruined by the removal of their customers. There is no compensation and little rehousing. But this local unpopularity, to which the railway company is indifferent, could not be defied by the local authority. It many acquire land for the future extension of its electric light ing works or the like; and in gradually clearing this land it no doubt takes care to deal with a few houses at a time in order to avoid the obligation to rehouse which becomes operative when ten houses are dealt with at one stroke; but even in this it has to proceed with a constant care to avoid "hardshipping" its constituents, whereas a commercial company will spread disaster through a whole ward without the least consciousness of what it is doing. This is only a striking instance of the inconvenience and suffering which the movements of commercial enterprise cause daily in crowded communities because they are wholly unconcerted. Municipal civilization is nothing but a struggle to get the operations of civic life better concerted. Meanwhile, the fact that the commercial speculator can with impunity be inconsiderate to a degree that would cost every municipal councillor his seat at the next election must be constantly borne in mind in any comparison of private with municipal enterprise.

Finally it must be admitted that until the municipality owns all the land within its boundaries, and is as free to deal with it and build upon it as our ground landlords are at present, the problem of housing cannot be satisfactorily solved.

IX
THE MUNICIPAL AUDIT

THERE are certain differences between the legal conditions of communal and commercial finance which must be taken into account in comparing them. These differences are mentioned here because, however wholesome they may be in the long run for municipal enterprise, they sometimes handicap it at the start.

A private company does not pay interest on its capital until its capital actually earns the interest. Nobody expects this to happen at once; and sometimes it does not happen at all. In any case the company treats its capital as a property to be held for ever. A municipality has to pay interest from the day the capital is borrowed; and it must not only treat that capital as a debt to be paid off, but the paying off must begin at once, concurrently with the interest. It is thus compelled to bequeath to posterity a freehold property and goodwill for which it has had to pay handsomely; and the result is that the Irishman's jesting question as to what posterity had done for him that he should do anything for posterity is becoming a serious question in the mouths of English ratepayers. The rough and ready reply that though the individual dies the community is immortal, and its life must be treated as infinitely continuous, is plausible; but even an immortal individual would starve if he invested all his income and spent none of it; and a community can sacrifice the present to the future in the same way. For instance, the immortality of the nation would not justify a Chancellor of the Exchequer in attempting to pay off the national debt in one year. If commercial traders and joint stock companies could set up industrial plant only on condition that they must form a sinking fund to pay off its cost within a period not greater than its lifetime, and often considerably less, the outcry would be heartrending; and the newspapers would be filled with demonstrations of the impossibility of trading on such terms.

Something of the kind is actually done at present when a concession is given to a private tramway company on condition that at the expiration of a term of years it shall hand over its lines to the municipality for their market value as scrap iron. But the difficulty about such contracts as these is that the courts will not enforce them. To a statesman or a socialist it is just as reasonable to compel a private company to buy itself out within a fixed period—for that is what such a condition comes to—as to place the same obligation on a municipality. Both have to make a present to posterity if anything is left at the expiry of the term. But there is nothing unprecedented in this. The inventor has to present his invention to posterity at the end of fourteen years, and the author his book at the end of forty-two years, or seven years after his death; whilst the London shopkeeper has to present his goodwill to his landlord at the end of his lease. And yet the same judge who will enforce the consequences of the expiry of a patent or copyright, and of the falling in of a lease, as if they were the most obviously natural and proper of arrangements, will refuse to enforce the scrap iron clause against a tramway company on the ground that it is inconceivable that Parliament could have contemplated anything so monstrous as its Act seems to imply. The result is that whereas a municipality is always held rigidly to its bargain, a commercial company can defy even an Act of Parliament if it is careful to conciliate all private opposition and attack nothing but the interests of the community. It is true that Acts of this description have sometimes driven too hard a bargain, as the electrical lighting companies succeeded in shewing when the term was lengthened from twenty-one to forty-two years. But municipal trade has suffered in the same way, many municipal projects having been abandoned or postponed because the term of repayment was too short.

In everyday practice, it is not so much the judge as the official auditor who is to be feared by the municipalities. It is not at present at all difficult to find a barrister who is thoroughly disaffected to municipal trading. If such a one were appointed by the Local Government Board to audit the accounts of a County Council, a London Borough Council, or an Urban District Council,[1] he might, on the very plausible ground of keeping it up to the mark commercially, insist on allowances for depreciation which, as the actual wear and tear is in practice made good out of revenue, and a reserve fund is maintained to replace scrapped machinery, might virtually load the enterprise with a second sinking fund, and enable the opponents of municipal trading to point to commercial companies which (having no sinking fund at all) could shew more economical and businesslike figures. On the other hand, if the auditor has not a formidable power of public criticism, the struggle which goes on in a local authority between the electric lighting committee in its efforts to hold over its profits under the head of reserve fund, and the rest of the council in its desire to distribute the profits among the ratepayers in the form of the always popular contribution in aid of the rates, may lead to the pillaging of the reserve fund for electioneering purposes, and even to such depreciation of plant as used to occur in the early days of continental State railways, when impecunious finance ministers swept the railway fares into the treasury and allowed the rolling stock, the permanent way, and the stations to decay. And yet if the auditor be empowered to dictate the financial management instead of simply to criticize it and check the items, he might discredit the most beneficial public enterprises by "simply looking at them as a man of business." He could not very well insist on street paving being put "on a sound business footing" by means of turnpikes and tolls which would make municipal paving "pay"; but he might, without shocking public opinion, insist on commercially profitable charges for water and light in addition to a double sinking fund (a double present to posterity) and thus enable the Industrial Freedom League to prove by figures that communal enterprise is less economical than commercial

[1] Municipal Corporations (except Tunbridge Wells, Bournemouth, and Southend-on-Sea) are not subject to the L.G.B. audit. The ratepayers elect two auditors and the Mayor nominates a third. In other words, the Municipal Corporations are not audited at all.

enterprise.

These possibilities are by no means fantastic. The report of the Commission on Municipal Trading (Blue Book No. 270, 23rd July 1903, 4s.) contains several sensible suggestions as to the auditing of municipal accounts; but as the recommendation "that the auditor should certify that separate accounts of all trading undertakings have been kept, and that every charge that each ought to bear has been duly debited," is not balanced by any consideration of the invisible credits of municipal trade, it may be inferred that Parliament is still disposed to apply the commercial test to communal enterprise; and it is not the business of the Local Government Board to be more enlightened than Parliament, though the Board is no doubt more exposed to the brute force of fact, which soon brings the most hardened commercial doctrinaires to their senses in the fairly obvious cases. The very municipalities themselves are dominated by the commercial view, and often encourage themselves rather childishly, keeping their accounts in such a way as to produce the utmost possible appearance of commercial prosperity by throwing as much as possible of the expenses on the general rate whilst crediting the receipts of each municipal service to its special department. There is, in fact, for the moment a serious menace to municipal enterprise in the cry for commercial auditing.

Fortunately, the demand is not a permanently practicable one. Experience soon reduces commercial auditing to absurdity when it is applied to municipal business, quite as much because it is too tolerant in some directions as because it is too exacting in others. Municipal auditing is technically a distinct branch not only of accountancy but of law; and it is no more the business of the ordinary accountant or barrister than pleading points of international law before the judicial committee of the Privy Council is the business of the ordinary Old Bailey practitioner. It will finally develop as a practically separate profession; and it is only in the meantime that we need be on our guard against the vulgar cry for treating a municipal enterprise like any other business, on sound business lines, etc., etc., etc.

The most commercially obsessed auditor, when he first touches municipal trade, is brought up standing by the novel fact that the duty of the municipality is to make as little profit as possible, whereas the duty of the commercial company is to make as much profit as possible. An electric lighting company paying a dividend of 10 per cent is a triumph of good management: a municipal electric lighting committee making profits at the same rate is guilty of social malversation, which the auditor should at once expose and challenge.

To understand this, the ratepayer must imagine himself in the position (if he does not already actually occupy it) of a consumer of municipal electric light. He pays at the usual commercial rate: say 6d. to 2d. per unit. At the end of the financial year he learns that the profit on municipal lighting has been so great that the electric lighting committee has been able to hand over a sum in aid of the general rate which reduces it by a penny in the pound. Is he gratified by the intelligence? Not at all: he indignantly demands what the municipality means by overcharging him for current in order to relieve the rates of his neighbors who burn gas or oil. And his protest is perfectly justified. The object of municipal trading is not relief of the rates: if it were, it might be manipulated so as to throw the entire burden of local taxation on certain classes of consumers exactly as the entire burden of local taxation in Monaco is thrown on the gamblers of Monte Carlo. Its object is to provide public services at cost price. This cost price, to make the service really economical in the wide sense of good municipal statesmanship, may include higher wages to unskilled labor than a private company would pay, and it of course includes interest on the capital raised by the general body of ratepayers. To this a cunning municipality will perhaps add some little bribe to the general ratepayer lest, when not expecting to be himself a consumer, he should refuse to trouble himself about the service, and vote for an avowed opponent of it. It will even retain a little profit to encourage itself; for the commercial habit is strong in the average councillor. But more than this the municipality has no right to charge except with the deliberate purpose of readjusting the burden of the rates by an obviously abusable method which should be challenged by a good auditor. The reckless way in which municipal trading is often recommended from the platform as a means of relieving the rates shews that some of its popular advocates understand it as little as its popular opponents; but the question comes up sharply enough in practice on the municipalities; and charges are kept as near to cost as is compatible with the excessive caution which characterizes municipal enterprise. This is done, not on principle, but because of the curious jealousies which exist between municipal committees, and between each committee and the whole council. Thus, when the electric lighting committee makes a profit it tries to keep it by crediting it to the reserve fund. A proposal to apply it to the reduction of the rates usually comes from the Finance and Rating Committee in the form of an amendment to the Electricity Committee's report. Furious hostility between the committees ensues; and if the amendment is carried, the Electricity Committee considers that the Finance Committee has plundered it, and takes care, next time, to reduce the price of current to the consumer so that there shall be no profits to be seized upon.

Thus the theoretically right course is taken even when the councillors do not understand the theory; and the practice is to avoid profits by keeping prices down to cost. The absence of profits is, in fact, a proof of the proper conduct of the enterprise. Such absence in a commercial company would be a proof of incompetence. An auditor therefore has to apply precisely opposite tests to municipal and commercial undertakings. His view of a commercial company is that the larger the profits, the sounder the undertaking. His view of a municipal supply is that the less the profit, the honester the finance of the borough. Above all, if he is to certify, as the Committee on Municipal Trading recommends, "that in his opinion the accounts present a true and correct [sic] view of the transactions and results of trading for the period under investigation" he must estimate not only the appropriated profits which would go to commercial shareholders as dividend, but the total social utility of the enterprise during the year to the ratepayers. And this is a sort of accounting which neither the Institute of Chartered Accountants nor the Incorporated Society of Accountants and Auditors yet profess.

X
THE MUNICIPAL REVENUE

ONE of the keenest grievances of the commercial man who sees profitable branches of his own trade undertaken by the municipality is that it is competing against him "with his own money," meaning that it forces him to pay rates, and then uses the rates to ruin him in his business. The effective platform reply to this is that the profitable municipal trades, far from costing the ratepayers anything, actually lighten their burden. The commercially unprofitable trades are left to the municipality without demur. The trades by which private contractors make profit and the municipality none are, as we have seen, mostly sweated or parasitic trades which in the long run add heavily to the ratepayer's public and private burdens.

But in any case the alleged grievance is far stronger as against commercial than as against communal competition. The private tradesman has to pay rent and interest as well as rates. Rent is the great original fund from which industrial capital is saved; and interest on that capital eventually forms a second capital fund of equal or greater magnitude; so that when a shopkeeper finds his business captured by a huge joint stock universal provider, he is being competed against "with his own money," paid by him to his landlord or to the capitalist from whom his capital is borrowed, just as much as when the new competitor is a municipality.

Nothing shews the economic superficiality and political ignorance of the ordinary citizen more than the fact that he submits without a word to the private appropriation of large portions of the proceeds of his business as rent by private landholders, whilst he protests furiously against every penny in the pound collected from him by the municipality for his own benefit. The explanation probably is that in signing his lease he has explicitly accepted the rent as inevitable, and at least has his house or shop to shew for it; whereas the rate collector strikes him as a predatory person who makes him pay for streets and lamps, schools and police stations, in which he has no sense of property.

Still, in dismissing the usual grievances on this subject as unreasonable, it must not be assumed that rating is a satisfactory method of raising revenue. A rate is simply a tax on houses: that is, a tax on an article of prime necessity. If it were shifted to bread there would be an overwhelming outcry about taxing the bread of the poor; and yet the poor suffer more from want of house room than from want of bread. What is more, the poor, under pressure, can contract their requirements of house room in the most disastrously unhealthy way. Eight people cannot live on a single ration of bread; but they can sleep in one room, and even take in a lodger.

We are all in the habit of estimating a man's means by the value of the house he lives in. Shopkeepers give credit to a good address much more readily than to a good man. The Income Tax Surveyor, making a guess at the income of an actor or journalist or artist, assesses his address, and can be brought down promptly by the modest admission, "I have only two rooms on the second floor." But scientific precision cannot be claimed for this method. A man living in a house worth £150 a year is pretty sure to be a well-to-do man if he uses the whole house as his private residence; but many people pay that rent in order to carry on the business of lodging-house keepers, in which case they live in the basement and the attics, and would not dream of taking a house for their own use at so high a rent as a third of that sum. The differences between business premises are as great as the differences between business and private premises. A single small room in Bond Street will accommodate a fashionable palmist who may be making a considerable income. Next door a manufacturer of motor cars, requiring a hundred times as much space, may be making no profits at all. In cheaper neighborhoods, the same contrast may occur between a watchmaker and a jobmaster or furniture remover. On the whole, there is very little to be said for our rating system as an index of what each individual ratepayer can afford to pay.

The only thing to be said for the system is that it is a rough way of taxing rent, since, theoretically, the rate falls on the landlord. It does so in fact as well as in theory when the tenant is rackrented to the last farthing; but then very few ratepaying tenants are so rackrented. If the tenant would at a pinch pay another £2 a year, say, sooner than move (a pretty common case, one guesses), he is from the economists' point of view enjoying £2 a year of the rent; and if his rates go up by £2 he will not be able to shift the increase on to his landlord: all that will happen is that his rent will become a rackrent instead of falling £2 short of it. The rate collector takes what the landlord spared. Thus the increase in local rates which has taken place of late years must to a great extent have fallen on the ratepaying tenants instead of on the landlords; and this explains why the tenants resist the rates so strenuously in spite of all abstract economic demonstrations that it is the landlord who pays in the long run.

The popular remedy is to rate site values directly, collecting from the tenant as usual, but empowering him to deduct from his rent *ad valorem*. Thus if the rate be a shilling in the pound on the site value, a shilling is deducted by the occupier from every pound he pays the leaseholder, and by the leaseholder from every pound he pays the ground landlord.

There is nothing impracticable or incomprehensible in this. The real objection to it, as Voltaire pointed out 150 years ago in L'Homme aux Quarante Écus, is that it throws the whole weight of local taxation on the proprietor of land, the most responsible and active sort of proprietor, and exempts the people who do nothing but order their banker to cash their dividend warrants and cut off their coupons for them. A landlord has to look after his property: in fact, some of the strongest arguments in favor of municipalization of land are drawn from a comparison of the handsome work done by great landlords in developing towns and districts, with the meaner results of petty proprietorship. The landlord, far from being the worst sort of proprietor, is the best. The admitted objection to property as an institution is that it inevitably creates an idle class of rich people. But in England this was faced cheerfully enough as long as property meant property in land, because even the most complete emancipation of the landlord from feudal duties left him still personally responsible for the prosperity of his estate; and when he neglected or mismanaged it (as no doubt he often did) at least he finally impoverished himself as well as others. It was not until the industrial revolution of the XVIII and XIX centuries developed the joint stock system that our manufactures began to throw vast quantities of money into the hands of shareholders who were completely cut off from the management of their property, and whose children grew up with the purse of Fortunatus and without exercising personal supervision or bearing personal responsibility of any kind in return for it. This is the explanation of the apparently anomalous incidence of the Income Tax, which, by sparing the poor and striking at the rich, recognizes the fact that personal industry is often in inverse ratio to income.

In the face of this social development the cry for concentration of local taxation on site values will recommend itself in principle to nobody except those whose income is derived exclusively from industrial dividends. Colossal as the phenomenon of "unearned increment" is in great cities, it differs in nothing but its obviousness from the incomes which result from it when it is invested in industrial enterprise. When a ground landlord sells an acre of land in the centre of London for a million, and invests that million in Consols which bring him in £25,000 a year, he does not exchange an unearned income for an earned one: he only exchanges a position of responsibility as a landholder strongly interested in keeping up the character of a London neighborhood, for a position of indifference to all public considerations whatsoever. To exempt him from rating at the expense of the purchaser of his acre would be to make the landlord a Jonah and throw him to the whale of Socialism. If any discrimination is made between classes of proprietors it should operate in the other direction. Lord Cadogan and the Dukes of Westminster, Bedford, Portland, etc., may with some plausibility claim that the difference between their properties and the surrounding ones is worth paying them for. Sir Gorgius Midas and his progeny have nothing to say for themselves at all. It may, of course, be politically convenient to enlist Sir Gorgius for the attack on the landlords, and then, when the battle is won, invite the landlords to revenge themselves by joining in the campaign for a graduated and differentiated Income Tax, exactly as the landlords revenged themselves for Free Trade by carrying the Factory Acts against the manufacturers. But this treatise is concerned not with parliamentary tactics, but with political science.

Perhaps the most urgently needed discrimination is between people who are able to pay rates on some scale or other and those who cannot afford to pay them at all. It is admitted that persons with incomes of less than £160 a year cannot afford to pay income tax; and we allow abatement even to people with as much as £699 a year. Now we have multitudes of small tradesmen and shopkeepers who make less than £160 a year, and are nevertheless left staggering under the burden of rates of from six to nine shillings in the pound on the valuation of their premises. These men resist the rates with desperation; and they are quite right. Everything that has been said in the preceding chapters as to the productiveness of municipal enterprise can be reduced to the single formula that municipal trade is a good investment. So is life insurance, for the matter of that; but suppose a man cannot afford the premium, what then?

Let us examine this point a little more closely. The cardinal difference between private and municipal enterprise for the capitalist is that investment in the one is voluntary, whilst investment in the other is compulsory. Let it be granted as a set-off to the compulsion that the municipal investment is unexceptional in point of soundness. What you get then is Compulsory Investment, which many rash people think must be a thrifty thing, because they identify investment with saving, and cannot conceive saving as wrong under any circumstances. As a matter of fact, for the majority of the unfortunate inhabitants of these islands, thrift in this sense is one of the most heartless and ruinous of all the vices. A poor woman who receives five shillings can always take it to the post office savings bank and refrain from spending it on the wants of the moment. Many well intentioned people who have been made hopelessly silly in money matters by large independent incomes, habitually urge working folk to take this course on all occasions, apparently under the impression that the wants of the moment for the poor refer exclusively to gin. But it is clear that if the woman's boots are falling to pieces, the purchase of a new pair will be a far more thrifty proceeding than the banking of the money. The lives of most poor women is a continual struggle to keep themselves and their children dryshod. I purposely leave the food question, the starving child, the aged father and so forth out of the question, because purchasers of half-crown books on Municipal Trading regard them as melodramatic figments, though they are the most constant and pressing realities to millions of poor people.

In short, saving and investment are quite secondary duties: the first and the hardest is expenditure on present needs. Saving, investment, life assurance, all of them most prudent and excellent operations for people who have had as much of present nourishment as they need, and still have something to spare, are, for heads of families in a state of privation, slow forms of suicide and murder; and those who preach them indiscriminately should be indicted for incitement to crime. When a bishop offends in this way, people who really understand the situation feel their blood rising almost to guillotining point. Yet, after all, the bishop does not force people to take his inconsiderate advice. But the municipality does. The London County Council, for instance, goes to many an unfortunate wretch grimly struggling with poverty in a little shop, underfed, underclothed, underhoused, and consequently desperately in want of more money to spend on himself and his family. Taking him by the scruff of the neck, it says to him, "Come: you must invest in the general prosperity of this magnificent metropolis, of which you are—or ought to be—proud to be a citizen. You must no longer cross the Thames in a wretched penny ferry boat: you must build a colossal Tower Bridge, with splendid approaches; or you must pass underneath in tubular triumphs of modern engineering. You must no longer walk through slums from the Strand to Oxford Street: you must make a new and lordly avenue flanked with imposing buildings. And you must cheer yourself up with parks and bands, and run delightful steamboats on the river for your recreation on summer evenings." Is it any wonder that the unhappy victim of this comprehensive civic patriotism turns savagely on his Progressive benefactors and asks them whether they suppose his name is Carnegie or Pierpont Morgan or Rothschild that he should be forced into the schemes of millionaires? And the irony of the proposals is the more biting as he well knows that if the improvements happen to affect his own business beneficially, his landlord will take the first opportunity to appropriate the increment by putting up his rent.

This grievance is one which cannot be argued away, and cannot without gross callousness be disregarded. There should clearly be complete exemption from rates for persons whose income is below a certain figure. We have no right to force on people conveniences that they cannot afford. The particular device by which this is to be effected need not be gone into here. It is enough to say that though a general reduction of rates would end in an equivalent increase of rents, and although the exemption of a particular class of tenants would enable the landlords to confiscate some of the relief exactly as the employers of pensioners manage to confiscate some of the pension by paying lower wages to the pensioner, yet an exemption applying only to particular and exceptional cases could not produce anything like an equivalent rise of rents.

The moral is that the relief of the ratepayer, whose burdens are heavy enough to crush all enthusiasm from municipal schemes that threaten to raise the rates, should be accomplished by taxation of income, heavily graduated and differentiated against unearned income. It could be collected by the Inland Revenue Department and distributed by the method of grants in aid. The grant in aid is an excellent device when it is made conditional on the efficiency of the services for which it is earmarked; and this, of course, implies control and criticism by a vigorous and capable Local Government Board.

On the continent, taxation of income for local purposes is freely resorted to; and each town has a custom house, or octroi, at every gate. There is an octroi at Newcastle-on-Tyne, and perhaps in some other English towns; and there is no valid theoretic objection to this means of raising local revenue, except the impracticable general objection to all indirect taxation. But as an octroi is an intolerable hindrance to people who are unaccustomed to it, and as taxation of income, and even ordinary rating, are far more scientific methods of raising local revenue, it is not likely to be resorted to unless an absolute refusal of the electorate to sanction sufficient direct taxation to meet the growing necessities of the municipal exchequer makes a crude resort to indirect taxation unavoidable.

There is another difficulty in municipal finance. When there is any work to be done by a municipality, the question presents itself, shall it be paid for out of the general rate for the half year, or shall it be paid for by a loan?

According to the popular view, the thrifty course is to pay as you go, and not add to "the burden of municipal debt." The correct financial theory is undoubtedly just the reverse: all expenditure on public works should be treated as capital expenditure. The capital should be raised in the cheapest market, and the rates used to pay the interest and sinking fund. When a municipality which can borrow at less than 4 per cent deliberately extorts capital for public works from tradesmen who have to raise it at from 10 to 40 per cent or even more, it is clearly imposing the grossest unthrift on its unfortunate constituents. In practice everything depends on the duration of the work. It would be absurd to pay for an electric lighting plant out of the half year's revenue. It would be silly to raise a loan to clear away a snowfall. But between these extremes there is much debateable ground on which the economic presumption is usually quite erroneously taken to be in favor of present payment. The result may be a rate so high that the struggling ratepayers (a large class in our cities) have to borrow the money to pay it, in which case they are clearly raising capital on their own private credit at comparatively exorbitant interest instead of on their public credit through the municipality. This is due solely to the habit of calling the capital of the municipality its debt. Municipal trading is the best cure for this habit; and one of its indirect advantages is that it trains councillors and auditors to take a much more intelligent and considerate view of the ratepayers' interest than they do at present.

In comparing municipal with commercial enterprise, the power of the municipality to make apparently unlimited calls on the ratepayers' pockets is generally classed with those advantages on the municipal side which are so overwhelming as to be called unfair, meaning only that they are advantages beyond the reach of commerce. In the same sense the competition of the mammoth universal provider with the petty shopkeeper is unfair; the competition of the electric light with gas or of the railway with the stage coach was unfair; and the use of rifles by civilized armies against Zulus armed with assegais is unfair. But it is easy to exaggerate the advantage of the municipality in this respect. Every additional penny in the pound is so fiercely contested by the ratepayer, who is also an elector, that far more mischief is done and money wasted by municipal impecuniosity than by municipal extravagance. In spite of the fact that our citizens get better value for their rates than for any other portion of their expenditure, they voluntarily give thousands to company promoters to make ducks and drakes of with a better grace than they give shillings to the rate collector for the most indispensable requirements of civilization. When the election comes round, woe to the party that has put up the rate! If any opponent of municipal trading really thinks that the ratepayers' pocket is the treasury of Rhampsinitis, let him become a municipal councillor and try.

XI
OUR MUNICIPAL COUNCILLORS

WHOEVER has grasped the full scope of the case for Municipal Freedom of Trade will see that the practicability of public enterprise is limited only by the capacity of its organizers and administrators. And this raises the question, where are we to find our municipal statesmen?

Let us first see what attractions the career of a municipal councillor offers, and what its drawbacks are.

As compared with a member of Parliament, a municipal councillor has an almost unbounded liberty of conscience and initiative. The party discipline which is a necessity in Parliament does not exist in municipal government, because the procedure of the councils differs widely from that of the House of Commons. There is no Cabinet, no Government, and no Opposition. There are, of course, Moderates and Progressives, Conservatives and Liberals, Labor members and Independents, Established Churchmen, Free Churchmen, and No Churchmen; and these form voting combinations, and carry their alliances and their feuds into the council chamber, appointing "whips," holding party meetings, and playing at party government by offering perfectly imaginary services to the real parliamentary parties in order to increase their sense of personal importance, and to establish a claim for their leaders on birthday honors and on adoption as parliamentary candidates, or at least on the fantastic orders of chivalry established by the Primrose League and its imitators. But all this is child's play, because there is no Government in the parliamentary sense, and consequently a vote against one's own party involves no ulterior consequences.

This will be better understood from a description of the organization of a municipality. The executive work is, of course, done departmentally by a paid permanent municipal staff. There is a sanitary department with the Medical Officer of Health as technical chief and a Chief Clerk as business chief. There is a Highways, Sewers and Public Works department (or some such title) under the Borough Engineer and a Chief Clerk. There is a Finance and Rating department under the Borough Treasurer or City Accountant and a Chief Clerk. There is perhaps an Electric Lighting Department, under the Electrical Engineer and a Chief Clerk. And so on, the central department being the General Business department under the Town Clerk, who is the head of the official hierarchy. On the parliamentary system, each of these departments would be presided over by a councillor selected on strict party lines; and these presiding councillors would be called Ministers and would form a Cabinet, the "first lord" of the General Business department being the Prime Minister and leader of the Council. All regular municipal legislation would be brought forward by this Cabinet; and on the rejection of any of their resolutions, or the carrying of a vote of censure against them, they would resign; a general election would take place in the borough, and a new Council be elected; and a new Cabinet would be formed. And the effect of this system would be that no member would be free to vote on any measure on its merits, because, as the effect of his defeating it would be to change the whole Government of the district (with the general policy of which he might be in cordial agreement) and transfer it to another party (the general policy of which he might consider ruinous), besides putting himself and the ratepayers to the heavy expense of an election, he would find himself repeatedly voting simply to keep his party in office without the slightest reference to the particular measure at stake, and would finally give up all pretence of discussion, and insist on being provided with a comfortable smoking room or library in which he could sit at his ease until a bell was rung to call him to the voting lobby.

There is, providentially, nothing of this sort in the municipal councils. Each department is controlled by a committee of councillors; and each committee elects its own chairman. The business of the department is brought before the committee by the Chief Clerk and the chief of the technical staff. The decisions of the committee are embodied in a series of resolutions. These resolutions form the report of the committee; and at the next meeting of the full Council, the chairman rises and "moves his report": that is, he moves all the resolutions of the committee; and the Council adopts them or not, as it pleases. It happens quite commonly that an amendment is moved and carried; or the resolution is referred back for further consideration; or it is flatly rejected. But nothing else happens. The chairman may be disappointed or indignant; but he does not resign. The committee may sulk for a while; but it goes on just as before. The chairmen do not form a Cabinet in any sense. They do not all belong necessarily to the same party even when they are elected on party lines; for the party that is in a majority in one committee may be in a minority on another. In many bodies the custom is to give every party its share of the chairmanships; and in almost all, old members are allowed sooner or later to have their turn in the chair without regard to their opinions and often without regard to their fitness for the duty, in which case the waste of time in committee is extremely trying to the more businesslike councillors. As to an appeal to the constituency by way of general election, it is out of the question. The councillors are elected for a fixed period; and no action of the council, short of a resolution accepting the simultaneous resignation of all its members—a plan outside practical politics—can shorten or lengthen its own term of office.

Under these circumstances independence of thought and character is not strangled in municipal public life as it is in the House of Commons. When a recruit has once mastered the procedure and taken the measure of a municipal council, he can, if he has ability enough, make himself as much of a Prime Minister in ten minutes as the senior alderman. He can indulge in cross voting without stint. He can get a chairmanship quite as soon as he knows enough to be something more than the puppet of the officials. No doubt, if his ambition is fashionable, he will find the House of Commons a better address than the Town Hall. But if he values useful public activity and freedom of conscience, he will find a municipality enormously superior to Parliament, unless his political talent or family influence is of a very unusual order.

It will now be asked why, under these tempting circumstances, it is so difficult to get efficient candidates for the municipal councils. The root cause is no doubt that insisted on long ago by Plato: namely, that capable men understand too well how difficult and responsible public work is, to be particularly anxious to undertake it; so that the first qualification for public life ought to be a strong reluctance to enter it. It is no exaggeration to say that the strongest man can kill himself with overwork even on a town council if he attempts to do everything there is for him to do. A wise insurance company would prefer a cabinet minister's life to a municipal chairman's, if the chairman shewed any disposition to do his work thoroughly and seriously.

On the other hand, nothing is easier than to sit on a council and do nothing. The claim of the House of Commons to be the best club in London is far more questionable than the claim of the municipal council to be the best club accessible to most of its members. It is possible for a councillor to be stupendously ignorant and shamelessly lazy, and yet to be not only popular with his fellow councillors, but—provided he is a tolerably entertaining speaker—with the ratepayers also. He passes for a very busy public man when he is really only a sociable one, by attending all his committees and doing nothing on them.

There is at present no way in which the municipal fainéant can be brought to book, even if a community which does not pay for his services had any right to make the attempt. Payment of directors' fees would not improve matters: the guinea-pig has been tried in private enterprise and found wanting. Still, there is a great deal to be said for payment of members of municipal bodies. It would make the voters much more jealous and exacting as to the personal qualifications and public industry of their representatives, besides producing some sort of consciousness that membership of a local authority really means useful work and not mere ceremonial. Far from substituting selfish motives for public ones, it would relieve municipal work from the reproach that men have no reasons but interested—not to say corrupt—reasons for undertaking it. It would give capable Labor leaders that training in public life without which they are apt to be socially dangerous in direct proportion to their ability and earnestness, and with which they stand so usefully for the whole community as well as for their own class against the sordidness and exclusiveness of the commercial classes and the social ignorance and thoughtlessness of the aristocracy. Labor representatives usually make excellent councillors, because they are much more severely criticized than their middle class colleagues. It is possible for a middle class councillor to sit on a municipality for twenty years in a condition of half-drunken stupor without exposure and defeat at the poll; but Labor councillors receive no such indulgence. As a rule they take their public business very seriously; are free from the social pressure which leads to so much reciprocal toleration of little jobs and venial irregularities among the middle class men of business; have the independence of professional men without their class prejudices; are exceptionally sensitive to the dignity of sobriety and respectable conduct; and, as they usually pay inclusive rents, never deliberately shelve necessary public work because it may mean an extra rate of an eighth of a penny in the pound. Thus, oddly enough, the municipal Labor member generally finds himself in alliance with the councillors who are too rich to be penny-wise and pound-foolish, and with the professional men whose livelihood has always depended on their own personal skill, in opposition to the petty shopkeepers and employers whose cramped horizon and short-sighted anxiety to keep down the rates at all costs are the main stumbling blocks in the way of municipal enterprise.

The tyranny of the petty tradesman is a serious evil in municipal life. The municipal constituency is small—only a ward; and the bigger and more important the city, the fewer votes will secure a seat, because of the difficulty of inducing busy or fashionable people to vote at all: in fact, it is easier to poll a village to the last man than to poll 50 per cent of the electors in a London ward. The squares and the slums have the same reason for not voting, because the city man, the laborer, and the artizan are alike in respect of not working at their homes; so that when they return home tired in the evening they will not turn out again in the raw November darkness, and trudge through the mud to the polling station at the request of that enthusiastic pest the canvasser. The result is that the smaller shopkeepers elect one another, since they can vote at any moment of the day by leaving their shops for a few minutes.

To canvass for this shopkeeping vote is an art in itself, and one which men of superior education and liberal ideas cannot be induced to study and practise. The small shopkeeper does not understand finance, nor banking, nor insurance, nor sanitary science. The social distinction between him and the working class is so small that he clings to it with a ferocity inconceivable by a peer, and will concede nothing to a laborer that is not either begged humbly as a favor or extorted by force of Trade Unionism. A proposal to give women living wages instantly brings before him a vision of "the girl at home," encouraged in uppishness, and asking another shilling a week. His pocket is so shallow that an extra penny in the pound appals him, not because it means an extra five or ten thousand pounds of revenue, but because it will cost him individually another half-crown or five shillings. The fate of an intelligent candidate who does not use his speech to conceal his thoughts may be imagined. Very much more reasonable men than Coriolanus are defeated at every election because they betray large views of municipal business instead of passionately affirming their own merits, vituperating their opponents recklessly, and flattering the follies of the most narrow-minded electors. And so, though a doctor may get in by the votes of his patients, and a minister of religion by those of his congregation and of his poor, the small shopkeeper is master of the municipal situation. His ideas rule all the urban local bodies. The twenty-eight London Borough Councils are completely in his hands. Even when he finds in his own ranks men of remarkable shrewdness and some capacity for large ideas, he keeps them rigidly under his thumb; and they, knowing that an appeal to the more liberal classes would not be responded to, accept their servitude and become what the Americans call "ward bosses." We do not condescend to name them at all, vestrydom being too little considered to be worth an English terminology.

One remedy for this is to make voting as easy for the city man as it is for the local tradesman. Our plan of making an election as great a nuisance as possible to everyone concerned gives an overwhelming advantage to the man who has nothing to do but "slip round the corner and vote" in the slack moments of a business that actually consists of interruptions and intrusions. The barrister, the doctor, the man of science, the author, the financier, the head of a large business, cannot be disturbed in this way. If he cannot vote by post, preserving the secrecy of the ballot by the familiar expedient of an outer and inner envelope, he will not vote at all. Even the laborer is now learning to meet the canvasser with "I will come if you send a carriage for me," thus creating a grievance for the candidate who has no carriages or carriage-keeping friends, and imposing an intolerable *corvée* on the people who do keep carriages, and whose friends borrow them for elections. A great deal of the apparent failure of democracy to secure the best available public representatives is really a failure to adapt our method of taking the vote to the convenience and susceptibilities of the more thoughtful and cultivated classes. We ignore the fact that what Plato said of the representative: that the reluctant and not the eager man—the man who feels the weight of a crown and not he who is dazzled by its glitter—should be chosen, has its application to the voter also. The partizan whom no weather and no distance can keep from the polling booth is not necessarily a better judge of a candidate than the man who has to be coaxed to undertake the very grave responsibility of choosing the government of the town for the next three years. Yet, far from coaxing him, we handicap him by arrangements which give a long start to political rancor, personal thickness of skin, and, above all, to the shop round the corner.

Still, there is something to be said for the petty tradesman. He is shrewd and effective enough when he is in his depth; and his local knowledge is indispensable. The policing and sanitation of a city consist largely of a running fight with petty nuisances and abuses to which the gossip of a street is a better guide than the most comprehensive municipal statesmanship. When the absurdity of the present municipal areas forces us to reconstruct our whole scheme of local government, there will still be a place for local committees to deal with the small change of municipal life; and on these local committees the petty shopkeeper will be as useful as he is noxious on bodies whose scope far transcends his homely little outlook.

XII
CONCLUSION

THE conclusion of this statement of the case for Municipal Trading leaves the reader still at the beginning of the subject, but, it is hoped, in an intelligent and unbewildered attitude. It will save him the trouble of a struggle with irrelevant rows of figures paraded to prove that municipal trade does not pay. It will also save him the trouble of reading ingenious attempts to confute these demonstrations from their own point of view; for he will understand that though the demonstrations may be erroneous in this or that instance, and though a Borough Treasurer may keep the municipal books in such a way as to give his accounts the utmost commercial plausibility, yet in the very cases where municipal trading is most profitable to the ratepayer, its departmental expenses are and ought to be greater, and its surpluses (if any) are and ought to be less than those of a private firm doing the same work —nay, that when the municipality undertakes at a heavy departmental loss work that has previously been carried on by commercial contractors at a tempting commercial profit, the ratepayers are probably saving more by this apparently bad bargain than by the municipal gas works and tram lines which not only do not cost them a farthing out of pocket, but actually contribute hard cash to the rates as well.

On the other hand he will see that municipal statesmanship, far from having been simplified by a safe Socialistic formula, now requires from its Councillors much more knowledge, ability, and character, than the old system, which had a really simple formula in the rule: Do nothing that can be left to private enterprise. In our reassurance at the discovery that the bogey of increasing municipal indebtedness is only the comfortable phenomenon of growing municipal capital, we must not forget that over-capitalization is as possible, if not as probable, in public as in private finance, and that a councillor must not only be in favor of, say, a municipal supply of electric light, but must, when that point is carried, have sense enough not to buy more horse-power than is necessary, nor lay a cable down a country road for the sole sake of the mayor's brother-in-law who has a villa at the far end, nor appoint a civil but unqualified young man as engineer merely because he is the sole support of his aged mother. On the other hand, he must not clamor for the municipalization of the section of a great trunk line of railway that happens to cross his borough, nor press the Parks Committee to undertake the municipal breeding of elephants for the sake of having a Jumbo for the children to ride on. Every proposal to municipalize lies somewhere on the scale between these extremes, and must be judged in council, not according to a Socialist or anti-Socialist canon, but according to its place on the scale, and always in view of the complicated social reactions analysed in the preceding pages.

Now this is not work for the political partizans and convivial vestrymen who still look on an alderman's robe or a mayor's chain as the crowning ornament of a successful commercial career, and on a Council as a Masonic Lodge where members can make useful acquaintances and put valuable pieces of business in one another's way. Complete disinterestedness is neither an attainable quality nor a desirable one; for it means complete indifference; and an attempt to "purify" politics by getting rid of all personal motives is apt to end like an attempt to purify card playing by abolishing the stakes: the keenest lovers of the game for its own sake are the first to insist on stakes in order to make the others play carefully. A very little practical experience will convince the youngest idealist that the way to set a man to work, in public as in private, is to give him an axe to grind, and that nothing gets done until it becomes a job for somebody. But there are axes and axes. One man, being a shopkeeper, seeks election because he hopes to establish a claim on the custom of the councillors (some of them heads of large establishments) with whom he will become intimate at the party meetings. When he is elected he will elect as mayor the man who will give the council two banquets a year, with champagne, rather than the strict teetotaller who will give one, with lemonade, or none. This naïve kind of interested motive is by far the commonest in English local public life. It does much more to stultify municipal politics than the rapacity of the slum landlord who seeks election to protect disorderly houses and to thwart the administration of the Housing and Public Health Acts, the chicanery of the country jerry-builder who aims at preventing the adoption or hindering the administration of sanitary by-laws, and the intrigues of the publican to get on the rating committee so as to mitigate the tendency to assess public houses on ruthlessly high valuations. As a matter of fact, in large cities, the better sort of builders and landlords of good house property have exceptionally strong personal interests in good municipal government; and a respectable and successful publican without either ability or character is almost an impossibility; for the first man to be demoralized and ruined by a public house is the publican himself if his character is vulnerable. The really dangerous men are those whose motives are so artless, petty, and familiar, that they are imperceptible; and it is these simple souls, incapable of mental effort or social comprehension, who stand blamelessly in the way of all far-reaching municipal action, whilst downright rogues will listen keenly to important proposals, and even support them vigorously if any pickings seem likely to come their way.

In short, for obstructive purposes, twenty sheep are more effective than fifty wolves. The moral is, not, of course, to elect rascals, but to prefer political motives, even when they are rooted in personal ambition, to commercial motives, convivial motives, snobbish motives, and especially to no motives at all. Purely political successes will serve the turn of a man who has the right temperament for public life quite well enough to make him work for the public good without any abnormal deficiency in selfishness, if the public will only let him. What really withholds capable and high-minded men from public life is the ignorance and intense recalcitrance of the people who vote, and the discouraging indifference of the people who dont. This will continue to make democracy intolerable until we deliberately and carefully teach citizenship to our children. One intelligent voter is worth a hundred persons who made bad Latin verses in their teens, or enjoyed for one day in their childhood a more or less accurate recollection of a more or less accurate statement in a schoolbook as to the principal products of Sumatra.

Finally, it has, I hope, been made clear that the infancy of modern local government must no longer be hampered by our ancient parochialism. The injury done us by foreign frontiers, with all their cannon and all their custom houses, is as nothing compared to the waste and hindrance set up by our absurd municipal frontiers. A relimitation of the areas and reconstitution of the units of local government is the most pressing requirement made by municipal trade upon our constructive statesmanship. We will no doubt ignore the existing deadlock as long as we can; for we are slow to frame ourselves to new occasions: we still nail telephone wires to chimneys and copings exactly as a laborer's wife stretches her clothes-line in the back yard; and the newest buildings so resolutely ignore the existence of the bicycle that it is positively easier to accommodate one in an XVIII century house than in a XX century one. But electricity is a potent force: it will shock British conservatism (a polite name for British laziness) out of its anachronisms if anything can.

THE SEVEN PLANS

(From The Intelligent Woman's Guide to Socialism and Capitalism)

TO EACH WHAT SHE PRODUCES

THE first plan: that of giving to every person exactly what he or she has made by his or her labor, seems fair; but when we try to put it into practice we discover, first, that it is quite impossible to find out how much each person has produced, and, second, that a great deal of the world's work is neither producing material things nor altering the things that Nature produces, but doing services of one sort or another.

When a farmer and his laborers sow and reap a field of wheat nobody on earth can say how much of the wheat each of them has grown. When a machine in a factory turns out pins by the million nobody can say how many pins are due to the labor of the person who minds the machine, or the person who invented it, or the engineers who made it, to say nothing of all the other persons employed about the factory. The clearest case in the world of a person producing something herself by her own painful, prolonged, and risky labor is that of a woman who produces a baby; but then she cannot live on the baby: the baby lives greedily on her.

Robinson Crusoe on his desert island could have claimed that the boats and shelters and fences he made with the materials supplied by Nature belonged to him because they were the fruit of nobody's labor but his own; but when he returned to civilization he could not have laid his hand on a chair or table in his house which was not the work of dozens of men: foresters who had planted the trees, woodmen who had felled them, lumbermen and bargemen and sailors and porters who had moved them, sawyers who had sawn them into planks and scantlings, upholsterers and joiners who had fashioned them into tables and chairs, not to mention the merchants who had conducted all the business involved in these transactions, and the makers of the shops and ships and all the rest of it. Anyone who thinks about it for a few minutes must see that trying to divide-up by giving each worker exactly what she or he has produced is like trying to give every drop of rain in a heavy shower exactly the quantity of water it adds to the supply in your cistern. It just cannot be done.

What can be done is to pay every person according to the time she or he spends at the work. Time is something that can be measured in figures. It is quite easy to pay a worker twice as much for two hours work as for one. There are people who will work for sixpence an hour, people who will work for eighteenpence an hour, people who will work for two guineas an hour, people who will work for a hundred and fifty guineas an hour. These prices depend on how many competitors there are in the trade looking for the work, and whether the people who want it done are rich or poor. You pay a sempstress a shilling to sew for an hour, or a laborer to chop wood, when there are plenty of unemployed sempstresses and laborers starving for a job, each of them trying to induce you to give it to her or him rather than to the next applicant by offering to do it at a price that will barely keep body and soul together. You pay a popular actress two or three hundred pounds a week, or a famous opera singer as much a night, because the public will pay more than that to hear her. You pay a famous surgeon a hundred and fifty guineas to cut out your appendix, or a famous barrister the same to plead for you, because there are so few famous surgeons or barristers, and so many patients and clients offering them large sums to work for them rather than for you. This is called settling the price of a worker's time, or rather letting it settle itself, by supply and demand.

Unfortunately, supply and demand may produce undesirable results. A division in which one woman gets a shilling and another three thousand shillings for an hour of work has no moral sense in it: it is just something that happens, and that ought not to happen. A child with an interesting face and pretty ways, and some talent for acting, may, by working for the films, earn a hundred times as much as its mother can earn by drudging at an ordinary trade. What is worse, a pretty girl can earn by vice far more than her plain sister can earn as an honest wife and mother.

Besides, it is not so easy to measure the time spent on a piece of work as it seems at first. Paying a laborer twice as much for two hours work as for one is as simple as twice one are two; but when you have to divide between an opera singer and her dresser, or an unskilled laborer and a doctor, you find that you cannot tell how much time you have to allow for. The dresser and the laborer are doing what any ablebodied person can do without long study or apprenticeship. The doctor has to spend six years in study and training, on top of a good general education, to qualify himself to do his work. He claims that six years of unpaid work are behind every minute of his attendance at your bedside. A skilled workman may claim in the same way that seven years of apprenticeship are behind every stroke of his hammer. The opera singer has had to spend a long time learning her parts, even when, as sometimes happens, she has never learnt to sing. Everybody acknowledges that this makes a difference; but nobody can measure exactly what the difference is, either in time or money.

The same difficulty arises in attempting to compare the value of the work of a clever woman with that of a stupid one. You may think that the work of the clever woman is worth more; but when you are asked how much more in pounds, shillings, and pence you have to give it up and fall back on supply and demand, confessing that the difference cannot be measured in money.

In these examples I have mixed up making things with doing services; but I must now emphasize this distinction, because thoughtless people are apt to think a brickmaker more of a producer than a clergyman. When a village carpenter makes a gate to keep cattle out of a field of wheat, he has something solid in his hand which he can claim for his own until the farmer pays him for it. But when a village boy makes a noise to keep the birds off he has nothing to shew, though the noise is just as necessary as the gate. The postman does not make anything: he only delivers letters and parcels. The policeman does not make anything; and the soldier not only does not make things: he destroys them. The doctor makes pills sometimes; but that is not his real business, which is to tell you when you ought to take pills, and what pills to take, unless indeed he has the good sense to tell you not to take them at all, and you have the good sense to believe him when he is giving you good advice instead of bad. The lawyer does not make anything substantial, nor the clergyman, nor the member of Parliament, nor the domestic servant (though she sometimes break things), nor the Queen or King, nor an actor. When their work is done they have nothing in hand that can be weighed or measured: nothing that the maker can keep from others until she is paid for it. They are all in service: in domestic service like the housemaid, or in commercial service like the shop assistant, or in Government service like the postman, or in State service like the King; and all of us who have fullsize consciences consider ourselves in what some of us call the service of God.

And then, beside the persons who make the substantial things there must be persons to find out how they should be made. Beside the persons who do things there must be persons who know how they should be done, and decide when they should be done, and how much they should be done. In simple village life both the making or the doing and the thinking may be done by the same person when he is a blacksmith, carpenter, or builder; but in big cities and highly civilized countries this is impossible: one set of people has to make and do whilst another set of people thinks and decides what, when, how much, and by whom.

Our villages would be improved by a little of this division of labor; for it is a great disadvantage in country life that a farmer is expected to do so many different things: he has not only to grow crops and raise stock (two separate arts to begin with, and difficult ones too), but to be a man of business, keeping complicated accounts and selling his crops and his cattle, which is a different sort of job, needing a different sort of man. And, as if this were not enough, he has to keep his dwelling house as part of his business; so that he is expected to be a professional man, a man of business, and a sort of country gentleman all at once; and the consequence is that farming is all a muddle: the good farmer is poor because he is a bad man of business; the good man of business is poor because he is a bad farmer; and both of them are often bad husbands because their work is not separate from their home, and they bring all their worries into the house with them instead of locking them up in a city office and thinking no more about them until they go back there next morning. In a city business one set of men does the manual work; another set keeps the accounts; another chooses the markets for buying and selling; and all of them leave their work behind them when they go home.

The same trouble is found in a woman's housekeeping. She is expected to do too many different things. She may be a very good housekeeper and a very bad cook. In a French town this would not matter, because the whole family would take all the meals that require any serious cooking in the nearest restaurant; but in the country the woman must do both the housekeeping and the cooking unless she can afford to keep a cook. She may be both a good housekeeper and a good cook, but be unable to manage children; and here again, if she cannot afford a capable nurse, she has to do the thing she does badly along with the things she does well, and has her life muddled and spoilt accordingly. It is a mercy both to her and the children that the school (which is a bit of Communism) takes them off her hands for most of the day. It is clear that the woman who is helped out by servants or by restaurants and schools has a much better chance in life than the woman who is expected to do three very different things at once.

Perhaps the greatest social service that can be rendered by anybody to the country and to mankind is to bring up a family. But here again, because there is nothing to sell, there is a very general disposition to regard a married woman's work as no work at all, and to take it as a matter of course that she should not be paid for it. A man gets higher wages than a woman because he is supposed to have a family to support; yet if he spends the extra money in drink or betting, the woman has no remedy against him if she is married to him. But if she is his hired housekeeper she can recover her wages at law. And the married man is in the same predicament. When his wife spends the housekeeping money in drink he has no remedy, though he could have a hired housekeeper imprisoned for theft if she did the very same thing.

Now with these examples in mind, how can an Intelligent Woman settle what her time is worth in money compared to her husband's? Imagine her husband looking at it as a matter of business, and saying "I can hire a housekeeper for so much, and a nursemaid for so much, and a cook for so much, and a pretty lady to keep company with for so much; and if I add up all this the total will be what a wife is worth; but it is more than I can afford to pay"! Imagine her hiring a husband by the hour, like a taxi cab!

Yet the income of the country has to be divided-up between husbands and wives just as it has between strangers; and as most of us are husbands and wives, any plan for dividing-up that breaks down when it is applied to husbands and wives breaks in the middle and is no use. The old plan of giving the man everything, and leaving the woman to get what she could out of him, led to such abuses that it had to be altered by the Married Women's Property Acts, under which a rich woman with a poor husband can keep all her property to herself whilst her husband is imprisoned for life for not paying her taxes. But as nine families out of ten have no property, they have to make the best of what the husband can earn at his trade; and here we have the strangest muddles: the wife getting nothing of her own, and the bigger children making a few shillings a week and having the difference between it and a living wage made up by the father's wage; so that the people who are employing the children cheaply are really sweating the father, who is perhaps being sweated badly enough by his own employer. Of this, more later on.

Try to straighten out this muddle on the plan of giving the woman and the children and the man what they produce each by their own work, or what their time is worth in money to the country; and you will find the plan nonsensical and impossible. Nobody but a lunatic would attempt to put it into practice.

TO EACH WHAT SHE DESERVES

THE second plan we have to examine is that of giving to each person what she deserves. Many people, especially those who are comfortably off, think that this is what happens at present: that the industrious and sober and thrifty are never in want, and that poverty is due to idleness, improvidence, drink, betting, dishonesty, and bad character generally. They can point to the fact that a laborer whose character is bad finds it more difficult to get employment than one whose character is good; that a farmer or country gentleman who gambles and bets heavily, and mortgages his land to live wastefully and extravagantly, is soon reduced to poverty; and that a man of business who is lazy and does not attend to it becomes bankrupt. But this proves nothing but that you cannot eat your cake and have it too: it does not prove that your share of the cake was a fair one. It shews that certain vices and weaknesses make us poor; but it forgets that certain other vices make us rich. People who are hard, grasping, selfish, cruel, and always ready to take advantage of their neighbors, become very rich if they are clever enough not to overreach themselves. On the other hand, people who are generous, public-spirited, friendly, and not always thinking of the main chance, stay poor when they are born poor unless they have extraordinary talents. Also, as things are today, some are born poor and others are born with silver spoons in their mouths: that is to say, they are divided into rich and poor before they are old enough to have any character at all. The notion that our present system distributes wealth according to merit, even roughly, may be dismissed at once as ridiculous. Everyone can see that it generally has the contrary effect: it makes a few idle people very rich, and a great many hardworking people very poor.

On this, Intelligent Lady, your first thought may be that if wealth is not distributed according to merit, it ought to be; and that we should at once set to work to alter our laws so that in future the good people shall be rich in proportion to their goodness and the bad people poor in proportion to their badness. There are several objections to this; but the very first one settles the question for good and all. It is, that the proposal is impossible. How are you going to measure anyone's merit in money? Choose any pair of human beings you like, male or female, and see whether you can decide how much each of them should have on her or his merits. If you live in the country, take the village blacksmith and the village clergyman, or the village washerwoman and the village schoolmistress, to begin with. At present the clergyman often gets less pay than the blacksmith: it is only in some villages he gets more. But never mind what they get at present: you are trying whether you can set up a new order of things in which each will get what he deserves. You need not fix a sum of money for them: all you have to do is to settle the proportion between them. Is the blacksmith to have as much as the clergyman? or twice as much as the clergyman? or half as much as the clergyman? or how much more or less? It is no use saying that one ought to have more and the other less: you must be prepared to say exactly how much more or less in calculable proportion.

Well, think it out. The clergyman has had a college education; but that it is not any merit on his part: he owes it to his father; so you cannot allow him anything for that. But through it he is able to read the New Testament in Greek; so that he can do something the blacksmith cannot do. On the other hand, the blacksmith can make a horse-shoe, which the parson cannot. How many verses of the Greek Testament are worth one horse-shoe? You have only to ask the silly question to see that nobody can answer it.

Since measuring their merits is no use, why not try to measure their faults? Suppose the blacksmith swears a good deal, and gets drunk occasionally! Everybody in the village knows this; but the parson has to keep his faults to himself. His wife knows them; but she will not tell you what they are if she knows that you intend to cut off some of his pay for them. You know that as he is only a mortal human being he must have some faults; but you cannot find them out. However, suppose he has some faults that you can find out! Suppose he has what you call an unfortunate manner; that he is a hypocrite; that he is a snob; that he cares more for sport and fashionable society than for religion! Does that make him as bad as the blacksmith, or twice as bad, or twice and a quarter as bad, or only half as bad? In other words, if the blacksmith is to have a shilling, is the parson to have a shilling also, or is he to have sixpence, or five pence and one-third, or two shillings? Cleverly these are fool's questions: the moment they bring us down from moral generalities to business particulars it becomes plain to every sensible person that no relation can be established between human qualities, good or bad, and sums of money, large or small. It may seem scandalous that a prize-fighter, for hitting another prize-fighter so hard at Wembley that he fell down and could not rise within ten seconds, received the same sum that was paid to the Archbishop of Canterbury for acting as Primate of the Church of England for nine months; but none of those who cry out against the scandal can express any better in money the difference between the two. Not one of the persons who think that the prize-fighter should get less than the Archbishop can say how much less. What the prize-fighter got for his six or seven minutes boxing would pay a judge's salary for two years; and we are all agreed that nothing could be more ridiculous, and that any system of distributing wealth which leads to such absurdities must be wrong. But to suppose that it could be changed by any possible calculation that an ounce of archbishop or three ounces of judge is worth a pound of prizefighter would be sillier still. You can find out how many candles are worth a pound of butter in the market on any particular day; but when you try to estimate the worth of human souls the utmost you can say is that they are all of equal value before the throne of God. And that will not help you in the least to settle how much money they should have. You must simply give it up, and admit that distributing money according to merit is beyond mortal measurement and judgment.

TO EACH WHAT SHE CAN GRAB

THE third plan: that of letting everyone have what she can lay her hands on, would produce a world in which there would be no peace and no security. If we were all equally strong and cunning we should all have an equal chance; but in a world where there are children and old people and invalids, and where able-bodied adults of the same age and strength vary greatly in greediness and wickedness, it would never do: we should get tired of it in no time. Even pirate crews and bands of robbers prefer a peaceful settled understanding as to the division of their plunder to the Kilkenny cat plan.

Among ourselves, though robbery and violence are forbidden, we still allow business to be conducted on the principle of letting everyone make what he can out of it without considering anyone but himself. A shopkeeper or a coal merchant may not pick your pocket; but he may overcharge you as much as he likes. Everyone is free in business to get as much and give as little for his money as he can induce his customers to put up with. House rent can be raised without any regard to the cost of the houses or the poverty of the tenant. But this freedom produces such bad results that new laws are continually being made to restrain it; and even when it is a necessary part of our freedom to spend our money and use our possessions as seems best to us, we still have to settle how much money and what possessions we should be given to start with. This distribution must be made according to some law or other. Anarchy (absence of law) will not work. We must go on with our search for a righteous and practicable law.

OLIGARCHY

THE fourth plan is to take one person in every ten (say), and make her rich without working by making the other nine work hard and long every day, giving them only enough of what they make to keep them alive and enable them to bring up families to continue their slavery when they grow old and die. This is roughly what happens at present, as one-tenth of the English people own nine-tenths of all the property in the country, whilst most of the other nine-tenths have no property, and live from week to week on wages barely sufficient to support them in a very poor way. The advantage claimed for this plan is that it provides us with a gentry: that is, with a class of rich people able to cultivate themselves by an expensive education; so that they become qualified to govern the country and make and maintain its laws; to organize and officer the army for national defence; to patronize and keep alive learning, science, art, literature, philosophy, religion, and all the institutions that distinguish great civilizations from mere groups of villages; to raise magnificent buildings, dress splendidly, impose awe on the unruly, and set an example of good manners and fine living. Most important of all, as men of business think, by giving them much more than they need spend, we enable them to save those great sums of spare money that are called capital, and are spent in making railways, mines, factories full of machinery, and all the other contrivances by which wealth is produced in great quantities.

This plan, which is called Oligarchy, is the old English plan of dividing us into gentry living by property and common people living by work: the plan of the few rich and the many poor. It has worked for a long time, and is still working. And it is evident that if the incomes of the rich were taken from them and divided among the poor as we stand at present, the poor would be only very little less poor; the supply of capital would cease because nobody could afford to save; the country houses would fall into ruins; and learning and science and art and literature and all the rest of what we call culture would perish. That is why so many people support the present system, and stand by the gentry although they themselves are poor. They see that if ten women can produce only £110 a year each by their labor, it may be wiser for nine of them to be content with £50 apiece, and make the other one an educated lady, mistress, and ruler by giving her £540 a year without any obligation to work at all, or any inducement to work except the hope of finding how to make their work more fruitful for her own benefit, rather than to insist on having £110 a year each. Though we make this sort of arrangement at present because we are forced to, and indeed mostly without knowing that we are making it, yet it is conceivable that if we understood what we were doing and were free to carry it out or not as we thought best, we might still do it for the sake of having a gentry to keep up finer things in the world than a miserable crowd all equally poor, and all tied to primitive manual labor.

But the abuses that arise from this plan are so terrible that the world is becoming set against it. If we decide to go on with it, the first step is to settle who is to be the tenth person: the lady. How is that to be decided? True, we could begin by drawing lots; and after that the gentry could intermarry and be succeeded by their firstborns. But the mischief of it is that when we at last got our gentry established we should have no guarantee that they would do any of the things we intended them to do and paid them to do. With the best intentions, the gentry govern the country very badly because they are so far removed from the common people that they do not understand their needs. They use their power to make themselves still richer by forcing the common people to work still harder and accept still less. They spend enormous sums on sport and entertainment, gluttony and ostentation, and very little on science and art and learning. They produce poverty on a vast scale by withdrawing labor from production to waste it in superfluous menial service. They either shirk military duties or turn the army into a fashionable retinue for themselves and an instrument of oppression at home and conquest abroad. They corrupt the teaching in the universities and schools to glorify themselves and hide their misdeeds. They do the same with the Church. They try to keep the common people poor and ignorant and servile so as to make themselves more indispensable. At last their duties have to be taken out of their hands and discharged by Parliament, by the Civil Service, by the War Office and the Admiralty, by city corporations, by Poor Law Guardians, by County and Parish and District Councils, by salaried servants and Boards of paid directors, by societies and institutions of all kinds depending on taxation or on public subscription.

When this occurs, as it actually has occurred, all the cultural and political reasons for the maintenance of a gentry vanish. It always does occur when city life grows up and takes the place of country life. When a peeress resides on her estates in a part of the country where life is still very simple, and the nearest thing to a town is a village ten miles from the railway station, the people look to her ladyship for everything that is not produced by their daily toil. She represents all the splendor and greatness and romance of civilization, and does a good deal for them which they would not know how to do for themselves. In this way a Highland clan, before Scotland became civilized, always had a chief. The clansmen willingly gave him the lion's share of such land and goods as they could come by, or of the plunder they took in their raids. They did this because they could not fight successfully without a leader, and could not live together without a lawgiver. Their chief was to them what Moses was to the Israelites in the desert. The Highland chief was practically a king in his clan, just as the peeress is a queen on her estates. Loyalty to him was instinctive.

But when a Highland chief walked into a city he had less power than the first police constable he met: in fact it sometimes happened that the police constable took him in charge, and the city authorities hanged him. When the peeress leaves her estate and goes up to London for the season, she becomes a nobody except to her personal acquaintances. Everything that she does for her people in the country is done in London by paid public servants of all sorts; and when she leaves the country and settles in America or on the Continent to evade British income tax she is not missed in London: everything goes on just as before. But her tenants, who have to earn the money she spends abroad, get nothing by her, and revile her as a fugitive and an Absentee.

Small wonder then that Oligarchy is no longer consented to willingly. A great deal of the money the oligarchs get is now taken back from them by taxation and death duties; so that the old families are being reduced very rapidly to the level of ordinary citizens; and when their estates are gone, as they will be after a few generations more of our present heavy death duties, their titles will only make their poverty ridiculous. Already many of their most famous country houses are occupied either by rich business families of quite ordinary quality, or by Co-operative Societies as Convalescent Homes or places for conference and recreation, or as hotels or schools or lunatic asylums.

You must therefore face the fact that in a civilization like ours, where most of the population lives in cities; where railways, motor cars, posts, telegraphs, telephones, gramophones and radio have brought city ways and city culture into the country; and where even the smallest village has its parish meeting and its communal policeman, the old reasons for making a few people very rich whilst all the others work hard for a bare subsistence have passed away. The plan no longer works, even in the Highlands.

Still, there is one reason left for maintaining a class of excessively rich people at the expense of the rest; and business men consider it the strongest reason of all. That reason is that it provides capital by giving some people more money than they can easily spend; so that they can save money (capital is saved money) without any privation. The argument is that if income were more equally distributed, we should all have so little that we should spend all our incomes, and nothing would be saved to make machinery and build factories and construct railways and dig mines and so forth. Now it is certainly necessary to high civilization that these savings should be made; but it would be hard to imagine a more wasteful way of bringing it about.

To begin with, it is very important that there should be no saving until there has been sufficient spending: spending comes first. A nation which makes steam engines before its little children have enough milk to make their legs strong enough to carry them is making a fool's choice. Yet this is just what we do by this plan of making a few rich and the masses poor. Again, even if we put the steam engine before the milk, our plan gives us no security that we shall get the steam engine, or, if we get it, that it will be set up in our country. Just as a great deal of the money that was given to the country gentlemen of England on the chance of their encouraging art and science was spent by them on cock-fighting and horse-racing; so a shocking proportion of the money we give our oligarchs on the chance of their investing it as capital is spent by them in self-indulgence. Of the very rich it may be said that they do not begin to save until they can spend no more, and that they are continually inventing new and expensive extravagances that would have been impossible a hundred years ago. When their income outruns their extravagance so far that they must use it as capital or throw it away, there is nothing to prevent them investing it in South America, in South Africa, in Russia, or in China, though we cannot get our own slums cleaned up for want of capital kept in and applied to our own country. Hundreds of millions of pounds are sent abroad every year in this way;

and we complain of the competition of foreigners whilst we allow our capitalists to provide them at our expense with the very machinery with which they are taking our industries from us.

Of course the capitalists plead that we are none the poorer, because the interest on their capital comes back into this country from the countries in which they have invested it; and as they invest it abroad only because they get more interest abroad than at home, they assure us that we are actually the richer for their export of capital, because it enables them to spend more at home and thus give British workers more employment. But we have no guarantee that they will spend it at home: they are as likely to spend it in Monte Carlo, Madeira, Egypt, or where not? And when they do spent it at home and give us employment, we have to ask what sort of employment? When our farms and mills and cloth factories are all ruined by our importing our food and cloth from abroad instead of making them ourselves, it is not enough for our capitalists to shew us that instead of the farms we have the best golf courses in the world; instead of mills and factories splendid hotels; instead of engineers and shipwrights and bakers and carpenters and weavers, waiters and chambermaids, valets and ladies' maids, gamekeepers and butlers and so forth, all better paid and more elegantly dressed than the productive workers they have replaced. We have to consider what sort of position we shall be in when our workers are as incapable of supporting themselves and us as the idle rich themselves. Suppose the foreign countries stop our supplies either by a revolution followed by flat repudiation of their capitalistic debts, as in Russia, or by taxing and supertaxing incomes derived from investments, what will become of us then? What is becoming of us now as taxation of income spreads more and more in foreign countries? The English servant may still be able to boast that England can put a more brilliant polish on a multi-millionaire's boots than any foreigner can; but what use will that be to us when the multi-millionaire is an expropriated or taxed-out pauper with no boots to have polished?

We shall have to go into this question of capital more particularly later on; but for the purposes of this chapter it is enough to shew that the plan of depending on oligarchy for our national capital is not only wasteful on the face of it, but dangerous with a danger that increases with every political development in the world. The only plea left for it is that there is no other way of doing it. But that will not hold water for a moment. The Government can, and to a considerable extent actually does, check personal expenditure and enforce the use of part of our incomes as capital, far less capriciously and more efficiently than our oligarchy does. It can nationalize banking, as we shall see presently. This leaves oligarchy without its sole economic excuse.

DISTRIBUTION BY CLASS

NOW for the fifth plan, which is, that though everybody should work, society should be divided into as many classes as there are different sorts of work, and that the different classes should receive different payment for their work: for instance, the dustmen and scavengers and scullerymaids and charwomen and ragpickers should receive less than the doctors and clergymen and teachers and opera singers and professional ladies generally, and that these should receive less than the judges and prime ministers and kings and queens.

You will tell me that this is just what we have at present. Certainly it happens so in many cases; but there is no law that people employed in different sorts of work should be paid more or less than one another. We are accustomed to think that schoolmistresses and clergymen and doctors, being educated ladies and gentlemen, must be paid more than illiterate persons who work with their hands for weekly wages; but at the present time an engine driver, making no pretension to be a gentleman, or to have had a college education, is paid more than many clergymen and some doctors;

and a schoolmistress or governess is very lucky indeed when she is as well off as a firstrate cook. Some of our most famous physicians have had to struggle pitiably against insufficient means until they were forty or fifty; and many a parson has brought up a family on a stipend of seventy pounds a year. You must therefore be on your guard against the common mistake of supposing that we need nowadays pay more for gentility and education than for bodily strength and natural cunning, or that we always do pay more. Very learned men often make little money or none; and gentility without property may prove rather a disadvantage than otherwise to a man who wants to earn a living. Most of the great fortunes are made in trade or finance, often by men without any advantages of birth or education. Some of the great poverties have been those of saints, or of geniuses whose greatness was not recognized until they were dead.

You must also get rid of the notion (if you have it: if not, forgive me for suspecting you of it) that it costs some workers more than others to live. The same allowance of food that will keep a laborer in health will keep a king. Many laborers eat and drink much more than the King does; and all of them wear out their clothes much faster. Our King is not rich as riches go nowadays. Mr Rockefeller probably regards His Majesty as a poor man, because Mr Rockefeller not only has much more money, but is under no obligation to spend it in keeping up a great establishment: that is, spending it on other people. But if you could find out how much the King and Mr Rockefeller spend on their own personal needs and satisfaction, you would find it came to no more than is now spent by any other two persons in reasonably comfortable circumstances. If you doubled the King's allowance he would not eat twice as much, drink twice as much, sleep twice as soundly, build a new house twice as big as Buckingham Palace, or marry another queen and set up two families instead of one. The late Mr Carnegie, when his thousands grew to hundreds of thousands and his hundreds of thousands to millions, gave his money away in heaps because he already had everything he cared for that money could buy for himself or his household.

Then, it may be asked, why do we give some men more than they need and some less? The answer is that for the most part we do not give it to them: they get it because we have not arranged what anyone shall get, but have left it to chance and grab. But in the case of the King and other public dignitaries we have arranged that they shall have handsome incomes because we intend that they shall be specially respected and deferred to. Yet experience shews that authority is not proportionate to income. No person in Europe is approached with such awe as the Pope; but nobody thinks of the Pope as a rich man: sometimes his parents and brothers and sisters are very humble people, and he himself is poorer than his tailor or grocer. The captain of a liner sits at table every day with scores of people who could afford to throw his pay into the sea and not miss it; yet his authority is so absolute that the most insolent passenger dares not treat him disrespectfully. The village rector may not have a fifth of the income of his farmer churchwarden. The colonel of a regiment may be the poorest man at the mess table: everyone of his subalterns may have far more than double his income; but he is their superior in authority for all that. Money is not the secret of command.

Those who exercise personal authority among us are by no means our richest people. Millionaires in expensive cars obey policemen. In our social scale noblemen take precedence of country gentlemen, country gentlemen take precedence of professional men, professional men of traders, wholesale traders of retail traders, retail traders of skilled workmen, and skilled workmen of laborers; but if social precedence were according to income all this would be completely upset; for the tradesmen would take precedence of everybody; and the Pope and the King would have to touch their hats to distillers and pork packers.

When we speak of the power of the rich, we are speaking of a very real thing, because a rich man can discharge anyone in his employment who displeases him, and can take away his custom from any tradesman who is disrespectful to him. But the advantage a man gets by his power to ruin another is a quite different thing from the authority that is necessary to maintain law and order in society. You may obey the highwayman who puts a pistol to your head and demands your money or your life. Similarly you may obey the landlord who orders you to pay more rent or take yourself and your brats into the street. But that is not obedience to authority: it is submission to a threat. Real authority has nothing to do with money; and it is in fact exercised by persons who, from the King to the village constable, are poorer than many of the people who obey their orders.

LAISSER-FAIRE

AND now, what about leaving things just as they are? That is just what most people vote for doing. Even when they dont like what they are accustomed to, they dread change, lest it should make matters worse. They are what they call Conservative, though it is only fair to add that no Conservative statesman in his senses ever pretends (except perhaps occasionally at election times, when nobody ever tells the truth) that they can conserve things by simply letting them alone.

It seems the easiest plan and the safest; but as a matter of hard fact it is not only difficult but impossible. When Joshua told the sun to stand still on Gibeon, and the moon in the valley of Ajalon, for a trifle of twentyfour hours, he was modest in comparison with those who imagine that the world will stay put if they take care not to wake it up. And he knew he was asking for a miracle.

It is not that things as they are are so bad that nobody who knows how bad they are will agree to leave them as they are; for the reply to that may be that if they dont like them they must lump them, because there seems to be no way of changing them. The real difficulty is that things will not stay as they are, no matter how careful you are not to meddle with them. You might as well give up dusting your rooms and expect to find them this time next year just as they are now. You might as well leave the cat asleep on the hearthrug and assume that you would find her there, and not in the dairy, when you came back from church.

The truth is that things change much faster and more dangerously when they are let alone than when they are carefully looked after. Within the last hundred and fifty years the most astounding changes have taken place in this very business that we are dealing with (the production and distribution of the national income) just because what was everybody's business was nobody's business, and it was let run wild. The introduction of machinery driven by steam, and later on of electric power distributed from house to house like water or gas, and the invention of engines that not only draw trains along the ground and ships over and under the sea, but carry us and our goods flying through the air, has increased our power to produce wealth and get through our work easily and quickly to such an extent that there is no longer any need for any of us to be poor. A labor-saving house with gas stoves, electric light, a telephone, a vacuum cleaner, and a wireless set, gives only a faint notion of a modern factory full of automatic machines. If we each took our turn and did our bit in peace as we had to do during the war, all the necessary feeding and clothing and housing and lighting could be done handsomely by less than half our present day's work, leaving the other half free for art and science and learning and playing and roaming and experimenting and recreation of all sorts.

This is a new state of things: a change that has come upon us when we thought we were leaving things just as they were. And the consequence of our not attending to it and guiding and arranging it for the good of the country is that it has actually left the poor much worse off than they used to be when there was no machinery at all, and people had to be more careful of pence than they now are of shillings; whilst the rich have become rich out of all reason, and the people who should be employed in making bread for the hungry and clothes for the naked, or building houses for the homeless, are wasting their labor in providing service and luxuries for idle rich people who are not in the old sense of the words either gentle or noble, and whose idleness and frivolity and extravagance set a most corrupting moral example.

Also it has produced two and a half revolutions in political power, by which the employers have overthrown the landed gentry, the financiers have overthrown the employers, and the Trade Unions have half overthrown the financiers. I shall explain this fully later on; meanwhile, you have seen enough of its effects in the rise of the Labor Party to take my word for it that politics will not stand still any more than industry merely because millions of timid old-fashioned people vote at every election for what they call Conservatism: that is, for shutting our eyes and opening our mouths.

If King Alfred had been told that the time would come in England when one idle family would have five big houses and a steam yacht to live in whilst hard-working people were living six in a room, and half starving at that, he would have said that God would never allow such things to happen except in a very wicked nation. Well, we have left God out of the question and allowed it to happen, not through wickedness, but through letting things alone and fancying that they would let themselves alone.

Have you noticed, by the way, that we no longer speak of letting things alone in the old-fashioned way? We speak of letting them slide; and this is a great advance in good sense; for it shews that we at last see that they slide instead of staying put; and it implies that letting them slide is a feckless sort of conduct. So you must rule out once for all the notion of leaving things as they are in the expectation that they will stay where they are. They wont. All we can do in that line is to sit idly and wonder what will happen next. And this is not like sitting on the bank of the stream waiting for the water to go by. It is like sitting idly in a carriage when the horse is running away. You can excuse it by saying "What else can I do?"; but your impotence will not avert a smash. People in that predicament must all think hard of some way of getting control of the horse, and meanwhile do all they can to keep the carriage right side up and out of the ditch.

The policy of letting things alone, in the practical sense that the Government should never interfere with business or go into business itself, is called Laisser-faire by economists and politicians. It has broken down so completely in practice that it is now discredited; but it was all the fashion in politics a hundred years ago, and is still influentially advocated by men of business and their backers who naturally would like to be allowed to make money as they please without regard to the interests of the public.

HOW MUCH IS ENOUGH?

WE seem now to have disposed of all the plans except the Socialist one. Before grappling with that, may I call your attention to something that happened in our examination of most of the others. We were trying to find out a sound plan of distributing money; and every time we proposed to distribute it according to personal merit or achievement or dignity or individual quality of any sort the plan reduced itself to absurdity. When we tried to establish a relation between money and work we were beaten: it could not be done. When we tried to establish a relation between money and character we were beaten. When we tried to establish a relation between money and the dignity that gives authority we were beaten. And when we gave it up as a bad job and thought of leaving things as they are we found that they would not stay as they are.

Let us then consider for a moment what any plan must do to be acceptable. And first, as everybody except the Franciscan Friars and the Poor Clares will say that no plan will be acceptable unless it abolishes poverty (and even Franciscan poverty must be voluntary and not compelled) let us study poverty for a moment.

It is generally agreed that poverty is a very uncomfortable misfortune for the individual who happens to be poor. But poor people, when they are not suffering from acute hunger and severe cold, are not more unhappy than rich people: they are often much happier. You can easily find people who are ten times as rich at sixty as they were at twenty; but not one of them will tell you that they are ten times as happy. All the thoughtful ones will assure you that happiness and unhappiness are constitutional, and have nothing to do with money. Money can cure hunger: it cannot cure unhappiness. Food can satisfy the appetite, but not the soul. A famous German Socialist, Ferdinand Lassalle, said that what beat him in his efforts to stir up the poor to revolt against poverty was their wantlessness. They were not, of course, content: nobody is; but they were not discontented enough to take any serious trouble to change their condition. It may seem a fine thing to a poor woman to have a large house, plenty of servants, dozens of dresses, a lovely complexion and beautifully dressed hair. But the rich woman who has these things often spends a good deal of her time travelling in rough places to get away from them. To have to spend two or three hours a day washing and dressing and brushing and combing and changing and being messed about generally by a lady's maid is not on the face of it a happier lot than to have only five minutes to spend on such fatigues, as the soldiers call them. Servants are so troublesome that many ladies can hardly talk about anything else when they get together. A drunken man is happier than a sober one: that is why unhappy people take to drink. There are drugs that will make you ecstatically happy whilst ruining you body and soul. It is our quality that matters: take care of that, and our happiness will take care of itself. People of the right sort are never easy until they get things straight; but they are too healthy and too much taken up with their occupations to bother about happiness. Modern poverty is not the poverty that was blest in the Sermon on the Mount: the objection to it is not that it makes people unhappy, but that it degrades them; and the fact that they can be quite as happy in their degradation as their betters are in their exaltation makes it worse. When Shakespear's king said

> Then happy low, lie down:
> Uneasy lies the head that wears a crown,

he forgot that happiness is no excuse for lowness. The divine spark in us flashes up against being bribed to submit to degradation by mere happiness, which a pig or a drunkard can achieve.

Such poverty as we have today in all our great cities degrades the poor, and infects with its degradation the whole neighborhood in which they live. And whatever can degrade a neighborhood can degrade a country and a continent and finally the whole civilized world, which is only a large neighborhood. Its bad effects cannot be escaped by the rich. When poverty produces outbreaks of virulent infectious disease, as it always does sooner or later, the rich catch the disease and see their children die of it. When it produces crime and violence the rich go in fear of both, and are put to a good deal of expense to protect their persons and property. When it produces bad manners and bad language the children of the rich pick them up no matter how carefully they are secluded; and such seclusion as they get does them more harm than good. If poor and pretty young women find, as they do, that they can make more money by vice than by honest work, they will poison the blood of rich young men who, when they marry, will infect their wives and children, and cause them all sorts of bodily troubles, sometimes ending in disfigurement and blindness and death, and always doing them more or less mischief. The old notion that people can "keep themselves to themselves" and not be touched by what is happening to their neighbors, or even to the people who live a hundred miles off, is a most dangerous mistake. The saying that we are members one of another is not a mere pious formula to be repeated in church without any meaning: it is a literal truth; for though the rich end of the town can avoid living with the poor end, it cannot avoid dying with it when the plague comes. People will be able to keep themselves to themselves as much as they please when they have made an end of poverty; but until then they will not be able to shut out the sights and sounds and smells of poverty from their daily walks, nor to feel sure from day to day that its most violent and fatal evils will not reach them through their strongest police guards.

Besides, as long as poverty remains possible we shall never be sure that it will not overtake ourselves. If we dig a pit for others we may fall into it: if we leave a precipice unfenced our children may fall over it when they are playing. We see the most innocent and respectable families falling into the unfenced pit of poverty every day; and how do we know that it will not be our turn next?

It is perhaps the greatest folly of which a nation can be guilty to attempt to use poverty as a sort of punishment for offences that it does not send people to prison for. It is easy to say of a lazy man "Oh, let him be poor: it serves him right for being lazy: it will teach him a lesson". In saying so we are ourselves too lazy to think a little before we lay down the law. We cannot afford to have poor people anyhow, whether they be lazy or busy, drunken or sober, virtuous or vicious, thrifty or careless, wise or foolish. If they deserve to suffer let them be made to suffer in some other way; for mere poverty will not hurt them half as much as it will hurt their innocent neighbors. It is a public nuisance as well as a private misfortune. Its toleration is a national crime.

We must therefore take it as an indispensable condition of a sound distribution of wealth that everyone must have a share sufficient to keep her or him from poverty. This is not altogether new. Ever since the days of Queen Elizabeth it has been the law of England that nobody must be abandoned to destitution. If anyone, however undeserving, applies for relief to the Guardians of the Poor as a destitute person, the Guardians must feed and clothe and house that person.

They may do it reluctantly and unkindly; they may attach to the relief the most unpleasant and degrading conditions they can think of; they may set the pauper to hateful useless work if he is able-bodied, and have him sent to prison if he refuses to do it; the shelter they give him may be that of a horrible general workhouse in which the old and the young, the sound and the diseased, the innocent girl and lad and the hardened prostitute and tramp are herded together promiscuously to contaminate one another; they can attach a social stigma to the relief by taking away the pauper's vote (if he has one), and making him incapable of filling certain public offices or being elected to certain public authorities; they may, in short, drive the deserving and respectable poor to endure any extremity rather than ask for relief; but they must relieve the destitute willy nilly if they do ask for it. To that extent the law of England is at its root a Communistic law. All the harshnesses and wickednesses with which it is carried out are gross mistakes, because instead of saving the country from the degradation of poverty they actually make poverty more degrading than it need be; but still, the principle is there. Queen Elizabeth said that nobody must die of starvation and exposure. We, after the terrible experience we have had of the effects of poverty on the whole nation, rich or poor, must go further and say that nobody must be poor. As we divide-up our wealth day by day the first charge on it must be enough for everybody to be fairly respectable and well-to-do. If they do anything or leave anything undone that gives ground for saying that they do not deserve it, let them be restrained from doing it or compelled to do it in whatever way we restrain or compel evildoers of any other sort; but do not let them, as poor people, make everyone else suffer for their shortcomings.

Granted that people should not on any account be allowed to be poor, we have still to consider whether they should be allowed to be rich. When poverty is gone, shall we tolerate luxury and extravagance? This is a poser, because it is much easier to say what poverty is than what luxury is. When a woman is hungry, or ragged, or has not at least one properly furnished room all to herself to sleep in, then she is clearly suffering from poverty. When the infant mortality in one district is much greater than in another; when the average age of death for fully grown persons in it falls far short of the scriptural threescore-and-ten; when the average weight of the children who survive is below that reached by well-fed and well-cared-for children, then you can say confidently that the people in that district are suffering from poverty. But suffering from riches is not so easily measured. That rich people do suffer a great deal is plain enough to anyone who has an intimate knowledge of their lives. They are so unhealthy that they are always running after cures and surgical operations of one sort or another. When they are not really ill they imagine they are. They are worried by their property, by their servants, by their poor relations, by their investments, by the need for keeping up their social position, and, when they have several children, by the impossibility of leaving these children enough to enable them to live as they have been brought up to live; for we must not forget that if a married couple with fifty thousand a year have five children, they can leave only ten thousand a year to each after bringing them up to live at the rate of fifty thousand, and launching them into the sort of society that lives at that rate, the result being that unless these children can make rich marriages they live beyond their incomes (not knowing how to live more cheaply) and are presently head over ears in debt. They hand on their costly habits and rich friends and debts to their children with very little else; so that the trouble becomes worse and worse from generation to generation; and this is how we meet everywhere with ladies and gentlemen who have no means of keeping up their position, and are therefore much more miserable than the common poor.

Perhaps you know some well-off families who do not seem to suffer from their riches. They do not overeat themselves; they find occupations to keep themselves in health;

they do not worry about their position; they put their money into safe investments and are content with a low rate of interest; and they bring up their children to live simply and do useful work. But this means that they do not live like rich people at all, and might therefore just as well have ordinary incomes. The general run of rich people do not know what to do with themselves; and the end of it is that they have to join a round of social duties and pleasures mostly manufactured by West End shopkeepers, and so tedious that at the end of a fashionable season the rich are more worn out than their servants and tradesmen. They may have no taste for sport; but they are forced by their social position to go to the great race meetings and ride to hounds. They may have no taste for music; but they have to go to the Opera and to the fashionable concerts. They may not dress as they please nor do what they please. Because they are rich they must do what all the other rich people are doing, there being nothing else for them to do except work, which would immediately reduce them to the condition of ordinary people. So, as they cannot do what they like, they must contrive to like what they do, and imagine that they are having a splendid time of it when they are in fact being bored by their amusements, humbugged by their doctors, pillaged by their tradesmen, and forced to console themselves unamiably for being snubbed by richer people by snubbing poorer people.

To escape this boredom, the able and energetic spirits go into Parliament or into the diplomatic service or into the army, or manage and develop their estates and investments instead of leaving them to solicitors and stockbrokers and agents, or explore unknown countries with great hardship and risk to themselves, with the result that their lives are not different from the lives of the people who have to do these things for a living. Thus riches are thrown away on them; and if it were not for the continual dread of falling into poverty which haunts us all at present they would refuse to be bothered with much property. The only people who get any special satisfaction out of being richer than others are those who enjoy being idle, and like to fancy that they are better than their neighbors and be treated as if they were. But no country can afford to pamper snobbery. Laziness and vanity are not virtues to be encouraged: they are vices to be suppressed. Besides, the desire to be idle and lazy and able to order poor people about could not be satisfied, even if it were right to satisfy it, if there were no poor people to order about. What we should have would be, not poor people and rich people, but simply people with enough and people with more than enough. And that brings up at last the knotty question, what is enough?

In Shakespear's famous play, King Lear and his daughters have an argument about this. His idea of enough is having a hundred knights to wait on him. His eldest daughter thinks that fifty would be enough. Her sister does not see what he wants with any knights at all when her servants can do all he needs for him. Lear retorts that if she cuts life down to what cannot be done without, she had better throw away her fine clothes, as she would be warmer in a blanket. And to this she has no answer. Nobody can say what is enough. What is enough for a gipsy is not enough for a lady; and what is enough for one lady leaves another very discontented. When once you get above the poverty line there is no reason why you should stop there. With modern machinery we can produce much more than enough to feed, clothe, and house us decently. There is no end to the number of new things we can get into the habit of using, or to the improvements we can make in the things we already use. Our grandmothers managed to get on without gas cookers, electric light, motor cars, and telephones; but today these things are no longer curiosities and luxuries: they are matter-of-course necessities; and nobody who cannot afford them is considered well-off.

In the same way the standard of education and culture has risen. Nowadays a parlormaid as ignorant as Queen Victoria was when she came to the throne would be classed as mentally defective. As Queen Victoria managed to get on very well in spite of her ignorance it cannot be said that the knowledge in which the parlormaid has the advantage of her is a necessity of civilized life any more than a telephone is; but civilized life and highly civilized life are different: what is enough for one is not enough for the other. Take a half-civilized girl into a house; and though she may be stronger and more willing and goodnatured than many highly civilized girls are, she will smash everything that will not stand the roughest handling. She will be unable to take or send written messages; and as to understanding or using such civilized contrivances as watches, baths, sewing machines, and electric heaters and sweepers, you will be fortunate if you can induce her to turn off a tap instead of leaving the water running. And your civilized maid who can be trusted with all these things would be like a bull in a china shop if she were let loose in the laboratories where highly trained scientific workers use machines and instruments of such delicacy that their movements are as invisible as that of the hour hands of our clocks, handling and controlling poisons and explosives of the most dangerous kind; or in the operating rooms where surgeons have to do things in which a slip of the hand might prove fatal. If every housemaid had the delicacy of touch, the knowledge, and the patience that are needed in the laboratories and operating threatres (where they are unfortunately not always forthcoming), the most wonderful changes could be made in our housekeeping: we could not only have the present work done much more quickly, perfectly, and cleanly, but we could do a great deal that is now quite impossible.

Now it costs more to educate and train a laboratory worker than a housemaid, and more to train a housemaid than to catch a savage. What is enough in one case is not enough in another. Therefore to ask baldly how much is enough to live on is to ask an unanswerable question. It all depends on what sort of life you propose to live. What is enough for the life of a tramp is not enough for a highly civilized life, with its personal refinements and its atmosphere of music, art, literature, religion, science, and philosophy. Of these things we can never have enough: there is always something new to be discovered and something old to be bettered. In short, there is no such thing as enough civilization, though there may be enough of any particular thing like bread or boots at any particular moment. If being poor means wanting something more and something better than we have—and it is hard to say what else feeling poor means—then we shall always feel poor no matter how much money we have, because, though we may have enough of this thing or of that thing, we shall never have enough of everything. Consequently if it be proposed to give some people enough, and others more than enough, the scheme will break down; for all the money will be used up before anybody will be content. Nobody will stop asking for more for the sake of setting up and maintaining a fancy class of pampered persons who, after all, will be even more discontented than their poorer neighbors.

The only way out of this difficulty is to give everybody the same, which is the Socialist solution of the distribution problem. But you may tell me that you are prepared to swallow this difficulty rather than swallow Socialism. Most of us begin like that. What converts us is the discovery of the terrible array of evils around us and dangers in front of us which we dare not ignore. You may be unable to see any beauty in equality of income. But the least idealistic woman can see the disasters of inequality when the evils with which she is herself in daily conflict are traced to it; and I am now going to shew you the connexion.

WHAT WE SHOULD BUY FIRST

TO test the effects of our unequal division of the nation's income on our national institutions and on the life and prosperity of the whole people we must view the industry of the country, and see how it is affected by inequality of income. We must view one by one the institution of marriage, the working of the courts of justice, the honesty of our Houses of Parliament, the spiritual independence of the Church, the usefulness of our schools, and the quality of our newspapers, and consider how each of them is dependent on the way in which money is distributed.

Beginning with industry, we are at once plunged into what we call political economy, to distinguish it from the domestic economy with which we are all only too familiar. Men find political economy a dry and difficult subject: they shirk it as they shirk housekeeping; yet it means nothing more abstruse than the art of managing a country as a housekeeper manages a house. If the men shirk it the women must tackle it. The nation has a certain income to manage on just as a housekeeper has; and the problem is how to spend that income to the greatest general advantage.

Now the first thing a housekeeper has to settle is what things are wanted most, and what things can be done without at a pinch. This means that the housekeeper must settle the order in which things are desirable. For example, if, when there is not enough food in the house, she goes out and spends all her money on a bottle of scent and an imitation pearl necklace, she will be called a vain and silly woman and a bad mother. But a stateswoman would call her simply a bad economist: one who does not know what should come first when money has to be spent. No woman is fit to have charge of a household who has not sense and selfcontrol cnough to scc that food and clothing and housing and firing come first, and that bottles of scent and pearl necklaces, imitation or real, come a long way afterwards. Even in the jeweller's shop a wrist watch comes before a necklace as being more useful. I am not saying that pretty things are not useful: they are very useful and quite right in their proper order; but they do not come first. A Bible may be a very proper present to give to a child; but to give a starving child a Bible instead of a piece of bread and a cup of milk would be the act of a lunatic. A woman's mind is more wonderful than her flesh; but if her flesh is not fed her mind will perish, whereas if you feed her flesh her mind will take care of itself and of her flesh as well. Food comes first.

Think of the whole country as a big household, and the whole nation as a big family, which is what they really are. What do we see? Half-fed, badly clothed, abominably housed children all over the place; and the money that should go to feed and clothe and house them properly being spent in millions of bottles of scent, pearl necklaces, pet dogs, racing motor cars, January strawberries that taste like corks, and all sorts of extravagances. One sister of the national family has a single pair of leaking boots that keep her sniffing all through the winter, and no handkerchief to wipe her nose with. Another has forty pairs of high-heeled shoes and dozens of handkerchiefs. A little brother is trying to grow up on a penn'orth of food a day, and is breaking his mother's heart and wearing out her patience by asking continually for more, whilst a big brother, spending five or six pounds on his dinner at a fashionable hotel, followed by supper at a night club, is in the doctor's hands because he is eating and drinking too much.

Now this is shockingly bad political economy. When thoughtless people are asked to explain it they say "Oh, the woman with the forty shoes and the man drinking at the night club got their money from their father who made a fortune by speculating in rubber; and the girl with the broken boots, and the troublesome boy whose mother has just clouted his head, are only riffraff from the slums". That is true; but it does not alter the fact that the nation that spends money on champagne before it has provided enough milk for its babies, or gives dainty meals to Sealyham terriers and Alsatian wolf-hybrids and Pekingese dogs whilst the infant mortality rate shews that its children are dying by thousands from insufficient nourishment, is a badly managed, silly, vain, stupid, ignorant nation, and will go to the bad in the long run no matter how hard it tries to conceal its real condition from itself by counting the pearl necklaces and Pekingese dogs as wealth, and thinking itself three times as rich as before when all the pet dogs have litters of six puppies a couple. The only way in which a nation can make itself wealthy and prosperous is by good housekeeping: that is, by providing for its wants in the order of their importance, and allowing no money to be wasted on whims and luxuries until necessities have been thoroughly served.

But it is no use blaming the owners of the dogs. All these mischievous absurdities exist, not because any sane person ever wanted them to exist, but because they must occur whenever some families are very much richer than others. The rich man, who, as husband and father, drags the woman with him, begins as everyone else begins, by buying food, clothing, and a roof to shelter them. The poor man does the same. But when the poor man has spent all he can afford on these necessaries, he is still short of them: his food is insufficient; his clothes are old and dirty; his lodging is a single room or part of one, and unwholesome even at that. But when the rich man has fed himself, and dressed himself, and housed himself as sumptuously as possible, he has still plenty of money left to indulge his tastes and fancies and make a show in the world. Whilst the poor man says "I want more bread, more clothes, and a better house for my family; but I cannot pay for them", the rich man says "I want a fleet of motor cars, a yacht, diamonds and pearls for my wife and daughters, and a shooting box in Scotland. Money is no object: I can pay and overpay for them ten times over." Naturally men of business set to work at once to have the cars and the yacht made, the diamonds dug out in Africa, the pearls fished for, and the shooting lodge built, paying no attention to the poor man with his crying needs and empty pockets.

To put the same thing in another way, the poor man needs to have labor employed in making the things he is short of: that is, in baking, weaving, tailoring, and plain building; but he cannot pay the master bakers and weavers enough to enable them to pay the wages of such labor. The rich man meanwhile is offering money enough to provide good wages for all the work required to please him. All the people who take his money may be working hard; but their work is pampering people who have too much instead of feeding people who have too little; therefore it is misapplied and wasted, keeping the country poor and even making it poorer for the sake of keeping a few people rich.

It is no excuse for such a state of things that the rich give employment. There is no merit in giving employment: a murderer gives employment to the hangman; and a motorist who runs over a child gives employment to an ambulance porter, a doctor, an undertaker, a clergyman, a mourning-dressmaker, a hearse driver, a gravedigger: in short, to so many worthy people that when he ends by killing himself it seems ungrateful not to erect a statue to him as a public benefactor. The money with which the rich give the wrong sort of employment would give the right sort of employment if it were equally distributed; for then there would be no money offered for motor cars and diamonds until everyone was fed, clothed, and lodged, nor any wages offered to men and women to leave useful employments and become servants to idlers. There would be less ostentation, less idleness, less wastefulness, less uselessness; but there would be more food, more clothing, better houses, more security, more health, more virtue: in a word, more real prosperity.

POSITIVE REASONS FOR EQUALITY

SO far, we have not found one great national institution that escapes the evil effects of a division of the people into rich and poor: that is, of inequality of income. I could take you further; but we should only fare worse. I could shew you how rich officers and poor soldiers and sailors create disaffection in the army and navy: how disloyalty is rampant because the relation between the royal family and the bulk of the nation is the relation between one rich family and millions of poor ones; how what we call peace is really a state of civil war between rich and poor conducted by disastrous strikes; how envy and rebellion and class resentments are chronic moral diseases with us. But if I attempted this you would presently exclaim "Oh, for goodness' sake dont tell me everything or we shall never have done." And you would be quite right. If I have not convinced you by this time that there are overwhelming reasons of State against inequality of income, I shall begin to think that you dislike me.

Besides, we must get on to the positive reasons for the Socialist plan of an equal division. I am specially interested in it because it is my favorite plan. You had therefore better watch me carefully to see that I play fairly when I am helping you to examine what there is to be said for equality of income over and above what there is to be said against inequality of income.

First, equal division is not only a possible plan, but one which has been tested by long experience. The great bulk of the daily work of the civilized world is done, and always has been done, and always must be done, by bodies of persons receiving equal pay whether they are tall or short, fair or dark, quick or slow, young or getting on in years, teetotallers or beer drinkers, Protestants or Catholics, married or single, short tempered or sweet tempered, pious or worldly: in short, without the slightest regard to the differences that make one person unlike another. In every trade there is a standard wage; in every public service there is a standard pay; and in every profession the fees are fixed with a view to enable the man who follows the profession to live according to a certain standard of respectability which is the same for the whole profession. The pay of the policeman and soldier and postman, the wages of the laborer and carpenter and mason, the salary of the judge and the member of Parliament, may differ, some of them getting less than a hundred a year and others five thousand; but all the soldiers get the same, all the judges get the same, all the members of Parliament get the same; and if you ask a doctor why his fee is half a crown or five shillings, or a guinea or three guineas, or whatever it may be, instead of five shillings or ten shillings, or two guineas or six guineas or a thousand guineas, he can give you no better reason than that he is asking what all the other doctors ask, and that they ask it because they find they cannot keep up their position on less.

Therefore when some inconsiderate person repeats like a parrot that if you gave everybody the same money, before a year was out you would have rich and poor again just as before, all you have to do is to tell him to look round him and see millions of people who get the same money and remain in the same position all their lives without any such change taking place. The cases in which poor men become rich are most exceptional; and though the cases in which rich men become poor are commoner, they also are accidents and not ordinary everyday circumstances. The rule is that workers of the same rank and calling are paid alike, and that they neither sink below their condition nor rise above it. No matter how unlike they are to one another, you can pay one of them two and sixpence and the other half a crown with the assurance that as they are put so they will stay, though here and there a great rogue or a great genius may surprise you by becoming much richer or much poorer than the rest. Jesus complained that he was poorer than the foxes and birds, as they had their holes and nests whilst he had not a house to shelter him; and Napoleon became an emperor; but we need take no more account of such extraordinary persons in forming our general plan than a maker of ready made clothes takes of giants and dwarfs in his price list. You may with the utmost confidence take it as settled by practical experience that if we could succeed in distributing income equally to all the inhabitants of the country, there would be no more tendency on their part to divide into rich and poor than there is at present for postmen to divide into beggars and millionaires. The only novelty proposed is that the postmen should get as much as the postmasters, and the postmasters no less than anybody else. If we find, as we do, that it answers to give all judges the same income, and all navy captains the same income, why should we go on giving judges five times as much as navy captains? That is what the navy captain would like to know; and if you tell him that if he were given as much as the judge he would be just as poor as before at the end of a year he will use language unfit for the ears of anyone but a pirate. So be careful how you say such things.

Equal distribution is then quite possible and practicable, not only momentarily but permanently. It is also simple and intelligible. It gets rid of all squabbling as to how much each person should have. It is already in operation and familiar over great masses of human beings. And it has the tremendous advantage of securing promotion by merit for the more capable.

MERIT AND MONEY

THAT last sentence may puzzle even the most Intelligent Woman if she has never before given her mind seriously to the subject; so I had better enlarge on it a little.

Nothing hides the difference in merit between one person and another so much as differences in income. Take for example a grateful nation making a parliamentary grant of twenty thousand pounds to a great explorer, or a great discoverer, or a great military commander (I have to make my example a man: women get only statues after their death). Before he has walked half way down the street on his way home to tell his wife about it he may meet some notorious fool or scandalous libertine, or some quite ordinary character, who has not merely twenty thousand pounds but twenty thousand a year or more. The great man's twenty thousand pounds will bring him in only a thousand a year; and with this he finds himself in our society regarded as "a poor devil" by tradesmen and financiers and quacks who are ten times as rich because they have never in their lives done anything but make money for themselves with entire selfishness, possibly by trading in the vices or on the credulity of their fellow-countrymen. It is a monstrous thing that a man who, by exercising a low sort of cunning, has managed to grab three or four millions of money selling bad whiskey, or forestalling the wheat harvest and selling it at three times its cost, or providing silly newspapers and magazines for the circulation of lying advertisements, should be honored and deferred to and waited on and returned to Parliament and finally made a peer of the realm, whilst men who have exercised their noblest faculties or risked their lives in the furtherance of human knowledge and welfare should be belittled by the contrast between their pence and the grabbers' pounds.

Only where there is pecuniary equality can the distinction of merit stand out. Titles, dignities, reputations do more harm than good if they can be bought with money. Queen Victoria shewed her practical common sense when she said that she would not give a title to anyone who had not money enough to keep it up; but the result was that the titles went to the richest, not to the best. Between persons of unequal income all other distinctions are thrown into the background. The woman with a thousand a year inevitably takes precedence of women with only a hundred, no matter how inferior she may be to them; and she can give her children advantages qualifying them for higher employments than those open to poor children of equal or greater natural capacity.

Between persons of equal income there is no social distinction except the distinction of merit. Money is nothing: character, conduct, and capacity are everything. Instead of all the workers being levelled down to low wage standards and all the rich levelled up to fashionable income standards, everybody under a system of equal incomes would find her and his own natural level. There would be great people and ordinary people and little people; but the great would always be those who had done great things, and never the idiots whose mothers had spoiled them and whose fathers had left them a hundred thousand a year; and the little would be persons of small minds and mean characters, and not poor persons who had never had a chance. That is why idiots are always in favor of inequality of income (their only chance of eminence), and the really great in favor of equality.

MISCELLANEOUS

IMPRISONMENT

(*From Doctors' Delusions, Crude Criminology, Sham Education*)

FOREWORD

WHEN I was a boy in my teens in Dublin I was asked by an acquaintance of mine who was clerk to a Crown Solicitor, and had business in prisons, whether I would like to go through Mountjoy Prison, much as he might have asked me whether I would like to go through the Mint, or the cellars at the docks. I accepted the invitation with my head full of dungeons and chains and straw pallets and stage gaolers: in short, of the last acts of Il Trovatore and Gounod's Faust, and of the Tower of London in Richard III. I expected the warders to look like murderers, and the murderers like heroes. At least I suppose I did, because what struck me most was that the place was as bright and clean as whitewash and scrubbing and polish could make it, with all the warders looking thoroughly respectable, and all the prisoners ruffianly and degenerate, except one tall delicate figure tramping round in the exercise ring, a Lifer by the color of his cap, who had chopped up his family with a hatchet, and been recommended to mercy on account of his youth. I thought, and still think, imprisonment for life a curious sort of mercy. My main impression of the others, and the one that has stuck longest and hardest, was that as it was evidently impossible to reform such men, it was useless to torture them, and dangerous to release them.

I have never been imprisoned myself; but in my first years as a public speaker I had to volunteer for prison martyrdom in two Free Speech conflicts with the police. As my luck would have it, on the first occasion the police capitulated on the eve of the day on which I had undertaken to address a prohibited meeting and refuse to pay a fine; and on the second a rival political organization put up a rival martyr, and, on a division, carried his election over my head, to my great relief. These incidents are not very impressive now; but the fact that my acquaintance with the subject of the following essay began with the sight of an actual prison, and that twice afterwards I was for a week or so firmly convinced that I was about to spend at least a fortnight and possibly a month in the cells, gave me an interest in the subject less perfunctory than that of the ordinary citizen to whom prison is only a reference in the police news, denoting simply a place where dishonest and violent people are very properly locked up.

This comfortable ignorance, by the way, is quite commonly shared by judges. A Lord Chief Justice of England, grieved at hearing from a lady of social importance that her son had been sent to prison as a Conscientious Objector, told her that he hoped she would get to see him often, and keep up his spirits with frequent letters, and send him in nice things to eat. He was amazed to learn from her that he might just as well have suggested a motor ride every afternoon and a visit to the opera in the evening. He had been sentencing people all through his judicial career to terms of imprisonment, some of them for life, without knowing that it meant anything more than being confined to the house and wearing a dress with broad arrows all over it. No doubt he thought, quite rightly, that such confinement was bad enough for anybody, however wicked.

I had no such illusions about prison life. My political activities often brought me into contact with men of high character and ability who had been victims of modern forms of persecution under the very elastic headings of treason, sedition, obstruction, blasphemy, offences against press laws, and so forth. I knew that Karl Marx had declared that British prisons were the cruellest in the world; and I thought it quite probable that he was right. I knew Prince Peter Kropotkin, who, after personal experience of the most villainous convict prisons in Siberia and the best model prison in France, said that they were both so bad that the difference was not worth talking about. What with European "politicals" and amnestied Irish Fenians, those who, like myself, were in the way of meeting such people could hardly feel easy in their consciences about the established methods of handling criminals.

Also I was in occasional touch with certain efforts made by the now extinct Humanitarian League, and by a little Society called the Police and Public Vigilance Society, to call attention to the grievances of prisoners. The League dealt with punishments: the Society, which was really an agitation conducted by one devoted man with very slender means, the late James Timewell, tried to obtain redress for people who alleged that they had been the victims of petty frame-ups by the police. But the witnesses on whose testimony these two bodies had to proceed were mostly either helpless creatures who could not tell the truth or scoundrels who would not tell it. The helpless creatures told you what they wanted to believe themselves: the scoundrels told you what they wanted you to believe.

Anyone who has tried to find out what war is like from our demobilized soldiers will understand. Their consciousness is limited and utterly uncritical; their memory is inaccurate and confused; their judgment is perverted by personal dislikes and vanities; and as to reflection, reason, self-criticism, and the rest of the intellectual counterchecks, they have no more of them than a mouse has of mathematics. If this is the case with normal men like soldiers, even less is to be expected from subnormal men like criminals. Neither the Humanitarian League nor Mr Timewell could rouse general public compunction with such testimony, or attract special subscriptions enough to enable them to conduct a serious investigation. And John Galsworthy had not then arisen to smite our consciences with such plays as The Silver Box and Justice.

This situation was changed by the agitation for Votes for Women and the subsequent war of 1914–18, both of which threw into prison an unprecedented number of educated, critical, public-spirited, conscientious men and women who under ordinary circumstances would have learnt no more about prisons than larks learn about coal mines. They came out of prison unembittered by their personal sufferings: their grievance was the public grievance of the whole prison system and its intense irreligiousness. In prison they had been capable of observing critically what they saw; and out of prison they were able to describe it. The official whitewash of the Prison Commissioners could not impose on them. They and their friends had money enough to take an office and engage a secretarial staff, besides supplying some voluntary educated labor. They formed a committee with Lord Olivier as chairman, which investigated the condition of English prisons and incidentally read some interesting reports of American ones. Eventually they issued their report as a volume entitled English Prisons Today, edited by Stephen Hobhouse and Fenner Brockway, who had both been in prison during the war.

I was a member of that committee; and the essay which follows was written as a preface to the report. But I did not find it possible to keep a thorough sifting of the subject within the limits of the sixth commandment, on which Mr Hobhouse took an uncompromising stand. Fortunately my friends Sidney and Beatrice Webb were just then reinforcing the work of the committee by issuing the volume of their monumental history of English Local Government which deals with prisons. By transferring my preface to their book I was able to secure the intended publicity for it, and to please everybody concerned, myself included.

I give this history of the essay lest it should be taken as a fanciful exercise by a literary man making up the subject out of his own head. I have not made a parade of facts and figures because my business is to change the vindictive attitude towards criminals which has made the facts possible; but I know the facts better, apparently, than the Prison Commissioners, and relevant figures quite as well.

However, the matter did not stop with the issue of Mr and Mrs Webb's Prisons Under Local Government. That work, though read throughout the civilized world by serious students of political science, has a specialized circulation. Fortunately, my preface to it attracted the attention of the Department of Christian Social Service of the National Council of the Protestant Episcopal Church in the United States. That body put it into general circulation in America.

[It now appears among my own works for the first time in the British Isles, 1931.] G. B. S.

Madeira, January 1925.

THE SPIRIT IN WHICH TO READ THIS ESSAY

Imprisonment as it exists today is a worse crime than any of those committed by its victims: for no single criminal can be as powerful for evil, or as unrestrained in its exercise, as an organized nation. Therefore, if any person is addressing himself to the perusal of this dreadful subject in the spirit of a philanthropist bent on reforming a necessary and beneficent public institution, I beg him to put it down and go about some other business. It is just such reformers who have in the past made the neglect, oppression, corruption, and physical torture of the old common gaol the pretext for transforming it into that diabolical den of torment, mischief, and damnation, the modern model prison.

If, on the contrary, the reader comes as a repentant sinner, let him read on.

THE OBSTACLE OF VINDICTIVENESS

The difficulty in finding repentant sinners when this crime is in question has two roots. The first is that we are all brought up to believe that we may inflict injuries on anyone against whom we can make out a case of moral inferiority. We have this thrashed into us in our childhood by the infliction on ourselves of such injuries by our parents and teachers, or indeed by any elder who happens to be in charge of us. The second is that we are all now brought up to believe, not that the king can do no wrong, because kings have been unable to keep up that pretence, but that Society can do no wrong. Now not only does Society commit more frightful crimes than any individual, king or commoner: it legalizes its crimes, and forges certificates of righteousness for them, besides torturing anyone who dares expose their true character. A society like ours, which will, without remorse, ruin a boy body and soul for life for trying to sell newspapers in a railway station, is not likely to be very tender to people who venture to tell it that its laws would shock the Prince of Darkness himself if he had not been taught from his earliest childhood to respect as well as fear them.

Consequently we have a desperately sophisticated public, as well as a quite frankly vindictive one. Judges spend their lives consigning their fellow-creatures to prison; and when some whisper reaches them that prisons are horribly cruel and destructive places, and that no creature fit to live should be sent there, they only remark calmly that prisons are not meant to be comfortable, which is no doubt the consideration that reconciled Pontius Pilate to the practice of crucifixion.

THE OBSTACLE OF STUPIDITY

Another difficulty is the sort of stupidity that comes from lack of imagination. When I tell people that I have seen with these eyes a man (no less a man than Richard Wagner, by the way) who once met a crowd going to see a soldier broken on the wheel by the crueller of the two legalized methods of carrying out that hideous sentence, they shudder, and are amazed to hear that what they call medieval torture was used in civilized Europe so recently. They forget that the punishment of half-hanging, unmentionably mutilating, beheading, and quartering, was on the British statute book within my own memory. The same people will read of a burglar being sentenced to ten years' penal servitude without turning a hair. They are like Ibsen's Peer Gynt, who was greatly reassured when he was told that the pains of hell are mental: he thought they cannot be so very bad if there is no actual burning brimstone. When such people are terrified by an outburst of robbery with violence, or Sadistically excited by reports of the White Slave traffic, they clamor to have sentences of two years' hard labor supplemented by a flogging, which is a joke by comparison. They will try to lynch a criminal who illtreats a child in some sensationally cruel manner; but on the most trifling provocation they will inflict on the child the prison demoralization and the prison stigma which condemn it for the rest of its life to crime as the only employment open to a prison child. The public conscience would be far more active if the punishment of imprisonment were abolished, and we went back to the rack, the stake, the pillory, and the lash at the cart's tail.

BLOOD SPORTS DISGUISED AS PUNISHMENT ARE LESS CRUEL THAN IMPRISONMENT BUT MORE DEMORALIZING TO THE PUBLIC

The objection to retrogression is not that such punishments are more cruel than imprisonment. They are less cruel, and far less permanently injurious. The decisive objection to them is that they are sports in disguise. The pleasure to the spectators, and not the pain to the criminal, condemns them. People will go to see Titus Oates flogged or Joan of Arc burnt with equal zest as an entertainment. They will pay high prices for a good view. They will reluctantly admit that they must not torture one another as long as certain rules are observed; but they will hail a breach of the rules with delight as an excuse for a bout of cruelty. Yet they can be shamed at last into recognizing that such exhibitions are degrading and demoralizing; that the executioner is a wretch whose hand no decent person cares to take; and that the enjoyment of the spectators is fiendish. We have then to find some form of torment which can give no sensual satisfaction to the tormentor, and which is hidden from public view. That is how imprisonment, being just such a torment, became the normal penalty. The fact that it may be worse for the criminal is not taken into account. The public is seeking its own salvation, not that of the lawbreaker. For him it would be far better to suffer in the public eye; for among the crowd of sightseers there might be a Victor Hugo or a Dickens, able and willing to make the sightseers think of what they are doing and ashamed of it. The prisoner has no such chance. He envies the unfortunate animals in the zoo, watched daily by thousands of disinterested observers who never try to convert a tiger into a Quaker by solitary confinement, and would set up a resounding agitation in the papers if even the most ferocious maneater were made to suffer what the most docile convict suffers. Not only has the convict no such protection: the secrecy of his prison makes it hard to convince the public that he is suffering at all.

HOW WE ALL BECOME INURED TO IMPRISONMENT

There is another reason for this incredulity. The vast majority of our city populations are inured to imprisonment from their childhood. The school is a prison. The office and the factory are prisons. The home is a prison. To the young who have the misfortune to be what is called well brought up it is sometimes a prison of inhuman severity. The children of John Howard, as far as their liberty was concerned, were treated very much as he insisted criminals should be treated, with the result that his children were morally disabled, like criminals. This imprisonment in the home, the school, the office, and the factory is kept up by browbeating, scolding, bullying, punishing, disbelief of the prisoner's statements and acceptance of those of the official, essentially as in a criminal prison. The freedom given by the adult's right to walk out of his prison is only a freedom to go into another or starve: he can choose the prison where he is best treated: that is all. On the other hand, the imprisoned criminal is free from care as to his board, lodging, and clothing: he pays no taxes, and has no responsibilities. Nobody expects him to work as an unconvicted man must work if he is to keep his job: nobody expects him to do his work well, or cares twopence whether it is well done or not.

Under such circumstances it is very hard to convince the ordinary citizen that the criminal is not better off than he deserves to be, and indeed on the verge of being positively pampered. Judges, magistrates, and Home Secretaries are so commonly under the same delusion that people who have ascertained the truth about prisons have been driven to declare that the most urgent necessity of the situation is that every judge, magistrate, and Home Secretary should serve a six months' sentence incognito; so that when he is dealing out and enforcing sentences he should at least know what he is doing.

COMPETITION IN EVIL BETWEEN PRISON AND SLUM

When we get down to the poorest and most oppressed of our population we find the conditions of their life so wretched that it would be impossible to conduct a prison humanely without making the lot of the criminal more eligible than that of many free citizens. If the prison does not underbid the slum in human misery, the slum will empty and the prison will fill. This does in fact take place to a small extent at present, because slum life at its worst is so atrocious that its victims, when they are intelligent enough to study alternatives instead of taking their lot blindly, conclude that prison is the most comfortable place to spend the winter in, and qualify themselves accordingly by committing an offence for which they will get six months. But this consideration affects only those people whose condition is not defended by any responsible publicist: the remedy is admittedly not to make the prison worse but the slum better. Unfortunately the admitted claims of the poor on life are pitifully modest. The moment the treatment of the criminal is decent and merciful enough to give him a chance of moral recovery, or, in incorrigible cases, to avoid making bad worse, the official descriptions of his lot become so rosy that a clamor arises against thieves and murderers being better off than honest and kindly men; for the official reports tell us only of the care that is taken of the prisoner and the advantages he enjoys, or can earn by good conduct, never of his sufferings; and the public is not imaginative or thoughtful enough to supply the deficiency.

What sane man, I ask the clamorers, would accept an offer of free board, lodging, clothing, waiters in attendance at a touch of the bell, medical treatment, spiritual advice, scientific ventilation and sanitation, technical instruction, liberal education, and the use of a carefully selected library, with regular exercise daily and sacred music at frequent intervals, even at the very best of the Ritz Hotels, if the conditions were that he should never leave the hotel, never speak, never sing, never laugh, never see a newspaper, and write only one sternly censored letter and have one miserable interview at long intervals through the bars of a cage under the eye of a warder? And when the prison is not the Ritz Hotel, when the lodging, the food, the bed, are all deliberately made so uncomfortable as to be instruments of torture, when the clothes are rags promiscuously worn by all your fellow-prisoners in turn with yourself, when the exercise is that of a turnspit, when the ventilation and sanitation are noisome, when the instruction is a sham, the education a fraud, when the doctor is a bully to whom your ailments are all malingerings, and the chaplain a moral snob with no time for anything but the distribution of unreadable books, when the waiters are bound by penalties not to speak to you except to give you an order or a rebuke, and then to address you as you would not dream of addressing your dog, when the manager holds over your head a continual threat of starvation and confinement in a punishment cell (as if your own cell were not punishment enough), then what man in his senses would voluntarily exchange even the most harassed freedom for such a life, much less wallow luxuriously in it, as the Punch burglar always does on paper the moment anyone suggests the slightest alleviation of the pains of imprisonment?

GIVING THEM HELL

Yet people cannot be brought to see this. They ask, first, what right the convict has to complain when he has brought it on himself by his own misconduct, and second, what he has to complain of. You reply that his grievances are silence, solitude, idleness, waste of time, and irresponsibility. The retort is, "Why call that torture, as if it were boiling oil or red hot irons or something like that? Why, I have taken a cottage in the country for the sake of silence and solitude; and I should be only too glad to get rid of my responsibilities and waste my time in idleness like a real gentleman. A jolly sight too well off, the fellows are. I should give them hell."

Thus imprisonment is at once the most cruel of punishments and the one that those who inflict it without having ever experienced it cannot believe to be cruel. A country gentleman with a big hunting stable will indignantly discharge a groom and refuse him a reference for cruelly thrashing a horse. But it never occurs to him that his stables are horse prisons, and the stall a cell in which it is quite unnatural for the horse to be immured. In my youth I saw the great Italian actress Ristori play Mary Stuart; and nothing in her performance remains more vividly with me than her representation of the relief of Mary at finding herself in the open air after months of imprisonment. When I first saw a stud of hunters turned out to grass, they reminded me so strongly of Ristori that I at once understood that they had been prisoners in their stables, a fact which, obvious as it was, I had not thought of before. And this sort of thoughtlessness, being continuous and unconscious, inflicts more suffering than all the malice and passion in the world. In prison you get one piled on the other: to the cruelty that is intended and contrived, that grudges you even the inevitable relief of sleep, and makes your nights miserable by plank beds and the like, is added the worse cruelty that is not intended as cruelty, and, when its perpetrators can be made conscious of it at all, deludes them by a ghastly semblance of pampered indulgence.

THE THREE OFFICIAL AIMS OF IMPRISONMENT

And now comes a further complication. When people are at last compelled to think about what they are doing to our unfortunate convicts, they think so unsuccessfully and confusedly that they only make matters worse. Take for example the official list of the results aimed at by the Prison Commissioners. First, imprisonment must be "retributory" (the word vindictive is not in official use). Second, it must be deterrent. Third, it must be reformative.

THE RETRIBUTION MUDDLE

Now, if you are to punish a man retributively, you must injure him. If you are to reform him, you must improve him. And men are not improved by injuries. To propose to punish and reform people by the same operation is exactly as if you were to take a man suffering from pneumonia, and attempt to combine punitive and curative treatment. Arguing that a man with pneumonia is a danger to the community, and that he need not catch it if he takes proper care of his health, you resolve that he shall have a severe lesson, both to punish him for his negligence and pulmonary weakness and to deter others from following his example. You therefore strip him naked, and in that condition stand him all night in the snow. But as you admit the duty of restoring him to health if possible, and discharging him with sound lungs, you engage a doctor to superintend the punishment and administer cough lozenges, made as unpleasant to the taste as possible so as not to pamper the culprit. A Board of Commissioners ordering such treatment would prove thereby that either they were imbeciles or else they were hotly in earnest about punishing the patient and not in the least in earnest about curing him.

When our Prison Commissioners pretend to combine punishment with moral reformation they are in the same dilemma. We are told that the reformation of the criminal is kept constantly in view; yet the destruction of the prisoner's self-respect by systematic humiliation is deliberately ordered and practised; and we learn from a chaplain that he "does not think it is good to give opportunity for the exercise of Christian and social virtues one towards another" among prisoners. The only consolation for such contradictions is their demonstration that, as the tormentors instinctively feel that they must be liars and hypocrites on the subject, their consciences cannot be very easy about the torment. But the contradictions are obvious here only because I put them on the same page. The Prison Commissioners keep them a few pages apart; and the average reader's memory, it seems, is not long enough to span the gap when his personal interests are not at stake.

PLAUSIBILITY OF THE DETERRENCE DELUSION

Deterrence, which is the real object of the courts, has much more to be said for it, because it is neither simply and directly wicked like retribution, nor a false excuse for wickedness like reformation. It is an unquestionable fact that, by making rules and forcing those who break them to suffer so severely that others like them become afraid to break them, discipline can be maintained to a certain extent among creatures without sense enough to understand its necessity, or, if they do understand it, without conscience enough to refrain from violating it. This is the crude basis of all our disciplines: home discipline, school discipline, factory discipline, army and navy discipline, as well as of prison discipline, and of the whole fabric of criminal law. It is imposed not only by cruel rulers, but by unquestionably humane ones: the only difference being that the cruel rulers impose it with alacrity and gloat over its execution, and the humane rulers are driven to it reluctantly by the failure of their appeals to the consciences of people who have no conscience. Thus we find Mahomet, a conspicuously humane and conscientious Arab, keeping his fierce staff in order, not by unusual punishments, but by threats of a hell after death which he invented for the purpose in revolting detail of a kind which suggests that Mahomet had perhaps too much of the woman and the artist in him to know what would frighten a Bedouin most. Wellington, a general so humane that he sacrificed the exercise of a military genius of the first order to his moral horror of war and his freedom from its illusions, nevertheless hanged and flogged his soldiers mercilessly because he had learnt from experience that, as he put it, nothing is worse than impunity. All revolutions have been the work of men who, like Robespierre, were sentimental humanitarians and conscientious objectors to capital punishment and to the severities of military and prison discipline; yet all the revolutions have after a very brief practical experience been driven to Terrorism (the proper name of Deterrence) as ruthless as the Counter-Revolutionary Terror of Sulla, a late example being that of the Russian revolution of 1917. Whether it is Sulla, Robespierre, Trotsky, or the fighting mate of a sailing ship with a crew of loafers and wastrels, the result is the same: there are people to be dealt with who will not obey the law unless they are afraid to disobey it, and whose disobedience would mean disaster.

CRIME CANNOT BE KILLED BY KINDNESS

It is useless for humanitarians to shirk this hard fact, and proclaim their conviction that all law-breakers can be reformed by kindness. That may be true in many cases, provided you can find a very gifted practitioner to take the worst ones in hand, with unlimited time and means to treat them. But if these conditions are not available, and a policeman and an executioner who will disable the wrongdoer instantaneously are available, the police remedy is the only practicable one, even for rulers filled with the spirit of the Sermon on the Mount. The late G. V. Foote, President of the English National Secular Society, a strenuous humanitarian, once had to persuade a very intimate friend of his, a much smaller and weaker man, to allow himself to be taken to an asylum for lunatics. It took four hours of humanitarian persuasion to get the patient from the first floor of his house to the cab door. Foote told me that he had not only recognized at once that no asylum attendant, with several patients to attend to, could possibly spend four hours in getting each of them downstairs, but found his temper so intolerably strained by the unnatural tax on his patience that if the breaking point had been reached, as it certainly would have been in the case of a warder or asylum attendant, he would have been far more violent, not to say savage, than if he had resorted to force at once, and finished the job in five minutes.

From resorting to this rational and practically compulsory use of kindly physical coercion to making it so painful that the victim will be afraid to give any trouble next time is a pretty certain step. In prisons the warders have to protect themselves against violence from prisoners, of which there is a constant risk and very well founded dread, as there are always ungovernably savage criminals who have little more power of refraining from furious assaults than some animals, including quite carefully bred dogs and horses, have of refraining from biting and savaging. The official punishment is flogging and putting in irons for months. But the immediate rescue of the assaulted warder has to be effected by the whole body of warders within reach; and whoever supposes that the prisoner suffers nothing more at their hands than the minimum of force necessary to restrain him knows nothing of prison life and less of human nature.

Any criticism of the deterrent theory of our prison system which ignores the existence of ungovernable savages will be discredited by the citation of actual cases. I should be passed over as a sentimentalist if I lost sight of them for a moment. On any other subject I could dispose of the matter by reminding my critics that hard cases make bad law. On this subject I recognize that the hard cases are of such a nature that provision must be made for them. Indeed hard cases may be said to be the whole subject matter of criminal law; for the normal human case is not that of the criminal, but of the law-abiding person on whose collar the grip of the policeman never closes. Only, it does not follow that the hardest cases should dictate the treatment of the relatively soft ones.

THE SEAMY SIDE OF DETERRENCE

Let us now see what are the objections to the Deterrent or Terrorist system.

1. It necessarily leaves the interests of the victim wholly out of account. It injures and degrades him; destroys the reputation without which he cannot get employment; and when the punishment is imprisonment under our system, atrophies his powers of fending for himself in the world. Now this would not materially hurt anyone but himself if, when he had been duly made an example of, he were killed like a vivisected dog. But he is not killed. He is, at the expiration of his sentence, flung out of the prison into the streets to earn his living in a labor market where nobody will employ an ex-prisoner, betraying himself at every turn by his ignorance of the common news of the months or years he has passed without newspapers, lamed in speech, and terrified at the unaccustomed task of providing food and lodging for himself. There is only one lucrative occupation available for him; and that is crime. He has no compunction as to Society: why should he have any? Society having for its own selfish protection done its worst to him, he has no feeling about it except a desire to get a bit of his own back. He seeks the only company in which he is welcome: the society of criminals; and sooner or later, according to his luck, he finds himself in prison again. The figures of recidivism shew that the exceptions to this routine are so few as to be negligible for the purposes of our argument. The criminal, far from being deterred from crime, is forced into it; and the citizen whom his punishment was meant to protect suffers from his depredations.

OUR PLAGUE OF UNRESTRAINED CRIME

It is, in fact, admitted that the deterrent system does not deter the convicted criminal. Its real efficacy is sought in its deterrent effect on the free citizens who would commit crimes but for their fear of punishment. The Terrorist can point to the wide range of evil-doing which, not being punished by law, is rampant among us; for though a man can get himself hanged for a momentary lapse of self-control under intolerable provocation by a nagging woman, or into prison for putting the precepts of Christ above the orders of a Competent Military Authority, he can be a quite infernal scoundrel without breaking any penal law. If it be true, as it certainly is, that it is conscience and not the fear of punishment that makes civilized life possible, and that Dr Johnson's

> How small, of all that human hearts endure,
> That part that laws or kings can cause or cure!

is as applicable to crime as to human activity in general, it is none the less true that commercial civilization presents an appalling spectacle of pillage and parasitism, of corruption in the press and in the pulpit, of lying advertisements which make people buy rank poisons in the belief that they are health restorers, of traps to catch the provision made for the widow and the fatherless and divert it to the pockets of company promoting rogues, of villainous oppression of the poor and cruelty to the defenceless; and it is arguable that most of this could, like burglary and forgery, be kept within bearable bounds if its perpetrators were dealt with as burglars and forgers are dealt with today. It is, let us not forget, equally arguable that if we can afford to leave so much villainy unpunished we can afford to leave all villainy unpunished. Unfortunately, we cannot afford it: our toleration is threatening our civilization. The prosperity that consists in the wicked flourishing like a green bay tree, and the humble and contrite hearts being thoroughly despised, is a commercial delusion. Facts must be looked in the face, rascals told what they are, and all men called on to justify their ways to God and Man up to the point at which the full discharge of their social duties leaves them free to exercise their individual fancies. Restraint from evil-doing is within the rights as well as within the powers of organized society over its members; and it cannot be denied that the exercise of these powers, as far as it could be made inevitable, would incidentally deter from crime a certain number of people with only marginal consciences or none at all, and that an extension of the penal code would create fresh social conscience by enlarging the list of things which law-abiding people make it a point of honor not to do, besides calling the attention of the community to grave matters in which they have hitherto erred through thoughtlessness.

DETERRENCE A FUNCTION OF CERTAINTY, NOT OF SEVERITY

But there is all the difference in the world between deterrence as an incident of the operation of criminal law, and deterrence as its sole object and justification. In a purely deterrent system, for instance, it matters not a jot who is punished provided somebody is punished and the public persuaded that he is guilty. The effect of hanging or imprisoning the wrong man is as deterrent as hanging or imprisoning the right one. This is the fundamental explanation of the extreme and apparently fiendish reluctance of the Home Office to release a prisoner when, as in the Beck case, the evidence on which he was convicted has become discredited to a point at which no jury would maintain its verdict of guilty. The reluctance is not to confess that an innocent man is being punished, but to proclaim that a guilty man has escaped. For if escape is possible deterrence shrinks almost to nothing. There is no better established rule of criminology than that it is not the severity of punishment that deters, but its certainty. And the flaw in the case of Terrorism is that it is impossible to obtain enough certainty to deter. The police are compelled to confess every year, when they publish their statistics, that against the list of crimes reported to them they can set only a percentage of detections and convictions. And the list of reported crimes can form only a percentage, how large or small it is impossible to say, but probably small, of the crimes actually committed; for it is the greatest mistake to suppose that everyone who is robbed runs to the police: on the contrary, only foolish and ignorant or very angry people do so without very serious consideration and great reluctance. In most cases it costs nothing to let the thief off, and a good deal to prosecute him. The burglar in

Heartbreak House, who makes his living by breaking into people's houses, and then blackmailing them by threatening to give himself up to the police and put them to the expense and discomfort of attending his trial and giving evidence after enduring all the worry of the police enquiries, is not a joke: he is a comic dramatization of a process that is going on every day. As to the black sheep of respectable families who blackmail them by offering them the alternative of making good their thefts and frauds, even to the extent of honoring their forged cheques, or having the family name disgraced, ask any experienced family solicitor.

Besides the chances of not being prosecuted, there are the chances of acquittal; but I doubt whether they count for much except with very attractive women. Still, it is worth mentioning that juries will snatch at the flimsiest pretexts for refusing to send people who engage their sympathy to the gallows or to penal servitude, even on evidence of murder or theft which would make short work of a repulsive person.

SOME PERSONAL EXPERIENCES

Take my own experience as probably common enough. Fifty years ago a friend of mine, hearing that a legacy had been left him, lent himself the expected sum out of his employers' cash; concealed the defalcation by falsifying his accounts; and was detected before he could repay. His employers angrily resented the fraud, and had certainly no desire to spare him. But a public exposure of the affair would have involved shock to their clients' sense of security, loss of time and consequently of money, an end to all hope of his ever making good the loss, and the unpleasantness of attendance in court at the trial. All this put any recourse to the police out of the question; and my friend obtained another post after a very brief interval during which he supported himself as a church organist. This, by the way, was a quite desirable conclusion, as he was for all ordinary practical purposes a sufficiently honest man. It would have been pure mischief to make him a criminal; but that is not the present point. He serves here as an illustration of the fact that our criminal law, far from inviting prosecution, attaches serious losses and inconveniences to it.

It may be said that whatever the losses and inconveniences may be, it is a public duty to prosecute. But is it? Is it not a Christian duty not to prosecute? A man stole £500 from me by a trick. He speculated in my character with subtlety and success; and yet he ran risks of detection which no quite sensible man would have ventured on. It was assumed that I would resort to the police. I asked why. The answer was that he should be punished to deter others from similar crimes. I naturally said, "You have been punishing people cruelly for more than a century for this kind of fraud; and the result is that I am robbed of £500. Evidently your deterrence does not deter. What it does do is to torment the swindler for years, and then throw him back upon society, a worse man in every respect, with no other employment open to him except that of fresh swindling. Besides, your elaborate arrangements to deter me from prosecuting are convincing and effective. I could earn £500 by useful work in the time it would take me to prosecute this man vindictively and worse than uselessly. So I wish him joy of his booty, and invite him to swindle me again if he can." Now this was not sentimentality. I am not a bit fonder of being swindled than other people; and if society would treat swindlers properly I should denounce them without the slightest remorse, and not grudge a reasonable expenditure of time and energy in the business. But to throw good money after bad in setting to work a wicked and mischievous routine of evil would be to stamp myself as a worse man than the swindler, who earned the money more energetically, and appropriated it no more unjustly, if less legally, than I earn and appropriate my dividends.

I must however warn our thieves that I can promise them no immunity from police pursuit if they rob me. Some time after the operation just recorded, an uninvited guest came to a luncheon party in my house. He (or she) got away with an overcoat and a pocketful of my wife's best table silver. But instead of selecting my overcoat, he took the best overcoat, which was that of one of my guests. My guest was insured against theft; the insurance company had to buy him a new overcoat; and the matter thus passed out of my hands into those of the police. But the result, as far as the thief was concerned, was the same. He was not captured; and he had the social satisfaction of providing employment for others in converting into a strongly fortified obstacle the flimsy gate through which he had effected an entrance, thereby giving my flat the appearance of a private madhouse.

On another occasion a drunken woman obtained admission by presenting an authentic letter from a soft-hearted member of the House of Lords. I had no guests at the moment; and as she, too, wanted an overcoat, she took mine, and actually interviewed me with it most perfunctorily concealed under her jacket. When I called her attention to it she handed it back to me effusively; begged me to shake hands with her; and went her way.

Now these things occur by the dozen every day, in spite of the severity with which they are punished when the thief is dealt with by the police. I daresay all my readers, if not too young to have completed a representative experience, could add two or three similar stories. What do they go to prove? Just that detection is so uncertain that its consequences have no really effective deterrence for the potential offender, whilst the unpleasant and expensive consequences of prosecution, being absolutely certain, have a very strong deterrent effect indeed on the prosecutor. In short, all the hideous cruelty practised by us for the sake of deterrence is wasted: we are damning our souls at great expense and trouble for nothing.

JUDICIAL VENGEANCE AS AN ALTERNATIVE TO LYNCH LAW

Thus we see that of the three official objects of our prison system: vengeance, deterrence, and reformation of the criminal, only one is achieved; and that is the one which is nakedly abominable. But there is a plea for it which must be taken into account, and which brings us to the root of the matter in our own characters. It is said, and it is in a certain degree true, that if the Government does not lawfully organize and regulate popular vengeance, the populace will rise up and execute this vengeance lawlessly for itself. The standard defence of the Inquisition is that without it no heretic's life would have been safe. In Texas today the people are not satisfied with the prospect of knowing that a murderer or ravisher will be electrocuted inside a gaol if a jury can resist the defence put up by his lawyer. They tear him from the hands of the sheriff; pour lamp oil over him; and burn him alive. Now the burning of human beings is not only an expression of outraged public morality: it is also a sport for which a taste can be acquired much more easily and rapidly than a taste for coursing hares, just as a taste for drink can be acquired from brandy and cocktails more easily and rapidly than from beer or sauterne. Lynching mobs begin with negro ravishers and murderers; but they presently go on to any sort of delinquent, provided he is black. Later on, as a white man will burn as amusingly as a black one, and a white woman react to tarring and feathering as thrillingly as a negress, the color line is effaced by what professes to be a rising wave of virtuous indignation, but is in fact an epidemic of Sadism. The defenders of our penal systems take advantage of it to assure us that if they did not torment and ruin a boy guilty of sleeping in the open air, an indignant public would rise and tear that boy limb from limb.

Now the reply to such a plea, from the point of view of civilized law, cannot be too sweeping. The government which cannot restrain a mob from taking the law into its own hands is no government at all. If Landru could go to the guillotine unmolested in France, and his British prototype who drowned all his wives in their baths could be peaceably hanged in England, Texas can protect its criminals by simply bringing its civilization up to the French and British level. But indeed the besetting sin of the mob is a morbid hero worship of great criminals rather than a ferocious abhorrence of them. In any case nobody will have the effrontery to pretend that the number of criminals who excite popular feeling enough to provoke lynching is more than a negligible percentage of the whole. The theory that the problem of crime is only one of organizing, regulating, and executing the vengeance of the mob will not bear plain statement, much less discussion. It is only the retributive theory over again in its most impudent form.

THE HARD CASES THAT MAKE BAD LAW

Having now disposed of all the official theories as the trash they are, let us return to the facts, and deal with the hard ones first. Everyone who has any extensive experience of domesticated animals, human or other, knows that there are negatively bad specimens who have no consciences, and positively bad ones who are incurably ferocious. The negative ones are often very agreeable and even charming companions; but they beg, borrow, steal, defraud, and seduce almost by reflex action: they cannot resist the most trifling temptation. They are indulged and spared to the extreme limit of endurance; but in the end they have to be deprived of their liberty in some way. The positive ones enjoy no such tolerance. Unless they are physically restrained they break people's bones, knock out their eyes, rupture their organs, or kill them.

Then there are the cruel people, not necessarily unable to control their tempers, nor fraudulent, nor in any other way disqualified for ordinary social activity or liberty, possibly even with conspicuous virtues. But, by a horrible involution, they lust after the spectacle of suffering, mental and physical, as normal men lust after love. Torture is to them a pleasure except when it is inflicted on themselves. In scores of ways, from the habitual utterance of wounding speeches, and the contriving of sly injuries and humuliations for which they cannot be brought to book legally, to thrashing their wives and children or, as bachelors, paying prostitutes of the hardier sort to submit to floggings, they seek the satisfaction of their desire wherever and however they can.

POSSIBILITIES OF THERAPEUTIC TREATMENT

Now in the present state of our knowledge it is folly to talk of reforming these people. By this I do not mean that even now they are all quite incurable. The cases of no conscience are sometimes, like Parsifal's when he shot the swan, cases of unawakened conscience. Violent and quarrelsome people are often only energetic people who are underworked: I have known a man cured of wife-beating by setting him to beat the drum in a village band; and the quarrels that make country life so very unarcadian are picked mostly because the quarrelers have not enough friction in their lives to keep them goodhumored.

Psycho-analysis, too, which is not all quackery and pornography, might conceivably cure a case of Sadism as it might cure any of the phobias. And psycho-analysis is a mere fancy compared to the knowledge we now pretend to concerning the function of our glands and their effect on our character and conduct. In the nineteenth century this knowledge was pursued barbarously by crude vivisectors whose notion of finding out what a gland was for was to cut it violently out and see what would happen to the victim, meanwhile trying to bribe the public to tolerate such horrors by promising to make old debauchees young again. This was rightly felt to be a villainous business; besides, who could suppose that the men who did these things would hesitate to lie about the results when there was plenty of money to be made by representing them as cures for dreaded diseases? But today we are not asked to infer that because something has happened to a violently mutilated dog it must happen also to an unmutilated human being. We can now make authentic pictures of internal organs by means of rays to which flesh is transparent. This makes it possible to take a criminal and say authoritatively that he is a case, not of original sin, but of an inefficient, or excessively efficient, thyroid gland, or pituitary gland, or adrenal gland, as the case may be. This of course does not help the police in dealing with a criminal: they must apprehend and bring him to trial all the same. But if the prison doctor were able to say "Put some iodine in this man's skilly, and his character will change," then the notion of punishing instead of curing him would become ridiculous. Of course the matter is not so simple as that; and all this endocrinism, as it is called, may turn out to be only the latest addition to our already very extensive collection of pseudo-scientific mares' nests; still, we cannot ignore the fact that a considerable case is being made out by eminent physiologists for at least a conjecture that many cases which are now incurable may be disposed of in the not very remote future by inducing the patient to produce more thyroxin or pituitrin or adrenalin or what not, or even administering them to him as thyroxin is at present administered in cases of myxœdema. Yet the reports of the work of our prison medical officers suggest that hardly any of them has ever heard of these discoveries, or regards a convict as anything more interesting scientifically than a malingering rascal.

THE INCORRIGIBLE VILLAINS

It will be seen that I am prepared to go to lengths which still seem fantastic as to the possibility of changing a criminal into an honest man. And I have more faith than most prison chaplains seem to have in the possibilities of religious conversion. But I cannot add too emphatically that the people who imagine that all criminals can be reformed by setting chaplains to preach at them, by giving them pious books and tracts to read, by separating them from their companions in crime and locking them up in solitude to reflect on their sins and repent, are far worse enemies both to the criminal and to Society than those who face the fact that these are merely additional cruelties which make their victims worse, or even than those who frankly use them as a means of "giving them hell." But when this is recognized, and the bigoted reformers with their sermons, their tracts, their horrors of separation, silence, and solitude to avoid contamination, are bundled out of our prisons as nuisances, the problem remains, how are you to deal with your incorrigibles? Here you have a man who supports himself by gaining the confidence and affection of lonely women; seducing them; spending all their money; and then burning them in a stove or drowning them in a bath. He is quite an attractive fellow, with a genuine taste for women and no taste at all for murder, which is only his way of getting rid of them when their money is spent and they are in the way of the next woman. There is no more malice or Sadism about the final operation than there is about tearing up a letter when it is done with, and throwing it into the waste paper basket. You electrocute him or hang him or chop his head off. But presently you have to deal with a man who lives in exactly the same way, but has not executive force or courage enough to commit murder. He only abandons his victims and turns up in a fresh place with a fresh name. He generally marries them, as it is easier to seduce them so.

Alongside him you have a married couple united by a passion for cruelty. They amuse themselves by tying their children to the bedstead; thrashing them with straps; and branding them with red-hot pokers. You also have to deal with a man who on the slightest irritation flings his wife under a dray, or smashes a lighted kerosene lamp into her face. He has been in prison again and again for outbursts of this kind; and always, within a week of his release, or within a few hours of it, he has done it again.

Now you cannot get rid of these nuisances and monsters by simply cataloguing them as subthyroidics and superadrenals or the like. At present you torment them for a fixed period, at the end of which they are set free to resume their operations with a savage grudge against the community which has tormented them. That is stupid. Nothing is gained by punishing people who cannot help themselves, and on whom deterrence is thrown away. Releasing them is like releasing the tigers from the Zoo to find their next meal in the nearest children's playing ground.

THE LETHAL CHAMBER

The most obvious course is to kill them. Some of the popular objections to this may be considered for a moment. Death, it is said, is irrevocable; and after all, they may turn out to be innocent. But really you cannot handle criminals on the assumption that they may be innocent. You are not supposed to handle them at all until you have convinced yourself by an elaborate trial that they are guilty. Besides, imprisonment is as irrevocable as hanging. Each is a method of taking a criminal's life; and when he prefers hanging or suicide to imprisonment for life, as he sometimes does, he says, in effect, that he had rather you took his life all at once painlessly, than minute by minute in long-drawn-out torture. You can give a prisoner a pardon; but you cannot give him back a moment of his imprisonment. He may accept a reprieve willingly in the hope of a pardon or an escape or a revolution or an earthquake or what not; but as you do not mean him to evade his sentence in any way whatever, it is not for you to take such clutchings at straws into account.

Another argument against the death penalty for anything short of murder is the practical one of the policeman and the householder, who plead that if you hang burglars they will shoot to avoid capture on the ground that they may as well be hanged for a sheep as for a lamb. But this can be disposed of by pointing out, first, that even under existing circumstances the burglar occasionally shoots, and, second, that acquittals, recommendations to mercy, verdicts of manslaughter, successful pleas of insanity and so forth, already make the death penalty so uncertain that even red-handed murderers shoot no oftener than burglars—less often, in fact. This uncertainty would be actually increased if the death sentence were, as it should be, made applicable to other criminals than those convicted of wilful murder, and no longer made compulsory in any case.

THE SACREDNESS OF HUMAN LIFE FROM THE WARDER'S SIDE

Then comes the plea for the sacredness of human life. The State should not set the example of killing, or of clubbing a rioter with a policeman's baton, or of dropping bombs on a sleeping city, or of doing many things that States nevertheless have to do. But let us take the plea on its own ground, which is, fundamentally, that life is the most precious of all things, and its waste the worst of crimes. We have already seen that imprisonment does not spare the life of the criminal: it takes it and wastes it in the most cruel way. But there are others to be considered beside the criminal and the citizens who fear him so much that they cannot sleep in peace unless he is locked up. There are the people who have to lock him up, and fetch him his food, and watch him. Why are their lives to be wasted? Warders, and especially wardresses, are almost as much tied to the prison by their occupation, and by their pensions, which they dare not forfeit by seeking other employment, as the criminals are. If I had to choose between a spell under preventive detention among hardened criminals in Camp Hill and one as warder in an ordinary prison, I think I should vote for Camp Hill. Warders suffers in body and mind from their employment; and if it be true, as our examination seems to prove, that they are doing no good to society, but very active harm, their lives are wasted more completely than those of the criminals; for most criminals are discharged after a few weeks or months; but the warder never escapes until he is superannuated, by which time he is an older gaolbird than any Lifer in the cells.

THE PRICE OF LIFE IN COMMUNITIES

How then does the case stand with your incurable pathological case of crime? If you treat the life of the criminal as sacred, you find yourself not only taking his life but sacrificing the lives of innocent men and women to keep him locked up. There is no sort of sense or humanity in such a course. The moment we face it frankly we are driven to the conclusion that the community has a right to put a price on the right to live in it. That price must be sufficient self-control to live without wasting and destroying the lives of others, whether by direct attack like a tiger, parasitic exploitation like a leech, or having to be held in a leash with another person at the end of it. Persons lacking such self-control have been thrust out into the sage-brush to wander there until they die of thirst, a cruel and cowardly way of killing them. The dread of clean and wilful killing often leads to evasions of the commandment "Thou shalt not kill" which are far more cruel than its frank violation. It has never been possible to obey it unreservedly, either with men or with animals; and the attempts to keep the letter of it have led to burying vestal virgins and nuns alive, crushing men to death in the press-yard, handing heretics over to the secular arm, and the like, instead of killing them humanely and without any evasion of the heavy responsibility involved. It was a horrible thing to build a vestal virgin into a wall with food and water enough for a day; but to build her into a prison for years as we do, with just enough loathsome food to prevent her from dying, is more than horrible: it is diabolical. If no better alternatives to death can be found than these, then who will not vote for death? If people are fit to live, let them live under decent human conditions. If they are not fit to live, kill them in a decent human way. Is it any wonder that some of us are driven to prescribe the lethal chamber as the solution for the hard cases which are at present made the excuse for dragging all the other cases down to their level, and the only solution that will create a sense of full social responsibility in modern populations?

THE SIXTH COMMANDMENT

The slaughtering of incorrigibly dangerous persons, as distinguished from the punitive execution of murderers who have violated the commandment not to kill, cannot be established summarily by these practical considerations. In spite of their cogency we have not only individuals who are resolutely and uncompromisingly opposed to slaying under any provocation whatever, we have nations who have abolished the death penalty, and regard our grim retention of it as barbarous. Wider than any nation we have the Roman Catholic Church, which insists literally on absolute obedience to the commandment, and condemns as murder even the killing of an unborn child to save the mother's life. In practice this obligation has been evaded so grossly—by the Inquisition, for example, which refused to slay the heretic, but handed him over to the secular arm with a formal recommendation to mercy, knowing that the secular arm would immediately burn him—that the case of the Church might be cited to illustrate the uselessness of barring the death penalty. But it also illustrates the persistence and antiquity of a point of conscience which still defies the argument from expediency. That point of conscience may be called a superstition because it is as old as the story of Cain and Abel, and because it is difficult to find any rational basis for it. But there is something to be said for it all the same.

Killing is a dangerously cheap way out of a difficulty. "Stone dead hath no fellow" was a handy formula for Cromwell's troops in dealing with the Irish; still, that precedent is not very reassuring. All the social problems of all the countries can be got rid of by extirpating the inhabitants; but to get rid of a problem is not to solve it. Even perfectly rational solutions of our problems must be humane as well if they are to be accepted by good men: otherwise the logic of the inquisitor, the dynamiter, and the vivisectionist would rule the world for ever as it unfortunately does to far too great an extent already. It may also be argued that if society were to forgo its power of slaying, and also its practice of punishment, it would have a stronger incentive to find out how to correct the apparently incorrigible. Although whenever it has renounced its power to slay sane criminals it has substituted a horribly rigorous and indeed virtually lethal imprisonment, this does not apply to homicidal lunatics, the comparatively lenient treatment of whom could obviously be extended to sane murderers. The Oxford Dictionary owes several of its pages to a homicide who was detained at Broadmoor (the English Asylum for Criminal Lunatics) during the pleasure of the Crown. As to the cases which, when not disposed of by the lethal method, involve caging men as tigers are caged, can they not be dealt with by the padded room? Granted that it is questionable whether the public conscience which tolerates such caging is really more sensitive or thoughtful than that which demands the lethal solution, and that at the present time executions, and even floggings, do not harden the authorities and lower the standard of humanity all through our penal system as much as continuing penalties do, yet the reluctance to kill persists. The moment it is pointed out that if we kill incurable criminals we may as well also kill incurable troublesome invalids, people realize with a shock that the urge of horror, hatred, and vengeance is needed to nerve them—or unnerve them—to slay. When I force humane people to face their political powers of life and death apart from punishment as I am doing now, I produce a terrified impression that I want to hang everybody. In vain I protest that I am dealing with a very small class of human monsters, and that as far as crime is concerned our indiscriminate hanging of wilful murderers and traitors slays more in one year than dispassionate lethal treatment would be likely to slay in ten. I am asked at once who is to be trusted with the appalling responsibility of deciding whether a man is to live or die, and what government could be trusted not to kill its enemies under the pretence that they are enemies of society.

GOVERNMENTS MUST PRESUME OR ABDICATE

The reply is obvious. Such responsibilities must be taken, whether we are fit for them or not, if civilized society is to be organized. No unofficial person denies that they are abused: the whole effect of this essay is to shew that they are horribly abused. I can say for my own part as a vehement critic and opponent of all the governments of which I have had any experience that I am the last person to forget that governments use the criminal law to suppress and exterminate their opponents whenever the opposition becomes really acute, and that the more virtuous the revolutionist and the more vicious the government, the more likely it is to kill him, and to do so under pretence of his being one of the dangerous persons for whom the lethal treatment would be reserved. It has been pointed out again and again that it is in the very nature of power to corrupt those to whom it is entrusted, and that to God alone belongs the awful prerogative of dismissing the soul from the body. Tolstoy has exhausted the persuasions of literary art in exhorting us that we resist not evil; and men have suffered abominable persecutions sooner than accept military service with its chief commandment, Thou shalt kill.

All this leaves the problem just where it was. The irresponsible humanitarian citizen may indulge his pity and sympathy to his heart's content, knowing that whenever a criminal passes to his doom there, but for the grace of God, goes he; but those who have to govern find that they must either abdicate, and that promptly, or else take on themselves as best they can many of the attributes of God. They must decide what is good and what evil; they must force men to do certain things and refrain from doing certain other things whether individual consciences approve or not; they must resist evil resolutely and continually, possibly and preferably without malice or revenge, but certainly with the effect of disarming it, preventing it, stamping it out, and creating public opinion against it. In short, they must do all sorts of things which they are manifestly not ideally fit to do, and, let us hope, do with becoming misgiving, but which must be done, all the same, well or ill, somehow and by somebody. If I were to ignore this, everyone who has had any experience of government would throw these pages aside as those of an inexperienced sentimentalist or an Impossibilist Anarchist.

Nevertheless, certain lines have to be drawn limiting the activities of governments, and allowing the individual to be a law unto himself. For instance, we are obliged (if we are wise) to tolerate sedition and blasphemy to a considerable extent because sedition and blasphemy are nothing more than the advocacy of changes in the established forms of government, morals, and religion; and without such changes there can be no social evolution. But as governments are not always wise, it is difficult enough to secure this intellectual anarchy, or as we call it, freedom of speech and conscience; and anyone who proposed to extend it to such actions as are contemplated by the advocates of lethal treatment would be dismissed as insane. No country at peace will tolerate murder, whether it is done on principle or in sin. What is more, no country at war will tolerate a refusal to murder the enemy. Thus, whether the powers of the country are being exercised for good or evil, they never remain in abeyance; and whoever proposes to set to those powers the limit of an absolute obedience to the commandment "Thou shalt not kill," must do so quite arbitrarily. He cannot give any reason that I can discover for saying that it is wickeder to break a man's neck than to cage him for life: he can only say that his instinct places an overwhelming ban on the one and not on the other; and he must depend on the existence of a similar instinct in the community for his success in having legal slaying ruled out.

THE RUTHLESSNESS OF THE PURE HEART

In this he will have little difficulty as long as the slaying is an act of revenge and expiation, as it is at present: that is why capital punishment has been abolished in some countries, and why its abolition is agitated for in the countries which still practise it. But if these sinful elements be discarded, and the slaying is made a matter of pure expediency, the criminal being pitied as sincerely as a mad dog is pitied, the most ardent present advocate of the abolition of capital punishment may not only consent to the slaying as he does in the case of the mad dog, but even demand it to put an end to an unendurable danger and horror. Malice and fear are narrow things, and carry with them a thousand inhibitions and terrors and scruples. A heart and brain purified of them gain an enormous freedom; and this freedom is shewn not only in the many civilized activities that are tabooed in the savage tribe, but also in the ruthlessness with which the civilized man destroys things that the savage prays to and propitiates. The attempt to reform an incurably dangerous criminal may come to be classed with the attempt to propitiate a sacred rattlesnake. The higher civilization does not make still greater sacrifices to the snake: it kills it.

I am driven to conclude, that though, if voluntary custodians can be found for dangerous incorrigibles, as they doubtless can by attaching compensating advantages to their employment, it is quite possible to proceed with slaying absolutely barred, there is not enough likelihood of this renunciation by the State of the powers of life and death to justify me in leaving lethal treatment out of the question. In any case it would be impossible to obtain any clear thinking on the question unless its possibilities were frankly faced and to some extent explored. I have faced them frankly and explored them as far as seems necessary; and at that I must leave it. Nothing that I have to say about the other sorts of criminals will be in the least invalidated if it should be decided that killing is to be ruled out. I think it quite likely that it may be ruled out on sentimental grounds. By the time we have reached solid ground the shock of reintroducing it (though this has been effected and even clamored for in some countries) may be too great to be faced under normal conditions. Also, as far as what we call crime is concerned, the matter is not one of the first importance. I should be surprised if, even in so large a population as ours, it would ever be thought necessary to extirpate one criminal as utterly unmanageable every year; and this means, of course, that if we decide to cage such people, the cage need not be a very large one.

I am not myself writing as an advocate one way or the other. I have to deal with European and American civilization, which, having no longer than a century ago executed people for offences now punished by a few months or even weeks of imprisonment, has advanced to a point at which less than half a dozen crimes are punishable by death: murder, piracy, rape, arson, and (in Scotland) vitriol throwing. The opponents of capital punishment usually believe, naturally enough, that the effect of abandoning the notion of punishment altogether as sinful (which it is) will sweep away the scaffold from these crimes also, and thus make an end of the death penalty. No doubt it will; but I foresee that it will reintroduce the idea of killing dangerous people simply because they are dangerous, without the least desire to punish them, and without specific reference to the actions which have called attention to their dangerousness. That extremity may be met with an absolute veto, or it may not. I cannot foresee which side I should take: a wise man does not ford a stream till he gets to it. But I am so sure that the situation will arise, that I have to deal with it here as impersonally as may be, without committing myself or anyone else one way or the other.

THE SOFT CASES THAT WE TURN INTO HARD ONES

Now let us look at the other end of the scale, where the soft cases are. Here we are confronted with the staggering fact that many of our prisoners have not been convicted of any offence at all. They are awaiting their trial, and are too poor and friendless to find bail; whilst others have been convicted of mere breaches of bye-laws of which they were ignorant, and which they could not have guessed by their sense of right and wrong; for many bye-laws have no ethical character whatever. For example, a boy sells a newspaper on the premises of a railway company, and thereby infringes a bye-law the object of which is to protect the commercial monopoly of the newsagents who have paid the company for the right to have a bookstall on the platform. The boy's brother jostles a passenger who is burdened with hand luggage, and says "Carry your bag, sir?" These perfectly innocent lads are sent to prison, though the warders themselves admit that a sentence of imprisonment is so ruinous to a boy's morals that they would rather see their own sons dead than in prison.

But let us take the guilty. The great majority of them have been convicted of petty frauds compared to which the common practices of the commercial world are serious crimes. Herbert Spencer's essays on the laxity of the morals of trade have called no trader successfully to repentance. It is not too much to say that any contractor in Europe or America who does not secure business by tenders and estimates and specifications for work and materials which he has not the smallest intention of doing or putting in, and who does not resort to bribery to have the work and materials he actually does do and put in passed by anybody whose duty it is to check them, is an exceptional man. The usage is so much a matter of course, and competition has made it so compulsory, that conscience is awakened only when the fraud is carried to some unusual length. I can remember two cases which illustrate what I mean very well. A builder of high commercial standing contracted to put up a public building. When the work began he found that the clerk of the works, whose business it was to check the work on behalf of the purchaser, lived opposite the building site. The contractor immediately protested that this was not part of the bargain, and that his estimate had been obtained on false pretences. The other is the case of the omnibus conductors of London when the alarum punch was invented and introduced. They immediately struck for higher wages, and got them, frankly on the ground that the punch had cut off the percentage they had been accustomed to add to their wages by peculation, and that it should be made up to them.

Both these cases prove that dishonesty does not pay when it becomes general. The contractor might just as well estimate for the work he really does and the material he actually uses; for, after all, since his object is to tempt the purchaser by keeping prices down, he has to give him the benefit of the fraud. If the purchaser finds him out and says, for example, "You estimated for galvanized pipes; and you have put in plain ones," the contractor can reply, "If I had put in galvanized pipes I should have had to charge you more." In the same way, the bus conductors might just as well have struck for an increase of wage as stolen it: the event proved they could have got it. But they thought they could secure employment more easily by asking for a low wage and making it up to their needs surreptitiously. It is one of the grievances of clerks in many businesses that they have to connive at dishonest practices as part of the regular routine of the office; but neither they nor their employers are any the richer, because business always finally settles down to the facts, and is conducted in terms not of the pretence but of the reality.

MOST PRISONERS NO WORSE THAN OURSELVES

We may take it, then, that the thief who is in prison is not necessarily more dishonest than his fellows at large, but mostly only one who, through ignorance or stupidity, steals in a way that is not customary. He snatches a loaf from the baker's counter and is promptly run into gaol. Another man snatches bread from the tables of hundreds of widows and orphans and simple credulous souls who do not know the ways of company promoters; and, as likely as not, he is run into Parliament. You may say that the remedy for this is not to spare the lesser offender but to punish the greater; but there you miss my present point, which is, that as the great majority of prisoners are not a bit more dishonest naturally than thousands of people who are not only at liberty, but highly pampered, it is no use telling me that society will fall into anarchic dissolution if these unlucky prisoners are treated with common humanity. On the contrary, when we see the outrageous extent to which the most shamelessly selfish rogues and rascals can be granted not only impunity but encouragement and magnificent remuneration, we are tempted to ask ourselves have we any right to restrain anyone at all from doing his worst to us. The first prison I ever saw had inscribed on it CEASE TO DO EVIL: LEARN TO DO WELL;

but as the inscription was on the outside, the prisoners could not read it. It should have been addressed to the self-righteous free spectator in the street, and should have run ALL HAVE SINNED, AND FALLEN SHORT OF THE GLORY OF GOD.

We must get out of the habit of painting human character in soot and whitewash. It is not true that men can be divided into absolutely honest persons and absolutely dishonest ones. Our honesty varies with the strain put on it: this is proved by the fact that every additional penny of income tax brings in less than the penny preceding. The purchaser of a horse or motor-car has to beware much more carefully than the purchaser of an article worth five shillings. If you take Landru at one extreme, and at the other the prisoner whose crime is sleeping out: that is to say, whose crime is no crime at all, you can place every sane human being, from the monarch to the tramp, somewhere on the scale between them. Not one of them has a blank page in the books of the Recording Angel. From the people who tell white lies about their ages, social positions, and incomes, to those who grind the faces of the poor, or marry whilst suffering from contagious disease, or buy valuable properties from inexperienced owners for a tenth of their value, or sell worthless shares for the whole of a widow's savings, or obtain vast sums on false pretences held forth by lying advertisements, to say nothing of bullying and beating in their homes, and drinking and debauching in their bachelorhood, you could at any moment find dozens of people who have never been imprisoned and never will be, and are yet worse citizens than any but the very worst of our convicts. Much of the difference between the bond and the free is a difference in circumstances only: if a man is not hungry, and his children are ailing only because they are too well fed, nobody can tell whether he would steal a loaf if his children were crying for bread and he himself had not tasted a mouthful for twenty-four hours. Therefore, if you are in an attitude of moral superiority to our convicts: if you are one of the Serve Them Right and Give Them Hell brigade, you may justly be invited, in your own vernacular, either to Come Off It, or else Go Inside and take the measure you are meting out to others no worse than yourself.

GOOD SOLDIERS OFTEN BAD CITIZENS, AND BAD CITIZENS GOOD PRISONERS

The distinction between the people the criminal law need deal with and those it may safely leave at large is not a distinction between depravity and good nature: it is a distinction between people who cannot, as they themselves put it, go straight except in leading strings, and those who can. Incurable criminals make well-behaved soldiers and prisoners. The war of 1914–18 almost emptied our prisons of able-bodied men; and in the leading strings of military discipline these men ceased to be criminals. Some soldiers who were discharged with not only first-rate certificates of their good conduct as soldiers, but with a Victoria Cross "For Valor," were no sooner cast adrift into ordinary civil life than they were presently found in the dock pleading their military services and good character as soldiers in mitigation of sentences of imprisonment for frauds and thefts of the meanest sort. When we consider how completely a soldier is enslaved by military discipline, and how abhorrent military service consequently is to civically capable people, we cannot doubt, even if there were no first-hand testimony on the subject, that many men enlist voluntarily, not because they want to lead a drunken and dissolute life (the reason given by the Iron Duke), or because they are under any of the romantic illusions on which the recruiting sergeant is supposed to practise, but because they know themselves to be unfit for full moral responsibility, and conclude that they had better have their lives ordered for them than face the effort (intolerably difficult for them) of ordering it themselves.

This effort is not made easier by our civilization. A man who treated his children as every laborer treated them as a matter of course a hundred years ago would now be imprisoned for neglecting them and keeping them away from school. The statute book is crammed with offences unknown to our grandfathers and unintelligible to uneducated men; and the list needs startling extension; for, as Mr H. G. Wells has pointed out, its fundamental items date from the Mosaic period, when modern Capitalism, which involves a new morality, was unknown. In more obvious matters we notice how the standard of dress, manners, and lodging which qualifies a man socially for employment as a factory hand or mechanic has risen since the days when no person of any refinement could travel, as everybody now travels, third-class.

REMEDIES IN THE ROUGH

We may now begin to arrange our problem comprehensively. The people who have to be dealt with specially by the Government because for one reason or another they cannot deal satisfactorily with themselves may be roughly divided into three sections. First, the small number of dangerous or incorrigibly mischievous human animals. With them should be associated all hopeless defectives, from the idiot children who lie like stranded jellyfish on asylum floors, and have to be artificially fed, to the worst homicidal maniacs. Second, a body of people who cannot provide for or order their lives for themselves, but who, under discipline and tutelage, with their board and lodging and clothing provided for them, as in the case of soldiers, are normally happy, well-behaved, useful citizens. (There would be several degrees of tutelage through which they might be promoted if they are fit and willing.) Third, all normal persons who have trespassed in some way during one of those lapses of self-discipline which are as common as colds, and who have been unlucky enough to fall into the hands of the police in consequence. These last should never be imprisoned. They should be required to compensate the State for the injury done to the body politic by their misdeeds, and, when possible, to compensate the victims, as well as pay the costs of bringing them to justice. Until they have done this they cannot complain if they find themselves distrained upon; harassed by frequent compulsory appearances in court to excuse themselves; and threatened with consignment to the second class as defectives. It is quite easy to make carelessness and selfishness or petty violence and dishonesty unremunerative and disagreeable, without resorting to imprisonment. In the cases where the offender has fallen into bad habits and bad company, the stupidest course to take is to force him into the worst of all habits and the worst of all company: that is, prison habits and prison company. The proper remedies are good habits and good company. If these are not available, then the offender must be put into the second class, and kept straight under tutelage until he is fit for freedom.

DIFFICULTY OF THE UNDISCIPLINED

The difficulty lies, it will be seen, in devising a means of dealing with the second class. The first is easy: too easy, in fact. You kill or you cage: that is all. In the third class, summoning and fining and admonishing are easy and not mischievous: you may worry a man considerably by badgering him about his conduct and dunning him for money in a police court occasionally; but you do not permanently disable him morally and physically thereby. It is the offender of the second class, too good to be killed or caged, and not good enough for normal liberty, whose treatment bothers us.

THE INDETERMINATE SENTENCE

Any proposal to place men under compulsory tutelage immediately raises the vexed question of what is called "the indeterminate sentence." The British Parliament has never been prevailed on to create a possibility of a criminal being "detained preventively" for life: it has set a limit of ten years to that condition. This is inevitable as long as the tutelage is primarily not a tutelage but a punishment. In England there is a law under which a drunkard, politely called an inebriate, can voluntarily sentence himself to a term of detention for the sake of being restrained from yielding to a temptation which he is unable to resist when left to himself. Under existing circumstances nobody is likely to do that twice, or even once if he has any knowledge of how the unfortunate inebriates are treated. The only system of detention available is the prison system; and the only sort of prisoner the officials have any practice in dealing with is the criminal. Every detained person is therefore put through the dismal routine of punishment in the first place, deterrence in the second place, and reform in the very remote third place. The inebriate volunteer prisoner very soon finds that he is being treated as a criminal, and tries in vain to revoke his renunciation of his liberty.

Otherwise, say the authorities very truly, they would be overwhelmed with volunteers. This reminds us of the Westminster Abbey verger who charged a French gentleman with brawling in church. The magistrate, inquiring what, exactly, the foreigner had done, was told that he had knelt in prayer. "But," said the magistrate, "is not that what a church is for?" The verger was scandalized. "If we allowed that," he said, "we should have people praying all over the place." The Prison Commissioners know that if prisons were made reasonably happy places, and thrown open to volunteers like the army, they might speedily be overcrowded. And this, with its implied threat of an enormous increase of taxation, seems a conclusive objection.

THE ECONOMY ASPECT

But if its effect would be to convert a large mass of more or less dishonest, unproductive or half productive, unsatisfactory, feckless, nervous, anxious, wretched people into good citizens, it is absurd to object to it as costly. It would be unbearably costly, of course, if the life and labor of its subjects were as stupidly wasted as they are in our prisons; but any scheme into which the conditions of our present system are read will stand condemned at once. Whether the labor of the subject be organized by the State, as in Government dockyards, post offices, municipal industries and services and so forth, or by private employers obtaining labor service from the authorities, organized and used productively it must be; and anyone who maintains that such organization and production costs the nation more than wasting the labor power of able-bodied men and women either by imprisonment or by throwing criminals on the streets to prey on society and on themselves, is maintaining a monstrous capitalistic paradox. Obviously it will not cost the nation anything at all: it will enrich it and protect it. The real commercial objection to it is that it would reduce the supply of sweatable labor available for unscrupulous private employers. But so much the better if it does. Sweating may make profits for private persons here and there; but their neighbors have to pay through the nose for these profits in poor rates, police rates, public health rates (mostly disease rates), and all the rest of the gigantic expenditure, all pure waste and mischief, which falls on the ratepayer and taxpayer in his constant struggle with the fruits of the poverty which he is nevertheless invited to maintain for the sake of making two or three of his neighbors unwholesomely and unjustly rich.

It is not altogether desirable that State tutelage should be available without limit for all who may volunteer for it. We can imagine a magistrate's court as a place in which men clamoring to be literally "taken in charge" are opposed by Crown lawyers and court officials determined to prove, if possible, that these importunate volunteers are quite well able to take care of themselves if they choose. Evidence of defective character would be sternly demanded; and if these were manufactured (as in the not uncommon case of a poor woman charging her son with theft to get him taken off her hands and sent to a reformatory) the offender would be ruthlessly consigned to my third division, consisting of offenders who are not to be taken in charge at all, but simply harried and bothered and attached and sold up until they pay the damages of their offences.

But as a matter of experience men do not seek the avowed tutelage of conditions which imply deficiency of character. Most of them resent any sort of tutelage unless they are brought up to it and therefore do not feel it as an infringement of their individuality. The army and navy are not overcrowded, though the army has always been the refuge of the sort of imbecile called a ne'er-do-well. Indeed the great obstacle to the realization of the Socialist dream of a perfectly organized and highly prosperous community, without poverty or overwork or idleness, is the intense repugnance of the average man to the degree of public regulation of his life which it would involve. This repugnance is certainly not weaker in England and America than elsewhere. Both Americans and Englishmen are born Anarchists; and, as complete Anarchism is practically impossible, they seek the minimum of public interference with their personal initiative, and overshoot the mark so excessively that it is no exaggeration to say that civilization is perishing of Anarchism. If civilization is to be saved for the first time in history it will have to be by a much greater extension of public regulation and organization than any community has hitherto been willing to submit to. When this extension takes place it will provide the discipline of public service for large masses of the population who now look after themselves very indifferently, and are only nominally free to control their own destinies; and in this way many people of the sort that now finds itself in prison will be kept straight automatically. But in any case there is no danger of a tutelary system being swamped by a rush of volunteers qualifying themselves for it by hurling stones through shop windows or the like.

All this does not mean that we must have indeterminate sentences of tutelage. The mischief of the present system is not that the criminal under preventive detention must be released at the end of ten years, but that if he relapses he is sent to penal servitude instead of being simply and sensibly returned to Camp Hill. What it does mean is that if the tutelage be made humane and profitable, the criminal, far from demanding his discharge, will rather threaten the authorities with a repetition of his crime if they turn him out of doors. The change that is needed is to add to the present power of the detaining authorities to release the prisoner at any time if they consider him fit for self-responsibility, the power of the prisoner to remain if he finds himself more comfortable and safe under tutelage, as voluntary soldiers feel themselves more comfortable in the army, or enclosed nuns in a convent, than cast on the world on his own resources.

WHITHER THE FACTS ARE DRIVING US

So much for the difficulty of the indeterminate sentence, which is quite manageable. Its discussion has led us to the discovery that in spite of the unchristian spirit of our criminal law, and the cruelty of its administration, the mere logic of facts is driving us to humane solutions. Already in England no judge or magistrate is obliged to pass any sentence whatever for a first offence except when dealing with a few extraordinary crimes which have affected our imagination so strongly that we feel bound to mark our abhorrence of them by special rigor not only to those convicted of them, but to those accused of them: for example, persons accused of high treason were formerly not allowed the help of counsel in defending themselves. And when the account of the English system of preventive detention at Camp Hill is studied in connection with the remarkable series of experiments now being made in America, it will be seen that nothing stands between us and humanity and decency but our cruelty, vindictiveness, terror, and thoughtless indifference.

CRIME AS DISEASE

It must not be imagined that any system will reach every anti-social deed that is committed. I have already shewn that most crime goes undetected, unreported, and even unforbidden; and I have suggested that if our system of dealing with crime were one with which any humane and thoughtful person could conscientiously co-operate, if we compensated injured persons for bringing criminals to justice instead of, as at present, making the process expensive and extremely disagreeable and even terrifying to them, and if we revised our penal laws by striking out of their list of criminal acts a few which ought not to be there and adding a good many which ought to be there, we might have a good many more delinquents to deal with than at present unless we concurrently improved the education and condition of the masses sufficiently to do away with the large part of law-breaking, which is merely one of the symptoms of poverty, and would disappear with it. But in any case we should diligently read Samuel Butler's Erewhon, and accustom ourselves to regard crime as pathological, and the criminal as an invalid, curable or incurable. There is, in fact, hardly an argument that can be advanced for the stern suppression of crime by penal methods that does not apply equally to the suppression of disease; and we have already an elaborate sanitary code under which persons neglecting certain precautions against disease are not only prosecuted but in some instances (sometimes quite mistaken ones, as the history of vaccination has proved) persecuted very cruelly. We actually force parents to subject their children to surgical operations, some of which are both dangerous and highly questionable. But we have so far stopped short of making it a punishable offence to be attacked by smallpox or typhus fever, though no legal assumption is more certain than that both diseases can be extinguished by sanitation more completely than crime by education. Yet there would be no greater injustice in such punishment than there is in the imprisonment of any thief; and the sanctimonious speech in which the judge in Erewhon, sentencing a man for phthisis, recapitulated the career of crime which began with an accident in childhood, and ended with pulmonary tuberculosis, was not a whit more ridiculous than the similar speeches made at every session by our own judges. Why a man who is punished for having an inefficient conscience should be privileged to have an inefficient lung is a debatable question. If one is sent to prison and the other to hospital, why make the prison so different from the hospital?

But I make the parallel here because it brings out the significance of the fact that we admit without protest that we have to put up with a good deal of illness in the world, and to treat the sufferers with special indulgence and consideration, instead of turning on them like a herd of buffaloes and goring them to death, as we do in the case of our moral invalids. We even punish people very severely for neglecting their invalids or treating them in such a way as to make them worse instead of better: that is, for doing to them exactly what we should do ourselves if instead of doing wrong in body and losing health they had gone wrong in mind and stolen a handkerchief. There are people in the world so incredibly foolish that they expect their children to be always perfectly truthful and perfectly obedient; but even these idiots do not expect their children to be perfectly well always, nor thrash them if they catch cold. In short, if crime were not punished at all, the world would not come to an end any more than it does now that disease is not punished at all. The real gist of the distinction we make is that the consequences of crime, if unpunished, are pleasant, whereas the consequences of catching a chill are its own punishment; but this will not bear examination. A bad conscience is quite as uncomfortable as a bad cold; and though there are people so hardily constituted in this respect that they can behave very selfishly without turning a hair, so are there people of such hardy physical constitution that they can abuse their bodies with impunity to an extent that would be fatal to ordinary persons. Anyhow, it is not proposed that abnormal subjects should be unrestrained.

On the other hand avoidable illnesses are just like avoidable crimes in respect of being the result of some form of indulgence, positive or negative. For all practical purposes the parallel between the physical and moral invalid holds good; only, we may have to reconsider the absolute sacredness of the physical invalid's life. I shall not here attempt to prejudge the result of that consideration; but it is clear that if we decide that this sacredness must be maintained at all costs, and that the idiot in Darenth, who lies there having food poured into it so that its heart may continue to beat and its lungs to breathe automatically (for it can do nothing voluntarily), must be preserved from death much more laboriously than Einstein, then we must hold the criminal equally fetish unless we are to keep the whole subject in its present disastrous confusion.

REFORMING OUR CONSCIENCES

The change in the public conscience which is necessary before these considerations can take effect in abolishing our villainous system of dealing with crime will never be induced by sympathy with the criminal or even disgust at the prison. The proportion of the population directly concerned is so small that to the great majority imprisonment is something so unlikely to occur—indeed, so certain statistically never to occur—that they cannot be persuaded to take any interest in the matter. As long as the question is only one of the comfort of the prisoner, nothing will be done, because as long as the principle of punishment is admitted, and the Sermon on the Mount ridiculed as an unpractical outburst of anarchism and sentimentality, the public will always be reassured by learning from the judges (none of whom, by the way, seems to know what really happens to a prisoner after he leaves the dock) that our prisons are admirable institutions, and by the romances of Prison Commissioners like Du Cane and Sir Evelyn Ruggles-Brise, who arrange prisons as children build houses with toy bricks, and finally become so pleased with their arrangements that they describe them in terms which make us wonder that they do not commit serious crimes to qualify themselves for prolonged residence in their pet paradises. I must therefore attack the punitive position at another angle by dealing with its psychological effect on the criminal.

EXPIATION AND MORAL ACCOUNTANCY

No ordinary criminal will agree with me for a moment that punishment is a mistake and a sin. His opinions on that point are precisely those of the policeman who arrests him; and if I were to preach this gospel of mine to the convicts in a prison I should be dismissed as a hopeless crank far more summarily than if I were to interview the Chief Commissioner at Scotland Yard about it.

Punishment is not a simple idea: it is a very complex one. It is not merely some injury that an innocent person inflicts on a guilty one, and that the guilty one evades by every means in his power. It is also a balancing of accounts with the soul. People who feel guilty are apt to inflict it on themselves if nobody will take the job off their hands. Confessions, though less common than they would be if the penalties were not so soul-destroying, are received without surprise. From the criminals' point of view punishment is expiation; and their bitterest complaints of injustice refer, not to their sentences, but to the dishonesty with which society, having exacted the price of the crime, still treats the criminal as a defaulter. Even so sophisticated a man of the world as Oscar Wilde claimed that by his two years' imprisonment he had settled accounts with the world and was entitled to begin again with a clean slate. But the world persisted in ostracizing him as if it had not punished him at all.

This was inevitable; but it was dishonest. If we are absurd enough to engage in a retributive trade in crime, we should at least trade fairly and give clean receipts when we are paid. If we did, we should soon find that the trade is impracticable and ridiculous; for neither party can deliver the goods. No discharge that the authorities can give can procure the ex-prisoner an eligible situation; and no atonement that a thief or murderer can make in suffering can make him any the less a thief or murderer. And nobody shirks this demonstration as much as the thief himself. Human self respect wants so desperately to have its sins washed away, however purgatorially, that we are willing to go through the most fantastic ceremonies, conjurations, and ordeals to have our scarlet souls made whiter than snow. We naturally prefer to lay our sins on scapegoats or on the Cross, if our neighbors will let us off so easily; but when they will not, then we will cleanse ourselves by suffering a penalty sooner than be worried by our consciences. This is the real foundation of the criminal law in human superstition. This is why, when we refuse to employ a discharged prisoner, he invariably pleads that what he did is paid for, and that we have no right to bring it against him after he has suffered the appointed penalty.

As we cannot admit the plea, we should consider whether we should exact the penalty. I am not arguing that the plea should be admitted: I am arguing that the bargain should never have been made. I am more merciless than the criminal law, because I would destroy the evildoer's delusion that there can be any forgiveness of sin. What is done cannot be undone; and the man who steals must remain a thief until he becomes another man, no matter what reparation or expiation he may make or suffer. A punishment system means a pardon system: the two go together inseparably. Once admit that if I do something wicked to you we are quits when you do something equally wicked to me and you are bound to admit also that the two blacks make a white. Our criminal system is an organized attempt to produce white by two blacks. Common sense should doggedly refuse to believe that evil can be abolished by duplicating it. But common sense is not so logical; and thus we get the present grotesque spectacle of a judge committing thousands of horrible crimes in order that thousands of criminals may feel that they have balanced their moral accounts.

FAMILIAR FRAUDS OF THE TRADE IN SIN

It is a game at which there is plenty of cheating. The prisoner pleads Not Guilty, and tries his best to get off, or to have as light a sentence as possible. The commercial brigand, fining himself for his plunderings by subscribing to charities, never subscribes as much as he stole. But through all the folly and absurdity of the business, and the dense mental confusion caused by the fact that it is never frankly faced and clearly stated, there shines the fact that conscience is part of the equipment of the normal man, and that it never fails in its work. It is retributive because it makes him uncomfortable; it is deterrent because detection and retribution are absolutely certain; and it is reformative because reformation is the only way of escape. That is to say, it does to perfection by divine methods what the Prison Commissioners are trying to do by diabolical methods without hope or even possibility of success.

REVENGE THE DESTROYER OF CONSCIENCE

The effect of revenge, or retribution from without, is to destroy the conscience of the aggressor instantly. If I stand on the corn of a man in the street, and he winces or cries out, I am all remorse, and overwhelm him with heartfelt apologies. But if he sets about me with his fists, the first blow he lands changes my mind completely; and I bend all my energies on doing intentionally to his eyes and nose and jaw what I did unintentionally to his toes. Vengeance is mine, saith the Lord; and that means that it is not the Lord Chief Justice's. A violent punishing, such as a flogging, carries no sense of expiation with it: whilst its effect lasts, which is fortunately not very long, its victim is in a savage fury in which he would burn down the gaol and roast the warders and the governor and the justices alive in it with intense satisfaction if he could.

Imprisonment, on the other hand, gives the conscience a false satisfaction. The criminal feels that he is working off his crime, though he is doing it involuntarily, and would escape at any moment if he could. He preserves his sense of solvency without ceasing to be a thief, as a gambler preserves it by paying his losses without ceasing to be a gambler.

THE SENTIMENTALITY OF REVENGE

There is a mysterious psychological limit to punishment. We somehow dare not kill a hopelessly diseased or dangerous man by way of punishment for any offence short of murder, though we chloroform a hopelessly diseased or dangerous dog by way of kindness without the least misgiving. Until we have purged our souls of malice, which is pure sentiment, we cannot get rid of sentimentality; and the sentimentality which makes us abominably cruel in one direction makes us foolishly and superstitiously afraid to act sternly in others. Homicidal lunatics say in their asylums "They cannot hang *us*." I could give here, but refrain for obvious reasons, simple instructions by carrying out which any person can commit a murder with the certainty, if detected, of being sent to an asylum instead of to the gallows. They ought to have just the contrary effect; for the case of the homicidal lunatic is the clearest case for judicial killing that exists. It is the killing of the sane murderer that requires consideration: it should never be a matter of course, because there are murders which raise no convincing presumption that those who commit them are exceptionally likely to commit another. But about a chronically homicidal lunatic there should be no hesitation whatever as long as we practise judicial killing at all; and there would not be if we simply considered without malice the question of his fitness to live in society. We spare him because the gallows is a punishment, and we feel that we have no right to punish a lunatic. When we realize that we have no right to punish anybody, the problem of disposing of impossible people will put itself on its proper footing. We shall drop our moral airs; but unless we rule killing out absolutely, persons who give more trouble than they are worth will run the risk of being apologetically, sympathetically, painlessly, but effectually returned to the dust from which they sprung.

MAN IN SOCIETY MUST JUSTIFY HIS EXISTENCE

This would at least create a sense of moral responsibility in our citizens. We are all too apt to take our lives as a matter of course. In a civilized community life is not a matter of course: it can be maintained only on complicated artificial conditions; and whoever enlarges his life by violating these conditions enlarges it at the expense of the lives of others. The extent to which we tolerate such vital embezzlement at present is quite outrageous: we have whole classes of persons who waste, squander, and luxuriate in the hard-earned income of the nation without even a pretence of social service or contribution of any kind; and instead of sternly calling on them to justify their existence or go to the scrap heap, we encourage and honor them, and indeed conduct the whole business of the country as if its object were to produce and pamper them. How can a prison chaplain appeal with any effect to the conscience of a professional criminal who knows quite well that his illegal and impecunious modes of preying on society are no worse morally, and enormously less mischievous materially, then the self-legalized plutocratic modes practised by the chaplain's most honored friends with the chaplain's full approval? The moment we cease asking whether men are good or bad, and ascertain simply whether they are pulling their weight in the social boat, our persistent evildoers may have a very unpleasant surprise. Far from having an easy time under a Government of soft-hearted and soft-headed sentimentalists, cooing that "to understand everything is to pardon everything," they may find themselves disciplined to an extent at present undreamed of by the average man-about-town.

CIVILIZED MAN IS NOT BORN FREE

And here it will occur to some of my readers that a book about imprisonment should be also a book about freedom. Rousseau said that Man is born free. Rousseau was wrong. No government of a civilized State can possibly regard its citizens as born free. On the contrary, it must regard them as born in debt, and as necessarily incurring fresh debt every day they live; and its most pressing duty is to hold them to that debt and see that they pay it. Not until it is paid can any freedom begin for the individual. When he cannot walk a hundred yards without using such a very expensive manufactured article as a street, care must be taken that he produces his share of its cost. When he has paid scot and lot his leisure begins, and with it his liberty. He can then say boldly, "Having given unto Cæsar the things that are Cæsar's I shall now, under no tutelage or compulsion except that of my conscience, give to God the things that are God's." That is the only possible basis for civil liberty; and we are unable to attain it because our governments corruptly shirk the duties of Cæsar; usurp the attributes of God; and make an unholy mess of which this horrible prison system of ours is only one symptom.

OUR NATURE NOT SO BAD AS OUR PRISON SYSTEM

We must, however, be on our guard against ascribing all the villainy of that system to our cruelty and selfish terrors. I have pointed out how the operation of the criminal law is made very uncertain, and therefore loses the deterrence it aims at, by the reluctance of sympathetic people to hand over offenders to the police. Vindictive and frivolous as we are, we are not downright fiends, as we should be if our modern prison system had been deliberately invented and constructed by us all in one piece. It has grown upon us, and grown evilly, having evil roots; but its worst developments have been well meant; for the road to hell is paved with good intentions, not with bad ones. The history of it is too long to be told here in detail; but a word or two of it is needed to save the reader from closing the volume in despair of human nature.

THE HISTORY OF OUR PRISONS

Imprisonment was not originally a punishment any more than chaining up a dog, cruel as that practice is, is a punishment. It was simply a method of detention. The officer responsible for the custody of an offender had to lock or chain him up somewhere to prevent him from running away, and to be able to lay his hand on him on the day of trial or execution. This was regarded as the officer's own affair: the law looked to him for the delivery of the offender, and did not concern itself as to how it was effected. This seems strange nowadays; but I can remember a case of a lunatic on a battleship, who had one man told off to act as his keeper. The lunatic was violent and troublesome, and gave his keeper plenty of severe exercise; but the rest of the crew looked on with the keenest enjoyment of the spectacle, and gave the lunatic the strictest fair play by letting his keeper fight it out with him unaided. And that is what the law did mostly in England until well into the nineteenth century. To this day there is no prison in some of the Virgin Islands. The prisoner is tied by the leg to a tree, and plays cards with the constable who guards him.

The result was that the provision of lock-ups became a private commercial speculation, undertaken and conducted for the sake of what could be made out of it by the speculator. There was no need for these places to be lock-ups: the accused could be chained up or gyved or manacled if no safe prison was available; and when lock-ups came to be provided as a matter of business, the practice of chaining was continued as a matter of tradition, and formed a very simple method of extorting money from prisoners by torture. No food was provided by the State: what the prisoner ate was charged against him as if he were in a hotel; and it often happened that when he was acquitted he was taken back to prison as security for his bill and kept there until he had paid it.

Under these circumstances the prison was only a building into which all classes and sorts of detained persons were thrown indiscriminately. The rich could buy a private room, like Mr Pickwick in the Fleet; but the general herd of poor criminals, old and young, innocent and hardened, virgin and prostitute, mad and sane, clean and verminous, diseased and whole, pigged together in indescribable promiscuity. I repeat: nobody invented this. Nobody intended it. Nobody defended it except the people who made money by it. Nobody else except the prisoners knew about it: they were as innocent as Mr Pickwick of what went on inside the prison walls. And, as usual in England, nobody bothered about it, because people with money could avoid its grossest discomforts on the negligibly rare occasions when they fell into the hands of the officers of the law. It was by the mere accident of being pricked for sheriff that John Howard learned what the inside of a gaol was like.

HOWARD'S GOOD INTENTIONS

As a result of Howard's agitation prisons are now State prisons: the State accepts full responsibility for the prisoner from the moment of his arrest. So far, so good. But in the meantime imprisonment, instead of being a means of detention, has become not only a punishment, but, for the reasons given at the outset of this essay, *the* punishment. And official shallowness, prevailing against the poet Crabbe's depth, has made it an infernal punishment. Howard saw that the prisoners in the old gaol contaminated one another; and his remedy was to give them separate cells in which they could meditate on their crimes and repent. When prisons with separate cells were built accordingly, the prison officials soon found that it saved trouble to keep the prisoners locked up in them; and the philanthropists out-Howarded Howard in their efforts to reform criminals by silence, separation, and the wearing of masks, lest they should contaminate one another by the expression of their faces. Until 1920 the convicts in Belgian prisons wore iron masks. Our own convicts wore cloth masks for some time, and would probably be wearing them still had not our solicitude for their salvation killed and driven them mad in such numbers that we were forced to admit that thorough segregation, though no doubt correct in principle (which is just where it is fatally incorrect), does not work. Frightful things in the way of solitude, separation, and silence, not for months, but for many years at a time, were done in American prisons.

The reader will find as much as he can stand in English Prisons Under Local Government, by Sidney and Beatrice Webb, and a good deal more in English Prisons Today, edited by Stephen Hobhouse and Fenner Brockway, in which the system is described from the prison cells, not by common criminals, but by educated and thoughtful men and women who, as agitators for Votes for Women or as Conscientious Objectors to military service, have been condemned to imprisonment of late years. Our horror at their disclosures must not blind us to my immediate point, which is that our prison system is a horrible accidental growth and not a deliberate human invention, and that its worst features have been produced with the intention, not of making it worse, but of making it better. Howard is not responsible: he warned us that "absolute solitude is more than human nature can bear without the hazard of destruction and despair." Elizabeth Fry saw nothing but mischief in prison silence and prison solitude. Their followers were fools: that is all.

THE SO-CALLED CRIMINAL TYPE

Perhaps the most far-reaching service done by the Brockway-Hobhouse report is the light it throws on the alleged phenomenon of a Criminal Type. The belief in this has gone through several vicissitudes. At first a criminal was supposed to be a beetle-browed, bulldog-jawed person for whom no treatment could be too bad. This suited the prison authorities, as nothing is so troublesome to them as waves of public sympathy with criminals, founded on imaginative idealizations of them. But the authorities changed their note when a scientific account of the type was put forward by Lombroso and a body of investigators calling themselves psychiatrists. These gentlemen found that criminals had asymmetrical features and other stigmata (an effective word). They contended that the criminals were the victims of these congenital peculiarities, and could not help themselves. As the obvious conclusion was that they were not morally responsible for their actions, and therefore should not be punished for them, the prison authorities saw their occupation threatened, and denied that there was any criminal type, always excepting the beetle-brows and bulldog-jaws which the criminal was assumed to have imposed on his naturally Grecian features by a life of villainy. They were able to point out that everybody has asymmetrical features, and that the alleged stigmata of the Lombrosic criminal are as characteristic of the Church, the Stock Exchange, the Bench, and the Legislature as of Portland and Dartmoor. That settled the matter for the moment. The criminal type was off.

But nobody who has ever visited a prison has any doubt that there is a prison type, and a very marked one at that. And if he is saturated with the teachings of the Natural Selectionists, according to which changes of type are the result of the slow accumulation of minute variations, and therefore cannot be visibly produced in less than, say, a million years, he will conclude, like Lombroso, that the criminal is a natural species, and therefore incorrigible.

HOW TYPES ARE MANUFACTURED

But twentieth-century observation has lately been knocking nineteenth-century science into a cocked hat by shewing that the types that were said to take a million years to produce can be produced in five. I have in my hand number seventy-four of the privately printed opuscula issued by the Society which calls itself the Set of Odd Volumes. It is entitled The Influence Which Our Surroundings Exert On Us, and is the work of Sir William Arbuthnot Lane, one of our most distinguished surgeons. In it he shews that by keeping a man at work as a deal porter, a coal trimmer, a shoemaker or what not, you can, within a period no longer than that spent in prison by typical criminals, produce a typical deal porter, coal trimmer and so on, the changes involved being visible grotesque skeletal changes for which Huxley or Owen would have demanded a whole evolutionary epoch. No Bolshevik has yet written so revolutionary a pamphlet as this little record of a recent after-dinner speech.

What it means is that the criminal type is an artificial type, manufactured in prison by the prison system. It means that the type is not one of the accidents of the system, but must be produced by imprisonment no matter how normal the victim is at the beginning, or how anxious the authorities are to keep him so. The simple truth is that the typical criminal is a normal man when he first enters a prison, and develops the type during his imprisonment.

PSYCHIATRISTS AND ENDOCRINISTS

This does not mean that no other types are to be noted in prison. By all means let the endocrinists go on dividing abnormal people, in prison and out, into hyper and sub pituitaries and thyroidics and adrenals. They need not, as the habit of the scientific world is, quarrel furiously with me for remarking that another type can be externally imposed on their pituitaries and thyroidics and adrenals impartially. The fact that a man has an excessive adrenal secretion may be a reason for trying to check it instead of punishing him. It does not alter the fact that if you keep one adrenal in penal servitude and another in the House of Lords for ten years, the one will shew the stigmata of a typical convict, and the other of a typical peer, in addition to the stigmata of adrenalism.

To realize the importance of this, we must recall the discredit into which Lombroso fell when it was pointed out that by his diagnosis everybody was more or less a criminal. I suggest that this was not quite so complete a *reductio ad absurdum* as it seemed. I have already accounted for the curious insensibility of the public to the misery they are inflicting on their prisoners by the fact that some of the most mischievous and unhappy conditions of prison life are imposed on all respectably brought-up children as a matter of course. It is arguable that what Lombroso took to be criminal stigmata were genuine prison stigmata, and that their prevalence among respectable people who have never been in gaol is due to the prison conditions to which such people are conventionally subjected for the first twenty years of their life.

THE CASE OF QUEEN VICTORIA

I take up another much discussed and most readable modern book: Queen Victoria, by Lytton Strachey. It contains some shocking pages, made bearable by the comedic power of the author, but still ghastly reading. Queen Victoria was very carefully brought up. When she was eighteen they came to her and told her that she was Queen of England. She asked whether she could really do what she liked; and when this was reluctantly admitted by her careful mother, Victoria considered what wonderful and hitherto impossible happiness she could confer on herself by her new powers. And she could think of nothing more delightful than an hour of separate solitary confinement. She had never been alone before, never been unwatched by people whose business it was to see that she behaved herself, and to rebuke her and punish her if she did anything they disapproved of. In short, she had been treated as a dangerous criminal, unfit to be trusted with any initiative or moral responsibility.

It would carry me too far to trace the effects of this monstrous bringing-up on the course of history. The book should be given to every prisoner who finds his solitary confinement every day from half-past four in the afternoon to next morning more than he can bear. He will find that there are worse things than solitude when the only company available is that of the warders and governor. And he will understand why the next thing the queen did was to turn her mother practically out of the house. She was, as he would put it, getting a bit of her own back. Let him then, if he is an intellectually curious prisoner, and has not been long enough in prison to have his intellect atrophied, make a list of the miseries that are common to the lot of our little Queen Victorias out of prison and our thieves and murderers in prison. Confinement, obedience, silence at associated work, continual supervision by hostile guardians reporting every infraction of rule for punishment, regulation of every moment of one's life from outside, compulsory exercise instead of play, systematic extirpation of initiative and responsibility, uncongenial and sometimes impossible tasks, and a normal assumption that every original and undictated action will be a wrong action. This is the lot of the well-brought-up child, whether heiress to a throne or heir to a country rector, like Samuel Butler, who was beaten by his father until he acquired and retained until his death some of the stigmata of a chained dog. The British statesman Mr Winston Churchill, a duke's grandson, tells us in his reminiscences that when he was a child of seven he was sent to an expensive school where the discipline was more ferocious than would be permitted in a Reformatory for young criminals of twice that age.

PREVALENCE OF CRIMINAL CHARACTERISTICS IN POLITE SOCIETY

Butler, a man of exceptionally strong character which reacted violently against his training, would have been what the Prison Commissioners call a bad prisoner, and therefore does not illustrate the normal social effect of the system. Even Queen Victoria, with all her characteristic prison transitions from tutelage to tyranny, and her inability to understand or tolerate any other conditions, was too energetic, uneducated, and original, not to react vigorously against her circumstances. It is when we look at modern civilization in bulk that we are forced to admit that child training (or rather taming), as we practise it, produces moral imbecility. About a dozen millions of persons, on whose education enormous sums had been spent publicly and privately, went like sheep to the slaughter in 1914–18; and the survivors are making elaborate arrangements to go again. A glance at the newspapers which cater specially for the classes which go through the respectable routine of preparatory school, public school, and university, will shew that the ideals of those classes, their points of honor, their sense of humor, their boasts, their anticipations of future exploits, are precisely those of criminals. They always are ready (Steady, boys, steady) to fight and to conquer again and again. Ned Kelly, Charles Peace, Dick Turpin and Claude Duval, the Black Prince, Harry the Fifth, Robin Hood, Paul Jones, Clive, Nelson and Captain Kidd, Cortez and Lord Roberts, were not all on the side of the law; but their morality was the same: they all held that pugnacity, the will to conquer, and the sort of courage that makes pugnacity and the will to conquer effective, are virtues so splendid that they sanctify plunder, devastation, and murder in direct proportion to the magnitude of these operations. The relaxations of the operators are love affairs and luxurious banquets. Now pray what else is the romance of the thieves' kitchen and of the surreptitious conversations of the prison exercise ring and associated labor shop? The difference is no more essential than that between whiskey and champagne, between an ounce of shag and a box of Havanas, between a burglary and a bombardment, between a jemmy and a bayonet, between a chloroformed pad and a gas shell, between a Browning pistol bought at a pawnbroker's and a service revolver. Gild the reputable end of it as thickly as we like with the cant of courage, patriotism, national prestige, security, duty, and all the rest of it: smudge the disreputable end with all the vituperation that the utmost transports of virtuous indignation can inspire: such tricks will not induce the divine judgment, by which all mankind must finally stand or fall, to distinguish between the victims of these two bragging predatory insects, the criminal and the gentleman.

The gentleman beats the criminal hollow in the magnitude of his operations and the number of people employed in them. For the depredations of the criminal are negligibly small compared to the military holocausts and ravaged areas, the civic slums, the hospitals, the cemeteries crowded with the prematurely dead, and the labor markets in which men and women are exposed for sale for all purposes, honorable and dishonorable. These are the products of criminal ideas imposed on the entire population. The common thief and burglar, miserably sweated by the receiver to whom he has to sell his plunder, steals a few spoons or diamonds at a monstrous risk, and gets less than a tenth of their value from a rascal who runs no risk worth considering; and the poor wretch is content with the trumpery debauch his hard-earned percentage brings him. The gentleman steals a whole country, or a perpetual income for himself and his descendants, and is never satisfied until he has more conquests and more riches to boast of. What is more, the illicit thief does not defend his conduct ethically. He may cry "To hell with the parsons and with honesty and white-livered respectability!" and so forth; but he does so as a defier of God, a public enemy, a Satanic hero. The gentleman really believes that he is a creator of national prestige, a defender of the faith, a pillar of society; and with this conviction to strengthen him he is utterly unscrupulous in his misplaced pride and honor, and plays the wholesaler in evil to the criminal's petty retail enterprises.

THE ROOT OF THE EVIL

And what is at the bottom of it all? Just the belief that virtue is something to be imposed on us from without, like the tricks taught to a performing animal, by the whip. Such manufactured virtue has no ethical value whatever, as appears promptly enough when the whip is removed. All communities must live finally by their ethical values: that is, by their genuine virtues. Living virtuously is an art that can be learnt only by living in full responsibility for our own actions; and as the process is one of trial and error even when seeking the guidance of others' experience, society must, whether it likes it or not, put up with a certain burden of individual error. The man who has never made a mistake will never make anything; and the man who has never done any harm will never do any good. The disastrous people are the indelicate and conceited busybodies who want to reform criminals and mould children's characters by external pressure and abortion. The cowards who refuse to accept the inevitable risks of human society, and would have everybody handcuffed if they could lest they should have their pockets picked or their heads punched, are bad enough; and the flagellomaniacs who are for ever shrieking the exploded falsehood that garotting was put down by flogging, and that all crimes, especially the sexually exciting ones, can be put down by more flogging, are worse; but such obvious cases of phobia and libido soon make themselves ridiculous if they are given a free platform. It is the busybody, the quack, the pseudo God Almighty, the Dr Moreau of Mr H. G. Wells's ghastliest romance, continually lusting to lay hands on living creatures and by reckless violation of their souls and bodies abort them into some monster representing their ideal of a Good Man, or a Model Citizen, or a Perfect Wife and Mother: he is the irreconcilable enemy, the ubiquitous and iniquitous nuisance, and the most difficult to get rid of because he has imposed his moral pretensions on public opinion, and is accepted as just the sort of philanthropist our prisons and criminals should be left to, whereas he (or she) is really the only sort of person who should never be admitted to any part of a prison except the gallows on which so many less mischievous egotists have expired. No one who has not a profound instinctive respect for the right of all living creatures to moral and religious liberty: that is, to liberty of moral and religious experiment on themselves, limited only by their obligations not to become unduly burdensome to others, should be let come within ten miles of a child, a criminal, or any other person in a condition of tutelage. Indelicacy on this point is the most conclusive of social disqualifications. When it is ignorant and short-sighted it produces criminals. When it is worldly-wise and pompous it produces Prison Commissioners.

RECAPITULATION

For the reader's mental convenience, I recapitulate the contentions presented above.

1. Modern imprisonment: that is, imprisonment practised as a punishment as well as a means of detention, is extremely cruel and mischievous, and therefore extremely wicked. The word extremely is used advisedly because the system has been pushed to a degree at which prison mortality and prison insanity forced it back to the point at which it is barely endurable, which point may therefore be regarded as the practicable extreme.

2. Although public vindictiveness and public dread are largely responsible for this wickedness, some of the most cruel features of the prison system are not understood by the public, and have not been deliberately invented and contrived for the purpose of increasing the prisoner's torment. The worst of these are (*a*) unsuccessful attempts at reform, (*b*) successful attempts to make the working of the prison cheaper for the State and easier for the officials, and

(*c*) accidents of the evolution of the old privately owned detention prison into the new punitive State prison.

3. The prison authorities profess three objects: (*a*) Retribution (a euphemism for vengeance), (*b*) Deterrence (a euphemism for Terrorism), and (*c*) Reform of the prisoner. They achieve the first by simple atrocity. They fail in the second through lack of the necessary certainty of detection, prosecution, and conviction; partly because their methods are too cruel and mischievous to secure the co-operation of the public; partly because the prosecutor is put to serious inconvenience and loss of time; partly because most people desire to avoid an unquestionable family disgrace much more than to secure a very questionable justice; and partly because the proportion of avowedly undetected crimes is high enough to hold out reasonable hopes to the criminal that he will never be called to account. The third (Reform) is irreconcilable with the first (Retribution); for the figures of recidivism, and the discovery that the so-called Criminal Type is really a prison type, prove that the retributive process is one of uncompensated deterioration.

4. The cardinal vice of the system is the anti-Christian vice of vengeance, or the intentional duplication of malicious injuries partly in pure spite, partly in compliance with the expiatory superstition that two blacks make a white. The criminal accepts this, but claims that punishment absolves him if the injuries are equivalent, and still more if he has the worse of the bargain, as he almost always has. Consequently, when absolution on his release is necessarily denied him, and he is forced back into crime by the refusal to employ him, he feels that he is entitled to revenge this injustice by becoming an enemy of Society. No beneficial reform of our treatment of criminals is possible unless and until this superstition of expiation and this essentially sentimental vice of vengeance are unconditionally eradicated.

5. Society has a right of self-defence, extending to the destruction or restraint of lawbreakers. This right is separable from the right to revenge or punish: it need have no

more to do with punishment or revenge than the caging or shooting of a man-eating tiger. It arises from the existence of (A) intolerably mischievous human beings, and (B) persons defective in the self-control needed for free life in modern society, but well behaved and at their ease under tutelage and discipline. Class A can be painlessly killed or permanently restrained. The requisite tutelage and discipline can be provided for Class B without rancor or insult. The rest can be treated not as criminals but as civil defendants, and made to pay for their depredations in the same manner. At present many persons guilty of conduct much viler than that for which poor men are sent to prison suffer nothing worse than civil actions for damages when they do not (unhappily) enjoy complete impunity.

6. The principle to be kept before the minds of all citizens is that as civilized society is a very costly arrangement necessary to their subsistence and security they must justify their enjoyment of it by contributing their share to its cost, and giving no more than their share of trouble, subject to every possible provision by insurance against innocent disability. This is a condition precedent to freedom, and justifies us in removing cases of incurable noxious disability by simply putting an end to their existence.

7. An unconquerable repugnance to judicial killing having led to the abolition of capital punishment in several countries, and to its reservation for specially dangerous or abhorrent crimes in all the others, it is possible that the right to kill may be renounced by all civilized States. This repugnance may be intensified as we cease to distinguish between sin and infirmity, or, in prison language, between crime and disease, because of our fear of being led to the extirpation of the incurable invalid who is excessively troublesome as well as to that of the incurable criminal.

On the other hand, the opposite temperament, which is not squeamish about making short work of hard cases, and which is revolted by the daily sacrifice of the lives of prison officials, and of relatives and nurses, to incurable criminals and invalids, may be reinforced by the abandonment of ethical pretentiousness, vengeance, malice, and all uncharitableness in the matter, and may become less scrupulous than at present in advocating euthanasia for all incurables.

Whichever party may prevail, punishment as such is likely to disappear, and with it the ear-marking of certain offences as calling for specially deterrent severities. But it does not follow that lethal treatment of extreme cases will be barred. On the contrary, it may be extended from murder to social incompatibility of all sorts. If it be absolutely barred, sufficient restraint must be effected, not as a punishment but as a necessity for public safety. But there will be no excuse for making it more unpleasant than it need be.

8. When detention and restraint are necessary, the criminal's right to contact with all the spiritual influences of his day should be respected, and its exercise encouraged and facilitated. Conversation, access to books and pictures and music, unfettered scientific, philosophic, and religious activity, change of scene and occupation, the free formation of friendships and acquaintances, marriage and parentage: in short, all the normal methods of creation and recreation, must be available for criminals as for other persons, partly because deprivation of these things is severely punitive, and partly because it is destructive to the victim, and produces what we call the criminal type, making a cure impossible. Any specific liberty which the criminal's specific defects lead him to abuse will, no doubt, be taken from him; but if his life is spared his right to live must be accepted in the fullest sense, and not, as at present, merely as a right to breathe and circulate his blood. In short, a criminal should be treated, not as a man who has forfeited all normal rights and liberties by the breaking of a single law, but as one who, through some specific weakness or weaknesses, is incapable of exercising some specific liberty or liberties.

9. The main difficulty in applying this concept of individual freedom to the criminal arises from the fact that the concept itself is as yet unformed. We do not apply it to chil-

dren, at home or at school, nor to employees, nor to persons of any class or age who are in the power of other persons. Like Queen Victoria, we conceive Man as being either in authority or subject to authority, each person doing only what he is expressly permitted to do, or what the example of the rest of his class encourages him to consider as tacitly permitted. The concept of the evolving free man in an evolving society, making all sorts of experiments in conduct, and therefore doing everything he likes as far as he can unless there are express prohibitions to which he is politically a consenting party, is still unusual, and consequently terrifying, in spite of all the individualist pamphlets of the eighteenth and nineteenth centuries. It will be found that those who are most scandalized by the liberties I am claiming for the convict would be equally scandalized if I claimed them for their own sons, or even for themselves.

The conclusion is that imprisonment cannot be fully understood by those who do not understand freedom. But it can be understood quite well enough to have it made a much less horrible, wicked, and wasteful thing than it is at present.

AYOT ST LAWRENCE,
Dec.–Jan. 1921–22.

KILLING FOR SPORT

(Preface from the book by Henry S. Salt)

SPORT is a difficult subject to deal with honestly. It is easy for the humanitarian to moralize against it; and any fool on its side can gush about its glorious breezy pleasures and the virtues it nourishes. But neither the moralizings nor the gushings are supported by facts: indeed they are mostly violently contradicted by them. Sportsmen are not crueller than other people. Humanitarians are not more humane than other people. The pleasures of sport are fatigues and hardships: nobody gets out of bed before sunrise on a drizzling wintry morning and rides off into darkness, cold, and rain, either for luxury or thirst for the blood of a fox cub. The humanitarian and the sportsman are often the self-same person drawing altogether unaccountable lines between pheasants and pigeons, between hares and foxes, between tame stags from the cart and wild ones from the heather, between lobsters or *paté de foie gras* and beefsteaks: above all, between man and the lower animals; for people who are sickened by the figures of a *battue* do not turn a hair over the infantile deathrate in Lisson Grove or the slums of Dundee.

Clearly the world of sport is a crystal palace in which we had better not throw stones unless we are prepared to have our own faces cut by the falling glass. My own pursuits as a critic and as a castigator of morals by ridicule (otherwise a writer of comedies) are so cruel that in point of giving pain to many worthy people I can hold my own with most dentists, and beat a skilful sportsman hollow. I know many sportsmen; and none of them are ferocious. I know several humanitarians; and they are all ferocious. No book of sport breathes such a wrathful spirit as this book of humanity. No sportsman wants to kill the fox or the pheasant as I want to kill him when I see him doing it. Callousness is not cruel. Stupidity is not cruel. Love of exercise and of feats of skill is not cruel. They may and do produce more destruction and suffering than all the neuroses of all the Neros. But they are characteristic of quite amiable and cheerful people, mostly lovers of pet animals. On the other hand, humane sensitiveness is impatient, angry, ruthless, and murderous. Marat was a supersensitive humanitarian, by profession a doctor who had practised successfully in genteel circles in England. What Marat felt towards marquesses most humanitarians feel more or less towards sportsmen. Therefore let no sportsman who reads these pages accuse me of hypocrisy, or of claiming to be a more amiable person than he. And let him excuse me, if he will be so good, for beginning with an attempt to describe how I feel about sport.

To begin with, sport soon bores me when it does not involve killing; and when it does, it affects me much as the murder of a human being would affect me, rather more than less; for just as the murder of a child is more shocking than the murder of an adult (because, I suppose, the child is so helpless and the breach of social faith therefore so unconscionable), the murder of an animal is an abuse of man's advantage over animals: the proof being that when the animal is powerful and dangerous, and the man unarmed, the repulsion vanishes and is replaced by congratulation. But quite humane and cultivated people seem unable to understand why I should bother about the feelings of animals. I have seen the most horrible pictures published in good faith as attractive in illustrated magazines. One of them, which I wish I could forget, was a photograph taken on a polar expedition, shewing a murdered bear with its living cub trying to make it attend to its maternal duties. I have seen a photograph of a criminal being cut into a thousand pieces by a Chinese executioner, which was by comparison amusing. I have also seen thrown on a screen for the entertainment of a large audience a photograph of an Arctic explorer taking away a sledge dog to shoot it for food, the dog jumping about joyously without the least suspicion of its human friend's intentions. If the doomed dog had been a man or a woman, I believe I should have had less sense of treachery. I do not say that this is reasonable: I simply state it as a fact. It was quite evident that the lecturer had no suspicion of the effect the picture was producing on me; and as far as I could see, his audience was just as callous; for if they had all felt as I felt there would have been at least a very perceptible shudder, if not an articulate protest. Now this was not a case of sport. It was necessary to shoot the dog: I should have shot it myself under the same circumstances. But I should have regarded the necessity as a horrible one; and I should have presented it to the audience as a painful episode, like cannibalism in a crew of castaways, and not as a joke. For I must add that a good many people present regarded it as a bit of fun. I absolve the lecturer from this extremity of insensibility. The shooting of a dog was a trifle to what he had endured; and I did not blame him for thinking it by comparison a trivial matter. But to us, who had endured nothing, it might have seemed a little hard on the dog, and calling for some apology from the man.

I am driven to the conclusion that my sense of kinship with animals is greater than most people feel. It amuses me to talk to animals in a sort of jargon I have invented for them; and it seems to me that it amuses them to be talked to, and that they respond to the tone of the conversation, though its intellectual content may to some extent escape them. I am quite sure, having made the experiment several times on dogs left in my care as part of the furniture of hired houses, than an animal who has been treated as a brute, and is consequently undeveloped socially (as human beings remain socially undeveloped under the same circumstances) will, on being talked to as a fellow-creature, become friendly and companionable in a very short time. This process has been described by some reproachful dog owners as spoiling the dog, and sincerely deplored by them, because I am glad to say it is easier to do than to undo except by brutalities of which few people are capable. But I find it impossible to associate with animals on any other terms. Further, it gives me extraordinary gratification to find a wild bird treating me with confidence, as robins sometimes do. It pleases me to conciliate an animal who is hostile to me. What is more, an animal who will not be conciliated offends me. There is at the Zoo a morose maned lion who will tear you to pieces if he gets half a chance. There is also a very handsome maneless lion with whom you may play more safely than with most St. Bernard dogs, as he seems to need nothing but plenty of attention and admiration to put him into the best of humors. I do not feel towards these two lions as a carpenter does towards two pieces of wood, one hard and knotty, and the other easy to work; nor as I do towards two motor bicycles, one troublesome and dangerous, and the other in perfect order. I feel towards the two lions as I should towards two men similarly diverse. I like one and dislike the other. If they got loose and were shot, I should be distressed in the one case whilst in the other I should say "Serve the brute right!" This is clearly fellow-feeling. And it seems to me that the plea of the humanitarian is a plea for widening the range of fellow-feeling.

The limits of fellow-feeling are puzzling. People who have it in a high degree for animals often seem utterly devoid of it for human beings of a different class. They will literally kill their dogs with kindness whilst behaving to their servants with such utter inconsideration that they have to change their domestic staff once a month or oftener. Or they hate horses and like snakes. One could fill pages with such inconsistencies. The lesson of these apparent contradictions is that fellow-feeling is a matter of dislikes as well as of likes. No man wants to destroy the engine which catches him in its cog-wheels and tears a limb from him. But many a man has tried to kill another man for a very trifling slight. The machine, not being our fellow, cannot be loved or hated. The man, being our fellow, can.

Let us try to get down to the bottom of this matter. There is no use in saying that our fellow-creatures must not be killed. That is simply untrue; and the converse proposal that they must be killed is simply true. We see the Buddhist having his path swept before him lest he should tread on an insect and kill it; but we do not see what that Buddhist does when he catches a flea that has kept him awake for an hour; and we know that he has to except certain poisonous snakes from his forbearance. If mice get into your house and you do not kill them, they will end by killing you. If rabbits breed on your farm and you do not exterminate them, you will end by having no farm. If you keep deer in your park and do not thin them, your neighbors or the authorities will finally have to save you the trouble. If you hold the life of a mosquito sacred, malaria and yellow fever will not return the compliment. I have had an interview with an adder, in the course of which it struck repeatedly and furiously at my stick; and I let it go unharmed; but if I were the mother of a family of young children, and I found a cobra in the garden, I would vote for "*La mort sans phrase*," as many humane and honorable persons voted in the case, not of a serpent, but of an anointed king.

I see no logical nor spiritual escape from the theory that evolution (not, please observe, Natural Selection) involves a deliberate intentional destruction by the higher forms of life of the lower. It is a dangerous and difficult business; for in the course of natural selection the lower forms may have become necessary to the existence of the higher; and the gamekeeper shooting everything that could hurt his pheasants or their chicks may be behaving as foolishly as an Arab lunatic shooting horses and camels. But where Man comes, the megatherium must go as surely as where the poultry farmer comes the fox must go unless the hunt will pay for the fox's depredations. To plead for the tiger, the wolf, and the poisonous snake, is as useless as to plead for the spirochete or the tetanus bacillus: we must frankly class these as early and disastrous experiments in creation, and accept it as part of the mission of the later and more successful experiments to recognize them as superseded, and to destroy them purposely. We should, no doubt, be very careful how we jump from the indisputable general law that the higher forms of life must exterminate or limit the lower, to the justification of any particular instance of the slaughter of non-human animals by men, or the slaughter of a low type of man by a high type of man. Still, when all due reservations are made, the fact remains that a war of extermination is being waged daily and necessarily by man against his rivals for possession of the earth, and though an urban humanitarian and vegetarian who never has occasion to kill anything but a microbe may shudder at the callousness with which a farmer kills rats and rabbits and sparrows and moles and caterpillars and ladybirds and many more charming creatures, yet if he were in the farmer's place he would have to do exactly the same, or perish.

In that case why not make a pleasure of necessity, and a virtue of pleasure, as the sportsmen do? I think we must own that there is no objection from the point of view of the animals. On the contrary, it is quite easy to shew that there is a positive advantage to them in the organization of killing as sport. Fox hunting has saved the existing foxes from extermination; and if it were not for the civilization that makes fox hunting possible, the fox would still be hunted and killed by packs of wolves. I am so conscious of this that I have in another place suggested that children should be hunted or shot during certain months of the year, as they would then be fed and preserved by the sportsmen of the counties as generously and carefully as pheasants now are; and the survivors would make a much better nation than our present slum products. And I go further. I maintain that the abolition of public executions was a very bad thing for the murderers. Before that time, we did exactly as our sportsmen now do. We made a pleasure of the necessity for exterminating murderers, and a virtue of the pleasure. Hanging was a popular sport, like racing. Huge crowds assembled to see it and paid large prices for seats. There would have been betting on the result if it had been at all uncertain. The criminal had what all criminals love: a large audience. He had a procession to Tyburn: he had a drink: he was allowed to make a speech if he could; and if he could not, the speech was made for him and published and sold in great numbers. Above all, such fair play as an execution admits of was guaranteed to him by the presence of the public, whereas now he perishes in a horrible secrecy which lends itself to all the abuses of secrecy. Whether the creature slain be man or what we very invidiously call brute, there is no case to be made against sport on its behalf. Even cruelty can justify itself, as far as the victim is concerned, on the ground that it makes sport attractive to cruel people, and that sport is good for the quarry.

The true objection to sport is the one taken by that wise and justly famous Puritan who objected to bear baiting not because it gave pain to the bear but because it gave pleasure to the spectators. He rightly saw that it was not important that we should be men of pleasure, and that it was enormously important that we should be men of honor. What the bear would have said if it had had any say in the matter can only be conjectured. Its captors might have argued that if they could not have made money by keeping it alive whilst taking it to England to be baited, they would have killed it at sight in the Pyrenees; so that it owed several months of life, with free board and lodging, to the institution of bear baiting. The bear might have replied that if it had not been for the bear pit in England they would never have come to hunt for it in the Pyrenees, where it could have ended its days in a free and natural manner. Let us admit for the sake of a quiet life that the point is disputable. What is not disputable by any person who has ever seen sport of this character is that the man who enjoys it is degraded by it. We do not bait bears now (I do not quite know why); but we course rabbits in the manner described in one of the essays in this book. I lived for a time on the south slope of the Hog's Back; and every

Sunday morning rabbits were coursed within earshot of me. And I noticed that it was quite impossible to distinguish the cries of the excited terriers from the cries of the sportsmen, although ordinarily the voice of a man is no more like the voice of a dog than like the voice of a nightingale. Sport reduced them all, men and terriers alike, to a common denominator of bestiality. The sound did not make me more humane: on the contrary, I felt that if I were an irresponsible despot with a park of artillery at my disposal, I should, (especially after seeing the sportsmen on their way to and from their sport) have said: "These people have become subhuman, and will be better dead. Be kind enough to mow them down for me."

As a matter of fact there is always a revulsion against these dehumanizing sports in which the killing can be seen, and the actual visible chase shared, by human beings: in short, the sports in which men revert to the excitements of beasts of prey. Several have been abolished by law: among them bear baiting and cock fighting: both of them sports in which the spectators shared at close quarters the excitement of the animals engaged. In the sports firmly established among us there is much less of this abomination. In fox hunting and shooting, predatory excitement is not a necessary part of the sport, and is indeed abhorred by many who practise it. Inveterate foxhunters have been distressed and put off their hunting for days by happening to see a fox in the last despairing stage of its run from the hounds: a sight which can be avoided, and often is, by the hunters, but which they may happen upon some day when they are not hunting. Such people hunt because they delight in meets and in gallops across country as social and healthy incidents of country life. They are proud of their horsemanship and their craftiness in taking a line. They like horses and dogs and exercise and wind and weather, and are unconscious of the fact that their expensive and well equipped hunting stables and kennels are horse prisons and dog prisons. It is useless to pretend that these ladies and gentlemen are fiends in human form: they clearly are not. By avoiding being in at the death they get all the good out of hunting without incurring the worst of the evil, and so come out with a balance in their favor.

Shooting is subtler: it is a matter of skill with one's weapons. The expert at it is called, not a good chicken butcher, but a good shot. When I want, as I often do, to pick him off, I do so not because I feel that he is cruel or degraded but because he is a nuisance to me with the very disagreeable noise of his explosions, and because there is an unbearable stupidity in converting an interesting, amusing, prettily colored live wonder like a pheasant into a slovenly unhandsome corpse. But at least he does not yap like a terrier, and shake with a detestable excitement, and scream out frantic bets to bookmakers. His expression is that of a man performing a skilled operation with an instrument of precision: an eminently human expression, quite incompatible with the flush of blood to the eyes and the uncovering of the dogtooth that makes a man like a beast of prey. And this is why it is impossible to feel that skilled shooting or foxhunting are as abominable as rabbit coursing, harehunting with beagles, or otter-hunting.

And yet shooting depends for its toleration on custom as much as on the coolness with which it has to be performed. It may be illogical to forgive a man for shooting a pheasant and to loathe him for shooting a seagull; but as a matter of plain fact one feels that a man who shoots seagulls is a cad, and soon makes him feel it if he attempts to do it on board a public ship, whereas the snipe shooter excites no such repulsion. And "fair game" must be skilfully shot if the maximum of toleration is to be enjoyed. Even then it is not easy for some of us to forget that many a bird must have been miserably maimed before the shooter perfected his skill. The late King Edward the Seventh, immediately after his recovery from a serious operation which stirred the whole nation to anxious sympathy with him, shot a stag, which got away to die of just such internal inflammation as its royal murderer had happily escaped. Many people read the account without the least emotion. Others thought it natural that the King should be ashamed, as a marksman, of his failure to kill, but rejected as sentimental nonsense the notion that he should feel any remorse on the stag's behalf. Had he deliberately shot a cow instead, everyone would have been astounded and horrified. Custom will reconcile people to any atrocity; and fashion will drive them to acquire any custom. The English princess who sits on the throne of Spain goes to bullfights because it is the Spanish fashion. At first she averted her face, and probably gave offence by doing so. Now, no doubt, she is a *connoisseuse* of the sport. Yet neither she nor the late King Edward can be classed as cruel monsters. On the contrary, they are conspicuous examples of the power of cruel institutions to compel the support and finally win the tolerance and even the enjoyment of persons of full normal benevolence.

But this is not why I call shooting subtle. It fascinates even humane persons not only because it is a game of skill in the use of the most ingenious instrument in general use, but because killing by craft from a distance is a power that makes a man divine rather than human.

> "Oft have I struck
> Those that I never saw, and struck them dead"

said the statesman to Jack Cade (who promptly hanged him); and something of the sense of power in that boast stimulates every boy with a catapult and every man with a gun. That is why there is an interest in weapons fathoms deeper than the interest in cricket bats and golf clubs. It is not a question of skill or risk. The men who go to Africa with cameras and obtain photographs and even cinematographs of the most dangerous animals at close quarters, shew much more skill and nerve than the gentlemen who disgust us with pictures of themselves sitting on the body of the huge creatures they have just killed with explosive bullets. Shooting "big game," like serving as a soldier in the field, is glorified conventionally as a proof of character and courage, though everyone knows that men can be found by the hundred thousand to face such ordeals, including several who would be afraid to walk down Bond Street in an unfashionable hat. The real point of the business is neither character nor courage, but ability to kill. And the greater cowards and the feebler weaklings we are, the more important this power is to us. It is a matter of life and death to us to be able to kill our enemies without coming to handgrips with them; and the consequence is that our chief form of play is to pretend that something is our enemy and kill it. Even to pretend to kill it is some satisfaction: nay, the spectacle of other people pretending to do it is a substitute worth paying for. Nothing more supremely ridiculous as a subject of reasonable contemplation could be imagined than a sham fight in Earls Court between a tribe of North American Indians and a troop of cowboys, both imported by Buffalo Bill as a theatrical speculation. To see these grown-up men behaving like children, galloping about and firing blank cartridges at one another, and pretending to fall down dead, was absurd and incredible enough from any rational point of view; but that thousands of respectable middle-aged and elderly citizens and their wives, all perfectly sober, should pay to be allowed to look on, seems flat madness. Yet the thing not only occurred in London, but occurs now daily in the cinema theatres and yearly at the Military Tournaments. And what honest man dare pretend that he gets no fun out of these spectacles? Certainly not I. They revived enough of my boyish delight in stage fights and in the stories of Captain Mayne Reid to induce me to sit them out, conscious as I was of their silliness.

Please do not revile me for telling you what I felt instead of what I ought to have felt. What prevents the sport question and every other question from getting squarely put before us is our habit of saying that the things we think should disgust us and fill us with abhorrence actually do disgust us and fill us with abhorrence, and that the persons who, against all reason and decency, find some sort of delight in them, are vile wretches quite unlike ourselves, though, as everyone can see, we and they are as like as potatoes. You may not agree with Mr. Rudyard Kipling about war, or with Colonel Roosevelt about sport; but beware how you pretend that war does not interest and excite you more than printing, or that the thought of bringing down a springing tiger with a well-aimed shot does not interest you more than the thought of cleaning your teeth. Men may be as the poles asunder in their speculative views. In their actual nervous and emotional reactions they are "members one of another" to a much greater extent than they choose to confess. The reason I have no patience with Colonel Roosevelt's tedious string of rhinoceros murders in South Africa is not that I am not interested in weapons, in marksmanship, and in killing, but because my interest in life and creation is still greater than my interest in death and destruction, and because I have sufficient fellow-feeling with a rhinoceros to think it a frightful thing that it should be killed for fun.

Consider a moment how one used to feel when an Irish peasant shot his landlord, or when a grand duke was blown to pieces in Russia, or when one read of how Charlotte Corday killed Marat. On the one hand we applauded the courage, the skill, the resolution of the assassin; we exalted in the lesson taught to tyrants and in the overthrow of the strong oppressor by the weak victim; but we were horrified by the breach of the law, by the killing of the accused at the decree of an irresponsible Ribbon Lodge under no proper public control, by the execution of the grand duke without trial and opportunity of defence, by the suspicion that Charlotte Corday was too like Marat in her lust for the blood of oppressors to have the right to kill him. Such cases are extremely complicated, except for those simple victims of political or class prejudice who think Charlotte Corday a saint because she killed a Radical, and the Ribbonmen demons because they were common fellows who dared to kill country gentlemen. But however the cases catch us, there is always that peculiar interest in individual killing, and consequently in the means and weapons by which individuals can kill their enemies, which is at the root of the sport of shooting.

It all comes back to fellow-feeling and appetite for fruitful activity and a high quality of life: there is nothing else to appeal to. No commandment can meet the case. It is no use saying "Thou shalt not kill" in one breath, and, in the next "Thou shalt not suffer a witch to live." Men must be killed and animals must be killed: nay, whole species of animals and types of men must be exterminated before the earth can become a tolerable place of habitation for decent folk. But among the men who will have to be wiped out stands the sportsman: the man without fellow-feeling, the man so primitive and uncritical in his tastes that the destruction of life is an amusement to him, the man whose outlook is as narrow as that of his dog. He is not even cruel: sport is partly a habit to which he has been brought up, and partly stupidity, which can always be measured by wastefulness and by lack of sense of the importance and glory of life. The horrible murk and grime of the Pottery towns is caused by indifference to a stupid waste of sunlight, natural beauty, cleanliness, and pleasant air, combined with a brutish appetite for money. A *battue* is caused by indifference to the beauty and interest of bird life and song, and callousness to glazed eyes and blood-bedabbled corpses, combined with a boyish love of shooting. All the people who waste beauty and life in this way are characterized by deficiency in fellow-feeling: not only have they none of St. Francis's feeling that the birds are of our kin, but they would be extremely indignant if a loader or a gamekeeper asserted any claim to belong to their species. Sport is a sign either of limitation or of timid conventionality.

And this disposes of the notion that sport is the training of a conquering race. Even if such things as conquering races existed, or would be tolerable if they did exist, they would not be races of sportsmen. The red scalp-hunting braves of North America were the sportingest race imaginable; and they were conquered as easily as the bisons they hunted. The French can boast more military glory to the square inch of history than any other nation; but until lately they were the standing butt of English humorists for their deficiencies as sportsmen. In the middle ages, when they fought as sportsmen and gentlemen, they were annihilated by small bodies of starving Englishmen who carefully avoided sportsmanlike methods and made a laborious business (learnt at the village target) of killing them. As to becoming accustomed to risks, there are plenty of ways of doing that without killing anything except occasionally yourself. The motor-cyclist takes more trying risks than the foxhunter; and motor-cycling seems safety itself compared to aviation. A dive from a high springboard will daunt a man as effectually as a stone wall in the hunting field. The notion that if you have no sportsmen you will have no soldiers (as if more than the tiniest fraction of the armies of the world had ever been sportsmen) is as absurd as the notion that burglars and garrotters should be encouraged because they might make hardier and more venturesome soldiers than honest men; but since people foolishly do set up such arguments they may as well be mentioned in passing for what they are worth.

The question then comes to this: which is the superior man? the man whose pastime is slaughter, or the man whose pastime is creative or contemplative? I have no doubt about the matter myself, being on the creative and contemplative side by nature. Slaughter is necessary work, like scavenging; but the man who not only does it unnecessarily for love of it but actually makes as much of it as possible by breeding live things to slaughter, seems to me to be little more respectable than one who befouls the streets for the pleasure of sweeping them. I believe that the line of evolution leads to the prevention of the birth of creatures whose lives are not useful and enjoyable, and that the time will come when a gentleman found amusing himself with a gun will feel as compromised as he does now when found amusing himself with a whip at the expense of a child or an old lame horse covered with sores. Sport, like murder, is a bloody business; and the sportsmen will not always be able to outface that fact as they do at present.

But there is something else. Killing, if it is to give us heroic emotions, must not be done for pleasure. Interesting though the slaying of one man by another may be, it is abhorrent when it is done merely for the fun of doing it (the sportsman's way) or to satisfy the envious spite of the worse man towards the better (Cain's way). When Charlotte Corday stabbed Marat, and when Hamilton of Bothwellhaugh shot the Regent Murray, they were stung by intolerable social wrongs for which the law offered them no redress. When Brutus and his fellow-conspirators killed Cæsar, they had persuaded themselves that they were saving Rome. When Samson slew the lion, he had every reason to feel convinced that if he did not, the lion would slay him. Conceive Charlotte Corday stabbing Marat as an exercise of manual and anatomical skill, or Hamilton bringing down the Regent as a feat of marksmanship! Their deeds at once become, not less, but more horrifying than if they had done them from a love of killing. Jack the Ripper was a madman of the most appalling sort; but the fascination of murder for him must have been compounded of dread, of horror, and of a frightful perversion of an instinct which in its natural condition is a kindly one. He was a ghastly murderer; but he was a hot-blooded one. The perfection of callousness is not reached until a life is sacrificed, and often cruelly sacrificed, solely as a feat of skill. Peter the Great amusing himself by torturing his son to death was a revolting monster; but he was not so utterly inhuman in that crime as he was when, on being interested by a machine for executing criminals which he saw in a museum on his travels, he proposed to execute one of his retinue to see how the machine worked, and could with difficulty be brought to understand that there was a sentimental objection to the proceeding on the part of his hosts which made the experiment impossible. When he tortured his son he knew that he was committing an abomination. When he wanted to try an experiment at the cost of a servant's life he was unconscious of doing anything that was not a matter of course for any nobleman. And in this he was worse than abominable: he was deficient, imbecile, less than human. Just so is the sportsman, shooting quite skilfully and coolly without the faintest sense of any murderous excitement, and with no personal feeling against the birds, really further from salvation than the man who is humane enough to get some sense of wickedness out of his sport. To have one's fellow-feeling corrupted and perverted into a lust for cruelty and murder is hideous; but to have no fellow-feeling at all is to be something less than even a murderer. The man who sees red is more complete than the man who is blind.

The triviality of sport as compared with the risk and trouble of its pursuit and the gravity of its results makes it much sillier than crime. The idler who can find nothing better to do than to kill is past our patience. If a man takes on himself the heavy responsibility of killing, he should not do it for pastime. Pastimes are very necessary; for though a busy man can always find something to do, there comes a point at which his health, his sanity, his very existence may depend on his doing nothing of the smallest importance; and yet he cannot sit still and twiddle his thumbs: besides, he requires bodily exercise. He needs an idle pastime. Now "Satan finds some mischief still for idle hands to do" if the idler lets his conscience go to sleep. But he need not let it go to sleep. There are plenty of innocent idle pastimes for him. He can read detective stories. He can play tennis. He can drive a motor-car if he can afford one. He can fly. Satan may suggest that it would be a little more interesting to kill something; but surely only an outrageous indifference to the sacredness of life and the horrors of suffering and terror, combined with a monstrously selfish greed for sensation, could drive a man to accept the Satanic suggestion if sport were not organized for him as a social institution. Even as it is, there are now so many other pastimes available that the choice of killing is becoming more and more a disgrace to the chooser. The wantonness of the choice is beyond excuse. To kill as the poacher does, to sell or eat the victim, is at least to act reasonably. To kill from hatred or revenge is at least to behave passionately. To kill in gratification of a lust for death is at least to behave villainously. Reason, passion, and villainy are all human. But to kill, being all the time quite a good sort of fellow, merely to pass away the time when there are a dozen harmless ways of doing it equally available, is to behave like an idiot or a silly imitative sheep.

Surely the broad outlook and deepened consciousness which admits all living things to the commonwealth of fellow-feeling, and the appetite for fruitful activity and generous life which come with it, are better than this foolish doing of unamiable deeds by people who are not in the least unamiable.

March, 1914.

THE AMAZING CASE OF THE GENERAL MEDICAL COUNCIL VERSUS THE LATE DR AXHAM

From The Times, 23 *October* 1925

THE difficulty about Dr Axham does not seem to be understood. Dr Axham, when he acted as anæsthetist for the patients of Sir Herbert Barker, did his clear duty as a member of a profession devoted to the relief of human suffering by every means within the competence of a physician, and to the encouragement and aid of every extension of those means. The public has benefited by his action and owes him its protection. Yet it has allowed him to be stigmatized for his services as guilty of infamous professional conduct and struck off the register. The striking-off will not hurt him nowadays, when unregistered practitioners are at a heavy premium because they have mastered the modern techniques of which registration guarantees ignorance; but at eighty-seven he is past practising, and the stigma is deeply felt and justly resented by him.

Meanwhile, Sir Herbert Barker, whom he was one of the first to recognize as a great manipulative surgeon, has been knighted in public recognition of his eminence at the instance of four famous surgeons, who petitioned the Prime Minister on the subject. The G.M.C. holds that they were guilty of infamous professional conduct, in which they were abetted by the King; but it does not act on its view, because the King and his advisers are not so helpless as Dr Axham was. Only by continuing the victimization of Dr Axham can it make its opinion quite clear, and intimidate every registered practitioner who would like to follow his admirable example.

Obviously it is useless to appeal to the G.M.C. But what about the really responsible bodies who are supposed to represent the nation in the matter—the Privy Council and the universities and the Government? It is they who, in gross neglect of their duty, and in spite of the plain provisions in the Act for public and scientific representation, have thrown the control of the profession, including powers which no political ruler in the civilized world now enjoys or would dream of claiming, into the hands of practising doctors, with the inevitable result that the Council has become a trade union of the worst type—namely, the type in which the entry to the trade and the right to remain in it are at the mercy of the union. Not only is the type the worst, but in this particular instance it is at the crude stage of preoccupation with professional earnings and sullen defiance of public opinion, which produced the Manchester and Sheffield outrages in working-class trade unionism in the last century. Within the last month or two a distinguished doctor has written to the Press declaring naïvely that the first duty of the G.M.C. is to protect the livelihood of the registered practitioners. He would be quite right if the G.M.C. were a trade union *de jure* as well as *de facto*; but as it is, on the contrary, a constitutional authority, its first duty is to protect the public and secure to it the advantages of all the latest developments in medicine and surgery. It has become in effect a trade union solely through the carelessness or superstition of the controlling bodies representing us poor laymen who are so vitally interested as patients, as well as disinterested science.

It seems hopeless, however, to make people understand this. My own efforts to call attention to it result only in what I must call editorial imbecilities to the effect that I have "a down on doctors," and that every quack would have to be registered if Sir Herbert Barker were registered, which is about as sensible as saying that because Brahms was made a Doctor of Music without doing the curricular exercises in counterpoint the universities are logically bound to confer degrees on all our street piano men. As a matter of fact, few persons can have had more or better doctor friends than I; indeed, that is why my utterances have been so well informed; but they may not speak for themselves, whereas I, being free to open my mouth without being ruined and stigmatized as infamous, can act occasionally as the mouthpiece of a gagged profession. Leaving that aside, I have my own interests and grievances as a citizen. My wife suffered from a laming traumatic dislocation for eight years. Thanks to the obsolete training maintained by the G.M.C., the registered surgeons were unable to correct it. They did not pretend to: the final verdict was: "You must go to Barker." But the G.M.C. said: "If you go to that blackleg, you shall howl for it, as we will ruin any man who dares administer an anæsthetic." And, in fact, the operation, which was completely successful, was performed without an anæsthetic, though I hasten to add that this was an effect of my wife's curiosity rather than of any serious difficulty in circumventing the trade union.

Later on, in an accident, I displaced one of my own bones rather badly; and again, though nothing could exceed the kindness of the registered medical gentlemen on the spot, they were unable to replace it for want of a perfectly well-known technique which every qualified surgeon should have at his fingers' ends. It took me ten days to get to Birmingham, where an American D.O. (doctor of osteopathy), also classed as a blackleg by the G.M.C., set me right after seventy-five minutes' skilled manipulation. Had the process been an unbearably painful one, which it fortunately was not, any anæsthetist saving me the pain would have done so under penalty of being rattened (as the term went in Sheffield) to the extent of being deprived of his livelihood.

No wonder I am overwhelmed with requests from the medical societies in all the medical schools in London to lecture to them on the situation. But I have nothing more to say than I have already said often and clearly enough; and I simply dare not use the language that the ablest leaders of the profession pour out on it. All I assert is that if the constitutional authorities will only do their duty by getting rid of the practitioners from the G.M.C. (save as assessors in case of need), and replace them with representatives of the public and of disinterested hygienic science, Dr Axham will be reinstated almost automatically, and the conquest of Harley Street by the unregistered, now in active progress, may be checked. For there is really nothing that the unregistered practitioners do that cannot be done by registered ones if only they are apprenticed to the techniques of today instead of to those of a century ago.

From The Times, 12 November 1925

Dr Axham has not been "covering," nor was it for covering that he was struck off the register. I happen to know what covering means: my uncle was a doctor. Real covering, which is not uncommon, and, in the cases which have come under my observation or to my knowledge, has been practised with impunity and with hardly a pretence of concealment, arises in the following way:

A registered doctor—usually a country doctor—finds that he is getting more patients than he can attend to. Obviously he should take another registered doctor into partnership. But this means inviting a rival on to his ground, and sharing fees with him. It is better business to engage an unregistered assistant, who will work as an employee at a modest salary, and who can never capture the practice and set up for himself. It is not difficult to find such assistants. There are always men in the market with a taste for doctoring, who, through poverty, age, or lack of the necessary sort of application and memory, are unable to pass examinations. Some of them, by superior clinical instinct and dexterity, are better doctors than their registered employers, and are preferred by the patients. Employment of such unregistered assistants is "covering." I have never heard it defended in principle, and I should be surprised if I heard Dr Axham or Sir Herbert Barker defend it either in practice or principle.

Covering is always the maintenance under false colors of an unregistered practitioner by a registered one, and cannot in its own nature be the converse. If Dr Axham, being a registered practitioner, and being called in as such to perform a surgical operation, had handed over the patient to "one Herbert Atkinson Barker," unregistered, but assumed by the patient on the strength of his connection with Dr Axham to be registered, then Dr Axham would have been guilty of covering.

What actually happened was just the opposite. A patient with a dislocated knee, finding, after many expensive experiments, that neither Dr Axham nor any other available registered surgeon could set it right, and that one Herbert Atkinson Barker, unregistered, and not pretending to be registered, had become famous by his success in such cases, naturally called in the said Herbert to cure him, as he had a perfect right to do without molestation or intimidation from the G.M.C. or anyone else. He asked—Would it hurt? On learning that it would, he called in Dr Axham to anæsthetize him, which again he had a perfect right to do. Dr Axham, having convinced himself that the operation, though neither he nor any of his registered colleagues could perform it, was a surgical one in the technical sense, and that Herbert Atkinson Barker had mastered it, was under the most sacred professional obligation to give the desired relief. There was no covering whatever in the transaction.

To make this clear, let us suppose that the victim of a railway collision lies pinned down beneath the wreckage in such a way that he can be released only by a skilled breakdown gang using compressed air drills, oxy-acetylene jets, cranes, and so forth, and that its operations are so unbearably painful that it is doubtful whether the victim can survive them. Let us suppose further that Dr Graham Little and Sir Bryan Donkin are present, rendering what aid they can. The distracted wife of the victim asks Dr Graham Little to anæsthetize him. Dr Graham Little is sympathetic, but regrets that, as the members of the breakdown gang are not on the medical register, he would be guilty of covering, and would be struck off the register for infamous professional conduct, if he relieved the sufferer in any way. If, however, his registered friend Sir Bryan Donkin will be good enough to undertake the salvage operations, he will be happy to act. Sir Bryan Donkin says that he would be only too delighted to be of use, but that, as he does not know how to handle compression drills and oxy-acetylene jets, the first effect of his interference would probably be to disembowel the patient and burn his head off. In these circumstances both gentlemen are very sorry, but nothing can be done, as it is evident that if eminent registered doctors were allowed to "cover" railway mechanics wholly ignorant of anatomy the nation must presently perish.

I must apologize to Dr Graham Little and Sir Bryan

Donkin for this monstrous supposition. I have not the slightest doubt that when it came to the point they would act precisely as Dr Axham acted. Perhaps they will forgive me in consideration of my having cleared up their minds on the subject of covering.

I am quite opposed to real covering, and wish the G.M.C. would stop it. Take a typical case. A patient, suffering from the very distressing pain called neuritis, calls in a registered doctor. It is clearly a case for some sort of manipulation rather than for the bottle. Possibly massage, the doctor thinks. As he knows nothing about massage, his duty is to call in a skilled Kellgren masseur. If he did, the masseur would at once tell him that massage is contra-indicated in such cases and would only aggravate the illness and give intense pain. But as, if the doctor called in a Kellgren masseur (who has to put in two years of finger training before he is considered manually qualified), he would share the fate of Dr Axham, he hands the patient over to a nurse who has spent a few hard-earned guineas on twelve lessons in massage from the local apothecary, with results that may be imagined. This procedure is tolerated by the G.M.C.; yet, if it is not covering, what is covering? The official answer is, apparently, any offence against the trade union. Offences against the patients are not only winked at, but in some of the worst instances practically imposed on the practitioner by forbidding him to call in competent assistance. Incompetent assistance is privileged.

May I say that I do not hold any brief for osteopathy, or Kellgren massage, or naturopathy or homeopathy, or Christian Science, or herbalism, or peculiarism, or for the few gifted individuals who, like Sir Herbert Barker, have developed and cultivated, by a course of intensive self-training which could not be imposed on any student, a personal technique which is practically incommunicable, and which they therefore do not pretend to teach to all comers any more than I pretend to teach all comers to write plays. My brief is for the public, the patient, the consumer, the victim who pays the piper in purse and person without being allowed to call the tune. My case is that the G.M.C. has been suffered to become a trade union of the most anti-social type, whereas it was meant to be, and if the constituent authorities will only do their plain duty can become, a public body protecting us against medical trade unionism (which is quite permissible in its proper place and under proper control by the community) as well as giving us a trustworthy guarantee that a practitioner who can produce its credentials has had a certain minimum of instruction and training, kept carefully up to date by representatives interested in scientific hygiene and not in the spread of lucrative hypochondria. Instead of this, the G.M.C. deliberately and openly addresses itself to the anti-social task of preventing the public from calling in any unregistered practitioner who is in competition with those on the register, whilst at the same time allowing the qualification for that register to remain in many respects not merely useless and out of date, but positively poisonous and murderous.

I have plenty of medical support for this view; but it will not appear in your columns, because a doctor cannot join in a Press campaign over his own name and address except at the risk of being struck off the register for "advertizing." If a doctor wishes to add to his income by writing critical articles in the lay Press, as some of our most eminent Churchmen do, he has to remove his name from the register and renounce clinical practice to secure freedom of utterance. I am not defending medical advertisement, registered or unregistered; I am simply explaining why any appeal for the reform of the General Medical Council must be conducted by laymen without avowed medical support. The situation is intolerable, and the remedy obvious.

HOW WILLIAM ARCHER IMPRESSED BERNARD SHAW

From a volume entitled Three Plays, by William Archer (Constable & Co., 1927)

WILLIAM ARCHER, though the most lucid and unequivocal of writers, was in person and manner probably the most deceptive man of his time. Nobody could have been less of an impostor in character; yet he took in all his contemporaries, even those who were fairly intimate with him. One of the cleverest of our younger essayists has described him as a dour Scot, without the slightest sense of humor, hard, logical, with an ability that was always in cold storage. This was not a stranger's deduction from his writings. It was a personal impression so strong that no study of his writings could quite dispel it. Not until the last London journalist who has met him has perished will William Archer be judged by his writings; and even in them there is an emotional reticence that will leave an incomplete picture of the man, though they will do him more justice than he ever did to himself. For the present, there is a fabulous Archer who is extremely unlike the real Archer, and much less amiable.

Had the fabulous Archer been the real one, our long friendship would have been impossible: indeed any friendship with him would have been impossible. Fortunately the real Archer was, like myself, the victim of an unsleeping and incorrigible sense of humor: the very quality (or fault) which the fabulous Archer utterly lacked. No doubt when we first met as young men of the same age some forty-five years ago, I interested him as a person free from certain superstitions that had been oppressive to him; but I interested him still more by being so laughably free, not only from superstitions recognized by him as such, but from many conventions which he had never dreamt of challenging, that I appealed irresistibly to him as an incarnate joke. The Shavianismus tickled him enormously; and he was never tired of quoting not only my jokes, but my heresies and paradoxes, many of which have by this time become platitudes. The way to get on with Archer was to amuse him: to argue with him was dangerous. The invaluable precept of Robert Owen: "Never argue: repeat your assertion," established me with Archer on the footing of a privileged lunatic, and made quarrels impossible.

Archer had the air of a stoic: he was really a humorist to whom a jest was worth more than most of the things common men prize. For instance, he was unlucky enough to have trouble with one of his eyes. He went to an oculist, and returned so radiant that I concluded that the oculist had cured him. On the contrary, the oculist had diagnosed amblyopia. "What is amblyopia?" said Archer. "Well," said the oculist, "the eye is quite perfect. There is no lesion or defect of any sort. A first-class eye. Only, it does not see anything." Archer found this so funny that he thought half his sight well lost for the fun of repeating it to me and everyone else.

Another instance, in which money was at stake. Though a thoroughbred Scot, he was usually so indifferent to it, so untouched by vulgar ambition or by the least taint of snobbery, so sensibly unpretentious in his habits, so content to go to the pit when he paid to enter a theatre or even in the steerage when he made a long voyage, that nothing but a stroke of luck could ever have made him rich; but when he got married he conscientiously set to work to accumulate savings; and by doing too much journalism he succeeded in making some provision for family contingencies. Unfortunately, on the best advice, he invested it all in Australian banks; and Australian banks presently went smash. I have known men reduced to fury and despair by less serious losses. Archer was sustained and even elated by our friend John Mackinnon Robertson. Robertson, not at that time the Right Honorable (he had not yet entered on the distinguished parliamentary career which he managed to combine so oddly with an equally distinguished literary activity), had just written an economic treatise entitled The Fallacy of Saving. He sent a copy to Archer; and it arrived simultaneously with the bad news from Australia. Archer at once sat down and wrote, "My dear Robertson: I am already completely convinced of the fallacy of saving, thank you." He came to me to tell me the story, chuckling with the enjoyment of a man who had just heard that his uncle had died in Australia and left him a million. Had he been a giggling fribble, incapable of his own distress, I should have had no patience with him. But, as I shall presently shew, never was there a man less a trifler than William Archer. He laughed at his misfortunes because things of the mind were important to him (humor is purely mental), and things of the body and of the pocket, as long as they stopped short of disablement and painful privation, relatively trivial. The sight of one eye did not matter provided he could see with the other; and he, who set very little store by what people call good living, could hardly be expected to feel much concern about savings whilst he could pay his way with earnings: a comic speech consoled him for both losses.

Why was it, then, that he produced so strong an impression of dourness, unbending Puritan rigidity, and total lack of humor?

The explanation is that in spite of his lifelong preoccupation with the theatre, he was not a dramatic, self-expressive person. Physically he was a tall upstanding well-built good-looking Scot, keeping his figure and bearing to the last. He had an agreeable voice and unaffected manners, and no touch of malice in him. But nobody could tell from any external sign what he was thinking about, or how he felt. The amblyopic eye may have contributed to this air of powerful reserve; but the reserve was real: it was a habit that had become first nature to him. In modern psycho-pathological terms it was a repression that had become a complex. Accustomed as I was to this, he amazed even me once. He had just completed his translation of Ibsen's Little Eyolf; and he read it to two or three friends of whom I was one. His reading was clear, intelligent, cold, without a trace of emotion, and rather wooden in the more moving passages. When he came to the last pages he suddenly handed me the book, and said, formally and with a marked access of woodenness, "Shaw: I must ask you to finish the reading for me. My feelings will not allow me to proceed." The contrast between the matter and the manner of this speech would have been irresistibly comic had any doubt of the sincerity of his distress been possible. I took the proof-sheets in silence, and finished the reading as desired. We were face to face with a man in whom dissimulation had become so instinctive that it had become his natural form of emotional expression. No wonder he seemed a monster of insensibility to those who did not know him very intimately.

To explain this, I must cast back to the year 1730 as a date in religious history. In that year, just before Wesley began Methodism in England, a Scots minister named John Glas was cast out by the General Assembly of the Kirk in Scotland as a Congregationalist heretic. Glas thought this was so much the worse for the Kirk in Scotland. Bible in hand, and strong in the Protestant right to private judgment, he founded one of the innumerable Separatist sects that arose in the eighteenth century. Shakespear would have called him a Brownist. He maintained that any group of persons organized according to the instructions of St Paul to Timothy, and qualified as godly according to the prescription of Matthew, was independent of any Kirk or General Assembly or ecclesiastical authority whatsoever, and was answerable to God alone. The aim of his own group was the realization of Christ's kingdom as defined in the famous reply to Pilate, "My kingdom is not of this world." Glas's son-in-law, Sandeman, carried this doctrine to England, where the groups became known as Sandemanians.

Now of Separation there is no end until every human being is a Separate Church, for which there is much to be said.

The Separatists continue to separate. In 1804 John Walker, Bachelor of Divinity (for so I construe the letters B.D.) and Fellow of Trinity College, Dublin, separated himself from the Episcopal Church of Ireland, and founded a sect called by him The Church of God, and by the profane The Walkerites. Its tenets resembled those of the Glasites so closely that there was talk of an amalgamation; but the Glasites were Sabbatarians; the Walkerites held that Christ had discarded the Sabbath; and so they could not agree. Anyhow Walkerism was superfluous in Scotland, where its numbers were often so small that worship among them was a family affair conducted by the head of the household, assisted by such male members of the sect as happened to be present. As the Glasites had flourishing congregations in many centres, Walkerite children would be sent to a Glasite Meeting when there was no Walkerite Meeting to send them to.

In the second generation of Walkerites, a Miss Walker married a Mr Archer. And one of their sons complicated the faith by marrying a daughter of James Morison, one of the shining lights of Glasism. From that exogamous alliance William Archer sprang. If ever there was a doubly predestined heir of grace, William, one would think, was he. And, on the whole, he lived up to his antecedents. But God fulfils Himself in many ways, and often in extremely unexpected ones. As William grew up, he felt obliged to pursue his hereditary Separatism to the point of separating himself not only from the Separatists, but from the curious fetish worship of the Bible, and the idolization of Christ, with which all the sects and Churches were still saturated.

This looks like a complete explanation of the reserve that was a second nature with him. But, if you are an English reader, do not infer too much from your ignorance of Scoto-Norwegian Separatism. Long before Archer's views had formed themselves sufficiently to threaten a schism in the family if he gave voice to them, he had profited, without the smallest friction, by the fact that both Walkerites and

Glasites regarded religion as too sacred to be made a subject of private conversation. They actually barred private prayer, and not only neither asked their children controversial questions nor permitted them to put any, but would not allow even a catechism to come between them and their God. In their view, you were either damned or saved by your own nature and the act of God; and any attempt to force God's hand in the transaction was sedition in His kingdom. Thus William was never driven to lie about his beliefs or about the family beliefs. He was simply not allowed to talk about either. He was, however, expected to go to Meeting when there was a meeting (Walkerite or Glasite) within reach, and not to laugh when his sense of humor got the better of the solemnity of the occasion. In the latter observance the Archer children were by no means uniformly successful. In William as in Mark Twain, the meetings had a marked homeopathic effect.

Another feature of Separatism which favored his freedom of thought was its anti-clericalism. The common English association of clericalism with piety is often misleading. The revolt against institutional religion which moved George Fox to regard a priest of any denomination as Mr Winston Churchill regards a Bolshevist, and to revile a church as a steeple house, has produced all the Separatist sects, and has in our day invaded even the Church of England in the person of the most intellectually eminent of its dignitaries. William Archer's father would have been surprised if anyone had called him an anti-clerical; but he had the Separatist habit of assuming that parsons are inadmissible acquaintances. The family atmosphere, if not explicitly anti-clerical, was, to say the least, not prelatical.

Archer's brother and collaborator in their translation of Peer Gynt tells me that he never heard his father say a word of any kind on any religious subject. This gives in a single sentence a vision of the extraordinary reserve imposed by the Separatism of Glas and Walker, surviving as a habit long after the original impulse had lost its fervor, and had even provoked a reaction. The reaction in William Archer carried him to a Modernism which would have been taken by Glas and Walker as unmistakeable evidence of his predestined damnation; but the habit of reserve remained.

It was reinforced as he grew older by the clash of his political opinions with those of the Glasites, who interpreted Christ's declaration that His kingdom was not of this world as implying a duty of unquestioning submission to all duly constituted secular authority. This view had settled down into simple political Conservatism; and when Archer's inner light led him to a vigorous Radicalism, it became necessary for him to extend his reserve from religion to politics, or else grieve his people very sorely, a cruelty of which he was quite incapable. He was hereditarily affectionate, and even suffered from a family inability to control his diaphragm (I borrow this quaint diagnosis from an expert) which made it impossible for him to command his voice when he was deeply moved, which explains both why he could not finish reading Little Eyolf and why up to the moment of relinquishing the attempt he had had to constrain himself so rigidly as to seem a wooden image rather than a very emotional man.

He was not himself conscious of the extent to which the Glasite diathesis influenced him. I do not believe that he knew or cared anything about the constitution or origin of Glasism: all he could tell me to satisfy my curiosity as a connoisseur in religious beliefs was that the performance, as he called it, consisted mainly in his grandfather reading the Bible phrase by phrase, and extracting from every phrase some not immediately obvious significance, the more far-fetched and fantastic the better. The grandson was interested neither in Kirk nor Conventicle, but in the theatre. He was prepared to attend to Shakespear, but not to Glasite hermeneutics. He had a certain admiration for his grandfather's ingenuity as an exegete, and was rather proud of him; but he soon learnt to defend himself from his expositions by an acquirement that often stood him in good stead in the theatre later on. He could slip his finger under the next page of his open Bible; go fast asleep; and turn the page without waking up when the rustling of all the other Bibles as their readers turned over struck on his sleeping ear and started a reflex action.

If I had known this when I attempted to read my first play to him I might not have abandoned it for years as an unfinished failure. He was utterly contemptuous of its construction; but this I did not mind, as I classed constructed plays with artificial flowers, clockwork mice, and the like. Unfortunately, when I came to the second act, something—possibly something exegetic in my tone—revived the old protective habit. He fell into a deep slumber; and I softly put the manuscript away and let him have his sleep out. When I mentioned this to our friend Henry Arthur Jones he reminded me of a member of the *Comédie Française*, who, on being remonstrated with for sleeping whilst an author was reading a play, said "Sleep is a criticism." This was my own view of the case; and I might never have meddled with the stage again had not Archer unconsciously discounted the incident one day by telling me the tale of his famous grandfather.

Thus he never came to know what his grandfather's religion was. He dismissed it, and most of Scriptural theology with it, as flat nonsense. And from this estimate he never to the end of his days retreated. It may seem strange that a man whose literary bent was so strong that he made literature his profession, whose ear was so musical that he could write excellent verse, and whose judgment was so respected that he was accepted as the most serious critic of his day, should be able to read the dregs of Elizabethan drama and not to read the Bible; but the fact remains that when I was writing my preface on Christianity (to Androcles and the Lion) and, having just read the New Testament through, asked him whether he had read the Gospels lately, and what he made of them he replied that he had tried, but "could not stick it." The doctrine was nonsense to him; and he had no patience with it because he took no interest in it. I pleaded that though Matthew had muddled his gospel by stringing sayings together in the wrong order, a more intelligible arrangement of them could be discovered by reading the other evangelists; but this produced no impression on him: the subject simply bored him; and he rather resented any attempt on my part to give the slightest importance to it. This was a very natural consequence of dosing a clever child prematurely with mental food that Ecumenical Councils have before now failed to digest; and parents and school committees will do well to make a careful note of it; but in Archer's case the intolerance it produced became a quality, as his book on India proves. There was no morbid nonsense about understanding everything and pardoning everything in the Archer family. The glimpses I had of them were quite convincing as to their being healthy-minded sensible open-air colonially rejuvenated people who, having to keep an inherited form of worship from making social life impossible, instinctively avoided sophistry and speculation, and took their intellectual course simply and downrightly. When, in what was then called The Conflict Between Religion and Science, William Archer took the side of Science, he broke away as cleanly and confidently as Glas had broken away from the Assembly or Walker from the Church of Ireland. He expressly denied having ever had any internal struggle or qualm. His only difficulty was to maintain his convictions without making his parents unhappy; and the Separatist reserve made it quite easy to do this whilst he lived with them.

When he came to London and began to write for the Secularist press, thus breaking the Separatist silence, he resorted to a *nom de plume*, for which, in those days, there were other reasons than family ones. A then future president of the National Secular Society had been actually imprisoned for a year for publishing in The Freethinker, his weekly journal, a picture of Samuel anointing Saul, in which the costumes and accessories were those of a modern hairdresser's shop; and until the expiration of the sentence Archer had to help with a monthly review which the victim of persecution edited for his more scholarly and fastidious followers. The leaders of the Secularist movement, including at that time Mrs Besant, were delighted to welcome Archer as a brilliant young recruit, and were somewhat taken aback when he would not enter into intimate social relations with them lest they should meet his parents, and quite simply told them so in his most expressionless manner. But for the strained relations which ensued, and for his preoccupation with the theatre, he might, like Robertson, have become a familiar figure in the pulpit of South Place Chapel, and been as definitely associated with Rationalism as Mr Edward Clodd. As it was, his position was sufficiently affirmed to make me ask him one day what his parents had to say about it. His reply was that the subject was never mentioned between them, but that he supposed they must have noticed that he did not attend any place of worship. Clearly there was no bitterness nor bigotry in the matter; and the fact that there was no resistance to break down made it impossible for a man of Archer's affectionate sensitiveness not to shield his father and mother from every contact with his heresy and its associations that could possibly be avoided without a sacrifice of his convictions.

Presently another interest came into his life. One showery day I was in New Oxford Street, probably going to or from the British Museum reading room, when I saw Archer coming towards me past Mudie's, looking much more momentous than usual. He seemed eight feet high; and his aspect was stern and even threatening, as if he were defying all Oxford Street, buses and all, to take the smallest liberty with him. His air of formidable height was partly due, perhaps, to his having draped himself in a buff-colored mackintosh which descended to his calves. But it was quaintly aided by the contrast of his inches with those of a lady who clung to his arm to keep pace with his unmerciful strides. She had a small head and a proportionately small comely face, winsome and ready to smile when not actually smiling. I had never seen Archer with a woman on his arm before, nor indeed concerning himself with one in any way; and, as the future author of Man and Superman, I feared the worst. And, sure enough, I was immediately introduced to the lady as his selection for the destiny of being Mrs Archer.

The marriage seemed a great success. Mrs Archer fitted herself into the simple and frugal life of her husband quite naturally, caring no more for fashion or manufactured pleasures and luxuries than he did. There came a wonderful son: he who figures in the correspondence of Robert Louis Stevenson as Tomarcher. Mrs Archer found the world paradise enough first with her Willie, and then with her man and her boy. She tolerated me and indulged me as an incarnate joke because he did; and I saw rather more of him after his marriage than before it, instead of less: a rare privilege for a bachelor friend.

But the more Archer's slender means obliged him to put Mrs Archer and the boy first, and literature comparatively nowhere, the more I, having among my budget of novels that nobody would publish a book called The Irrational Knot (meaning the marriage tie), began to doubt whether domesticity was good for his career. At last I read an anonymous article on onc of Archer's subjects which seemed to me a poor one. I was on the point of abusing it roundly to him one day when, to my consternation, he said, just in time, that he had written it. My concern was not becausc I thought the article unsatisfactory: every writer produces unsatisfactory articles occasionally. But that, good or bad, I had not recognized it as his: a failure unprecedented so far, proved to me that he had lost some of the brilliancy and unmistakeable individuality of style which had attracted me in his articles in The London Figaro long before I made his acquaintance. I knew that the way to make money in journalism is to turn out rapidly great quantities of undistinguished stuff; and I knew also that when a man marries he gives up his right to put quality of work first, and income second. I did not conceive it possible at that time that I should ever become a married man myself. With an artistic recklessness which shocks me in retrospect I told Archer that Mrs Archer was spoiling him, and that he would be a lost man unless he broke loose. He said, with that wooden formality which was the surest sign that he was deeply moved, that he must ask me not to visit his house whilst I held opinions so disparaging to Mrs Archer.

I was not in the least offended. Indeed I never was offended by anything Archer ever said to me or wrote about me, though he sometimes expressed a quite unnecessary remorse for speeches or articles which he supposed must have been painful to me. For some time I remained under his interdict, and saw nothing of Mrs Archer. Then the unexpected happened. Archer did not break loose; but Mrs Archer did. Let me not be misunderstood. There was no gentleman in the case. It was much more interesting than that.

I forget how long Mrs Archer remained a dropped subject between us; but it was Archer himself who resumed it. I found him in a state of frank anxiety which in him indicated considerable distress of mind; and he told me that Mrs Archer fancied that there was something the matter with her, though she was, as he believed, in perfect health. Now Mrs Archer, like her husband, was not at all the sort of person her appearance suggested. She seemed dainty, unassuming, clinging. Really, she was a woman of independent character, great decision and pertinacity, and considerable physical hardihood. This I had half guessed that day in Oxford Street, but I kept the guess to myself, as it might have been taken as a wanton paradox until the sequel bore it out. When Archer told me of his perplexity I shared it, and could think of nothing to suggest.

To the rescue of this male helplessness came a remarkable lady from America, Miss Annie Payson Call, authoress of a book entitled Power through Repose, and of a system, partly manipulative, partly sympathetic, of straightening

out tangled nerves. Miss Call had the same sort of amiability as Mrs Archer, and the same overflow of energy for which selfishness was not enough. She tackled Mrs Archer; she tackled me; she tackled everybody; and as she was a charming person, nobody objected. But she found in Mrs Archer something more than the passive subject of a cure. She found a pupil, a disciple, and finally an apostle in England. Mrs Archer's vocation also was for healing sore minds and wandering wits. With what seems to me in retrospect a staggering suddenness, though in fact she had to see Tom through to his independent manhood first, she created the nerve training institution at King's Langley which survives her. Literary people in the eighteen-nineties used to write futile sequels to Ibsen's Doll's House: Mrs Archer found a real and perfectly satisfactory sequel. She became an independent professional woman most affectionately married to an independent professional man, the two complementing instead of hampering each other; for in practical matters he was full of inhibitions and diffidences from which she was vigorously free. Incidentally I ceased to be one of Willie's bachelor encumbrances. Mrs Archer, having developed considerably more practical initiative and ability than ever I possessed, took me in hand fearlessly on her new footing, and admitted me, I think, to as much of her friendship as I deserved.

Thus Archer's domesticity ceased to be a problem; and you may set him down for good and all as fortunate in his marriage. But to suggest all that his marriage meant for him I must return to the child Tom Archer. The extraordinary companionship which Archer found in his little son could not have existed but for a double bond between them. First, Archer had retained much more of his own childhood than even his most intimate friends suspected. He must have been a very imaginative child; and he had retained so much of a child's imagination and fun that it was for some time a puzzle to me that he could be so completely fascinated as he was by Ibsen's imagination, and that yet, when I produced

my Quintessence of Ibsenism, he dismissed much of the specifically adult and worldly part of it precisely as he had dismissed the Scriptural exegetics of his grandfather. This devoted Ibsenite, who translated the Master's works so forcibly and vividly, was never in the least an Ibsenist: he delighted in Ibsen's plays just as a child delights in The Arabian Nights without taking in anything of the passages which Captain Burton left unexpurgated. It was this innocence that limited his own excursions into dramatic literature; he could not see that the life around him, including his own, was teeming with dramatic material, and persisted in looking for his subjects either in literature or in fairyland.

Now it happened that Tom Archer, though so entirely his mother's son in most respects that, save for an occasional fleeting revelation in his expression, he was not a bit like Archer, had a prodigious imagination. Having no derisive brothers and sisters to make him sensitive and secretive about it, but, on the contrary, a father who took it with the tenderest seriousness, and in fact became an accomplice in all its extravagances, Tom was able to let himself go gloriously. He invented a *pays de Cocagne* which he called Peona, which went far beyond the garret-forest in The Wild Duck, as it had no contact with limited mechanical realities. I heard much of Peona and its inhabitants at second hand, and even a little at first hand, on which occasions I swallowed every adventure with a gravity not surpassed by Archer's own. I am sure that Archer, whose youth as one of a large and robust family enjoyed no such protection, could never have felt this delicacy had he not remembered his own youth, and recognized his own imagination in his son's.

There was another experience from which he was determined to protect Tom; and that was the British boarding school, or boy farm, as William Morris called it. It was useless to romance to him about the character-forming virtues and historic glories of Eton and Harrow, Winchester and Rugby and Marlborough: he anticipated the opinions of Sanderson of Oundle, who heartily agreed with me when I

expressed my opinion that these places should be razed to the ground, and their foundations sown with salt. Archer had taken his own schooling as a dayboy, and was convinced, with good reason, that this arrangement, however inconvenient for the parents, was much more wholesome for the child. Accordingly, Tom spent his childish schooldays with his people in a Surrey cottage on the façade of which Mr Edward Rimbault Dibdin inscribed the name Walden (a compliment to Thoreau) in highly artistic lettering. When he outgrew the educational resources of that primitive neighborhood the family moved to Dulwich and sent him to the college there.

Meanwhile my comment on Tom was that he was a second Rudyard Kipling; for, as I happened to know from William Morris, Mr Kipling had been a great Peoneer in his nonage. The years in which Archer and Tom explored Peona together passed as fast as real years in a real country until at last the once inexhaustible subject of Tom dropped so completely that I actually had to ask Archer about him. To my amazement he conveyed to me, with a manner that would have done credit to a piece of mahogany, that the firm of Archer & Son of Peona had dissolved partnership. Tom, he explained, had been ill; and Archer opined that the illness had affected his character, which, he said, was totally changed. This theory of the alleged change was too summary and too surgical to convince me. But I forbore to probe; and the truth came out gradually. The child Tom, developing into the incipient man, emerged from Peona a most unnatural son. He was as keen about the glories of public schools as if he were indeed the author of Stalky and Co. He distinguished himself at Dulwich by the facility with which he turned out Latin verses, becoming Captain of the Classical Side. He joined the Officers' Training Corps, and actually made his father enlist in the Inns of Court Volunteers, a trial which Archer supported because, being a private, and having to salute Tom, who was an officer, the situation appealed to his sense of humor as well as to his conscientious public spirit. In short, he dragged Archer out of Peona with him, and imposed public schools ideals on him. Military romance alone survived from fairyland; and even that took the fashionable imperialist shape.

Up to this time Archer had, without knowing it, been a true Glasite in the essential sense. His kingdom had not been of this world. But now, what with the son grasping with all his imaginative power at conventional military ideals, and this world beginning to treat the father with more and more of the distinguished consideration which his work earned and his unworldly character commanded, Archer had to adapt himself as far as he could to the responsibilities of his celebrity, and to set himself to make the best of convention instead of criticizing it with the independence of a young and comparatively unknown man. Every free-lance who makes a reputation has to go through this phase; but Archer was under the special emotional pressure of having to adapt himself to Tom's Kiplingesque war mentality in and out of season. He became as conventional as it was in his nature to be, and indeed, for Tom's sake, perhaps a little more, though the public school had taken away his playmate.

Presently Tom's boyhood passed like his childhood, and left him a young man, still his mother's son in respect of being under average military size and considerably over average military vigor of mind and practical initiative. Oxford, where he had expected to distinguish himself because he had done so at Dulwich, did not suit him. True, his aptitude for classical exercises did not desert him. He took honors in law, and was in no sense a failure. But Oxford was something of a failure for him. The struggle for life was not real enough there for a youth who had a passion for the military realism of soldiering. When he left Oxford to begin adult life, he worked as a solicitor for a couple of years in London. Then an opening in America, with a promise of a speedy return to rejoin his family at home, took him across the Atlantic.

Two months later the gulf of war opened at the feet of our young men. Tom rushed back to hurl himself into it. Amid the volcanoes of Messines he was serving as a lance-corporal in "the dear old G Company" of the London Scottish. Invalided home, he accepted a commission, and for a year was able to do no more than sit on the brink of the gulf in the Ordnance until his strength returned, when he volunteered afresh for the firing line as lieutenant in the King's Own Scottish Borderers. In February 1918 he married Alys Morty, cousin to a comrade-at-arms fallen at Messines, and had a deliriously happy honeymoon in Ireland. Then, the war still dragging on, he hurled himself into the gulf again; and this time, at Mount Kemmel, it closed on him, and his father saw him no more. He left his young widow to take his place in his parents' affections, the newly found beloved daughter succeeding to the newly lost beloved son. Yet Archer was loth to let the son go. He renewed an old interest in super-rational research; investigated dreams and the new psycho-analysis; and even experimented unsuccessfully in those posthumous conversations in which so many of the bereaved found comfort. And so, between daughter and son, the adventure of parentage never ended for Archer.

When the war broke out he was past military age, and had to confine his part in it to countering the German propaganda service and doing some of our own, an employment in which his knowledge of languages stood him in good stead. When the Armistice made an end of that, his own bent reasserted itself and took him back to the theatre, and (save where his memories of Tom were concerned) to militant Rationalism.

His great work of translating Ibsen had by this time been brought to an end by Ibsen's death. I am myself a much-translated author; and I know how hard the lot of a translator is if he is sensitive to frantic abuse both by rival or would-be rival translators, and by literary men inflamed by an enthusiasm for the author (gained from the translations they abuse) which convinces them that his opinions are their own, and that the translator, not seeing this, has missed the whole point of the work. I use the word frantic advisedly: the lengths to which these attacks go are incredible. At one time it was the fashion in the literary cliques to dismiss Archer's translations as impossible. I told them it was no use: that Archer-Ibsen had seized the public imagination as it had seized theirs, and would beat any other brand of Ibsen in English. And it was so. Whenever a translation was produced without the peculiar character that Archer gave to his, it had no character at all, no challenge, at best only a drawing room elegance that was a drawback rather than an advantage. When Mr Anstey burlesqued Ibsen in Punch, he did it by burlesquing Archer: without Archer the plays would not have bitten deep enough to be burlesqued. Even in the case of Peer Gynt, which moved several enthusiasts to attempt translations following the rhymes and metres of the original (I began one myself, with our friend Braekstad translating for me literally, line by line, and got as far as a couple of pages or so), the unrhymed translation by Archer and his brother Colonel Charles Archer held its own against the most ingenious and elaborate rival versions. Whenever Peer Gynt was quoted it was always in the Archer version. I have already given the explanation. Archer understood and cared for Ibsen's imagination. For his sociological views he cared so little that he regarded them mostly as aberrations when he was conscious of them. Thus, undistracted by Ibsen's discussions, he went straight for his poetry, and reproduced every stroke of imagination in a phraseology that invented itself *ad hoc* in his hands. As nothing else really mattered, the critics who could not see this, and would have it that everything else mattered, neither made nor deserved to make any permanent impression. Besides, the air of Norway breathed through his versions. He had breathed it himself from his childhood during his frequent visits, beginning at the age of three, to the Norwegian home of his grandparents, where he had two unmarried aunts who exercised his tenderness and powers of admiration very beneficently. As to the few lyrics which occur in Ibsen's plays, and which would have baffled a prosaic translator, they gave Archer no trouble at all: he was at his best in them. If it had been possible for the father of a family to live by writing verse in the nineteenth century, Archer would probably have done more in that manner on his own account.

How far he sacrificed a career as an original playwright to putting the English-speaking peoples in possession of Ibsen is an open question. In my opinion he instinctively chose the better part, because the theatre was not to him a workshop but part of his fairyland. He never really got behind the scenes, and never wanted to. The illusion that had charmed his youth was so strong and lasting that not even fifty years of professional theatre-going in London could dispel it. Inevitably then he liked the theatre as he found it at first: the theatre of the French "well-made play." But the attraction of this school of theatrical art for him did not lie in its ingenuities and neatnesses of construction, though he sometimes wrote as if it did. He liked it because it also lived in fairyland. Sophisticated as it was, yet was its kingdom not of this world. Archer, though he approached it as a reformer, did not want to reform it out of existence: he wanted to strengthen it by giving some sort of subsistence to its make-believe, which had worn thin and stale, ignorant and incredible. He did not want to drag the heroine from her fairyland; but how could he believe in her if she had an obviously impossible solicitor and butler and lady's maid? If she lived in a world totally exhausted of ideas, created by authors who, outside their little theatrical clique, knew nothing of their country, and conceived it as a complete vacuum in respect of the things it had most at heart: business, sport, politics, and religion, how could a man of any strength of mind or sense of verisimilitude take her seriously? That was why Archer cried out in one breath for naturalness in the theatre and for artifice in dramatic authorship. In the novel, which raises no question of technique, he welcomed the most uncompromising naturalness, making me read De Maupassant's Une Vie, applauding Zola, and coming into my rooms one day full of his discovery of a new novelist of our own, who had burst on the world with a naturalistic novel entitled A Mummer's Wife. I was so impressed with his account of it that I eagerly asked the name of the author; but when he told me it was George Moore I burst into irreverent laughter, knowing the said George personally as an inveterate romancer, whose crimson inventions, so far delivered orally for private circulation only, suggested that he had been brought into the world by a union of Victor Hugo with Ouida. But Archer insisted on my reading the book, as he had insisted on my reading Une Vie; and I stood rebuked for my incredulity.

I never read Archer's one novel, a youthful exploit called The Doom of the Destroyed, which had been published serially in a Scottish newspaper, and was one of his favorite jokes. I gathered that in point of romance it left George Moore's unpublished *quasi* autobiographical tales of adventure nowhere; but it is certain that Archer's adult taste in novels was for merciless realism. Therefore when one day he proposed that we two should collaborate in writing a play, he to supply the constructional scaffolding or scenario, and I to fill in the dialogue, I assumed that I might be as realistic as Zola or De Maupassant with his entire sympathy. But he was always upsetting my assumptions as to his sympathies; and he did so signally on this occasion.

It happened in this way. Archer had planned for two heroines, a rich one and a poor one. The hero was to prefer the poor one to the rich one; and in the end his disinterestedness was to be rewarded by the lucrative discovery that the poor one was really the rich one. When I came to fill in this scheme I compressed the two heroines into one; but I made up the one out of two models, whom I will now describe.

Once, when I was walking homewards at midnight through Wigmore Street, taking advantage of its stillness and loneliness at that hour to contemplate, like Kant, the starry heaven above me, the solitude was harshly broken by the voices of two young women who came out of Mandeville Place on the other side of the street a couple of hundred yards behind me. The dominant one of the pair was in a black rage: the other was feebly trying to quiet her. The strained strong voice and the whimpering remonstrant one went on for some time. Then came the explosion. The angry one fell on the other, buffeting her, tearing at her hair, grasping at her neck. The victim, evidently used to it, cowered against the railings, covering herself as best she could, and imploring and remonstrating in a carefully subdued tone, dreading a police rescue more than the other's violence. Presently the fit passed, and the two came on their way, the lioness silent, and the lamb reproachful and rather emboldened by her sense of injury. The scene stuck in my memory, to be used in due time.

Also I had about this time a friendship with a young independent professional woman, who enjoyed, as such, an exceptional freedom of social intercourse in artistic circles in London. As she was clever, goodnatured, and very good-looking, all her men friends fell in love with her. This had occurred so often that she had lost all patience with the hesitating preliminaries of her less practised adorers. Accordingly, when they clearly longed to kiss her, and she did not dislike them sufficiently to make their gratification too great a strain on her excessive goodnature, she would seize the stammering suitor firmly by the wrists, bring him into her arms by a smart pull, and saying "Let's get it over," allow the startled gentleman to have his kiss, and then proceed to converse with him at her ease on subjects of more general interest.

I provided Archer with a heroine by inventing a young woman who developed from my obliging but impatient friend in the first act to the fury of Wigmore Street in the second: such a heroine as had not been seen on the London stage since Shakespear's Taming of the Shrew. And my shrew was never tamed.

Now Archer was not such a simpleton as to be unaware that some women are vulgar, violent, and immodest according to Victorian conceptions of modesty. He would probably have assented to the proposition that as vulgarity, violence, and immodesty are elements in human nature, it is absurd to think of them as unwomanly, unmanly, or unnatural. But he also knew that a character practically free from these three vices could be put on the stage without any departure from nature, for the excellent reason that his own character was most unusually free from them, even his strong Scottish sense of humor being, like his conversation, entirely clean. Why, then, impose them wantonly on his charming and refined heroine? He repudiated all complicity in such an outrage. He reproached me for my apparent obsession with abominably ill-tempered characters, oversexed to saturation. My way in the theatre was evidently not his way; and it was not until, at my third attempt as a playwright, I achieved a play (Mrs Warren's Profession) which appealed to his sense of Zolaistic naturalism, that he ceased to dissuade me from pursuing the occupation into which he had innocently tempted me.

I must mention that his decisive and indignant retirement from the collaboration occurred whilst the play was still in shorthand, and therefore quite illegible by him, and not legible enough by myself to admit of my reading it aloud to him tolerably. But I had made demands on him which betrayed my deliberate and unconscionable disregard of his rules of the art of play construction. His scenario had been communicated to me *viva voce*; and when I told him I had finished the first act, and had not yet come to his plot, asking him to refresh my memory about it, he felt as the architect of a cathedral might if the builder had remarked one day that he had finished the nave and transepts according to his own fancy, and, having lost the architect's plans, would like to have another copy of them before he tackled the tower, the choir, and the lady chapel. I managed to appease my architect by arguing that it was not until the second act that a well-made play came to business seriously, and that meanwhile I had fulfilled his design by making the river Rhine the scene of the meeting of the lovers in the first act. But when, having written some pages of the second act, I said I had used up all his plot and wanted some more to go on with, he retired peremptorily from the firm. He was of course quite right: I was transmogrifying not only his design but the whole British drama of that day so recklessly that my privilege as a paradoxical lunatic broke down under the strain; and he could no longer with any self-respect allow me to play the fool with his scenario. For it was not a question of this particular scenario only. He did not agree with me that the form of drama which had been perfected in the middle of the nineteenth century in the French theatre was essentially mechanistic and therefore incapable of producing vital drama. That it was exhausted and, for the moment, sterile, was too obvious to escape an observer of his intelligence; but he saw nothing fundamentally wrong with it, and to the end of his life maintained that it was indispensable as a form for sound theatrical work, needing only to be brought into contact with life by having new ideas poured into it. I held, on the contrary, that a play is a vital growth and not a mechanical construction; that a plot is the ruin of a story and therefore of a play, which is essentially a story; that Shakespear's plays and Dickens's novels, though redeemed by their authors' genius, were as ridiculous in their plots as Goldsmith's hopelessly spoilt Goodnatured Man: in short, that a play should never have a plot, because, if it has any natural life in it, it will construct itself, like a flowering plant, far more wonderfully than its author can consciously construct it.

On such terms collaboration between us was impossible: indeed my view practically excludes collaboration. His view does not; and we shall presently see him returning to it after an interval of many years, during which I had become an established playwright, possibly wrong in my theory, but beyond all question successful in my practice.

He had already written plays single-handed. I remember a one-act play called Clive, dealing with the failure of that hero's attempt at suicide, and his conclusion that Heaven had other views for him. As this has disappeared, he may have destroyed it as puerile; but I thought it promising, and more alive than a play about a prima donna who lost her voice, a theme frankly taken from George Eliot's Armgart. George Eliot's reputation was then enormous, in spite of the protests of Ruskin, and of the alliterative vituperations of Swinburne; and it was very far from being undeserved. When I read Middlemarch in my teens I was impressed by it as by a masterpiece of a new order; and I have no doubt that Archer was equally impressed, though I do not remember discussing George Eliot with him. But the impression she made was not encouraging. The effect of the fatalistic determinism into which the scientific thought of that day had driven her was distinctly depressing and laming. Her characters seemed the helpless victims of their environment and inherited dispositions, contributing nothing except a few follies and weaknesses to the evolutionary struggle, if the word struggle can be used where there is no real resistance to what Darwin called natural selection. Now a fatalist, as George Eliot proved, can write so well that a capable man of letters like the late Lord Bryce, in a public eulogy of Tolstoy, could think of nothing more complimentary to say of him than that as a novelist he was second only to George Eliot. But, for all that, she discouraged many noble spirits; and I think she disabled Archer to some extent, directly or indirectly. The last drop of dramatic vitality in her school was drained by Ibsen; and when Archer had translated Ibsen there was nothing left for the translator.

Archer had various theories as to this disablement: as, for instance, that he could not write dialogue, which was nonsense; but the fact was that a George Eliotish philosophy of life, and a mechanistic limitation of the possibilities of the theatre, combined with his natural and very amiable diffidence and his unconsciously Glasite unworldliness, kept him back from the newly broken and rather unsightly ground in which alone a new drama could germinate.

At last, quite late in life, he had a dream; and the dream was a good story about an Asiatic Rajah made cynical by a Western education, and a Green Goddess who had to be propitiated by blood sacrifices, some English captives becoming available for that purpose. The result proved that the complexes which inhibited him from writing effective plays when he was awake, did not operate when he was asleep. When he turned his dream into a play it was prodigiously successful, first in America and then in England; and Archer ceased at last to be a much underpaid man. I had urged at every opportunity that the great national services he had done by his Englishing of Ibsen should be acknowledged by a pension (a title without one is only a source of expense); but I was always met with the difficulty that in this Philistine country parliamentary grants are made only to generals, pro-consuls, and Polar explorers. Literature and art have nothing to look for but an occasional knighthood or a civil list pension; and to obtain the pension it is necessary to assert that the postulant is in straitened circumstances. For Ashton Ellis, the translator of Richard Wagner's voluminous prose works, it had been possible, when he was almost destitute, to obtain a wretched pittance of £80 a year; but Archer was at no time at a loss for his livelihood. After the success of The Green Goddess a pension was more than ever out of the question; and Archer never had any official recognition of his public service, out of which, by the way, he steadfastly refused to make money through translator's performing fees, lest he should compromise his disinterestedness as a critic.

Here let me say, parenthetically, that Archer was incorruptible as a critic. In his day there were various methods of amiable corruption in vogue. One was called simply Chicken

& Champagne, which explains itself. It includes various degrees of blandishment; and some of them were tried on Archer; but they were hopelessly thrown away on him, because he never had the least suspicion of their nature, and either accepted them in unconquerable innocence at their face value, or declined them because they bored him. Another way was available if the critic was known to have written a play. The manager asked for it; put it on the shelf; promised production at some future unspecified time; and offered an advance on account of author's fees. A third method was almost a routine. An actor-manager would write to a critic to say that he wanted to consult him as an expert. An interview would follow. The manager would explain that he had acquired the performing right of some foreign play, and was thinking of attempting a part in it. Would the critic advise him about the translation? Would he care to undertake the translation? If so, would he sell a six months' option on the translation for, say, £50? If the critic was amenable, the £50 changed hands; and nothing more was heard of the play or the translation. If not, he recommended another translator; the manager shrugged his shoulders; and the two parted smiling. The managers did this, I believe, rather because it was the fashion, and almost the due of a leading critic, than with any sense that the proposal was in any way improper. Certainly the actor-managers who made it to me when I was a critic thought no worse of it than of tipping a waiter, and probably considered it rather unsocial on my part to evade the transaction.

Notwithstanding Archer's reputation as a translator, no such proposals were made, as far as I know, to him. His integrity was unassailed because it was so obviously impregnable. I doubt if he even knew the game as a usage, though he must have been aware of instances in which dealings in options had been followed by marked accesses of eulogy. After all, the instances were exceptional; besides, he went his own way so completely as a matter of course that he passed through the theatrical world without noticing all its aberrations, as indeed he passed through the kingdom of this world in general. He was much too scrupulous in the matter of the Ibsen translations; but the position of a critic who is also a proprietor of performing rights of any kind is certainly a very delicate one; and it was characteristic of Archer to carry his delicacy too far rather than accept a commercial interest in the plays of an author whom his critical conscience obliged him to recommend with all his might.

Diffident to the last, Archer had no sooner constructed The Green Goddess according to rule, and finished the two main acts, than he lost self-confidence, and perhaps patience, over the dénouement in the third act, and asked me to finish the play for him on the old ground that he could not write dialogue. I overwhelmed him with denunciations of his laziness; told him he could finish it perfectly well for himself if he chose to; and threatened that if I did the work I would make the lady get the better of the wicked Rajah in the vein of Captain Brassbound's Conversion. This threat was effectual; and he turned to Arthur Pinero to finish the play for him. Pinero, with great tact, made an alternative suggestion which opened Archer's eyes to the fact that if it was not worth his while to write the last act because it was to be hack work, he should offer it to a hack writer. Archer thereupon finished the play himself, and was, I hope, delivered by the result from all further misgivings as to his own competence. But it was too late in the day to begin life anew as a fashionable playwright; and The Green Goddess stands, by no means as the crown of his career, but rather as a proof that the inhibitions which prevented him from achieving this sort of worldly success earlier were not due, as he himself feared, to lack of faculty, but to Providence, which had other fish for him to fry.

In his predestined work I do not include the whole of his huge output of notices of theatrical performances, nor even the plans for a national theatre, which he prepared in collaboration with Harley Granville-Barker, then the most wonderful of the younger generation knocking at our doors. Journalistic criticism, after the first years, becomes necessarily for the most part repetitive bread-winning; and the theatre planning was rather like building sand castles in the face of a flood tide, a pastime to which Granville-Barker was much addicted as a refuge from his proper business of writing plays. Archer's essays on the censorship, on Diderot's Paradox (Masks or Faces?), and on Macready, with his reprints of the theatrical criticisms of Lewes and Forster, are all valuable and readable; but they lay in his path as a professional critic of the theatre, and are therefore not so significant as the excursions to which his spirit drove him.

In 1906 a Spanish educationalist and philanthropist who was also strongly anti-clerical (meaning really anti-obscurantist), and was therefore supposed by the officers of the Spanish army to be in his nature essentially diabolical, and in his habits an assassin of all royal persons, had the misfortune to fall into the hands of a court-martial in Barcelona, where he was shamefully ill-used whilst in custody, and finally shot. It was a monstrous case of class ignorance and vindictive bigotry; and Archer willingly accepted a journalistic commission to visit Spain and investigate it. He exposed it so effectually that the biographical dictionaries and encyclopædias now refer to him as their authority for their accounts of the martyrdom—for that is what it came to—of Ferrer.

His subsequent visit to India, though it had no such sensational provocation, produced his remarkable book on the subject. At that time it was the fashion for literary European travellers returning from Asia to display their susceptibilities to the call of the East by depicting an India of boundless and magical fascination, lit up with Bengal lights, saturated with the charm of Pierre Loti's romances, adorned with the temples of a living religion more profound than our own, and inhabited by Rabindranath Tagores and dark-eyed enchantresses, with Mahatmas in the mountain background. These enthusiasts were more Indian than any Indian; and

their readers, who had never been in India, began where they left off, and went much further into an imaginary East. Archer went to see for himself, and instantly and uncompromisingly denounced the temples as the shambles of a barbarous ritual of blood sacrifice, and the people as idolaters with repulsive rings through their noses. He refused to accept the interest of Indian art and the fictions of Indian romance as excuses. He remained invincibly faithful to Western civilization, and told the Indians flatly what a civilized Western gentleman must think of them and feel about some of their customs. Had he been able to get behind the scenes of Indian domestic life as Katherine Mayo did some years later, his book might have made as great a sensation as hers.

In writing thus he did India the only service in his power. If Western civilization is not more enlightened than Eastern we have clearly no right to be in India. When once the British conqueror and master of India comes to think that suttee is a touching and beautiful act of wifely sacrifice, he had better abdicate, come home, and introduce suttee in England. When he ceases to treat the car of Juggernaut precisely as he would treat a motor-bus driven to the public danger, his mission in India is over. What we owe to the Roman occupation of Britain we do not know: in fact there is too much ground for Mr George Trevelyan's conclusion that we relapsed the moment the Romans left us to ourselves; but we should certainly owe nothing at all if the Romans had had the slightest doubt that the augur represented a less grossly superstitious religion than the Druid, and that Roman law and Roman civilization were higher than British. They may have been as hasty and superficial as Sir John Woodroffe declares Archer to have been; but they did not think so; and anyhow the sole justification of their conquest and occupation was that they were right. We shall have to clear out of India some day as the Romans had to clear out of Britain: perhaps the sooner the better for both parties. But it is certain that if, after that happens, the

Indians are ever to say "It was a good thing for us that the westerners came and taught us something," it will be because the English criticism of India was Archer's criticism, and not that of the occidental renegades who swell the heads of our Indian students by assuring them that we are crude barbarians compared to them. Archer would have been the last man to deny that we are shocking barbarians according to our own standards; that white women with small earrings cannot logically despise brown women with large noserings; and that the Fundamentalist who prosecutes a school teacher for refusing to bow the knee to the god to whom Jephthah sacrificed his daughter can hardly hope to impose himself on an educated Hindu as a pioneer of thought. All the same, the Fundamentalist does not sacrifice his daughter or even his calf, and would send anyone who did to the electric chair or the lunatic asylum; and the Eastern toleration of noserings is not justified by the Western toleration of earrings. People who make the one an excuse for the other will never do anything to lighten the load of human superstition; and as this was really Archer's appointed task in life he wrote one of the most useful because one of the most resolutely unsympathetic books on India produced in his generation. It is not all unsympathetic or anti-Indian: very far from it. But it was the unsympathetic part that was needed and effective. If you like, he wrote about the Indians as John Glas would have written about the heathen. But why not rather put it that he wrote about the Indians as Dickens wrote about the Americans? And does anyone now doubt that Dickens told the Americans what they needed to be told, and that his honesty did not prevent his becoming more popular with them than any of their romantic flatterers?

I have no more to say about William Archer that matters enough to be printed. Looking back as far as the days when, finding me full of literary ability but ridiculously incapable of obtaining literary employment and desperately in need of it, he set me on my feet as a critical journalist by simply handing me over a share of his own work, and making excuses for

having deputed it until the Pall Mall Gazette and The World, then in the van of fashionable journalism, accepted the deputy as a principal, I am conscious that many of our contemporaries must have seen him much oftener than I, and that this sketch of him must be incomplete and perhaps in some points misleading. And there is the other possibility: that I may have been too close to him, and known him too early, to realize his full stature. But I am sure that I never could get him to think as well of himself as I thought of him. I leave it to others to compose a proper full-dress literary portrait of him: all I have tried to do here is to give some sort of life to a sketch of a friend of whom, after more than forty years, I have not a single unpleasant recollection, and whom I was never sorry to see or unready to talk to.

One day I received from him the following letter:

27, Fitzroy Square, W.1.

My dear G. B. S. *17th December* 1924.

Since I wrote you, I have learnt that I shall have to undergo an operation one of these days—I go into a nursing home tomorrow. I don't know that the operation is a very serious one, and as a matter of fact I feel as fit as a fiddle, so I suppose my chances are pretty good. Still, accidents will happen; and this episode gives me an excuse for saying, what I hope you don't doubt—namely, that though I may sometimes have played the part of all-too candid mentor, I have never wavered in my admiration and affection for you, or ceased to feel that the Fates had treated me kindly in making me your contemporary and friend. I thank you from my heart for forty years of good comradeship.

Whatever happens, let it never be said that I did not move in good society—I lunched today with the King of Norway and Prince Olaf.

Very kind regards to Mrs Shaw, and all good wishes for 1925.—Ever yours, W. A.

I was not seriously alarmed, and presently sailed for Madeira. On landing there, the first words that caught my eye on the news bulletin in the hall of Reid's Hotel were "Death of Mr William Archer." They threw me into a transport of fury. The operation had killed him. I am unfashionable enough to hold that an operation which does not justify itself by its promised results should always be the subject of a stringent inquest; for I have never been able to regard a death caused by an operation as a natural death. My rage may have been unjust to the surgeons; but it carried me over my first sense of bereavement. When I returned to an Archerless London it seemed to me that the place had entered on a new age in which I was lagging superfluous.

I still feel that when he went he took a piece of me with him.

OSCAR WILDE

A Letter to Frank Harris, published by him in his Life of Wilde, 1918

MY DEAR HARRIS:—

Why was Wilde so good a subject for a biography that none of the previous attempts which you have just wiped out are bad? Just because his stupendous laziness simplified his life almost as if he knew instinctively that there must be no episodes to spoil the great situation at the end of the last act but one. It was a well-made life in the Scribe sense. It was as simple as the life of Des Grieux, Manon Lescaut's lover; and it beat that by omitting Manon and making Des Grieux his own lover and his own hero.

Des Grieux was a worthless rascal by all conventional standards; and we forgive him everything. We think we forgive him because he was unselfish and loved greatly. Oscar seems to have said: "I will love nobody: I will be utterly selfish; and I will be not merely a rascal but a monster; and you shall forgive me everything. In other words, I will reduce your standards to absurdity, not by writing them down, though I could do that so well—in fact, *have* done it—but by actually living them down and dying them down."

However, I mustnt start writing a book to you about Wilde: I must just tumble a few things together and tell you them. To take things in the order of your book, I can remember only one occasion on which I saw Sir William Wilde, who, by the way, operated on my father to correct a squint, and overdid the correction so much that my father squinted the other way all the rest of his life. To this day I never notice a squint: it is as normal to me as a nose or a tall hat.

I was a boy at a concert in the Antient Concert Rooms in Brunswick Street in Dublin. Everybody was in evening dress; and—unless I am mixing up this concert with another (in which case I doubt if the Wildes would have been present)—the Lord-Lieutenant was there with his courtiers in blue facings. Wilde was dressed in snuffy brown; and as he had the sort of skin that never looks clean, he produced a dramatic effect beside Lady Wilde (in full fig) of being, like Frederick the Great, Beyond Soap and Water, as his Nietzschean son was beyond Good and Evil. He was currently reported to have a family in every farmhouse; and the wonder was that Lady Wilde didnt mind—evidently a tradition from the Travers case, which I did not know about until I read your account, as I was only eight in 1864.

Lady Wilde was nice to me in London during the desperate days between my arrival in 1876 and my first earning of an income by my pen in 1885, or rather until, a few years earlier, I threw myself into Socialism and cut myself contemptuously loose from everything of which her at-homes—themselves desperate affairs enough, as you saw for yourself—were part. I was at two or three of them; and I once dined with her in company with an ex-tragedy queen named Miss Glynn, who, having no visible external ears, reared a head like a turnip. Lady Wilde talked about Schopenhauer; and Miss Glynn told me that Gladstone formed his oratorical style on Charles Kean.

I ask myself where and how I came across Lady Wilde; for we had no social relations in the Dublin days. The explanation must be that my sister, then a very attractive girl who sang beautifully, had met and made some sort of innocent conquest of both Oscar and Willie. I met Oscar once at one of the at-homes; and he came and spoke to me with an evident intention of being specially kind to me. We put each other out frightfully; and this odd difficulty persisted between us to the very last, even when we were no longer mere boyish novices and had become men of the world with plenty of skill in social intercourse. I saw him very seldom, as I avoided literary and artistic coteries like the plague, and refused the few invitations I received to go into society with burlesque ferocity, so as to keep out of it without offending people past their willingness to indulge me as a privileged lunatic.

The last time I saw him was at that tragic luncheon of yours at the Café Royal; and I am quite sure our total of meetings from first to last did not exceed twelve, and may not have exceeded six.

I definitely recollect six: (1) At the at-home aforesaid. (2) At Macmurdo's house in Fitzroy Street in the days of the Century Guild and its paper The Hobby Horse. (3) At a meeting somewhere in Westminster at which I delivered an address on Socialism, and at which Oscar turned up and spoke. Robert Ross surprised me greatly by telling me, long after Oscar's death, that it was this address of mine that moved Oscar to try his hand at a similar feat by writing The Soul of Man Under Socialism. (4) A chance meeting near the stage door of the Haymarket Theatre, at which our queer shyness of one another made our resolutely cordial and appreciative conversation so difficult that our final laugh and shakehands was almost a reciprocal confession. (5) A really pleasant afternoon we spent together on catching one another in a place where our presence was an absurdity. It was some exhibition in Chelsea: a naval commemoration, where there was a replica of Nelson's Victory and a set of P. & O. cabins which made one seasick by mere association of ideas. I dont know why I went or why Wilde went; but we did; and the question what the devil we were doing in that galley tickled us both. It was my sole experience of Oscar's wonderful gift as a raconteur. I remember particularly an amazingly elaborate story which you have no doubt heard from him: an example of the cumulation of a single effect, as in Mark Twain's story of the man who was persuaded to put lightning conductor after lightning conductor at every possible point on his roof until a thunderstorm came and all the lighting in the heavens went for his house and wiped it out.

Oscar's much more carefully and elegantly worked out

story was of a young man who invented a theatre stall which economized space by ingenious contrivances which were all described. A friend of his invited twenty millionaires to meet him at dinner so that he might interest them in the invention. The young man convinced them completely by his demonstration of the saving in a theatre holding, in ordinary seats, six hundred people, leaving them eager and ready to make his fortune. Unfortunately he went on to calculate the annual saving in all the theatres of the world; then in all the churches of the world; then in all the legislatures; estimating finally the incidental and moral and religious effects of the invention until at the end of an hour he had estimated a profit of several thousand millions: the climax of course being that the millionaires folded their tents and silently stole away, leaving the ruined inventor a marked man for life.

Wilde and I got on extraordinarily well on this occasion. I had not to talk myself, but to listen to a man telling me stories better than I could have told them. We did not refer to Art, about which, excluding literature from the definition, he knew only what could be picked up by reading about it. He was in a tweed suit and low hat like myself, and had been detected and had detected me in the act of clandestinely spending a happy day at Rosherville Gardens instead of pontificating in his frock-coat and so forth. And he had an audience on whom not one of his subtlest effects was lost. And so for once our meeting was a success; and I understood why Morris, when he was dying slowly, enjoyed a visit from Wilde more than from anybody else, as I understand why you say in your book that you would rather have Wilde back than any friend you have ever talked to, even though he was incapable of friendship, though not of the most touching kindness on occasion.

Our sixth meeting, the only other one I can remember, was the one at the Café Royal. On that occasion he was not too preoccupied with his danger to be disgusted with me because I, who had praised his first plays handsomely, had turned traitor over The Importance of Being Earnest. Clever as it was, it was his first really heartless play. In the others the chivalry of the eighteenth-century Irishman and the romance of the disciple of Théophile Gautier (Oscar was old-fashioned in the Irish way, except as a critic of morals) not only gave a certain kindness and gallantry to the serious passages and to the handling of the women, but provided that proximity of emotion without which laughter, however irresistible, is destructive and sinister. In The Importance of Being Earnest this had vanished; and the play, though extremely funny, was essentially hateful. I had no idea that Oscar was going to the dogs, and that this represented a real degeneracy produced by his debaucheries. I thought he was still developing; and I hazarded the unhappy guess that The Importance of Being Earnest was in idea a young work written or projected long before under the influence of Gilbert and furbished up for Alexander as a potboiler. At the Café Royal that day I calmly asked him whether I was not right. He indignantly repudiated my guess, and said loftily (the only time he ever tried on me the attitude he took to John Gray and his more abject disciples) that he was disappointed in me. I suppose I said, "Then what on earth has happened to you?" but I recollect nothing more on that subject except that we did not quarrel over it.

When he was sentenced I spent a railway journey on a Socialist lecturing excursion to the North drafting a petition for his release. After that I met Willie Wilde at a theatre which I think must have been the Duke of York's, because I connect it vaguely with St Martin's Lane. I spoke to him about the petition, asking him whether anything of the sort was being done, and warning him that though I and Stewart Headlam would sign it, that would be no use, as we were two notorious cranks, and our names would by themselves reduce the petition to absurdity and do Oscar more harm than good. Willie cordially agreed, and added, with maudlin pathos and an inconceivable want of tact: "Oscar was NOT a man of bad character: you could have trusted him with a woman anywhere." He convinced me, as you discovered later, that signatures would not be obtainable; so the petition project dropped; and I dont know what became of my draft.

When Wilde was in Paris during his last phase I made a point of sending him inscribed copies of all my books as they came out; and he did the same to me.

In writing about Wilde and Whistler, in the days when they were treated as witty triflers, and called Oscar and Jimmy in print, I always made a point of taking them seriously and with scrupulous good manners. Wilde on his part also made a point of recognizing me as a man of distinction by his manner, and repudiating the current estimate of me as a mere jester. This was not the usual reciprocal-admiration trick: I believe he was sincere, and felt indignant at what he thought was a vulgar underestimate of me; and I had the same feeling about him. My impulse to rally to him in his misfortune, and my disgust at "the man Wilde" scurrilities of the newspapers, was irresistible: I dont quite know why; for my charity to his perversion, and my recognition of the fact that it does not imply any general depravity or coarseness of character, came to me through reading and observation, not through sympathy. I have all the normal violent repugnance to homosexuality—if it be really normal, which nowadays one is sometimes provoked to doubt.

Also, I was in no way predisposed to like him: he was my fellow-townsman, and a very prime specimen of the sort of fellow-townsman I most loathed: to wit, the Dublin snob. His Irish charm, potent with Englishmen, did not exist for me; and on the whole it may be claimed for him that he got no regard from me that he did not earn.

What first established a friendly feeling in me was, unexpectedly enough, the affair of the Chicago anarchists, whose Homer you constituted yourself by your story called The Bomb. I tried to get some literary men in London, all heroic rebels and sceptics on paper, to sign a memorial asking for the reprieve of these unfortunate men. The only signature I got was Oscar's. It was a completely disinterested act on his part; and it secured my distinguished consideration for him for the rest of his life.

To return for a moment to Lady Wilde. You know that there is a disease called giantism, caused by "a certain morbid process in the sphenoid bone of the skull—viz., an excessive development of the anterior lobe of the pituitary body" (this is from the nearest encyclopedia). "When this condition does not become active until after the age of twenty-five, by which time the long bones are consolidated, the result is acromegaly, which chiefly manifests itself in an enlargement of the hands and feet." I never saw Lady Wilde's feet; but her hands were enormous, and never went straight to their aim when they grasped anything, but minced about, feeling for it. And the gigantic splaying of her palm was reproduced in her lumbar region.

Now Oscar was an overgrown man, with something not quite normal about his bigness: something that made Lady Colin Campbell, who hated him, describe him as "that great white caterpillar." You yourself describe the disagreeable impression he made on you physically, in spite of his fine eyes and style. Well, I have always maintained that Oscar was a giant in the pathological sense, and that this explains a good deal of his weakness.

I think you have affectionately underrated his snobbery, mentioning only the pardonable and indeed justifiable side of it; the love of fine names and distinguished associations and luxury and good manners. You say repeatedly, and *on certain planes*, truly, that he was not bitter and did not use his tongue to wound people. But this is not true on the snobbish plane. On one occasion he wrote about T. P. O'Connor with deliberate, studied, wounding insolence, with his Merrion Square Protestant pretentiousness in full cry against the Catholic. He repeatedly declaimed against the vulgarity of the British journalist, not as you or I might, but as an expression of the odious class feeling that is itself the vilest vulgarity. He made the mistake of not knowing his place. He objected to be addressed as Wilde, declaring that he was Oscar to his intimates and Mr Wilde to others, quite unconscious of the fact that he was imposing on the men with whom, as a critic and journalist, he had to live and work, the alternative of granting him an intimacy he had no right to ask or a deference to which he had no claim. The vulgar hated him for snubbing them; and the valiant men damned his impudence and cut him. Thus he was left with a band of devoted satellites on the one hand, and a dining-out connection on the other, with here and there a man of talent and personality enough to command his respect, but utterly without that fortifying body of acquaintance among plain men in which a man must move as himself a plain man, and be Smith and Jones and Wilde and Shaw and Harris instead of Bosie and Robbie and Oscar and Mister. This is the sort of folly that does not last forever in a man of Wilde's ability; but it lasted long enough to prevent Oscar laying any solid social foundations.

Another difficulty I have already hinted at. Wilde started as an apostle of Art; and in that capacity he was a humbug. The notion that a Portora boy, passed on to T.C.D. and thence to Oxford and spending his vacations in Dublin, could without special circumstances have any genuine intimacy with music and painting, is to me ridiculous. When Wilde was at Portora, I was at home in a house where important musical works, including several typical masterpieces, were being rehearsed from the point of blank amateur ignorance up to fitness for public performance. I could whistle them from the first bar to the last as a butcher's boy whistles music-hall songs, before I was twelve. The toleration of popular music—Strauss's waltzes, for instance—was to me positively a painful acquirement, a sort of republican duty.

I was so fascinated by painting that I haunted the National Gallery, which Doyle had made perhaps the finest collection of its size in the world; and I longed for money to buy painting materials with. This afterwards saved me from starving: it was as a critic of music and painting in The World that I won through my ten years of journalism before I finished up with you on The Saturday Review. I could make deaf stockbrokers read my two pages on music, the alleged joke being that I knew nothing about it. The real joke was that I knew all about it.

Now it was quite evident to me, as it was to Whistler and Beardsley, that Oscar knew no more about pictures than anyone of his general culture and with his opportunities can pick up as he goes along. He could be witty about Art, as I could be witty about engineering; but that is no use when you have to seize and hold the attention and interest of people who really love music and painting. Therefore, Oscar was handicapped by a false start, and got a reputation for shallowness and insincerity which he never retrieved until too late.

Comedy: the criticism of morals and manners *viva voce*, was his real forte. When he settled down to that he was great. But, as you found when you approached Meredith about him, his initial mistake had produced that "rather low opinion of Wilde's capacities," that "deep-rooted contempt for the showman in him," which persisted as a first impression and will persist until the last man who remembers his æsthetic period has perished. The world has been in some ways so unjust to him that one must be careful not to be unjust to the world.

In the preface on education, called Parents and Children, to my volume of plays beginning with Misalliance, there is a section headed Artist Idolatry, which is really about Wilde. Dealing with "the powers enjoyed by brilliant persons who are also connoisseurs in art," I say, "the influence they can exercise on young people who have been brought up in the darkness and wretchedness of a home without art, and in whom a natural bent towards art has always been baffled and snubbed, is incredible to those who have not witnessed and understood it. He (or she) who reveals the world of art to them opens heaven to them. They become satellites, disciples, worshippers of the apostle. Now the apostle may be a voluptuary without much conscience. Nature may have given him enough virtue to suffice in a reasonable environment. But this allowance may not be enough to defend him against the temptation and demoralization of finding himself a little god on the strength of what ought to be a quite ordinary culture. He may find adorers in all directions in our uncultivated society among people of stronger character than himself, not one of whom, if they had been artistically educated, would have had anything to learn from him, or regarded him as in any way extraordinary apart from his actual achievements as an artist. Tartufe is not always a priest. Indeed, he is not always a rascal: he is often a weak man absurdly credited with omniscience and perfection, and taking unfair advantages only because they are offered to him and he is too weak to refuse. Give everyone his culture, and no one will offer him more than his due."

That paragraph was the outcome of a walk and talk I had one afternoon at Chartres with Robert Ross.

You reveal Wilde as a weaker man than I thought him: I still believe that his fierce Irish pride had something to do with his refusal to run away from the trial. But in the main your evidence is conclusive. It was part of his tragedy that people asked more moral strength from him than he could bear the burden of, because they made the very common mistake—of which actors get the benefit—of regarding style as evidence of strength, just as in the case of women they are apt to regard paint as evidence of beauty. Now Wilde was so in love with style that he never realized the danger of biting off more than he could chew: in other words, of putting up more style than his matter would carry. Wise kings wear shabby clothes, and leave the gold lace to the drum major.

I was at your Saturday Review lunch at the Café Royal when Wilde came in just before the trial. He said he had come to ask you to go into the witness box next day and testify that Dorian Gray was a highly moral work. Your answer was something like this: "For God's sake, man, put everything on that plane out of your head. You dont realize what is going to happen to you. It is not going to be a matter of clever talk about your books. They are going to bring up a string of witnesses that will put art and literature out of the question. Clarke will throw up his brief. He will carry the case to a certain point; and then, when he sees the avalanche coming, he will back out and leave you in the dock. What you have to do is to cross to France tonight. Leave a letter saying that you cannot face the squalor and horror of a law case; that you are an artist and unfitted for such things. Dont stay here clutching at straws like testimonials to Dorian Gray. *I tell you I know*. I know what is going to happen. I know Clarke's sort. I know what evidence they have got. You must go."

It was no use. Wilde was in a curious double temper. He made no pretence either of innocence or of questioning the folly of his proceedings against Queensberry. But he had an infatuate haughtiness as to the impossibility of his retreating, and as to his right to dictate your course. Oscar finally rose with a mixture of impatience and his grand air, and walked out with the remark that he had now found out who were his real friends.

What your book needs to complete it is a portrait of yourself as good as your portrait of Wilde. Oscar was not combative, though he was supercilious in his early pose. When his snobbery was not in action, he liked to make people devoted to him and to flatter them exquisitely with that end. Mrs Calvert, whose great final period as a stage old woman began with her appearance in my Arms and the Man, told me one day, when apologizing for being, as she thought, a bad rehearser, that no author had ever been so nice to her except Mr Wilde.

Pugnacious people, if they did not actually terrify Oscar, were at least the sort of people he could not control, and whom he feared as possibly able to coerce him. You suggest that the Queensberry pugnacity was something that Oscar could not deal with successfully. But how in that case could Oscar have felt quite safe with you? You were more pugnacious than six Queensberrys rolled into one. When people asked, "What has Frank Harris been?" the usual reply was, "Obviously a pirate from the Spanish Main."

Oscar, from the moment he gained your attachment, could never have been afraid of what you might do to him, as he was sufficient of a connoisseur in Blut Bruderschaft to appreciate yours; but he must always have been mortally afraid of what you might do or say to his friends.

You had quite an infernal scorn for nineteen out of twenty of the men and women you met in the circles he most wished to propitiate; and nothing could induce you to keep your knife in its sheath when they jarred on you. The Spanish Main itself would have blushed rosy red at your language when classical invective did not suffice to express your feelings.

It may be that if, say, Edmund Gosse had come to Oscar when he was out on bail, with a couple of first-class tickets in his pocket, and gently suggested a mild trip to Folkestone, or the Channel Islands, Oscar might have let himself be coaxed away. But to be called on to gallop *ventre à terre* to Erith—it might have been Deal—and hoist the Jolly Roger on board your lugger, was like casting a light comedian and first lover for Richard III. Oscar could not see himself in the part.

I must not press the point too far; but it illustrates, I think, what does not come out at all in your book: that you were a very different person from the submissive and sympathetic disciples to whom he was accustomed. There are things more terrifying to a soul like Oscar's than an as yet unrealized possibility of a sentence of hard labor. A voyage with Captain Kidd may have been one of them. Wilde was a conventional man: his unconventionality was the very pedantry of convention: never was there a man less an outlaw than he. You were a born outlaw, and will never be anything else.

That is why, in his relations with you, he appears as a man always shirking action—more of a coward (all men are cowards more or less) than so proud a man can have been. Still this does not affect the truth and power of your portrait. Wilde's memory will have to stand or fall by it.

You will be blamed, I imagine, because you have not written a lying epitaph instead of a faithful chronicle and study of him; but you will not lose your sleep over that. As a matter of fact, you could not have carried kindness further without sentimental folly. I should have made a far sterner summing up. I am sure Oscar has not found the gates of heaven shut against him: he is too good company to be excluded; but he can hardly have been greeted as "Thou good and faithful servant." The first thing we ask a servant for is a testimonial to honesty, sobriety, and industry; for we soon find out that these are the scarce things, and that geniuses and clever people are as common as rats. Well, Oscar was not sober, not honest, not industrious. Society praised him for being idle, and persecuted him savagely for an aberration which it had better have left unadvertized, thereby making a hero of him; for it is in the nature of people to worship those who have been made to suffer horribly: indeed I have often said that if the Crucifixion could be proved a myth, and Jesus convicted of dying of old age in comfortable circumstances, Christianity would lose ninety-nine per cent of its devotees.

We must try to imagine what judgment we should have passed on Oscar if he had been a normal man, and had dug his grave with his teeth in the ordinary respectable fashion, as his brother Willie did. This brother, by the way, gives us some cue; for Willie, who had exactly the same education and the same chances, must be ruthlessly set aside by literary history as a vulgar journalist of no account. Well, suppose Oscar and Willie had both died the day before Queensberry left that card at the Club! Oscar would still have been remembered as a wit and a dandy, and would have had a niche beside Congreve in the drama. A volume of his aphorisms would have stood creditably on the library shelf with La Rochefoucauld's Maxims. We should have missed the Ballad of Reading Gaol and De Profundis; but he would still have cut a considerable figure in the Dictionary of National Biography, and been read and quoted outside the British Museum reading room.

As to the Ballad and De Profundis, I think it is greatly to Oscar's credit that, whilst he was sincere and deeply moved when he was protesting against the cruelty of our present system to children and to prisoners generally, he could not write about his own individual share in that suffering with any conviction or sympathy. Except for the passage where he describes his exposure at Clapham Junction, there is hardly a line in De Profundis that he might not have written as a literary feat five years earlier. But in the Ballad, even in borrowing form and melody from Coleridge, he shews that he could pity others when he could not seriously pity himself. And this, I think, may be pleaded against the reproach that he was selfish. Externally, in the ordinary action of life as distinguished from the literary action proper to his genius, he was no doubt sluggish and weak because of his giantism. He ended as an unproductive drunkard and swindler; for his repeated sales of the Daventry plot, in so far as they imposed on the buyers and were not transparent excuses for begging, were undeniably swindles. For all that, he does not appear in his writings a selfish or base-minded man. He is at his worst and weakest in the suppressed part of De Profundis; but in my opinion it had better be published, for several reasons. It explains some of his personal weakness by the stifling narrowness of his daily round, ruinous to a man whose proper place was in a large public life. And its concealment is mischievous because, first, it leads people to imagine all sorts of horrors in a document which contains nothing worse than any record of the squabbles of two touchy men on a holiday; and, second, it is clearly a monstrous thing that one of them should have a torpedo launched at him and timed to explode after his death.

Now that you have written the best life of Oscar Wilde, let us have the best life of Frank Harris. Otherwise the man behind your works will go down to posterity as the hero of my very inadequate preface to The Dark Lady of the Sonnets.

MR ARNOLD BENNETT THINKS PLAY-WRITING EASIER THAN NOVEL WRITING

THE AUTHOR'S CRAFT. By Arnold Bennett. (Hodder & Stoughton.)

From The Nation, 11 *March* 1916

I DID not at first understand why the Editor of The Nation sent me Mr Bennett's book as one which I might like to review. Mr Bennett talks shop and debits harmless tosh about technique for the entertainment of literary amateurs in a very agreeable and suggestive manner, as he has every right to do, being so distinguished a master of the craft. But why on earth should I join in the conversation and snatch a professional job from some young reviewer whose week's board and lodging it would provide?

I found the solution of the enigma on page 76, which begins with the words, "One reason why a play is easier to write than a novel." That fetched me. I did not want to know "one reason" for so outrageous a stroke of novelist's bluff. But the impetus of my reading carried me on, in spite of the shock; and so I learnt that this one reason is "that a play is shorter than a novel." It is; and so is the Bible shorter than the London Directory. "Excuse the length of my letter," said Pascal: "I had no time to write a short one."

Now, I am not going to argue. I never do. I will simply take one of the shortest, most intense, and most famous scenes in English dramatic literature, and rewrite it as a chapter in a novel in the style of my friends Bennett and Galsworthy when they are too lazy to write plays:

MACBETH

A PLAY. By William Shakespear. *Act V. Scene* 8

The precinct of Macbeth's Castle on Dunsinane Hill

Enter Macbeth

MACB. Why should I play the Roman fool, and die

On mine own sword? Whiles I see lives, the gashes
Do better upon *them*.

Enter Macduff

MACD. Turn, hell-hound, turn.
MACB. Of all men else I have avoided thee;
But get thee back: my soul is too much charg'd
With blood of thine already.
MACD. I have no words,
My voice is in my sword, thou bloodier villain
Than terms can give thee out! (*They fight.*)
MACB. Thou losest labor.
As easy may'st thou the intrenchment air
With thy keen sword impress, as make me bleed.
Let fall thy blade on vulnerable crests:
I bear a charmed life, which must not yield
To one of woman born.
MACD. Despair thy charm;
And let the angel whom thou still hast serv'd
Tell thee, Macduff was from his mother's womb
Untimely ripp'd.
MACB. Accurséd be that tongue that tells me so;
For it hath cow'd my better part of man.
And be these juggling fiends no more believ'd
That palter with us in a double sense;
That keep the word of promise to our ear,
And break it to our hope. I'll not fight with thee.
MACD. Then yield thee, coward;
And live to be the show and gaze o' the time.
We'll have thee, as our rarer monsters are,
Painted upon a pole; and, underwrit,
"Here may you see the tyrant."
MACB. I'll not yield,
To kiss the ground before young Malcolm's feet,
And to be baited with the rabble's curse.
Though Birnam wood *be* come to Dunsinane,
And thou oppos'd, being of no woman born,
Yet I will try the last: before my body

I throw my warlike shield. Lay on, Macduff;
And damn'd be him that first cries, "Hold! Enough!"
(*Exeunt fighting.*)

MACBETH

A Novel. By Arnold Bennett, John Galsworthy, or Anybody. The Last Chapter

He was to fail, after all, then. The day was going against him. His men were not really fighting. They had conveyed to Old Siward that they were open to an offer of quarter; and the hint had not been lost on that ancient campaigner, whose son he had just slain.

What was the use of killing? Duncan, Banquo, the Macduff people: he had waded through their blood; and how much better would it not be if it were all a dream and they were alive and kind to him?

How the martins were singing! Banquo, always a bit of a fool, had been sentimental about the martins. Gruach, the dear dead wife whom the southrons persisted in calling Lady Macbeth, had argued with Banquo about them, telling him that their habits were insanitary, and that they were infested with small bugs which got into the castle, already too rich in insect life. But Duncan had agreed with Banquo; and when Gruach became queen she would not let the martins' nests be broken down, being anxious to copy Duncan's tastes in every way, lest anyone should say that the Macbeths did not know how kings lived. And so the martins were singing, singing, always singing when they were not fly-catching.

It came to him, with a twist at the heart, that he had never told Gruach the truth about Banquo. He had left her to believe that he had killed him because the witches had foretold that his posterity should be kings. But the real reason was that Banquo had given himself moral airs. That is hard to bear at any time; but when you are within ten minutes of committing a murder, it is insufferable. Morality is easy for a man who does not intend to do anything; but a man of action cannot stand on scruples. These idle thanes who sat down on their little patrimonies and had no ambition: they had invented this moral twaddle to excuse their laziness.

What an exquisite morning it was! Was there anything so blue as a blue sky, anything so white as a white cloud, any gold so golden as the gold of the gorse? From the summit of Dunsinane he could see almost to the Roman wall on the south and to the Forth Bridge on the north. The wind had backed a little to the north: perhaps it would rain later. But no such foreboding troubled the wood pigeon that now called to him, "Tak two coos, Taffy: tak two coos, Taffy." He smiled grimly. He had taken from first to last not less than a thousand coos; and this funny bird kept on exhorting him to take two. And yet he did not throw a stone at it as he once would have done. It seemed all so useless. You strove and strove, and killed and killed, and made journeys to consult witches; and at the end of it all the wood pigeon had no more to say to you than before; and the sky was no bluer, the cloud no whiter, the whins no yellower. Curse the sky! Curse the whins! Doubly damn the wood pigeon! Why not make an end of it, like the Roman fool at Philippi? He stood his claymore on its hilt on the flags and bent over the point. Just to lean on it, and let it go through him: then the wood pigeon might coo itself black in the face: Macbeth would be at rest with Duncan. Where had he heard about Philippi? It seemed unlikely that he could have learned Roman history; and yet he found that he did know. Do men know everything before death? He shuddered. Strange, that he, who rather enjoyed killing other people, should feel an intense repugnance to kill himself! Yet there was one canny thing about killing yourself: it relieved you of all concern for the future. You could kill as many other people as you liked first without considering the consequences. He would, please God, spit a few more of his enemies on that sword before his own turn came. He tossed it into the air by the point, and caught the hilt as it came down. He no longer heard the wood pigeon.

And yet, what was that? Had the wood pigeon called him a hell-hound? He turned, and saw Macduff there, between him and the sun, glaring at him. If the sun had been in his eyes, he could not have glared. It was clever of him to come that way and get the advantage of the sun.

Macduff! Yes, Macduff: the man of whom the spirit called up by the witches had bade him beware. The man whose wife and child he had slaughtered. Could he blame him for glaring? Would not any man glare after such an experience? Banquo had glared even after his death, but with no speculation in his eyes. There was speculation enough in Macduff's: he was speculating on the sun being in the eyes of his adversary.

How the martins were singing! How fresh the air tasted! How good life was! How many pleasant paths there were on those hillsides, paths that had led his feet and Macduff's to this one spot of all spots in the world? Well, if Macduff had not come by one path he would have come by another. That was life, always inscrutable, sometimes a little ironical. The wind dropped: the banner had ceased to flap, and hung inert. A number of birds and crickets, no longer scared into silence by its flapping, joined the concert of the martins. Again came the wood pigeon's incitement, "Tak two coos, Taffy: tak——" What was that? A sharp, rasping sound called Macbeth from the landscape. He looked again at the man against whom he had been warned.

Macduff had stooped to sharpen his claymore on the flags. He was squatting down in an attitude which brought his boney knees into prominence just below his kilt, and drawing his blade to and fro with a harsh, rhythmical grating on the granite. By the mere instinct of imitation, Macbeth did the same. His knees were fleshier; and it was harder for him to stoop; but he did it. It is never easy for a king to stoop; but Fate will have it so sometimes. Now there were two blades scraping. The birds stopped singing, and listened in astonished suspicious silence. Only a jay laughed.

Macbeth heard it. Something stirred in him, and distorted his lips into a grin. It seemed to him that he suddenly opened a book that had always been sealed to him. When Gruach was dying he had asked the doctor for some physic for the mind; and the doctor had failed him. Then he had asked the porter, because he had noticed that the porter, alone among all the men of his acquaintance, was light-hearted, and would laugh, even when nobody was being hurt or ridiculed, and seemed to despise ambition. And the porter had told him that life is not so bad if you can see the fun of it. Old Siward had nailed the porter to the door that morning because he refused to open it to the enemy. Did he see the fun of that, Macbeth wondered? Yet here, as he squatted before Macduff, and they both sharpened their blades on the flags, a dim sense of something laughable in the situation touched him, though, God knows, there was nothing to laugh at if the warning of the witches were trustworthy. The spirits had said that no man born of woman should harm Macbeth. That seemed pretty conclusive. But they had also said that he would not be vanquished until Birnam Wood came to Dunsinane. That also seemed conclusive; yet the thing had happened: he had seen the wood walking.

He decided to give Macduff a chance. He was tired of killing people named Macduff. He said so. He advised Macduff to go away.

Macduff tried to speak; gulped; and came on. His voice was in his sword.

Macbeth was not afraid, though he knew he was not the man he had been. He had drunk heavily since he seized the throne: the Scots expected that from a king. But he could fight as well as ever for forty-five seconds; and then he could clinch, and try to get in his dirk somewhere. After all, Macduff was no teetotaller, if one might judge by his nose, which was red and swollen. Only, the doubt came: was the redness and the swelling from drink, or from weeping over his slaughtered family? With that thought came Macduff's first blow: a feint, followed by a vicious thrust at the groin.

Macbeth was quick enough to drop his targe and stop the thrust, even while he guarded the blow that did not come. That reassured him, and took some of the bounce out of Macduff. He was equally successful the next time, and the next. He became elated. At last his pride in his charmed life got the better of his prudence. He told Macduff that he was losing his labor, and told him why.

The effect was exactly the contrary of what he had anticipated. A gleam of savage delight came into Macduff's eyes.

What did it mean?

Macbeth was not left long in doubt. He stood petrified, whilst a tale poured from Macduff's lips such as had never before blasted the ears of mortal man. It cannot be repeated here: there is such a thing as the library censorship. Let it suffice that it was a tale of the rude but efficient obstetric surgery of those ancient times, and that it established beyond all question the fact that Macduff had never been born.

After that, Macbeth felt that he simply could not fight with him. It was not that he was afraid, even now. Nor was it that he was utterly disgusted at the way the witches had let him down again. He just could not bring himself to hack at a man who was not natural. It was like trying to eat a cat. He flatly refused further combat.

Of course, Macduff called him Coward. He did not mind that so much; for he had given his proofs, and nobody would believe Macduff; nor, indeed, would any reasonable Scot expect him to fight an unborn adversary. But Macduff hinted at unbearable things: at defeat, disgrace, the pillory even.

There was a lark singing now. Far down the hillside, where the rugged road wound up to the barbican, the last of Birnam Wood was still on the march. A hawk hovered motionless over a walking oak: he could see the glint of the sun on its brown back. The oak's legs must be those of an old soldier, he thought, who had cunningly taken the heaviest tree so that he might be late for the fighting. But, old or young, the soldier was now anxious lest he should be late for the plunder and the other sequels to the sack of a castle; for the oak was coming up at a rattling pace. There were nests in it, too. Curious, to wonder how those nesting pairs took their moving!

A surge of wrath went through Macbeth. He was, above all things, a country gentleman; and that another country gentleman should move his timber without acquiring any rights infuriated him. He became reckless. Birnam Wood —*his* wood—had been taken to Dunsinane: was that a thing he could be expected to stand? What though Macduff had not been properly born: was it not all the more likely that he had a weak constitution and could not stick it out if he were pressed hard in the fight? Anyhow, Macbeth would try. He braced himself; grasped his claymore powerfully; thrust his shield under the chin of his adversary; and cried, "Lay on, Macduff."

He could not have chosen a more unfortunate form of defiance. When the news had come to Macduff of the slaughter of his wife and boy, he had astonished the messenger by exclaiming, "What! All my pretty chickens and their dam at one fell swoop!" Accustomed from his earliest youth to deal with horses, he knew hardly anything of poultry, which was a woman's business. When he applied the word dam, properly applicable only to a mare, to a hen, Malcolm, though deeply moved by his distress, had a narrow escape of a fit of hysterics; for the innocent blunder gave him an impulse of untimely laughter. The story had been repeated; and something of it had come to Macduff's ears. He was a highly-strung man, exquisitely sensitive to ridicule. Since that time the slightest allusion to chickens had driven him to transports of fury. At the words, "Lay on," he saw red. Macbeth, from the instant those fatal words passed his lips, had not a dog's chance.

In any case, he would not have been ready to meet a sudden attack. All his life he had been subject to a strange discursiveness which sent his mind wandering to the landscape, and to the fauna and flora of the district, at the most exciting crises of his fate. When he meant to tell Gruach that he had arranged to have Banquo killed, he had said to her, instead, "Light thickens; and the crow makes wing to the rooky wood." His attention had already strayed to the wood pigeon when Macduff's yell of fury split his ears; and at the same moment he felt his foe's teeth snap through his nose and his foe's dirk drive through his ribs.

When Malcolm arrived, there was little left of Macbeth but a pile of mince. Macduff was panting. "That will teach him," he said, and stopped, exsufflicate.

They laid Macbeth beside Gruach in God's quiet acre in the little churchyard of Dunsinane. Malcolm erected a stately tomb there, for the credit of the institution of kingship; and the epitaph, all things considered, was not unhandsome. There was no reproach in it, no vain bitterness. It said that Macbeth had "succeeded Duncan."

The birds are still singing on Dunsinane. The wood pigeon still coos about the coos; and Malcolm takes them frankly and generously. It is not for us to judge him, or to judge Macbeth. Macbeth was born before his time. Men call him a villain; but had the press existed in his day, a very trifling pecuniary sacrifice on his part would have made a hero of him. And, to do him justice, he was never stingy.

Well! Well!

THE END

There! that is what is called novel writing. I raise no idle question as to whether it is easy or not. Fine art of any sort is either easy or impossible. But that sort of thing I can write by the hundred thousand words on my head. I believe that if I turned my attention to mechanics for a month or two, I could make a typewriter attachment that would do it, like the calculating attachment that has lately come into use. The odd thing is that people seem to like it. They swallow it in doses of three hundred pages at a time; and they are not at all keen on Shakespear. Decidedly, when my faculties decay a little further, I shall go back to novel writing. And Arnold Bennett can fall back on writing plays.